A Companion to Bioethics

Blackwell Companions to Philosophy

This outstanding student reference series offers a comprehensive and authoritative survey of philosophy as a whole. Written by today's leading philosophers, each volume provides lucid and engaging coverage of the key figures, terms, topics, and problems of the field. Taken together, the volumes provide the ideal basis for course use, representing an unparalleled work of reference for students and specialists alike.

Already published in the series:

Also under contract:

A Companion to Bioethics

Second edition

Edited by

Helga Kuhse and Peter Singer

WILEY-BLACKWELL

A John Wiley & Sons, Ltd., Publication

This second edition first published 2009
© 2009 Blackwell Publishing Ltd
Except chapter 18 © Gregory E. Pence
Edition history: Blackwell Publishing Ltd (1e, 1998)

Blackwell Publishing was acquired by John Wiley & Sons in February 2007. Blackwell's
publishing program has been merged with Wiley's global Scientific, Technical, and Medical
business to form Wiley-Blackwell.

Registered Office
John Wiley & Sons Ltd, The Atrium, Southern Gate, Chichester, West Sussex, PO19 8SQ,
United Kingdom

Editorial Offices
350 Main Street, Malden, MA 02148-5020, USA
9600 Garsington Road, Oxford, OX4 2DQ, UK
The Atrium, Southern Gate, Chichester, West Sussex, PO19 8SQ, UK

For details of our global editorial offices, for customer services, and for information about
how to apply for permission to reuse the copyright material in this book please see our
website at www.wiley.com/wiley-blackwell.

The right of Helga Kuhse and Peter Singer to be identified as the authors of the editorial material in this
work has been asserted in accordance with the Copyright, Designs and Patents Act 1988.

Wiley also publishes its books in a variety of electronic formats. Some content that appears in print
may not be available in electronic books.

Designations used by companies to distinguish their products are often claimed as trademarks.
All brand names and product names used in this book are trade names, service marks, trademarks
or registered trademarks of their respective owners. The publisher is not associated with any product
or vendor mentioned in this book. This publication is designed to provide accurate and authoritative
information in regard to the subject matter covered. It is sold on the understanding that the publisher
is not engaged in rendering professional services. If professional advice or other expert assistance is
required, the services of a competent professional should be sought.

Library of Congress Cataloging-in-Publication Data
A companion to bioethics / edited by Helga Kuhse and Peter Singer. — 2nd ed.
      p. cm. — (Blackwell companions to philosophy ; 15)
   Includes bibliographical references and index.
   ISBN 978-1-4051-6331-6 (hardcover : alk. paper)
1. Bioethics.   2. Medical ethics.   I. Kuhse, Helga.   II. Singer, Peter, 1946–

   R724.C616 2009
   174.2—dc22
                                                                2009007422

A catalogue record for this book is available from the British Library.

Set in 10/12.5pt Photina by Graphicraft Limited, Hong Kong
Printed and bound in Singapore by Fabulous Pte Ltd

01   2009

For Brent

Contents

Contributors

John D. Arras, University of Virginia

Margaret Pabst Battin, University of Utah

Joseph Boyle, University of Toronto

Peter Braude, King's College London

Dan W. Brock, Harvard Medical School, Boston

Alexander Morgan Capron, University of Southern California, Los Angeles

Ruth Chadwick, Cardiff University, Wales

James F. Childress, University of Virginia

Angus Clarke, Cardiff University, Wales

Jan Crosthwaite, University of Auckland, New Zealand

Norman Daniels, Harvard University, Boston

Govert den Hartogh, University of Amsterdam, The Netherlands

Carl Elliott, University of Minnesota, Minneapolis

Segun Gbadegesin, Howard University, Washington, DC

Lynn Gillam, University of Melbourne

Raanan Gillon, Imperial College London

Eric Gregory, Princeton University

R. M. Hare, Deceased

John Harris, University of Manchester

Roger Higgs, King's College School of Medicine and Dentistry, London

Nils Holtug, University of Copenhagen

Eike-Henner W. Kluge, University of Victoria, Canada

Michael Kottow, University of Chile, Santiago

Donald W. Light, University of Medicine and Dentistry of New Jersey

Christopher Lowry, The Chinese University of Hong Kong

Florencia Luna, University of Buenos Aires

Ruth Macklin, Albert Einstein College of Medicine, Bronx, New York

Jeff McMahan, Rutgers University, New Brunswick

Paul Ulhas Macneill, University of Sydney

Rita C. Manning, San José State University, California

Sarah Marchand, St Paul, Minnesota

Jonathan D. Moreno, University of Pennsylvania

Justin Oakley, Monash University, Australia

Kevin Outterson, Boston University, Boston

Gregory Pence, University of Alabama at Birmingham

Laura M. Purdy, Wells College, Aurora, New York

James Rachels, Deceased

Janet Radcliffe Richards, University of Oxford

Bernard E. Rollin, Colorado State University

Julian Savulescu, University of Oxford

Udo Schüklenk, Queen's University, Kingston, Ontario

Michael J. Selgelid, The Australian National University, Canberra

Daniel K. Sokol, Imperial College London

Bonnie Steinbock, State University of New York

Brian Stoffell, Flinders University, South Australia

Janet L. Storch, University of Victoria, Canada

Peter A. Sy, University of the Philippines, Quezon City

Michael Tooley, University of Colorado at Boulder

Verena Tschudin, University of Surrey, UK

Wibren van der Burg, Erasmus University, Rotterdam

Mary Warnock, Axford, Wiltshire, UK

Mary Anne Warren, San Francisco State University, San Francisco, California

Daniel Wikler, Harvard University, Boston

Dr Robert Young, La Trobe University, Melbourne

Acknowledgments

For encouraging us to take on the first edition of this project, we wish to thank Alyn Shipton – although we had some doubts along the way that we would ever finish what turned out to be a mammoth task.

In revising the book, we were ably assisted by Brent Howard. Our contributors will be well aware of the thoroughness with which he went through each essay, and of his ability to make valuable suggestions for improving not only the style, but also in many cases the substance of the argument. Sadly, Brent's health problems meant that he could not assist us with the last few essays, and he did not live to see the volume in print. Thank you, Brent.

Helga Kuhse and Peter Singer

Part I

Introduction

1

What Is Bioethics?
A Historical Introduction

HELGA KUHSE AND PETER SINGER

Since the 1960s ethical problems in health care and the biomedical sciences have gripped the public consciousness in unprecedented ways. In part, this is the result of new and sometimes revolutionary developments in the biomedical sciences and in clinical medicine. Dialysis machines, artificial ventilators, and organ transplants offer the possibility of keeping alive patients who otherwise would have died. *In vitro* fertilization and related reproduction techniques allow a range of new relationships between parents and children, including the birth of children who are not genetically related to the women who bear them. The development of modern contraceptives, prenatal testing, and the availability of safe abortions have given women and couples increased choices about the number and kinds of children they are going to have. Groundbreaking developments in genetics and the possibility of genetic enhancement add a further dimension to these choices. Technological breakthroughs, however, have not been the only factor in the increasing interest in ethical problems in this area. Another factor has been a growing concern about the power exercised by doctors and scientists, which shows itself in issues about "patients' rights" and the rights of the community as a whole to be involved in decisions that affect them. This has meant greater public awareness of the value-laden nature of medical decision-making, and a critical questioning of the basis on which such decisions are made. It has become patently obvious during the past three or four decades that, to give just one example, someone has to decide whether to continue life-support for patients who will never regain consciousness. This is not a technical decision that only doctors are capable of making, but an ethical decision, on which patients and others may have views no less defensible than those of doctors.

It was in the climate of such new ethical issues and choices that the field of inquiry now known as "bioethics" was born. The word was not originally used in this sense. Van Rensselaer Potter first proposed the term for a "science of survival" in the ecological sense – that is, an interdisciplinary study aimed at ensuring the preservation of the biosphere (Potter 1970). This terminology never became widely established, however, and instead "bioethics" came to refer to the growing interest in the ethical issues arising from health care and the biomedical sciences. It is to bioethics in this latter sense that the present volume forms a *Companion*.

Although the term itself is new, and the prominence of bioethics owes much to recent developments in the biomedical sciences, bioethics can also be seen as a modern version of a much older field of thought, namely medical ethics. Undoubtedly, bioethics claims medical ethics as part of its province, but in many ways it takes a distinctly different approach. Traditionally, medical ethics has focused primarily on the doctor–patient relationship and on the virtues possessed by the good doctor. It has also been very much concerned with relations between colleagues within the profession, to the extent that it has sometimes seemed to exemplify George Bernard Shaw's remark that "all professions are conspiracies against the laity." Bioethics, on the other hand, is a more overtly critical and reflective enterprise. Not limited to questioning the ethical dimensions of doctor–patient and doctor–doctor relationships, it goes well beyond the scope of traditional medical ethics in several ways. First, its goal is not the development of, or adherence to, a code or set of precepts, but a better understanding of the issues. Second, it is prepared to ask deep philosophical questions about the nature of ethics, the value of life, what it is to be a person, the significance of being human. Third, it embraces issues of public policy and the direction and control of science. In all these senses, bioethics is a novel and distinct field of inquiry. Nevertheless, its history must begin with the history of medical ethics.

Medical Ethics

Medical ethics has a long and varied history (Reich 1995: 1439–646). While it is often thought that it had its beginning in the days of Hippocrates, in ancient Greece, it is in fact much older. Even tribal societies, without a written language, already had more or less well-articulated values that directed the provision of health care by shamans, exorcists, witches, sorcerers, and priests, as well as by midwives, bonesetters, and herbalists. One of the earliest written provisions relating to the practice of medicine is from the Code of Hammurabi, written in Babylon in about 1750 BC. It stipulates that if a doctor uses a bronze lancet to perform a major operation on a member of the nobility that results in death or leads to the loss of an eye, the doctor's hand will be cut off (Pritchard 1969). Other early provisions of medical ethics were embedded in a religious tradition. A monument in the sanctuary of Asclepius, for example, tells doctors to be "like God: savior equally of slaves, of paupers, of rich men, of princes, and to all a brother, such help he would give" (Etziony 1973); and the Daily Prayer of a Physician, often attributed to the twelfth-century Jewish doctor Moses Maimonides (but now thought to date from the eighteenth century), condemns not only "thirst for profit" but also "ambition for renown and admiration" (Veatch 1989: 14).

The ancient ethical codes were often expressed in the form of oaths. The best-known medical oath in the Western tradition is the Oath of Hippocrates, commonly assumed to be from the fifth century BC, and often regarded as the very foundation of Western medical ethics. Despite the oath's continuing appeal, its origins are clouded in mystery. Around 500 BC many different schools of medical practice coexisted, each of them reflecting somewhat different medical, philosophical, and religious beliefs. One of these medical schools, on the island of Cos, was headed by the physician Hippocrates. The Hippocratic School produced a large body of writings on medicine, science, and ethics. The date of the oath, however, is unknown, with estimates ranging from the sixth century BC to the beginning of the Christian era (Edelstein 1967). The oath's significance in the history of Western medical ethics is twofold. In affirming that "I will use dietetic measures to the use and profit of the sick according to my capacity and understanding. If any danger and hurt threatens, I will endeavor to avert it," the oath establishes the principles of beneficence and nonmaleficence, that is, that doctors must act so as to benefit their patients and seek to prevent harm. In addition, the oath's prohibition on giving a potion to produce an abortion, or giving any poison to end the life of a patient, is consonant with the view of the sanctity of human life that has dominated medical ethics under Christendom. Other aspects of the oath – like the injunction to honor one's teacher like a parent, "to share his fate and if occasion arise supply him with the necessaries of life" – are less frequently referred to in modern discussions of medical ethics.

While some scholars hold that the increasing importance of the Hippocratic Oath is linked to the rise of Christianity, this is disputed by others who believe that there are significant differences and tensions in the ethical precepts on which Hippocratic and Christian medicine were built. One obvious difference lies in the two traditions' religious commitment. At different times, various modifications were thus introduced to make the Hippocratic Oath acceptable to Christians. One of the earliest of these dates from the tenth or eleventh century. It is entitled "From the Oath According to Hippocrates Insofar as a Christian May Swear it." This oath no longer required Christian doctors to swear to Greek gods and goddesses; rather, those taking the oath addressed themselves to "God the Father of our Lord Jesus Christ" (Jones 1924: 23).

Perhaps one of the most significant moral influences of Christianity relates to its emphasis on love for one's neighbor and compassion for the ill. Religious institutions, such as monasteries, began to set up "hospitals" for the ill and destitute, and Christian teaching emphasized that doctors must cultivate the virtues of compassion and charity. A treatise, probably dating from the early twelfth century, exhorts doctors not to heal "for the sake of gain, nor to give more consideration to the wealthy than to the poor, or to the noble than the ignoble" (MacKinney 1952: 27), and in the thirteenth century Thomas Aquinas considered it a sin if a doctor demanded an excessive fee, or if he refused to give gratuitous treatment to a patient who would die for want of it.

If greed and lack of charity were regarded as sins, so were other practices as well. Navarrus, a leading sixteenth-century canonist, provided a clear statement that condemned euthanasia as sinful, even if motivated by pity. In this, he followed St Augustine's earlier pronouncement, in *The City of God*, that Christians must not choose suicide to escape illness; and Thomas Aquinas' condemnation of the practice on the grounds that it was unnatural and a usurpation of God's prerogative to give and take life.

When it came to another topic still central to contemporary bioethical debate – that of abortion – the historical position of the Church has been somewhat ambiguous. While the practice was standardly condemned in the early Christian literature, its wrongness was often regarded as a matter of degree. Following Aristotle, various thinkers – including Thomas Aquinas – thought that only the abortion of an animated fetus constituted homicide. Animation was presumed to occur at 40 days for male fetuses, and 90 days for female fetuses. By and large, this view remained dominant until 1869, when Pius IX declared all direct abortions homicide, regardless of the fetal stage of development.

5

Over the millennia, many different religious groups have attempted to formulate the central virtues and duties of doctors in various ways, and to articulate their particular responses to issues within medical ethics. The Roman Catholic Church is thus not the only Christian Church to have well-developed views on a range of issues in medical ethics; there are a number of Protestant Churches with distinct positions as well. In addition, there are of course extensive non-Christian religious teachings. Jewish and Islamic medical ethics, for example, articulate the duties and responsibilities of Jewish or Islamic doctors, and in East Asia and the Indian subcontinent, traditions of medical ethics are intertwined with Taoism, Confucianism, Buddhism, Shintoism, and Hinduism.

Over the centuries, medical practitioners themselves continued to reflect on the qualities that the virtuous doctor should possess, in particular in his relationship with patients. While these reflections were typically intertwined with prevailing religious trends and teachings, the seventeenth and eighteenth centuries brought some changes. John Gregory, a prominent eighteenth-century Scottish doctor-philosopher, drew on prevailing Enlightenment philosophies to articulate his view that doctors must be "sympathetic," in the sense developed by the great Scottish philosopher David Hume. In other words, the doctor was to develop "that sensibility of heart which makes us feel for the distresses of our fellow creatures, and which, of consequence, incites us in the most powerful manner to relieve them" (Gregory 1817: 22).

Gregory's reflections on the role of doctors and the doctor–patient relationship are still highly relevant today. Not only was he possibly the first doctor who sought to develop a universal moral basis for medical ethics – one that was free from narrow religious and parochial concerns – but his view of the central role played by care and sympathy in the doctor–patient relationship may also be read as one of the first articulations of an "ethics of care." In recent times, care approaches to ethics have played an important role in feminist and nursing approaches to ethics.

Nursing Ethics

Medical ethics has not been the only source of ethics relating to health care. Professional nursing had its beginning in nineteenth-century England, where Florence Nightingale established the first school of nursing and laid down some of the ethical precepts that would shape the practice of nursing for a long time. Emphasis was placed on the character of the nurse. Above all else, a good nurse must be a good woman, as Florence Nightingale put it.

By the early 1890s nurses had begun seriously to discuss ethical issues in nursing. In 1899 the International Council of Nurses was established, professional journals, such as *The American Journal of Nursing*, sprang up and in 1901 Isabel Hampton Robb, a leader of nursing at the time, wrote one of the first books on nursing ethics, entitled *Nursing Ethics for Hospitals and Private Use* (Robb 1901). The vast majority of nurses are women and, until fairly recently, the vast majority of doctors have been men. Not surprisingly, the relationship between doctors and nurses reflected the different roles of women and men, and their relative status in society. One of the manifestations of this was the assumption that the primary responsibility of nurses was to doctors rather than to patients, and that nurses had to show absolute obedience to their medical colleagues. As one American nursing leader put it in 1917: "The first and most helpful criticism I ever received from a doctor was when he told me that I was supposed to be simply an intelligent machine for the purpose of carrying out his order" (Dock 1917: 394).

The view that the nurse's primary responsibility was to the doctor prevailed until the 1960s, and was still reflected in the 1965 version of the *International Code of Nursing Ethics*. Item 7 of the *Code* states: "The nurse is under an obligation to carry out the physician's orders intelligently and loyally." The revival of feminist thinking in the late 1960s paralleled the developing self-consciousness and self-assertiveness of nurses, and in the 1973 *International Council of Nurses' Code for Nurses*, the nurse's "primary responsibility" is no longer seen to be to doctors but to patients – "to those people who require nursing care."

This questioning by nurses of their traditional role and their relationship with doctors and patients eventually converged with a movement by feminist philosophers that challenged the traditional (and therefore male-dominated) view of ethics as a matter of abstract, impartial, and universal principles or rules. Instead of this conception of ethics, feminist philosophers like Nel Noddings (1984) conceived of ethics as a fabric of care and responsibility arising out of personal relationships. Building on this "female" approach to ethics, both philosophers and nurses sought to construct a new ethics for nurses based on the concept of care. Jean Watson, a nurse and a prominent proponent of a nursing ethics of care, applies to the nursing situation Noddings's view that an ethics of care "ties us to the people we serve and not to the rules through which we serve them" (Watson 1988: 2).

Bioethics

Perhaps the first "modern" work of bioethics was Joseph Fletcher's *Morals and Medicine*, published in 1954. Fletcher was an American Episcopalian theologian whose controversial "situation ethics" approach to ethical questions had more in common with consequentialist ethics than with traditional Christian views. In keeping with this, he later abandoned his religious belief. Although Fletcher did much to stimulate early discussions of ethical issues in medicine, it was only in the 1960s that bioethics really began to take shape as a field of study. This period was one of important cultural and social changes. The civil rights movement focused attention on issues of justice and inequality; the Cuban missile crisis and the Vietnam War led to a renewed questioning of war and nuclear weapons; and the resurgence of feminism, coupled with the availability of safe abortions and modern contraceptives, raised questions about women's reproductive rights. For much of the late 1960s and early 1970s, university authorities were besieged by students, initially in opposition to the Vietnam War, but later also demanding that their courses be relevant to the larger social issues of the day. These changes had their effect on the practice of philosophy too, sparking a renewed interest in normative and applied ethics. While the prevailing orthodoxy among English-speaking moral philosophers throughout the 1960s was that philosophy deals with the analysis of moral terms rather than with practical issues, this attitude began to shift in the 1970s. Increasingly, moral philosophers began to address themselves to such practical ethical issues as abortion and euthanasia, the ethics of war and of capital punishment, the allocation of scarce medical resources, animal rights, and so on. They frequently dared to question what had not been questioned before. Since some of these issues related to practices in health care and the biological sciences, this movement in philosophy helped to establish bioethics as a critical discipline.

The other major impetus to the growth of the field was the development of new medical technology that threw up questions no one had needed to answer before. One of the first high-profile bioethics issues in the United States shows this clearly. The first machines that could dialyze patients who had suffered kidney failure dramatically saved the lives of patients who would otherwise have been dead in a matter of days; but the machines were very expensive, and there were many more patients who were suffering from renal disease than there were machines. In 1962 the artificial kidney centre in Seattle, Washington, set up a committee to select patients for treatment. Its life-and-death decisions earned it the name of "the God committee," and focused attention on the criteria it used. A study that showed a bias toward people of the same social class and ethnic background as the committee itself eventually led to further discussion about the best way to solve such problems.

Of all the medical breakthroughs of this period, the most widely publicized was the first heart transplant, performed by the South African surgeon Christiaan Barnard in 1967. The patient's death 18 days later did not dampen the spirits of those who hailed a new era of medicine – with its attendant ethical dilemmas. The ability to perform heart transplants was linked to the development of respirators, which had been introduced to hospitals in the 1950s. Respirators could save many lives, but not all those whose hearts kept beating ever recovered any other significant functions. In some cases, their brains had ceased to function altogether. The realization that such patients could be a source of organs for transplantation led to the setting up of the Harvard Brain Death Committee, and to its subsequent recommendation that the absence of all "discernible central nervous system activity" should be "a new criterion for death" (Rothman 1991). The recommendation has subsequently been adopted, with some modifications, almost everywhere.

If the availability of respirators and other powerful life-extending technology raised questions about the time when a patient should be declared dead, it also brought to the forefront questions about the proper limits of employing this technology in attempts to save or prolong a patient's life. While it had generally been accepted that competent patients must not be treated against their will, the situation of incompetent patients was far less clear. This was true not only with regard to patients who had been rendered incompetent by illness, accident, or disease, but also the treatment of seriously disabled or premature newborn infants. The question was simply this: if a patient is unable to say "no," does this mean that his or her life must always be prolonged for as long as possible, even if the patient's prospects are very poor?

In 1973 a leading US medical journal, the *New England Journal of Medicine*, published a study by two pediatricians on the ethical dilemmas they encountered in the special care nursery (Duff and Campbell 1973). The doctors, Raymond Duff and A. G. M. Campbell, did not think that all severely ill or disabled infants should receive life-prolonging treatment. They thought it important to break down "the public and professional silence on a major taboo," and indicated that out of 299 infants in the special-care nursery, 43 had died as a consequence of a non-treatment decision. A central question was whether these non-treatment decisions were morally and legally sound.

Questions about the limits of treatment for those who are unable to decide for themselves were raised not only in the United States but in other countries as well. Australian and British doctors, for example, had begun publishing their views on the selective non-treatment of infants born with spina bifida, and thereby contributed to an ongoing debate about the appropriateness of a "quality of life" or a "sanctity of life" approach in the practice of medicine (Kuhse and Singer 1985).

It was not until 1976 that a landmark US case – that of Karen Ann Quinlan – lent support to the view that doctors had no legal duty to prolong life in all circumstances. Karen Ann Quinlan, who had become comatose in 1975, was attached to a respirator to assist her breathing. Her condition was described as "chronic persistent vegetative state." When the treating doctor refused to honor the family's wishes that Karen be removed from the respirator, the case eventually came before the New Jersey Supreme Court, which decided that life-support could be discontinued without the treating doctor being deemed to have committed an act of unlawful homicide. The case had implications for future thinking about various issues relating to medical end-of-life decisions, such as the moral and legal relevance of the distinction between so-called ordinary and extraordinary means of treatment, the role of parents or guardians in medical end-of-life decisions, the validity or otherwise of a now incompetent patient's previously expressed wishes regarding life-sustaining treatment, and so on.

Important ethical issues had already been raised in the United States with regard to the ethics of human experimentation by writers such as Henry K. Beecher (1966). It had become known that patients at the Jewish Chronic Disease Hospital in Brooklyn had been injected with live cancer cells, without their consent; that, from 1965 to 1971, mentally retarded children at Willowbrook State Hospital in New York had been inoculated with the hepatitis virus; and that a 1930 study aimed at determining the "natural history" of syphilis in untreated black men continued in Tuskegee, Alabama, until the early 1970s.

The public attention directed at these cases led to important changes in the scrutiny that US agencies henceforth directed at medical research. In 1973 the US Congress established the National Commission for the Protection of Human Subjects of Biomedical and Behavioral Research, whose members were charged with the task of drawing up regulations that would protect the rights and interests of subjects of research. While the Commission's role was only temporary, its influence was not. Most of the Commission's recommendations became regulatory law, and one of its reports – the Belmont Report – clearly articulated the ethical principles that should, in the Commission's view, govern research: respect for persons, beneficence, and justice. Subsequently, principles such as these have been influential in bioethics through their incorporation into a widely used bioethics text, now in its sixth edition – *Principles of Biomedical Ethics* (Beauchamp and Childress 2009).

By the end of the 1960s, mounting ethical problems in medicine, research, and the health-care sciences had already led to the establishment in the United States of the first institutions and centers for bioethics. One of the best known of these centers – the Institute of Society, Ethics and the Life Sciences (the Hastings Center) – was founded by Daniel Callahan and Willard Gaylin in 1969, and its publication, the *Hastings Center Report*, was one of the first publications exclusively directed toward the newly emerging discipline of bioethics.

Almost from the beginning, bioethics was an interdisciplinary enterprise. While ethics had been the near-exclusive domain of moral philosophers and religious thinkers, bioethics crossed the boundaries not only of medicine, nursing, and the biomedical sciences, but of law, economics, and public policy as well. Bioethics in this broad, interdisciplinary sense has since become firmly established as a field of inquiry and of learning – first in the United States, and since then in many other countries as well. It is now taught at universities at both undergraduate and postgraduate levels, and many nursing and medical schools regard bioethics as an integral part of their curriculum. Today there are many bioethics research centers throughout the world, and bioethicists are often consulted by government commissions, law reform bodies, and professional organizations. Many countries have their own national bioethics associations and the International Association of Bioethics (IAB) links bioethicists from all parts of the world. A number of highly regarded scholarly bioethics journals emanate from different continents, and international congresses on bioethics are now a frequent phenomenon. In short, while bioethics had its beginning in the United States, it is now a global field of inquiry.

Bioethics is now also becoming more global in its focus. As Michael Selgelid points out in his contribution to this volume (chapter 36), 90 percent of medical research resources are spent on diseases that account for only 10 percent of the global burden of disease – the diseases that people in rich countries are likely to suffer from. This is in part because pharmaceutical corporations have no incentive to develop drugs to treat people who will not be able to afford to buy them, and in part because the government research funds of rich nations are also mostly directed toward finding treatments for the diseases that afflict the citizens of those nations. There is, therefore, comparatively little research into finding treatments for the diseases from which people in poorer nations are likely to suffer. That fact itself, of course, poses an ethical question – do the people of the rich nations, through their governments or through private philanthropy, have an obligation to reverse this imbalance? Bill and Melinda Gates clearly believe there is. The website of the Gates Foundation says that one of their key values is "All lives – no matter where they are being led – have equal value" and the research they are funding is directed against diseases like malaria, which kill millions of people every year, virtually all in developing countries.

But there has also been a 10/90 problem in bioethics itself – in fact, until the 1990s, probably much less than 10 percent of the work of bioethicists was focused on bioethical issues raised by 90 percent of the global burden of disease. This is now changing. *Developing World Bioethics*, a journal devoted to bioethical issues relating to the developing world, is one example of this change. The IAB has made a deliberate effort to encourage bioethics in developing countries. As discussed elsewhere in this volume, much more attention is being paid to bioethical issues raised by infectious diseases, including, but not limited to, HIV/AIDS. In this revised edition, we have also increased the number of articles dealing with global bioethical issues and issues that particularly face developing countries. It remains true, unfortunately, that the majority of articles dealing with specific issues focus on bioethical issues in affluent countries. That reflects the state of the field today – although it is moving in the right direction, as far as increasing its focus on problems outside affluent nations is concerned, it is moving slowly and there are still very few people working in bioethics in developing countries, and writing about the issues those countries face.

References

Beauchamp, T. L. and Childress, J. F. (2009) [1979]. *Principles of Biomedical Ethics*, 6th edn. New York: Oxford University Press.

Beecher, H. K. (1966). Ethical and clinical research. *New England Journal of Medicine* 274: 1354–60.

Dock, S. (1917). The relation of the nurse to the doctor and the doctor to the nurse. *American Journal of Nursing* 17.

Duff, R. S. and Campbell, A. G. M. (1973). Moral and ethical problems in the special-care nursery. *New England Journal of Medicine* 279: 890–4.

Edelstein, L. (1967). The Hippocratic Oath: text, translation and interpretation. In O. Temkin and C. L. Temkin (eds.), *Ancient Medicine: Selected Papers of Ludwig Edelstein*. Baltimore, MD: Johns Hopkins Press, pp. 3–63.

Etziony, M. B. (1973). *The Physician's Creed: An Anthology of Medical Prayers, Oaths, and Codes of Ethics Written by Medical Practitioners Throughout the Ages*. Springfield, IL: Charles C. Thomas.

Fletcher, J. (1954). *Morals and Medicine: The Moral Problems of the Patient's Right to Know the Truth, Contraception, Artificial Insemination, Sterilization, Euthanasia*. Boston: Beacon.

Gregory, J. (1817). *Lectures and Duties on the Qualifications of a Physician*. Philadelphia: M. Carey.

Jones, W. H. S. (1924). *The Doctor's Oath: An Essay in the History of Medicine*. New York: Cambridge University Press.

Kuhse, H. and Singer, P. (1985). *Should the Baby Live? The Problem of Handicapped Infants*. Oxford: Oxford University Press.

MacKinney, L. C. (1952). Medical ethics and etiquette in the early Middle Ages: the persistence of Hippocratic ideals. *Bulletin of the History of Medicine* 26: 1–31.

Noddings, N. (1984). *Caring: A Feminine Approach to Ethics and Moral Education*. Berkeley: University of California Press.

Potter, V. R. (1970). Bioethics, science of survival. *Biology and Medicine* 14: 127–53.

Pritchard, J. B. (1969). *Ancient Near Eastern Texts Relating to the Old Testament*, 3rd edn. Princeton, NJ: Princeton University Press.

Reich, W. T. (ed.) (1995). *Encyclopedia of Bioethics*. London: Simon & Schuster and Prentice Hall International.

Robb, I. H. Hampton (1901). *Nursing Ethics for Hospitals and Private Use*. Cleveland, OH: J. B. Savage.

Rothman, D. (1991). *Strangers at the Bedside*. New York: Basic Books.

Veatch, R. M. (1989). *Medical Ethics*. Boston: Jones and Bartlett.

Watson, J. (1988). Introduction: an ethic of caring/curing/nursing *qua* nursing. In J. Watson and M. A. Ray (eds.), *The Ethics of Care and the Ethics of Cure: Synthesis in Chronicity*. New York: National League for Nursing.

Part II

Questions About Bioethics

2

Ethical Theory and Bioethics

JAMES RACHELS

What is the relation between bioethics and ethical theory? Since bioethics deals with the moral issues that come up in particular cases, and ethical theory deals with the standards and principles of moral reasoning, it is natural to think the relation between them might be something like this:

> *The straightforward-application model.* The ethical theory is the starting-point, and we apply the theory to the case at hand in order to reach a conclusion about what should be done.

Utilitarianism is the leading example of an ethical theory that might be thought to solve bioethical problems by the straightforward application of its ideas. Utilitarianism says that in any situation we should do what will have the best overall consequences for everyone concerned. If this is our theory, and we want to decide what should be done in a particular case, we simply calculate the likely effects of various actions and choose the one that produces the greatest benefit for the greatest number of people.

But many bioethicists reject this model. In the first place, anyone who approaches an ethical problem by announcing "I hold such-and-such a theory; therefore my conclusion is so-and-so" will be unlikely to get much of a hearing. We want to know what really is best, not just what this or that theory says. Moreover, many investigators doubt that there can be a satisfactory ethical theory of the kind that philosophers have traditionally sought, because, they say, morality cannot be codified in a set of rules. Instead, living morally is a matter of cultivating virtuous habits of action, including, perhaps, the kind of "caring" behavior that some feminist writers have argued is central (see chapter 11, "A Care Approach"). And in any case, it is said, bioethical controversies are too complicated to be resolved by the simple application of a theory. Theories are general and abstract, while real life is messy and detailed.

If we reject the straightforward-application model, where do we turn for an alternative? One of the most popular options is an approach that focuses on "case studies" – detailed investigations of specific cases that make use of whatever analytical ideas and principles seem most promising in the circumstances at hand. The case-study approach suggests a different conception of the relation between ethical theory and bioethics:

The physics/car-mechanic model. The relation between ethical theory and bioethics is like the relation between physics and automobile repair. Cars operate according to the laws of physics, to be sure; but one doesn't have to know physics to be a good mechanic, and one certainly does not "apply" the laws of physics to fix cars. The mechanic's reasoning does not begin with "For every action, there is an equal and opposite reaction." Instead, it begins with something like: "The problem is either electrical or fuel-related. If it's electrical . . ."

So, like the car mechanic, the bioethicist will rely on mid-level principles, ignoring the lofty but unhelpful pronouncements of high-level theory.

Case Studies and Mid-level Principles

At first blush, the case-study approach seems to permit bioethicists to make progress without resorting to ethical theory. But this turns out to be an illusion. In ethics, theoretical issues crop up everywhere. Deciding about abortion requires that we think about the nature of persons; the allocation of health-care resources raises questions of distributive justice; and arguments about euthanasia make critical assumptions about the meaning and value of human life. Without the resources of ethical theory, we could make little progress in dealing with such matters. It is also an illusion to think that mid-level principles can, by themselves, yield definitive answers to ethical questions.

Consider the case of Theresa Ann Campo Pearson, an anencephalic infant known as "Baby Theresa," who was born in Florida in 1992. There are about 1,000 such infants – babies without brains – born each year in the United States, so Baby Theresa's story would not have been newsworthy except for an unusual request by her parents. Knowing that their baby could not live long and that, even if she could, she would never have a conscious life, Baby Theresa's parents volunteered her organs for transplant. They thought her kidneys, liver, heart, lungs, and eyes should go to other children who could benefit from them. The physicians believed this was a good idea, but Florida law would not allow it. So after nine days Baby Theresa died, and by then her organs had deteriorated too much to be transplanted. Other children died as well – the ones who would have received the transplants – but because we do not know which children they were, we tend not to think of their deaths as real costs of the decision.

The newspaper stories about Baby Theresa prompted a great deal of public discussion. Would it have been right to remove the infant's organs, thereby causing her immediate death, to save the other children? A number of professional bioethicists joined the debate, but surprisingly few of them agreed with the parents and physicians. Instead they appealed to various principles to support letting all the children die. "It just seems too horrifying to use people as means to other people's ends," said one expert. Another explained, "It is unethical to kill in order to save. It's unethical to kill person A to save person B." And a third added: "What the parents are really asking for is: kill this dying baby so that its organs may be used for someone else. Well, that's really a horrendous proposition."

Here we see mid-level principles at work (see chapter 7, "A Principle-based Approach"). ("It is unethical to kill in order to save" is a typical mid-level principle.)

Compared to the abstract pronouncements of ethical theory, mid-level principles are much more like everyday moral rules. They express our commonsense understanding of right and wrong. Therefore, it may be argued, we can have greater confidence in decisions that are supported by widely shared mid-level principles than decisions based on general theories, which are more remote from everyday life and inevitably more controversial.

Of course, these principles are called "mid-level" because they are derived from, or justified by, higher-level principles. So aren't we just ignoring an important part of the picture if we are content with only the mid-level rules? To this there are two replies. First, it may be maintained that mid-level principles are not derived from higher considerations. They may be viewed as a collection of independent moral principles each of which is valid in itself. (Someone taking this view might like the sort of general ethical theory championed by W. D. Ross in the 1930s.) The problem, however, is that within this approach one has no way of adjudicating conflicts between the independent rules. Suppose a different bioethicist, looking at the case of Baby Theresa, felt that the mid-level rule "save as many children as possible" has priority? Or suppose she favored the rule "saving the life of a child with the potential for a satisfying human life is more important than respecting the life of a child without a brain?" Then, of course, the conclusion would be that Theresa's organs should be taken. So the mid-level rules alone cannot provide a definitive answer to the question of what we should do.

Second, and more interesting, it could be pointed out that the same mid-level rules may be endorsed by *more than one* higher-level principle. Kantians, for example, take it as an ultimate principle that people should always be treated as ends in themselves; so they would naturally insist that "It is wrong to kill person A to save person B." But utilitarians might also endorse this mid-level principle. They might see it as a useful rule of thumb because following it will have generally good consequences, just as following other familiar rules – don't lie, don't steal, and so on – have generally good consequences. Thus these theorists may arrive at the same mid-level rules, despite their different starting-points. If so, we do not need to worry about which starting-point is correct. On the contrary, our confidence in the mid-level principle is increased by the fact that many outlooks endorse it.

Once again, however, a problem arises about how to adjudicate conflicts. Both Kantians and utilitarians would also endorse, as a mid-level rule, that we should save as many children as possible. But when there is a conflict, they might have different recommendations about which mid-level rule should be given priority. By establishing priorities, each theory gives an answer to the question of what should be done. But if they ultimately lead to different answers, we cannot avoid the larger issue of which theory is correct.

Of course, the failure to reach a definite conclusion need not be regarded as a defect. There is a way to avoid choosing between theories: when different lines of reasoning lead to different outcomes, we can conclude that we are faced with an unresolvable dilemma. This may appeal to those who dislike appearing dogmatic. "Not all dilemmas have easy solutions," it may be said, and the doctors and scientists may be left to fend for themselves, with the bioethicist wishing them good luck. According to taste, this may be considered a realistic acknowledgment of the complexity of an issue or a failure of nerve.

The following episode illustrates an additional way in which ethical theory can aid in the analysis of particular cases. In 1995 an international medical team fought an outbreak of ebola – a devastating virus that destroys cells and causes disintegration of the internal organs as it spreads throughout the body – in Kikwit, Zaire, in which 244 people died. As the epidemic was winding down, a nurse who had worked throughout the crisis was stricken, and the Zairian doctors formulated a desperate plan to save her. This particular strain of ebola did not kill everyone who became infected; one in five victims survived. So the Zairian physicians proposed to save the nurse by transfusing whole blood from one of the survivors, in the hope that whatever antibodies had saved him would be transferred to her.

The foreign doctors adamantly opposed this plan. The donor blood might contain HIV, or hepatitis, or some other harmful agent, they said. And suppose the diagnosis is mistaken – what if she only has malaria or typhoid? By transfusing the blood we might actually be giving her ebola, not curing her of it. Besides, in a similar procedure using animals, the treatment had failed.

The Zairian physicians met privately to discuss these objections. They dismissed the worries about giving the nurse HIV or typhoid; after all, she already had ebola. As for the possibility that the diagnosis was mistaken, this was also dismissed. "We shouldn't doubt our diagnosis," said one doctor, "we've seen so many cases." They concluded that, although their chances of helping the nurse in this way were slight, it was better than nothing.

With the nurse's consent, the transfusion was given, and she recovered. Eight more patients were then given similar transfusions, and seven of them also recovered. These were the last cases in the epidemic. The foreign doctors did not, however, concede that the treatment had worked. "We'll never know," said a physician from the Centers for Disease Control in Atlanta. Other possible explanations for the recoveries were offered – late in the epidemic the virus may have become less deadly, or people may have been getting smaller viral loads when infected.

At first glance, it seems that there was little difference in principle between the views of the Zairian physicians and the foreigners. Both groups were concerned, in a straightforward way, with the welfare of the patients: they merely differed about what strategy would stand the best chance of accomplishing their common goal. Yet, on reflection, we can detect a subtle difference between them. The difference concerned their respective attitudes about action versus inaction. In explaining their unanimous decision to proceed with the transfusion, the head of the Zairian team said "We felt compelled to try *something*." And before the procedure was undertaken, he challenged the European and American physicians: "Tell us if there is something else we can do, and we'll do it." The one thing not acceptable to them was to do nothing: they couldn't just let the nurse die.

The foreigners, by contrast, were more conservative. When in doubt, their preference was not to act, but to wait and see what would happen. The traditional first principle of medical ethics is "Do no harm," and the foreign doctors seem to have been strongly motivated by this thought. It is as though they were thinking: *it is worse to cause harm than merely to allow it to happen.* Or perhaps: *one bears greater responsibility for the consequences of one's actions than for the consequences of one's inactions.* The question of who was right, the Zairians or the foreigners, is partly a question about the soundness of these mid-level principles.

A benefit of doing case studies is that they help us to identify the intuitive principles that influence people. Once exposed, such principles may be subjected to critical examination. Are they, in fact, sound? In practice, however, the critical examination is often skipped, and it is assumed that any principle that seems intuitively plausible is a "relevant factor" to be taken into account in analyzing issues. The chief danger of the case-studies approach is that it can degenerate into nothing more than a systematic description of what people happen to believe.

The mid-level principles we have mentioned – that we may not kill one person in order to save another, that we should save as many as possible, and that it is worse to cause harm than to allow it to happen – are among the items often found in the bioethicist's kit-bag. Here is a small sample of additional principles that might be invoked as case studies are pursued:

- that people are moral equals – that no one's welfare is more important than anyone else's;
- that personal autonomy, the freedom of each individual to control his or her own life, is especially important;
- that people should always be treated as ends in themselves, and never as mere means;
- that personal relationships, especially kinship, confer upon people special rights and responsibilities with regard to other people;
- that a person's intention, in performing a given action, is relevant to determining whether the action is right;
- that we may not do evil that good may come; and
- that what is "natural" is good and what is "unnatural" is bad.

Obviously, different bioethicists will be attracted to different combinations of these ideas; each investigator will accept some of them and reject others. But on what grounds will they be accepted or rejected? Once again, it is an argument for the relevance of ethical theory that a well-supported theory would provide principled evidence or argument concerning which of these are worthy of acceptance and which are not. Each item on this list can be rationally assessed; it need not be judged simply on its intuitive appeal. But such assessments quickly take one into the more abstract matters of ethical theory.

Justifying the Choice of an Ethical Theory

There are other reasons why bioethicists have doubted the value of ethical theory. Some doubts are prompted by the number of theories available. It is not as though there were only one theory on which everyone agrees. Instead, there are numerous theories that conflict with one another. Confronted with such an array, what is the bioethicist to do? Is there any principled way to choose between the competing theories? Or is the choice merely arbitrary?

This issue was raised in the eighteenth century by David Hume, who argued that morals are ultimately based on "sentiment, not reason." Hume knew that moral judgments require reasons in their support, but he pointed out that every chain of reasoning leads back to some first principle that is unjustified. If we ask for a justification

19

of that principle, perhaps one can be given, but only by appealing to still another unjustified assumption, and so on forever. We can never justify all our assumptions; reasoning must begin somewhere. A utilitarian might begin by assuming that what is important is maximizing welfare. Someone else, with a different cast of mind, might make a different assumption. But reason alone cannot justify the choice of one starting-point over another.

Hume is not the only philosopher who has objected to exaggerated claims about what unaided reason can accomplish. A more recent critic, Alasdair MacIntyre, advances a different sort of objection. MacIntyre argues that "rationality" has meaning only within a historical tradition. The idea of impartial reason justifying norms of conduct binding on all people is, he says, an illusion fostered by the Enlightenment. In reality, historical traditions set standards of inquiry for those working within them. But the standards of rational thinking differ from tradition to tradition, and so we cannot speak of "what reason requires" in any universal sense. In his *Whose Justice? Which Rationality?* MacIntyre writes:

> What the enlightenment made us for the most part blind to and what we now need to recover is . . . a conception of rational inquiry as embodied in a tradition; a conception according to which the standards of rational justification themselves emerge from and are part of a history in which they are vindicated by the way in which they transcend the limitations of and provide remedies for the defects of their predecessors within the history of that same tradition. (1988: 6–7)

Thus, in MacIntyre's view, the reasons that would be adduced by a modern liberal in arguing, say, that slavery is unjust, would not necessarily be acceptable to an Aristotelian, whose standards of rationality are different; and the search for standards that transcend the two traditions is a fool's quest. No such tradition-neutral standards exist, except, perhaps, for purely formal principles such as non-contradiction, which are too weak to yield substantive results.

What are we to make of all this? If these arguments are correct, then no ethical theory can be anything more than an expression of the theorist's sentiments or the historical tradition he or she represents. But before we accept such discouraging conclusions, there are some additional points that should be kept in mind.

First, even if "reason alone" cannot determine what ultimate principles we should accept, this does not mean the choice must be arbitrary. There are numerous constraints on what principles we may choose, and these constraints provide grounds for hoping that reasonable people will be able to reach agreement. All people have the same basic needs – food, warmth, friendship, protection from danger, meaningful work, to name only a few. We all suffer pain and we are all susceptible to disease. All of us are products of the same evolutionary forces, which have made us at least partially altruistic beings. And we are social animals who live in communities, so we must accept the rules that are necessary for social living. Together, these facts, and others like them, impose striking limits on what sort of principles it is rational for us to accept.

Second, it may be true, as MacIntyre says, that the standards of rational thinking differ from one historical tradition to another. But this does not mean that traditions are immune from criticism. Some moral traditions depend on theological assumptions that are inconsistent or arbitrary. Others make assumptions about the nature of the world that are at odds with what we have learned from modern science. Still others are based on untenable views about human nature. Thus there is no need to assume that all traditions are equal. At the very least, those that do not depend on what Hume called "superstition and false religion" are preferable to those that do.

Bearing these points in mind, we might be a little more optimistic about what reason can accomplish. We might hope to discover ethical arguments that appeal to rational people generally and not just to some subset of people who have agreeable sentiments or form part of an agreeable tradition. But abstract considerations will take us only so far; the real proof that such arguments are possible is to display one. A test case might be slavery, which, as we have noted, is condemned by modern liberal culture but accepted within other traditions. Is there an argument against slavery that must be acknowledged by every reasonable person, regardless of the tradition of which he or she is a part?

The primary argument against slavery is this: all forms of slavery involve treating some people differently from the rest, depriving them of liberty and subjecting them to a host of evils. But it is unjust to set some people apart for different treatment unless there is something about them that justifies setting them apart – unless, that is, there is a *relevant difference* between them and the others. But there are no such differences between humans that could justify setting some of them apart as slaves; therefore slavery is unjust.

Should this argument be compelling, not only to modern liberals, but to those who live in different sorts of societies, with different sorts of traditions? Consider a slave society such as Aristotle's Athens. According to one estimate, there were as many slaves in Athens, in proportion to the population, as there were in the slave states of America before the civil war. Aristotle himself defended slavery, arguing that some people are "slaves by nature" because of their inferior rationality. Yet the resources available within Aristotle's own tradition seem to have been sufficient for an appreciation of slavery's injustice. Aristotle reports that "some regard the control of a slave by a master as contrary to nature. In their view the distinction of master and slave is due to law or convention; there is no natural difference between them: the relation of master and slave is based on force, and being so based has no warrant in justice" (1253b21).

Aristotle did not share this enlightened view. Plainly, though, he accepted the principle that differences in treatment are unjustified unless there are relevant differences between people. In fact, this is just a modern version of an idea that he advances in the *Nicomachean Ethics*, namely that like cases should be treated alike and different cases differently. That is why he felt it necessary to defend slavery by contending that slaves possess an inferior degree of rationality. But this is a claim that can be shown to be false by evidence that should be counted as evidence as much by him as by us. Therefore, even on Aristotle's own terms, slavery should be recognizable as unjust. And in saying this we are not simply transporting our standards of rationality back into a culture that was "different."

Perhaps, then, we may hope for an ethical theory that will specify norms acceptable to all reasonable people. Justifying such a theory, however, will not be easy. (But then, why should it be? Why should justifying a general theory in ethics be easier than justifying a general theory in, say, physics or psychology?) The process will include assessing our intuitions about particular cases; looking at a host of arguments about individual behavior and social policy; identifying and evaluating mid-level principles; bringing to bear what we know about human nature and human social systems; considering the claims of religion; and then trying to fit it all together in one unified scheme of understanding. If there is indeed one best overall ethical theory, it is likely to appear as many lines of inquiry converge. The fact that there is still so much disagreement among ethical theorists may be due not to the impossibility of the project but to its complexity, and to the fact that secular ethical theory is still a young subject.

What does this mean for the question with which we started, about the relation between ethical theory and bioethics? We have seen that the physics/car-repair model won't do, because case studies cannot be conducted independently of theoretical concerns. We are now in a position to appreciate more fully why the simple-application model won't do either. It is not that ethical theory is useless, or that real life is too messy and complicated to be approached using its tools. Rather, it is that the simple-application model represents the relation between ethical theory and bioethics as a one-way affair. In reality, however, bioethics contributes to ethical theory as well as benefiting from it. In studying cases and identifying and analyzing mid-level principles, bioethicists are pursuing one of the many lines of inquiry that contribute to the development of ethical theory. In this sense, bioethics is part of ethical theory. One flows into the other.

Considering all this, we might try a different analogy that provides a more satisfactory way of understanding the relation between ethical theory and bioethics.

The biology/medicine model. The relation between ethical theory and bioethics is like the relation between biology and medicine. A physician who knew nothing of biology, but who approached her patients in the spirit of a car mechanic with a kit-bag of practical techniques, might do a generally serviceable job. But she would not be as good as the physician who did know the relevant sciences. The difference would come out when new or tricky problems arose, requiring more than the rote application of already familiar techniques. To deal with the difficult problems, she might find herself turning to scientific researchers for help, or even turning temporarily to more fundamental research herself. And what she learns from the cases she encounters in her practice might, in turn, have significance for the further development of the sciences.

At its best, bioethics does not operate independently of ethical theory; but neither does it proceed by simply "applying" a theory to particular cases. Instead there is an interplay between theory and case study that benefits both.

References

Aristotle (1946). *The Politics*, trans. Ernest Barker. London: Oxford University Press.
Briggs, D. (1992). Baby Theresa case raises ethics questions. *Champaign-Urbana News Gazette*, March 31: A6.
Halpern, E. and Jacobovici, S. (1966). Plague fighters. *Nova* (Public Broadcasting System), February 6.

Hume, D. (1751). *An Inquiry Concerning the Principles of Morals*, Appendix I.
MacIntyre, A. (1988). *Whose Justice? Which Rationality?* Notre Dame, IN: University of Notre Dame Press.
Ross, W. D. (1930). *The Right and the Good.* Oxford: Oxford University Press.

Further reading

Beauchamp, T. L. and Childress, J. F. (2009 [1979]). *Principles of Biomedical Ethics*, 6th edn. New York: Oxford University Press.
Brody, B. A. (ed.) (1988). *Moral Theory and Moral Judgments in Medical Ethics*. Dordrecht: Kluwer.
Jonsen, A. R. and Toulmin, S. (1988). *The Abuse of Casuistry: A History of Moral Reasoning.* Berkeley: University of California Press.
Various authors (1995). Theories and methods in bioethics: principlism and its critics. *Kennedy Institute of Ethics Journal* 5 (September).

3

Culture and Bioethics

SEGUN GBADEGESIN

What *Is* Culture?

We may identify two senses of culture. In one sense, culture is the activity of cultivating or tending nature, which is supposedly its raw material. Humans need this activity of tending or cultivating in order to move beyond the limitations imposed by nature. This is the sense in which we talk of a cultured person. It is this sense of culture that Alain Locke focuses our attention on when he declares that, "the highest intellectual duty is the duty to be cultured" (Locke 1989: 176). Elaborating further, Locke observes that culture is "the capacity for understanding the best and most representative forms of human expression, and of expressing oneself, if not in similar creativeness, at least in appreciative reactions and in progressively responsive refinement of tastes and interests" (Locke 1989: 177). A cultured person is a refined person, who has been worked upon by culture and so to some extent liberated from nature. Here, culture takes the sense of civilization: to be cultured is to be civilized.

In a second sense, popularized by E. B. Tylor, culture is the complex of values, customs, beliefs, and practices which constitute the way of life of a specific group of people. For Tylor, this complex includes "knowledge, belief, art, morals, law, custom, and any other capabilities and habits acquired by man as a member of society" (1958: 1; see also Eagleton 2000: 34). Terry Eagleton reminds us that this sense of the concept is traceable to Herder and the German Idealists. While the first sense of culture is identified with the Enlightenment in which culture has some appeal to universalism, in the Herderian sense, culture "means not some grand, unilinear narrative of universal humanity, but a diversity of specific life-forms, each with its own peculiar laws of evolution" (Eagleton 2000: 12).

Of course, the Herderian sense of culture as a way of living is a revolt against the Enlightenment sense of culture as civilization, a revolt against the notion that the European ideals of civility can be transported to the whole world. As Eagleton puts it, "[Herder] is out to oppose the Eurocentrism of culture-as-universal-civilization with the claims of those 'of all the quarters of the globe' who have not lived and perished for the dubious honor of having their posterity made happy by a speciously superior European culture" (Eagleton 2000: 12).

24

Culture in the Herderian sense is primitive, organic, and authentic. This concept of culture is sympathetic to treating all cultures as equal. For if there is no basis for evaluating ways of living as superior or inferior, good or bad, it follows that any hierarchy of cultures is unfounded. It would also follow that there is no justification for elevating one culture over another, and giving it greater moral weight. It is easy to see that this position elides a problem. The assertion that no way of living can be shown to be better or worse than any other fails to consider that there are tensions between ways of living: consider the life of the slave master versus the life of the enslaved. If every way of living is good to its practitioner, can it be equally good to all, including its victims? In what follows, I will address this question with regard to the intersection of culture and bioethics. Using the Herder–Tylor sense of culture as my point of departure, I raise the question whether or not, in spite of the multiplicity of cultures, there cannot be a universal foundation for bioethics.

Bioethics Today: Present Realities

In the autumn of 1994, I had an interesting experience in my Health Care Ethics Discussion Group at the Howard University College of Medicine. The course had about 300 students from all health-related disciplines. Faculty members were drawn from various disciplines, with groups of two or three faculty to handle 12–15 students in discussion sections after a 30-minute lecture. On this particular day, the discussion was on "suicide and the refusal of life-sustaining treatment." To initiate the discussion, I asked the question: "What, if anything, is wrong with suicide, and what will you do if you are confronted with a case of a suicidal patient?" The discussion was lively, with the majority of the students insisting on appealing to the principle of autonomy, and ensuring that the decision of the patient was rational and well informed. However, one of the students, a middle-aged woman, insisted on the rightness of an appeal to the "principle of paternalism," arguing that, in her view, a community that allows suicide cannot survive and that human beings are not just atoms in the void, they are anchored in a system of relations. It took some persuasive reasoning to get her to accept that the principle of paternalism to which she appealed, and the reason she was giving (communal survival), were quite distinct. The appeal to the principle of paternalism would reject the wishes or desires of the patient on account of what it considers the best interest of the patient. So in our case, the paternalist, unconvinced about the rationality of the patient's decision to refuse life-sustaining treatment, would reject her wishes as not being in her best interests. The important point here is that the reason or justification has to do with the patient's best interest, which is determined to be at variance with the patient's current wishes and desires. It has nothing to do with the survival of the community, which was the reason that the woman gave: no society would survive if it allows suicide.

The woman protested angrily against what she considered to be a collaborated attempt by the rest of the group to discredit her position. She thought that the group was promoting a Western liberal perspective, whereas she came from a society which placed a high value on community and that, being a Muslim from the Middle East, her religious morality was at variance with liberal individualism. It was clear to me then

25

that her objection to the principle of autonomy as the basis for resolving the case of the patient was grounded in her religion. But it is relevant here because, according to the working definition of culture that I have adopted from Tylor, religion is a component of culture. The woman was upset, maintaining that the other students were intolerant of her views and that each time she made a contribution they were ready to attack her. I intervened to assure her that the other students were not attacking her personally, but that we were all engaged in a philosophical exploration of the issues. She was not convinced.

At the end of the period, the woman approached me with the same complaint. She told me that, though she was originally a Muslim from the Middle East, she has become an American in every other respect, being married to a white American with children. She thought that the students were attacking her position on the basis of their assumption that she did not understand American culture and morality. Her defense against this alleged assumption was that she was herself American by marriage and citizenship. Now the fact that this woman is also an American (and her story resonates with millions of Americans who share common citizenship but different cultural traditions) shows that intercultural disagreements are part of the fabric of American bioethics in particular and, by extension, Western bioethics in general. In other words, the idea that bioethics provides a neat demarcation between Western and non-Western cultures, while preserving a uniform Western cultural approach, is challenged by such an incident as this. Therefore, the issue of the intersection of culture and bioethics, while it has been discussed by reference to non-Western versus Western cultures, is more general and more complex. Yet, mythical as the idea of a single distinctive non-Western culture vis-à-vis a unique Western culture is, there is no denying the fact that this perception is, for many, a reality.

Bioethics is seen by many people from non-Western cultures as a Western phenomenon. This perception is not limited to general populations with traditional orientations; some scholars are also suspicious of the narrow cultural foundations and directions of contemporary bioethics. Enrico Chiavacci has suggested that, "each people and each culture finds its own dignity within its own cultural identity," and that "cultural identities, if properly respected and understood, can offer new richness of thought to the whole human family" (1992: 99). Cultural pluralism casts a shadow over the idea of a purely rational, and therefore universal, ethics. Recognizing, as Edmund Pellegrino (1992: 191) does, that culture and ethics "are inextricably bound to each other," is not enough to clear that shadow.

Here is another anecdote. I once wrote an article on "The ethics of polygyny" in which I argued that the principles of "respect for persons," "fairness," and "interest" should be applied to judging the morality of polygyny in its various manifestations, and I cautioned against an absolute justification or condemnation of the practice. To my surprise, one of the anonymous readers of the paper for a specialized journal to which I had sent it disagreed with my basic framework on the ground that I was applying a Western philosophical paradigm to assess a non-Western practice. In other words, I was charged with the crime of imposing a Western moral view on an African cultural practice. Naturally, I am sensitive to this kind of allegation. I am a Yoruba who relocated to the United States in the late 1980s, after having studied in Wisconsin during the previous decade. I lived in Yorubaland for more than 45 years and fully imbibed its culture. My father was a polygamist because my mother, his first wife, had only one child. My father wanted more children, and therefore married a second, and then a third and then a fourth wife. And while he tried to make it work, it was not easy. Therefore in the published version of the paper, I defended my position. Since I believe that my response in that article is relevant to what I will argue here, I would like to quote from that paper:

> Clearly, these principles [respect for persons, fairness, and interest] rely on a Western framework and the question is whether such a framework is in fact adequate for evaluating the institutions and practices of other cultures. African institutions, for instance, it may be argued, ought to be evaluated by African moral standards . . . I sympathize with this point of view. . . . However, it is very easy to carry the objection too far in this area. It is possible to assume, for instance, that the principles we have discussed thus far, do not feature at all in traditional African moral discourse. But this would be exaggerating cultural differences beyond reason. Traditional Africans – men and women – had their own misunderstandings. The communal structure of society does not guarantee a completely harmonious relationship. People, as human beings, occasionally fight. Elders are called upon to resolve disputes, either between husband and wife or between co-wives or between brothers. On such occasions, the elders listen carefully to all sides of the dispute and then, thoughtfully, they point out the faults on the part of each of the parties to the dispute by appealing to the appropriate moral standards. They say, for instance, "my son, what you have done is wrong because you treat your wife badly. Don't you realize that she has feelings? What do you think her family will think of us?" In other words, the elders appeal to considerations that give meaning to the principles of interest, fairness and respect. It would therefore be wrong to suggest that these principles are exclusively Western. True, they are formulated by Western philosophers in their philosophical discourse, but they are also universally recognized principles applicable to interpersonal relationships. (Gbadegesin 1993: 13–14)

The problem we face with regard to the present reality of bioethics does not appear to me to be insurmountable. There is the perception that bioethics is a Western, liberal-individualist, empiricist ethos, as Pellegrino (1992) puts it. There seems to be a conflict between focus on what is of concern to the West with its technological breakthroughs, and what is of interest to non-Western cultures. There is a need to resolve these apparent conflicts, and this is the challenge of transcultural bioethics: underscoring the universality of bioethics without undermining the significance of cultural identities.

The Universality of Bioethics

Every culture *must* develop a response to the new technologies in health-care systems. This response may be a rejection or an acceptance of these technologies with their consequences. This rejection or acceptance may be based on traditional norms or on a modification of those norms in the face of the requirements of the new technologies. To suggest that bioethics is universal is simply to point to the universality of this imperative. The technology may be as simple as a vaccine against smallpox or as complex as that of organ transplantation. What choice to make in such contexts becomes a moral issue, since human interests are at stake. Therefore issues raised in bioethics are universal issues. This is not the problem; the universality of the question is not denied. It is the universality of the answers that is challenged, and this may be at three levels: the level of principle, the level of rules, and the level of practice.

At the level of principle there are challenges to the universal validity of the principles of autonomy, individualism, and secularism. These principles, which are generally regarded as being at the heart of Western bioethics, have been challenged at several points by non-Western cultures still proud of their communal relations and spiritualistic ethos. It is not that the concept of autonomy is totally alien to non-Western cultures; only that while the West emphasizes individual autonomy, non-Western cultures place greater stress on cultural, communal, or family autonomy. Thus, for example, the decision as to the choice of medical procedure is frequently left to the family, not the individual. But as we have seen earlier, there is also a pluralism of cultures in Western societies, and quite a good number of such cultures also emphasize family or communal autonomy. African American families living in the rural south of the United States are a good example. It is also true of some Mediterranean cultures.

At the level of rules, the rationality of a procedure or belief is differently conceived, and derives from what principles and values are upheld as sound. The Yoruba accident victim, who objects to amputation of both legs on the ground that it is better to die than to live without legs, may be operating on the principle that "death is better than (a perceived) loss of dignity." This would make sense in a culture in which such a principle is widely accepted.

Finally, on the level of practice, there are challenges to the Western focus on high-profile biomedical technology which seems to be the driving force of bioethics in the West. This is simply a matter of aiming one's theoretical focus on society's most pressing practical issues. Non-Western cultures are pressed by the prevalence of poverty-generated diseases, and the shortage of health-care facilities. Therefore, issues of justice in the allocation of basic health-care resources, and a focus on primary health care and preventative medicine, seem more important than consideration of the ethics of when to discontinue life-support systems or how to allocate organs for transplantation.

The Challenge of Transcultural Bioethics

If the above analysis is correct, and we may speak of differences at the levels of principles, rules, and practice, it would seem that we have located the challenge these differences pose for transcultural bioethics; that is, for the derivation of bioethical principles and practices that are applicable to all human cultures. The idea of transcultural bioethics in this sense is anchored in the desirability and possibility of universal standards in bioethics. The rationale for moving towards a transcultural bioethics in the sense explained seems clear: bioethical issues arise in and for all cultures because health-care issues which provide the raw material for bioethics are universal. The differences between cultures are in regard to the resources available for dealing with the health-care issues in different cultural settings, as well as the understanding of those issues in different cultures. In order to facilitate understanding, and to get around the challenge of differences in resources plus cultural diversity, there have to be genuine efforts on the part of bioethicists to cross cultural boundaries for the purpose of understanding the outlook and challenges of each culture. This facilitation of understanding across cultures is a prerequisite for the development of principles that truly embrace all cultures and thus make possible the establishment of transcultural bioethics. The question remains though: what are the conditions for the possibility of transcultural bioethics and how, if at all, is it different from bioethics today?

We have suggested that bioethical issues and questions cut across cultures, though the answers – principles, rules, and practice – vary from culture to culture. The challenge to the development of transcultural bioethics would seem to be posed at the level of principles, rules, and practice.

Practice

I start with the easiest: the level of practice. Transcultural bioethics will have to facilitate the research focus of bioethicists from various nations and cultures on activities of most pressing need in their cultures, and serve as a coordinating forum for the transcultural dialogue on these activities. It may be difficult for scholars from, say, Africa to even contemplate any kind of research activities without the active support of international organizations and research institutions. The urgent need for political stability, democratic institutions, and economic advancement is all too demanding. But justice in the allocation of resources to the health-care sector is equally demanding. If no one is able to investigate the present realities, we will not be informed, and people who may be willing to take steps to improve the situation cannot act. Therefore, at the level of practice, the prospect of transcultural dialogue is not a remote one. But it cannot be achieved by an exportation of the research interests of Western bioethicists to non-Western countries where other interests may be dictated by the realities they face. Such realities may also include the need to mediate the conflict between the demands of biomedical technology and the beliefs and moral systems of local cultures and religious traditions.

Principles and Rules

The most difficult challenge occurs at the level of principles and rules. It is here that the conflict between philosophically inspired ethics and culturally motivated moral intuitions and beliefs appears most clearly. Of course, this way of putting it already signifies a bias in favor of the former. After all, the idea of a culturally motivated intuition suggests that something is lacking – the blessing of philosophy. It is on this assumption that the most difficult problem arises: how do we approach the various conflicting principles and rules to enhance the possibility of a transcultural dialogue? In other words, in the light of these conflicting principles and rules, what are the conditions for the possibility of a transcultural bioethics? Three responses/approaches to this question may be sketched:

1 Defend and retain "Western" values and impose them on other cultures for universal application as principles and rules. This is the method of cultural imperialism and value absolutism.
2 Reject the universal validity of Western values and recognize a plurality of values as the basis for principles and rules in different cultures. Transcultural bioethics is, then, respect for cultural identities without the need for common morality. This is the method of value relativism.
3 Examine, meta-culturally, Western and non-Western principles, rules and practices based on them, with all their internal complexities, looking out for common foundational values which transcend cultures and which could be used to formulate common bioethical principles. This is the method of transculturalism and value reciprocity.

Cultural Imperialism and Value Absolutism

We now know that the idea of a uniformity of cultural values in Western societies, or in any other societies, is a myth. We are aware of cultural differences within Western societies. Within the Western divide of the cultural landscape, there are varieties of cultural differences. Thus the African American and Native American cultures in North America differ significantly from the Euro-American majority culture. But there are predominant cultural values that have been identified with the West. Those values were presented to other societies as universal values and this process has been historically described as cultural imperialism by non-Western cultures. There is a warrant for this reaction especially when one recalls the arrogance of colonial administrators and the concept of the "white man's burden" which they championed. Therefore, it is obvious that no stance that takes as absolute either Western values or the values of any specific culture can be an adequate foundation for transcultural ethics. And the suspicion of non-Western cultures about bioethics today is simply an understandable reaction based on this historical experience. The fact that value bigotry usually accompanies value absolutism does not help matters either. Therefore transcultural bioethics must seek a more solid foundation than can be provided by cultural imperialism. This is not to suggest that Western values are necessarily inadequate. The point is that for them to ground principles that are universal, their adequacy cannot be based on their cultural specificity or superiority.

Cultural Pluralism and Value Relativism

Consider the following dialogue between the value relativist (VR) and the universalist (UN):

VR: Bioethics is a Western phenomenon. As a discipline, it has its origin in the West; it concerns itself with Western issues in medicine and biomedical research; it appeals to a Western moral paradigm and its rational agency to resolve such issues.

UN: Bioethics is a universal phenomenon. It has been brought alive by new developments in medicine and biomedical research which are not confined to Western societies. It deals with these issues from a philosophical perspective, which is the perspective of reason, not that of any one culture. Indeed, it is the same traditional ethics applied to the realm of biomedical research.

VR: I agree that bioethics could be universal, but I do not believe that it now is. For, in order to be universal, it has to (i) deal with or show interest in issues relevant to non-Western cultures; and (ii) accept non-Western moral paradigms and rational agency as valid.

UN: I understand your charge in (i): not all issues raised by biomedical research are of particular interest to all societies whose priorities may be somewhere else (the ethics of organ transplantation may not be of interest to a society in which it is not technologically feasible). But the charge in (ii) is difficult to understand, and it seems to me to be the core of your complaint. For the challenge to accept non-Western moral standards as morally valid could mean (a) accept them as morally valid after they have been rationally scrutinized and found to measure up, or (b) accept them even when they are known by a Westerner to be wrong. But you know that reason must be the arbiter in this matter, and reason has no cultural bias.

VR: You appeal to reason as if it is so simple. But judgment of rationality is not a straightforward matter. Consider the following cases:

(a)   A woman refused surgical operation for the treatment of her breast cancer because it would leave her without a breast.
(b)   A man committed suicide because a bad automobile accident left him paralyzed from the waist down.
(c)   The daughter of a 90-year-old woman would not give approval for a surgical operation to be performed on her mother because she was, in her view, old enough to die peacefully in her own home.
(d)   The relatives of an aged dying woman, concerned about her incoherent utterances bordering on "confessions" about past "wickedness," decided to kill her on their own.

There is a standard here, in each of these cases, which can be understood by an average Yoruba person. It is captured in the Yoruba concept of "*ikuyajesin*" – death is preferable to loss of dignity. Is this understandable in the same way as a valid standard by the Western universalist? Or will it be subjected to "rational" critique beyond the concept of *ikuyajesin?*

The value relativist's position is the opposite of cultural imperialism. The position of the cultural pluralist appears to be non-controversial: there is a plurality of culture groups, and each of them deserves respect. Indeed, the values derived from these cultures are legitimate objects of respect. This is the point of Enrico Chiavacci's observation that "each people and each culture finds its own dignity within its own cultural identity . . . therefore each culture and religion, with its own ethical perspectives, must be respected and appreciated" (1992: 99). On the other hand, the value relativist moves from the harmless idea that there is a plurality of cultures to the problematic inference that there is

31

no objective basis for a cross-cultural judgment of values. But granted that the value relativist is motivated by the desire for cross-cultural tolerance, it seems clear that she cannot at once motivate a coherent notion of cross-cultural tolerance unless this is also a value that all cultures already affirm; otherwise it can have no basis.

It is important, however, not to throw away the baby of cultural pluralism with the bathwater of value relativism. The point of the cultural pluralist is that it is important to understand and respect differences with regard to ways of life and belief systems; and to avoid jumping too quickly into judgment of rationality. There is hardly a cultural belief or practice that has no rational basis as far as the group is concerned. There is always a standard as in the above cases: *ikuyajesin* – death is preferable to loss of dignity. The cultural pluralist would call for understanding and explain that there is at least consistent and intelligible thinking behind the four cases, even if she would not ultimately defend the underlying principle of death before indignity as ethical. She would urge the universalist to try and understand the thinking of the Yoruba people.

The distinction we have made between cultural pluralism and value relativism is crucial. Though the latter appears to ride on the back of the former, we may affirm cultural pluralism while we reject value relativism. The fact of cultural differences and the importance of understanding it and bearing it in mind before we make judgments of rationality and morality are the emphasis of cultural pluralism. The thesis of value relativism is stronger, moving from the observation that there are cultural differences to the inference that there can be no valid cross-cultural standards for evaluating conduct or judging values. The position of the cultural pluralist is compatible with the view that we need fully to understand and appreciate the viewpoint of a particular standard before we judge it as inadequate.

Transculturalism and the Idea of Shared Values

An adequate response to the challenge of transcultural bioethics should reject the arrogance of cultural imperialism, which absolutizes the dominant values of any cultural tradition (be it Western, Eastern, Northern, or Southern), and the skepticism of ethical relativism which absolutizes the parochial values of ethnic and culture groups. On the positive side of the response, emphasis must be placed on (a) serious effort to understand the cultures and values of other peoples; (b) development of a compendium of values and belief systems across cultures; (c) promotion of intercultural dialogue on the critical analysis of those values and belief systems; (d) identification of a set of common values that transcend particular cultures; and (e) utilization of this set of common values in the development of bioethical principles and standards that all cultures can embrace.

What appears to be the main obstacle to transcultural bioethics is the suspicion that, in its present form, it projects only the dominant values of the West: autonomy, individualism, secularism, and privacy. There may, in fact, be no warrant for this charge. However, the fact that bioethics today developed in the West in response to the impact of developments in biomedical technology on health-care delivery, seems to lend credence to the suspicion. What is needed is a dialogue across cultures on the values that must inform the project of bioethics in a world that is becoming smaller day by day. Such a dialogue should bring out the commonality of shared values and reconcile the apparent differences in world outlooks. It may well be that the values of autonomy, individualism, and privacy are not totally beyond the understanding of non-Western cultures. Even though African cultures have been characterized as placing emphasis on community at the expense of individual autonomy, the matter is more complex than an either/or analysis suggests. For instance, most African cultures have beliefs that parallel, or share substantial similarities with, the following beliefs of the Yoruba traditional culture:

1　Individuals are creatures of Olodumare (the Yoruba supreme deity) and are endowed with dignity and worth, with a capacity for moral reflection and virtuous life.
2　It is wrong to cause unnecessary harm to a creature of Olodumare, including non-humans.
3　A person who is a member of a community must not be sacrificed to the deities of the community.
4　Personhood is constituted by communal relationships through the articulation of values shared with other members and the actualization of individual potentials in response to, and by active participation in, the community.

Empirically speaking, once we look beyond the different terms for the deity, some of these beliefs are not radically different from Judeo-Christian beliefs or indeed from Islamic beliefs. It is a fundamental belief in Christianity that God creates human beings and endows them with dignity and makes them equal by virtue of the spirit that God breathes into them. Christians also share the belief that it is wrong to cause unnecessary harm to any of God's creatures. The last Yoruba belief is about the constitution of person-hood by communal relationships through the articulation of values shared with other members and the actualization of individual potentials in response to, and by active participation in, the community. The woman who refused a surgical operation to remove a cancerous breast is articulating the values of the community concerning death with dignity. And while it is difficult to see how the belief on the dignity of death relates to actualizing one's potential and participating in the community, the Yoruba do not see a conflict. Death is not the end of life; it is only a transition from one form of existence to another. The world of the dead is an extension of the world of the living and the dead commune with, and participate in the life of, the community of the living. The point here then is that if we look carefully at the various cultures, we are very likely to find commonalities of outlook which can sustain a transcultural approach to bioethics. Of course, there will always remain some hard nuts of difference. Some of those differences are inevitable. But they may not be crucial. Differences in customs of aesthetic experience and the judgments that are based on them may have no serious impact on ethics or bioethics. However, where crucial differences occur, there has to be a principle of adjudication in order to move toward the goal of transcultural bioethics.

I would like to suggest the principle of human flourishing for the adjudication of conflicts between cultural beliefs and practices that impact on ethics in general, and bioethics in particular. This is based on the belief that the moral weight of culture in ethics and bioethics is *relative* to its effect on human flourishing (Gbadegesin 2007). The core of morality is the promotion of human flourishing, and therefore a critical standard for evaluating a civil ethos is the extent to which it promotes or negates human flourishing. If a cultural practice truly enhances human flourishing, the moral weight of the culture is heavy and it deserves careful attention. On the other hand, the moral weight of a cultural practice which negates or retards human flourishing is very light and may indeed be nil.

One common objection to this principle is that there is a variety of ideas of human flourishing across cultures. A short answer to this claim is that it misconstrues the idea of human flourishing. For the notion does not lend itself to cultural determination. Human flourishing is individual human flourishing, and this requires an individual to be able to do certain things and be a certain kind of a person. An individual flourishes when he or she is not hampered not only from satisfying his or her basic needs but also from aspiring to higher levels of attainment. An individual flourishes when he or she is capable of participating in the affairs of the community as a free person with human dignity. Even if we grant the influence of culture on conceptions of human flourishing, it does not follow that cultures cannot come to an agreement on a thin conception of human flourishing that can serve as a principle of adjudication. Thus I agree with Thomas Pogge that "though disagreements about what human flourishing consists in may prove ineradicable, it may well be possible to bypass them by agreeing that nutrition, clothing, shelter, and certain basic freedoms, as well as social interaction, education, and participation, are important means to it – means which just social institutions must secure for all" (Pogge 1999: 342). This eliminates certain practices, for instance the practice of human sacrifice, which clearly negates the flourishing of the individual victim and has no redeeming social value. If the belief is that the sacrifice would pacify the gods and bring the much-needed rainfall, we know that it is misplaced, and it is useless to defend the belief on the ground that it works for the people, because it does not. Moreover, it does a disservice to the common humanity that we lay claim to by suggesting that the people are the best judge in that situation.

If, however, a cultural practice has a negative impact on individual human flourishing and it has a redeeming social value, say, in the survival of the society, then the moral weight of the culture is consequential. An example here is the case of a just war, if war can be described as a cultural practice. In this case, however, the sacrifice it entails for individuals must be distributed fairly across the social spectrum. Other examples may not lend themselves to easy answers. But on such occasions, rational people must enter into rational dialogue. An essential condition here is the need for mutual respect for the humanity and equality of all parties. A cultural practice is not self-justifying. Thus, while it is true that every cultural practice deserves a prima facie equal consideration, where there is a conflict in the practices of cultures, we must appeal to a principle of adjudication. An adequate principle of adjudication is the principle of human flourishing. Therefore, a cultural practice that negates human flourishing does not deserve equal consideration. This must be the message of transcultural bioethics.

References

Chiavacci, E. (1992). From medical deontology to bioethics: the problem of social consensus of basic issue within western culture and beyond it in the human family. In E. Pellegrino, P. Mozzarella, and P. Corsi (eds.), *Transcultural Dimensions in Medical Ethics*. Frederick, MD: University Publishing Group, pp. 91–103.

Eagleton, T. (2000). *The Idea of Culture*. Malden, MA: Blackwell Publishing.

Gbadegesin, S. (1993). The ethics of polygyny. *Quest: Philosophical Discussions* 7/2: 3–29.

Gbadegesin, S. (2007). The moral weight of culture in ethics. In L. J. Prograis, Jr and E. Pellegrino (eds.), *African American Bioethics: Culture, Race, and Identity*. Washington, DC: Georgetown University Press.

Locke, A. (1989). The ethics of culture. In Leonard Harris (ed.), *The Philosophy of Alain Locke: Harlem Renaissance and Beyond*. Philadelphia: Temple University Press, pp. 176–85.

Pellegrino, E. (1992). Intersections of Western biomedical ethics and world culture: problematic and possibility. *Cambridge Quarterly Journal of Healthcare Ethics* 3: 191–6.

Pogge, T. (1999). Human flourishing and universal justice. In E.F. Paul, F. Miller, Jr, and J. Paul (eds.), *Human Flourishing*, vol. 16. Cambridge: Cambridge University Press, pp. 331–6.

Tylor, E. B. (1958). *Primitive Culture*. New York: Harper.

Further reading

Engelhardt, H. T. (1991). *Bioethics and Secular Humanism: The Search for a Common Morality*. Philadelphia: Trinity Press International.

Flack, H. (1992). The confluence of culture and bioethics. In H. Flack and E. Pellegrino (eds.), *African American Perspectives on Biomedical Ethics*. Washington, DC: Georgetown University Press, pp. xi–xx.

Hoffmaster, B. (1992). Can ethnography save the life of medical ethics? *Social Science and Medicine* 35: 1421–31.

Ingstad, B. and Whyte, S. R. (1995). *Disability and Culture*. Berkeley: University of California Press.

Leisinger, K. (1993). Bioethics here and in poor countries: a comment. *Cambridge Quarterly Journal of Healthcare Ethics* 2: 5–8.

Marshall, P., Thomasma, D., and Bergsma, J. (1994). Intercultural reasoning: the challenge for international bioethics. *Cambridge Quarterly Journal of Healthcare Ethics* 3: 321–8.

Meleis, A. I. and Jonsen, A. R. (1983). Ethical crises and cultural differences. *Western Journal of Medicine* 138: 889–93.

Murray, R. F. (1992). Minority perspectives on biomedical ethics. In E. Pellegrino, P. Mozzarella, and P. Corsi (eds.), *Transcultural Dimensions in Medical Ethics*. Frederick, MD: University Publishing Group, pp. 35–42

Oshuntokun, B. O. (1992). Biomedical ethics in the developing world: conflicts and resolutions. In E. Pellegrino, P. Mozzarella, and P. Corsi (eds.), *Transcultural Dimensions in Medical Ethics*. Frederick, MD: University Publishing Group, pp. 105–43.

Prograis, L. J., Jr and Pellegrino, E. (2007). *African American Bioethics: Culture, Race, and Identity*. Washington, DC: Georgetown University Press.

Veatch, R. M. (1989). *Cross Cultural Perspectives in Medical Ethics: Readings*. Boston: Jones and Bartlett.

4

Gender and Bioethics

JAN CROSTHWAITE

The professions and disciplines from which bioethics emerged – medicine, theology, philosophy, and law – have long been male-dominated, male-focused, and sometimes misogynist. Early bioethical writings, even when addressing issues of primary concern to women, such as abortion, rarely considered women's views specifically or engaged with feminist thinking on these issues. They showed little awareness of the patriarchal character of institutions within which bioethical issues arose, or of the possible impact on bioethical issues of cultural assumptions about differences between women and men. Nor was the possibility of gender bias in ethical theorizing itself considered. That fundamental conceptions of human norms and the processes of ethical deliberation might reflect a particular gendered perspective went largely unremarked. Bioethical debate and the principles underlying it were assumed to be open to all rational minds and uncontaminated by such contingencies as gender.

While women have not been absent from bioethical discussions, it is in the last decades of the twentieth century that women's voices have been heard as making a distinctive contribution. This largely reflects the increasing recognition of feminist thinking as an important contributor to critical reflection on intellectual traditions and social institutions. The contributions of women and feminists can be both disturbing and enriching: disturbing because they are often critical of health-care institutions and practices, and also of bioethics and its reflections on these; enriching (and essential) because they are disturbing and because they bring to debates the diverse but often distinctive experiences, interests, and values of women.

Feminism and Gender

It is feminism which allows the significance of women's voices to be understood. Feminism is not a single viewpoint; feminist thinking is informed by different disciplinary backgrounds, different political frameworks, different race, class, cultural, and individual experiences, and different understandings of feminism itself. (Tong (1989) provides a helpful introduction to a variety of feminisms.) Indeed, a recurrent issue for feminists is whether there is anything which can be held to unify the different feminist voices without thereby disrespectfully diminishing their differences and effectively silencing some.

36

I think there is a unifying theme distinctive of feminism: the concern to understand and eliminate the oppression of women in all its guises. This underpins feminist concerns to document women's experiences, preferably in their own voices, and to provide theoretical analyses of these experiences, their origins and implications, as the basis for a critique of social institutions. It does not, however, yield a single answer to either the basis of such oppression or the appropriate means for addressing it.

Feminist concern with the oppression of women provides the framework for understanding the significance of gender. "Gender" refers to the social elaboration of a biological difference between male and female into two distinct kinds of people, men and women. Feminists have identified both the existence of gender differences and their particular construction in Western civilization as contributing to the oppression of women. Feminist writers in the 1970s distinguished sex, the biological differentiation of male and female, from gender, the social differentiation of masculine and feminine individuals in terms of roles, behavior, and psychological traits. More recent feminists have been critical of the conceptualization and use of any sex/gender distinction. They argue that it presents a false dichotomy, and that accounts of gender often privilege a particular cultural/historical perspective at the expense of recognizing the diversity of ways of understanding differences between men and women to be found across different times, cultures, and classes. Emphasis on gender *simpliciter* also obscures the contribution of other factors (including race and class) to the life experiences, social relationships, and sense of self, of individual women and men.

How to accommodate the multifarious and cross-cutting differences between women (and between social groups in general) is a major issue in contemporary feminist thinking. Recognition of difference complicates feminist social analysis and feminist attempts to eliminate women's oppression, but it also promotes more sophisticated analysis and political theorizing. In addressing multiplicities of difference, and the impact of diverse cultural frameworks on an overall understanding of issues of justice and oppression, feminism has developed conceptual and methodological tools of use to bioethicists in the multicultural and global context of contemporary issues (Tong 2001).

Whatever the theoretical standing of the concept of gender, attention to differences between men and women (both assumed and actual) is important to understanding and ethically evaluating any social practice, including health care. It reveals unjust differences in distribution of, or access to, rights and goods, and it reveals the existence and operation of oppressive relationships and social structures. Attention to gender enriches bioethical understanding and evaluation. It encourages attention to the operation of power relations more generally in health-care institutions and practices, and to the impact of health-related issues on the oppression of social groups. It forces bioethicists to attend more to the political and social contexts of the moral issues they consider and to the practice of bioethics itself within such contexts.

Gender and Health Care

Feminists have drawn attention to gender inequality and discrimination within health-care professions, and have pointed out the gendered division of labor and status in health-care institutions (e.g., Miles 1991: ch. 5). Activities of "care" are women's work, while "curing" (and the scientific expertise which backs it) is men's province and more valued. This reflects traditional Western stereotypes of femininity and masculinity. It also reinforces a distorted conception (characteristically expressed in war metaphors) of health care as the (masculine) conquest of disease through technological wizardry and the valiant battles of physicians and surgeons against invading organisms and unruly organs.

Feminists have also documented a history of exploitation and abuse of women patients, from unnecessary hysterectomies to genital reconstructions performed without women's knowledge (Scully 1980). Even within the practice of beneficent medicine, there are disturbing ethical failures in the treatment of women. Research suggests that women may receive a lesser quality of health care than men with similar conditions (Muller 1990). But women's most frequent complaints concern failures of respect: not being taken seriously as authorities on their own experience and preferences; not being properly informed about their condition and treatment options; and generally not being accorded the rights of competent adults to decide about their own health care. Gender stereotypes and behavior patterns foster these failures and reinforce the inequalities inherent in physician–patient encounters. Yet while bioethics has been centrally concerned with issues of patient autonomy and power imbalances between health-care professionals and their clients, it has had relatively little to say about the impact of gender on these issues.

The protection of research subjects is also a major concern of bioethics, but it is feminists who have primarily drawn attention to unethical experimentation on women, including the therapeutic use of drugs which have not been adequately tested for effects on women. Women have been under-represented in, and excluded from, studies concerning illnesses which affect them as well as men (Bird 1994; Bartlett et al. 2005). Sometimes gender differences are explicitly used as a reason for excluding women, because incorporating such factors as women's hormonal cycles and the possibility of pregnancy complicates research and adds to its cost. Therapies and illnesses may affect women differently from men, and their exclusion or under-representation in research is medically, scientifically, and ethically problematic. Exploring the extent to which this occurs, and requirements to prevent it, requires explicit focus on gender as a category of research analysis.

Feminists have attributed much gender bias in health care and research to the assumption that women's health issues are primarily reproductive, a reflection of a long tradition of identifying women with their reproductive biology. They have discerned also the effects of Western culture's identification of human norms with men and men's experience and values (usually men of a particular race and class). Even in those areas where women's physiology and experience are unique – their reproductive biology – traces of an assumption that women are deviations from the human (i.e., male) norm can be found. Women's normal functioning is seen as medically problematic; menopause becomes an "estrogen deficiency disease." Prophylactic removal of healthy but supposedly "useless" reproductive organs from older women also suggests a narrowly reproductive focus on women's bodies and lives, particularly when not accompanied by any consideration of other possible functions (e.g., in sexual response) of such organs. Feminists have also argued that research into some diseases in women

38

(e.g. HIV/AIDS) has been more concerned with the implications of women's illness for men and babies than for women themselves (Faden et al. 1996). Such attitudes can be seen as reflecting and reinforcing oppressive views of women as fundamentally bearers of men's children.

Feminists have criticized medicine as an agent of social control of women. In areas which significantly affect women's reproductive lives, predominantly male medical professionals control information and access to technologies, and dominate individual and social decision-making. In these areas, and in mental health, medicine has sustained women's oppression through control of their bodies and behavior, and through its articulation and enforcement of gender roles and characteristics. Gynecological surgery of various kinds has been used to 'cure' behavior deemed inappropriate for women. Psychiatry, and access to reproductive technology (both conceptive and contraceptive), have both been used to enforce socially acceptable (hetero)sexual and maternal behavior and roles (Miles 1991; Scully 1980).

Such analyses are of course disputed. Health-care professionals are rarely motivated in the therapies they offer or the research they undertake by the wish to deliberately harm or exploit women. Hence, accusations of oppression can be shocking and painful. Moreover, differential treatment of women and men may be justified in terms of the sex-differentiated distribution and implications of diseases (as Mertz et al. (1996) argue in response to feminist accusations of bias in AIDS research). However, feminist analysis is concerned less with conscious motivations than with discerning underlying assumptions, and patterns of thinking and of practices, of which people may be quite unaware. Feminists draw attention to systemic effects of what may be individually well-motivated actions. Nor do all feminists agree about analyses, implications, or acceptability of particular health-care practices or policies.

Feminist criticism of health-care professions, practices, and policies provides important data for bioethical reflection. The defense of actions and practices against such criticism is therapeutic in that it requires that feminist concerns be explicitly addressed and that gender become a category of analysis. Relations of dominance between social groups are ethical concerns and should be part of bioethical deliberation. Feminist analyses provide distinctive ways of understanding and evaluating social practices and institutions, including those concerned with health care (e.g., Dodds 2005), and feminist debates stimulate reflection on issues which might otherwise go unattended. (See also Parts IV, "Before Birth," and V, "Issues in Reproduction.")

Gender and Ethics

As significant work in feminist bioethics has made clear (e.g., Sherwin 1992; Wolf 1996), the importance for bioethics of feminist attention to gender goes beyond the critique of specific health-care practices and institutions. It prompts reflection also on the possibility of gender biases in the theoretical frameworks of bioethics, particularly in conceptions of the nature of moral agents and moral deliberation.

Feminist approaches to ethics, and consequently to bioethics, are varied. Though sometimes mistakenly identified with feminine ethics of care, they reflect a range of theoretical positions. What they share is the fundamental feminist concern with understanding and eliminating women's oppression, and with ensuring proper attention is paid to women's experiences and interests. These concerns underpin feminist critiques of ethical (and bioethical) theorizing. But feminist ethics moves beyond critique to articulating alternative theories and approaches to moral deliberation. (See also Part III, "Ethical Approaches," particularly chapter 11, "A Care Approach.")

Such theories often incorporate elements of the ethic of care described by Carol Gilligan (1982). Gilligan claimed to hear a distinctive "ethic of care or responsibility" in women's moral deliberations. It is characterized by an emphasis on maintaining connection and relationships, on care for others (and self), and on avoiding harm. Care-thinkers focus on the particular features and contextual location of moral problems, rather than attempting to abstract features which would allow these to be subsumed under general rules or principles. They seek to resolve problems through communication, appealing to shared understanding of relationships and needs, and prefer the creative exploration of options that might dissipate conflicts to the consistency of universal rules.

Gilligan contrasted this "moral orientation" with the "ethic of justice" she saw as dominant in contemporary moral discourse. She argued that the voices of care and justice are gender inflected, though neither uniquely nor universally found in women and men respectively. An ethic of justice emphasizes values of fairness and equal respect for individuals (particularly their rights to self-determination). It focuses on the impartial adjudication of conflicting claims or obligations through appeal to rationally derived and universally applicable principles. While this does not adequately reflect the range or subtlety of Western ethical theorizing, it does capture certain dominant themes, themes which emerge strongly in bioethical debates.

Both the content of an ethic of care and its presentation as an alternative to dominant moral theorizing throw into question the claims of traditional ethical theories to present universal, impartial, and gender-neutral moral thinking. This, together with its resonance with many women's experience and values, makes care ethics of particular interest to feminists. But care's characterization as a feminine ethic is problematic given feminist concern with gender and oppression. A feminine morality embedded in nurturance, close personal attachments, and emotional response to others recalls demeaning characterizations of women as morally inadequate. Ideas of women as emotional, lacking a sense of justice, and incapable of objective and impartial rationality have been used in Western culture to justify their exclusion from public life and their subordination to men. Feminists are also justifiably cautious about any ethic generated within a situation of subordination. The inclusion of women's moral thinking in a feminist ethic must be moderated by critical awareness of gender and of the location of women's experiences and values within (usually patriarchal) social structures and contexts.

Many feminists wish to transcend a justice–care dichotomy. They endorse certain aspects of feminine ethics of care, but also appeal to justice values to ground their critique of oppression. Indeed, feminist analyses of oppression suggest reconceptualizing and extending our understandings of justice beyond the dominant focus on distributive justice (Young 1990). Care-oriented values also support feminist advocacy of individual empowerment as a means of counteracting unequal and oppressive relationships.

Like care ethics, feminist ethics emphasizes the importance of attention to context, particularly social context, and to the unique properties of specific individuals and moral problems. They argue too that human relationships, emotional responses, and individuals' understandings of themselves and their situations are essential components of moral reflection and should not be seen as antithetical to it (Sherwin 1992). Such emphases favor a different account of the nature of moral deliberation and of human beings as moral agents from those dominant in Western ethical and political thinking.

Moral Persons and Moral Deliberation

Susan Wolf partly attributes bioethics' failure to engage with feminism to its "early embrace of a liberal individualism largely inattentive to social context" and "its emphasis on deduction from ethical principles rather than induction from concrete cases" (1996: 5). Liberal individualism gives priority to respect for individual self-determination or autonomy. It sees fairness and equality of treatment as requiring impartial application of universal principles which abstract essential commonalities from the messy specificities of real individuals. This yields a notion of abstract individuals as fundamentally autonomous agents, aware of their own preferences and values, and motivated by rational self-interest (though not necessarily selfish). Their connections to one another are primarily through voluntary contractual relationships mediated by reason-determined codes of rights and obligations. The imposition of any particular conception of what is good or valuable is a failure of respect for the essentially self-determining nature of such individuals. Such a conception has difficulty recognizing the complex relationships between individuals and social groups, except as these emerge in individual preferences.

Against such abstract ciphers, many feminists present a richer conception of persons as historically and culturally located, socially related, and essentially embodied (e.g., Diprose 1994). Individuals are located in and formed by specific relationships (chosen and unchosen) and ties of affection and responsibility. Their preferences and possibilities are affected by membership of social groups with specific concrete and symbolic properties. Such a conception of socially embedded selves refocuses thinking about autonomy, shifting the emphasis from independent self-determination toward ideals of integrity within relatedness. It demands an approach to moral deliberation which does not require detachment from others, nor the idea of a self-transparent "self." Respecting autonomy becomes less a matter of protecting individuals from "coercive" influences than of positive empowerment, recognizing people's interdependence, and supporting individuals' development of their own understanding of their situation and options.

Attention to social groups also shifts ethical emphasis on individual judgment more toward ideals of communicative and collaborative decision-making. The understanding and judgments of concrete individuals are particular rather than universal, and are constrained by personal situation and experience. Many feminists reject the possibility of an unsituated epistemological or moral perspective, arguing that knowledge and morality are products of social negotiation. Debates in feminist epistemology and feminist ethics address the possibility of recognizing and valuing diverse perspectives without embracing a relativism that would limit the possibility of shared social life and moral standards and undercut the ground from which to condemn oppression.

Against the ideal of objective and impartial moral rationality, many feminists emphasize an engaged moral response. Moral perception and response involve some form of empathic engagement with specific others, rather than detached application of abstract principles. This, together with recognition of the moral significance of emotions and affective relationships, calls into question ideals of impartiality in ethics. While there are clearly contexts in which it is wrong to favor particular others, certain professional and personal relationships may permit, or even morally require, such preferential treatment. Health professionals are increasingly feeling the tension between obligations to their own patients and the impartiality required of custodians of scarce public resources.

Distinguishing proper responsiveness to the needs of particular others from distorting bias (and harmful self-sacrifice) requires a carefully nuanced understanding of the nature and demands of the variety of interconnected human relationships – personal, professional, and political – and a sense of how these fit into a wider social framework. Feminist thinking, with its concern to understand oppression and the many faces of power, both personal and institutional, helps provide such a perspective. The focus on women's lived experience has also provided possible alternative organizing concepts to the ideas of autonomy and justice which have been so significant in bioethics. See, for example, work which takes the characteristically feminine activity of mothering as the foundation point for defining ethical relationships (Kittay 1999; Ruddick 1989).

Bioethical Self-reflection

As a profession with responsibilities for the ethical evaluation of major social institutions, bioethics must be prepared to engage in critical reflection on its own social position, assumptions, and practices. Its dominant theoretical frameworks, including the "four principles," have come under critical scrutiny, from inside and outside (Gudorf 1994). The resultant self-examination is necessary and beneficial, though its outcome is far from clear. But it is clear that the process will benefit from exploring some of the directions and implications of feminist approaches to ethics (and to epistemology).

All professions tend to reflect socially dominant perspectives and values, yet bioethics often needs to represent the interests of those who will be affected by healthcare policies and practices, particularly socially disadvantaged groups. The professional context of bioethics makes it difficult for marginalized groups to speak for themselves. Bioethical deliberations are frequently debates between "experts," carried out in committees, and professional or academic institutions and journals. The ethical (and epistemological) problems of speaking for others are obvious and need to be consciously addressed.

Bioethics in the twenty-first century is aware of the need to include the perspectives and experiences of marginalized social groups, and frequently includes feminist commentaries in its discussion of issues. However, merely presenting such perspectives is not yet integrating them into the framework of bioethics, and work remains to be done on providing the theoretical structures which can move from multiple, sometimes conflicting, perspectives to defensible resolutions of moral issues.

There is obvious overlap in interests, and possibility for fruitful interaction, between bioethics and feminism. Feminist bioethics is a contributor to reflection on bioethical issues and on bioethical reflection itself. Without an understanding of the complex social implications of gender, ethical discussion of prenatal sex selection would be sadly impoverished. Nor can we hope to deal successfully with the issues raised by genetic technologies without a robust awareness of the differential impacts of gender characterizations and roles on conceptions of human potential and desirable attributes. Both feminist thinking and attention to gender offer new conceptual frameworks within which bioethics can address both perennial and new issues.

References

Bartlett, C., Doyal, L., Ebrahim, S., Davey, P., Bachmann, M., Egger, M., and Dieppe, P. (2005). The causes and effects of socio-demographic exclusions from clinical trials. *Health Technology Assessment (Winchester, England)* 9/38: iii–iv, ix–x, 1–152.

Bird, C. E. (1994). Women's representation as subjects in clinical studies: A pilot study of research published in JAMA in 1990 and 1992. In A. Mastroianni, R. Faden, and D. Federman (eds.), *Women and Health Research: Ethical and legal issues of Including Women in Clinical Studies*, vol. 2. Workshop and commissioned papers. Washington, DC: National Academy Press, pp. 151–73.

Diprose, R. (1994). *The Bodies of Women: Ethics, Embodiment and Sexual Difference*. London and New York: Routledge.

Dodds, S. (2005). Gender, ageing, and injustice: social and political contexts of bioethics. *Journal of Medical Ethics* 31/5: 285–598.

Faden, R., Kass, N., and McGraw, D. (1996). Women as vessels and vectors: lessons from the HIV Epidemic. In S. M. Wolf (ed.), *Feminism and Bioethics: Beyond Reproduction*. New York and Oxford: Oxford University Press, pp. 252–81.

Gilligan, C. (1982). *In a Different Voice: Psychological Theory and Women's Development*. Cambridge, MA: Harvard University Press.

Gudorf, C. E. (1994). A feminist critique of biomedical principlism. In E. R. DuBose, R. P. Hamel, and L. J. O'Connell (eds.), *A Matter of Principles? Ferment in US Bioethics*. Valley Forge, PA: Trinity Press International, pp. 164–81.

Kittay, E. F. (1999). *Love's Labor: Essays on Women, Equality and Dependency*. New York: Routledge.

Mertz, D., Sushinsky, M. A., and Schüklenk, U. (1996). Women and AIDS: The ethics of exaggerated harm. *Bioethics* 10/2: 92–113.

Miles, A. (1991). *Women, Health and Medicine*. Milton Keynes and Philadelphia: Open University Press.

Muller, C. F. (1990). *Health Care and Gender*. New York: Russell Sage Foundation.

Ruddick, S. (1989). *Maternal Thinking: Toward a politics of peace*. Boston, MA: Beacon Press.

Scully, D. (1980). *Men who Control Women's Health: The Miseducation of Obstetrician-Gynecologists*. Boston: Houghton Mifflin.

Sherwin, S. (1992). *No Longer Patient: Feminist Ethics and Health Care*. Philadelphia: Temple University Press.

Tong, R. (1989). *Feminist Thought: A Comprehensive Introduction*. Boulder, CO, and San Francisco, CA: Westview Press.

Tong, R. (2001). Toward a feminist global bioethics: addressing women's health concerns worldwide. *Health Care Analysis* 9: 229–46.

Wolf, S. M. (ed.) (1996). *Feminism and Bioethics: Beyond Reproduction.* New York and Oxford: Oxford University Press.

Young, I. M. (1990). *Justice and the Politics of Difference.* Princeton, NJ: Princeton University Press.

Further reading

Alcoff, L. and Potter, E. (eds.) (1993). *Feminist Epistemologies.* New York and London: Routledge.

Cole, E. B. and Coultrap-McQuin, S. (eds.) (1992). *Explorations in Feminist Ethics: Theory and Practice.* Bloomington and Indianapolis: Indiana University Press.

Cook, R. J. (1994). Feminism and the four principles. In R. Gillon and A. Lloyd (eds.), *Principles of Health Care Ethics.* Chichester: John Wiley, pp. 193–206.

Dally, A. (1991). *Women under the Knife: A History of Surgery.* London: Hutchinson Radius, 1991.

DeBruin, D. (1994). Justice and the inclusion of women in clinical studies: a conceptual framework. In A. Mastroianni, R. Faden, and D. Federman (eds.), *Women and Health Research: Ethical and Legal Issues of Including Women in Clinical Studies,* vol. 2. Workshop and commissioned papers. Washington, DC: National Academy Press, pp. 127–50.

Donchin, A. and Purdy, L. M. (eds.) (1999). *Embodying Bioethics: Recent Feminist Advances.* Lanham: Rowman and Littlefield.

Doyal, L. (1995). *What Makes Women Sick: Gender and the Political Economy of Health.* New Brunswick, NJ: Rutgers University Press.

Foster, P. (1995). *Women and the Health Care Industry: An Unhealthy Relationship?* Buckingham and Philadelphia: Open University Press.

Held, V. (ed.) (1995). *Justice and Care: Essential Readings in Feminist Ethics.* Boulder, CO, and Oxford: Westview Press.

Holmes, H. B. and Purdy, L. M. (eds.) (1992). *Feminist Perspectives in Medical Ethics.* Bloomington and Indianapolis: Indiana University Press. (A collection of articles from *Hypatia* 4/2 and 4/3 (1989), special issues on feminist ethics and medicine, and ethics and reproduction.)

Jaggar, A. M. (1992). Feminist ethics. In L. Becker and C. Becker (eds.), *Encyclopedia of Ethics.* New York and London: Garland, pp. 361–70.

Mackenzie, C. and Stoljar, N. (eds.) (2000). *Relational Autonomy in Context: Feminist Perspectives on Autonomy, Agency and the Social Self.* New York: Oxford University Press.

Mahowald, M. B. (2000). *Genes, Women, Equality.* New York: Oxford University Press.

More, E. S. and Milligan, M. A. (eds.) (1994). *The Empathic Practitioner: Empathy, Gender and Medicine.* New Brunswick, NJ: Rutgers University Press.

Noddings, N. (1984). *Caring: A Feminine Approach to Ethics and Moral Education.* Berkeley: University of California Press.

Petchesky, R. and Judd, K. (eds.) (1998). *Negotiating Reproductive Rights: Women's Perspectives Across Countries and Cultures.* London: Zed Books.

Rawlinson, M. C. (2001). The concept of a feminist bioethics. *Journal of Medicine and Philosophy* 26/4: 405–16.

Rawlinson, M. C. and Donchin, A. (2005). The quest for universality: reflections on the Universal Draft Declaration on Bioethics and Human Rights. *Developing World Bioethics* 5/3: 258–66.

Rogers, W. (2004). Evidence based medicine and justice: a framework for looking at the impact of EBM upon vulnerable or disadvantaged groups. *Journal of Medical Ethics* 30/2: 141–5.

Rogers, W. A. (2006). Feminism and public health ethics. *Journal of Medical Ethics* 32/6: 351–4.

Russell, D. (1995). *Women, Madness, and Medicine.* Cambridge: Polity.

Sherwin, S., Baylis, F., Bell, M., et al. (1998). *The Politics of Women's Health: Exploring Agency and Autonomy.* Philadelphia: Temple University Press.

Todd, A. D. (1989). *Intimate Adversaries: Cultural Conflict Between Doctors and Women Patients.* Philadelphia: University of Pennsylvania Press.

Tong, R. (1997). *Feminist Approaches to Bioethics: Theoretical Reflections and Practical Applications.* Boulder, CO: Westview Press.

Tong, R. (2002). Love's labor in the health care system: working toward gender equity. *Hypatia* 17/3: 200–13.

5

Religion and Bioethics

ERIC GREGORY

The origins of the contemporary discipline of bioethics in the 1960s and 1970s owe much to religious discussions of issues like euthanasia, research on human subjects, organ transplants, the distribution of health-care resources, *in vitro* fertilization, and various dimensions of patient care. Histories of bioethics, for example, often cite the pioneering work of theologians such as Joseph Fletcher, Paul Ramsey, Richard McCormick, and James Gustafson. Moreover, in the United States at least, religious adherents play a significant political role in public debate and grassroots mobilization on matters related to bioethics. Yet professional bioethics in the English-speaking world often contrasts the rigor of analytic moral philosophy with outdated, sectarian, or dogmatic modes of religious reasoning. Religious ethics is thought to be less capable of fruitfully engaging the moral implications of unprecedented technological developments in pluralist societies.

Many religiously oriented ethicists continue, nevertheless, to contribute to contemporary bioethics. Some argue that the particularity of religious traditions (e.g., Judaism, Roman Catholicism, and Buddhism) supplies visions of goodness and rightness that give shape to diverse approaches in bioethics. As systems of beliefs, narratives, and ritual practices, these same traditions also support broader attitudes towards health, the body, aging, medicine, vulnerability, and suffering, on this view. Even so, many religious ethicists point to important analogues between religious thought and various secular moralities in order to advance agreement on practical conclusions required in setting public policy and passing laws. Yet some also criticize mainstream bioethics for limiting moral inquiry to the formal resolution of "conflicts between interests in order to secure social cooperation without appeal to robust views of the good" (McKenny 1997: 8), or for complicity in "dominant cultural narratives of liberal individualism, scientific progress, and the market" (Cahill 2005: 6). A full account of these interdisciplinary debates and the prospects of a common morality is beyond the scope of this essay, but it is important to register this contested background as a cautionary note when bringing these themes into conversation.

Such caution is particularly relevant in light of the so-called return of religion in the twenty-first century. Despite various predictions and theories of secularization, religions continue to offer intellectual and social practices that actively sustain diverse ways of life for many people across the globe. These traditions play an ongoing role in moral debates given a desire to respond to practical issues in the life of their various communities. Hospitals, government commissions, medical associations, and universities continue to draw upon ethicists with knowledge of religious traditions to inform their bioethical discussions. In fact, one prominent bioethicist notes "signs of growing interest in attention to religion and theology in bioethics in general" (Childress 2003: 48). It is not possible to provide a complete survey of these traditions and their bioethical reflection. While reference will be made to other religions, this essay primarily focuses on Christian ideals of conduct, character, and community, and some modern disputes over their interpretations and applications in bioethics. The structure of the essay, however, addresses more general questions about the role of religion in contemporary bioethics. My aim is to be illustrative rather than comprehensive.

Problems and Arguments

One way to think about religious traditions like Christianity is to see them as historically constituted by internal arguments concerning the appropriate expressions of their values and principles. On this view, a tradition is most dynamic when it "embodies continuities of conflict" (MacIntyre 1981: 222). In fact, while religious communities work hard to achieve agreement on matters of doctrine and practice, they often work just as hard to achieve clarity on the nature of their disagreements. These disagreements usually involve more fundamental disagreements regarding the interpretation of various sources for moral deliberation. The definition of these sources, and the appropriate inferences to be made by their use in specific moral judgments, are contested realms in religion and ethical theory (Cahill and Childress, 1996). Many Christian communities, either explicitly or tacitly, identify four sources as the building blocks or the basic grammar of their moral language: Scripture, reason, tradition, and experience.

"Scripture" refers to the canonical texts accepted as authoritative revelation about God and God's purposes for humanity. For Christians, these books are commonly referred to as the Old and New Testaments. Important passages include the Decalogue (Exodus 20:2–17), the parable of the Good Samaritan (Luke 10:25–37), the Golden Rule (Mathew 7:12), and prophetic admonitions to "do justice" (Micah 6:8) and "love your neighbor as yourself" (Matthew 22:39). These passages figure centrally in the development of Western law and morality, especially with regard to respect for life, universalizability, and impartiality (values embraced by many who reject their theological justifications). "Reason" refers to the human capacity to form concepts, reflect and deliberate, and freely pursue intelligible human goods. This source is particularly important for an approach in Roman Catholic bioethics known as "natural law." Appeals to natural law in applied ethics emphasize the non-relative and incommensurable features of human flourishing. They aspire to provide a universal ethic for any rational person and draw heavily from non-theological sources such as philosophy and the social sciences. Notably, several philosophers have argued for a "new natural law theory" that does not deduce moral norms from metaphysical theses about the existence of God or from observations about human nature (George 1994). Many Protestant traditions also have developed accounts of natural law, but they have tended to be critical of any preoccupation with the formal analysis of moral action that neglects theological attention to character and virtues. "Tradition" refers both to official church teachings and statements as well as less formal practices and customs. Finally, "experience" refers most broadly to the concrete knowledge afforded through the lived reality of the world as persons in community with God and others. Major traditions within Christianity develop and employ these sources in various ways. Characteristically, for example, Roman Catholicism trades heavily on tradition and reason as resources for interpreting Scripture while evangelical Protestantism elevates the authority of Scripture.

It is perhaps most helpful to examine various appeals in particular cases, highlighting distinctive elements not likely to be found in strictly philosophical surveys. Attention to cases is not an accidental feature of Christian bioethics. "Casuistry" is a longstanding approach in Christian ethics that involves case-based reasoning similar to methods of interpretation by appeal to precedent in Jewish and Islamic law. It considers paradigmatic cases ("murder" or "lying") in order to further develop norms which bear upon moral evaluation of obligations and values in particular circumstances. In Christian ethics, casuistry often serves to resolve problems of "conscience," and arose out of medieval confessional practices and pastoral counseling (Jonsen and Toulmin 1988). Taken together, consideration of the following cases will illustrate modes of reasoning implicit in Christian ethics in the last quarter-century.

Euthanasia

Christian reflection on saving and killing, suffering and death, and illness and health continue to inform contemporary decision-making at the end of life. Today's debates tend to focus on a narrow context brought about by achievements in medical technology. This technology has postponed or prolonged the dying process in ways that cause many no longer to see death as something always to be avoided. The paradigmatic case for moral and legal discussions of euthanasia is that of a person suffering from a medically classifiable disease who chooses to end his or her life in order to shorten the period of pain and suffering. I here focus on cases of voluntary euthanasia and physician-assisted suicide, rather than on non-voluntary or involuntary euthanasia. In voluntary cases, a person chooses to die and asks others (specifically those in the medical profession) to help. Secular debates often hinge on the relative merits of a compassionate respect for this autonomous choice as contrasted with social concerns regarding the character of medical practice and slippery slope arguments about manipulation and abuse. In Christian ethics, however, the moral question is often put this way: what does love for a dying person require, permit, or forbid? As with most issues in bioethics, Christian support for a wide range of positions on euthanasia can be found. Despite this characteristic diversity, however, a few general observations can be made given common Christian affirmations of the "sanctity of life."

The Roman Catholic tradition offers the most developed and systematic Christian opposition to active euthanasia and assisted suicide. Its discussions typically invoke two sets of familiar distinctions: "active" versus "passive" euthanasia and "ordinary" versus "extraordinary" means of life support. Some religious and secular moralists have heavily challenged or abandoned these distinctions for both philosophical and medical reasons. Many Roman Catholic moralists, however, maintain that these descriptive differences continue to have normative significance. In concert with the Principle of Double Effect, they are used to justify the prudent refusal of certain "heroic" life-prolonging treatments as well as limited forms of indirect action, like pain medication, that may hasten the underlying process of death. In some cases, death is accepted as a foreseen but unintended side effect of an act that itself is not "intrinsic-ally evil." On this view, the strict intention of an act is revealed by the act itself rather than what one happens to take as a motive for action ("compassion"). The intention ("killing" or "letting die") is manifest in the act, not the psychology of the agent. Critics of active or intentional euthanasia argue that it tempts one to commit injustice ("murder") in the name of mercy. The key element in Roman Catholic opposition to euthanasia is the exceptionless moral norm against directly and intentionally killing an innocent human. This prohibition can also be found in statements on euthanasia in Orthodox Judaism, Islam, and Buddhism.

From where is this norm against taking innocent life derived? Christianity teaches that life is a gift from a God who became incarnate as a human being. Seen through both Genesis 1 and John 1, life is understood as both good and sacred; concomitantly, life is denigrated when it is seen as a value to be measured against other values. It is not a self-possession to be abandoned in the face of a "poor quality of life." This view is sometimes linked to claims that secular evaluations do not take into account the theological significance of suffering – while suffering is not a good in itself, it may be, on Christian terms, a potential means of transformation and fellowship with God. Some are also quick to point out that much suffering at the end of life is bound up with, and can be prevented by attention to, structures of "social sin" (e.g., does the dying person have access to good palliative care? Do women seek euthanasia because they have been socialized into a role that requires them to always be the caregivers and never the "burden"?). Christian support for the hospice movement coheres with this commitment to communal caring for patients even when illness resists medical treatment or cure, and this embodied care-giving has particular theological resonance in a Christian context, as it draws on the embodied care that Jesus came to give humanity. Many Christian ethicists emphasize a moral commitment to individual patients, rather than to treatment of disease or the species as a whole (Ramsey 1970). They frequently claim that requests for death are, in fact, often an expression of fear of abandonment through the dying process.

At the same time, however, Christian ethicists point out that life is not an absolute and unconditional good. Physical existence is not to be worshipped as an idol. Respect for life does not mean denying the reality of death, especially if the onset of death so threatens both body and spirit that it also threatens one's capacity to be related to God and others. Indeed, accepting death may be a profound recognition of one's status as a mortal creature. These considerations have led some to revisit even traditional Catholic moral theology in order to open the door, in extreme circumstances, to voluntary euthanasia as a morally viable last resort. On this view, "death for the Christian is never an unambiguous good, but it is sometimes a lesser evil than the evil of suffering" (Cahill 1987: 450). As we see in the final section, however, such a devel-opment in moral doctrine need not imply a specific judgment on the legalization of euthanasia.

Abortion

Recognizing all human life as a fragile "gift" is a deep feature of Christian opposition to abortion on demand. Abortion is seen as a violation of something sacred, a concept also found in some non-theological writings in bioethics (Dworkin 1993). While sanctity and dignity are often associated terms, moral critics of abortion sometimes distinguish between notions of unmerited "sanctity" and secular notions of achieved "dignity" (Jackson 2005). On this view, the fetus bears the "image of God," a value that resides in the embodied creature. The fetus does not need to justify itself or be assigned value by the powerful based on some achievement or capacity. It is not an aggressor or mere tissue. Opponents of abortion also cite biblical passages that suggest God's intimate formation of all life (e.g., Isaiah 44:2, Psalm 139:13; Luke 1), though there are historical disputes regarding theological interpretation of "personhood" that mirror similar disputes in philosophy. Moral opposition to abortion causes intense social and political conflict, especially when efforts are made to criminalize its practice and exercise coercive state control over women's bodies. Political efforts to transcend the rhetorical contrast between rival "pro-life" and "pro-choice" camps seem unable to move the debate beyond stalemate. Moral and legal evaluation of abortion also sharply divides Christian churches.

Some argue that abortion presents such a fundamental dilemma – a choice between the rights and welfare of women versus the protection of innocent human life – that it cannot be resolved. Others find that salient differences between abortion and infanticide are recognized even by opponents of abortion who exempt cases, again under the Principle of Double Effect, where the life of the mother is threatened. This distinction at least suggests the possibility of moral analysis under the rubric of legally justified killing. Still others argue that religious communities need to abandon the conventional liberal terms on which abortion is discussed by advocating broader social support for both women and children. This criticism coincides with calls to create counter-cultural religious communities that welcome children and women (Hauerwas 1981). As with arguments concerning the death penalty, respect for life admits a plurality of competing claims and pulls many Christians (and non-Christians) in different directions. The difficulty of abortion, however, remains distinctive precisely because pregnancy is a unique phenomenon of total physical dependency.

Abortion is most often thought of as a moral problem because of the "potentiality" issue. Some argue that Christians must err on the side of inclusiveness as a matter of social justice, including the fetus as a person regardless of size, location, or neocortex development. Christians refer to biblical injunctions to protect vulnerable outsiders not afforded respect by society and unable to protect themselves (Matthew 25:40). It is not simply virtuous to provide bodily assistance; on this view, it is an obligation stemming from the prohibition against murder which overrides otherwise compelling interests in autonomy and other goods. In addition to the prohibition against unjust killing, Paul Ramsey emphasized the "promise-keeping" or "covenantal" relation that follows from voluntary sexual intercourse. When a man and a woman freely have sex, they tacitly promise to support and protect any life, however "unwanted," they might be conceiving. Others, however, claim that while the fetus may elicit moral concern or respect, it is not deserving of the same absolute respect otherwise afforded human persons.

They criticize "pro-life" arguments for rigid commitment to a moral rule rather than concrete concern for actual persons faced with often intolerable circumstances such as pregnancy following rape or incest. Feminist theologians have also linked opposition to reproductive rights with patriarchal Christian attitudes toward procreation, sexuality, and the equal participation of women in society (Harrison and Cloyes 1994).

Stem cells, embryos, and new reproductive technologies

Many hope to find a way of talking about bioethics that avoids the shrill and polarizing history of abortion debates or the simplistic opposition of religion and science which contributes to high levels of social distrust. The ethics of stem cell research is a good test case, especially because even for religious conservatives it does not pose as direct and immediate a conflict of lives. Most Christian ethicists accept somatic cell gene therapy as an extension of non-genetic medical therapies which seek to cure or reduce the effects of disease. However, they also express reservations about a "technological imperative" that risks crossing the line between therapy and enhancement in prideful search of human perfection. Enhancement, it is argued, reflects a Promethean effort to improve the human genetic pool through morally questionable means and for morally questionable purposes. Christian ethics shares with other moralities a commitment to healing, but it also argues that human beings can be tainted by pernicious motives even in the cause of good. This fear is popularly expressed by the slogan "playing God."

The Roman Catholic Church does not oppose stem cell research as such, but it officially opposes research that involves harvesting stem cells through the intentional destruction of embryonic life. For this community, embryos do not differ in kind from other human persons, and the prohibition of murder grounds their opposition to obtaining stem cells through the killing of embryos. Many Roman Catholics, however, dissent from this teaching, typically by taking a more developmental view of human personhood which supports less restrictive judgments about embryonic research. Embryos may deserve respect as bodies, but they are not persons in the relevant sense and so their use in research (especially existing embryos bound to be discarded rather than embryos cultivated for research) should not be rejected given the potential benefits. In fact, such research is supported by religious affirmations of the responsible use of human creativity and scientific discovery. Protestant positions on stem cell research range dramatically, but, like many issues in bioethics, the debate is generally similar to Catholic arguments.

In vitro fertilization is opposed by the Roman Catholic Church on the grounds that it separates the unitive and procreative goods of marriage, but it is at least tacitly endorsed by most Protestant denominations (especially when the gametes used are the couple's own). Protestant moralists tend to argue that the complex goods of marriage should characterize the *overall* course of the marital relationship rather than each individual act of sexual intercourse. A distinctive feature of the Catholic debate has emerged in response to the growing numbers of frozen embryos derived from *in vitro* fertilization procedures, and the prospect of transferring and "adopting" genetically unrelated embryos. This practice creates the possibility of distinguishing biological, gestational, and social motherhood. The Roman Catholic Church has yet to issue a clear teaching on the emerging practice of "embryo adoption," but the issue divides ethicists who otherwise affirm the Catholic vision of a "culture of life" (Weaver and Brakman 2007). The debate focuses on the proper description of the practice; namely, is it a kind of "making" that violates Catholic teachings on surrogacy, gamete donation, and other forms of assisted reproductive technology? Or, is it a kind of virtuous "rescue" that coheres with Catholic teachings on hospitality and respect for life? This debate is a good example of how religious traditions grapple with new biotechnologies and scientific possibilities that raise previously unasked questions.

This final example also raises a broader concern. Apart from analyzing the intrinsic morality of actions, religious ethicists often express general concerns about the commercialization of the life-science industry. These include worries about the commodification of human bodies, but also concerns about power and distributive justice in the biotechnology marketplace (Cahill 2005). This concern may lead some to argue for greater public funding of scientific research in order to alleviate further disparities of unequal access to health care and resources generated by private research.

Religion and Bioethics: A Distinctive Contribution?

Those who advocate greater attention to religion in bioethics do so for many different reasons. One motivation responds to a pragmatic need given the *actual* role of religion in public life (as opposed to normative claims about its *proper* role). For example, comparative studies in religion and bioethics, drawing from disciplines like anthropology and sociology, aim to provide greater cross-cultural understanding and self-critical reflection (LaFleur 1992). Many scholars in religious studies challenge the assumption that there is a universal essence to all religions which can be identified and distinguished from other spheres of culture. This assumption, it is argued, betrays a contingent Western understanding, one that reflects the inheritance of predominantly Christian categories about transcendence and the sacred (Asad 1993; Masuzawa 2005). Religion, in this sense, is an artificial invention – a claim that would complicate how many secular bioethicists understand appeals to the category of "religion." Others claim that inclusion of religious traditions offers welcome additions to conventional discussions of principles (autonomy, beneficence, nonmaleficence, and justice) or dominant moral theories (consequentialism and absolutism). They argue that the repertoire of theological concepts enriches what can often be a mechanical application of secular principles and theories in bioethics. As mentioned, some religious ethicists argue that professional bioethics too often takes for granted the assumptions of a particular version of political and economic liberalism. They contrast substantive considerations of human virtue with the formalism of approaches to bioethics that are preoccupied with fictional examples, legal process, or economic utility (Evans 2002).

Attention to religion may also further discussions in normative theory that are connected with applied ethics. Notably, religious ethicists have offered critical works on sometimes neglected themes in the foundations of ethics, including attention to divine commands, abomination, moral faith, and notions of well-being and excellence (Adams 1999). In addition, religious traditions provide sources for reflection on the status of moral dilemmas and the prospect of tragedy in the moral life (Santurri 1988). Christians divide on this theoretical issue for different reasons. For example, some argue that God could not order the world so as to allow for competing moral claims that yield genuine moral dilemmas. That is, apparent moral dilemmas may reflect weakness of will or epistemic difficulty rather than a deeply tragic human condition. Others argue that the world in which we live structurally contains moral dilemmas that occasion both moral regret and guilt. Nevertheless, this world is the best of all possible worlds for fulfilling God's intention that humanity become friends with God. A second example follows from religious beliefs about the significance of God-relatedness for morality. Some argue that belief in God limits the demandingness of our moral obligations. For example, appeals to notions like divine providence or vocation are employed to criticize consequentialist forms of reasoning that attempt to maximize the overall good of the world. Religious bioethics is often an ethics of drawing lines between various motives and forms of action rather than of weighing and balancing effects. At the same time, however, this same theological belief can generate a kind of realism that overrides deontological constraints and admits "doing evil" by appeal to notions of divine grace and human finitude.

Finally, developments in cognitive psychology, neuroscience, and molecular biology may revive interest in broadly religious themes given their potentially fundamental alteration of views about the neural structure of human mental states. Empirical study of various religious practices, including prayer and meditation, is a much publicized feature of these developments. Such experiments may contribute to materialistic con-clusions which are thought to be at odds with belief in God or the existence of a "soul." Moreover, ethical issues related to personal identity and moral agency will assume a new shape given the best of recent neurobiology and pharmacology. These develop-ments raise specific issues like the use of drugs to suppress memories of traumatic stress. But they also raise general questions about the normative implications of empirical findings about how the brain works. Some philosophers, for example, have turned to new psychological research as a resource for both understanding moral intuitions and evaluating various ethical proposals. To the extent that these studies address philosophical questions in metaphysics and epistemology, and ethics, religious responses will con-tinue to be a part of the conversation (Wolpe 2005).

Religion, Bioethics, and Liberal Society

Given the facts of pluralism, the proper role of religion in liberal societies is a prominent theme in contemporary legal, political, and social philosophy. Issues related to public bioethics often provide case studies for these discussions, especially as they relate to state funding, regulatory policy, and constitutional interpretation. One legal example involves religious accommodation in clinical settings. Jehovah's Witnesses, for example, may object to medical practices such as blood transfusions for children; or, as with some Native Americans and Orthodox Jews, religious citizens might challenge neurological definitions of "whole brain death" and request that patients remain on costly respiratory life-support (Olick 1991). The question of whether or not religion should get "special treatment" in these and other cases continues to be a matter of legal and clinical debate.

It is noteworthy that while a distinction between legality and morality is often identified with modern liberalism, it can also be found throughout many religious

53

traditions. For example, Christians speak of exercising distinctive virtues (e.g., *agape*) that cannot, and should not, be subject to legal enforcement. Legal coercion, moreover, does not follow from that fact that one considers something to be morally right or wrong. A number of practical and principled considerations enter into decisions to criminalize or regulate a practice. This accounts for why it is intelligible to argue that active euthanasia may be moral, but it should remain illegal; and, on the other hand, elective abortion may be immoral, but should remain legal.

Appeals to religious liberty raise philosophical questions about the very possibility of neutrality in public bioethics. Many religious citizens support liberal political arrangements that respect the rights of religious and non-religious citizens by not privileging any one tradition, ethical theory, or vision of the good life. Nevertheless, religious citizens often argue that dominant forms of social contract liberalism imply a secularist perspective on reality, a worry that can radicalize religious opposition to public bioethics. An important aspect of these debates is the appropriate role of religious speech in political argument, especially given the massive influence of John Rawls's "idea of public reason," which places moral restrictions on reasoning from religious convictions in certain contexts (Rawls 1996). Religious defenders of "natural law" approaches in bioethics often support this account of the ethics of citizenship. Recent philosophical writings, however, cast doubt on the availability of shared, publicly accessible reasons that can do this work of common justification (Eberle 2002; Stout 2005). They suggest a more permissive notion of rationality that still offers moral constraints on democratic speech, but it does not take account of whether or not such speech is "religious." These philosophical debates will continue, and may harbor significant political ramifications, especially as bioethics assumes an increasingly global perspective. One conclusion might be advocated: greater literacy about religion and bioethics will be necessary to further the work of reason-giving in professional bioethics that aspires to be just, humane, and democratic.

References

Adams, R. M. (1999). *Finite and Infinite Goods: A Framework for Ethics*. Oxford: Oxford University Press.

Asad, T. (1993). *Genealogies of Religion: Discipline and Reasons of Power in Christianity and Islam*. Baltimore: The Johns Hopkins University Press.

Cahill, L. S. (1987). A "natural law" reconsideration of euthanasia. In S. Lammers and A. Verhey (eds.), *On Moral Medicine: Theological Perspectives in Medical Ethics*. Grand Rapids: Eerdmans Publishing Company, pp. 445–53.

Cahill, L. S. (2005). *Theological Bioethics: Participation, Justice, and Change*. Washington, DC: Georgetown University Press.

Cahill, L. S. and Childress, J. F. (eds.) (1996). *Christian Ethics: Problems and Prospects*. Cleveland, OH: The Pilgrim Press.

Childress, J. F. (2003). Religion, theology and bioethics. In F. G. Miller (ed.), *The Nature and Prospects of Bioethics: Interdisciplinary perspectives*, Totowa, NJ: Humana Press, pp. 43–67.

Dworkin, R. (1993). *Life's Dominion: An Argument About Abortion, Euthanasia, and Individual Freedom*. New York: Alfred A. Knopf.

Eberle, C. J. (2002). *Religious Convictions in Liberal Politics*. Cambridge: Cambridge University Press.

Evans, J. H. (2002). *Playing God? Human Genetic Engineering and the Rationalization of Public Bioethical Debate*. Chicago: University of Chicago Press.

George, R. (ed.) (1994). *Natural Law Theory: Contemporary Essays*. Oxford: Oxford University Press.

Harrison, B. and Cloyes, S. (1994). Theology and morality of procreative choice. In L. Daly (ed.), *Feminist Theological Ethics*. Louisville, KY: Westminster/John Knox Press, pp. 213–32.

Hauerwas, S. (1981). *A Community of Character: Toward a constructive Christian Social Ethic*. Notre Dame: University of Notre Dame Press.

Jackson, T. P. (2005). The image of God and the soul of humanity: reflections on dignity, sanctity, and democracy. In T. Cuneo (ed.), *Religion in the Liberal Polity*. Cambridge: Cambridge University Press, pp. 43–72.

Jonsen, A. R. and Toulmin, S. (1988). *The Abuse of Casuistry: A History of Moral Reasoning*. Berkeley: University of California Press.

LaFleur, W. (1992). *Liquid Life: Abortion and Buddhism in Japan*. Princeton: Princeton University Press.

MacIntyre, A. (1981). *After Virtue: A Study in Moral Theory*. Notre Dame: University of Notre Dame Press.

Masuzawa, T. (2005). *The Invention of World Religions: Or, How European Universalism Was Preserved in the Language of Pluralism*. Chicago, IL: University of Chicago Press.

McKenny, G. P. (1997). *To Relieve the Human Condition: Bioethics, Technology, and the Body*. Albany, NY: State University of New York.

Olick, R. S. (1991). Brain death, religious freedom, and public policy: New Jersey's landmark initiative. *Kennedy Institute Ethics Journal* 1/4: 275–92.

Ramsey, P. (1970). *The Patient as Person: Explorations in Medical Ethics*. New Haven, CT: Yale University Press.

Rawls, J. (1996). *Political Liberalism*. New York: Columbia University Press.

Santurri, E. (1988). *Perplexity in the Moral Life: Philosophical and Theological Considerations*. Charlottesville: University of Virginia Press.

Stout, J. (2005). *Democracy and Tradition*. Princeton, NJ: Princeton University Press.

Weaver, D. F. and Brakman, S. V. (eds.) 2007. *The Ethics of Embryo Adoption and the Catholic Tradition*. Berlin-Dordrecht: Springer.

Wolpe, P. R. (2005). Religious responses to neuroscientific questions. In J. Illes (ed.), *Neuroethics: Defining the Issues in Theory, Practice, and Policy*. Oxford: Oxford University Press, pp. 289–96.

Further reading

Atighetchi, D. (2006). *Islamic Bioethics: Problems and Perspectives*. Berlin-Dordrecht: Springer.

Cavanaugh, T. A. (2006). *Double-Effect Reasoning: Doing Good and Avoiding Evil*. Oxford: Oxford University Press.

Farley, M. (2002). *Compassionate Respect: A Feminist Approach to Medical Ethics and Other Questions*. Mahwah, NJ: Paulist Press.

Guinn, D. E. (ed.) (2006). *Handbook of Bioethics and Religion*. Oxford: Oxford University Press.

Jonsen, A. R. (2003). *The Birth of Bioethics*. Oxford: Oxford University Press.

Keown, D. (2001). *Buddhism and Bioethics*. New York: Macmillan.

Mackler, A. L. (2003). *Introduction to Jewish and Catholic Bioethics: A Comparative Analysis*. Washington, DC: Georgetown University Press.

Outka, G. (2002). The ethics of human stem cell research. *Kennedy Institute of Ethics Journal* 12/2: 175–213.

6

Law and Bioethics

WIBREN VAN DER BURG

There is probably no other field in which law and ethics are so strongly intertwined as in biomedicine. Legal and ethical doctrines on topics like informed consent have been developed through close cooperation between lawyers and ethicists. The work of ethicists is in many ways both oriented toward the law and influenced by the law. Ethicists act as expert witnesses in courts or as advisors on legislative issues, for example, on the regulation of embryo research. In countries where ethics committees or review boards are legally recognized, they seem to have a semi-judicial status. Conversely, legal concepts, like the right to privacy, dominate moral discussions.

Because bioethics and health law are so strongly connected, every bioethicist must have a basic understanding of law. For instance, when an ethicist is asked for advice on legislation, he or she should take account of the institutional character of law, which has its own dynamics, restraints, and societal functions. Take, for example, a discussion of prostitution in the context of AIDS policies. Here the practical problems of enforcement and the possible side effects of legal prohibition alone might produce such bad consequences that the more principled arguments against legal moralism become superfluous.

Law

A general and neutral definition of law seems to be impossible because in various respects law is a highly variable and diverse phenomenon. Of course, a number of defining characteristics have been suggested, especially some criteria that would distinguish law from morality. Among those criteria are the connection of law with political authority or with sanctions, the existence of certain kinds of procedures, and the emphasis on external acts rather than on motives. However, as Judith Shklar (1964) has argued, none of the differential features suggested is found in all legal systems or practices, nor are they always absent in morality.

Nevertheless, these and other less than general characteristics are important for a full understanding of the phenomenon of law. When they are present in concrete legal systems – and only insofar as they are present – they influence the internal dynamics and societal functioning of law. Most of these features have to do with the institutionalized character of law, which takes different forms in different historical contexts.

56

One example may suffice to show the importance of taking these institutional characteristics into account. Law emphasizes, partly for reasons of proof, external acts rather than internal intentions, whereas many ethical theories do the reverse. This difference explains why the distinction between "active" and "passive" euthanasia is usually deemed more important in law than in moral theory. A Dutch criminal case against a gynecologist in Alkmaar, who was accused of the swift, active euthanasia of a severely handicapped and suffering neonate, illustrates this difference in approach. In my view, the crucial moral issue in cases like this is whether or not to start medical treatment when non-treatment will result in the baby's death within months. This is the real decision about life or death. However, the lower court considered this issue to be within the realm of professional autonomy and therefore of no legal relevance. (I should add that the appeal court took a more sophisticated stance.) The legal discussion focused on a different point in the decision process – namely swift, active euthanasia. If the doctor had chosen to let the baby die a "natural" but slow and painful death, or even if he had intentionally hastened death by administering increasing doses of painkillers, he would not have been prosecuted. Because he actively administered swift euthanasia, however, he was prosecuted for murder. (In the end he was not convicted.) Most ethicists agreed that, once the non-treatment decision had been taken, this was the most humane way of acting to avoid further suffering for the baby. Thus the ethical and legal discussions focus on different points in the decision process: the non-treatment decision and the swift, active euthanasia, respectively. This relative emphasis on external acts rather than intentions is only one of the characteristics of law with a more general, though not universal, nature. There are many others that are connected only to specific legal cultures or to fields of law in specific phases of their development. This wide variety of characteristics possessed by law in different cultures and fields makes it almost impossible to make general statements about law and bioethics. Positive law takes a different shape in every country and, even if statutory rules seem identical, the differences in legal cultures often result in different interpretations.

A major difference among Western legal cultures is that between the "common law" countries (the Anglophone world), where judicial precedent constitutes the main body of law, and "civil law" countries (roughly the countries of the European continent and their former colonies) where codification and statutory law form the core of the law. In the common law tradition, the basic attitudes toward statutes and legal rules, and hence the interpretative strategies, are generally more restrictive than those in civil law countries. A statute on patient rights will therefore be more restrictively interpreted in England and Wales than in the Netherlands; hence an identical statute (or an international treaty) may have different effects in the two different traditions. The existence of major non-Western legal traditions, like those of Chinese law and Middle Eastern law, leads to an additional variation.

There is even variation within a legal culture. For example, the possibilities and limitations of legal change through adjudication are different from those of change through legislation. Case law can offer flexible, incremental change but is sometimes unable to deal systematically with comprehensive social concerns; legislation can produce clear and prospective rules, but its mistakes may also have more comprehensive consequences (Dworkin 1996). Or, to take another source of variation, legal thought and attitudes in the field of contract law differ from those in criminal law. Reference to morality in criminal law is, for instance, generally considered more acceptable if it results in the acquittal of the defendant than if its purpose is to broaden the scope of a legal prohibition. The fact that health law is an amalgam of various fields of law therefore creates many internal tensions and inconsistencies.

There is also a more fundamental plurality in the concept of law. There are two perspectives on law that cannot be consistently grasped in one theory, just as an electron can be seen as a particle and as a wave, but not as both at the same time.

The first approach regards law as a product, as law in the books. Law is, for instance, structured as a collection of statutes, judicial decisions, and customary rules, or as a system of rules and principles. This approach to law is, in a sense, the most natural one. Legislators produce law in the form of statutes; judges decide cases on the basis of their understanding of the legal rules and principles. The second approach regards law as a process, as an activity (or, rather, a cluster of processes). Law is seen as an interpretative and argumentative practice (Dworkin 1978) and legislation as a purposive enterprise (Fuller 1969).

Both views on law are connected and presuppose each other. Law as a process is in many ways oriented to and structured by law as a product. Law as a product only makes sense because it is continuously interpreted, reconstructed, changed, and applied in a great many processes. Interdependent as they may be, it is nevertheless impossible to combine both perspectives at the same time. A unifying theory cannot be found by bringing both dimensions of law under one heading; it can be found only by acknowledging the dialectic interplay between them. This unavoidable, but rarely explicitly recognized, multitude of perspectives inherent in the phenomenon of law itself is, in my view, a major cause of the misunderstandings and quarrels between the various schools of jurisprudence, like natural law and legal positivism.

The distinction between the two perspectives has important practical consequences. In a product view (which is dominant in many legal textbooks), many standard distinctions can be defended, like that between existing law (law as it is) and ideal law (law as it ought to be from a critical point of view) or between law and morality – the product is usually easily identifiable by some test of pedigree. But in a process view, the legal and moral arguments cannot be so neatly separated, as Ronald Dworkin (1978) has argued. When discussing the legality of euthanasia in court, we have no simple criteria to say this argument is a moral one and that one is strictly legal. The two categories fuse, because law is an open system which means that in principle every moral argument can be legally relevant. And as soon as we regard law as a dynamic, ongoing process of competing interpretations, we realize that our views on what "the law on euthanasia" is are always partly determined by, and open to our normative views on, what the law on euthanasia ought to be. We should therefore lay aside the simple, static image of existing or positive law in favor of a more dynamic concept in which views on law as it is, and views on law as it should be, are continually merging into views on law as it is becoming.

Morality

In ethics, a largely analogous distinction can be made between a product view of morality and a practice view. (Process and practice are not fully equivalent, which is largely due to the institutional character of law.) A product approach in ethics focuses on normative theories, principles, and guidelines – for instance, on protocols and guidelines regarding medical experiments. We can also regard morality as a practice, as an activity in which we are continually interpreting, reconstructing, and realizing our central moral values – for instance, our ideal of being a good doctor or nurse.

Here again, my suggestion would be that we need these two perspectives of product and practice, but cannot take both at the same time. The choice of perspective has important consequences. In a product view, Hart's (1963) distinction between positive and critical morality is a clear-cut one. However, if we reflect from within ethics on ethics as an interpretative practice, this distinction becomes a dialectical interplay, simply because we have no Archimedean point for our critical morality. Our view of ideal morality is always partly determined by our positive morality; and at the same time our positive morality includes the possibility of self-criticism and justification in the light of ideal or critical morality.

From Morality to Law

After this preparatory work, we can now turn to the central theme of this article: the relationships between morality and law in the field of biomedicine. Morality influences law in many ways. Moral opinions on issues like abortion are often expressed in legislation or reflected in judicial decisions. This raises the question: when is it justified to transform morality into law, or at least to give legal effect to it? It should be noted that if we phrase the question in this standard way, we implicitly take a product view of both law and morality. We are asking when a moral rule or principle should be incorporated into the law. In a process or practice view, the distinction between law and morality is less strict and therefore the question would acquire a vaguer and less tangible character.

I will cluster the major issues under three headings.

The integrity of the law (and of its constitutive fields and processes), with its special function and character, should be taken into account. For instance, when discussing euthanasia, we should recognize that law has special problems of enforcement and proof, and that legal rules should be general. It seems impossible to make general rules that fully cover the morally acceptable cases of euthanasia, and to set corresponding standards of proof which only acceptable cases can meet. This implies, in my view, that even though we should legalize some forms of euthanasia, we will be forced to prosecute certain morally acceptable cases in order to avoid tolerating unacceptable cases. Embryo experimentation presents another example: even if, from a moral point of view, individuation at 14 days after conception were only an arbitrary line, it might be a defensible one in legislation, just because legal rules have to be simple and clear.

Both the intended effects and the unwanted side-effects should be estimated (Skolnick 1968; Cotterrell 1992: esp. ch. 2). Moreover, we should be realistic about the intended effects: legislation is not always effective in influencing people's behavior. The unpredicted and undesirable side effects of legislation sometimes outweigh the beneficial effects. The US prohibition of alcohol in the 1920s is a classic example: it allowed the Mafia to flourish, and it led to corruption, blackmail, and selective law-enforcement. The modern "war on drugs" has similar effects; if we take these into account, we should doubt whether criminalization is a good strategy. A strict prohibition of abortion usually has undesirable consequences, like women dying after undergoing illegal abortions.

The side effects of a law can yield arguments both for and against legalization of specific practices. Laws against euthanasia may result in a completely uncontrolled, secret medical practice of euthanasia; legalization of euthanasia may make some older people feel that they are under social pressure to request it.

The third cluster of topics is straightforwardly *normative*. According to most normative political theories, some forms of behavior that are considered morally wrong should nevertheless not be the subject of legal prohibition; but just when and why this is so is an issue of controversy. Some theories construe the sphere of morality in which the law has no business broadly, on the basis of classic ideas like safeguarding private spheres or fundamental rights. Apart from their controversial character, these normative theories seem to be only partly relevant to the reality of modern societies, where states play an active role and where law is a crucial instrument for policy purposes. Moreover, a serious limitation of most of these theories, even of Feinberg's celebrated four-volume analysis and defense of such an approach (Feinberg 1984–90) is that they deal only with criminal law. In modern states, however, other forms of law may be more important. Medical malpractice rarely leads to criminal cases; the threat of private lawsuits is more substantial. Consider the practice of surrogate pregnancy, for example. (See also chapter 17, "Assisted Reproduction.") Law can deal with surrogacy in many ways other than blanket prohibition: it may establish family relationships and inheritance rights between the child and either the surrogate mother or the commissioning couple; it may give or withhold legal effect to specific surrogacy contracts; and internal hospital regulations can make assisted insemination for such purposes impossible. In modern societies, many morally sensitive issues concern contract or administrative law rather than criminal law. This variety makes it impossible to suggest simple criteria for deciding which part of morality is to be legally regulated, or the way in which this should be done. Even an outline of a normative theory on this broader theme is still lacking.

From Law to Morality

Conversely, law also influences morality in various respects. Legal styles of argument can influence the style of moral reasoning. If a legal system focuses on cases, morality will probably be *case-oriented* as well. Civil law legal cultures naturally focus on statutory rules; we may therefore expect moral reasoning in these countries to be more rule-oriented than in the more casuistic common law countries. (See also chapter 12, "A Case Approach.")

Furthermore, legal concepts sometimes influence the structure of moral debates. When the theme of abortion is legally structured in terms of conflicting rights, it will be more difficult to encourage an open moral debate in terms other than rights, for example, on whether abortion based on gender of the fetus is acceptable. If there is a threat of a conservative backlash against legalized abortion, citizens may be unwilling to give up the liberal rights framework, even if it is not adequate for more subtle moral questions.

Finally, law may directly influence the contents of popular morality. For example, legal rules on informed consent may, directly or in the long run, mold medical practice and moral opinion.

A different normative issue is whether law gives rise to moral obligations. Especially in rapidly developing fields such as those of bioethics, the law often cannot keep up with the pace of change. Is a health-care professional morally obliged to obey a law that is inadequate or unjust, like an illiberal abortion law? This theme of political obligation and civil disobedience has elicited a rich literature (Greenawalt 1989). A word of caution might be in place. Law is more than a set of statutory rules: most legal systems have means (like the defense of necessity) for allowing acts that, though against the letter of the law, are morally justified. It may therefore be unclear whether an act like euthanasia or abortion is really illegal, precisely because moral argument is relevant in interpreting the law (Dworkin 1978).

Converging Law and Morality

The relations between morality and law usually have the character of mutual interaction rather than that of a one-way influence. We can distinguish three typical developmental phases or models in the interaction between health law and bioethics in most Western countries (Van der Burg 1997). In the first phase, the emphasis is on ethical practice; only a small number of legal rules exist as a codification of this practice. In the second, law and ethics converge in a product approach and cooperate closely in changing the traditional practice; in the third, they diverge again.

Until the 1960s, neither bioethics nor health law were independent disciplines; guidelines and rules (the "product") were almost non-existent. The medical profession was largely autonomous and free from external legal regulation; medical ethics was primarily an ethics of good medical practice. The few legal rules that existed usually reflected positive morality, like rules prohibiting abortion, euthanasia, and certain sexual activities. In this setting, the relationships between law and morality were primarily discussed under the headings of legal moralism and paternalism. We may therefore call this the moralistic-paternalistic model. The best critical analysis of problems with this model can be found in Feinberg's work, to which reference has already been made (see also Dworkin 1994).

This moralistic-paternalistic model has, in most countries, gradually been replaced by a different one, which I shall call the liberal model. Health law and bioethics have developed into flourishing disciplines that are closely connected. They have a common mission: the search for adequate answers to the many new problems that arise and the struggle to make biomedical practice comply with norms shared by ethics and health law. In interdisciplinary cooperation, ethicists and lawyers are developing doctrines of euthanasia and abortion. Legal case materials are used for illustration in bioethics textbooks; ethical literature is quoted in legal texts and court decisions.

This convergence has been facilitated by a number of closely connected factors that characterize the new liberal model. First, both health law and bioethics take a product view (exemplified in the principlism of Beauchamp and Childress (2009; see also chapter 7, "A Principle-based Approach"), trying to develop new theories for the new problems that arise (or for old problems that are seen in a new light) such as the plight of psychiatric patients and the possibilities and risks of new technologies. Second, both use the same conceptual categories: rules, principles, rights, procedures. As a result, translation from legal to moral analysis, and vice versa, seems (at least superficially) simple, which is a precondition for successful cooperation. Third, both focus on what is minimally necessary for decent medical practice rather than on the ideal situation; formulating and realizing minimum standards seems to be a major achievement itself. The fourth factor is closely connected to the other three: both use the same liberal substantive theory, in which autonomy and patient rights are central.

These four factors not only facilitate cooperation between the two disciplines, but also contribute to their effectiveness. In modern pluralist societies, an overlapping consensus can more easily be reached on procedures, minimum rules, and rights than on the good life. The liberal model offers simple legal solutions to intricate problems like abortion and euthanasia by entrusting individuals with the responsibility for moral dilemmas. The problems that were most urgent in the early years of bioethics and health law – patient rights, abortion, medical experiments – can thus all be fruitfully addressed in the context of a product-oriented liberalism (at least, with respect to abortion, if one starts from the assumption that the fetus does not count as a full person). Moreover, scarce intellectual resources and weak societal powers are thus combined.

Of course, this liberal model has not been equally effective everywhere; in fact, no country has yet fully implemented it. In strongly pluralist societies, like the United States and the Netherlands, it has been much more influential than in, for example, Ireland. There are even differences within one country. The United States has adopted an extremely liberal stance on patient rights, whereas, so far, it has taken a more moralistic position on various issues in the field of human sexuality.

Diverging Law and Morality: Beyond the Liberal Model

The liberal model has now gained broad support in many countries. Central elements have been legally recognized and sometimes codified in constitutional rights, statutes and international treaties. (Although, of course, this process of legal recognition is in many countries still far from completion.) Bioethics and health law have become established fields in many universities. The very success of the liberal model, however, now leads to its decline: the advantages become less important and the disadvantages become more visible. Although the criticisms are quite diverse, they have a common implication: developments in health law and bioethics should no longer be parallel and connected. To put it simply: health law is criticized as being too dominant, too rigid and not sensitive enough to the complex problems of health-care practice; bioethics is criticized as being reduced to a minimum rights-oriented morality that neglects broader ethical dimensions. Precisely because, and in so far as, the liberal model has been realized, we are now in a position to go beyond it.

Trying to predict future developments would be too speculative. Therefore I can only make some tentative suggestions for the way in which a new, post-liberal model of the relations between health law and bioethics should be construed. First, the liberal model has undeniably brought progress; its achievements, especially in health law, should not be discarded lightly. Patient rights, legal abortion, informed consent, and so on should be preserved. It should, however, be supplemented, and in some respects corrected, on the basis of a proper understanding of the specific roles and characteristics of law and ethics, and of the differences between them.

With regard to bioethics, we should acknowledge that the four factors responsible for the liberal success have resulted in a certain one-sidedness. These characteristics have been challenged by a host of critics in modern ethics, ranging from MacIntyre (1981) to the advocates of an ethics of care (Gilligan, 1982). (See chapters 10, "A Virtue Ethics Approach," and 11, "A Care Approach.") To compensate for this one-sidedness, we should supplement them with a richer view of ethics rather than do away with them. Many current topics simply cannot be discussed adequately in terms of the liberal model: we should discuss both product and practice, both the minimally decent and the excellent doctor. When we discuss experiments with human embryos or sex selection, references to autonomy and rights are not sufficient. A full ethical analysis of prenatal diagnosis requires a discussion of topics like society's attitude toward persons with a handicap, and this inevitably leads us to issues that are connected to more personal and even religious conceptions of the good life. These are examples of the ways in which, in ethics, we must go beyond the liberal model.

For health law, the situation is different, and here we should largely stick to the liberal model. Legislating virtues, let alone legislating the full richness of the good life, is not possible and not desirable. Therefore health law can only partly follow bioethics in its reorientation toward practice and toward ideals of good health care. But it should, at least, not hinder this ethical reorientation and therefore it should show more self-restraint. Legal rules are sometimes too rigid and general to do justice to the intricate details of health-care practice. As the rise of "legally defensive medicine" – for example, ordering additional tests primarily in order to minimize the risk of being sued – illustrates, legal rules can adversely influence health care. After a period of rapid expansion of health law, it may therefore now be time for a more modest attitude of legal self-restraint and for the reduction of legal interventions.

As a result, law and ethics will diverge. Precisely because the close cooperation between law and ethics has been so fruitful in the past, it is now time to loosen the bonds in the interests of law and of morality, but especially in the interest of good health-care practice.

References

Beauchamp, T. L. and Childress, J. F. (2009 [1979]). *Principles of Biomedical Ethics*, 6th edn. New York: Oxford University Press.

Cotterrell, R. (1992). *The Sociology of Law: An Introduction*. London: Butterworths.

Dworkin, G. (ed.) (1994). *Morality, Harm, and the Law*. Boulder, CO: Westview Press.

Dworkin, R. (1978). *Taking Rights Seriously*. Cambridge, MA: Harvard University Press.

Dworkin, R. B. (1994). *Limits: The Role of Law in Bioethical Decision Making*, Bloomington: Indiana University Press.

Feinberg, J. (1984). *The Moral Limits of the Criminal Law*. Vol. 1: *Harm to Others*. New York: Oxford University Press.

Feinberg, J. (1985). *The Moral Limits of the Criminal Law.* Vol. 2: *Offence to Others.* New York: Oxford University Press.

Feinberg, J. (1986). *The Moral Limits of the Criminal Law.* Vol. 3: *Harm to Self.* New York: Oxford University Press.

Feinberg, J. (1990). *The Moral Limits of the Criminal Law.* Vol. 4: *Harmless Wrongdoing.* New York: Oxford University Press.

Fuller, L. L. (1969). *The Morality of Law.* New Haven: Yale University Press.

Gilligan, C. (1982). *In a Different Voice.* Cambridge, MA: Harvard University Press.

Greenawalt, K. (1989). *Conflicts of Law and Morality.* New York: Oxford University Press.

Hart, H. L. A. (1963). *Law, Liberty and Morality.* Oxford: Oxford University Press.

Hart, H. L. A. (1994). *The Concept of Law.* Oxford: Clarendon Press.

MacIntyre, A. (1981). *After Virtue.* Notre Dame, IN: University of Notre Dame Press.

Shklar, J. N. (1964). *Legalism: Law, morals, and political trials.* Cambridge, MA: Harvard University Press.

Skolnick, J. H. (1968). Coercion to virtue. *Southern California Law Review* 41: 588–641.

Van der Burg, W. (1997). Bioethics and law: a developmental perspective. *Bioethics* 11/2: 91–114.

Further reading

Blom-Cooper, L. and Drewry, G. (1976). *Law and Morality.* London: Duckworth.

Clouser, K. D. (1994). Morality vs. principlism. In R. Gillon (ed.), *Principles of Health Care Ethics.* Chichester: John Wiley, pp. 251–66.

Devlin, P. (1965). *The Enforcement of Morals.* London: Oxford University Press.

Dickens, B. M. (1994). Legal approaches to health care ethics and the four principles. In R. Gillon (ed.), *Principles of Health Care Ethics.* Chichester: John Wiley, pp. 305–17.

Dworkin, R. (ed.) (1977). *The Philosophy of Law.* Oxford: Oxford University Press.

Mason, J. K. et al. (2006). *Mason and McCall Smith's Law and Medical Ethics.* Oxford: Oxford University Press.

Raz, J. (1979). *The Authority of Law: Essays on Law and Morality.* Oxford: Clarendon Press.

Schneider, C. E. (1994). Bioethics in the language of the law. *Hastings Center Report* 24/4: 16–22.

Skolnick, J. H. (1992). Rethinking the drug problem. *Dædalus: Journal of the American Academy of Arts and Sciences* 121/3: 133–59.

Part III

Ethical Approaches

7

A Principle-based Approach

JAMES F. CHILDRESS

This chapter will analyze and assess several principle-based approaches to ethics, with particular attention to bioethics. It will explore the various forms they take, the kinds of principles they accept, and the different ways they relate those principles to particular judgments in concrete situations.

A principle-based approach must, at a minimum, hold that some general moral norms or action guides are central in moral reasoning. Some of these may be construed as principles, others as rules. Both principles and rules are "general action guides specifying that some type of action is prohibited, required, or permitted in certain circumstances" (Solomon 1978: 408). Although I will sometimes use the term "principles" as well as the term "norms" to encompass both principles and rules, I will also construe principles as more general norms and rules as more specific norms. Principles often provide warrants for more specific rules, while rules specify more concretely the type of prohibited, required, or permitted action.

The Variety of Principle-based Approaches

No single approach can be called *the* principles approach. Hence, the criticisms directed against one principle-based approach may not apply to other such approaches. For instance, criticisms aimed at a deontological theory that is principle-based may not be effective against a consequentialist theory that is also principle-based. And yet the language of "principles" is sometimes mistakenly restricted to deontological theories, that is, to theories holding that some inherent or intrinsic features of actions, such as lying or truthfulness, make them right or wrong. This restriction is a mistake, because consequentialist theories, which focus on the probable consequences or effects of actions, may also be principle-based. Utilitarianism, the most prevalent contemporary consequentialist theory, invokes the principle of utility in assessing actions or rules (see, among others, the writings of Joseph Fletcher, R. M. Hare, Richard Brandt, and Peter Singer (1993, 1996)).

Act utilitarians apply the principle of utility directly to different possible acts in a situation to determine which act would probably produce the greatest good; that act is then right and obligatory. They further insist that principles or rules other than utility can only function as maxims or rules of thumb without prescriptive, binding power. Such principles or rules can help agents see the tendencies of different acts to produce good or bad consequences. By contrast, rule utilitarian theories appeal to the principle of utility to shape other principles and rules, which then determine the rightness or wrongness of particular acts. A rule utilitarian might, for instance, defend such rules as truthfulness and confidentiality on the grounds that physicians' adherence to these rules over time will produce the greatest good. Physicians would then follow such rules rather than directly applying the principle of utility. However, they could appeal to the principle of utility to resolve conflicts between such rules as truthfulness and confidentiality in particular situations. According to act utilitarians, rule utilitarians and rule deontologists are more alike than different – both make too much of principles and rules (other than the principle of utility itself) and too little of the consequences of particular acts.

Some principle-based approaches attempt to include both consequentialist and deontological or non-consequentialist principles, without reducing one to, or deriving one from, the other, and without appealing to any overarching principle (see, for example, Beauchamp and Childress 2009). Various deontological and consequentialist moral principles appear in bioethical debates. For example, the influential US National Commission for the Protection of Human Subjects of Biomedical and Behavioral Research (1978) justified its policy recommendations by three major principles: respect for persons (which includes respect for autonomy), beneficence (which includes nonmaleficence) and justice (see also Childress et al. 2005). Most moral justifications of research involving human subjects invoke such non-consequentialist principles as respect for autonomy (expressed in rules of informed consent) and justice (expressed in the fair selection of research subjects), along with such consequentialist considerations as the research's probable chance of producing generalizable knowledge and its probable benefits to the subject and others, balanced against its risks to the subject.

More broadly, in the literature of bioethics, principles represent the following sorts of general moral considerations: obligations to respect the wishes of competent persons (respect for persons or autonomy); obligations not to harm others, including not killing them or treating them cruelly (nonmaleficence); obligations to benefit others (beneficence); obligations to produce a net balance of benefits over harms (utility); obligations to distribute benefits and harms fairly (justice); obligations to keep promises and contracts (fidelity); obligations of truthfulness; obligations to disclose information; and obligations to respect privacy and to protect confidential information (confidentiality).

In various ethical frameworks, some of these obligations appear as principles, others as rules; some as primary and fundamental, others as secondary and derivative. For example, in *Principles of Biomedical Ethics* (2009, as well as earlier editions), Beauchamp and Childress identify four primary principles – respect for autonomy, nonmaleficence, beneficence (including utility), and justice – and several derivative rules – "tell the truth," "keep your promises," "protect the privacy of others," and "do not pass on to others information given to you in confidence" – along with various other rules, such as the requirement to obtain the informed consent of a patient or prospective research subject. On this view, rules are derivative, because they are grounded in the primary principles. "Tell the truth," for example, can be derived from the principle of respect for autonomy because people cannot make autonomous decisions without accurate information. (This approach is sometimes called the "four principles approach" by defenders (Gillon 2003) and "principlism" by critics (Clouser and Gert 1990 and Gert et al. 2006).)

Robert Veatch's list of principles in *A Theory of Medical Ethics* (1981) and *The Basics of Bioethics* (2000) – which consists of beneficence, contract-keeping, autonomy, honesty, avoiding killing, and justice – is similar in important respects but differs in others. He also recognizes several moral rules or intermediate moral formulations, such as informed consent. In a much shorter list, formulated for secular morality among strangers, H. Tristram Engelhardt's *Foundations of Bioethics* (1995) only recognizes principles of permission (what he had earlier called "autonomy") and of beneficence, while reducing justice to these two considerations. However, it also recognizes several derivative obligations.

In short, one major difference among principle-based approaches is how they sort out different obligations. Some may encompass several obligations under a few general headings, while others may view them as distinct and even separable obligations. And some theories favor the language of rights over the language of obligations.

Variety also marks the justification of different ethical principles. To some, the language of principles suggests a strictly rationalist theory that appeals to non-historical foundations, such as natural law. And they argue that principle-based approaches pay inadequate attention to history, convention, community, tradition, and the like. Certainly, some principle-based approaches do in fact appeal to universal moral norms based on natural law (see, for instance, Pope John Paul II, *Evangelium Vitae*, 1995). However, rationalistic conceptions of principles are not the only ones in ethics or bioethics. For instance, Beauchamp and Childress (2009) appeal to the "common morality," that is, to principles discerned in laws, policies, and practices. There are particularistic and universalistic versions of appeals to "common morality," but all of them refrain from drawing norms from abstract human reason or human nature.

Connecting General Principles to Particular Judgments about Cases

Principles need bridges to concrete, particular judgments. The same principle may point in different directions – for example, the principle of benefiting the patient may offer ambiguous directives. And any relevant principle may conflict with other relevant principles – for example, the principle of benefiting the patient may conflict with the principle of respecting the patient's autonomous choices. In the light of such ambiguities and conflicts, Henry Richardson (1990 and 2005) identifies three major ways to connect principles to case judgments: (1) application, which involves the deductive application of principles and rules; (2) balancing, which weighs conflicting principles to determine which has priority in the situation, and (3) specification, which proceeds by "qualitatively tailoring our norms to cases" through specifying such circumstances as who, what, and when.

Despite its prominence, the metaphor of *application*, as in *applied ethics*, cannot illuminate all, or even most, significant relations between principles and particular judgments. Not all cases involve the rational deduction of particular judgments from general principles, and particular case judgments may even modify the way principles are formulated and interpreted. Hence, most principle-based approaches reject the metaphor of application as misleading insofar as it suggests a deductivist, mechanical method that appears to flounder in cases of conflict.

Two other possible ways of connecting principles and particular judgments – specification and balancing – address two distinct (but inseparable) dimensions of norms – their meaning, range, and scope, on the one hand, and their weight or strength, on the other.

Specifying norms' meaning, range, and scope

We regularly specify the meaning, range, and scope of moral norms. First of all, as R. M. Hare (1989: 54) notes, "any attempt to give content to a principle involves specifying the cases that are to fall under it. . . . Any principle, then, which has content goes some way down the path of specificity." Second, specifications often take the form of rules that provide more concrete guidance. For instance, rules of voluntary, informed consent often specify the principle of respect for personal autonomy. And rules of confidentiality specify the requirements of several principles, including respect for autonomy and utility, the latter because of the value of confidential relations for the provision of effective health care. Third, apparent cases of conflict between principles (and rules) may evaporate when the relevant principles (and rules) are more fully specified.

To take one example, different specifications play a role in different definitions and assessments of lying. On the one hand, "lying" is sometimes defined as making an intentionally deceptive statement. According to this definition, a physician in the US tells a lie when he or she greatly exaggerates the severity of the patient's medical problems in order to obtain full insurance coverage for the patient. The moral debate about such a case would then focus on whether the rule against deception could be overridden in this case by a principle of patient benefit or of utility. Whatever the conclusion about this particular case, few if any ethical theories consistently hold that lying, so defined, is absolutely wrong, because it is easy to imagine circumstances where lying would prevent a terrible harm or injustice.

On the other hand, "lying" is sometimes defined not simply as making an intentionally deceptive statement, but as intentionally deceiving, or withholding information from, *someone who has a right to the truth*. Under such a definition, the moral debate would focus on whether the physician in the case above actually lied, and the answer would depend in part on whether the insurance company had a right to accurate information, especially if its policies appeared to be unjust. On this second definition of lying, the rule against lying could be viewed as absolute, but all the difficult moral questions would be answered, and all the exceptional cases handled, by determining who has a right to the truth rather than by balancing the prohibition of lying against other moral considerations.

A process of specification pervades the papal encyclical *Evangelium Vitae* ("The Gospel of Life") (John Paul II, 1995), which focuses on different ways of taking human life from the perspective of the biblical commandment "Thou shalt not kill." It would be difficult to defend the prohibition against killing as absolute, and, even in the Bible, it coexists with the divine authorization to kill in self-defense, in warfare, and in capital punishment. The Christian tradition over time specified this broad principle in the following rule: Do not directly take the life of an innocent human being. Hence, Roman Catholicism has prohibited active euthanasia and, based on its convictions about when human life begins, abortion as well.

In general, then, various principle-based approaches specify their principles in more specific, concrete, and detailed rules. Often these are quite uncontroversial – for example, specifying the principle of respect for autonomy in rules requiring informed consent or refusal. One important question is whether moral rules can stand on their own and provide sufficient guidance without reference to more general principles. Clouser and Gert (1990; see also Gert et al. 2006) reject moral principles altogether in favor of more specific rules along with some ideals. However, it is not clear that all that is important in moral principles, such as those identified by Beauchamp and Childress (2009 and earlier editions), can be fully captured in the 10 rules Gert (2004) offers in their place. The rules are: don't kill, don't cause pain, don't disable, don't deprive of freedom, don't deprive of pleasure, don't deceive, keep your promises, don't cheat, obey the law, and do your duty. These rules specify the harms that are to be avoided under the requirement – what others might call the principle – of nonmaleficence. All are negative except for promise-keeping, obedience of law, and performance of duty (mainly role-related duty). Gert and colleagues find the principles of respect for autonomy, beneficence, and justice in principlism more problematic. Yet they bring part of what others include under a principle of beneficence under their ideals, which include such positive actions as relieving pain, preventing death, and helping the needy (Clouser and Gert 1990; Gert et al. 2006). But such actions thereby become praiseworthy rather than prima facie obligatory, as claimed by some principle-based approaches. Furthermore, some argue that the omitted principles perform important moral functions not completely discharged by the rules; for instance, respect for personal autonomy goes well beyond these specific rules in expressing an important moral obligation.

However, Clouser and Gert (1990) and Gert et al. (2006), among other critics, charge that the principles identified by Beauchamp and Childress do not adequately determine action because they are so general and vague. One attempt within principlism to address these charges further extends the role of specification; examples include "specified principlism" (DeGrazia 1992; contrast Strong 2000) or the combination of specification with constrained balancing (Beauchamp and Childress 2009). Still some critics wonder whether specification, which is intended to reduce intuitive judgments, actually falls prey to the same problems its proponents find in efforts to balance moral norms (Arras 1994).

Balancing moral norms

Balancing moral norms is another way to try to resolve moral dilemmas and conflicts. Balancing presupposes a certain conception of the weight or strength of moral norms. Four main conceptions of norms' weight or strength appear on a spectrum: (a) using maxims or rules of thumb as merely illuminative; (b) balancing prima facie binding principles and rules; (c) ranking principles in lexical or serial order; and (d) adhering to absolute principles and rules. It is possible that all four conceptions play some role in ethics and bioethics, and much of the debate focuses on which general moral considerations should have how much weight or strength.

71

At one end of the spectrum are absolutists, who maintain that some moral principles and rules bind moral agents regardless of the circumstances, including countervailing moral factors. However, even absolutists generally recognize only a few absolute principles and often define and specify them in such a way as to reduce or eliminate irresolvable moral dilemmas. To take one example, Paul Ramsey (1968 and 1970) often handled hard cases not by overriding or rebutting moral rules but, rather, by deepening their meaning. Hence, he could view some cases of justified deception – for example, to save a life – not as "exceptions," but rather as implicit within a deeper understanding of the rule against lying (1968).

It is important to distinguish the debate about *which* principles or rules are absolute from the debate about *whether* there are absolutes. Skepticism about construing some principle, such as sanctity of life, or truthfulness, as absolute, often leads to a general challenge to absolutism. Nevertheless, some principles and rules, particularly specified negative rules, may be absolute or virtually absolute – plausible candidates include moral rules against rape, cruelty, and murder. But much of the moral work appears in setting the criteria for these categories – for instance, which kind of acts count as murder. Once the criteria are set, no competing moral considerations can justify the acts in question.

At the other end of the spectrum, an act utilitarian may recognize only one absolute principle – utility – and then view all other principles and rules as mere maxims or rules of thumb. They are all parallel to the maxim in tennis, "don't aim very close to the line on second service," which advises rather than obligates players. Principles and rules other than utility merely identify the tendencies of actions, based on past experience, to produce or subvert good consequences. They are illuminative, not prescriptive. A more thoroughgoing situational or contextual ethic might even reject the overarching moral principle of utility in favor of particular judgments based on intuition or conscience.

One intermediate conception of the weight and strength of moral norms views norms as prima facie or presumptively binding, rather than as either absolutely binding or merely advisory. For example, Beauchamp and Childress (2009) argue that their four primary principles – respect for autonomy, nonmaleficence, beneficence (including utility or proportionality), and justice – along with such derivative rules as veracity, fidelity, privacy, and confidentiality, are only prima facie binding. That is, they are binding at first impression and are sufficient to establish the rightness or wrongness of an act unless they are outweighed or overridden. Insofar as an act embodies the characteristics or features identified by the relevant principles or rules, it is morally right or obligatory. However, acts may have several morally relevant features, such as truthfulness and causing harm, which represent conflicting principles or rules. As prima facie binding, all relevant principles and rules have to be weighed and balanced in situations of conflict. However, for Beauchamp and Childress, in contrast to act utilitarians, the moral agent has to justify departures from any of these principles – because they are prescriptive, not merely illuminative – by showing that, in the situation, some other principle has more weight or greater stringency. The assignment of weights or priorities occurs in the situation, not through abstract, a priori formulations.

This approach suffers from the limitations of any pluralistic approach that does not assign, in advance, weights or priorities to various principles and rules: it appears to be excessively intuitive. While conceding that intuitive judgments cannot be totally eliminated in balancing principles in actual situations, Beauchamp and Childress (2009) propose, in addition to specification, a decision procedure to reduce the reliance upon intuition. They contend that the logic of prima facie duties imposes conditions that prevent just any judgment based on a relevant principle from being acceptable in a conflict. The constraining conditions include: good reasons can be offered to act on the overriding norm rather than on the infringed norm; the moral objective justifying the infringement has a realistic prospect of achievement; no morally preferable alternative actions are available; the lowest level of infringement, commensurate with achieving the primary goal of the action, has been selected; any negative effects of the infringement have been minimized; all affected parties have been treated impartially. They contend that a stronger decision procedure finds no warrant in moral experience and moral theory.

Some critics doubt that balancing moral norms, even within such constraints, can always yield the right conclusion in a serious conflict – for example, between promoting societal welfare through research involving human subjects and protecting the rights of potential research subjects through voluntary, informed consent. But they are also suspicious of the rule utilitarian's appeal to the ultimate principle of utility in order to adjudicate conflicts among those principles and rules. Instead, they offer a set of priority rules that rank different principles and rules in advance of concrete situations.

The work of Robert Veatch (1981, 2000, and 2005) represents a major effort to develop a lexical or serial order for principles: all the deontological or non-consequentialist principles have lexical priority over the principle of beneficence. However, when the deontological or non-consequentialist principles themselves conflict, Veatch employs a "balancing strategy." He thus finds "a solution to the inevitable unacceptable tension between Hippocratic individualism and the utilitarian drive toward aggregate net benefit" (1981). This solution "comes from the articulation of other non-consequentialist principles that will necessarily have a bearing on medical ethical decisions: contract keeping, autonomy, honesty, avoiding killing, and justice" and from assigning them collective priority over the production of good consequences for individuals (Hippocratic individualism) or society (utilitarianism). Non-consequentialist principles are given "coequal ranking" in relation to each other and "lexical ranking" over the principle of beneficence. Similarly Engelhardt (1995) gives the principle of permission priority over the principle of beneficence because, in a pluralistic society, we lack a consensus about harms and benefits. Critics of such attempts to provide a lexical order challenge what amounts to an absolute ranking, in the abstract, of one principle over another or others, contending that it inevitably runs afoul of actual human experience in real situations.

Critiques

In light of the wide variety of principle-based positions, it is not surprising that their supporters are regularly in strong disagreement with each other. Beyond these intramural disputes, other critics challenge several or all principle-based approaches.

73

First, the advocates of case-based approaches sometimes rail against the "tyranny of principles" on behalf of the primacy of particular judgments (Toulmin 1981; Jonsen and Toulmin 1988). However, when their claims are examined carefully, these casuists, as they are frequently termed, mainly oppose certain kinds of principles: that is, principles that are absolute, invariant, eternal, and so forth. Many principle-based approaches also reject such conceptions of principles and can accept several of the casuists' other claims. For instance, recognizing principles does not imply that moral knowledge is fundamentally general rather than particular. Even if particular case judgments are primary, those particular case judgments imply similar judgments for relevantly similar cases. The requirement of universalizability or generalizability, many philosophers argue, entails that moral agents extend their moral judgment that "X is wrong" to all relevantly similar "Xs." Hence, particular judgments, even if they are primary, still give rise to principles and rules, which can then guide further action. Defenders of general moral norms often stress, against the casuists, that norms are important in identifying relevant similarities and differences between cases. One approach that views both particular case judgments and general moral norms as important in moral reasoning holds that they are dialectically or dialogically related – each one may potentially modify and correct the other in an effort to achieve greater coherence (Beauchamp and Childress 2009). Finally, principle-based approaches can recognize the importance of settled cases, so-called paradigm cases about which there is a strong moral consensus, and can reason analogically from such cases to new or controversial ones, just as casuists do.

Casuists often admit that principles and rules are appropriate, and even necessary, in interactions among strangers in contrast to relations between intimates and friends (Toulmin 1981). Hence, a fundamental question in bioethics is whether patients and health-care professionals interact as intimates and friends or as strangers. Holding that, at least in the West, such interactions largely involve moral strangers, Engelhardt (1995) propounds a theory of bioethics for peaceable, secular, pluralistic societies with primary attention to the principle of permission (see also Wildes 2000).

Several critics of principle-based approaches, particularly what has been called principlism, lament the tiresome invocation of the mantra of principles (Clouser and Gert 1990; Arras 1994; Harris 2003). This criticism sometimes suggests that some principle-based approaches distort bioethics by offering relatively abstract categories, such as respect for autonomy and nonmaleficence, which tempt novices to suppose that they have become experts in ethics because they can chant the mantra. Then these novices mechanically apply the principles. Proponents of principle-based approaches retort that there is good and bad scholarship in ethics and bioethics, whichever approach is taken, and that it is important to compare the best representations of each approach, as well as to criticize deficient versions.

Other critics charge that principle-based approaches reduce ethics and bioethics to the analysis and resolution of moral quandaries and dilemmas. However, principle-based approaches recognize that much, even most, of the moral life is a matter of doing what one recognizes to be right, obligatory or good, without any perplexity about what one ought to do and without direct appeal to principles. Nevertheless, when conflicts or novel situations arise, as they sometimes do, principles are important.

A closely related criticism contends that principle-based (and also case-based) approaches err in concentrating on "What ought I/we to *do?*" rather than on the more fundamental question "What ought I/we to *be?*" The latter question directs us to virtue and character. Proponents of the primacy of virtue and character usually hold that a virtuous professional can *discern* the right course of action in the situation without reliance on principles and rules and/or that a virtuous person will *desire* to do what is right. Defenders of principles respond that there is no assurance that good people will discern what is right, especially in novel situations or conflicts. Also, people who are generally good might not always desire to do what is right. Consequently, in many cases, it is simply unclear what a virtuous physician or other health professional would do. Thus, supporters of principles and rules believe that these moral tenets can, especially when backed by sanctions, helpfully guide conduct. Furthermore, principles of action also help to determine which virtues should be developed, particularly because many virtues correlate with principles and rules – for example, benevolence with beneficence, and truthfulness with veracity. Several other virtues – such as conscientiousness and courage – are important for morality as a whole, including action in accordance with principles.

In conclusion, these several critiques offer major challenges to principle-based approaches to ethics and bioethics, but many proponents of principle-based approaches believe that they can accommodate the most important and cogent criticisms without abandoning their principles.

References

Arras, J. D. (1994). Principles and particularity: the role of cases in bioethics. *Indiana Law Journal* 69: 983–1014.

Beauchamp, T. L. and Childress, J. F. (2009). *Principles of Biomedical Ethics*, 6th edn. New York: Oxford University Press. (Earlier editions appeared in 1979, 1983, 1989, 1994, and 2001.)

Childress, J. F., Meslin, E. M., and Shapiro, H. T. (eds.) (2005). *Belmont Revisited: Ethical Principles for Research with Human Subjects.* Washington, DC: Georgetown University Press.

Clouser, K. D. and Gert, B. (1990). A critique of principlism. *Journal of Medicine and Philosophy* 15: 219–36.

DeGrazia, D. (1992). Moving forward in bioethical theory: theories, cases, and specified principlism. *Journal of Medicine and Philosophy* 17: 511–39.

Engelhardt, H. T. (1995). *Foundations of Bioethics*, 2nd edn. New York: Oxford University Press.

Gert, B. (2004). *Common Morality: Deciding What To Do.* New York: Oxford University Press.

Gert, B., Culver, C. M., and Clouser, K. D. (2006). *Bioethics: A Systematic Approach*, 2nd edn. New York: Oxford University Press.

Gillon, R. (2003). Ethics needs principles – four can encompass the rest – and respect for autonomy should be "first among equals." *Journal of Medical Ethics* 29/5: 307–12.

Hare, R. M. (1989). Principles. In *Essays in Ethical Theory.* Oxford: Clarendon Press, pp. 49–65.

Harris, J. (2003). In defense of unprincipled ethics. *Journal of Medical Ethics* 29/5: 303–6.

John Paul II, Pope (1995). *Evangelium Vitae.* Rome: The Vatican.

Jonsen, A. R. (1995). Casuistry: An alternative or complement to principles? *Kennedy Institute of Ethics Journal* 5: 237–51.

Jonsen, A. R. and Toulmin, S. (1988). *The Abuse of Casuistry: A History of Moral Reasoning.* Berkeley: University of California Press.

National Commission for the Protection of Human Subjects of Biomedical and Behavioral Research (1978). *The Belmont Report: Ethical Guidelines for the Protection of Human Subjects of Research*. DHEW Publication No. (OS) 78-00. Washington, DC: Department of Health Education and Welfare.

Ramsey, P. (1968). The case of the curious exception. In G. Outka and P. Ramsey (eds.), *Norm and Context in Christian Ethics*. New York: Charles Scribner's Sons.

Ramsey, P. (1970). *The Patient as Person*. New Haven, CT: Yale University Press.

Richardson, H. (1990). Specifying norms as a way to resolve concrete ethical problems. *Philosophy and Public Affairs* 19: 279–320.

Richardson, H. (2005). Specifying, balancing, and interpreting bioethical principles. In J. F. Childress et al. (eds.), *Belmont Revisited: Ethical Principles for Research with Human Subjects*. Washington, DC: Georgetown University Press, pp. 205–27.

Singer, P. (1993). *Practical Ethics*, 2nd edn. Cambridge: Cambridge University Press.

Singer, P. (1996). *Rethinking Life and Death: The Collapse of our Traditional Ethics*. New York: St Martin's Griffin.

Solomon, W. D. (1978). Rules and principles. In W. T. Reich (ed.), *Encyclopedia of Bioethics*, vol. 1. New York: Free Press, pp. 407–13.

Strong, C. (2000). Specified principlism: what is it, and does it really resolve cases better than casuistry? *Journal of Medicine and Philosophy* 25: 324–41.

Toulmin, S. (1981). The tyranny of principles. *Hastings Center Report* 11/6: 31–9.

Veatch, R. M. (1981). *A Theory of Medical Ethics*. New York: Basic Books.

Veatch, R. M. (2000). *The Basics of Bioethics*. Upper Saddle River, NJ: Prentice Hall.

Veatch, R. M. (2005). Ranking, balancing, or simultaneity. In J. F. Childress et al. (eds.), *Belmont Revisited: Ethical Principles for Research with Human Subjects*. Washington, DC: Georgetown University Press, pp. 184–204.

Wildes, K. Wm., S. J. (2000). *Moral Acquaintances: Methodology in Bioethics*. Notre Dame, IN: Notre Dame University Press.

Further reading

DuBose, E. R., Hamel, R., and O'Connell, L. J. (eds.) (1994). *A Matter of Principles: Ferment in US Bioethics*. Valley Forge, PA: Trinity Press International.

Dworkin, R. B. (ed.) (1994). Symposium: emerging paradigms in bioethics. *Indiana Law Journal* 69: 945–1122.

Gillon, R. (ed.) (1994). *Principles of Health Care Ethics*. New York: John Wiley and Sons.

Hooker, B. (2002). *Ideal Code, Real World: A Rule-Consequentialist Theory of Morality*. Oxford: Oxford University Press.

Savulescu, J. (ed.) (2003). Festschrift edition of the *Journal of Medical Ethics* in honor of Raanan Gillon. Introduction by R. Gillon. *Journal of Medical Ethics* 29/5: 265–312.

Spicer, C. M. (ed.) (1995). Special issue: theories and methods in bioethics: principlism and its critics. *Kennedy Institute of Ethics Journal* 5: 181–286.

8

Exceptionless Rule Approaches

JOSEPH BOYLE

Several approaches to moral decision-making are recognized by their proponents and others as incorporating exceptionless rules or norms, "moral absolutes" as they are often called. Examples of the kind of exceptionless norms essential to these approaches are the biblically based prohibitions against adultery and other sexual behavior, the Catholic prohibition against intentionally killing the innocent, and the Augustinian and Kantian prohibitions against lying. These well-known examples of moral absolutes are norms that are taken as holding without exception, that is, the actions of the kind specified in the rule are judged impermissible simply in virtue of their being of that kind. Further morally relevant information about the particular action cannot alter the judgment of impermissibility. Exceptionless rules of this kind play a role in a number of moral approaches that are reasonably understood as forms of "traditional morality" (Oderberg 2000: vii–ix, 33, 68–9). Some of these approaches are based on theological conviction; some are based on philosophical ethical theories, such as natural law or virtue ethics (Pellegrino 2005: 469–86). Debates continue as to the soundness of these approaches and of the exceptionless rules they incorporate and apply in bioethics, as recent discussions about mercy killing, artificial reproduction, and truth-telling in clinical and research contexts reveal. So the topic of this essay is important for understanding and engaging in a central feature of the traditional moral outlook of many health-care professionals, religious people, and others.

The Idea of an Exceptionless Moral Norm

A moral norm is exceptionless if and only if what the rule prescribes is morally decisive and cannot be overridden by other considerations. This idea is plain enough: one is to follow an exceptionless rule no matter what; such rules are not defeated by other moral considerations.

But various sorts of moral statements are reasonably considered rules, and they can all be absolute or exceptionless in the sense indicated above. Most of these kinds of absolute rules do not, upon reflection, contribute to distinctive approaches to moral decision-making as are evoked by the tag "exceptionless rule approaches." These approaches are characterized by a claim about the exceptionlessness of a specific kind of rule which I will call a *precept*, namely a universal prescription which directs that an action of a kind characterized in descriptive, non-moral terms may, should, or should not be done.

On this conception of a precept, several kinds of morally interesting sentences or "rules" are not precepts and so cannot be exceptionless rules in the sense to be considered here. First and most importantly, universal moral *principles* – for example, the principle of utility or the categorical imperative – are not precepts, but grounds for precepts and for any other moral considerations they justify. Moral principles make reference to all human actions, whereas precepts refer only to actions of a specifically described kind. Within some ethical approaches, a universal principle may have absolute weight in relation to all other moral considerations. This does not make the principle a precept and does not imply that any precept it grounds will be absolute.

Within some moral theories dominated by a single, supreme normative principle, some exceptionless precepts will be justified, but even in these cases it is useful to distinguish ground and precept. A precept requires, in addition to its normative ground, a description of a kind of action (Donagan 1977: 66–8). Thus, if deception in medical experimentation is held to violate the Kantian principle of respect for rational creatures, the act of deceiving a research subject must be described so as to reveal its incompatibility with that respect. If that incompatibility is revealed as holding for all cases of deception, then the resulting precept will be exceptionless. As this example suggests, there is disagreement among proponents of absolute rule approaches to ethics concerning which prohibitions are exceptionless.

Second, prescriptions of actions already characterized by moral evaluations are ordinarily not precepts but tautologies. I say ordinarily because there are precepts bearing upon actions already morally characterized whose purpose is to round out the moral evaluation of already approved or condemned actions. Calling an act parricide presupposes it is wrongful killing but adds something needed for a full moral evaluation. It is sometimes unclear whether the characterization of the action that is the subject of a prescription or a given moral statement is a precept or a tautology. Nevertheless, the role of exceptionless rules in moral decision-making is reduced to nearly zero if they are no more than a set of tautologies in which we are reminded of the wrongfulness of actions already characterized as wrongful. So, I will not regard as precepts such rules as "Murder (understood as wrongful killing) is wrong" or "Lying (understood as deceiving those who have a right to the truth) is wrong." Any exceptionlessness such norms might have is simply a function of their tautologous character (Finnis 1991: 4–6).

The contrast between precepts and other exceptionless rules points to the sense in which precepts might be distinctively and interestingly exceptionless: a precept is exceptionless if and only if it prescribes that an action of a descriptively (not evaluatively) characterized kind should not be done and that its being of that kind guarantees that no further, true description of the action and its circumstances will remove its impermissibility (Chappell 1998: 78). In other words, a negative precept, a prohibition of a kind of action, is exceptionless when one knows not only that the action as one has characterized it is wrong, but also that anything else one might discover about that action, its circumstances, and consequences will not alter that negative evaluation of the action.

The idea can be exemplified by the traditional precept against killing humans as formulated in the Catholic tradition: no one should intentionally kill an innocent human. In this precept, the subject is not killing but intentional killing, and it is the intentional killing of innocents, not humans as such, that is prohibited. Innocents are not defined as those it is wrong to kill but, very roughly, as those not engaged in or convicted of wrongdoing that seriously threatens the common good (Finnis et al. 1987: 86–91; Finnis 1991: 2). One who understands this precept as an exceptionless rule will judge that when one knows that an act is an act of intentionally killing an innocent human being, then one knows that the act is wrong, and is wrong in such a way that anything further one might discover about the action will not change its moral valence from impermissible to permissible. As this example indicates, the route from precept to final moral verdict is much quicker and more direct when the precept is absolute than when it is not. The absolute prohibition establishes the basic moral verdict: an action of a kind excluded by a moral absolute simply cannot morally be done.

Traditional moralists acknowledge that other precepts than prohibitions are in some sense exceptionless. For example, Kantian imperfect duties can be considered absolute in the sense that they are always in force even though they sometimes cannot prescribe that a particular action should be done. Moreover, they can be formulated as prohibitions against failing to form and act on some plan of self-perfection and beneficence (Donagan 1991: 500). Still, the absoluteness of such precepts is not the same as the exceptionlessness of some prohibitions of specifically described actions. The latter, not the former, are what provide the distinctive approach to moral decision-making found in natural law thinking and in other forms of traditional morality. For exceptionless prohibitions of actions like lying and intentional killing of the innocent tell us that some definite things we might have reason to do are simply out of the question morally. Our serious duties to improve ourselves and help others simply do not have this sort of relationship to any definite thing we might choose to do.

The Role of Exceptionless Precepts in Moral Thinking

As already suggested, exceptionless rule approaches to moral decision-making do not limit moral rules to exceptionless prohibitions. Their defenders believe that there are relatively few moral absolutes and that the principles grounding them also ground other precepts. For example, natural law principles enjoining rational concern for human good not only absolutely exclude a small set of actions which harm people, they also enjoin positive initiatives to support people and their goods (Finnis 1991: 1–3; Murphy 2001: 198–212). Thus we are obliged not only to not intentionally kill, slander, and so on, but reasonably to avoid harming the goods protected by these prohibitions, even when the goods are damaged incidentally to other worthwhile projects, and to promote these goods in ourselves and others.

In short, exceptionless precepts are understood by those who accept them as playing a distinctive role in moral thinking within a larger scheme of moral norms and precepts (Anscombe 1981: 34). A key feature of that role has been noted above: knowing that a proposed action is forbidden by a moral absolute ends moral deliberation about doing that action (though not necessarily the temptation to do it) and immediately establishes the person's moral verdict on the action. Thus, even though exceptionless precepts have fuzzy edges and generate borderline cases that are difficult to decide, they do provide fixed points in the normative landscape. Since abiding by exceptionless precepts can be difficult, they do not simplify moral life, but their accessibility as fixed points can help those who wish to avoid rationalization and moral confusion.

Other precepts do not work this way: reflection on the various aspects of an individual action can turn up morally relevant features which can change one's moral evaluation of the action (Grisez 1983: 256–9; 1997: 858–67). The classical example is that we are ordinarily obliged to return property to the owner upon demand, but not when we discover that the owner intends to use it for seditious purposes. The analogous case of promise-keeping is more applicable to bioethics: promises generally involve an obligation to carry out what is promised. But sometimes it is unreasonable to keep one's promise, since keeping it would be unfair to others or harmful to one's moral self.

Exceptionless Rules and Consequentialism

The functioning of moral absolutes within moral deliberation provides a significant block to the introduction of consequentialist considerations into a moral approach which includes them (Anscombe 1981: 34). Consequentialist considerations cannot overturn an exceptionless prohibition, even if those considerations would justify the action were it not absolutely excluded. In other words, moral absolutes might be said to dominate the larger moral schemes they are part of because, being exceptionless, they trump other moral precepts.

Donagan has argued that this dominance is justified as structurally necessary in a moral system having as its normative basis the Kantian principle of respect for rational creatures. He claims that this dominance is what is expressed in the Pauline principle that evil is not to be done that good may come of it – that is, that exceptionless precepts are not to be violated so that otherwise mandatory goods can be achieved:

> The Pauline principle, therefore, is not an external stipulation, like the serial ordering adopted by contractarian theorists, for getting rid of conflicts between perfect and imperfect duties. It is nothing but a general statement of a condition implicit in every precept of imperfect duty that is validly derivable from the fundamental principle of morality itself. It is structurally necessary. And it manifestly entails that the precepts of imperfect duty – the precepts that flow from the principles of culture and beneficence – cannot be inconsistent with the prohibitory principles. (Donagan 1977: 155)

Donagan's Kantian argument can be reformulated as a requirement for a kind of goods-based ethics, such as is found in natural law theory. A rational regard for the good of rational creatures is its basic normative principle. But natural law is not consequentialist; its proponents never supposed that determination of the best state of affairs was the proper conception of rational regard for the good.

That view of practical rationality has been supported by two distinct positions about practical rationality and the good. The first of these is that human goods and their instances are incommensurable in their rational desirability (Finnis et al. 1987: 254–60; Murphy 2001: 198–212; Boyle 2005: 11–25). This view casts doubt on the possibility of making characteristically consequentialist judgments, namely, those moral directives based on a determination of what is simply or unconditionally better or best: wherever and to whatever extent moral directives based on comparative value judgments are not possible, the perspective of moral absolutism becomes more plausible: in all such cases, the greater good does not provide a rational basis for setting aside exceptionless prohibitions themselves based on a concern for how each of us should rationally respond to what affects the good of human beings.

An alternative view having the same implications for consequentialism and exceptionless rule approaches is that the demand the goods make on our practical reason is for respect and non-violation as well as promotion (Chappell 1998: 74–82). If goods are not only to be pursued but respected and not violated, practical reason endorses the Pauline principle's rejection of consequentialism, since that principle rejects the violation of human goods.

On either of these conceptions of the good and of practical reason, there is independent philosophical support for the traditional theistic view that one must not do evil in order that good might come about. Traditional theism holds that humans have a real but limited part to play within divine providence, namely, to live their lives responsibly in accord with the precepts which define their role in the divine plan, accepting that overall outcomes are beyond human reckoning and so are God's responsibility (Finnis 1991: 12). These conceptions of the good and of practical reason support the conclusion of this theistic view of human responsibility, and they do so independently of the theistic premises.

Plainly, the preceding account is no more than a sketch of some opening moves in a complex philosophical dialectic. The point is simply that the anti-consequentialism of moral absolutism need not be simply a relic of its religious origins or a combination of mistakes and confusions, but is part of a coherent, although admittedly controversial, moral view.

The Casuistry of Exceptionless Rule Approaches

It is sometimes unclear whether an action one is evaluating is prohibited by an exceptionless precept. For example, it is often unclear whether a decision to act or forgo action which will hasten or cause death is a violation of the absolute prohibition against intentionally killing the innocent. Consequently, the fixed points in the moral landscape which exceptionless rules provide are not always defined by bright, clear borders. These precepts have fuzzy edges and there are borderline cases that are difficult to settle. Thus, within exceptionless rule approaches there is a need for casuistry to determine whether or not a certain kind of action falls within a kind prohibited by a moral absolute. The purpose of this kind of moral analysis is not consequentialist determination of the overall good an action or its alternatives might achieve, but the conceptual clarification needed to know whether a borderline case is an action of a kind prohibited by a moral absolute (Anscombe 1981: 36). Thus, although the structure of moral absolutist theories is deductive, since precepts are justified in the light of moral principles to which they are connected by action descriptions, much of the philosophical work of absolutist ethics lies in the non-deductive conceptual clarification that is needed to reveal precisely the moral kind of the action being evaluated (Donagan 1977: 71–4).

The casuistry of moral absolutism comes in several varieties which, in contrast to other forms of casuistry, have in common the control of the process of comparing and clarifying actions by a basic moral principle having the potential to generate exceptionless precepts. Donagan develops a distinctive strategy. He seeks to derive prohibitory precepts from the Kantian basic principle that one should never fail to respect rational nature as an end in itself by specifying actions which generally violate that principle. He then considers putative exceptions with a view toward determining whether or not they are inconsistent with the basic principle. Those inconsistent with the basic principle are included within the kind of action prohibited and the others are set aside. So the action absolutely excluded cannot be, for example, killing or lying as such, but killing or lying "at will," that is, except in those circumstances in which killing or lying is shown to be consistent with the basic principle (Donagan 1977: 72–3). Here the casuistry is presupposed for the formulation of the absolute precept.

More widespread than Donagan's indirect derivation of precepts is the direct approach of Catholic natural law according to which certain well-formulated absolute precepts – for example, the prohibition against intentionally killing the innocent or against using falsehoods to deceive – are derived directly from moral principles. Cases arise in which it is unclear whether a given act is or is not an act of the prohibited kind: whether some ambiguous communications are or are not lies or whether some defensive killings are intentional killings of the innocent. Casuistry seeks to settle such questions.

Casuistry of this kind is well known in bioethics and applied ethics more generally probably because of the influence of natural law casuistry on traditional moral thinking generally. Much of this casuistry centers on the application of the controversial doctrine of the double effect. The distinction between what is often called "indirect" killing and direct or intentional killing is perhaps the most influential of these applications of double effect in bioethics and in other areas of applied ethics, such as just war theory.

This doctrine presupposes that a distinction can be made between what is done intentionally and what is voluntarily brought about as a side effect of an intentional action. It maintains that this distinction has a special moral significance: states of affairs it would be absolutely wrong to bring about intentionally may, if other conditions are met, voluntarily be brought about as side effects. In other words, the absolute prohibition applies only to the intentional action (Anscombe 1981: 21).

This doctrine is not an ad hoc device developed by Catholic moralists to mitigate the disagreeable consequences of the acceptance of exceptionless precepts; its applications are sometimes disagreeable (or not) in both what they allow and what they permit. Double effect permits a hysterectomy on a pregnant woman with cancer, and also various other "indirect" abortions, but it cannot be used to block the application of the exceptionless prohibition against intentional killing to any abortion aimed at ending fetal life. Similarly, in end-of-life decisions, double effect allows that life-sustaining treatment may be removed if it constitutes a significant burden on the patient or others. But double effect has no tendency to allow withholding treatment for the sake of ending a life judged no longer worth living. These cases are not differentiated by the level of comfort or discomfort people sometimes see in moral judgments about them.

More likely, double effect is an essential element in the traditional morality within which exceptionless precepts function. A possible explanation is that a non-consequentialist concern for the goods of persons plausibly leads to absolute prohibitions of some voluntary harmings. Intentional harmings can be prohibited, since one can always refrain from intentional action. But not all harms brought about as side effects can be prohibited, since, frequently, whatever a person chooses to do, he or she will bring about harm as a side effect (Boyle 1991: 486–8; 2004: 55–7).

As in casuistry generally, the results of absolutist casuistry are likely to be fallible and controversial. But within its absolutist framework, such mistakes can be corrected and, as Anscombe noted, the mistakes of casuistry can cause one to stretch a point on the circumference, but they do not allow one to destroy the center (Anscombe 1981: 36).

Traditional approaches to ethics that incorporate exceptionless precepts are not fashionable nowadays, in bioethics or elsewhere. But being out of fashion is not the same as being philosophically disreputable, and much of this contribution is meant to suggest that exceptionless rule approaches to ethics are not based on superstition or confusion. There is another reason for taking exceptionless rule approaches to ethics seriously in bioethics. Many distinctions, arguments, and analyses originally developed within these approaches have become important elements within bioethical discussions. Questions about the intelligibility of these elements, whether within or independently of their original, traditional, and absolutist framework, can hardly be answered without taking that framework seriously.

References

Anscombe, E. (1981). Modern moral philosophy. In *Ethics, Religion and Politics: Collected Papers*, vol. III. Minneapolis: University of Minnesota Press.

Anscombe, E. (2005). Action, intention and "double effect." In M. Geach and L. Gormally (eds.), *Human Life, Action and Ethics*. Exeter: Imprint Academic.

Boyle, J. (1991). Who is entitled to double effect? *Journal of Medicine and Philosophy* 16: 475–94.

Boyle, J. (2004). Medical ethics and double effect: the case of terminal sedation. *Theoretical Medicine and Bioethics* 25: 51–60.

Boyle, J. (2005). Being reasonable in choosing among incommensurable goods. *Vera Lex* 6: 11–34.

Chappell, T. D. J. (1998). *Understanding Human Goods: A Theory of Ethics*. Edinburgh: Edinburgh University Press.

Donagan, A. (1977). *The Theory of Morality*. Chicago and London: University of Chicago Press.

Donagan, A. (1991). Moral absolutism and the double effect exception: reflections on Joseph Boyle's "Who is entitled to double effect?" *Journal of Medicine and Philosophy* 16: 495–509.

Finnis, J. (1991). *Moral Absolutes: Tradition, Revision, and Truth*. Washington, DC: Catholic University of America Press.

Finnis, J., Boyle, J., and Grisez, G. (1987). *Nuclear Deterrence, Morality and Realism*. Oxford: Oxford University Press.

Grisez, G. (1983). *The Way of the Lord Jesus.* Vol. I: *Christian Moral Principles.* Chicago: Franciscan Herald Press.

Grisez, G. (1997). *The Way of the Lord Jesus.* Vol. III: *Difficult Moral Questions.* Quincy, IL: Franciscan Press.

Murphy, M. (2001). *Natural Law and Practical Rationality.* Cambridge: Cambridge University Press.

Oderberg, D. S. (2000). *Moral Theory: A Non-consequentialist Approach.* Oxford: Blackwell.

Pellegrino, E. D. (2005). Some things ought never to be done: moral absolutes in clinical ethics. *Theoretical Medicine and Bioethics* 26: 469–86.

9

A Utilitarian Approach

R. M. HARE

The main constituents of any utilitarian theory may be called *consequentialism*, *welfarism* (Sen and Williams 1982: 3) and *aggregationism*. Consequentialism can be defined, roughly at first, as the view that the consequences of an act are what make it right or wrong. But this by itself is unclear. There is one sense of "consequences" in which nobody who thinks carefully about the question can help being a consequentialist. That is the sense used here.

A *consequentialist* is somebody who thinks that what determines the moral quality of an action (that is, determines whether it is right or wrong) are its consequences. A contrast is sometimes drawn between theories which determine the moral quality of actions by their observance or non-observance of rules, and those which determine it by whether they promote valued consequences. But it is obvious that, as we shall see, it is determined by both, and that any adequate theory will take both consequences and rules into account. We normally judge the rightness or wrongness of actions by their conformity to rules or principles, and the principles themselves are judged by the consequences of observing them. If the actions are intentional, we praise or blame the agent for them.

An action is the making of some difference to what happens – to the history of the world. If I make no difference to what happens, I have done no action. In the widest sense, even if I do nothing (do not move a finger), I have done an action (what is sometimes called an act of omission).

I can of course be blamed for doing nothing: someone might say "You were to blame for not saving the life of the patient when you could have." It made a difference to the history of the world that I did nothing. We are, in other words, *responsible* for what we fail to do as well as for what we actively do. Suppose, then, that my gun is pointing at somebody and I pull the trigger, and he dies. We say. "I have killed him." Killing him was what I did – my act. If I did wrong, what made it wrong was the consequence of my pulling the trigger, namely that I killed him. In the light of this example, it is hard to see how people can deny that consequences, in *this* sense, are what make actions right or wrong, and make the people who do them, if the actions are intentional, good or bad. So, in this sense, consequentialism is hard to reject. The people who reject it no doubt have some other sense of "consequentialism" in mind; but it is seldom clear what sense.

The second constituent of utilitarianism is *welfarism*. Utilitarians think that the consequences that are relevant to the morality of actions are consequences that increase or diminish the welfare of all those affected. This means, for a utilitarian, the welfare of all those affected considered impartially. We may define "welfare" as "the obtaining to a high or at least reasonable degree of a quality of life which on the whole a person wants, or prefers to have."

The word "prefer" is very important, but also ambiguous. It can be used, and normally is used by economists, to mean a pattern of behavior. In this sense, we are said to prefer one sort of thing to another if we habitually and intentionally choose the first sort of thing when we have the choice. On the other hand, it can be used to mean an introspectable mental state of liking one thing more than another. Economists tend to use the first sense, because it makes it possible to determine empirically, by observing people's behavior, what they prefer. The ambiguity normally causes no trouble, because what we prefer in the introspectable sense we usually also prefer in the behavioral sense; but there can be exceptions where the uses diverge. For example, many people (and not only neurotics) try unsuccessfully to shake off habits which they wish they did not have; so their behavior does not tally with their introspectable preferences.

There is also a problem about whether, for a utilitarian, *all* preferences have to be counted, or only some. For example, suppose that some child now prefers to go on eating sweets, although it will tend to make him obese, which he will later prefer not to be. This is a fairly easy case to deal with: the utilitarian will aim at the child's preference satisfaction as a whole; its enjoyment of the sweets will count for something, but probably its suffering later from the disadvantages that fat people cannot avoid will count for more.

But there are more difficult problems. How about so-called "external" preferences? These are preferences that states of affairs should obtain which will never enter into the experience of the preferrer (see Dworkin 1977: 234). I prefer, say, that in my country people should not indulge in homosexual acts even in private and even if I never see them doing it. Does this preference of mine count for *anything* against the enjoyment they get? There have been many disputes on this point, but it is simplest to say that this and other external preferences do not count (see Hajdin 1990).

The biggest problem of all about preferences is the problem of *when* the preferences are to be had, if they are to count. It is convenient to use the terms "now-for-now," "then-for-then," and "now-for-then preferences" (Hare 1981: 101ff.). A now-for-now preference is a preference now for what should happen now; a then-for-then preference is a preference at some later time for what should happen at that time; a now-for-then preference is a preference now for what should happen at some later time. Suppose that I have a preference now that I should not be kept alive if I am seriously handicapped; but that when the time comes I very much want to live. So my now-for-then preference conflicts with my then-for-then preference. Which ought utilitarians to satisfy, if they cannot satisfy both? It seems simplest to say that now-for-then preferences do not count (Hare 1981: 101ff.; Brandt 1989).

Moral philosophers dispute about whether preferences of all sentient creatures are to count, or only the preferences of humans. A thoroughgoing utilitarian will take the former view, and defend it by just the same arguments as are used to defend utilitarianism in general (Singer 1993: ch. 3).

So far, then, we have, as constituents of utilitarianism, consequentialism – that is, the view that it is their consequences that determine the morality of actions – and welfarism – that is, the view that the consequences that we have to attend to are those that conduce to the welfare of those affected or the opposite. The remaining constituent is a view about the *distribution* of this welfare. It is the view that when, as usually, we have a choice between the welfare of one lot of people and the welfare of another lot, we should choose the action which maximizes the welfare (i.e., maximally promotes the interests) of all *in sum*, or *in aggregate*. We may call this constituent *aggregationism*.

Aggregationism implies that we should ignore the *distribution* of the welfare that we are bringing about, and simply maximize its total sum in aggregate. That is, if one outcome will produce more welfare, but distribute it very unequally, and another will produce less, but distribute it more equally, it is, according to aggregationism, the first outcome that we ought to choose. This often leads to objections to aggregationism, and therefore to utilitarianism itself, by people of an egalitarian bent, who think that equality of distribution matters in itself, as an independent value, and must not be sacrificed to the maximization of the total welfare.

There are also objections of a different, even opposite kind; it is often held that we have particular duties to, say, a patient or a family member, that we do not have to people in general, and that this person has rights to our attention that other people do not have.

But before we discuss these objections to aggregationism, we must point out that it certainly *seems* to be a simple consequence of a view that is held by many people, including many opponents of utilitarianism, namely the view that in making moral judgments we have to be *impartial* between the interests of the people affected by our judgments. This impartiality is what Bentham was getting at in his famous dictum "Everybody to count for one, nobody for more than one" (cited in Mill 1861: ch. 5). It is also what is implied by a requirement, which a great many anti-utilitarians (e.g. Dworkin 1977: 182) hold dear, that we should show "equal concern and respect" for all. It is hard to see what it would be to show equal concern and respect, if not to respect their interests equally. But if we respect their interests equally, we shall give the same weight to the equal interests of each of them. So, for example, if one of them wants some outcome more than the other wants to avoid it, we shall think we ought to bring that outcome about. But this leads directly to aggregationism.

It is easy to see this. If I give as much weight to the interests of person A as to those of person B, and the same weight again to those of person C, what happens when the interests of A and B, on the one hand, preponderate in sum over the interests of C on the other? Obviously, it would seem, the interests of A and B ought to weigh more with us than those of C. If we said anything but this, we should *not* be giving equal weight to the interests of A, B, and C, and therefore not showing equal concern and respect for A, B, and C. So, if one outcome will promote the interests of A and B, and the other will promote the interests of C, and the interests of all these individuals are equal, and we cannot produce both outcomes, it is the first outcome that we ought to produce, if we are to show all three equal concern and respect.

It is therefore surprising that so many anti-utilitarians, who profess to believe that we ought to show equal concern and respect to all those affected, object to aggregationism. The argument just given could be put by saying that if the interests of A and

B are stronger *in aggregate* than those of C, we should promote the former rather than the latter. Yet it was based on the requirement to give equal concern and respect to all three.

Another argument commonly used against aggregationism is also hard to understand (Rawls 1971: 27). This is the objection that utilitarianism "does not take seriously the distinction between persons." To explain this objection: it is said that, if we claim that there is a duty to promote maximal preference satisfaction regardless of its distribution, we are treating a great interest of one as of less weight than the lesser interests of a great many, provided that the latter add up in aggregate to more than the former. For example, if I can save five patients moderate pain at the cost of not saving one patient severe pain, I should do so if the interests of the five in the relief of their pain is greater in aggregate than the interest of the one in the relief of his (or hers).

But to think in the way that utilitarians have to think about this kind of example is *not* to ignore the difference between persons. Why should anybody want to say this? Utilitarians are perfectly well aware that A, B, and C in my example are different people. They are not blind. All they are doing is trying to do *justice* between the interests of these different people. It is hard to see how else one could do this except by showing them all equal respect, and that, as we have seen, leads straight to aggregationism.

It must be admitted that often utilitarians argue that we should treat other people's interests as if they were all our own interests. This is a way of securing impartiality. It is implied both by the Christian doctrine of *agape* and by the Kantian categorical imperative, as Kant explicitly says (Kant 1785: BA69 = 430). But this is not to ignore the difference between persons. It is merely to give equal weight to the interests of all persons, as we would do if we gave to all of them the same weight as we give to our own interests; and this is what *agape*, and treating everybody as ends as Kant says we should, require.

This objection belongs to a class of objections to utilitarianism that rest on appeal to common moral convictions or intuitions. In the case we have just been considering, it seems counterintuitive to say that an enormous harm to one person can be outweighed in moral thinking by a larger number of small gains to other people. There is also a tedious number of other objections to utilitarianism based on appeals to intuition. They are to be answered by recognizing that moral thinking occurs at two levels, the critical and the intuitive, and that intuition operates at the latter level, but utilitarianism at the former level, so that the two do not conflict.

We have already mentioned some examples of this kind of objection, such as the objection that we sometimes think we ought to attach an independent value to equality in distribution, or that we ought to favor those near to us, even when utility is not thereby maximized. Other well-worn examples are the alleged requirement of utilitarianism that the sheriff should execute the innocent man to prevent a riot; that one should save an important person from an air crash rather than one's own son if one cannot save both; that one should break promises when even the slightest advantage in preference satisfaction is produced thereby; and that one should kidnap one person, kill him, and extract his organs for transplants in order to save the lives of many. (On such objections, see Hare 1981: chs. 8–9.)

They are all easily answered once we realize the importance for moral practice of having firm principles or rules that we do not readily depart from. We cannot often predict the future well enough to be sure what act would maximize utility; and even if we have the information, we do not often have time to consider it fully, and without bias in our own favor. These sound general rules form the basis of our general moral convictions and intuitions, and it is unwise to depart from them lightly. If we do, we shall often be in danger of not acting for the best.

These rules have to be general or unspecific enough to be manageable. For one thing, if they are too complicated we shall not be able to teach them to our children or even learn them ourselves. Also, if they are too specific they may not be of much use. The point – or one of the points – of having moral rules is to cover a lot of cases which, though different in detail, resemble one another in important features.

So there is a good case for having simple general rules. We need therefore some way of putting a limit to the specificity that our rules can have. By "specificity," I mean the opposite of "generality." It is important to notice that generality, in the sense in which it is the opposite of specificity, is not the same as universality (Hare 1972). Principles can be highly specific but still universal, in the sense of containing no references to individuals. But this is not yet a sufficient answer to the objections we have been considering – the objections from counterintuitiveness. What shall we do in unusual cases, where we find ourselves wanting to make exceptions to the rules for good moral reasons, as they seem to us?

The way to get over this difficulty is to allow two levels of moral thinking. At the intuitive level we have the general rules, which are simple enough to master. But there will be conflicts between these simple rules. These conflicts are really the source of the objections from counterintuitiveness. For example, there is a simple rule which bids doctors to do the best they can to cure their patients, and another which forbids them to murder people in order to extract their organs. The rules may conflict in unusual cases. If they do, we need a higher level of thinking, which can be much more specific and deal in detail with these cases.

It will be found that real cases, such as we might encounter in practice, are not so difficult to handle as the cases in philosophers' examples. The former will generally be much more complex than the latter, and the additional information available will enable us to reconcile our intuitions with utilitarianism. For example, the abandonment of the rule forbidding murder will inevitably have such serious evil consequences that no saving of patients' lives by giving them murdered people's organs will compensate for the harm done. These murders will not long remain secret; and there can be better ways of securing organs for transplant. And the sheriff will do well to think what will happen in real life if sheriffs do not maintain the rule of law and justice, and so preserve people's rights. Rights certainly have a place in moral thinking, but it is a place easily preserved for them by consequentialism and utilitarianism (Hare 1981: ch. 9; Sumner 1987). Similarly, there are utilitarian reasons why a substantial degree of equality in society is good for everybody (Hare 1981: ch. 9), and why doctors and parents should look after their own patients and children respectively (Hare 1981: ch. 8). These partial and egalitarian principles at the intuitive level can be justified by impartial reasoning at the higher or critical level.

It is good enough if utilitarianism tallies with our intuitions in real cases; they do not have to fit cases which are unlikely ever to arise. If such cases do arise in unusual circumstances, most people on reflection will decide that they ought to act for the best (that is, as utilitarianism bids), even if this involves breaking one of the conflicting intuitive rules in order to observe the other.

References

Brandt, R. B. (1989). Fairness to happiness. *Social Theory and Practice* 15.

Dworkin, R. (1977). *Taking Rights Seriously.* Cambridge, MA: Harvard University Press.

Hajdin, M. (1990). External and now-for-then preferences in Hare's theory. *Dialogue* 29.

Hare, R. M. (1972). Principles. *Aristotelian Society* 73. (Reprinted in *Essays in Ethical Theory.* Oxford: Oxford University Press, 1989.)

Hare, R. M. (1981). *Moral Thinking.* Oxford: Oxford University Press.

Kant, I. (1785). *Groundwork of the Metaphysic of Morals*, cited from the translation by H. J. Paton, *The Moral Law.* London: Hutchinson, 1948, p. 92. (References are to pages of original editions and to the Royal Prussian Academy edition.)

Mill, J. S. (1861). *Utilitarianism.*

Rawls, J. (1971). *A Theory of Justice.* Cambridge, MA: Harvard University Press.

Sen, A. and Williams, B. (1982). *Utilitarianism and Beyond.* Cambridge: Cambridge University Press.

Singer, P. (1993). *Practical Ethics.* Cambridge: Cambridge University Press.

Sumner, L. W. (1987). *The Moral Foundation of Rights.* Oxford: Oxford University Press.

10

A Virtue Ethics Approach

JUSTIN OAKLEY

A common way of expressing admiration or condemnation of another's behavior is by saying "What sort of person would do a thing like that?" Going out of one's way to help a needy stranger can be seen not only as providing help but as acting generously, and overcoming fearsome obstacles to reach an important goal can be regarded not just as displaying strength of will but as acting courageously. Similarly, adverse judgments of how someone acted can express a bewilderment not only at harm done or at any rights infringed, but at the sort of person who would do such a thing. For instance, inflicting suffering upon another may in certain circumstances be thought malevolent or malicious, in addition to being harmful or disrespectful. An important feature of act-evaluations like generous, courageous, malevolent, and malicious is that they necessarily include reference to the character or dispositions from which the person acts. Virtue ethics is an approach that picks up on these common ways of judging actions. It holds that actions cannot be properly judged as right or wrong without reference to considerations of character.

Over the past three or four decades, there has been a revitalization in ethics of the ancient notion of virtue. The origins of this renewed philosophical interest in the virtues can be traced back to Elizabeth Anscombe's article, "Modern Moral Philosophy," published in 1958, but the bulk of work on virtue-based approaches to ethics did not begin to appear until the early 1980s, mainly in the writings of Philippa Foot, Bernard Williams, and Alasdair MacIntyre. The twenty-first century has seen a further intensification of activity in virtue ethics, as more detailed and sophisticated expressions of the approach have been developed. Virtue ethics has now reached the stage where it is widely recognized as offering a coherent and plausible alternative to consequentialist and Kantian approaches. This revival of virtue ethics has led to a corresponding development of virtue ethics perspectives on issues in bioethics.

The Rise of Virtue Ethics

While a virtue-based approach to ethics has its intrinsic merits, the turn toward virtue ethics has to a significant extent been motivated by dissatisfaction with certain aspects of mainstream ethical theories. One general complaint which advocates of virtue ethics have made about consequentialist and Kantian theories is that they place too much emphasis on questions about what we ought to *do*, at the expense of dealing with more basic questions about what sort of person we ought to be and what sort of life we ought to lead. Another general criticism which proponents of virtue ethics make of consequentialist and Kantian theories is that they are deficient even as ethics of action, for they are excessively abstract and thus say too little about what agents ought to do in concrete circumstances. A related charge is that these mainstream theories evaluate all acts in terms of "right," "wrong," "obligatory," or "permissible," and in doing so leave us with an impoverished moral vocabulary. A virtue ethics approach, by contrast, employs such evaluative terms as "courageous," "callous," "honest," and "just" – as well as the more familiar "right" and "wrong" – and thereby provides a much richer and more fine-grained range of evaluative possibilities. More specifically, many have argued that the impartiality characteristic of both consequentialist and Kantian approaches to ethics devalues the ethical importance of personal relationships such as friendship, and that the duty-based approaches of Kantianism and deontology lead to an objectionably minimalist conception of a good life.

The development of a virtue ethics approach to bioethics, in particular, while inspired by these general dissatisfactions with standard ethical theories, has also drawn impetus from some more localized targets. To some extent, virtue-based approaches to bioethics have been developed as a reaction to the dominance of bioethics by utilitarianism, which some have thought oversimplifies certain issues in bioethics (see Hursthouse 1987). But some writers explain the rise of virtue theory in bioethics as a reaction not so much to utilitarianism in particular but, rather, as a response to the shortcomings of principle-based approaches to bioethics, which usually claim to be founded on common ground between utilitarian and Kantian or deontological approaches to bioethics. Principle-based approaches (and especially that taken by Beauchamp and Childress 2009) have become near-orthodoxy in discussions of many issues in bioethics (and patient-care issues in particular), but various writers have recently expressed doubts about whether such approaches adequately capture both the contextual nature of decisions in patient care, and the moral importance of a health professional's character (and these doubts echo some of the general criticisms noted above of consequentialism and Kantianism as ethical theories). However, it is misleading to contrast virtue-based and principle-based approaches to bioethics, since this implies that virtue-based approaches reject appeals to principles. There is no reason why a virtue ethics approach cannot endorse certain principles, both generally – such as "we ought to repay our debts" – and in relation to patient care – such as "a good general practitioner normally gives priority to his or her own patients over those of other doctors."

Essential Features of Virtue Ethics

As a theory of right action, the most fundamental claim made by virtue ethics is that reference to character and virtue are essential in the justification of right action (see Hursthouse 1999: 28–31; Oakley and Cocking 2001; Slote 1992; Zagzebski 2006). A virtue ethics criterion for right action can be stated initially in broad terms as follows (see Hursthouse 1991: 225; 1996: 22):

V: An action is right if and only if it is what an agent with a virtuous character would do in the circumstances.

Most contemporary forms of virtue ethics provide a criterion of this type, or something very like it. **V** states that a right action is one that accords with what a virtuous person would do in the circumstances, and what *makes* the action right is that it is what a person with a virtuous character would do here. For example, it is right to save another's life, where continued life would still be a good to that person, because this is what a person with the virtue of benevolence would do. And it is ordinarily right to keep a promise made to someone on their deathbed, even though living people would benefit from its being broken, because that is what a person with the virtue of justice would do (see Foot 1977: 106; Hursthouse 1996: 25; 1999: 36). Some virtue ethicists have recently introduced certain qualifications to **V**. For example, in addressing the concern that even virtuous agents might occasionally act wrongly when, say, they act contrary to their virtuous characters, Rosalind Hursthouse (1999: 28) stipulates that the virtuous exemplar in **V** must be construed as acting *in character*. Further varieties of virtue ethics are also emerging that specify the link between virtue and right action in terms that appear somewhat different from **V**. Thus, Christine Swanton eschews justification via virtuous exemplars in developing her "target-centered" approach, whereby virtuous actions are those that hit the target (i.e. realize the proper goal) of the virtue relevant to the context, and right actions are those that are overall virtuous in the circumstances the actual agent finds themselves in (2003: 228–40). Nevertheless, **V** is the formulation that has thus far been used as the basis for developing most virtue ethics approaches to bioethics.

Of course, as it stands, **V** is very general, and if virtue ethics is to guide and justify actions, this criterion needs to be supplemented by an account of *which* character traits are virtues. (Similarly, a rule-utilitarian criterion of right action in terms of acting in accordance with certain rules needs to be supplemented by an account of *which* universally adopted rules maximize utility.) Nevertheless, this formulation already highlights a key difference between virtue ethics and standard Kantian and Utilitarian approaches, whereby the rightness of an act is determined by whether the act is in accordance with universalizable principles, or by whether it maximizes expected utility, respectively. For neither of those approaches, as standardly defined, makes reference to character essential to the justification of right action.

Before explaining in more detail how the dispositions of the virtuous agent in **V** might be derived, we need to clarify how **V** is to be used in evaluating actions. For as it stands, **V** could be interpreted as stating a purely *external* criterion of right action, which could be met no matter what motives or dispositions one acts from, so long as one has a good idea of what a virtuous agent would do in the circumstances. Or **V** could be taken as incorporating certain *internal* requirements, whereby one acts rightly only if one acts from the kinds of motives and dispositions that a virtuous agent would act from in the circumstances. Most virtue ethicists understand **V** in the second of these ways – that is, doing what the virtuous agent would do involves not merely the performance of certain acts, but also requires acting from certain dispositions and (in many cases) certain motives. For example, acting as someone with the virtue of benevolence would act involves not only providing assistance to another but also includes having and acting from a genuine concern for the well-being of that person, and a disposition to have and to act from that concern in particular kinds of situations. As Aristotle (1980: VI, 13, 1144b26–9) put it: "It is not merely the state in accordance with the right rule, but the state that implies the *presence* of the right rule, that is virtue." Acting as the virtuous agent would act typically involves acting from certain motives, though with the virtue of justice one can act justly from a variety of motives, so long as one acts from a *disposition* that incorporates an appropriate sense of justice. Indeed, every virtue can be thought to embody a *regulative ideal*, involving the internalization of a certain conception of excellence such that one is able to adjust one's motivation and conduct so that they conform to that standard. Thus, while most but not all virtues are motive-dependent, all virtues are plausibly thought to involve regulative ideals and so include internal requirements of some sort. (Swanton's target-centered virtue ethics seems to be an exception to this: her pluralistic approach allows for the possibility that one can hit the target of a particular virtue from no relevant inner state at all, so Swanton (2003: 294, 245–6) seems to reject the idea that hitting the target of the contextually relevant virtue always requires acting from a particular virtuous motive or disposition – though she thinks it usually requires at least the absence of *vicious* motives.)

Indeed, a striking difference between virtue ethics and standard utilitarian and Kantian ethical theories is the close connection typically made by virtue ethics between motive and rightness. Most forms of utilitarianism and Kantianism which are not merely theoretical possibilities hold that, generally speaking, one can act rightly, whatever one's motivation – so long as one maximizes expected utility or acts in accordance with duty, one has done the right thing, whether one's motives were praise-worthy, reprehensible, or neutral. As we have seen, however, virtue ethics typically holds that acting rightly, in many situations, requires acting from a particular sort of motivation, since this is part of what is involved in doing what a virtuous person would do in the circumstances. And, apart from its links with Aristotle's ethics, this strong connection between motive and rightness has considerable intuitive plausibility. Many people believe, for instance, that the rightness of giving a gift to a friend depends partly on whether one acts from motives appropriate to the occasion, like affection and friendly feeling – giving out of a sense of duty may not actually be the right thing to do here. This is not to say that virtue ethics approaches usually take the rightness of an act to depend *entirely* on its motivation.

However, Michael Slote (2001; 2007) has argued that virtue ethics is most plaus-ibly developed along such lines. In contrast to Swanton's target-centered account, where it is sometimes possible to hit the target of a virtue without any specific motivation at all, Slote develops an "agent-based" virtue ethics, whereby an action is right if and only if it is done from a virtuous motive, such as benevolence. (This approach could be under-stood as endorsing a form of **V**, whereby "doing what the virtuous agent would do" is entirely a matter of one acting from a virtuous motive, such as benevolence, when one acts.) For Slote though, acting from the virtuous motive of benevolence, is not simply acting to help another from a warm-hearted feeling toward them, but involves seek-ing via empathy to understand their plight, and monitoring one's action to see that it is actually helping. Without those features, Slote argues, one's motivation to help does not constitute genuine benevolence. Thus, Slote's account is closer than it may first seem to many other contemporary forms of virtue ethics, where well-motivated acts that fail to uphold the regulative ideal relevant to a particular virtue are seen as failing to meet the criterion of right action stated in **V**.

Another key difference between virtue ethics and classical forms of utilitarianism is that many contemporary virtue ethicists argue that virtues are intrinsic goods that are plural, and so the goodness of the virtues cannot be reduced to a single underlying value, such as utility. The good of integrity, for example, does not consist simply in the utility (e.g. pleasure) that the agent or others gain from this. (This irreducible plurality of the virtues is not incompatible with the notion of an underlying unity of the virtues, a concept held by many ancient Greek philosophers; however, many modern virtue ethicists reject the idea of a unity between the different virtues.) This commitment to evaluative pluralism can sometimes make it difficult to determine what ought to be done. What if, for instance, the honest thing to do seems to conflict with the kind thing to do, as when a friend asks you whether his wife is having an affair, and you happen to know that she is? Hursthouse argues:

> [S]omeone hesitating over whether to reveal a hurtful truth . . . thinking it would be kind but dishonest or unjust to lie, may need to realize, with respect to these particular circumstances, not that kindness is more (or is less) important than honesty or justice, and not that honesty or justice sometimes requires one to act unkindly or cruelly, but that one does people no kindness by concealing this sort of truth from them, hurtful though it may be. (1991: 231)

Further, in cases of genuine conflict between two virtues, where, for example, kindness does seem to demand dishonesty, or where honesty would be unkind, virtue ethics can allow that acting in accordance with either of these virtues may be right. For it recognizes that there can be circumstances where not all virtuous people (acting in character) would necessarily act in the same way. The evaluative pluralism of contemporary virtue ethics acknowledges that determining what is right can involve taking account of competing ethical considerations, and looking toward what a moral exemplar would do can be particularly instructive here, for an exemplar has taken account of the competing considerations and reached an all-things-considered judgment about what is to be done. Thus, the appeal to what a virtuous agent would do not only emphasizes the importance of motivation in right action, but also acknowledges how exemplars can point the way to sound ethical judgment in circumstances where the plural values that are the virtues conflict. In a later work on virtue ethics, however, Hursthouse (1999) argues that appeals to exemplars can be of limited practical use, and she suggests that rules of thumb, or "V-rules," such as "do what is honest," are more helpful as concrete guides to action than consulting a virtuous "oracle."

Some contemporary variants of Kantian and utilitarian approaches themselves allow that reference to character could play an essential role in justifying actions. For example, Barbara Herman (1993) has argued that the rightness of an act could be determined by reference to whether a good Kantian agent, whose character is regulated by a commitment to not acting impermissibly, would have performed such an act. And some utilitarians have argued that to act rightly is to act as the good utilitarian agent would, where such an agent is disposed to follow rules, or to have aversions or inclinations toward act-types, that – when followed or had by people generally – maximize expected utility (see, e.g., Brandt 1989; see also Hooker 1990). Sometimes these suggestions are put simply as theoretical possibilities, rather than fully worked out ethical theories, with their implications for practice spelled out. Nevertheless, distinguishing virtue ethics from these contemporary versions of Kantian and utilitarian views requires filling in the details about what character traits count as virtues (see Oakley 1996). So, just as Kantians and utilitarians need to detail their general criteria of rightness by specifying what rules we are to act in accordance with, or what expected utility consists in, virtue ethicists must likewise provide details about what the virtues are. For virtue ethics to be capable of guiding action, the criterion of right action in **V** needs to be completed with an account of the virtues.

The distinctiveness of virtue ethics compared to other theories is brought out more fully when we turn to the ways in which advocates of the approach ground the normative conceptions in the character of the virtuous agent. The approaches taken by contemporary virtue ethicists to filling out the notion of a virtuous character can be divided into two broad types. Many virtue ethicists (and most virtue ethics approaches to bioethics) take the Aristotelian view that the virtues are character traits which we need in order to live humanly flourishing lives. On this view, developed by Foot (1977; 2001) and Hursthouse (1987; 1999), benevolence and justice are virtues because they are part of an interlocking web of intrinsic goods – which includes friendship, integrity, and knowledge – without which we cannot have *eudaimonia*, or a flourishing life for a human being. According to Aristotle, the characteristic activity of human beings is the exercise of our rational capacity, and only by living virtuously is our rational capacity to guide our lives expressed in an excellent way. There is a sense, then, in which someone lacking the virtues would not be living a *human* life.

Another approach to grounding the virtues, developed principally by Michael Slote (1992), rejects the eudaimonist idea of Aristotle that the virtues are given by what humans need in order to flourish, and instead derives the virtues from our commonsense views about what character traits we typically find admirable – as exemplified in the lives of figures such as Albert Einstein and Mother Teresa – whether or not those traits help an individual to flourish. Slote's (2001; 2007) most recent work on this approach moves toward a Humean sentimentalist virtue ethics, which takes empathy and care as central. Linda Zagzebski (2006) also develops a non-eudaimonist form of virtue ethics, which she labels "exemplarism," where virtuous exemplars are basic in an explanatory sense and can be defined ostensively. Swanton's (2003) target-centered virtue ethics also rejects Aristotelian eudaimonism (while retaining certain other Aristotelian features), and moves toward an approach based on Nietzsche and other philosophers. Swanton (2003: 19) argues that virtues are dispositions to respond to morally significant features of objects in an excellent way, whether or not such dispositions are good for the person who has them. For example, a great artist's creative drive can be a virtue, Swanton (2003: 82–3) argues, even if this drive leads the artist to suffer bipolar disorder – while such a creative drive need not bring flourishing in this case, it is nevertheless an excellent way of responding to value, and can certainly result in a life that is justifiably regarded as successful in some sense (even if, perhaps, only posthumously).

Virtue Ethics Approaches to Bioethics

As the writings of its contemporary exponents demonstrate, virtue ethics has a great deal to contribute to bioethics. Virtue ethics provides distinctive new perspectives on many familiar issues in bioethics, and it addresses some important questions which standard utilitarian and deontological approaches have shown themselves ill-equipped to deal with, or have neglected altogether. Among the areas of bioethics which have received considerable attention from virtue ethicists are abortion, euthanasia, reproductive ethics, and the practice of health care.

An excellent example of a virtue ethics approach to bioethics is Rosalind Hursthouse's groundbreaking book on the ethics of abortion, *Beginning Lives* (1987). Hursthouse argues that the traditional debate about the competing rights of the mother and the fetus is fundamentally irrelevant to the morality of abortion. Individuals can exercise their rights virtuously or viciously, and Hursthouse argues that the morality of a woman's decision to have an abortion depends importantly on the sort of character which she manifests in deciding to have an abortion in her particular circumstances. For example, deciding to terminate a seven-month pregnancy in order to have a holiday abroad would be callous and self-centered, and aborting a fetus because one is fearful of motherhood is cowardly, if one is otherwise well-positioned to become a parent; however, an adolescent girl who has an abortion because she does not yet feel ready for motherhood would thereby show a proper humility about her present level of development. Hursthouse argues that these judgments are appropriate because "parenthood in general, and motherhood and childbearing in particular, are intrinsically worthwhile, [and] are among the things that can be correctly thought to be partially constitutive of a flourishing human life" (1991: 241; see also 1987: 168–9, 307–18). These virtue-based evaluations of women's abortion decisions also reflect the fact that terminating a pregnancy (unlike, say, having a kidney removed) involves cutting off a new human life, which in most circumstances should be regarded as a morally serious matter (Hursthouse 1991: 237; see also 1987: 16–25, 50–8, 204–17, 331).

Virtue ethics has also been applied in illuminating ways to other issues in reproductive ethics, such as embryo selection decisions in preimplantation genetic diagnosis (PGD). For example, Rosalind McDougall (2005; 2007) has argued that embryo selection decisions in PGD on the basis of sex or disability should be evaluated in terms of what a virtuous parent would do in the circumstances. And selecting an embryo simply because it is male or female, or because one wants a child to be deaf like oneself, McDougall argues, is contrary to the parental virtue of "acceptingness" of one's child.

Another example of a virtue ethics approach in bioethics is Philippa Foot's (1977) influential discussion of euthanasia (see also Van Zyl 2000). Foot analyzes the concept of euthanasia, and argues that wanting to die does not necessarily make death a good for that person; rather, death can be a good to a person only when their life lacks a minimum of basic human goods, such as autonomy, friendship, and moral support. Foot argues that the virtues of justice and charity allow one to fulfill a competent individual's request to be killed, where such basic human goods are absent. Foot also argues that analyzing end-of-life decisions in terms of these virtues can bring out an

97

important moral difference between killing and letting die. In normal circumstances, both justice and charity require us not to kill people, and both virtues require that we do not let people die when we could reasonably have helped them. Further, where someone whose life lacks a minimum of basic human goods expresses a sincere request to be killed, both justice and charity would permit such an action to be carried out. However, where such a person demands *not* to be killed and, say, wishes to be left to die in agony, the requirements of these virtues diverge – that is, justice would forbid us from carrying out the act of killing which charity would normally permit us to perform in such circumstances.

Because of its goal-directed or teleological structure, Aristotelian virtue ethics provides a natural basis for developing an ethic of various professional roles (see Oakley and Cocking 2001). In ordinary life the character traits that qualify as virtues are given by their connections with *eudaimonia*, the overarching goal of a good human life. The virtues in various professional contexts can be derived through a similar teleological structure. Thus, *health* is clearly a central goal of medicine, and which of a doctor's character traits count as professional virtues are those that help the doctor serve the goal of patient health. For example, medical beneficence would qualify as a virtue, as it focuses doctors on patients' own interests and curbs a tendency toward the unnecessary interventions found in defensive medicine. Similarly, trustworthiness helps with effective diagnosis and treatment by helping patients feel comfortable about revealing intimate details about themselves, and medical courage helps doctors work toward healing patients by facing risks of serious infection when necessary (Oakley and Cocking 2001: 93). Thus, a virtue ethics approach to medical ethics would hold that patients ought to be told the truth about their condition, not because truth-telling maximizes utility, nor because patients have a right to know this information, but because this is what is involved in a doctor having the virtue of truthfulness, and a disposition to tell patients the truth serves the medical goal of health without breaching the constraint (applying to a doctor as a professional) against violating the patient's autonomy. In highlighting the links between virtuous character traits and the proper goal(s) of the profession in question, virtue ethics also takes seriously the notion of professional integrity.

This virtue ethics approach has also been applied to other health professions, including psychiatry and nursing, and to other professions such as legal practice and business (see Swanton 2007). For example, Jennifer Radden (2007) argues that serving the proper psychiatric goals of mental health and healing requires psychiatrists to develop role-constituted virtues like self-knowledge, self-unity, and realism, along with "unselfing," which involves a "personally yet acutely attentive attitude" and control over self-presentation, so that proper boundaries are upheld in the therapist–patient relationship (p. 122). Radden argues that these and other virtues, such as integrity, are crucial in psychiatry, as patients are especially vulnerable to exploitation in this context. Alan Armstrong (2006) argues that compassion, courage, and respectfulness are role virtues in nursing practice (see also Van Hooft 1999), and virtue ethics' emphasis on the importance of professional integrity has been seen as an antidote to a "creeping privatization and managerialism" in nursing and health care generally (Sellman 2006: 107).

Indeed, virtue ethics offers a promising and insightful approach to many issues in patient care. Edmund Pellegrino and David Thomasma (1993) show how an account of the virtues in medical practice is necessarily based on a philosophy of medicine, in a way that demonstrates what goals are appropriate to and distinctive of medicine as an important human endeavor. Virtue ethics approaches to medical practice typically examine issues in patient care by looking at the doctor–patient relationship, and at the sorts of character traits which are crucial for a doctor in that relationship, such as honesty, compassion, integrity, and justice (see Drane 1988: 43–62; Girod and Beckman 2005; Jansen 2000; Pellegrino 1995; Shelp 1985; Thomasma 2004;). However, some who acknowledge the importance of virtuous character traits in good medical practice do not take a virtue-*based* approach, but rather see such accounts as providing a necessary practical supplement to a fundamentally deontological or utilitarian morality (see, e.g., Beauchamp and Childress 2009; Hare 1994; Pellegrino and Thomasma 1993).

Criticisms of Virtue Ethics

A number of criticisms have been made of virtue-based approaches. One concern is whether the notion of virtue is clear or detailed enough to serve as the basis of a criterion of rightness. Some argue that this criterion of rightness is too *vague* to be an acceptable basis of justification in ethics. What would a virtuous agent do in the great variety of situations in which people find themselves? There is a plurality of virtuous character traits, and not all virtuous people seem to have these traits to the same degree, so virtuous people might not always respond to situations in the same way. Is the right action in a given set of circumstances the action which would be done by an honest person, a kind person, or a just person? As Robert Louden puts it:

> Due to the very nature of the moral virtues, there is . . . a very limited amount of advice on moral quandaries that one can reasonably expect from the virtue-oriented approach. We ought, of course, to do what the virtuous person would do, but it is not always easy to fathom what the hypothetical moral exemplar would do were he in our shoes. (1984: 229)

Now, to the extent that the criticism here expresses a general worry about appeals to "what a certain person would do," it is worth remembering that such appeals are quite commonly and successfully used in justifications in a variety of areas. For example, novice doctors and lawyers being inducted into their professions sometimes justify having acted in a certain way by pointing out that this is how their professional mentor would have acted here. Also, courts often rely significantly on claims about what a reasonable person would have foreseen, in determining a person's legal liability for negligent conduct. Moreover, any general worry about such appeals would also apply to many consequentialist theories, which hold that the rightness of an action is determined partly by appealing to what consequences would have been foreseen by a reasonable person in the agent's position.

However, those who accept reliance on such appeals in other areas might well have misgivings about the particular sort of appeal to such a standard which is made by virtue ethics. For establishing what counts as having reasonable foresight of the consequences of actions may be far easier than establishing what counts as having a virtuous character. And it may be considerably more difficult to determine which of the variety of virtuous character traits a virtuous person would act on in a given situation than it is to determine which consequences of a given action a reasonable person would actually foresee (see Rachels and Rachels 2006).

Now, establishing the nature of a virtuous agent's character is indeed a complex matter, but it should be remembered that virtue ethics does not derive this from some prior account of right action. Rather, which character traits count as virtuous is determined by their involvement in human flourishing or their admirability or excellence, as explained above. It is true to say that virtue ethics does not deliver an "algorithm" of right action (as Aristotle put it), and that a virtue ethics criterion of rightness is perhaps less precisely specifiable and less easily applicable than that given by consequentialist theories (although perhaps not compared to those given by Kantian theories). But it is perhaps an overreaction to argue that this undermines virtue ethics' claim to provide an acceptable approach to ethical justification. For virtue ethicists often give considerable detail about what virtuous agents have done and would do in certain situations, and these details can help us to identify what it is right to do in a particular situation. (We might not gain any more precision from the directives of contemporary Kantian and consequentialist theories which advise us to do what a good Kantian or consequentialist agent would do.) And further, virtue ethics need not claim that there is only one true account of what a virtuous person would be and do, for it can allow that, sometimes, whichever of two courses of action one chooses, one would be acting rightly. In some situations, that is, whether one does what a kind person would have done, or what an honest person would have done, one would still have acted rightly (see Hursthouse 1996: 34; 1999).

Another criticism of virtue ethics focuses on the plausibility of a purely character-based criterion of rightness, such as that given by virtue ethics in **V** above. That is, some argue that (no matter how precisely specifiable and unitary virtuous character traits are) reference to what an agent with a virtuous character would do is not sufficient to justify actions. In support of this criticism, some argue that people with very virtuous characters can sometimes be led by a virtuous character trait to act wrongly. For example, a benevolent doctor may be moved to withhold a diagnosis of terminal cancer from a patient, although the doctor reveals the news to the patient's family, and asks them to join in the deception. Or a compassionate father might decide to donate most of the family's savings to a worthwhile charity, without sufficiently thinking through how his action is likely to result in severe impoverishment for his family in the long term. As Robert Veatch (1988: 445) puts the worry: "I am concerned about well-intentioned, bungling do-gooders. They seem to exist with unusual frequency in health care, law, and other professions with a strong history of stressing the virtue of benevolence with an elitist slant." If we agree that thoroughly virtuous people can some-times be led by their virtuous character traits to act wrongly, then this seems to cast strong doubt on the plausibility of virtue ethics' criterion of rightness in **V** above. Some critics have been led by such examples of moral ineptitude to claim that virtue ethics is incomplete, and must therefore be underwritten by a deontological or a utilitarian criterion of rightness (see Beauchamp and Childress 2009; Driver 1995; Frankena 1973: 63–71; Hare 1994; Pellegrino and Thomasma 1993; Rachels and Rachels 2006).

Now, some virtue theorists would question whether the agent does act wrongly in these sorts of cases (see, e.g., Slote 1992). However, suppose it is granted that the agent concerned does indeed act wrongly in some such cases. There is no reason to think that virtue ethics is committed to condoning such moral ineptitude. For most virtues are not simply a matter of having good motives or good dispositions, but have a practical component which involves seeing to it that one's action succeeds in bringing about what the virtue dictates. As Swanton (2003) puts it, acting virtuously involves hitting the target, or goal, of the virtue in question. Therefore, we might question the extent to which the agent really does have the virtuous character trait which we are assuming he does here. Is it really an act of benevolence to withhold a diagnosis of terminal cancer from a patient, leaving that patient to die in ignorance of his or her true condition? Alternatively, in cases where the action does not seem to call into question the degree to which the agent has the virtuous character trait under scrutiny, it might be that the agent was lacking in some other virtue which was appropriate here. Thus, the father seems to have an inadequate sense of loyalty toward his own family.

The above concern with **V** is that a person who is fully virtuous might nevertheless act wrongly. The converse problem has also been raised – that people deficient in virtue can act rightly, although their actions are not things that fully virtuous agents would do. It is therefore claimed that **V** fails to capture such oughts because virtuous agents in **V** are fully virtuous and so would not find themselves in such situations to begin with (Copp and Sobel 2004: 546; Cullity 1999: 280; Johnson 2003). As Robert Johnson puts it, there are clearly duties of self-improvement for people who are not fully virtuous, but what such duties require are things that would be *uncharacteristic* of a virtuous person. For example, Johnson (2003: 817) argues that an habitual liar ought to use strength of will to resist his temptation to lie, but it cannot be said that what the habitual liar ought to do here is something that a fully virtuous agent would do, as a fully virtuous agent would not be tempted to lie in the first place. But is it really so clear that there are cases where what one ought to do is something that no virtuous exemplar would ever in any circumstances do? Exemplars can still be action-guiding for agents who are not fully virtuous. This objection also seems to ignore how virtues might apply to role ethics, where what a virtuous professional (e.g. a virtuous criminal defense lawyer) ought to do might sometimes be uncharacteristic of what a virtuous person would do in everyday life, but virtue ethics can consistently recognize such role-differentiation (see Oakley and Cocking 2001). In specifying **V**, then, careful attention must be paid to what "in the circumstances" of the agent means.

There is also lively debate about the prospects for virtue ethics in light of certain studies in social psychology, which suggest that the variations in behavior displayed by different individuals in a given context are often better explained by minor situational variations than by the assumptions we commonly make about differences in character traits between those individuals (Campbell 1999; Doris 2002; Harman 1999). Summarizing these studies, John Doris comments that "Circumstance . . . often has an extraordinary influence on what people do, whatever sort of character they may *appear* to have" (2002: i). Some, however, dispute the conclusiveness of such studies, while others maintain that different virtuous character traits were actually exhibited by the research subjects (see Kamtekar 2004; Merritt 2000; Sabini and Silver 2005; Sreenivasan 2002). In any case, there are clearly some individuals who have very robust

101

virtuous character traits that are not easily undermined by situational factors. For instance, some whistleblowers have displayed great courage in overcoming all manner of obstacles to expose corrupt behavior in their organization (see discussion in Bolsin et al. 2005). Perhaps acting virtuously is rarer and less attainable than we sometimes like to think, but that by itself is no reason to abandon **V** as a criterion of right action.

Conclusion

Because contemporary virtue ethics is a relatively recent arrival in ethical theory and bioethics, it is difficult to fully assess its future prospects. Virtue ethics approaches have already made significant contributions in both areas, but more remains to be done to develop the approach itself, and to investigate its applications to ethical issues in health care, reproductive practices, and biotechnology. Nevertheless, it is already clear that the renaissance of virtue ethics has substantially enriched normative ethics and has irrevocably changed the ethical landscape, and the emergence of virtue-based approaches to issues in bioethics has created a very promising alternative to the more established approaches.

References

Anscombe, E. (1958). Modern moral philosophy. *Philosophy* 33/124.

Aristotle (1980). *The Nicomachean Ethics*, trans. W. D. Ross. Oxford: Oxford University Press.

Armstrong, A. E. (2006). Towards a strong virtue ethics for nursing practice. *Nursing Philosophy* 7/3: 110–24.

Beauchamp, T. L. and Childress, J. F. (eds.) (2009 [1979]). *Principles of Biomedical Ethics*, 6th edn. New York: Oxford University Press.

Bolsin, S., Faunce, T., and Oakley, J. (2005). Practical Virtue Ethics: healthcare whistleblowing and portable digital technology. *Journal of Medical Ethics* 31/10: 612–18.

Brandt, R. (1989). Morality and its critics. *American Philosophical Quarterly* 26/2.

Campbell, J. (1999). Can philosophical accounts of altruism accommodate experimental data on helping behaviour? *Australasian Journal of Philosophy* 77/4.

Copp, D. and Sobel, D. (2004). Morality and virtue: an assessment of some recent work in virtue ethics. *Ethics* 114/3: 514–54.

Cullity, G. (1999). Virtue ethics, theory, and warrant. *Ethical Theory and Moral Practice* 2/3: 277–94.

Doris, J. M. (2002). *Lack of Character: Personality and Moral Behavior*. New York: Cambridge University Press.

Drane, J. F. (1988). *Becoming a Good Doctor: The Place of Virtue and Character in Medical Ethics*. Kansas City: Sheed and Ward.

Driver, J. (1995). Monkeying with motives: agent-basing virtue ethics. *Utilitas* 7/2: 281–8.

Foot, P. (1977). Euthanasia. *Philosophy and Public Affairs* 6: 85–112. (Reprinted in Foot, *Virtues and Vices*, Berkeley: University of California Press, 1978.)

Foot, P. (2001). *Natural Goodness*. Oxford: Oxford University Press.

Frankena, W. (1973). *Ethics*, 2nd edn. Englewood Cliffs, NJ: Prentice-Hall.

Gardiner, P. (2003). A virtue ethics approach to moral dilemmas in medicine. *Journal of Medical Ethics* 29/5: 297–302.

Girod, J. and Beckman, A. W. (2005). Just allocation and team loyalty: a new virtue ethic for emergency medicine. *Journal of Medical Ethics* 31/10: 567–70.

Hare, R. M. (1994). Methods of bioethics: some defective proposals. *Monash Bioethics Review* 13/1: 34–47.

Harman, G. (1999). Moral philosophy meets social psychology: virtue ethics and the fundamental attribution error. *Proceedings of the Aristotelian Society* 99/3: 316–31.

Herman, B. (1993). *The Practice of Moral Judgment*. Cambridge, MA: Harvard University Press.

Hooker, B. (1990). Rule-consequentialism. *Mind* 99/393: 67–77.

Hurka, T. (2001). *Virtue, Vice, and Value*. Oxford: Oxford University Press.

Hursthouse, R. (1987). *Beginning Lives*. Oxford: Blackwell.

Hursthouse, R. (1991). Virtue theory and abortion. *Philosophy and Public Affairs* 20/3: 223–46.

Hursthouse, R. (1995). Applying virtue ethics. In R. Hursthouse, G. Lawrence, and W. Quinn (eds.), *Virtues and Reasons: Philippa Foot and Moral Theory: Essays in Honour of Philippa Foot*. Oxford: Clarendon Press, pp. 57–75.

Hursthouse, R. (1996). Normative virtue ethics. In Crisp, R. (ed.), *How Should One Live? Essays on the Virtues*. Oxford: Clarendon Press, pp. 19–36.

Hursthouse, R. (1999). *On Virtue Ethics*. Oxford: Oxford University Press.

Jansen, L. A. (2000). The virtues in their place: virtue ethics in medicine. *Theoretical Medicine* 21/3: 261–76.

Johnson, R. N. (2003). Virtue and right. *Ethics* 113/4: 810–34.

Kamtekar, R. (2004). Situationism and virtue ethics on the content of our character. *Ethics* 114/3: 458–91.

Louden, R. (1984). On some vices of virtue ethics. *American Philosophical Quarterly* 21/3: 227–36.

McDougall, R. (2005). Acting parentally: an argument against sex selection. *Journal of Medical Ethics* 31/10: 601–5.

McDougall, R. (2007). Parental virtue: a new way of thinking about the morality of reproductive actions. *Bioethics* 21/4: 181–90.

Merritt, M. (2000). Virtue ethics and situationist personality psychology. *Ethical Theory and Moral Practice* 3/4: 365–83.

Oakley, J. (1996). Varieties of virtue ethics. *Ratio* 9/2: 128–52.

Oakley, J. and Cocking, D. (2001). *Virtue Ethics and Professional Roles*. Cambridge: Cambridge University Press.

Pellegrino, E. D. (1995). Toward a virtue-based normative ethics for the health professions. *Kennedy Institute of Ethics Journal* 5/3: 253–77.

Pellegrino, E. D. (2007). Professing medicine, virtue-based ethics, and the retrieval of professionalism. In R. L. Walker and P. J. Ivanhoe (eds.), *Working Virtue: Virtue Ethics and Contemporary Moral Problems*. Oxford: Clarendon Press.

Pellegrino, E. D. and Thomasma, D. C. (1993). *The Virtues in Medical Practice*. New York: Oxford University Press.

Rachels, J. and Rachels, S. (2006). *The Elements of Moral Philosophy*, 5th edn. New York: McGraw-Hill.

Radden, J. (2007). Virtue ethics as professional ethics: the case of psychiatry. In R. L. Walker and P. J. Ivanhoe (eds.), *Working Virtue: Virtue Ethics and Contemporary Moral Problems*. Oxford: Clarendon Press.

Sabini, J. and Silver, M. (2005). Lack of character? Situationism critiqued. *Ethics* 115/3: 535–62.

Sellman, D. (2006). Review of *Virtue Ethics and Professional Roles* (by Justin Oakley and Dean Cocking). *Nursing Philosophy* 7/2: 106–7.

Shelp, E. (ed.) (1985). *Virtue and Medicine*. Dordrecht: Reidel.

Slote, M. (1992). *From Morality to Virtue*. New York: Oxford University Press.

Slote, M. (2001). *Morals from Motives*. Oxford: Oxford University Press.

Slote, M. (2007). *The Ethics of Care and Empathy*. London: Routledge.

Sreenivasan, G. (2002). Errors about errors: virtue theory and trait attribution. *Mind* 111/441: 47–68.

Swanton, C. (2003). *Virtue Ethics, A Pluralistic View*. Oxford: Oxford University Press.

Swanton, C. (2007). Virtue ethics, role ethics, and business ethics. In R. L. Walker and P. J. Ivanhoe (eds.), *Working Virtue: Virtue Ethics and Contemporary Moral Problems*. Oxford: Clarendon Press.

Thomasma, D. C. (2004). Virtue theory in philosophy of medicine. In G. Khushf (ed.), *Handbook of Bioethics: Taking Stock of the Field from a Philosophical Perspective*. Dordrecht: Kluwer.

Van Hooft, S. (1999). Acting from the virtue of caring in nursing. *Nursing Philosophy* 6/3: 189–201.

Van Hooft, S. (2006). *Understanding Virtue Ethics*. Chesham: Acumen.

Van Zyl, L. (2000). *Death and Compassion: A Virtue-Based Approach to Euthanasia*, Aldershot: Ashgate.

Veatch, R. (1988). The danger of virtue. *Journal of Medicine and Philosophy* 13/4.

Zagzebski, L. (2006). The admirable life and the desirable life. In T. Chappell (ed.), *Values and Virtues: Aristotelianism in Contemporary Ethics*. Oxford: Oxford University Press.

Further reading

Annas, J. (2007). Virtue ethics. In D. Copp (ed.), *The Oxford Handbook of Ethical Theory*. Oxford: Oxford University Press.

Baron, M., Pettit, P., and Slote, M. (1997). *Three Methods of Ethics: A Debate*. Oxford: Blackwell.

Crisp, R. (ed.) (1996). *How Should One Live? Essays on the Virtues*. Oxford: Clarendon Press.

Crisp, R. and Slote, M. (eds.) (1997). *Virtue Ethics*. Oxford: Oxford University Press.

Driver, J. (2001). *Uneasy Virtue*. Cambridge: Cambridge University Press.

Gardiner, S. (ed.) (2005). *Virtue Ethics: Old and New*. Ithaca: Cornell University Press.

MacIntyre, A. (1984). *After Virtue*, 2nd edn. Notre Dame, IN: University of Notre Dame Press.

Nussbaum, M. (1995). Aristotle on human nature and the foundations of ethics. In J. Altham and R. Harrison (eds.), *World, Mind, and Ethics: Essays on the Moral Philosophy of Bernard Williams*. Cambridge: Cambridge University Press.

Statman, D. (ed.) (1997). *Virtue Ethics*. Edinburgh: Edinburgh University Press.

Stohr, K. and Wellman, C. H. (2002). Recent work on virtue ethics. *American Philosophical Quarterly* 27/4: 49–72.

Walker, R. L. and P. J. Ivanhoe (eds.) (2007). *Working Virtue: Virtue Ethics and Contemporary Moral Problems*. Oxford: Clarendon Press.

Williams, B. (1973). A critique of utilitarianism. In J. J. C. Smart and B. Williams, *Utilitarianism: For and Against*. Cambridge: Cambridge University Press.

11

A Care Approach

RITA C. MANNING

An ethic of care is a way of understanding one's moral role, of looking at moral issues and coming to an accommodation in moral situations. In this chapter, I will outline my version of care ethics, provide an overview of some other important care theories, and suggest some ways to apply this theory to bioethics.

One Model of Care Ethics

Though humans have always included features of care in their constructive interactions with each other, it only emerged recently as a systematic moral perspective. Nel Noddings's very influential book, *Caring: A Feminine Approach to Ethics and Moral Education* (1984 and 2003), was the first contemporary work that described care in some detail as a moral orientation. Virginia Held (2005) has also been an influential defender of this perspective who has most recently extended care theory to the global arena. There are important differences and similarities in the various descriptions of an ethic of care, but in this first section, I will be defending my own particular conception of an ethic of care. (Manning 1992).

Care involves a basic human capacity to recognize and respond to the needs of others and to moderate our behavior in light of the good or harm it might cause to others. Martin Hoffman (2000) is a prominent moral psychologist who sees care as growing out of our natural capacity for empathy. This capacity is evident even in newborns, who cry when they hear another baby crying. Later in their development, children come to be motivated to help whenever they encounter others in distress. Finally, reflection allows us to build on our basic empathic distress at the suffering of others. We then can generalize beyond our immediate experience of someone's distress and imagine the distress of someone who is distant from us. In both cases, we feel impelled to help. Because there is a natural basis for care, care as a moral perspective can both be a strong motivation for doing the right thing and also provide a basis for recognizing right actions.

One way to think about moral perspectives is to see them as growing out of ideal ways to respond in a certain context. For example, if one thinks about what is involved in doing one's moral best in the context of a marketplace between relatively independent and self-interested strangers, the value of honesty and trust are central. When one thinks about what is involved in caring for someone who needs our help, the value of concern, competence and trust is central. The care perspective in moral philosophy grew out of looking systematically at what is required to be a responsible member of a flourishing relationship. Sara Ruddick (1989), for example, looked carefully at what is involved in being a good mother to dependent children. Many contemporary defenders of an ethic of care, and many historical antecedents such as David Hume and Adam Smith, think that one can generalize beyond relationships with our intimates. Thus, once we find out what values motivate a person to be an ideal caring person in an intimate relationship, we can apply those values to situations that involve distant strangers. When one understands what practices best allow us to apply these values in intimate relationships, one can extend these practices to other situations.

For care ethics, caring is a moral response to a variety of features of situations: harm, past promises, role relationships, etc. In the case of need, our obligation to respond in an appropriately caring way arises when we are able to respond to need. Need is mediated by a number of factors, including family, culture, economic class, gender and sexuality, disability, and illness. As a caring person responds to needs, she recognizes the vast differences in power that exist and shape the recognition and articulation of needs. Harm is another feature of moral situations. Most people understand that being the cause of harm to someone else creates an obligation to respond. But causation is a complex idea. We can be part of the causal story even when we don't think of ourselves as the primary cause. Suppose, for example, that you see the person sitting next to you cheating in an exam. If you simply look the other way, and later find out that a patient was seriously harmed because the practitioner really did not understand the procedure that should have been followed, and that this procedure was the very one the person was being tested on when you saw the cheating, you are partly responsible for the harm.

There are two other things that call up an obligation to care that are worth noting here: past promising and role-responsibility. When we make a promise, either explicit or implicit, we commit ourselves to a certain course of action. An ethic of care doesn't say that you are always committed to keeping a promise because sometimes doing so can be harmful to all concerned, but it does impose a moral obligation to respond. Similarly, being in a particular role, for example, health-care practitioner, comes with a set of general obligations.

There are four central processes in an ethic of care: moral attention, sympathetic understanding, relationship awareness, and harmony and accommodation.

Moral attention

Moral attention is the attention paid to the situation in all its complexity. When one is morally attentive, one wishes to become aware of all the details that will allow a sympathetic response to the situation. It is not enough to know that this is a case of a particular kind, say a case about lying or cruelty. In order to understand what our obligations are, we have to know all the details that might make a difference in our understanding and response to the particular situation at hand.

Sympathetic understanding

When one sympathetically understands the situation, one is open to sympathizing, and even identifying, with the persons in the situation. One tries to be aware of what the others in the situation would want one to do, what would most likely be in their best interests, and how they would like one to carry out their wishes and interests and meet their needs. Note that it is not at all clear that what one desires and what is actually in one's best interests are identical. Balancing these conflicts requires sensitive dialogue and negotiation. I call this sensitive attention to the best interests of others "maternalism." As one adopts this sympathetic attitude, one often becomes aware of what others want and need. Finally, as we respond to others, we look to satisfy their needs in ways that will preserve their sense of competence and dignity, while at the same time addressing their needs or alleviating their suffering.

Relationship awareness

There is a special kind of relationship awareness that characterizes caring. First, there is the most basic relationship, that of fellow creatures. Then there is the immediate relationship of need and ability to fill the need. Another relationship is created when you are the cause of harm to someone else. One might also be in some role relationship with the other that calls for a particular response, such as doctor–patient. One is aware of all these relationships as one surveys a situation from the perspective of care. But there is another kind of relationship awareness that is involved as well. One can be aware of the network of relationships that connect humans, and care about preserving and nurturing these relationships. As caring persons think about what to do, they try not to undermine these relationships but rather to nurture and extend the relationships that are supportive of human flourishing.

Accommodation and harmony

Related to the notion of relationship awareness is accommodation. Often there are many persons involved, and how best to respond is not obvious. The desire to nurture networks of care requires that one try to accommodate the needs of all, including oneself. It is not always possible, or wise, to do what everyone thinks they need, but it is important to give everyone concerned a sense of being involved and considered in the process. When we do this, we have a better chance of preserving harmony. Of course, not all harmony is worth preserving. The oppressive society may be pretty stable and harmonious, but at the price of those at the bottom. An ethic of care would be opposed to this type of superficial harmony, since it is dependent on treating some as though they do not deserve the same care as others.

An Overview of Care Ethics

One of the challenges of describing an ethic of care is that it is a moral perspective that has emerged through an organic process; it is empirical in the sense that it has its beginnings in Gilligan's description (1982) of the moral experience of real women, and it has very different features in the work of various theorists. In this section I will offer an overview and assessment of two different, but representative, care perspectives: those of Nel Noddings (2003) and Virginia Held (2005). I will then describe the work of Michael Slote (2003), who defends a related view that offers powerful insights for an ethic of care.

There are a number of themes that are common to Held and Noddings. The first is that a model of care can be constructed by theorizing about the characteristics of successful caring practices; the second is the prominent role of relationships; the third is the role of emotion in moral theory; the fourth is the rejection of moral principles; the fifth is that moral decisions are contextual; the sixth is a social ontology of persons. In addition to these shared themes, there are two areas where Held and Noddings disagree: the foundation of the obligation to care and whether care is a virtue. I begin with the similarities and then turn to the disagreements.

First is the view that care is best exemplified in caring interactions between intimates. Both Noddings and Held use maternal caring as their central example. I defend what I call maternalism, and note the importance of tailoring one's response to the particular kind of relationship one is in.

Second, care is situated within relationships. Care is not strictly voluntary or contractual – one finds oneself in various relationships that provide a context for understanding one's obligations. Held and Noddings focus on the relationships between intimates, though they both claim that their accounts can be extended to distant strangers. I argue for a broader conception of relationship.

Third, care appeals to emotion. The central emotion in care ethics is empathy. Empathy is a complex of emotional responses, conditioned responses, and reflective judgments about how one ought to respond. Martin Hoffman (2000) describes empathy as both a response to suffering and a proactive constraint on behavior. As a response to suffering, empathy provides a motive to alleviate suffering. As a constraint on behavior, empathy provides reason to avoid inflicting harm on others and a reason for providing redress to the victims of harm.

Held contrasts care with principle-based views by describing care as emotionally based, while principle-based views are cognitively based. I would argue that care is also reflective and empirically based. One cannot be appropriately caring independently of an assessment of the value of care and the specific demands of the particular relationships and situations one finds oneself in. We have a wealth of evidence about the world and about the concerns and interests of humans to guide us in filling out an account of caring obligation.

Fourth, care ethics is not a principle-based account – one doesn't discover one's obligations by reflecting on one's commitments to moral principles. Further, having an obligation toward or for someone doesn't imply that there is only one way of discharging the obligation. From the care perspective, the morally praiseworthy person acts directly on the motive of care and concern for others, and not on the motive of respect for moral principle. In fact, both Noddings and Held argue that we often use moral principles to distance ourselves from others. Although I agree that they can function this way, I think they can also serve the useful function of providing moral minimums when our ability to understand the situation is in some sense compromised or when we need a general rule to guide behavior in an institutional setting.

Fifth, for care ethics, the right action becomes clear only in the context of focused attention to the immediate situation. Noddings describes this as engrossment in the other, while Virginia Held describes moral responsiveness as the device by which one comes to understand one's obligations. I describe moral attention and sympathetic understanding as the process whereby one begins to understand one's particular obligations.

Sixth, an ethic of care assumes a relationship-centered social ontology and corresponding self-understanding. Care theorists assume that persons are at least partly defined by the relationships in which they participate. Nona Lyons (1983) argues that a social ontology is common to people who find care ethics more persuasive than some other moral theories, while those whose self-identify is more individualistic will gravitate to other moral theories. What Lyons calls "separate/objective selves" recognize moral dilemmas as those that involve a conflict between their principles and someone else's desires, needs, or demands. As such, they must mediate their interaction with others in terms of ground rules and procedures that can be accepted by all. At the same time, separate/objective selves recognize that interaction with others plays a role in one's satisfaction, so they value community and relationship insofar as these play a role in individual satisfaction. Connected selves, on the other hand, see themselves in terms of others, so relationship is central to self-identity, rather than seen as voluntary and incidental. The problem of interaction is not then conceived of as how to get others to interact with oneself on terms that would be acceptable to all, but how to protect the ties of affection and connection that are central to one's very self-identity.

I now turn to what I see as central differences among the three accounts: whether care is a virtue, and whether need is the only or primary foundation of obligation.

Care as a virtue

Held explicitly rejects the view that care is a virtue, while I think this is the most plausible way to understand it. Like other virtues, care is a general disposition to behave in a particular way. One argument for seeing care as a virtue is that, if we fail to do so, we will not be able to trust our natural feelings of empathy to lead us to do the right thing. There are two ways in which empathy can fail as a guide to moral action. The first is the failure to feel empathy in the presence of suffering or harm. Conscious avoidance of suffering and blaming the victim are very effective ways to avoid feeling empathy. But the failure to empathize is not always a conscious and deliberate action. Sometimes we are simply overwhelmed by the suffering of others and experience paralyzing empathic over-arousal. The second way that empathy can fail as a moral motive is bias toward the near and dear. Hoffman distinguishes here between two kinds of empathic bias: here-and-now bias, and familiarity bias. We are more likely to feel empathy for someone with whom we are in direct contact than with someone who is more distant, regardless of who is more in need of our help. So if Dorothy comes into your office and really needs your help, you are more likely to help her even if you've just been told that another patient, Jacques, is on the phone and also needs your help. Dorothy's distress calls up reactions that are, to a certain extent, simply hard-wired into your brain, while Jacques' predicament requires you to imagine how he is feeling. Familiarity bias has a similar, probably evolutionary, basis: the groups that survived to reproduce were those groups whose members learned to be altruistic towards each other. If we see care as a virtue, we will be able to explain why the caring person should avoid these failures of empathy. Like other virtues, care is a general disposition to behave in a particular way in all similar situations. If care is a virtue, the person who gives in to the above failures of empathy is an insufficiently caring or benevolent person. Further, ideally caring or benevolent persons would recognize these human failings and consciously work to extend their care to distant others.

The foundation of obligation

Annette Baier (1995) suggests that a care ethics would not need an account of obligation, because the concept of obligation implies coercion, while care implies affection as the basic motivation. She argues that we ought to supplant the concept of obligation with the concept of trust, conceiving of morality as based on trusting rather than coercing people. But I think there are two key distinctions that we can draw here. The first is between what we ought to do and what motives we ought to act upon. While care ethics privileges the motive of concern for others over the motive of concern for doing one's duty, it's not clear that this is incompatible with also recognizing obligations. The second distinction is between having an obligation and having a system for enforcing obligation. I think it is better to be able to trust people to carry out their obligations than to have to resort to coercion; one cannot even understand trust in this sense without assuming that we do in fact have obligations.

A stronger version of the idea that one doesn't need an account of obligation when one has the appropriate feelings of affection is that one shouldn't rely on one's sense of obligation when one could be relying on feelings of affection. There is a central confusion involved here – that ties of affection do all the motivational work. But this seems false. For example, I may have tremendous affection for my child and still need to rouse myself with a sense of my obligation as a parent before setting off for that conference with the principal.

Both Noddings and Held describe obligation as a response to need. I would argue that, although need plays a crucial role, there are other considerations that create obligations, including harm, promising, and role-responsibility. We recognize that a caring response to these obligation conditions is generally required of us, though, in carrying out our obligations in a given context, we are guided by our sense of what an ideally benevolent person would be motivated to do, and by a commitment to balance our obligations to intimates and distant others.

Slote's moral sentimentalism

Michael Slote describes his view as "moral sentimentalism," and it is an agent-based view: morality is understood entirely in terms of the motives of ideally benevolent agents. It doesn't follow that a benevolent agent's thinking something is good makes it good. The right sort of person still has choices and not all her actions express benevolence.

> Acts . . . don't count as admirable or virtuous . . . *merely because* they are or would be done by someone who is in fact admirable, or possessed of admirable inner states; they have to exhibit, express, or reflect such states or be such that they would exhibit, etc., such states if they occurred, in order to count as admirable or virtuous. (Slote 2003: 17)

110

Slote explicitly rejects principle-based motivation in favor of benevolence as characteristic of ideal agents: "Anyone who needs to make use of some overarching principle or rule in order to act in a 'balanced' way toward his children can be suspected of an unloving, or at least a less than equally loving, attitude toward those children" (2003: 68). For Slote, the ideal agent balances caring in the following way. One first balances care for one's intimates. Then one balances this intimate caring with two additional items: humanitarian caring about distant others and self-concern. Good people "will balance those larger concerns in something like the way that we have seen occurs when a person loves two individuals" (2003: 70). There is an important distinction between intimate caring and humanitarian caring to note here. Intimate caring is not aggregative, while humanitarian caring is.

Within this overall balanced caring for intimates and distant others, one is some-times required to make what Slote describes as a moral shift: "But one's special or greater concern for oneself and those near and dear to one . . . seem[s] morally to go out the window when significant public or political issues are at stake" (2003: 97). This moral shift can be justified in terms of need and role-responsibility.

Slote's account is contextual in the way that all virtue accounts are – while ideal moral agents will have the right sort of motivation, there are no common rules that they will all follow. On the other hand, Slote does make room for deontological con-siderations. He argues that the prime advantage of his view over utilitarianism is that his view is consistent with what he takes to be our correct intuition that some acts are always wrong: "An agent-based, sentimentalist account of deontology can hold that anyone willing to kill in order to save (a few) extra lives has morally bad or unacceptable overall motivation . . . and . . . can treat that claim as a ground floor ethical judgment" (2003: 82).

Care and Other Moral Perspectives

At this juncture, I want to make a meta-ethical point. I am not convinced that in some ethically preferred world, however one defines this, everyone would adopt the same moral theory or the same way of dealing with the moral realities of life. I am certainly not convinced that, in this world, everyone can do so. Rather, I think that each reasonably adequate moral theory has insight to offer and sheds light on a different aspect of our moral lives. I also think that each of us has a particular history and moral narrative that limits our ability to adopt new moral perspectives, regardless of how we may evaluate one moral theory against another. Finally, I think that when we try to make moral theories guides to action in the rough-and-tumble world of complex and difficult choices, we ought to take comfort where and when we can.

It is also important to distinguish between an ethic of care and an ethical approach to care-giving. One need not subscribe to an ethic of care as a moral perspective to realize that there are special issues that arise for any of us in our various roles as care-givers. I think that an ethic of care will shed light on a range of issues, certainly including the ethics of care-giving, but I am not committed to the view that moral theories are necessarily incompatible. They are often complementary. Care and Confucian ethics are similar in some important respects, for example. Ideal humanness (jen) and propriety (li) play a central role in Confucian ethics. Jen is analogous in some important respects to care, while li, like accommodation, reminds us that the good society must value harmony among its members (Tao 2000).

One helpful way to connect moral theories is to notice that they each focus primarily on a different component of our moral experience. An ethic of care reminds us of the importance of human relationships. It places moral value on communities as well as persons and asserts that our actions take place in the context of relationship – our decisions should consider existing relationships and are often carried out via social action. Doing the right thing and living the morally good life must be understood in the context of trust, reciprocity, and concern for others.

An ethic of care provides a corrective to some other ways of thinking about caring for patients. Kantian and utilitarian approaches are often seen as the gold standard in discussions of health care, but they are not quite up to every task. Patient autonomy and patient rights have a distinctly Kantian pedigree. We value patient autonomy because we see humans as rational moral agents who ought to be treated as ends in themselves and never merely as means. Patient rights provide the framework for our interactions with these autonomous persons. But if we rely exclusively on this perspective, we may lose sight of patients as needing care. When we are sick, we may not be up to the task of asserting our rights, and while we may value our autonomy we also value being cared for. Utilitarianism is most useful at the macro-level in discussions of social issues, reminding us of problems of cost and allocation. Care reminds us never to lose sight of actual persons.

There will be times when a care model appears to be in tension with a moral rights perspective. The patients' rights conception of the autonomous, competent patient is quite remote from the care conception of patients as primarily persons in need of maternal assistance. Still, these models can often work in tandem, and in my opinion ought to be so wedded. I envision the marriage of justice and care in the following way. First, we must be sensitive to the self-understanding of those entrusted to our care. Some patients will be aggressive about asserting their autonomy and privacy, while others will feel more comfortable making decisions collectively with their intimates and health-care team. Second, respecting rights is a minimal moral requirement, but we have not completely discharged our responsibilities until we treat others in a genuinely caring way. There is a further amendment to the rights model that must be made to make this a successful marriage. We should not assume that everyone is always capable of asserting and defending their rights in an autonomous way. Rather, we should recognize that sometimes people might be in need of care while temporarily (and in some cases permanently) unable to assert and defend their rights. In this case, we care for them and see returning them to full autonomy as part of our obligation rather than as an assumption about their present status.

Care and Bioethics

I now turn to the task of applying care ethics to bioethics. I begin with a review of the central features of care ethics and then move to a discussion of care in bioethics. Since I think that its application will differ in important ways in different contexts, I have divided the discussion there into three parts: care in the clinical setting, care in the research setting, and care in the allocation of health care. While what I say here will be sketchy and preliminary, I hope it provides a model for extending this theory further.

Summary of care ethics

While care ethics is much more nuanced than some other moral theories, it is still action guiding. When thinking about how to develop one's own moral character, it is important to develop one's empathy, since this will be an important guide to action. One needs to practice reasonable self-concern, both because one is deserving of care and because effective caring is impaired when one doesn't take adequate care of oneself. In interactions with patients one knows reasonably well, a practitioner with a well-developed empathic response can be guided by attending to the details of the situation with a commitment to viewing the patient sympathetically, noting the ongoing supportive relationships, and responding in such a way that the patient's best interest is served while preserving the harmonious relationships that support the patient. Since one will seldom have the luxury of enough time to provide ideal care to a single patient, one must balance concern between patients, while remaining sensitive to the importance of humanitarian caring and reasonable self-concern.

When one is not so familiar with the patient, or when one is developing guidelines for an institutional setting, one needs rules based on generalizations about the best way to be caring in interactions with patients. These rules function to set a moral minimum and some reasonable expectations about how others will behave. The rules will specify some actions as beyond the pale, as incompatible with a genuinely benevolent motivation. At the same time, support and encouragement should be given to help people to exceed this minimum and offer genuine caring support to patients. Institutions should be sensitive to the need to develop and sustain models of ideal caring practices. Finally, the conditions for developing empathy should be encouraged, while the dangers of empathic over-arousal, and familiarity, and here-and-now bias should be discouraged.

Caring for patients takes place in a setting that often makes it extremely difficult, if not impossible, to be our best caring selves. An ethic of care provides both a moral and political ideal. It is a moral ideal as it describes a way to structure one's moral interactions with others. It is a political ideal as it provides a powerful critique of existing institutions. In what follows, I am describing how care functions as a moral ideal. I will assume, just for the sake of description, that the institutional setting supports this ideal.

Care in the clinical setting

The clinical setting is perhaps the most natural setting for an ethic of care. Here the practitioner is responding to the needs of patients and doing so in a way that honors her commitment to her professional responsibilities and membership in a community dedicated to the well-being of patients. As she interacts with individual patients, she is morally attentive, sympathetically understanding, and sensitive to a set of relationships: between herself and the patient, between the patient and the other members of the health-care team, between the patient and her intimates and personal support team. Doing the right thing involves doing what is best for the patient, while respecting the patient's own sense of what this entails and preserving the harmony of all the supportive relationships involved.

Even in the most supportive institutional setting, one faces a conflict when one has to take care of more than a few patients. In this situation, one can appeal to the balancing metaphor that Slote offers. He describes the loving parent as the one who does not divide his attention in an arithmetically equal way between all his children, but rather the parent who is sensitive to the individual needs of his children. I would add that the ideally benevolent parent is also sensitive to the relationships between the children, and the perceptions that his children have of their relative importance to the parent. Even where one child is getting more attention because his needs are greatest, it is possible for the other children to feel that this is both fair and not a threat to their own relationship with the parent. Similarly, the health-care professional must balance his care between his patients, while at the same time striving to give them all a sense that they are receiving appropriate attention. The clinician can also experience a moral shift in the case of a pressing need. In the case of a natural catastrophe, for example, the clinician may be obligated temporarily to abandon her current patients in order to provide care for those affected by the natural disaster.

Care in the research setting

The research setting provides more of a challenge for an ethic of care because here the practitioner has obligations that can be in tension. On the one hand, she is responsible for the individuals under her care. On the other, she is responsible to future patients who may benefit from her research. Here I think we can appeal to Slote's view of the ideally benevolent agent – her care for immediate patients must be balanced by a humanitarian care for all. The concern for those in close connection, in this case those patients whose care she is supervising in the context of a clinical trial, must be individualistic in that she must give each of them what they need, insofar as this is possible. At the same time, though, she must be trying to create the best aggregative outcome for a large group of potential beneficiaries of her research. Again, a moral shift may take place that requires that she shift her concern in favor of the patients in the trial, or in favor of potential beneficiaries. Suppose, for example, that the patients in the trial began to suffer from a totally unexpected side effect of the clinical treatment. In this case, the moral shift is motivated both by the researcher's role in causing the harm and the extent of the harm.

Care and the allocation of health care

Some critics of care ethics argue that it is in the context of obligations toward strangers that care ethics fails. The problem is that if care requires an ongoing relationship and ties of affection, it cannot be extended to distant strangers. If care requires engrossment in the ends of the others, it will only be possible to care for a fairly small group of intimates. Here I think we can see the importance of viewing care as a virtue. If we see care as a general benevolent motivation, then there is no reason to assume that it cannot be extended to strangers. An ideally caring person would not be indifferent to the fact that distant others share the same needs, desires, and hopes that characterize one's intimates. If one's immediate obligations flow from the needs of others, as well as past harm, promising, and role-responsibility, then one will have obligations to strangers as well as intimates. I do think that care theorists are right to point out that we will have special commitments to intimates, and Slote is correct to point out the importance of love to the ideally benevolent agent. Still, I agree with Slote that it is hard to imagine describing a person as benevolent in the absence of concern for humanity as a whole.

As one focuses on the fair allocation of health care, one's concern is not limited to one's own patients. Rather, the concern is to extend health care in a fair way to the population as a whole. I would argue that equality would be a foundational value here since the basic reasons why we think persons are entitled to care – because they have needs and are capable of suffering – apply to all humans. The fact that we stand in a particular relationship to some humans shapes our obligations to them, but not their status as deserving of care.

One might also appeal to Slote's idea of balancing here. While concern for one's intimates is part of the motivation of the ideally benevolent agent, humanitarian concern is also a necessary condition of being an ideally benevolent agent. In the case of a parent, one's intimates include one's children, but an ideally benevolent person would also be concerned for the welfare of all children. In case of health care, there are a number of perspectives one might occupy. One might be in private practice and considering whether and how to include new un- or underinsured patients. Here, a caring person would balance concern for new un- or underinsured patients with concern for current patients. The caring person would also balance care for both groups with reasonable self-concern. Another perspective might be that of public policy-maker. Here the "intimates" might be one's fellow countrypersons and the distant others might be those in distant countries. Again, one balances concern for intimates with concern for distant others. As in the clinical and research setting, a catastrophe can require a moral shift towards intimates or distant others.

Conclusion

In this chapter, I have outlined a particular version of an ethic of care and given a general strategy for implementing it. I have also discussed some other representative care ethics and their similarities and differences. Finally, I have tried to provide some guidance for applying this perspective to bioethics. This perspective has already been the subject of useful criticism (Nelson 1992; Kuhse 1995), and generated important and insightful discussions of particular issues in bioethics, and I expect that it will continue to do so in the future.

References

Baier, A. (2005). *Moral Prejudices: Essays on Ethics*. Cambridge, MA: Harvard University Press.
Gilligan, C. (1982). *In a Different Voice*. Cambridge, MA: Harvard University Press.

Held, V. (2005). *The Ethics of Care: Personal, Political and Global*. Oxford: Oxford University Press.

Hoffman, M. (2000). *Empathy and Moral Development*. Cambridge: Cambridge University Press.

Kuhse, H. (1995). Clinical ethics and nursing: "yes" to caring, but "no" to a female ethics of care. *Bioethics* 9/3–4: 207–19.

Lyons, N. (1983). Two perspectives on self, relationship, and morality. *Harvard Educational Review*: 125–45.

Manning, R. (1992). *Speaking from the Heart: A Feminist Perspective on Ethics*. Lanham, MD: Rowman & Littlefield.

Nelson, H. (1992). Against Caring. *Journal of Clinical Ethics* 3/1: 8–15.

Noddings, N. (2003 [1984]). *Caring: A Feminine Approach to Ethics and Moral Education*, 2nd edn. Berkeley: University of California Press.

Ruddick, S. (1989). *Maternal Thinking: Toward a Politics of Peace*. Boston, MA: Beacon Press.

Slote, M. (2003). *Morals From Motives*. Oxford: Oxford University Press.

Tao Lai Po-Wah, J. (2000). Two perspectives of care: Confucian *ren* and feminist care. *Journal of Chinese Philosophy* 27/2: 215–40.

Further reading

Andre, J. (2001). *Bioethics as Practice*. Chapel Hill, NC: The University of North Carolina Press.

Benner, P. (1998). *Expertise in Nursing Practice: Caring, Clinical Judgment and Ethics*. New York: Springer.

Cates, D. F. and Lauritzen, P. (eds.) (2002). *Medicine and the Ethics of Care*. Washington, DC: Georgetown University Press.

Chakraborti, C. (2006). Ethics of care and HIV: a case for rural women in India. *Developing World Bioethics* 6/2: 89–94.

Dickenson, D. (2006). Gender and ethics committees: where's the "different voice"? *Bioethics* 20/3: 115–24.

Gelfand, S. and Shook, J. R. (eds.) (2006). *Ectogenesis: Artificial Womb Technology and the Future of Human Reproduction*. New York: Rodopi.

Kuhse, H. (1997). *Caring: Nurses, Women and Ethics*. Oxford: Blackwell.

Mahowald, M. (2006). *Bioethics and Women: Across the Life Span*. Oxford: Oxford University Press.

Tong, R. (1998). The ethics of care: a feminist virtue ethic for healthcare practitioners. *Journal of Medicine and Philosophy* 23: 131–52.

Wilkinson, T. M. (2005). Bioethics, bodies and (care)ful thinking. *Res Publica* 11/1: 75–83.

12

A Case Approach

JOHN D. ARRAS

Top-down vs Bottom-up

In its broadest definition, "casuistry" is the art of applying abstract principles, maxims, or rules to concrete cases. Our morality may tell us, for example, that "killing is wrong," but we are then left with the difficult task of determining, in concrete circumstances, whether a particular act amounts to a form of killing and, if so, whether the killing might possibly be excused or justified. Although just about every moral viewpoint will condemn the killing of an innocent child for selfish motives, for example, other more problematic cases challenge our understanding and deployment of this rule. Is disconnecting a patient from a ventilator a form of killing, or does it just amount to "letting die"? Is it permissible to kill an animal for food, a fetus for economic reasons, or a terminally ill cancer patient at her own request? To answer these more complicated questions we need to develop a complex "casuistical" account of the rule and its application to particular cases. Defined in this broad way, just about any traditional approach to morality – including Christian, Jewish, Kantian, utilitarian, or the "principlist" amalgam so dominant in contemporary bioethics (Beauchamp and Childress 2009) – will require a casuistical tradition by virtue of which its abstract norms are fitted to concrete cases.

Although casuistry has a long and controversial history as an approach to ethics (Jonsen and Toulmin 1988; Keenan and Shannon 1995; Leites 1988), it has emerged in recent bioethical discussions primarily as an alternative to more "top-down" or "theory-driven" methods. Thus, whereas the dominant approach to bioethics has tended to emphasize the importance of moral principles – such as beneficence, autonomy, and justice – or the application of moral theories (such as utilitarianism or Rawlsian contractarianism) to concrete dilemmas at the bedside or in social policy, the defenders of casuistry advocate an approach that works from the "bottom up," starting with our responses to concrete cases and then proceeding, as desirable or necessary, to the development of more abstract principles or moral rules. In this narrower sense, contemporary casuistry has much in common with other "particularist" or "interpretivist" criticisms of more principle- or theory-driven methods, such as feminism, pragmatism, hermeneutics, and virtue ethics (Arras 1994).

Core Elements of Casuistical Analysis

In order to explicate the more salient features of contemporary casuistry in bioethics, we shall begin with a case drawn from the experience of a neonatal intensive care unit:

> Baby Boy Johnson was the "lucky" one. Ten months ago, he and his twin brother had been born prematurely at 28 weeks to their drug-addicted mother. His brother had died shortly after birth, but Robert had survived, barely, languishing all this time in the neonatal intensive care unit (NICU). "Failure to thrive" is the generic medical description: born at a mere 2.6 pounds, he now weighed only 6.6 pounds.
>
> Robert was a flaccid, immobile encyclopedia of pediatric ailments. Early on, he had developed a severe lung disorder requiring mechanical ventilation, followed by the usual litany of neonatal catastrophe: a serious intracranial bleed, damaging strokes, seizures, episodes of sepsis, and failure to absorb nutrients. To address the latter problem, a gastrostomy tube was surgically inserted, but proved insufficient. Then the surgeon tried to bypass the failing gut with a catheter designed to deliver artificial nutrients directly into the bloodstream; but after two hours of pounding on Robert's skeletal frame, he gave up in frustration. A resident summed up the case: "No body mass, no lungs, no calories to the brain . . . no hope."
>
> Given Robert's dismal prognosis, the doctors began to feel that they were torturing him for no good reason. A nurse told the group that she had to apologize to Robert each time she had to stick him with a needle, which was all too frequently. In spite of the caregivers' desire to release Robert from his suffering, his poor, unsophisticated mother and father continued to hope for a "miracle" in this temple of high-tech medicine. The father asked, "Will my son play football?" The mother, perhaps haunted by the probability that her drug habit had damaged her son, asked, "When will my child get off the machine and come home?" Denying the inevitable, Robert's parents' steadfast demand of a horrified staff was that "everything be done" for their devastated child.

Paradigm, analogy, taxonomy

Rather than viewing such a case primarily as a site for the immediate deployment of various abstract bioethical principles, the modern casuist must first provide a robust and detailed description of the case, while fitting it under a certain rubric, such as "termination of treatment." This description will usually include an inventory of the likely moral reasons or "maxims" that might typically be invoked in such circumstances. Thus, the casuist would be attentive to what was going on in the case – that is, the interests and wishes of the various parties, the child's medical condition and prognosis, the distinct histories that brought each of the parties to this impasse – as well as to the variety of maxims or middle-level principles triggered by situations of this type, such as "Parents should normally make medical decisions for their children" and "Medically futile treatment need not be offered" (Jonsen 1991).

The next step is to fit the case as described into a *taxonomy*, a structured reservoir of responses to similar cases that contains various *paradigm cases* of conduct judged to be manifestly right or wrong, virtuous or shameful (Jonsen and Toulmin 1988; Jonsen 1991). The casuist argues that if moral certitude is to be located anywhere, it resides in our responses to such cases. We know, for example, that it is wrong to kill people without their consent. Indeed, such killing constitutes a paradigmatically wrongful act. We know this, moreover, with greater certitude than we know exactly *why* killing is wrong or which moral theory best explains why it is. Indeed, were a seemingly attractive principle to call for a response different from one of these paradigm cases, that would usually be a good reason to jettison the proposed principle. Thus, casuists are fond of saying that whatever moral certainty we have is to be found at the level of the case, not at the level of abstract principles or theory.

The casuist then tries to locate the new and problematic case on a continuum of cases stretching from a paradigm of acceptable conduct at one end of a spectrum to a paradigm of unacceptable conduct at the other end. Thus, in our case, she might fix on the standard sort of case involving well-educated, well-meaning parents who are generally agreed to have a right of parental decision-making. At the other end of the spectrum, she might conjure up the sort of case where the parents' putative right to make decisions might be effectively overridden. In this particular NICU, there was such a case. Several years before, a case involving a child with a fatal diagnosis (trisomy 18) and a horribly externalized gut (gastroschisis) had provided a defining moment for the unit's evolving moral taxonomy. The surgery to repair the gut would have involved significant and protracted pain and suffering for a child with an already fatal prognosis, but the child's parents had insisted on treatment, saying that surgery was "God's will." In this case, the entire medical team had reached consensus that they would not honor the usual maxim of deferring to parental wishes because the treatment would have been painful, futile, and unaccompanied by compensating benefit.

The crucial task of the casuist, then, is to determine where along this spectrum of paradigmatic cases the present case falls. Indeed, for the casuist, to say that someone "knows bioethics" is in large measure to say that he or she is thoroughly familiar with all the "big" or paradigmatic cases and knows how to reason from them to a suitable result in new and perplexing cases. This is done by means of *analogical thinking* (Jonsen 1991; Sunstein 1993). The casuist must compare the case at hand with the paradigm cases in order to determine how they are alike and how they differ in morally relevant respects. In our NICU case, the casuist asks whether the situation involving the patient is closer to the paradigm cases in which the parents' right of decision-making is honored, or rather to the case of the child with trisomy 18. In spite of the evident differences between the Johnson case and the trisomy case, the medical team felt that the similarities were powerful and outweighed the differences. In both cases, treatment was deemed both "medically futile" and extremely burdensome for the child. In this way, casuistical reasoning gives a concrete significance to the abstract criterion of "excessive burden."

This process of reasoning has much in common with the common law. In contrast to normative systems founded on explicit codes and pre-established principles, both the common law and casuistry work from the bottom up, inductively and incrementally developing new principles to deal with problematic cases. Accordingly, casuistry is often referred to as a kind of "common law morality."

119

The role of principles in casuistry

Casuists disagree about the normative status and derivation of principles in moral reasoning. Some espouse a radically particularist position, claiming that moral principles are mere inductive generalizations based upon our intuitive responses to cases (Toulmin 1982; 1988). These principles, it is claimed, merely raise our intuitions about cases to a higher level of abstraction and thus do not really tell us anything new. As such, principles have no independent normative force and thus cannot be used to criticize our fundamental responses to paradigmatic cases.

Other casuists, while acknowledging the dependence of principles on our history of moral experience, claim nevertheless that these principles can have an action-guiding or normative force (Jonsen 1995). For these more moderate casuists, paradigm cases are precisely those that most clearly, powerfully, and unambiguously embody the truth of a given moral principle or maxim. They argue that casuistry, properly understood, is not so much an alternative as a necessary complement to the development and deployment of principles (Arras 1991; Beauchamp and Childress 1994: 92–100).

In spite of this fundamental difference, both the radical particularists and the moderate casuists agree that whatever meaning a particular principle might have crucially depends upon the role it has played in the history of our previous interpretations. They agree that principles do not emerge from some celestial vault, fully articulated and ready for application to cases. Rather, their meaning is slowly developed and refined as we move from one set of important cases to another. Thus, the right to refuse medical treatment is not simply equivalent to an abstract right to liberty; its precise meaning is forged in the process of working through a large number of treatment refusal cases, each posing some new twist or nuance.

Likewise, both casuistical factions agree that the weight of any given principle cannot be determined in the abstract; like meaning, weight must be gauged in the context of the case. Casuists thus agree with the defenders of ethical "intuitionism" who reject the possibility of a pre-established hierarchy of values and principles. Eschewing any such "lexical ordering" (Rawls 1971: 42) of principles, casuists insist that the details of each case will determine the precise weight of all the relevant yet conflicting moral principles at stake. Thus, the principle of autonomy may prevail in one treatment refusal case where the patient's choice is deemed to be competent, well informed, and no threat to the welfare or resources of others; but it may be trumped in other cases where the claims of autonomy are weaker or the rival claims of others to scarce resources are stronger. Casuists caution that there is no rule that would allow us to determine, ahead of time, which value ought to prevail in any given case. Echoing a familiar Aristotelian theme, they insist that there is no substitute for good judgment (*phronesis*) based upon the particulars – the who, what, where, when, how much – of the case (Jonsen and Toulmin 1988: 19, 58–74).

Casuistry as rhetoric

In contrast, then, to methodological approaches that view ethics as a quasi-scientific enterprise bent on deductive demonstration of particular truths, casuistry emerges as a thoroughly *rhetorical* mode of inquiry (Jonsen and Toulmin 1988: 326; Jonsen

1995). Whereas the partisans of a geometric approach attempt to convince through long chains of reasoning finally punctuated by the claim, "You cannot think otherwise on pain of inconsistency!" casuists attempt to persuade by adducing numerous and often disparate considerations. Thus, instead of basing their argument for a right to health care on any single principle, such as utility, casuists typically invoke a cluster of complementary considerations including not just utility but also equal opportunity, communitarian themes, and the historical commitment of the medical profession to serve the poor. Although this method lacks the theoretical simplicity and aesthetic allure of more monistic approaches, it is much more likely to convince a larger number of people, many of whom may not embrace a theorist's preferred foundational principle. This kind of multifaceted, rhetorical appeal typically yields moral conclusions that are admittedly only probable, not apodictic; but the casuist argues, again following Aristotle, that this is the best we can hope for when arguing about particulars.

Advantages of a Casuistical Approach

Casuistry's close reliance on context gives it a distinct advantage over more theory-driven approaches in the practical worlds of policy formation and the medical clinic. It is a method of thinking especially well suited to busy physicians and nurses whose clinical outlook is already thoroughly case-oriented and who have neither the time nor the inclination to bother with too much theory. Although casuists must clearly presuppose a fair measure of social agreement on which to base their proposed solutions, they stress that usually there is no need for agreement at the level of deep theory or principle. Consensus can often be reached at a relatively low level of analysis between the invocation of "middle-level" principles (e.g., the principle of informed consent) and the particulars of the case (Jonsen and Toulmin 1988; Sunstein 1993). Thus, while the members of a bioethics commission might advance competing theories of *why* a certain practice, such as surrogate parenting, might be wrong, they may all be able to reason analogically to the conclusion that surrogate contracts constitute a form of "baby selling," and this might be all the agreement they need for the practical task at hand.

Like the common law, which also eschews appeals to deep theory, casuistry thus appears particularly well suited to the resolution of conflicts within a pluralistic, democratic society (Sunstein 1993). In the absence of a single, state-sponsored vision of the good life, casuistry seeks an "overlapping consensus" between groups with disparate and often conflicting views. But whereas a theorist like John Rawls (1993) seeks such consensus at the level of overarching, abstract principles, the casuist seeks it at the lower level of responses to paradigmatic cases, responses that might be explained or justified quite differently by different groups.

Seeking consensus at this lower, less theoretical level has an additional benefit for life in a pluralistic society. Whether the competing voices in a public debate take the high road of elevated principle or the low road of analogical reasoning, there are bound to be winners and losers. But if an issue is resolved at the lower level, the losers are likely to feel far less offended and aggrieved than if they had lost on the higher plane of their most cherished principles. In the area of abortion, for example, the so-called "pro-life" faction might have reacted in a much more temperate and measured fashion had the Supreme Court decided *Roe v. Wade* (1973) in a way that did not completely nullify their deeply held belief that all human life is somehow sacred. An approach more closely tailored to the factual circumstances of that case might have been less polarizing and thus more hospitable to future compromises.

Objections and Replies

Casuistry is insufficiently critical

A common objection to casuistical approaches is that, precisely because they work from the "bottom up" – because they begin already immersed in current intuitions, convictions, and practices, they are unable to provide a critical standpoint from which those very practices might be judged (Arras 1991; Wildes 1993; Tomlinson 1994). It may well be that some of our most strongly felt convictions, far from being obviously right, are actually the fruit of profoundly unjust social practices and institutions. If we could just step back and gain some critical distance, the injustice might become visible; but because casuistry anchors itself in paradigm cases, which are themselves based upon deeply entrenched social practices and attitudes, it will often leave such systemic injustices undetected and unchallenged.

In response, the casuist can and should admit that this approach, which is essentially backward-looking, may have some conservative tendencies. It remains true, however, that the overall direction of casuistical thought, whether conservative or progressive, will ultimately depend upon who is judging and which principles and values animate their analogical reasoning. Progressive social critics using progressive social norms will reason analogically to progressive conclusions.

Second, the casuist will note that most mature cultures will contain resources for robust self-criticism. Even at those moments when the values of the philistines, the hypocrites, and the unjust majority seem unshakeable, untapped resources for potentially subversive cultural criticism can often be identified (Walzer 1987; Kuczewski 1997). Martin Luther King, for example, spoke to white racists not as an outsider but, rather, as a fellow Christian, and he invoked values embedded in his culture's rich traditions and taxonomy to devastating effect.

It would also be fair for the casuist to respond here that even if casuistry is susceptible to the lure of common opinion and ideology, other rival methodological approaches often fare no better. Although principlists or theorists might think themselves better equipped than casuists to recognize and criticize lines of case judgments that deviate from the road of justice, they are often just as blind to the deeply entrenched prejudices of the day.

Reasoning by analogy is too indeterminate

A second criticism alleges that casuistry might work well within cultures featuring pervasive agreement on fundamental values, but that it must founder in highly pluralistic or even "postmodern" cultures like our own (Wildes 1993). Whether or not this criticism has merit, it does highlight the important fact that casuistry is more a method than a doctrine, more an engine of thought than a moral compass. The direction that this engine takes will invariably depend upon the value commitments of a community of inquirers (Kuczewski 1997). Thus, it makes perfect sense to talk about an Orthodox Jewish casuistry embedded in Halakah (Jewish law), a Roman Catholic casuistry, or even the casuistry of a particular NICU or hospital ethics committee.

The objection, then, is that casuistical reasoning depends upon deep-seated agreement on fundamental values and will necessarily fail to reach determinate conclusions when deployed in modern, pluralistic societies where such agreement is lacking. In contrast to the similar methodology of common law, which enjoys the advantages of having clearly defined decision-making authorities (judges) and paradigm cases that legally bind all subsequent interpreters (legal precedents), casuistry as practiced in secular, pluralistic societies features no clearly authoritative "moral experts" and its precedents (paradigms) are always subject to revision and reinterpretation at the hands of rival commentators.

In response, the casuist might first note the point made above: that casuistry may often be able to help forge consensus at the shallow level of responses to cases even when consensus at the deeper level of principle or theory is unlikely. Secondly, the casuist can resist the implication that modern societies are hopelessly Balkanized into small, hermetically sealed interpretive communities. In spite of the differences between regions and groups, modern societies are becoming increasingly *cosmopolitan*, increasingly marked by the overlap and interpenetration of disparate cultural and linguistic subgroups. Finally, it might be noted that, in spite of our manifest differences, the various interlocking communities of hospital clinicians, academics, judges and juries, medical societies, policy centers, and grassroots movements somehow manage to grope their collective way toward an overlapping consensus on a number of fronts in bioethics – even on the highly contested terrain of death and dying – largely with the aid of casuistical reasoning. While it would be overly sanguine to view casuistry as a kind of universal solvent for bioethical disputes, it would be overly pessimistic to ignore the ability of analogical reasoning at least to narrow the range of legitimate disagreement even when it cannot effect consensus.

Conclusion

Although casuistry has emerged in recent years as a rival approach to the dominant strain of principlism in contemporary bioethics, it is best viewed as a more modest but indispensable contribution to a more inclusive, holistic approach to ethical reasoning. Analogical thinking is usually a necessary component both in moral problem-solving and in the gradual development of moral principles and theories. Reasoning by means of paradigm and analogy provides the kind of specificity often lacking in more theory- or principle-driven approaches, allowing us to connect more abstract concepts with familiar fact patterns. And casuistical analysis also allows parties divided at the level of principle to converge on responses to specific paradigms and cases – a distinct advantage in pluralistic, democratic societies.

But casuistry also has familiar limitations that prevent it from being considered a self-sufficient method. Like the common law, it is inherently backward-looking and can be insufficiently attentive to a more systematic and scientific assessment of consequences (Tomlinson 1994; Posner 1995: 171–98). Likewise, because of its focus on proximate paradigms, casuistry can also fail to pay adequate attention to larger, overarching social questions, such as what kind of society we wish to live in (Arras 1991). And finally, relying as it does on settled convictions and common responses to cases, casuistry always risks a facile accommodation to the prejudices of the day. For these reasons, casuistry must be supplemented with an account of action-guiding principles and theories, with a concern for larger questions of the good life within a community, and with a critical eye for deep-seated and pervasive social injustices that distort our interpretation of cases.

References

Arras, J. D. (1991). Getting down to cases: the revival of casuistry in bioethics. *Journal of Medicine and Philosophy* 16: 29–51.

Arras, J. D. (1994). Principles and particularity: the roles of cases in bioethics. *Indiana Law Journal* 69: 983–1014.

Beauchamp, T. L. and Childress, J. F. (1994 [1979]). *Principles of Biomedical Ethics*, 4th edn. New York: Oxford University Press (6th edn. 2009).

Jonsen, A. R. (1991). Casuistry as methodology in clinical ethics. *Theoretical Medicine* 12: 295–307.

Jonsen, A. R. (1995). Casuistry: an alternative or complement to principles? *Kennedy Institute of Ethics Journal* 5: 237–51.

Jonsen, A. R. and Toulmin, S. (1988). *The Abuse of Casuistry: A History of Moral Reasoning.* Berkeley: University of California Press.

Keenan, J. F. and Shannon, T. (1995). *The Context of Casuistry.* Washington, DC: Georgetown University Press.

Kuczewski, M. G. (1997). *Fragmentation and Consensus: Communitarian and Casuist Bioethics.* Washington, DC: Georgetown University Press.

Leites, E. (ed.) (1988). *Conscience and Casuistry in Early Modern Europe.* Cambridge: Cambridge University Press.

Posner, R. (1995). *Overcoming Law.* Cambridge, MA: Harvard University Press.

Rawls, J. (1971). *A Theory of Justice.* Cambridge, MA: Harvard University Press.

Rawls, J. (1993). *Political Liberalism.* New York: Columbia University Press.

Sunstein, C. R. (1993). On analogical reasoning. *Harvard Law Review* 106: 741–91.

Tomlinson, T. (1994). Casuistry in medical ethics: rehabilitated, or repeat offender? *Theoretical Medicine* 15: 5–20.

Toulmin, S. (1982). The tyranny of principles. *Hastings Center Report* 11: 31–9.

Toulmin, S. (1988). The recovery of practical philosophy. *American Scholar* 57: 337–52.

Walzer, M. (1987). *Interpretation and Social Criticism.* Cambridge, MA: Harvard University Press.

Wildes, K. W. (1993). The priesthood of bioethics and the return of casuistry. *Journal of Medicine and Philosophy* 18: 33–49.

Further reading

Brody, B. A. (1988). *Life and Death Decision Making.* New York: Oxford University Press.

Miller, R. B. (1996). *Casuistry and Modern Ethics: A Poetics of Practical Reason.* Chicago: University of Chicago Press.

Strong, C. (1988). Justification in ethics. In B. A. Brody (ed.), *Moral Theory and Moral Judgments in Medical Ethics*. Dordrecht: Kluwer, pp. 159–84.

Sunstein, C. (1996). *Legal Reasoning and Political Conflict.* New York: Oxford University Press, pp. 35–61.

Wallace, J. (1996). *Authoritative Practice: The Case for Particularism in Ethics.* Ithaca, NY: Cornell University Press.

Part IV

Before Birth: Issues
Involving Embryos and Fetuses

13

Personhood

MICHAEL TOOLEY

Basic Moral Principles and the Concept of a Person

In everyday discourse, the term "person" is used in two rather different ways. Sometimes its meaning is purely biological, and it is used to refer simply to individuals belonging to our own species, *Homo sapiens*. Often, however, people refer to entities that are not humans – such as gods, angels, and possible extraterrestrials – as persons. Or they wonder whether certain animals, such as whales, dolphins, and primates, may not be persons. The term "person" is then being used in a very different way – namely, to refer, not to individuals belonging to a certain species, but, instead, to individuals who enjoy something comparable, in relevant respects, to the type of mental life that characterizes normal adult human beings.

It is the latter concept that has come to play a central role in ethics, and the reason is that a number of considerations strongly support the idea that the concept of a person is crucial for the formulation of many *basic* moral principles, including ones concerned with the morality of killing. For, first of all, consider two different fates that might befall one: on the one hand, being killed, and, on the other, having one's upper brain completely destroyed, while one's lower brain remains intact. Since the upper brain, consisting of the cerebral hemispheres, contains the neurophysiological basis not only of higher mental functions such as self-consciousness, deliberation, thought, and memory, but also of consciousness of even the most rudimentary sort, the destruction of the upper brain means the destruction of the capacity for any sort of mental life. But in addition, the upper brain also contains the basis of the specific memories, beliefs, attitudes, and personality traits that make one the unique person one is. Consequently, the destruction of the upper brain involves the destruction not only of certain general capacities, but also of the states that underlie personal identity. Provided that the lower brain, or brain stem, is not damaged, however, there will still be a living member of our species, since it is the lower brain that controls life processes, including respiration. In a case of killing, by contrast, one no longer has a living member of our species. Nevertheless, the two outcomes seem equally bad. Furthermore, if one considers someone's intentionally bringing about either outcome, each action seems as wrong as the other.

A second and related consideration involves the idea of reprogramming. Suppose that, rather than being killed, one undergoes *total* reprogramming in which all of one's memories, beliefs, attitudes, preferences, abilities, and personality traits are destroyed, and replaced with completely unrelated pseudo-memories, beliefs, attitudes, preferences, abilities, and personality traits. If this were done, an entity would still exist that would be not only a living member of our species, but also a psychologically normal, adult human being. But would this outcome be any less unwelcome from the point of view of the individual involved than the two just considered? Or would performing such an action be any less wrong than killing, or completely destroying the upper brain of, a normal, adult human being? Most people, it seems, do not think so, on the grounds that, though one is left, in the reprogramming case, with a living and quite possibly normal adult human being, the individual who once existed has been destroyed.

A third consideration is this. Suppose that, after one person destroys your upper brain, a second person, knowing that this has been done to you, proceeds to destroy the lower brain. Are you worse off as a result of the latter action, and has the person who performed that action done something that was morally on a par with what the first person did? In order to hold that you would be worse off, it would seem that one would have to hold that the destruction of all of someone's brain was morally worse than the destruction of just the upper brain. If, as many people feel, this consequence is not plausible, one is forced to conclude that although the action of the second person involves killing a living member of our species, while the action of the first person does not, it is the first action, and not the second, that is seriously wrong.

One can make sense of these intuitions only if one concludes, first, that it is a basic moral principle that the destruction of a person is at least prima facie seriously wrong and, secondly, that the wrongness of killing normal adult human beings derives from the fact that killing in such cases involves the destruction of a person. For when this view is adopted, one can explain, on the one hand, why having one's upper brain completely destroyed, or being completely reprogrammed, is morally on a par with being killed: all three acts involve the destruction of a person. One can also explain why one is not made worse off by the destruction of the lower brain, once one's upper brain has been destroyed – namely, that although this action results in the death of a living member of our species, it does not involve the destruction of a person.

The above considerations all turn upon cases involving human beings. The fourth and final line of thought focuses instead upon animals belonging to other species. One way of developing this final point is by raising the question of the morality of killing in the case of some animals with which we are actually acquainted. Thus one might focus, for example, on a chimpanzee that has learned sign language, and ask whether the painless killing of such an animal would be morally problematic, and, if so, to what extent. But given that what we are interested in are *basic* moral principles concerned with killing, there is another way of developing the argument. It arises because basic principles must apply not merely to situations of sorts that we have already encountered, but also to types of situations that, although they have not yet arisen, could very well do so. As a consequence, rather than confining one's consideration to species that are presently known to exist on earth, one can focus, instead, upon a possible extraterrestrial – one whose mental life is, by hypothesis, in no way inferior to our own. If there were such a being, would killing it be seriously wrong, or would it be morally comparable, instead, to killing, say, a plant, or an insect? Most people, it appears, feel that the killing of such a being who was not a member of our species, but who had a comparable or superior mental life, would be seriously wrong. If this view is right, then one is forced to conclude, once again, that a fundamental principle that is crucial for setting out an account of the morality of killing is that the destruction of persons is at least prima facie very seriously wrong.

Human Persons and Human Organisms

One might accept the concept of a person, and acknowledge that basic moral principles concerning the morality of killing need to be formulated in terms of that concept, but then go on to advance the claim – defended, for example, by Eric Olson (1997) – that a human person is identical with the relevant human organism. A number of very strong objections show, however, that the latter view is untenable.

The first objection turns upon a point made in the preceding section – namely, that having one's upper brain completely destroyed appears to be just as bad as being painlessly killed. But when a human person's upper brain is destroyed, there is still a living human organism. Accordingly, if human persons were identical with human organisms, no person would be destroyed when an upper brain was destroyed. But then how could it be the case that destruction of one's upper brain is as bad as being painlessly killed?

A second and closely related objection is this. Suppose that Bruce's upper brain is destroyed, but the rest of Bruce's body is unharmed, whereas Matt's body is completely destroyed, except for the upper brain, which is then transplanted into what had been Bruce's body. If human persons were identical with human organisms, and if one knew that one was going to be involved in a scenario of this sort, then, other things being equal, one should choose to be in Bruce's position, rather than Matt's, since the organism that survives is the organism that originally corresponded to Bruce. The vast majority of people, however, would prefer to be in Matt's position, which shows that they reject the view that a human person is identical with a certain organism.

A third objection is based on the idea of reprogramming. As noted earlier, people typically think that the complete reprogramming of a person's brain, so that all of the person's memories, beliefs, attitudes, preferences, abilities, and personality traits are destroyed, and replaced with completely unrelated pseudo-memories, beliefs, attitudes, preferences, abilities, and personality traits, is morally on a par with killing a human organism. But how could this be the case if human persons were identical with organisms, for, on that view, killing a human organism destroys a person, where complete reprogramming does not?

The fourth and final objection I shall mention is this. Suppose that A and B are two human organisms, that John is the person associated with organism A, and that Mary is the person associated with organism B. According to the contention that human persons are identical with human organisms, the person John is identical with organism A, and the person Mary is identical with organism B.

Suppose, now, that John's upper brain is removed from organism A, while Mary's upper brain is removed from organism B. The first of these is then transplanted into organism B, while the second is transplanted into organism A. All of John's beliefs, attitudes, memories, personality traits, and psychological capacities will now

131

be associated with organism *B*, while all of Mary's beliefs, attitudes, memories, personality traits, and psychological capacities will now be associated with organism *A*.

If John were identical with organism *A*, it would follow that John had undergone an extraordinary change with regard to his beliefs, attitudes, memories, personality traits, and psychological capacities. Similarly, given the claim that Mary is identical with organism *B*, Mary would have undergone an extraordinary change with regard to her beliefs, attitudes, memories, personality traits, and psychological capacities.

But neither of these things would be the case. What would have happened is not that John and Mary would have undergone extraordinary psychological changes, but, rather, that John would now be associated with organism *B*, while Mary would now be associated with organism *A*.

Given that human persons are not identical to human organisms, what is the relation between human persons and organisms? A very plausible answer, I suggest, is that a human organism at a time may *constitute* a human person at that time. A defense of this view would require, however, a long detour through the metaphysics of the constitution relation. Interested readers should turn to Lynne Rudder Baker's very interesting discussion (2000).

The Concept of a Person and the Wrongness of Killing

The principle that the destruction of persons is very seriously wrong is not itself very controversial: very few philosophically informed people, thoroughly acquainted with the sorts of considerations briefly sketched above, would wish to reject it. There are, however, a number of other issues, in the neighborhood of this principle, that are far from uncontroversial. One of the most important, for example, is the following. If something is a person, then, other things being equal, its destruction is seriously wrong, and intrinsically so. But, in addition, if one destroys a person, one does something wrong *to* the entity that one destroys. Is it only persons of which this is true? Or is person-hood a prima facie *sufficient* condition, but not a *necessary* condition, of an entity's possessing this sort of moral status?

What other types of entity might be thought to have the same moral status as that of persons? Two candidates that certainly need to be considered are suggested by discussions of the morality of abortion. First, there are potential persons – where the concept of a potential person is the concept of an entity that, though not a person, contains within itself all the positive factors that are needed in order for it to become a person. Secondly, there are entities that, though neither persons nor potential persons, belong to a species whose normal adult members are persons. (Examples of the latter are anencephalic human babies, which, because of severe congenital malformation of the brain resulting in the possession of at most rudimentary cerebral hemispheres, are in a permanent vegetative state, and thus are not even potential persons.)

A second controversial issue concerns the boundaries of personhood. For while there is widespread agreement that certain combinations of psychological properties – such as those that one finds in normal adult members of our own species – suffice to make something a person, there is considerable disagreement among philosophers both

132

concerning which of those properties are the morally significant ones, and concerning which properties constitute a *minimum* basis for personhood.

A final important issue is whether personhood is an all-or-nothing matter, so that all persons, *qua* persons, have precisely the same moral status, or whether, on the contrary, personhood admits of degrees. On this matter, by far the dominant view has been that personhood does not admit of degrees. As we shall see below, however, there are reasons for questioning this opinion.

What Makes Something a Person?

What properties suffice to make something a person? That certain clusters of properties are sufficient is almost universally accepted among philosophers. Consider, for example, a being that (1) possesses consciousness, (2) has preferences, (3) has conscious desires, (4) has feelings, (5) can experience pleasure and pain, (6) has thoughts, (7) is self-conscious, (8) is capable of rational thought, (9) has a sense of time, (10) can remember its own past actions and mental states, (11) can envisage a future for itself, (12) has non-momentary interests, involving a unification of desires over time, (13) is capable of rational deliberation, (14) can take moral considerations into account in choosing between possible actions, (15) has traits of character that undergo change in a reasonably non-chaotic fashion, (16) can interact socially with others, and (17) can communicate with others. Few would disagree that such an entity is a person. But what is one to make of this list of 17 properties? Some of the properties are rather closely related, so one may be able to shorten the list somewhat. One will still be left, however, with a large collection of significantly different properties. Are all of those properties relevant with respect to whether an entity is a person? Among those that are relevant, are any of them sufficient on their own to make something a person?

Once these questions are raised, quite different answers are likely to be advanced, and, on the whole, relatively little consensus is likely to exist. Thus, with regard to the issue of what properties, on their own, make something a person, some important alternative views are (1) that self-consciousness is sufficient, (2) that the capacity for rational thought is sufficient, (3) that being a moral agent is sufficient, (4) that being a subject of non-momentary interests is sufficient, (5) that having a mental life that involves an adequate amount of continuity, and connectedness via memory, is sufficient, and (6) that simple consciousness is sufficient. How is one to decide on the correctness of these claims? In this area, appeal to mere intuitions seems especially unpromising, and there would seem to be little hope of resolving this issue without making out a case for a systematic moral theory. The question, moreover, is a very pressing one. For while the choice among the first five views just mentioned might very well not make too much difference with regard to our present decisions, given that all five views would seem to entail that one does not have a person until one has an entity whose mental life is unified over time in quite significant ways, if it turned out that mere consciousness was sufficient to make something a person, that would obviously have very significant implications with regard to the moral acceptability of many of our present practices. For adult members of many animal species, and certainly including all mammals, would then have to be classified as persons, and so their use

133

either as a source of food, or in many scientific, medical, and commercial experiments, would be seriously wrong.

Another deeper issue that needs to be addressed by ethical theorists is whether the possession of certain general *capacities* – such as the capacity for self-consciousness or for rational thought – makes something a person. Many philosophers in the area of ethics have tended to assume, without offering any supporting argument, that this is so. Within philosophy of mind, however, it is often held that a person does not exist until there is a series of actual, conscious experiences that are psychologically interconnected in certain ways. If the latter view is correct, then neither the mere possession of certain unexercised capacities, nor even the combination of conscious experience plus unexercised capacities, suffices to make it the case that one has a person: it is crucial that the relevant capacities be ones that either have been, or are being, exercised.

But can one have, say, a capacity for thought that has never been exercised? It would seem that one can. For given that an organism will have a capacity for thought if it has a brain containing certain complex neuronal connections, it is possible that the necessary neurological development might be completed at a time when the organism is not conscious, so that there would be, at a certain time, a capacity for thought that had never been exercised in any way.

There is a genuine theoretical issue, accordingly, whether something becomes a person as soon as it acquires a relevant capacity, or only later, when it first exercises the capacity. Unlike the preceding issue, however, this one does not have substantial practical implications, as the question of killing rarely arises in situations where a capacity exists but has not yet been used. A satisfactory resolution of this issue is essential, however, if one is to have a comprehensive moral theory concerning the basis of personhood, and the morality of killing.

Is Personhood a Matter of Degree?

If, in thinking about personhood, one focuses only upon human persons, it is very easy to take it for granted that all persons, *qua* persons, have the same moral status. But once one considers the possibility of entities that have only some of the psychological properties possessed by normal adult human beings, or that have some of those properties only to a markedly lesser degree, it then becomes clear that it is important to ask whether all persons necessarily have the same moral status, or whether, on the contrary, personhood is a matter of degree.

This issue is also one that it may be very difficult to resolve in the absence of a general moral theory. One way of thinking about this question that may be helpful, however, in the absence of such a theory, is this. First, is the wrongness of destroying a person connected in some way with the value that an individual's life has, or potentially has, *for* that individual? Secondly, if it is, are there properties that make for personhood such that the extent to which one possesses those properties makes a difference with respect to the value that one's life has for oneself? If the answer to both of these questions is in the affirmative, then one has a reason for concluding that personhood is a matter of degree.

Assume, for illustration, that the ability to remember one's past actions and mental states, and the ability to envisage a future for oneself, and to pursue goals and projects, are properties that make for personhood. Organisms might vary greatly, presumably, in the extent to which they have those abilities. Imagine, then, having those abilities to a much more limited degree – so that, say, one could not remember more than a minute of one's prior life, nor envisage a future extending more than a minute beyond the present. What difference would such a change make to the value that an individual's life would have for that individual? If the answer is that the value would be significantly reduced, and if the wrongness of destroying a person is related to the value that life has, or could have, for the individual in question, then the destruction of a person with such very limited abilities to remember the past, and envisage a future, will not be as seriously wrong as the destruction of a person who possesses the much less limited abilities characteristic of normal human persons. Not all persons, then, would have the same moral status.

If this is right, there are some significant consequences. First, the fact that an animal belonging to another species has certain crucial characteristics only to a much lesser degree than normal human beings will not mean that the animal has no moral status at all. Secondly, within our own species, the acquisition of personhood may very well be a gradual process, and similarly for the loss of it, at least in some cases – such as, for example, Alzheimer's disease, which ultimately results in a permanent, degenerative, vegetative state.

Is Potential Personhood Morally Significant?

With regard to the question of whether there are non-persons that have the same moral status as persons, the most important candidates are potential persons. In considering this issue, it is crucial to distinguish between passive potentialities and active potentialities. Thus, while an unfertilized human ovum together with a neighboring, human spermatozoon are, in a sense, potentially a person, the potentiality is a passive one, since it requires outside intervention to start a process that will ultimately give rise to a person. By contrast, once the unfertilized human ovum is united with the spermatozoon, one has – or so, at least, it might initially seem – an active potentiality for personhood. A potential person is to be understood, therefore, as something that involves an active potentiality for personhood, and it is the destruction of such a potentiality that some have claimed is morally on a par with destroying a person.

Why should the small change in location involved in uniting the ovum and the spermatozoon make such a great moral difference? If this purely physical change were accompanied, for example, and as some people believe, by the creation of an immaterial, immortal soul that was attached to the fertilized human ovum, and which possessed, from the very beginning, the *capacity* for self-consciousness and rational thought, then it would be easy to see why one might hold that a morally significant change had taken place. But this line of thought, whatever its merits, has no connection with the claim that potential persons have the same moral status as persons, since it involves the idea that one really has a *person* – and not merely a potential person – from the very beginning of life.

135

Does the physical change in itself, then, have moral significance? There are at least three reasons for holding that it does not. First, compare the situation involving the unfertilized ovum and spermatozoon, with that of the fertilized ovum. In both cases, genetic material is present that will completely determine the genetic characteristics of any resulting individual. But what of the difference between a passive potentiality and an active one? The answer is that in neither case does one have a *fully* active potentiality – that is, a potentiality that will actualize itself if not interfered with. For unless the fertilized ovum is in an appropriate environment that supplies warmth, nutrients, etc., the development of the fertilized ovum is going to be very brief and very limited indeed. In both cases, accordingly, very significant outside assistance is required if a person is ultimately to come into being, and so it seems very implausible to assign a significantly different moral status to the two situations.

Secondly, consider the following case, where there *is* a fully active potentiality. An artificial womb has been perfected, and it now contains an unfertilized ovum, along with a spermatozoon. There is also a device, however, that will ensure that fertilization will soon take place, and that if there is no interference, the result will be the emergence, in nine months time, of a normal human baby, who will then receive appropriate care so that it can continue to develop. This situation involves, accordingly, a fully active potentiality, by contrast with the case of the isolated, fertilized human ovum. The crucial question, then, is this. What is the moral status of destroying the fully active potentiality by, say, turning off the machine before fertilization has taken place? Very few people, it seems, would hold that such an action is morally wrong. If this is right, then the destruction of a fully active potentiality for personhood, rather than being morally comparable to the destruction of a person, is not morally wrong at all.

Thirdly, consider a case where almost every one would agree that potentiality is morally significant – namely, the case where a person is in a temporary coma from which he or she will eventually emerge. Killing the human organism in question would be seriously wrong, and it might be suggested that the reason that it is wrong is that the organism has an active potentiality for recovering consciousness. But this conclusion is mistaken, as can be seen if one considers a slightly different case, in which a person is in a coma from which he or she will never emerge unless, say, an operation is performed to relieve increasing pressure within the brain. In the latter case, there is only a passive potentiality for recovering consciousness, but it is still seriously wrong to kill the human organism in question. The conclusion, accordingly, is that in cases where potentialities are clearly relevant to the morality of killing, both active and passive potentialities are relevant.

Is Species Membership Morally Significant?

A second suggestion that is sometimes advanced concerning entities that might have the same moral status as persons is that if something, while neither a person nor even a potential person, belongs to a species whose normal adult members are persons, such an entity has the same moral status as a person. On this view, then, the killing of an anencephalic human infant would be morally on a par with the destruction of a person.

This view appears unsatisfactory, however, for a number of reasons. First, it seems plausible to base an entity's moral status upon its intrinsic properties, rather than upon its relations to other individuals. Thus, for example, whether an entity is a person should not be a matter of how others do or do not regard it, or how they do or do not treat it. Nor should it be in any way dependent upon what other entities happen to exist. Moral status is intrinsic to an individual. But this would not be so if species membership could be sufficient to give one the same moral standing as a person.

Secondly, why should the purely physical relation of belonging to the same species make a difference with respect to one's moral status, when other purely physical properties and relations do not appear to do so?

Thirdly, it seems natural to connect having moral status with having interests that need to be protected. The term "interest," however, can be used in quite different ways. In one sense of the term, anything that contributes to the proper functioning of something is in that thing's interest. So interpreted, however, it applies to things that have no moral status, since in this sense of the term, it is, for example, in the interest of a computer not to be exposed to extremes of temperature.

The morally significant concept of interest is, by contrast, one that connects up with being a conscious entity, and with being capable of having desires. In this sense of "interest," an anencephalic human infant, for example, does not and cannot have any interests at all, since it can never be conscious. Accordingly, if moral status is connected with having interests in the relevant sense, species membership cannot suffice to bestow moral status.

Finally, the proposed principle is exposed to counterexamples. That is to say, there are cases that fall under the principle, and where it therefore implies that a certain entity would have the same moral status as a person, but where this is not intuitively plausible. Thus, for example, the principle implies that a member of our species whose upper brain has been completely destroyed has the same moral status as a person, and this seems incorrect. There would seem to be good reasons for concluding, then, that species membership is not itself morally significant.

If this conclusion is correct, it has some very important implications. The most immediate concerns anencephalic and severely brain-damaged humans. At present, such individuals are sometimes kept alive by medical intervention, and not infrequently at very substantial cost. If, however, species membership is not morally significant, there is no moral reason to prolong, often at great cost, the lives of individuals that neither are, nor ever can be, persons.

The Moral Status of Human Embryos, Fetuses, and Newborn Infants

If the preceding conclusions are correct, then neither the fact that human embryos, fetuses, and newborn infants belong to a certain species, nor the fact that they are potential persons gives them a special moral status. It would seem, then, that their moral status must turn on whether they are persons. In the case of human embryos, even the very modest claim that something cannot be a person unless it possesses, or has previously possessed, at least the capacity for rudimentary consciousness leads to the

137

conclusion that human embryos are not persons. In the case of human fetuses and newborn infants, the issue is less clear-cut; however, there are at least two lines of thought that may prove helpful. In the first place, once potentialities have been set aside, and the focus is upon the type of mental life that an entity is, or has been, capable of enjoying, it seems likely that any criterion of personhood that classified newborn human infants as persons would also classify adult animals of *many* other species as persons as well, and so would necessitate a very significant revision of our ordinary moral opinions. Secondly, many of the criteria of personhood that have been traditionally proposed entail that something is not a person unless it presently possesses, or has possessed, the capacity for thought, and this means that if any of those traditional criteria is even roughly correct, then human fetuses and newborn infants cannot be persons unless the capacity for thought is something that develops at some point prior to birth – a possibility that does not seem very likely, given our current knowledge of early human behavior and neurophysiological development.

The conclusion that normal newborn humans are not persons, if correct, has very important consequences concerning our responsibilities to newborn humans. For if potential personhood is not morally significant, and if normal newborn humans are not persons, then the intrinsic moral status of such individuals does not differ from that of anencephalic infants. This in turn means that if one considers the case of human infants that are neurologically normal, but physically severely disabled, the question arises as to whether painless termination of life may not be morally best in many such cases.

Summing Up: Ethics and the Concept of a Person

Many of the most controversial issues that society faces involve either killing, or letting die. These include such questions as that of how the concept of death is best defined, of when non-voluntary euthanasia is morally justified, of the moral status of abortion, and of our responsibilities with regard to newborn human infants – both anencephalic, and severely brain-damaged ones, and also ones that are neurologically normal, but severely disabled. A resolution of these problems is likely to remain very difficult until there is a more widespread appreciation of the fact that basic moral principles dealing with killing and letting die need to be formulated in terms of the concept of a person.

A final area where the concept of a person is obviously crucial concerns the moral status of animals belonging to other species. In some cases, given our increasing knowledge of the psychological capabilities of non-human animals, our present understanding of the concept of a person probably provides a sufficient basis for concluding that some non-human animals are persons. In other cases, however, where one is dealing with animals whose psychological capabilities are much more limited, a satisfactory answer may very well require a more subtle understanding of precisely what properties do, and do not, suffice to make something a person.

References

Baker, L. R. (2000). *Persons and Bodies: A Constitution View.* Cambridge: Cambridge University Press.

Blumenfeld, J. B. (1977). Abortion and the human brain. *Philosophical Studies* 32: 251–68.

Brandt, R. B. (1972). The morality of abortion. *Monist* 56: 503–26.

Brody, B. (1975). *Abortion and the Sanctity of Human Life: A Philosophical View.* Cambridge, MA: MIT Press.

Donceel, J. F. (1970). Immediate animation and delayed hominization. *Theological Studies* 31: 76–105.

Engelhardt, H. T. (1978). Medicine and the concept of a person. In T. Beauchamp and S. Perlin (eds.), *Ethical Issues in Death and Dying.* Englewood Cliffs, NJ: Prentice-Hall.

English, J. (1975). Abortion and the concept of a person. *Canadian Journal of Philosophy* 5: 233–43.

Gillespie, N. C. (1977). Abortion and human rights. *Ethics* 87: 237–43.

Glover, J. (1977). *Causing Deaths and Saving Lives.* Harmondsworth, UK: Penguin.

Hare, R. M. (1975). Abortion and the golden rule. *Philosophy and Public Affairs* 4: 201–22.

Ladd, J. (ed.) (1979). *Ethical Issues Relating to Life and Death.* New York: Oxford University Press.

McCloskey, H. J. (1975). The right to life. *Mind* 84: 403–25.

McMahan, J. (2001). *The Ethics of Killing: Problems at the Margins of Life.* Oxford: Oxford University Press.

Olson, E. T. (1997). *The Human Animal: Personal Identity Without Psychology.* New York: Oxford University Press.

Parfit, D. (1984). *Reasons and Persons.* Oxford: Clarendon Press.

Sumner, L. W. (1981). *Abortion and Moral Theory.* Princeton, NJ: Princeton University Press.

Tooley, M. (1972). Abortion and infanticide. *Philosophy and Public Affairs* 2: 37–65.

Tooley, M. (1979). Decisions to terminate life and the concept of a person. In J. Ladd (ed.), *Ethical Issues Relating to Life and Death.* New York: Oxford University Press.

Tooley, M. (1983). *Abortion and Infanticide.* Oxford: Oxford University Press.

Warren, M. A. (1973). On the moral and legal status of abortion. *Monist* 57: 43–61.

14

Abortion

MARY ANNE WARREN

The world remains divided between jurisdictions in which abortion is legal, at least in the first trimester, and those in which it is prohibited or narrowly restricted. Approximately 61 percent of the world's population has legal access with few restrictions as to reason, or on broadly inclusive health or socioeconomic grounds (Crane and Hord Smith 2006: 4). This is the case in most of the developed or rapidly developing nations, including China and India. In contrast, roughly 36 percent of the world's population live in countries where abortion is permitted only to save the woman's life or physical health (Crane and Hord Smith 2006: 4). These include many of the poorest nations of Africa, Asia, and Central and South America. The World Health Organization (WHO) estimates that about half of the 40–50 million abortions that occur annually are unsafe – that is, done by persons who lack the necessary training and medical resources. Each year about 70,000 women die from unsafe abortions (WHO 2003: 7), about 95 percent of them in developing nations where access to abortion is severely restricted (WHO 2003: 12). About one in five unsafe abortions results in infection of the reproductive tract, which can cause chronic health problems or permanent infertility (WHO 2003: 14).

Under these conditions, it is important to examine carefully the arguments for and against the moral permissibility of abortion. The moral status of abortion – whether it is permissible or impermissible – is the primary determinant of the legal status it should have. Of course, not all morally objectionable actions should be legally banned; some are too minor to justify legal coercion. But if abortion is a form of wrongful homicide, as many opponents believe, then it is too serious a moral wrong to be legally tolerated. Conversely, if abortion is morally permissible, then the toll taken on women's lives and health by the lack of access to safe and legal abortion is extremely difficult to justify.

I will begin with the arguments in support of a woman's right to terminate her pregnancy, at least in the earlier stages. The first group of arguments examines the consequences of denying women safe and effective means of controlling their fertility; the rest deal with the infringement of basic moral rights that this denial entails. Next, I consider the arguments against the moral permissibility of abortion. The most important is that human embryos and fetuses from conception onwards are human beings with the same moral right to life as other human beings. This is the position of the Roman Catholic Church, which holds that abortion is morally wrong even when it is the only way to save the woman's life. Another argument is that embryos and fetuses have a right to life because of their potential to *become* human beings. Some arguments are not based on the claim that embryos and fetuses have a right to life; for instance, it is sometimes said that easy access to abortion cheapens human life, or encourages promiscuity. I will consider these arguments in turn.

The Arguments for the Freedom to Choose

The consequentialist case for access to safe abortion must begin with the conditions that can make unwanted pregnancy difficult to avoid. In all parts of the world, the majority of women are involved in sexual relationships with men – with or without a marriage contract – during a substantial part of their fertile years. Such relationships are strongly desired by most heterosexual adults, and attempts to lower the rate of heterosexual activity through "abstinence only" sex education consistently fail. These relationships are often important to the woman's economic survival and her ability to support her children, because, while they usually have the primary responsibility for childrearing, women's earning power is usually less than men's. Although contraceptives reduce the risk of unwanted pregnancy, all of them have a significant failure rate. Moreover, millions of women do not have the freedom, knowledge, or material resources to make effective use of contraception. Even the least expensive contraceptives are beyond the economic reach of much of the world's population. In rural areas women may lack transportation to and from clinics where contraceptives can be obtained. Some men refuse to use condoms, or prevent their sexual partners from using other contraceptives. Some religions (notably Roman Catholicism) teach that artificial means of contraception are morally objectionable, and strive to make them unavailable, often successfully. Finally, some pregnancies are the result of rape or other forms of coercion.

Under these conditions, without access to safe abortion, women cannot decide whether to have children, how many to have, or when to have them. Without this freedom, they are less able to protect their own lives and health, and support the children they may already have. Women who give birth too frequently and who lack good nutrition and medical care are more likely to die in childbirth, and their children are more likely to die in infancy (Rosenfeld 1989). In some communities, single women face abuse – and sometimes death – if they become pregnant. Even in more tolerant societies, a woman who has children she cannot support may be condemning them to extreme poverty.

These are among the reasons why so many women experience unplanned pregnancies, and why they often judge it necessary to end them. The need is so compelling that, where abortion is illegal, many women risk criminal penalties, and death or permanent injury from clandestine surgical, pharmacological, or self-induced abortions.

It is not only individual women and families who suffer from the absence of safe abortion. Rapid population growth magnifies the difficulties that developing nations face in eradicating poverty and disease. Global biodiversity and the future ability of the planet to support human life are also at stake. Global warming makes it clearer than ever before that the earth can no longer support a rapidly growing human population.

141

Many countries' ability to support their populations at present levels is threatened by the increased incidence of catastrophic floods, droughts, and wildfires, the displacement of populations as a result of wars and natural disasters, and the loss of agricultural land to rising ocean levels, desertification, erosion, and commercial development. Species are being lost at an accelerating rate because of over-exploitation, habitat destruction, and human-caused climate changes. Yet many of the poorest nations are still experiencing rapid population growth – in large part because the lack of contraception and safe abortion forces many women to have more children than they otherwise would.

These are some of the consequentialist arguments for access to safe abortion. Equally important are the rights-based arguments, which focus upon the encroachments upon women's freedom that are inherent in the prohibition or restriction of access to abortion. The freedom to seek or reject particular medical interventions is a vital part of human liberty. If there are basic human rights, then this must be one of them, because without it other basic rights are negated. Children and mentally disabled persons are not always accorded this right, because they are presumed to be less able to make informed judgments about their medical needs than are competent adults. But pregnant women are entitled to the same freedom to decide what happens to their bodies as are other competent adults. To deny them the freedom to end a pregnancy is to infringe upon this vital freedom. It is also to deny them the freedom to protect their own life and health, control their own fertility, and pursue a good life for themselves and those for whom they are responsible (McCauley 1994). The freedom to decide whether to have (more) children would be important even if fetuses were not gestated in women's bodies, because parenthood brings with it responsibilities that can be impossible to fulfill, and that in the minds of many parents cannot be eliminated by surrendering the child for adoption. Most feminists and civil libertarians regard these infringements upon women's freedom as human rights violations. Such infringements cannot be justified by appealing to cultural traditions or religious doctrines; on the contrary, it is these that need reconsideration where they entail the violation of basic rights.

If embryos and fetuses do not have a moral right to life, then these arguments ought to be persuasive. However, someone who believes that embryos and fetuses have that right is unlikely to be persuaded by either consequentialist or rights-based arguments. It is at best morally problematic deliberately to kill individuals who have a right to life, even to prevent very bad consequences or to protect others' basic moral rights. While some homicides may be justified (e.g., those done in self-defense), no one is entitled to kill an innocent human being who has done nothing to waive or forfeit the right to life. But are there sound reasons to believe that embryos and fetuses have a full and equal right to life?

Fetal Life and Humanity

It is often said that human life begins at conception. The incorporation into the ovum of the DNA contained in the spermatozoon provides the fertilized ovum, or zygote, with a complete human genotype, which is essential for its development into a mature human being. From conception onwards, this development is gradual and continuous. Thus, it is argued, conception is the only time at which the life of a human being can rightly be said to begin. If this is true, and if all human beings have a right to life, then it follows that the zygote has this right. Neither its early stage of development, nor its social invisibility, nor its dependence upon the woman's body for life support can justify the denial of this right (Noonan 1970). If embryos and fetuses have a right to life, then they may not be killed except under conditions that would justify the killing of an older human being. We do not permit parents to kill already-born children because of economic need or threats to the parents' lives or health; and if embryos and fetuses have the right to life, then they should not be killed for such reasons either.

But is it true that human life begins at conception? This claim is highly ambiguous. If it means that the biological life of the ovum or sperm begins only at conception, then it is false. Sperm and ova are alive before they meet; or if they are not, then conception does not occur. In fact, ova are formed in the ovaries of female human fetuses before they are born, and have been alive for years before they are fertilized.

Perhaps the claim that life begins at conception means that the ovum becomes biologically human when it is fertilized. But this is also false. An unfertilized human ovum is as human as any other human cell. It differs from most human cells in being haploid rather than diploid (having 24 rather than 48 chromosomes); but this is standard for human sperm and ova, and does not belie their species membership. All the cells in our bodies that contain our human genome are, by definition, human. If their biological humanity were sufficient to endow them with a right to life, then brushing one's teeth would be the moral equivalent of mass homicide, since it inevitably destroys many living human cells, as well as many bacteria.

Another interpretation of the claim that life begins at conception is that a human individual comes into existence at that time. Most of the cells of which our bodies are composed are by definition not complete human individuals, but parts thereof. Fertilized ova are arguably different, because they are (usually) genetically unique; and at least some of them have the potential to develop into mature human beings. But are these sufficient reasons for regarding them as human beings?

The claim that a human individual comes into existence at conception can be disputed on empirical grounds. Some bioethicists argue that the early embryo cannot be identified with the embryo that develops later because, for approximately the first two weeks, it consists of a set of undifferentiated cells, each of which could give rise to a complete embryo under some circumstances. The early embryo may spontaneously divide, resulting in twins or triplets; alternatively, it may combine with another embryo, giving rise to a single embryo with a mosaic of genetic traits. Thus, it is concluded, the early embryo is not yet an individual human being (Ford 1988). Although most induced abortions occur later than 14 days from conception, the point is relevant to the abortion debate because some people suspect that hormonal contraceptives (such as the morning-after pill) can prevent the implantation of a fertilized ovum. If an embryo does not become a human individual until two weeks after conception, then the primary objections to abortion do not apply to this case.

Although very early embryos may not be human individuals, more developed embryos and fetuses presumably are. The question then becomes: do all human individuals have a right to life? It is not self-evident that they do. Human embryos and fetuses, especially in the earlier stages, are different from more developed human beings in ways that may be morally relevant. True, there are many physical resemblances between fetuses and infants; by the end of the first trimester a fetus has a face, hands, feet, and other physical features that are recognizably human. This makes it easy to believe that it is a thinking, feeling being; but appearances can be deceptive. Prior to the latter part of the second trimester, fetuses very probably lack the neurophysiological structures and functions that are necessary for the occurrence of pain and other conscious experiences, as well as for thought, self-awareness, and other mental activities (Burgess and Tawia 1996). And it is virtually certain that first-trimester fetuses have yet to develop these structures and functions. Consequently, they cannot suffer pain, unhappiness, or the loss of anything that they enjoy, desire, or value. They are biologically alive, but they do not have what James Rachels called a "biographical" life (1990: 208–9) – one that includes feelings and experiences. While *we* may value their lives, they cannot value their own present or future existence.

This difference casts doubt upon the claim that embryos and presentient fetuses have a right to life comparable to that of older human beings. If already-born human beings (and sometimes other animals) are thought of as having moral rights, while plants and microbes usually are not, this is in large part because there is no good reason to believe that plants and microbes can experience pain, suffering, or any other harm that matters to them. Their evident lack of sentience is the reason why we do not normally refer to them as *beings*, even though they are living organisms. Similarly, it may be appropriate to think of human embryos and presentient fetuses as biologically human individuals that have not yet become beings.

The Argument from Fetal Potential

Some argue that abortion is morally wrong not because embryos and fetuses are already human beings, but because they have the potential to become human beings. If the lives of all human beings have moral value, then, it is argued, entities that have the potential to develop into human beings must have the same value. One version of the argument points out that most of us value our futures, and suggests that it is the fact that we have valuable futures that gives us a right to life. Given that embryos and fetuses have the potential to develop into beings who will value their futures as much as we value ours, why should their valuable futures not give them the same right to life (Marquis 1989)?

One response to the argument from potential is that we often treat a particular property as sufficient for a certain right, without treating the potential to develop that property as also sufficient. For instance, the right to vote in political elections may be granted to citizens 18 years or older, but not to younger individuals – even though most of them have the potential to reach the age of 18. This discrimination is probably justified, because 18-year-olds as a group are apt to be better prepared to vote intelligently than are most younger persons. A line needs to be drawn, and this is probably as good a place as any to draw it. Similarly, there are differences between actual and potential human beings that may justify differences in their legal and moral rights.

Another response to the claim that potential human beings have a right to life is that this claim is subject to a *reductio* argument. For if it were true, then it would apply not only to human embryos and fetuses but also to unfertilized human ova, which also have the potential to become human beings. Of course, this cannot happen without the timely arrival of enough human spermatozoa to bring about fertilization. But this is only one of many biological and other conditions that are necessary for the birth of an infant. Thus, it is odd to say that the ovum acquires the potential to give rise to a human being only when it is fertilized. Thus, if potential human beings have a right to life, then not only is abortion morally wrong but it is also wrong to prevent an ovum from being fertilized, whether by using contraceptives or by deliberately avoiding sexual intercourse when conception is possible. If we wish to reject these extreme conclusions, then we must reject the claim that all potential human beings have a right to life. (See also the discussion of potential by Michael Tooley in chapter 13, "Personhood.")

The rejection of this claim does not imply that potential human beings have no value. If a pregnancy is wanted, then the embryo or fetus will be greatly valued. But if the pregnancy is unwanted or medically dangerous, or if the fetus is abnormal in ways incompatible with long-term survival, then its value as a potential human being may be outweighed by the needs of actual human beings. It is biologically impossible for all potential human beings to become actual. Human reproductive biology ensures that the great majority of human ova do not become zygotes; and it is possible that most zygotes never become viable embryos (Grobstein 1988). Moreover, it is good that this is so, since women's capacity to bear and raise children is limited, as is the earth's capacity to support more human beings.

Abortion and Fetal Development

The argument thus far suggests that neither the biological aliveness and humanity of the early fetus, nor its potential to become a human being provides a sound reason for according it a right to life. However, as a pregnancy progresses, it becomes more difficult to regard the fetus as only a *potential* human being. Not only does it come to look more like a baby, but it probably begins at some point before birth to have a rudimentary form of consciousness. It is fairly certain that first-trimester and early second-trimester fetuses are not sentient, since neither the sense organs nor the parts of the brain necessary for processing sensory information (including the cerebral cortex) are well enough developed. Electrical activity in the cerebral cortex has been reported as early as 20 weeks gestational age; however, the more organized patterns of electrical activity that are typical of waking and dreaming states seem not to appear before about 30 weeks (Burgess and Tawia 1996: 23). Thus, it seems quite likely that the beginnings of sentience lie either in the late second trimester or in the third trimester.

The possibility of sentience in the later states of fetal development is one reason for regarding early abortion as morally preferable to late abortion. The reader may wonder whether this claim does not imply that it is also morally problematic to kill sentient or possibly sentient animals of other species for food or for other human uses. I believe that it does. Killing sentient or possibly sentient beings is morally problematic because it deprives them of lives that they may have been consciously enjoying. While it is not wrong in every case, it requires justification in terms of some legitimate need,

145

for example, as a necessary means of self-defense, subsistence, or the protection of human or ecosystemic health.

Another reason to prefer early to late abortion is that it is medically less dangerous for the woman, and less emotionally traumatic for her and others. Most women are aware of these differences, and, where safe abortion is available, most abortions occur well before the end of the second trimester. In the United States, fewer than 2 percent of abortions are performed after 20 weeks (Columbia University Mailman School of Public Health 2007: 3). Nevertheless, circumstances can sometimes justify later abortions. These are most often done because the fetus has a disastrous abnormality, such as anencephaly (the absence of all or most of the brain), that guarantees that it will be stillborn or die soon after birth.

Making Abortion Difficult to Obtain

Some people doubt that fetuses have a right to life, but are still uncomfortable with a policy of "abortion on demand." They believe that if abortions are easy to obtain, then many will be done for morally inadequate reasons. Consequently, they favor making abortion difficult to obtain, for example, by permitting it only when there is an immediate medical danger to the woman, or an exceptional economic or personal hardship. They may also favor requiring the consent of the fetus's father or of the woman's parents, if she is a legal minor; or requiring the woman to undergo counseling aimed at changing her mind; or a mandatory waiting period before the abortion can be done.

One argument for making abortion difficult to obtain is that permitting it for just any reason devalues human life. On this view, a human life has value even when the individual has no right to life, and should not be ended for reasons that are less than compelling. This argument presumes that women who are free to choose will often end pregnancies for non-compelling reasons, perhaps for mere convenience. But the magnitude of a woman's personal stake in the decision makes this presumption implausible. Her life and the lives of those she is close to will be substantially altered by her course of action. Laws and regulations that restrict access to abortion make an already difficult personal situation even more difficult. Inevitably, such laws create the greatest hardships for women who are young, poor, disabled, abused, or otherwise vulnerable. If the goal is to express respect for human life by reducing the number of abortions, a fairer and more effective approach is to reduce the number of unwanted pregnancies through more adequate sex education, universal access to contraception, and the development of more effective and affordable contraceptives.

Ideological Bases of the Abortion Debate

Abortion is controversial not only because some people believe that it violates the rights of embryos and fetuses, but also because it is a symbol of ancient conflicts over sexual morality, birth rates, and the social roles of women. Abortion opponents are likely to fear that children, and society as a whole, will suffer if women and men abandon their traditional familial roles. They may believe that legal abortion undermines these gendered familial roles by making extramarital sex less perilous for women, and giving men an easy rationalization for not supporting their children. They may fear that a decline in birth rates will undermine the nation's military and economic strength. (This was the primary rationale for the prohibition of abortion in Stalin's Soviet Union and Ceausescu's Romania.) In contrast, supporters of legal abortion are less apt to believe that women must have a distinct social role; that sexual activity is morally objectionable absent a commitment to having children; or that a high birth rate is necessary for national security.

It is difficult to find evidence that access to safe abortion harms society. The bulk of the evidence points to the conclusion that it benefits women, families, and nations, and reduces the danger that future generations will inherit a devastated planet. The belief that it harms society, like belief in the moral equality of the presentient embryo and fetus, involves an element of faith – often (but not always) religious faith. The classical liberal view is that personal freedom should not be limited on the basis of religious or other beliefs that lack empirical support, and that are not accepted by a large majority of informed persons. Abortion cannot be shown to be morally objectionable on strictly secular grounds; and many people (a large majority, in many societies) are supportive of women's right to choose. For these reasons, access to abortion is essential to religious, as well as reproductive, freedom (Wenz 1994).

Conclusion

Women often have compelling reasons for choosing abortion, reasons that are sufficient to justify killing a presentient embryo or fetus. Late abortion is morally more problematic, and not something that many women want if they have the option of early abortion. Nevertheless, late abortion is justifiable in some cases, such as when the fetus is disastrously abnormal, or the woman's life or health is seriously endangered. Because abortion is at best an unpleasant experience, and because many people are deeply troubled by it, reducing the number of abortions is a legitimate societal goal. However, respect for women's autonomy and well-being demands that this reduction be brought about through means that empower women to avoid unwanted pregnancies, rather than through laws or regulatory practices that make safe abortion more difficult to obtain.

References

Burgess, J. A. and Tawia, S. A. (1996). When did you first begin to feel it? Locating the beginning of human consciousness. *Bioethics* 10/1: 1–26.

Columbia University Mailman School of Public Health (2007). Technical issues in reproductive health. Section IV. Available at: www.columbia.edu/itc/hs/pubhealth/modules/reproductiveHealth/.

Crane, B. B. and Hord Smith, C. E. (2006). *Access to Safe Abortion: An Essential Strategy for Achieving the Millennium Development Goals to Improve Maternal Health, Promote Gender Equality, and Reduce Poverty.* New York: United Nations Millennium Project. Available at: www.unmillenniumproject.org/documents/Crane_and_Hord-Smith-final.pdf.

Ford, N. (1988). *When Did I Begin?* Cambridge: Cambridge University Press.

Grobstein, C. (1988). *Science and the Unborn.* New York: Basic Books.

McCauley, A. P. et al. (1994). Opportunities for women through reproductive choice. *Population Reports* M/12: 1–39.

Marquis, D. (1989). Why abortion is immoral. *Journal of Philosophy* 86/4: 183–202.

Noonan, J., Jr (1970). An almost absolute value in history. In John Noonan, Jr (ed.), *The Morality of Abortion.* Cambridge, MA: Harvard University Press, pp. 51–9. (Reprinted in T. Beauchamp and L. Walters (eds.), *Contemporary Issues in Bioethics.* Belmont, CA: Wadsworth, 1994, pp. 279–82.)

Rachels, J. (1990). *Created From Animals: The Moral Implications of Darwinism.* Oxford: Oxford University Press.

Rosenfeld, A. (1989). Maternal mortality in developing countries: an ongoing but neglected "epidemic." *Journal of the American Medical Association* (21 July): 376.

Wenz, P. S. (1994). *Abortion Rights as Religious Freedom.* Philadelphia: Temple University Press.

WHO (2003). *Safe Abortion: Technical and Policy Guidance for Health Systems.* Geneva: World Health Organization. Available at: www.who.int/reproductive-health/publications/safe_abortion/safe_abortion.pdf.

15

Mother–Fetus Conflict

BONNIE STEINBOCK

Prior to the 1940s, the fetus within the uterus was considered to be largely protected from external harm. Today it is recognized that a range of behaviors by a pregnant woman can affect the developing fetus or the child after birth. For example, if the pregnant woman contracts rubella, the fetus may die *in utero*, or be born deaf, blind, or mentally retarded. If she fails to get proper nutrition or smokes cigarettes, the baby may be born with a low birth-weight, a condition correlated with a significantly higher infant mortality rate. Drinking alcohol, using illicit drugs, or even taking over-the-counter drugs can all adversely affect fetal health and development. Moreover, these adverse effects are most likely to happen during the early stages of fetal development. The recognition that maternal behavior during pregnancy can have detrimental effects, not only on the fetus *in utero*, especially early in gestation, but on the child after birth, raises the question: what obligations does a pregnant woman have to protect the health of the developing fetus?

This chapter attempts to provide a conceptual framework for thinking about mother–fetus conflict. I begin by distinguishing the issue from the abortion debate, arguing that women have prima facie moral obligations to avoid inflicting prenatal harm regardless of whether they have an obligation to refrain from abortion. I then apply the framework to illegal drug use during pregnancy, forced cesareans, and fetal surgery.

Abortion and Mother–Fetus Conflict

Abortion is often considered to be an example – even a paradigm example – of a mother–fetus conflict (Rhoden 1987). This makes sense only if it is assumed that abortion pits the interests of the fetus against those of the pregnant woman. However, many scholars reject the assumption that there can be a conflict of interests in the context of abortion, at least during early to mid-gestation, because they maintain that, at least during this period, the fetus, unlike the pregnant woman, does not have interests.

The reason fetuses are alleged not to have interests for a number of months is that, for most of their development, they are not conscious or aware or sentient. They cannot think or feel, experience anything, or want anything. They can be *killed*, as any living thing can be killed, but during the first trimester of gestation, they are not sentient because the cortical, subcortical, and peripheral centers necessary for awareness, of which pain is the most obvious sort, do not begin to develop until early in the second trimester (Glover and Fisk 1996). Of abortions carried out in the United States, 88 percent are done within the first 12 weeks (Guttmacher Institute 2006), when the possibility of the fetus feeling pain (much less fear or anguish) is so remote as to be easily dismissed. There is less consensus about the onset of sentience after the first trimester. Some experts (Lee et al. 2005) think that it does not occur until the beginning of the third trimester, while others (Glover and Fisk 1996) think that the fetus may begin to feel something as early as mid-gestation. On the principle that it is better to be safe than sorry, they recommend that, in later terminations, anesthesia should be delivered to the fetus, to ensure that the termination causes as little suffering as possible, while not compromising the woman's health. If this recommendation were followed, it would affect only a small percentage of induced abortions in the United States and other countries with similar rates of abortion, such as Canada and the countries of Western Europe (Guttmacher Institute 2006).

The restriction of interests to beings capable of wanting things stems from a certain conception of what it is to have interests, namely that interests are composed out of our desires, concerns, and goals. As Joel Feinberg (1974) suggests, interests are those things in which one has a stake. If we think of interests as stakes in things, and understand what we have a stake in as defined by our concerns or by what matters to us, then the connection between interests and the capacity for conscious awareness becomes clear. Without awareness, beings cannot care about anything. Without the ability to care about anything, beings cannot have desires, preferences, hopes, aims, and goals. Without desires, preferences, etc., they cannot have interests. There may be all kinds of reasons, including moral reasons, for preserving or protecting non-conscious beings, but such reasons cannot derive from *their* interests, since non-conscious beings do not have any interests. Accordingly, non-conscious, non-sentient fetuses do not have interests. Therefore abortion, throughout most of gestation, does not pit the interests of the pregnant woman against the interests of the fetus.

Admittedly, not everyone accepts this conception of interests, or its implications for the morality of abortion. Some philosophers (Regan 1976; Marquis 1989; 2007) maintain that beings that cannot have wants can nevertheless have interests and rights based on those interests. However, others, including me (Steinbock 1992), argue that sentience and the having of at least rudimentary wants (such as a desire to avoid pain) are a necessary condition for having any interests at all (Boonin 2003; Feinberg 1974; Singer and Kuhse 1986; Sumner 1981; Warren 1997. For related views, see McMahan 2002; Reiman 1999; 2007).

Once the fetus becomes sentient, probably toward the end of the second trimester, it has at least one interest, namely an interest in not being subjected to painful stimuli. At least some of the debate about late-term abortions focuses on the pain they allegedly cause sentient fetuses. Most people, even those who are fervently pro-choice, are distressed by late-term abortions, partly because of the risk of inflicting pain and partly because the late-gestation fetus is so close to being a full-term infant that all of the reasons for the social protection of infants are present (Rhoden 1986b). Yet sometimes such abortions are medically indicated. As Allan Rosenfield, Dean of the

Columbia School of Public Health, commented in an op-ed piece: "The anguished decision to use dilatation and extraction is usually reached when a woman's life or health would be jeopardized if the pregnancy is continued or if there is a fetal abnormality incompatible with life." The choice of method should be based on what is best for the patient and should be chosen by her doctor, not legislators.

Typically, such abortions are the tragic outcomes of wanted pregnancies. The women who have them are faced with the death of the baby and a risk to their own life or health, including future sterility, if they attempt to give birth. Every reasonable attempt should be made to ensure that the fetus does not experience pain during the procedure. If for some reason this is not possible, the long-term interests of the pregnant woman in preserving her life and health surely outweigh the interests of a doomed fetus in temporarily experiencing unavoidable pain.

Leaving aside rare late-term abortions which involve sentient fetuses, what are the implications of the abortion debate for mother–fetus conflict? First, a word about terminology. Those who oppose abortion call themselves "pro-life," while those who support liberal abortion laws call themselves "pro-choice." Neither term is entirely satisfactory; both beg the question in different ways. The "pro-life" label assumes that the kind of life to be protected is human life; rarely are "pro-lifers" vegetarians. The "pro-choice" label assumes that the choice is a morally permissible one, avoiding the question of the moral status of the fetus. Nevertheless, despite these deficiencies, I will use the terms "pro-lifers" and "pro-choicers" for two reasons. First, they are shorter and more graceful than the likely alternatives, such as "opponents of abortion" and "supporters of liberal abortion laws." Second, it shows respect to those who identify themselves by these terms to call them what they prefer to be called.

Pro-lifers, who regard embryos and fetuses as "pre-born children," consider pregnant women to have the same moral obligations to their fetuses as they do to their born children. Abortion is morally as wrong as killing a child would be. It is also morally wrong to engage in behaviors likely to result in fetal harm or death. Thus, pro-lifers will condemn behaviors such as using illicit drugs, abusing alcohol, or smoking during pregnancy, because of the risk these pose to the developing fetus, without providing any significant or morally important benefit to the pregnant woman.

Pro-choicers who view the early fetus as incapable of being harmed obviously cannot condemn such behaviors during pregnancy on the ground that these harm the early fetus. (They might condemn the behaviors on the ground that they could harm the late fetus, for example, by causing a miscarriage. I will say more below about whether death can be a harm to the late-gestation fetus.) Does this mean that pro-choicers should regard behavior during pregnancy as a matter of personal choice? Some pro-choicers in the United States have taken this position, vigorously opposing "fetal rights" legislation (limited, it appears, to US jurisdictions), often seeing it as part of a larger political agenda to make abortion illegal.

In my view, this ignores an important difference between the behavior of a pregnant woman who is going to term and the behavior of a pregnant woman who aborts her pregnancy during the first or second trimester. If a woman does not abort, her conduct during pregnancy may have adverse effects not only on the fetus, but on the future child. Whatever the status of the fetus, children have interests and rights, including the fundamental moral and legal right not to be injured. Thus, a child who

151

has learning disabilities, for example, as a result of his mother's binge-drinking during pregnancy, has been harmed. The risk of causing fetal alcohol syndrome exists throughout pregnancy, although it is greatest during the first trimester. Admittedly, the child who has been harmed by maternal behavior did not exist as a child at the time the injury was inflicted, but that does not lessen the obligation to avoid causing the child who is going to come into existence foreseeable injury.

Strictly speaking, then, the term "mother–fetus conflict" is misleading, since the obligation is not to the fetus per se, at least not to the early fetus, but to the future child. However, the term "mother–fetus conflict" emphasizes the fact that the conflict occurs when the woman is pregnant and the child still a fetus. Efforts to protect the fetus must be achieved through the body of the pregnant woman, raising the same sort of issues regarding privacy and bodily autonomy that are present in the abortion debate. Therefore, while it is important to distinguish abortion and mother–fetus conflict, it is equally important to acknowledge the similarities. Otherwise, we run the risk of forgetting the impact of restrictive measures on the pregnant woman, who is a person with her own needs and interests. We run the danger of treating her, as Annas (1986) has expressed it, as a "fetal container."

Some people profess to be baffled by the idea that a person can have obligations not to harm individuals who have not yet been born. However, this is not a bizarre idea. Examples abound both in law and in ordinary life. A wrongful act done today may harm someone in the future who is not yet born or even conceived. As one of the authors of a leading book on torts expresses it: "The improper canning of baby food today is negligent to a child born next week or next year, who consumes it to his injury" (Harper and James, 1956: 1030). Similarly, we can condemn a careless or selfish use of resources that will adversely affect our children or grandchildren. It is equally possible to ascribe responsibility on the part of pregnant women who plan to bear children to avoid behavior that is likely to injure them.

Others, who accept the idea of responsibility to not yet existing persons, are puzzled by the claim that women have moral obligations to prevent illness or disability in their "not-yet-born children" (Murray 1987), but no obligation to refrain from killing them. This seems paradoxical, since, ordinarily, death is a greater harm than illness or disability. However, the paradox is removed when it is remembered that the victim of the illness or disability is a child who will suffer from the injury, while the entity that is killed by abortion is a fetus that has no interests and cannot be harmed.

Pitting the mother against the fetus

Some people object to the characterization "mother–fetus" *conflict* as being unnecessarily adversarial. Undesirable behaviors, such as binge-drinking or drug-using, which endanger fetal health, also endanger maternal health. They recommend that health-care professionals treat both mother and fetus as a unit with common interests.

This objection to the "conflict characterization" has a great deal of truth to it. In most cases, there is no conflict between the pregnant woman and her fetus. Most women try to ensure that their babies will be born healthy. Because the interests of women and the children they will bear are most often inseparably entwined, some commentators object to the very phrase "mother–fetus conflict" as unnecessarily adversarial.

However, it must be recognized that a pregnant woman can have interests, including entirely legitimate interests, that may conflict with what will protect the life or health of her fetus. For example, cancer treatments that give a pregnant woman the best chance of survival may kill or deform her fetus. Fetal surgery which is the fetus's only chance of survival may impose considerable risks on the pregnant woman. It is wishful thinking to pretend that what is best for the pregnant woman is necessarily best for the fetus or future child, or that what is best for the fetus always promotes the pregnant woman's interests. The possibility of conflict remains.

Moral Obligations to the Unborn

The above analysis suggests that women have prima facie moral obligations to their future children to avoid inflicting prenatal harm. However, it does not follow that these moral obligations should be made into legal ones. The question of legal obligation and responsibility raises a host of additional questions, including the harms created by legal coercion and the effectiveness of a punitive approach in protecting future children. These considerations have led the majority of commentators to reject the legal prohibition of "prenatal child abuse" and forced medical treatment of pregnant women.

Confining ourselves to moral obligations, the next question is: what are their nature and extent? For example, are pregnant women morally required to avoid only behaviors that will cause harm to the surviving child, or can there be an obligation to avoid fetal death or stillbirth? The answer is obvious for those who consider fetuses to have the moral status of born children, but what should be the view of pro-choicers? It may seem that, to be consistent, pro-choicers should maintain that the woman's obligation is only to the child, if it survives. Behavior that results in fetal death is not wrong, since abortion is morally permissible. However, there are two complications which make this answer problematic. First, it is rarely possible to separate the risk of causing fetal death from the risk of causing postnatal harm. Smoking, for example, increases the risk of stillbirth and is also associated with learning disabilities. Probably any behavior that risks killing, but does not in fact kill the fetus, may harm the future child, and should be avoided for that reason.

A second complication concerns the developmental stage of the fetus. A first-trimester fetus lacks interests, but the same cannot be said of a third-trimester fetus that is conscious and sentient. Such a fetus presumably has all the interests ascribable to a newborn, including the interest in continued existence. Although some philosophers think that this is impossible (e.g., Tooley 1983), I maintain that sentient beings can have an interest in continued existence (Steinbock 1992: 57–8). A sentient being can experience pleasure as well as pain and therefore has an interest in having further pleasurable experiences, that is, in continued existence. For this reason, I maintain that both newborns and sentient fetuses ordinarily have an interest in continued existence. (The exception would be when continued existence provided little but suffering.) The refusal by a pregnant woman to have a cesarean section, resulting in a stillbirth, would, on this analysis, constitute a harm to the fetus.

If sentient fetuses have an interest in continued existence, it may be thought that it follows that they have a right to life, and that this precludes abortion. However, this does not follow. First, even if a fetal right to life is granted, this does not impose on the pregnant woman an obligation to allow the fetus to remain inside her body at the sacrifice of her own life or health (Thomson 1971), although it would presumably impose a moral obligation on her not to abort for less than pressing reasons. Second, one could argue that because the fetus is dependent on the pregnant woman for its existence, and because its presence in her body imposes certain burdens on the pregnant woman, a full-fledged right to life cannot be ascribed to the fetus, even after it becomes sentient and acquires interests.

The next question is the scope of a woman's obligations to her "not-yet-born child." The danger here is to sentimentalize the relationship between the pregnant woman and her fetus, as if the fact that the woman is pregnant is the only morally important thing about her, and to regard the pregnancy as trumping all other considerations. A better way to conceptualize women's obligations to their not-yet-born children is to think in terms of what is required of parents of born children. As Murray puts it: "Our moral obligations to our children may be particularly broad and deep, but they do not overwhelm all other moral considerations in all circumstances" (1991: 107). Moreover, we do not require parents to protect children from all risk of harm, only to take necessary steps to protect children from substantial risks of serious harm. Interpretation of all of these features is obviously something on which reasonable people can disagree. Consider, for example, drinking during pregnancy. There is no known minimum safe level of alcohol consumption. It is possible that any consumption of alcohol could harm the developing fetus. (Recent research suggests that consumption of any amount of alcohol at any time during pregnancy increases the risk – admittedly very small – of infant leukemia.) Therefore, many doctors recommend that women totally abstain from alcohol throughout pregnancy. Others believe that an occasional glass of wine, especially after the first trimester when the vital organs are being formed, is extremely unlikely to do any harm. Given the disagreement among experts and the low level of risk in any case, a moral obligation totally to abstain from alcohol during pregnancy cannot be established. Instead, low to moderate alcohol consumption is a matter of personal discretion, to be decided by the individual woman in conjunction with her physician.

By contrast, heavy and prolonged maternal alcohol abuse during pregnancy can cause fetal alcohol syndrome (FAS), which is typically marked by severe facial deformities and mental retardation. Drug use during pregnancy is also risky. The effects of fetal exposure to cocaine, for example, include growth retardation in the womb and subtle neurological abnormalities, leading to extraordinary irritability in infancy and learning disorders later. In more extreme cases, cocaine can cause brain-damaging strokes. The difficulty with maintaining that pregnant women have a moral obligation to stop abusing alcohol or using cocaine is that these are usually addictive behaviors and ones that are not fully voluntary. If it would be impossible, or extremely difficult, for pregnant addicts just to stop drinking or smoking crack without treatment, they cannot be said to have an obligation to do so. Instead, their moral obligation might be to enter into a treatment program. However, such help is often not available. Many in-patient alcohol rehabilitation programs in the United States exclude pregnant women, largely because of a fear of liability. The situation is even worse for drug addicts (Chavkin 1990). Therefore, even if we maintain that pregnant addicts have a moral obligation to do what they can to overcome their addictions for the sake of their not-yet-born babies, we should also recognize a societal obligation to provide treatment programs. In the absence of sufficient voluntary programs, calls for mandatory substance-abuse programs for pregnant women seem premature.

I have based women's obligations to their not-yet-born children on the decision not to terminate the pregnancy. But what if the failure to terminate is not a decision at all, but rather the result of lack of access to abortion? Does a woman have the same responsibility to safeguard fetal health if she would have chosen abortion, if available? Certainly risky behavior on the part of a woman who has chosen to bear a child is more callous and blameworthy than similar behavior from a woman who is undergoing a "compulsory" pregnancy. Nevertheless, the impact on the child is the same. For that reason, any woman who will bear a child, voluntarily or not, is morally required to avoid inflicting prenatal injury on it, if she can do so without sacrificing important interests of her own.

The Obstetrical Cases: Forced Cesareans

Most women are willing to undergo considerable risk and pain to ensure that their babies are born healthy. Occasionally, however, a woman rejects a medical intervention, such as a cesarean delivery, recommended by her doctor. Whether her refusal is morally permissible depends on the strength of her reasons. Certainly reasons that are normally trivial (like not wanting to have an ugly scar above the bikini line) would not justify letting a nearly-born fetus die. Refusals for such reasons are rare, if they exist at all. More typical are refusals based on religious or cultural beliefs, a fear of surgery or rejection of the doctor's prognosis. These are not necessarily unimportant or selfish reasons, and refusals based on such considerations are not obviously unjustified.

Traditionally, doctors have been able to override patient refusal if surgery is in the patient's best interest and the patient is incapable of giving or withholding consent. A determination of competence depends on the patient's ability to understand her condition, the proposed treatment, and the risks and benefits of treating or not treating. The mere fact that the patient refuses treatment her doctors consider necessary does not establish inability to give or refuse consent. However, the line between a competent but idiosyncratic refusal of treatment and an inability to consent is often a very fine one, as illustrated by a case in England. In March 1997, a British woman with a phobia about needles was forced to have her baby delivered by cesarean section after a highly unusual midnight emergency sitting of the Court of Appeal. Doctors told her that the baby could die or be brain-damaged if delivered vaginally. The woman at first agreed to have the anesthetic administered by needle, and then by mask, but changed her mind both times. Her doctors feared she was going into labor and asked the High Court to approve the operation. The judges accepted arguments that, because of her needle phobia, the woman was not mentally competent to make the decision, and ordered the cesarean to be performed. However, the court "confirmed that a competent woman has the absolute right to refuse intervention, even if she puts her own or her unborn child's life or health at risk. The court has no jurisdiction to sanction an operation to protect a fetus" (Dyer 1997).

Refusals of cesarean deliveries present physicians with a dilemma only if two conditions obtain. First, there must be a generally accepted right of competent patients

155

to refuse medical treatment deemed necessary for the welfare of the nearly-born child. If decisions about treatment are for doctors to make, then doctors can simply ignore refusals they consider to be harmful or irrational. In countries where physicians' paternalism is still the norm, the fact that the patient does not consent to a cesarean would scarcely be a consideration, much less an obstacle to proceeding. It would not occur to obstetricians in such societies to get a court order to override the woman's refusal. They would simply perform the cesarean they deemed necessary over the woman's objections. Secondly, the fetus must lack the status of a full legal person. In some countries (for example, Spain), the fetus is considered to be a person as regards treatment that is of benefit to it. Abortion is generally not permitted, except in the case of severe fetal deformity or to prevent a grave risk to the woman's life or health. Few Spanish obstetricians would permit a nearly-born fetus to die simply because its mother refused a cesarean delivery. Although this type of case has never reached the Spanish courts, it seems very likely that if such a case were to be heard, Spanish courts would rule in favor of the fetus.

Refusals of cesarean delivery pose agonizing dilemmas for physicians who respect the patient's right to refuse treatment, but who feel that they cannot sit back and let a nearly-born baby die or be born extremely damaged, especially if the woman's refusal seems irrational. Moreover, doctors are not "hired hands" who do whatever their clients want. They are supposed to use their professional judgment to determine the right way to manage a particular pregnancy, labor, and delivery. If a patient wants the doctor to do something contrary to good clinical practice, the doctor has no obligation to comply.

On the other side, there is increasing consensus, at least in the United States and Canada, among members of the legal profession, bioethicists, and professional medical societies that overriding a competent woman's refusal of a cesarean delivery is almost never justified. This consensus is based on several considerations. First, there is the risk to the woman. Cesarean deliveries, while quite safe, have a higher maternal morbidity and mortality than do vaginal deliveries. (The mortality rate for cesareans is approximately four times higher than for vaginal delivery.) Thus, if court-ordered cesareans are performed, increased physical risks are imposed on one person for the sake of another. No court has, for example, ever ordered a parent to surrender a kidney, bone marrow, or any other body part for donation to a child, another relative, or anyone else. In fact, it is doubtful that a parent could be legally compelled to donate a pint of blood necessary to save his or her child's life. If parents do not have a legal duty to take even minor health risks to benefit their children, why should a pregnant woman be compelled to undergo major surgery for the sake of the fetus?

Second, the imposition of compulsory surgery has unsettling implications for the doctor–patient relationship. What if the woman continues to refuse, even after a court order is obtained? Are doctors prepared to hold down, forcibly anesthetize, and cut open a non-consenting woman? A third factor is the possibility the doctors are wrong about the need for a cesarean. In a number of cases in the United States in which court-ordered cesarean sections were sought, the women delivered vaginally and the babies were born healthy (Rhoden 1986a). Compulsory cesareans therefore may subject women to unnecessary surgery.

Some doctors think that a case can be made for compulsory cesareans in one case: well-documented complete placenta previa. This is a serious condition that can result in the detachment of the placenta from the uterus, causing hemorrhaging and endangering the lives of both the mother and fetus. According to McCullough and Chervenak:

> the only obstetric management strategy consistent with promoting the social-role inter-ests of the fetus is cesarean delivery, because vaginal delivery dooms the social-role interests of the fetus, while cesarean delivery dramatically protects and promotes those interests. . . . [C]esarean delivery, despite its morbidity and mortality risks for the woman and despite its invasiveness, unequivocally produces net medical benefit for the pregnant woman. Any clinical judgment to the contrary borders on the irrational. (1994: 249–50)

McCullough and Chervenak acknowledge that there have been a few cases, even of allegedly well-documented complete placenta previa, when the doctors were wrong in their predictions of fetal death and a vaginal birth was successful. However, they dismiss this as irrelevant. There will always be errors in medicine. The question is not whether doctors can be *certain* that a cesarean is indicated, but whether their clinical judgment is *reliable*. All the evidence indicates that a cesarean delivery is indicated for well-documented complete placenta previa.

Moreover, they argue, the pregnant woman is ethically obligated to take reasonable risks on behalf of the fetus in the management of her pregnancy. Furthermore, if her refusal of surgery is based on an irrational fear, overriding her refusal does not violate her autonomy, because false beliefs and irrational fears are not an expression of auto-nomy. Nor is the woman being used as a mere means to save the fetus, as in the case of forced bone marrow or organ donations, since the surgery can be reliably predicted to benefit her as well as her baby.

However, as Justice Warren Burger, of the United States Supreme Court, said in his dissent in *Georgetown*, the right to refuse treatment is not limited to "*sensible* beliefs, *valid* thoughts, *reasonable* emotions, or *well-founded* sensations." Moreover, the claim that compulsory cesareans for complete placenta previa provide a "net benefit" to the woman is based solely on physical benefit. A Christian Scientist who has spiritual objec-tions to a cesarean delivery does not regard a compulsory cesarean as a "net benefit." The dangers implicit in allowing doctors to step in and weigh the risks of surgery for someone who has competently chosen to forgo them should lead us to reject even a carefully circumscribed exception to the doctrine of informed consent.

A better solution to the problem of mother–fetus conflict is to prevent its occurrence. A woman may fail to comply with medical advice, such as taking medication, because it makes her sick or because she does not understand the risk to her baby or herself. She may be unable to stay off her feet or remain in the hospital, as her doctors recommend, because of her obligations to her other children. A concerted effort on the part of health-care professionals and social workers to try to help her solve these prob-lems will often do more to protect her fetus than prosecuting her after the harm is done. Effective substance-abuse programs for pregnant women and the provision of adequate prenatal care for all women would be more likely to protect not-yet-born children than a punitive approach.

Fetal Surgery

In recent decades, there have been revolutionary developments in the diagnosis and treatment of fetal anatomical abnormalities. Prenatal surgery has saved some fetuses that would have died *in utero* (Harrison and Adzick 1991). At the same time, such surgery imposes considerable risks on the pregnant woman. Her womb must be cut open twice, first when the fetus is temporarily removed from the womb to be operated on, and again for a cesarean delivery. After the fetus is replaced in her womb, she must take powerful drugs daily to prevent labor. There is also the danger of uterine rupture because of the two operations. Moreover, there is no guarantee of a successful outcome for the fetus. Fetal mortality is high and some of the survivors will be born with serious defects.

If the case against forced cesareans is strong, the case against forced *in utero* surgery is much stronger. Most of the therapies are still experimental. They carry significant risks for the woman and, unlike cesarean delivery for complete placenta previa, there is no direct benefit to the pregnant woman. There is no guarantee of success, and the result may be a severely handicapped baby. The decision as to whether fetal therapy is "worth it" must remain a personal and individual one.

Conclusion

Women have moral obligations to avoid inflicting prenatal harm. Just as parents have obligations to avoid exposing their born children to substantial risks of serious harm, so pregnant woman have comparable obligations to the children they will bear. The avoidance of prenatal harm may require women to make sacrifices and take risks. However, the obligation to avoid prenatal harm should be balanced against other obligations and interests. While some behaviors, such as recreational use of crack cocaine, are clearly morally wrong, others, such as refusal of a cesarean because of a fear of surgery, are morally debatable, while still others, such as rejection of experimental fetal surgery, are clearly morally permissible. In resolving mother–fetus conflicts, women's rights to privacy, bodily integrity, and autonomy must be considered along with the welfare of the fetus and surviving child.

References

Annas, G. (1986). Pregnant women as fetal containers. *Hastings Center Report* 16: 13–14.

Boonin, D. (2003). *A Defense of Abortion.* Cambridge: Cambridge University Press.

Brazier, M. (1992). *Medicine, Patients and the Law,* 2nd edn. Harmondsworth, UK: Penguin (esp. ch. 11, "Pregnancy and Childbirth").

Chavkin, W. (1990). Drug addiction and pregnancy: policy crossroads. *American Journal of Public Health* 80: 483–7.

Dyer, C. (1997). Appeals court rules against compulsory cesarean sections. *British Medical Journal* 314: 993.

Feinberg, J. (1974). The rights of animals and unborn generations. In W. T. Blackstone (ed.), *Philosophy and Environmental Crisis.* Athens, GA: University of Georgia Press, pp. 43–68.

Feinberg, J. (1984). *Harm to Others.* New York: Oxford University Press.

Glover, V. and Fisk, N. (1996). Commentary: We don't know; better to err on the safe side from mid-gestation. *British Medical Journal* 13: 796.

Guttmacher Institute (2006). In brief. Facts on induced abortion in the United States. Available at: www.guttmacher.org/pubs/fb_induced_abortion.html (accessed August 8, 2007).

Harper, F. V. and James, F. (1956). *Law of Torts*, vol. 2. Boston, MA: Little Brown.

Harrison, M. R. and Adzick, N. S. (1991). The fetus as patient: surgical considerations. *Annals of Surgery* 213: 279–91.

Lee, S. J., Peter Ralston, H. J., Drey, E. A., Partridge, J. C., and Rosen, M. A. (2005). Fetal pain: a systematic multidisciplinary review of the evidence. *Journal of the American Medical Association* 294: 947–54.

McCullough, L. and Chervenak, F. (1994). *Ethics in Obstetrics and Gynecology.* New York and Oxford: Oxford University Press.

McMahan, J. (2002). *The Ethics of Killing: Problems at the Margins of Life.* New York: Oxford University Press.

Marquis, D. (1989). Why abortion is immoral. *Journal of Philosophy* 89: 183–202.

Marquis, D. (2007). Abortion revisited. In B. Steinbock (ed.) *The Oxford Handbook of Bioethics.* Oxford: Oxford University Press, pp. 395–415.

Murray, T. (1987). Moral obligations to the not-yet-born: the fetus as patient. *Clinics in Perinatology* 14: 329–43.

Murray, T. (1991). Prenatal drug exposure: ethical issues. *Future of Children* 1/1: 105–12.

Regan, T. (1976). Feinberg on what sorts of beings can have rights. *Southern Journal of Philosophy* 14: 485–98.

Reiman, J. (1999). *Abortion and the Ways We Value Human Life.* Lanham, MD: Rowman & Littlefield.

Reiman, J. (2007). *The Rich Get Richer and the Poor Get Prison*, 8th edn. Boston, MA: Pearson/Allyn and Bacon.

Rhoden, N. (1986a). The judge in the delivery room: the emergence of court-ordered cesareans. *California Law Review* 74: 1951–2040.

Rhoden, N. (1986b). Trimesters and technology: revamping *Roe* v. *Wade. Yale Law Journal* 95: 639–97.

Rhoden, N. (1987). Cesareans and Samaritans. *Law, Medicine and Health Care* 15: 118–25.

Singer, P. and Kuhse, H. (1986). The ethics of embryo research. *Law, Medicine and Health Care* 14: 133–8.

Steinbock, B. (1992). *Life Before Birth: The Moral and Legal Status of Embryos and Fetuses.* New York and Oxford: Oxford University Press.

Steinbock, B. (2007). Moral status, moral value, and human embryos: implications for stem cell research. In B. Steinbock (ed.) *The Oxford Handbook of Bioethics.* Oxford: Oxford University Press, pp. 416–40.

Sumner, L. W. (1981). *Abortion and Moral Theory.* Princeton, NJ: Princeton University Press.

Thomson, J. (1971). A defense of abortion. *Philosophy and Public Affairs* 1: 47–66.

Tooley, M. (1983). *Abortion and Infanticide.* Oxford: Clarendon Press.

Warren, M. A. (1997). *Moral Status: Obligations to Persons and Other Living Things.* Oxford: Clarendon Press.

Further reading

American Academy of Pediatrics, Committee on Biothics (1988). Fetal therapy: ethical considerations. *Pediatrics* 81: 898–9.

159

American College of Gynecologists and Obstetricians Committee Opinion Number 55 (1987). Patient-choice: maternal–fetal conflict.

Annas, G. J. (1982). Forced cesareans: the most unkindest cut of all. *Hastings Center Report* 12: 16–17.

Annas, G. J. (1988). She's going to die: the case of Angela C. *Hastings Center Report*, 18: 23–5.

Bays, J. (1990). Substance abuse and child abuse: impact of addiction on the child. *Pediatric Clinics of North America* 37: 881–904.

Daniels, C. R. (1993). *At Women's Expense: State Power and the Politics of Fetal Rights.* Cambridge, MA: Harvard University Press.

Elias, S. and Annas, G. J. (1987). *Reproductive Genetics and the Law.* Chicago: Yearbook Medical Publishers.

Fleischman, A. and Macklin, R. (1987). Fetal therapy: ethical considerations, potential conflicts. In William B. Weil and Martin Benjamin (eds.), *Ethical Issues at the Outset of Life.* Boston: Blackwell Scientific Publications, pp. 121–48.

Ginn, D. (1994). Pregnant women and consent to medical treatment. *Health Law in Canada* 15: 41–8.

Jackman, M. (1995). The status of the fetus under Canadian law. *Health Law in Canada* 15: 83–6.

Mathias, R. (1995). NIDA survey provides first national data on drug use during pregnancy. NIDA (National Institute on Drug Abuse) Notes, 10.

Mathieu, D. (1991). *Preventing Prenatal Harm: Should the State Intervene?* Dordrecht: Kluwer.

Moss, K. (1990). Substance abuse during pregnancy. *Harvard Women's Law Journal* 13: 278–99.

Nelson, L. J. and Milliken, N. (1988). Compelled medical treatment of pregnant women. *Journal of the American Medical Association* 259: 1060–6.

Nelson, L. J., Buggy, B. P., and Weil, C. J. (1986). Forced medical treatment of pregnant women: "compelling each to live as seems good to the rest." *Hastings Law Journal* 37: 703–63.

Robertson, J. A. (1982). The right to procreate and *in utero* fetal therapy. *Journal of Legal Medicine* 3: 333–66.

Robertson, J. A. (1994). Maternal–fetal conflict and *in utero* fetal therapy. *Albany Law Review* 57: 781–93.

Part V

Issues In Reproduction

16

Population

MARGARET PABST BATTIN

Issues concerning global population growth have been among the most vigorously argued of contemporary conflicts. On the one side, population theorists beginning with Malthus have warned that failure to limit population growth will mean environmental and hence human disaster; on the other, at least three traditional groups of critics – each with different reasons – have resisted these warnings of overpopulation as well as demands for population control. While rates of population growth and decline affect virtually all areas of health, bioethicists have so far given insufficient attention to such issues. Nevertheless, it is possible to see the outlines of at least a partial solution to population problems, though it is a controversial one.

The Malthusian Warning

In 1798, Thomas Malthus warned that human beings, like other species, may reproduce at a rate that outstrips the carrying capacity of the site they inhabit and so doom themselves to destruction (Malthus 1798). Malthus's idea is a simple one: since human beings can have more children than simply replace themselves, and since these children in turn can also have more children than replace themselves, the growth of the human population tends to be exponential; but their food resources are ultimately limited by the productive capacity of the land. When a species does exceed the carrying capacity of its site, according to Malthusian theory, it "crashes" or dies back, either partially or completely. Widespread starvation, epidemics of disease exacerbated by the poor nutritional status of the population, pathological or aggressive behavior aggravated by overcrowding, and other factors lead to dramatic, involuntary population loss.

In the year 10,000 BC, there were somewhere between 2 and 20 million people in the world; by AD 1, there were still only about a quarter billion people. By 1600 there were half a billion; 200 years later the population had doubled; and by 1930 it had doubled again. Paul Ehrlich raised a global alarm with the publication of *The Population Bomb* (1968), but by 1999 global population had doubled yet again, from 3 billion in 1959 to 6 billion. The 7 billion mark for the total global population is predicted to be reached between 2010 and 2015 (US Census Bureau).

Thanks both to development and to family planning programs, population growth rates have declined substantially in many parts of the world; especially in the developed countries, the public perception appears to be that the threat of population "explosion" is over. But slowed growth is still growth, and, due to population momentum as large numbers of young people reach reproductive age, total global population is still increasing. Population projections for the year 2050 have ranged from a low 7.78 billion estimate, representing the original goals of the United Nations International Conference on Population and Development held in Cairo in 1994, to a 2008 estimate of 9.2 billion (US Census Bureau), to a high-variant estimate of almost 11 billion if fertility rates are just half a child higher per woman than the medium estimate (United Nations Population Division 2007: 7).

Malthus himself did not advocate "population control" programs; he thought moral restraint might serve as some check, but, a pessimist, he also assumed that the human population, like any overproducing animal species, would go through cycles of expansion and die-back. But the so-called neo-Malthusians, following pioneer Paul Ehrlich's wake-up calls as population growth ballooned in the 1960s, pointed out that "die-back" means intense suffering and devastating loss of life for human beings. Many warned that the sole way to avoid such a cataclysm was the resolute practice of population control.

"Population Control" and its Critics

Active policy development dedicated to limiting population growth began in the 1960s, fortified by the development of "the Pill." Beginning with India's vasectomy-incentive program in the mid-1960s, family-planning programs have been developed in some 200 countries around the world – some desultory, some completely ineffectual, and some very aggressive, like China's one-child program. Early programs for what was often called "population control" relied primarily on permanent sterilization, either male or female; newer programs have stressed reversible contraception, including condoms, oral contraceptives (the Pill), transdermal patches, intrauterine devices (IUDs), subdermal implants (Norplant and its single-rod successors), depot injectibles (Depo-Provera and related forms), and other forms of fertility regulation, using contraception both to delay the onset of childbearing and to yield greater spacing between children as ways of decreasing total family size. However, population-control programs have been assailed by traditional critics of at least three different sorts (cf. Campbell 1998).

Religious critics

Among religious groups, two have been conspicuously opposed to population limitation: the Catholic Church and Islam. The bases of their opposition are rather different: Catholicism's opposition to population limitation is doctrinally rooted in opposition to contraception, based on Genesis 38; Islam's opposition is essentially pronatalist in character: it favors large family size. Drawing on earlier roots, but articulated in response to the development of the Pill, Catholic teaching, which permits sex only within marriage, insists that the marital act must be both "unitive" and "procreative" – that every act of sexual activity must be open to the transmission of new life (Pope Paul VI

1968). The use of all forms of "artificial" contraception is forbidden, as is sterilization. Catholics may licitly use only "natural family planning," that is, only rhythm methods (including calendar-based schedules and those involving temperature measurement and self-inspection of the cervical mucus), which rely on abstinence during the woman's fertile period. Because they involve periodic abstinence, these methods all require the cooperation of the male.

The teaching in *Humanae Vitae* (it is a teaching, not doctrine, and is not articulated as infallible) has had quite different consequences. When first promulgated in 1968, it produced what was described as "the month of theological anger" by clerics opposed to the Church's position. In much of Latin America, the Philippines, and elsewhere, however, it has heavily influenced public policy, and family-planning programs, abortion, sterilization, and the distribution of contraception have been prohibited, underfunded, or in other ways impeded by governments. In the United States and much of Western Europe, in contrast, it was largely ignored: Catholic women practice contraception at about the same rate as non-Catholic women. Yet Catholic opposition to population control has played a major role in international policy in two ways: it has at times influenced governments to discontinue funding for family-planning programs; but it has also reinforced attention to issues of unequal distribution of resources and disparate levels of development as a way of understanding how economic injustice can contribute to population pressures.

Islam too has been concerned about the permissibility of "artificial" contraception, though it clearly accepts the Holy Prophet's endorsement of *azl*, male withdrawal during intercourse. Some authorities allow modern contraception; some prohibit it; and some adopt a position of conditional acceptance, permitting it, for instance, only with the wife's consent or if a diaphragm or IUD is fitted by a woman physician. Spermicides and oral contraceptives or other hormonal methods are considered permissible only if it can be shown that they do not harm the woman. Islam has also strongly emphasized the importance of children.

Both Catholicism and Islam are undergoing considerable evolution in response to population issues. Although Catholicism still prohibits all "artificial" contraception and sterilization, it places increasing emphasis on responsible planning of family size, made possible through the use of natural methods of fertility control. Some Islamic countries, like Iran, Tunisia, Turkey, Bangladesh, and Indonesia, have had very successful family-planning programs, with dramatic drops in average family size; some are now at replacement in some areas of these countries. Others, particularly in the Middle East, have begun to introduce family-planning programs and to welcome non-governmental programs: several of these seek to introduce concepts of condom use and responsible family-size planning to males, rather than females, on the assumption that this is both more in accord with basic Islamic religious teachings and with the realities of reproductive choice in male-dominated societies.

For both religious traditions, critics often suggest that opposition to family planning and population control cloaks a politics of population size: the greater the population, it is assumed, the more adherents a religious group will have and the greater a nation's economic, military, and political strength. Skeptics denounce this as a merely political strategy; loyalists defend it as a way of defending the inherent value of continuation of the family, the religious tradition, and of society. But change is occurring:

while some religious groups continue to see strength in numbers, many countries, including India, are beginning to see it the other way round: too large a population is a liability, not an asset. This sets up a new tension: between countries as economic and political units, on the one hand, and, on the other, the majority religions which inform their cultures and guide the reproductive behavior of their peoples.

Feminist critics

Meanwhile, feminist critics like Betsy Hartmann (1987) have examined the nature and methods of programs designed to control population growth. Controlling population growth means controlling people, they have argued, and it means especially controlling women. Population programs have typically operated by targeting "acceptors" – women who can be pressured into accepting contraception or sterilization – and have paid little or no attention to women's subordinate situations in patriarchal societies, their precarious economic circumstances, their lack of education and familiarity with modern medicine, their compromised nutritional status, and their desperate need of other health care. Furthermore, the feminist critique adds, population-control programs have paid little attention to women's reproductive rights (Dixon-Mueller 1993; Women's Global Network for Reproductive Rights).

It is true that some of the early population control programs in India, Indonesia, and other developing countries have been conducted in sometimes inept, irresponsible ways. For instance, as feminist critics have pointed out, some programs encouraged the implantation of various kinds of long-acting contraceptives, especially the IUD and the subdermal implant, without regard to side effects and with no provisions for removal of the device should the woman experience side effects or wish to have a child: once it was in, there was nowhere to go to get it removed. Contraceptive testing, feminist critics have also claimed (though this is not documented), was sometimes conducted without informed consent or with placebo controls (the woman who gets the dummy pill risks a pregnancy she does not want). Other contraceptive testing has been conducted, the feminist critique continues, with drugs the long-term effects of which are not known, like the anti-fertility vaccines, or modalities easily abused, like quinacrine sterilization. Compounding the damage, feminists have argued, population-control programs seem to have committed a conceptual error as well: these programs appear to *blame* poor, uneducated women in the third world for unrestrained, "excess" fertility, as if problems of global population growth, including environmental degradation and immigration pressures on wealthy nations, were exclusively their fault.

Ineptly and irresponsibly managed population-control programs pursued in the absence of adequate health-care systems have been one target of feminist rage, and so has the specter of China's effectively imposed one-child policy. Although it contributed to a dramatic reduction in China's enormous growth rate (though because of population momentum, China's population continues to grow), the one-child policy has been condemned by feminists and others for its policies of required contraception, forced abortion, and mandatory sterilization (Gu et al. 2007). It has also been denounced for its consequences for women: in a cultural tradition with a pronounced preference for sons, China has seen widespread selective sex-based abortion, concealment and abandonment of female children, and, in some cases, female infanticide, all contributing to a stark imbalance in male–female gender ratios.

Cornucopian critics

In the debates over population among religious and feminist thinkers, a third school of researchers, usually dubbed the Cornucopians, has attempted to show that the supposed limits on population growth are not well founded and hence that population control is not needed. Cornucopianism claims that the earth's resources are not in danger of depletion or disruption by pollution to the point of failing to support the human population. The late Julian Simon was particularly vocal among this group, pointing out that there is no agreement on the actual "carrying capacity" of the globe and insisting that human ingenuity can be counted upon to develop new food-production techniques and new ways of exploiting and conserving resources (Simon 1981). Many researchers have focused on specific areas such as agriculture, fisheries, fresh water, fuels, air quality, and so on to try to demonstrate that substantial increases in global population can still be accommodated, but, as critics point out, it is irresponsible to rely on partial Cornucopianism – that is, to argue that some resources will not be depleted. Even if it were possible to produce food for 1,000 billion people, this does not entail that it is possible to dispose of the domestic and industrial wastes of 1,000 billion people and their engines; and even if there were adequate agricultural water supplies, this does not entail that there would be sufficient resources for fertilizer. Furthermore, some resources are affected by our uses of others. Cornucopianism is limited by the weakest essential link.

Observers also point out that many other factors exacerbate population pressures, leading to famine, urban crowding, immigration pressures, and so on. Chief among these are the inequitable distribution of goods and resources between the poor nations and the rich ones and differential political power can exacerbate problems of distribution of food and other goods, so that famine occurs as a result of inequitable political processes and the control of resources by powerful groups, not a genuine lack of food. Diversion of crops for biofuel has also played a recent role. Amartya Sen (1992) has argued that there has never been famine in any nation with a free press; yet the threat of famine and the failure of other resources looms large in the consciousness of many areas of the world, including monumental China and its equally populous regional neighbor, India, especially in times of rising food prices. Attention is now also focused on the risks of environmental pollution and global warming associated with population and consumption increase, as well as on the security implications of population growth and decline, and whether high fertility and international migration from some countries constitutes a threat to low-fertility countries elsewhere (Weiner and Teitelbaum 2001).

"Leveling Off": The Demographic Transition

Much thinking about population issues has been shaped by the assumption that global population growth will "level off" in the middle of the twenty-first century. It is assumed that current declines in growth rates will continue, that population momentum will be slowed, and that average total family size will stabilize at about 2.1 children per woman, on average, around the globe. This is the assumption; the question is whether it is a realistic prediction or an unsupported and dangerous fantasy. Furthermore, there continues to be disagreement about the predicted size of the global population when – or if – leveling off occurs.

The "leveling-off" assumption relies on projections concerning what has been known as the demographic transition, a pattern of four distinct stages that a society is said to go through in moving from an undeveloped, agrarian economy to an industrialized, developed one. In the first stage of the demographic transition, that characterizing premodern, undeveloped, non-industrial, agrarian economies, birth rates are high, but so are death rates: in the absence of modern medicine and many other factors, life is hard, infant mortality is high, maternal mortality in childbirth is also high, and the average lifespan is short. Thus population size remains comparatively stable: there are many births, but many early deaths. In the second stage, the introduction of immunization programs, clean water supplies, antibiotics, and other developments from the technologically advanced nations leads to a sharp drop in death rates, but traditional social patterns continue to favor high birth rates. With high birth rates and low death rates, the population soars. (This has been the picture in many developing countries, especially in sub-Saharan Africa). With increasing development, however, a third stage begins: as women are increasingly educated, as infant mortality drops and families find they do not need many children born to ensure that a few survive, as social insurance systems mean that parents do not need to rely on their children for support in their old age, and as additional children no longer mean an additional source of labor in tasks like wood-gathering, water-hauling, and farm work, but instead begin to represent a liability in schooling costs, clothing costs, entertainment, and supervision in an urban environment, birth rates begin to decline: thus population growth rates slow. In the fourth stage, which characterizes industrialized nations like those of Europe, both birth and death rates are low – births are fewer, but lifespans longer – and population size "levels off" or stabilizes. The population problem, it is widely assumed, will then be solved. Indeed, in some countries – notably Italy, Spain, Japan, the former Soviet East European states and Russia, fertility has dropped well below replacement rate.

Yet the issue is not just how high population growth can climb or how far it can decline, but at what level population size can be sustained over time. The assumption that population growth rates will stabilize during the middle of the twenty-first century and that declines in fertility in some developing countries will not stall above replacement level for a prolonged period has lulled many thinkers into concluding that there is no real problem. However, population futures are by no means easy to predict (Caldwell 2004; Demeny 2004). Indeed, the dramatic declines in growth rates already observable in many developed countries may to some extent be a mirage. As John Bongaarts (2002) has pointed out, fertility measures in many developed countries are temporarily depressed by a rise in the mean age of childbearing: as women shift childbearing to later ages, what looks like a drop in total fertility may turn out to be only a postponement, one that will be reflected in corresponding increases in apparent fertility rates when social patterns of postponement end and the timing of childbearing stabilizes or shifts back to earlier ages. Furthermore, in more than half of developing countries in sub-Saharan Africa, fertility declines that seemed well under-way have slowed or stalled (Bongaarts 2008). Thus the sense now widespread in the developed countries that the population "explosion" is over may be misinformed in two ways: it does not take account of population pressures in the still-developing world (the UN projects that the population of developing countries will rise from 5.4 billion in 2007 to 7.9 billion in 2050, reaching a level higher than the current population of the entire globe, while the population of the developed world will remain unchanged, though it would decline were it not for migration from the developing to the developed world); and it over-interprets its own current "birth dearth" (Vallin 2002).

There are two substantial problems with this conclusion. For one thing, the prospect of "population entrapment" suggests that, for some societies now experien-cing very high growth rates, societal infrastructures will fail very rapidly as the popu-lation outstrips their capacity, and will in effect reverse any prospects of development: it will become more difficult to assure food supplies, to provide education and health care, to offer jobs (especially to women), to maintain social security systems, and, as survival becomes increasingly threatened and people retreat to precarious rural and urban ("garbage dump") foraging lifestyles, people will have more children rather than fewer in the hope that some survive. Population entrapment is most likely in the least developed nations with most rapid current population growth and greatest population momentum, including some that Paul Kennedy (1993) predicted would be losers, not winners, in the twenty-first century. In these countries, it has been feared, the demo-graphic transition may not take place after all, and population growth will be limited by crash and die-back, especially if immigration restrictions are maintained by the wealth-ier nations.

A second problem challenging the assumption that the demographic transition will solve population problems lies in failure to fully attend to the mechanism of the transition, or to examine adequately the assumption that declines in birth rates are the result of economic development. In recent decades, economic development has been a strategy actively pursued as a means of population growth control. Goals associated with it have included increased education for both women and children – especially female children – lowering infant mortality rates, enhancing the status of women, the creation of jobs for women, etc.: these are the strategies explicitly favored in the Cairo proposals of 1994. There is a causal issue here about whether increases in the level of development *cause* declines in birth rates or are merely associated with them. But there are other issues as well. Economic development brings with it dramatic increases in rates of consumption: diets consisting of more fats and meats (less efficient foodstuffs than grains), more extensive energy uses, more uses of consumer and industrial pro-ducts that pollute or exhaust environmental resources. The specter here is sometimes pictured as more than a billion inhabitants of China (a fifth of the world's population), all having just one child, maybe two, but, like the inhabitants of the United States, all wanting refrigerators and automobiles. Emulating Western economic models may also mean emulating Western domestic models as well, with low family size but huge uses of resources. Economic development risks increasing, rather than decreasing, strains on the carrying capacity of humankind's site, the earth, and hence offers an enormously problematic solution to population problems.

The Ethics of Population Programs

Debate over population is focused not only on issues of maximal and optimal population size, but on what lowers average total family size and hence population growth. Most nations now have family-planning programs, though these vary tremendously in character, methods, and effectiveness; some are governmental, some are conducted by non-governmental organizations (NGSs); and some rely entirely on local private groups. They variously stress education and the provision of family-planning information, access to contraception, the provision of contraception, and various other strategies; they rely to differing degrees on local funding and international assistance; and they are subject in differing ways to interference or support from religious and cultural institutions (Sen et al. 1994). Many place considerable emphasis on voluntary choice, though whether largely in rhetoric but also in practice is less clear. Yet despite their enormous variety, virtually all of them face several basic ethical dilemmas about the methods they employ.

Incentives and disincentives

What moral limits are there on the use of incentives and disincentives to manage population size? Which are preferable? How strong may they be? Perhaps most notorious for its use of problematic incentives, India's vigorously pursued population-control policy of 1975–6 has been widely believed to have used transistor radios: though this may well be a myth and no documentation of the practice is available, they were allegedly offered to any man who would consent to a vasectomy on the spot. Financial incentives, however, were certainly offered to local officials who could persuade villagers to accept sterilization, often at the mobile "vasectomy camps" created around the country. At the same time, disincentives were also used to secure compliance with sterilization programs: fines, denial of benefits, denial of medical treatment for government officers, denial of governmental quarters for civil servants, denial of accommodations in housing projects for the public, and disqualification for most government scholarships. The use of incentives and disincentives to influence reproductive behavior has occurred in many other areas, in a wide variety of forms. The Nazis used bronze, silver, and gold medals to reinforce large family size for Aryan (but not Jewish) women: four, six, and eight children respectively. Ceausescu's Romania used a variety of harsh disincentives and penalties for abortion or failure to have an adequate number of children, set at five. Singapore's 1983 combination pronatalist/antinatalist program provided a wide array of benefits and preferences to encourage educated women to have large families, but also used incentive payments for sterilization to decrease fertility among uneducated women. And China's one-child program has used a wide range of incentives (better jobs, better housing, better pay) for couples with one child only, together with disincentives (fines, demotions, penalties, even house-burnings) to discourage those having more than the permitted number of children.

Both incentives and disincentives can violate fundamental principles of autonomy: incentives by being too big or too attractive to resist, especially for someone in precarious economic circumstances, disincentives by being too dangerous to incur. In both cases, a basic principle of reproductive liberty would require informed, voluntary choice about matters relevant to procreation, but the voluntariness of such choices can quite easily be infringed. India's notorious transistor radios, even if fictional, pose an example of incentives that compromise voluntary choice in two ways: not only would they have been too attractive to resist for poor villagers, but the "point-of-purchase" way in which they were allegedly offered would have undercut the possibility of reflective deliberation for a man or the possibility of discussion with his wife. Many contemporary population theorists now hold that incentives to have fewer children are unnecessary: since women in high-fertility societies typically say they would prefer to have had fewer children than they actually have, the provision of contraception and safe abortion, as well as removing social blocks to utilization of them, would be all that is necessary to result in lowered family size.

Contraception mandates vs. family size ceilings

At the same time, ethical issues are also posed by the differing uses of contraception mandates and family size ceilings. India's vasectomy program emphasized promoting contraception, loosely tied to family size; China's program, on the other hand, promulgated a family size limit, coupled with the supply and surveillance of contraception to maintain this limit. While in practice contraception mandates and family size ceilings are often intertwined, they are conceptually different. Contraception mandates may alter the decisional structure of childbearing choices, but still recognize individual preferences in choices about family size; family size limits may impose a ceiling, but can leave it to the couple to determine how to prevent childbearing so as to stay within the limit. Both are often used in ways that openly restrict reproductive liberty; the question is which form of interference is morally more tolerable? Contraceptive mandates seem particularly problematic where the contraceptive employed poses health risks to the user, involves unacceptable side effects, or is irreversible; family size limits are problematic where they are very severe (as in a one-child policy), are inequitably imposed, or are not necessitated by a country's demographic situation. Contraceptive mandates tend to impose burdens of restricted childbearing on just some individuals, the "acceptors"; family size limit policies often tend to punish violators after the fact.

However, both contraceptive mandates and family size limits may be acceptable in some situations. China provides a good example, it may be argued, of both: it has effectively mandated contraceptive use, though it employs methods appropriate to the user's situation – short-acting methods before childbearing, the IUD after the birth of the first child (so that if the first child is lost, an additional pregnancy can be initiated), and sterilization after the birth of a second or third child; and it has imposed these mandates on *all* women. At the same time, its family size ceiling has been comparatively egalitarian: the policy is one child for all couples (with the exception of two in some rural provinces and no ceiling in non-Han ethnic areas around China's perimeter), not, say, five children for Party members and no children for non-members. This policy has come to be seen by the populace as a demographic necessity and therefore understandable; one-child family size has come to be seen as normal (Nie 2005; Nie and Wyman 2005). Although officially still in force, the one-child policy is beginning to undergo some erosion, as well-to-do couples electively pay sometimes very large fines for having additional children. As China considers ways to move away from the one-child policy to a more stable, long-term one (2.1 children per couple is stabilization rate), it now permits couples who themselves have no siblings to have two children (Zeng 2007).

Targeting

Even in countries with less acute population problems, ethical issues may arise in family-planning programs. For example, they may be targeted at groups segregated by income, ethnicity, or race which are perceived to be at higher risk of excess childbearing – for instance, contraceptive programs targeted at inner-city, African American high-school girls in the United States. Even if targeted contraceptive programs do not violate canons of voluntary choice, they may be inequitable solely in view of their approach to people identified primarily as members of specific, often stereotyped subgroups, making assumptions about the members of a subgroup that are not true of all individuals in it. Other issues include adherence to veiled family-size limitations: target ceilings entertained by program officials or governments, but not known to recipients of family-planning services or available for public discussion. And family-planning programs may also violate canons of informed consent by withholding information about the contraceptive measures it makes available, including information about risks, reversibility, and side effects.

Objections to population programs per se

A recent, wholesale critique of population programs in general, of "a humanitarian movement gone terribly awry" (Connelly 2008), insists that it is "too late to simply call off the dogs of population control" where fertility is below replacement, and that the "entire edifice of institutions, policies, and programs" which form the "population control juggernaut" should be scrapped, along with the "nasty theory" that there are "*too many people*" (Mosher 2008). The Christian Right is said to see international population policy as "a horror story of devastation and destruction visited upon women and the 'natural family,'" focusing on human rights abuses like coerced abortion, especially in China, Peru, and Kosovo (Buss and Herman 2003: 63). These critics share an underlying commitment to value-of-life and family-values principles, a mistrust of government and of targeted programs, and the view that population increase is necessary for economic growth; but they also exhibit a tendency to exaggeration, to fail to see issues of unwanted fertility and its particular impact on poor women, to confuse a decline in growth rates with an absolute decline in total population, and to fail to consider what would have happened to global population had the family-planning programs put in place beginning in the 1960s not been instituted in the first place. They also fail to recognize what may be the consequences of current steep declines in foreign aid for family planning, from $723 million in 1955 to $442 million in 2004, and the implications that may have both for future fertility rates and for the precarious situation of women in severe economic or personal straits facing an unwanted pregnancy.

Despite continuing challenges, it is fair to say that there is now much greater awareness in global family-planning programs of the ethical issues they raise than in the early days of population-control programs, thanks in large measure to political surveillance and especially feminist critique. The kinds of abuses evident in many early programs appear to be diminishing, and there is much broader agreement both that practically every country still has an unmet need for contraception, and that voluntary choice in access to it is essential. Issues about abortion, however, remain divisive: some 70–80,000 women, almost all poor and/or residents of poor countries or countries where abortion is illegal, die from unsafe abortions each year.

Optimal Population Size: Fewer with More, or More with Less?

Dire predictions about overpopulation, about sustainable patterns of consumption, about future generations, and about the threat of die-back and crash presuppose a set of theoretical reflections most vigorously pursued in philosophy by Derek Parfit (1984), and in related versions in social-choice theory by Blackorby and collaborators (2005). Although Parfit's concern is presented in philosophically sophisticated form, the question he poses is at root a simple – though troublingly difficult – one. Which is to be preferred, when speaking of populations: that situation which yields the highest average level of welfare, or that which yields the greatest aggregate total of welfare? Put in another way, which is to be preferred: a situation in which there are fewer people though their quality of life is high, or one in which there is just as much happiness altogether, but there are more people although their quality of life is lower?

Translated into the context of the actual world, with its wide gaps between rich nations and very rich population subgroups within them, and desperately poor nations with populations enduring chronic hunger or starvation, the problem might look like this: would it be a better world in which everyone lives as the rich do – with houses, automobiles, refrigerators, and the ample use of resources? Then there would have to be many fewer of them, if the population is to survive. Or would it be better if the rich had much, much less, and lived at the levels of subsistence that the poor and very poor now do? Then there could be many, many more people alive, with just the same use of resources.

A Thought-Experiment About a Solution to the Population Problem

Neither coercive population control, nor cavalier acceptance of die-back, nor appeal to optimistic but unfounded cornucopian hopes, nor naive reliance on the assertion that population will simply "level off" by itself in the next decades is a satisfactory solution. The population issue is a real one, with massive human consequences. But I think there is at least a partial solution, an intuitively simple one, readily seen in the form of a conjecture or thought-experiment (Battin 1995; 1996; 1997). What if, we might ask, instead of continuing reproductive patterns in which fertile individuals either accept pregnancy as the consequence of sexual intercourse, or decide whether and how to practice contraception, or resort to abortion if unwanted pregnancy occurs – what if the default mode of human biology, so to speak, were such that conceiving or siring a child required a *positive* decision, followed by deliberate action intended to allow pregnancy to occur? This shift is what occurs with so-called long-acting reversible contraception, or LARC – like the intrauterine device or the subdermal implant – which maintains a condition in which a woman is infertile, or incapable of pregnancy, unless she has the contraceptive neutralized or removed. Of course, the actual technologies now available for women are far from perfect, and such technologies are not yet available at all for men, though research on long-term contraception for men is in progress in many countries, especially India and China (Turok 2007; Male Contraception Information Project 2008). But we can still entertain the conjecture: what if *everybody*, both male and female, were to use long-acting, reversible, "automatic" contraception, so that sustaining or contributing to pregnancy required a positive choice, rather than simply a negative choice to prevent it? Such a picture would of course be morally acceptable only with adequate guarantees of no-questions-asked reversibility and only if it were genuinely universal, not targeted at groups perceived to be over-reproducing, since it is only with these two guarantees that reproductive choice could be fully protected – one can always choose to have a child. It thus protects against the permanent end to childbearing options that many family-planning programs' reliance on sterilization has involved. But with the two guarantees of non-targeted universality and on-demand reversibility, we can imagine further development of contraceptive technologies of high safety, high reliability, and immediate reversibility, free of side effects, nuisance, or risks, technologies that would offer "automatic" but reversible contraception without requiring user compliance, but always permitting a positive choice of conception.

This is of course a thought-experiment and not a proposal; and it sidesteps the issue of how it might come to be that way. Yet the thought-experiment is a powerful one, eliciting a picture that on its face seems far preferable to our current difficulties with unwanted and unintended fertility. If *everyone* routinely used automatic contraception, then all childbearing would require a simultaneous choice by both male and female to try to produce a child. This is to make family planning as fully voluntary as possible: both parents must want the children they have, though they may have as many as they want. Nevertheless, since people will *accept having* more children than they would *choose to have*, reversing the default, so to speak, in choices about childbearing will mean that the greatest possible drop in unintended childbearing occurs that is consistent with full reproductive choice. It gives people of all backgrounds, educational, and wealth levels everywhere the freedom to make their own decisions about the size of their families; but still results in lowered fertility. This change might not solve all population problems, but it would go a long way indeed toward reducing growth without infringement of reproductive rights.

At the same time, population "emergencies" in the other direction could also occur: that of sharply declining birth rates or major die-offs, including both slow processes like declining fertility due to environmental toxins and rapid catastrophes like high-mortality infectious-disease pandemics (e.g. avian flu), or global nuclear or biological warfare. Population policy in many countries has emphasized permanent methods of fertility discontinuation – starting with India's emphasis on vasectomies for men and many other countries' reliance on tubal ligation or quinacrine cauterization for women. Voluntary sterilization has been the single most popular method in both the US and the UK. But these permanent methods are typically difficult and expensive to reverse, so they cannot be favored if it is uncertain whether population growth or population decline is the more serious risk. Here is where LARC, long-acting *reversible* contraception, has a dramatic advantage: childbearing can be resumed if people wish to do so not only in the event of a personal tragedy like losing a child, but also if some form of negative population emergency occurs.

Although bioethicists have been interested in contributory issues like immigration, environmental sustainability, aging and intergenerational justice, and life-extension technology, they have attended very little to the issues of population per se. But they might have a good deal to say about which is worse: unrestrained population growth, followed by crash and die-back; uncontrolled or forced population decline; or stringently imposed population control, limiting reproductive rights. Given that none of these alternatives is attractive, it remains to be seen whether there is still some other alternative. The thought-experiment presented here concerning long-acting, always-reversible, "automatic" contraception, in continuous use for both men and women except when they actively choose to have a child, can, I believe, go a long way toward showing us a route between these three undesirable alternatives, a route that can survive close ethical scrutiny in that it serves both essential objectives: reducing population growth *and* protecting reproductive rights.

References

Battin, M. P. (1995). Editorial: A better approach to adolescent pregnancy. *Social Science and Medicine* 41/9: 1203–5.

Battin, M. P. (1996). Roundtable. Adolescent pregnancy: when it is a problem, what is the solution? *Reproductive Health Matters* 8 (November): 110–12.

Battin, M. P. (1997). Sex and consequences: world population growth versus reproductive rights. *Philosophic Exchange* 27: 17–31.

Blackorby, C., Bossert, W., and Donaldson, D. (2005). *Population Issues in Social Choice Theory, Welfare Economics, and Ethics.* Cambridge and New York: Cambridge University Press.

Bongaarts, J. (2002). The end of the fertility transition in the developed world. *Population and Development Review* 28/3: 419–43.

Bongaarts, J. (2008). Fertility transitions in developing countries: progress or stagnation? *Studies in Family Planning* 39/2: 105–10.

Buss, D. and Herman, D. (2003). *Globalizing Family Values. The Christian Right in International Politics.* Minneapolis, MN, and London: University of Minnesota Press.

Caldwell, J. C. (2004). Demographic theory: a long view. *Population and Development Review* 30/2: 297–316.

Campbell, M. (1998). Schools of thought: an analysis of interest groups influential in international population policy. *Population and Environment* 19/6 (July): 487–512.

Campbell, M., Sahin-Hodoglugil, N. N., and Potts, M. (2006). Barriers to fertility regulation: a review of the literature. *Studies in Family Planning* 37/2: 87–98.

Cohen, Joel E. (1995). *How Many People Can the Earth Support?* New York and London: W. W. Norton.

Connelly, M. (2008). *Fatal Misconception. The Struggle to Control World Population.* Cambridge, MA, and London: Belknap/Harvard University Press.

Demeny, P. (2004). Population futures for the next three hundred years: soft landing or surprises to come? *Population and Development Review* 30/3: 507–17.

Dixon-Mueller, R. (1993). *Population Policy and Women's Rights: Transforming Reproductive Choice*. Westport, CN, and London: Praeger.

Ehrlich, P. R. (1968). *The Population Bomb*. New York: Ballantine Books.

Ehrlich, P. R. and Ehrlich, A. H. (1990). *The Population Explosion*. New York: Simon and Schuster.

Gee, E. M. and Gutman, G. M. (eds.) (2002). *The Overselling of Population Aging: Apocalyptic Demography, Intergenerational Challenges, and Social Policy*. Don Mills, Ontario: Oxford University Press.

Grant, L. (ed.) (2006). *The Case for Fewer People: The NPG Forum Papers*. Santa Ana, CA: Seven Locks Press.

Gu, B., Wang, F., Guo, Z., and Zhang, E. (2007). China's local and national fertility policies at the end of the twentieth century. *Population and Development Review* 33/1: 129–47.

Hartmann, B. (1995 [1987]). *Reproductive Rights and Wrongs: The Global Politics of Population Control*, rev. edn. Boston, MA: South End Press.

Kennedy, P. (1993). *Preparing for the Twenty-First Century*. New York: HarperCollins.

Male Contraception Information Project (MCIP) (2008). Online at www.malecontraceptives.org; http://NewmaleContraception.org (accessed June 3, 2008).

Malthus, T. R. (1798). *An Essay on the Principle of Population, as It Affects the Future Improvement of Society*. (Complete 1st edn and partial 7th edn (1872), reprinted in G. Himmelfarb (ed.), *On Population*. New York: Modern Library, 1960.)

Mosher, S. W. (2008). *Population Control. Real Costs, Illusory Benefits*. New Brunswick, NJ, and London: Transaction Publishers.

Nie, J.-B. (2005). *Behind the Silence: Chinese Voices on Abortion*. Lanham, MD: Rowman & Littlefield.

Nie, Y. and Wyman, R. J. (2005). The one-child policy in Shanghai: acceptance and internalization. *Population and Development Review* 31/2: 313–36.

Noonan, J. T., Jr (1986). *Contraception: A History of its Treatment by the Catholic Theologians and Canonists*, enlarged edn. Cambridge, MA, and London: Belknap/Harvard University Press.

Nussbaum, M. C. (1999). *Sex and Social Justice*. New York: Oxford University Press.

Parfit, D. (1984). *Reasons and Persons*. Oxford: Clarendon Press.

Pope Paul VI (1968). *Humanae Vitae*. Encyclical Letter of His Holiness Paul VI on the regulation of birth, July 25. Available online at www.vatican.va/holy_father/paul_vi/encyclicals/documents/hf_p-vi_enc_25071968_humanae-vitae_en.html (accessed June 9, 2008).

Potts, M. (2008). Review of *Fatal Misconception*. *Population and Development Review* 34/3: 547–81.

Sen, A. (1992). *Inequality Reexamined*. Cambridge, MA: Harvard University Press.

Sen, G., Germain, A., and Chen, L. C. (eds.) (1994). *Population Policies Reconsidered: Health, Empowerment, and Rights*. Harvard Series on Population and International Health. Cambridge, MA: Harvard School of Public Health and International Women's Health Coalition, distributed by Harvard University Press.

Simon, J. L. (1981). *The Ultimate Resource*. Princeton: Princeton University Press.

Turok, D. (2007). The quest for better contraception: future methods. *Obstetrics and Gynecology Clinics of North America* 34: 137–66.

United Nations Population Division (2007). *World Population Prospects: The 2006 Revision*. Available online at www.un.org/esa/population/publications/wpp2006/English.pdf (accessed June 9, 2008).

US Census Bureau. *World Population Information and Population Clocks*. Available online at www.census.gov/ipc/www/idb/worldpopinfo.html (accessed June 9, 2008).

Vallin, J. (2002). The end of the demographic transition: relief or concern? *Population and Development Review* 28/1: 105–20.

Weiner, M. and Teitelbaum, M. (2001). *Political Demography, Demographic Engineering*. New York: Berghahn Books.

Women's Global Network for Reproductive Rights (WGNRR), Amsterdam. Multiple newsletters. Available online at www.wgnrr.org/.

Zeng, Y. (2007). Options for fertility policy transition in China. *Population and Development Review* 33/2: 215–46.

17

Assisted Reproduction, Prenatal Testing, and Sex Selection

LAURA M. PURDY

Use of assisted reproduction (AR) has exploded in the 30 plus years since the birth of Louise Brown, the first baby born via *in vitro* fertilization (IVF) (Soini et al. 2006). This growth has been promoted by pronatalist social values and enabled by ever more powerful reproductive technologies.

"AR" denotes techniques for creating a baby other than by sexual intercourse between a woman and a man. Some involve only a couple (usually married), whereas others may involve singles or unmarried couples and utilize bodily products or services of third parties. Among the former are artificial insemination by husband (AIH), "standard" IVF and the related technologies of gamete intrafallopian transfer (GIFT), and zygote intrafallopian transfer (ZIFT), as well as intracytoplasmic sperm injection (ICSI) and preimplantation genetic diagnosis (PGD). Among the latter are insemination by donor (AID), IVF, and PGD using donor eggs or sperm, as well as various forms of contract pregnancy or "surrogacy." Some approaches require cryopreservation (freezing) or may involve precursor tissue such as ovarian tissue (*BioNews* 2005b; Robertson 1994; Spar 2006). There is already a huge range of possible permutations of these methods, raising new questions about family relationships. Still more options are on the horizon, such as cloning, eggs using material from more than one individual, artificial gametes and artificial wombs (Spar 2006).

Widespread social values promote AR. Many believe that having one's "own" biological children is a natural and important part of life, and, indeed, that women are unfulfilled unless they have gestated babies. Individuals unable to conceive on their own are thus encouraged to seek AR, preferably using their own gametes, but using donor services if necessary, before, or instead of, seeking to adopt. Some techniques (such as AID, egg donation, PGD, and prenatal testing followed by abortion) can also help parents select children who meet certain criteria, such as freedom from genetic diseases carried by one or both parties, having tissue that is compatible with that of a seriously ill sibling ("savior siblings") (*BioNews* 2005c), or being a particular sex. Other approaches, such as contract pregnancy, can protect women at special risk of harm from pregnancy.

The demand for AR still appears to be increasing rapidly. Infertility is quite common: it is estimated that about 15 percent of couples who attempt to become pregnant

178

worldwide fail to conceive. This failure is attributed to such factors as sexually transmitted diseases, poor health care, environmental pollution, unsafe illegal abortions, unnecessary hysterectomies, early sterilization, and education and employment patterns that lead women to delay childbearing (Warren 1988). Powerful new technologies, including genetic tests and MicroSort®, are also being developed that raise the possibility of selecting for or against particular characteristics, thus also increasing demand. And new technologies are prompting requests for still more innovative services. For example, postmenopausal women can now sometimes give birth at very advanced ages (67!) by using donor eggs (*BioNews* 2007a). It is even possible to gestate fetuses in brain-dead women or use sperm from dead men to create post-mortem babies.

General Assessments of Assisted Reproduction

Some people oppose AR in principle. This opposition may arise from conservative premises or from feminist (or, more generally, progressive) ones. Let us consider each in turn.

Conservative objections can be traced to two basic facts. One is that AR separates sex and reproduction. The other is that AR radically alters traditional relationships (Reich 1978). Resistance to separating sex and reproduction is generally based either on some version of natural law theory or on explicit religious principle, such as the view that non-procreative sex is sinful. Because natural law theory tends either to commit the naturalistic fallacy (i.e., assume that what is "unnatural" is bad or wrong) or beg questions, it cannot provide a strong moral basis for prohibiting the separation of sex and reproduction. Religious principles are, in turn, an unacceptable basis for social policy in pluralistic societies, although individuals who adhere to them are free, other things being equal, to live according to them. AR does alter tradition, but traditions can be less than optimal or even seriously harmful.

Feminist objections can ultimately be traced to the fear that AR will reinforce and promote sexism. Feminists emphasize that pronatalism, together with the emphasis on biological relationships, leads many women to undertake costly and potentially risky procedures to remedy infertility that would not otherwise trouble them or that they might be happy to alleviate via adoption. Furthermore, since men are still dominant in society, and are especially influential in science, technology, and medicine, AR adds to men's power over women. A few feminists have claimed that if additional techniques (such as ectogenesis or cloning) were perfected, men might seek to eliminate women from society altogether; other developments might also lead to morally objectionable forms of eugenics. Many feminists also believe it would be better to address sources of infertility, and eradicate the underlying sexism that makes it so problematic for women, especially in extremely patriarchal cultures. In their view, focusing on AR displaces these reforms (Spallone and Steinberg 1987). They, along with other progressives, are also concerned about possible harm to women and children from innovative therapies now being routinely offered without prior extensive research to establish safety and efficacy; these worries are exacerbated by the fact that, in the US, infertility treatment is now a highly profitable business, raising concerns about potential conflicts of interest. Elsewhere, regulation may further particular agendas, such as those espoused by the Vatican, rather than protecting women or children (Spar 2006). These claims deserve serious scrutiny. However, given the benefits of some forms of AR, and the practical impossibility of stopping it, the best hope is informed and democratic discussion, followed by intelligent regulation.

Because of the many forms of AR, only a few basic issues can be considered here.

Artificial insemination and egg donation

AR began with artificial insemination (AI). AIH first opened up the possibility of separating sex and reproduction; AID first involved a third party in the treatment without sexual intercourse. AID is widely accepted; it is estimated to produce some 30,000 babies yearly in the United States alone. Sperm banking has become big business, with more than 100 clinics in the US in 1999 (Spar 2006). AID per se does not appear to harm the individuals it produces, although it raises questions about non-traditional family relationships; it seems that the main risk of emotional harm comes not from the relationships themselves, but from secrecy and lies about them. However, inadequate screening for sexually transmitted diseases like AIDS (acquired immunodeficiency syndrome) or genetic disease could harm women or children; lack of screening capacity is the principal drawback of do-it-yourself AID. In theory, using a physician's services should provide such protection. However, in practice, it does not always do so, given lacunae in regulation and the potential for human error. Using physician AID is more costly than do-it-yourself AID, and raises the possibility of unjustifiable gate-keeping harmful to single women or lesbian couples. Physicians have also been caught using their own sperm without consent. AID could also theoretically cause marital problems if men are less attached to children to whom they are not genetically related. Poor regulation raises the specter of custody claims by donors or demands for financial support by recipients. Anonymity is another major issue: should children born of AID have a right to genetic or personal information about their biological fathers? In general, however, AID appears a beneficial practice that circumvents male infertility and can be used to prevent serious genetic disease (Mahowald 1993).

Egg donation is more physically and morally complicated. Whereas sperm for donation are obtained by masturbation, obtaining eggs is risky and unpleasant for donors. Women are usually hormonally stimulated to produce multiple eggs; frequent blood tests and sonograms are required to monitor their development. The resulting eggs are then retrieved by passing a needle through the vaginal wall. The risks include hormonal overstimulation, possible damage from the needle, and potentially harmful long-term effects of these procedures, including a suspected risk of cancer (Holmes 1988). In addition, because the procedure is relatively new (dating only to the early 1980s), in some countries there are few legal protections for participants.

Given these risks, one might well question whether it is in women's interest to donate eggs. Nonetheless, a flourishing market in eggs has developed in some countries, such as the US, where eggs from women considered the most desirable are advertised for as much as $50,000. Other countries, like Germany and Egypt, prohibit egg donation, and in some it is permitted but compensation is limited (Spar 2006). One would hope that safer techniques and stringent safety-oriented regulation will reduce risk in the future.

180

IVF and its relatives

IVF provides a way to detour around blocked or damaged fallopian tubes; GIFT and ZIFT are variants that raise most of the same moral issues. Women must either undergo egg retrieval or acquire a donor egg; then sperm and egg are united in a Petri dish (Walters and Singer 1982). Where a husband's sperm is known to be deficient in some way, intracytoplasmic sperm injection (ICSI) may be done, injecting a single sperm through the outer membrane of the egg wall. Fertilization may also be helped along with so-called "assisted hatching" (Spar 2006). After a few cell multiplications, embryos with apparent defects are discarded, and some or all of the rest are implanted in the woman's uterus. Physicians are now getting equally good results in some cases using single embryo transfer, which prevents the risks of multiple pregnancy (*BioNews* 2007b). If a woman becomes pregnant, she receives frequent injections of progesterone until the 12-week point. IVF raises the risk of ectopic pregnancy, miscarriage, and multiple births. Success rates have risen somewhat, but are still relatively low: around 25–30 percent overall – much higher in some groups, but much lower for others; the use of donor eggs has increased the success rate for women over the age of 40. Clinics have different success rates overall, and may measure "success" differently, in some cases focusing on the number of pregnancies rather than live births (Spar 2006: 56–7).

No procedures are acceptable that risk serious harm to future children. Some people believe that the right to life begins at conception. They believe that because IVF may lead to the production of "extra" individuals that may be discarded, it is tantamount to murder. As the status of embryos is discussed elsewhere in this volume (see chapters 13, 14, and 40), there is no need to enter the debate here. In the US, a Christian embryo adoption (the "snowflake Program") is now being offered to address this problem (Spar 2006).

However, concern about IVF harm to future children is appropriate even if one does not share the view that moral personhood begins at conception. Minor harms might be outweighed by the benefit to the child of existence; more serious ones should raise doubts about the morality of IVF. There is some evidence that IVF babies have roughly double the risk of birth defects from normal pregnancies, although different studies produce different results (Holmes 1988; Soini et al. 2006). Despite rapid growth, the procedure is still relatively new and so there can as yet be no evidence of its long-term safety. Perhaps the high rate of unsuccessful cycles of treatment and pregnancies is weeding out most serious health problems (Robertson 1994: ch. 5).

Women are also at risk from IVF. As we have seen, there is some risk in extracting eggs. IVF pregnancies are frequently ectopic, a life-threatening condition; "normal" ones frequently fail for other (mostly unknown) reasons as well. It usually requires several cycles of treatment to give birth, and even then many women do not achieve this goal. This state of affairs may entice women into endless treatments which are hard on them both physically and emotionally. IVF costs continue to increase, and, at best, costs are only partially covered by private insurance or national health insurance systems. In the US, people may pay from $66,000 to $240,000 per live birth; when the real costs of multiple pregnancy are included, they run into the millions for society as a whole. Furthermore, cesarean section rates are higher than average, in part because these pregnancies are regarded as "precious" and in need of especially close physician management. However, cesarean deliveries are riskier for women and more costly than vaginal deliveries; subsequent deliveries must usually also be cesareans. Given all these facts, one might question whether women who undertake IVF fully understand its risk–benefit ratio (Sherwin 1992).

Women's consent might also be questioned on specifically feminist grounds. Pronatalism is pervasive in human societies, as is the attitude that women who do not gestate babies are unfulfilled (or even worthless). These forces pressure women to produce children at almost any cost (Warren 1988). The onus of barrenness is so great for some that they will undertake IVF even when it is their partner who requires treatment. All this suggests that women considering IVF should at least have thorough counseling.

The risks and costs of IVF have elicited additional objections. Many people believe that adoption would be preferable to using scarce resources to create more children. Overpopulation is another concern. And, although adoption can be an excellent option, it raises moral questions of its own, as it may contribute to the exploitation of poor young women. Interracial adoptions pose special difficulties. In any case, there is a shortage of healthy, white babies because pregnancy rates have dropped and more women are keeping their babies. Adopting older children with serious problems may be extremely demanding, and it would be unfair to expect only the infertile to take on these children, while the fertile can ignore their plight and have any number of genetically related children. It is true that the human population is outstripping its ability to make sure that all people are even minimally provided for. Generally, reproductive rates go down when there is intelligent economic development but it isn't happening quickly enough to avoid further famines and environmental degradation. However, it is unfair to expect the infertile to bear the brunt of measures to reduce population growth because of negative social views of infertile women and inadequate government social security programs. Instead, schemes to reduce births must spread the burden more equally. A related issue is the scarce health-care resources used on IVF at a time when many people lack basic care, either because, as in Britain, their national insurance scheme is underfunded or because, as in the United States, there is no guarantee of even the most basic care. Progressives raise additional worries about the justice of access. Some argue against having the procedure available at all, whereas others lament that it should not be available to anyone if it is not available to all. Both arguments have some merit.

Overall, IVF means that the infertile do not have to accept their fate because there is always another procedure to try, and "giving up" means that they are perceived as responsible for their infertility. Women especially, propelled by society's sexism and pronatalism, may feel strongly pressured to pursue IVF and other ARs instead of getting on with their lives. Thus there needs to be much more democratic debate about the whole issue, alerting women to their options and empowering them to refuse IVF, or any invasive treatment (Sherwin 1992). It is true that some technologies become so entrenched as part of standard care that it is hardly possible to refuse them. For much of the world, the expense limits such pressures, although in some nations, like Denmark, IVF is much more accessible and therefore more difficult to refuse.

Some people also worry that IVF's existence could lead to a stringent eugenic program that examines every embryo before implantation. But the objection is then to the eugenic program, not IVF. Unfortunately, the mere development of any innovation could lead to its use being made mandatory by an oppressive state. A lingering question is why reproductive technologies like IVF continue their rapid deployment. While the extremist worry that men are plotting to replace women with artificial wombs seems untenable, the scientific and medical establishment does not have a particularly good record of meeting women's real needs. By focusing limited resources here, society emphasizes women's childbearing role at the expense of other desirable goals such as a better understanding of women's health. As with AI, an additional worry is that the increasing medicalization of reproduction will also increase dependence on the scientific and health-care establishments. This is worrisome in itself, and also because of the potential for the imposition of gate-keeping ethical views. Among them are the views that only married couples should have children, either because other relationships are disapproved of or because of (unsubstantiated) concern that others may be poor parents (Overall 1993). However, in some countries, like the US, market forces are countering such discrimination by creating clinics that do cater to the unmarried (Spar 2006).

Cryopreservation is still experimental in humans, and the long-term risks to children are unknown. In addition, storing embryos and other genetic materials may create opportunities for mix-ups, where the wrong material is used, and exacerbate problems about disposition and ownership. For example, couples may come to disagree about what to do with their materials if their situation changes or embryos may be "orphaned" because of unexpected deaths (Robertson 1994: 104–14). These problems can be reduced (but not eradicated) by detailed contracts.

IVF also vastly increases the frequency of multiple pregnancies, both twins and triplets, but also so-called "supertwins" (quadruplets through octuplets). These pregnancies, especially the higher-order ones, are risky both for pregnant women and their fetuses. Perinatal mortality is increased, and surviving babies are likely to suffer from serious disabilities, including blindness, or motor and learning problems (Nakajo et al. 2004; Armour and Callister 2005). Selective abortion of some of the fetuses can protect the remaining ones somewhat, although it slightly increases the risk of losing the whole pregnancy (Overall 1993).

IVF plus egg donation also opens up the potential for pregnancy in postmenopausal women. Many consider this practice immoral because it is unnatural and because elderly women might die before their children are self-sufficient. But postmenopausal pregnancy is no more unnatural than any form of AR, and few object to old men fathering children.

Despite all these issues, IVF should not be banned, since that would treat women as legal incompetents, damaging them more than unwise reproductive decisions would do. It would probably also give rise to medical tourism as the infertile seek treatment in less-regulated countries.

Surrogacy

"Surrogacy" involves one woman gestating a baby to be raised by another. Initially, women who acted as surrogates used their own eggs, but it is increasingly common for them to use client or donor eggs. Friends or relatives may carry babies for each other, or the transaction may be a commercial one. Most of the controversy revolves about this latter practice, although the former may involve morally problematic familial coercion (Narayan 1995).

"Old-fashioned" surrogacy (where the woman who is to be pregnant contributes her own egg) raises the question whether the process should be called surrogacy at all, as that suggests that the contracting man's sperm is more important than either her egg or gestational service. It would make more sense to use a more accurate term like "contract pregnancy." Such terminological issues are highlighted still more by "gestational" contract pregnancy that uses another woman's egg: who is a mother? The traditional concept of motherhood (involving genetic, gestational, and social relationships) is being deconstructed, potentially leading to serious conceptual tensions, especially for feminists and other progressives. Rearing relationships surely are central, although biological links should be neither devalued nor worshipped (Stanworth 1987). The more parties there are to the transaction, the more complicated the relationships and the legal difficulties when either too many or not enough people want to raise a given child (Alpern 1992). An example of the first was the notorious Baby M case, where Mary Beth Whitehead, who had both provided her egg and gestated the child, refused to give up custody. An example of the second happened when no one would take custody of a deformed baby (Spar 2006).

Thus it is clear that contract pregnancy raises important questions about the welfare of children resulting from it. It raises equally important questions about its effect on women, both as individuals and as a disadvantaged group, and about the integrity and harmony of families (Mahowald 1993).

As with AR generally, contract pregnancy has spread without the kind of careful research on its consequences that would help assure us that it is not seriously harmful. In the US, fears about contract pregnancy have led to quite strict regulation in some states, despite generally lax regulation of other ARs. However, such regulation may well reflect vague ethical fears or influential religious agendas rather than the real needs of women and children. The practice is highly regulated in some countries (e.g., the UK and Israel) and prohibited in others (e.g., Egypt, Germany, and Denmark) (Spar 2006).

In what additional ways might children be harmed? Gestational contract pregnancy exposes them to whatever risks might be inherent in the technologies used to create them. Both kinds of pregnancies (simple and gestational) might also lead to psychological or emotional problems. For example, children might be disturbed to think that they weren't born the "usual way," but it is plausible to believe that the more common the practice, the less of a problem that would be. Also, recent (albeit preliminary) studies show that children (and families) are doing well (MacCallum et al. 2007); others suggest that lack of openness about children's origins is more of a problem than those origins themselves (Golombok et al. 2006).

Some people believe that the potential for emotional upset implies that contract pregnancy is wrong. But many of the same people also believe that it is morally permissible to have children even when they are at risk of serious disease or disability, since otherwise they would not be alive. There is also concern about the effect of contract pregnancy on a woman's existing children, who may bond with the fetus and then have to watch the baby being given away. But surely it is possible to explain that

184

their mother is so delighted with motherhood that she wants to make it possible for others who could not have healthy children without her help. In any case, what needs to be emphasized is that, ultimately, rearing parents are "real" parents.

Would concern by some about the possibility of such emotional upset constitute sufficient grounds for banning contract pregnancy? Generally we do not bestow this kind of veto power on particular groups, but depend instead on some sort of moral cost-benefit analysis, taking into account the often intense unhappiness of the infertile and the desirability of other goals such as preventing serious disease in children or women (Purdy 1996). Also, many social problems may be attenuated by the increasing use of contracting women's own (or donor) eggs, although that may raise medical risks somewhat. Presumably, using their own (or donor) eggs makes it easier for women party to the contract to explain to the children that they merely needed or provided gestational services.

Another important line of argumentation objects to contract pregnancy on the grounds that it involves the commodification of human life, or baby-selling (Radin 1987). However, some would question whether there is anything wrong with commodification. Others would deny the charge, contending that what is at issue is the rental of gestational services and/or the sale of a right to a parental relationship to a child.

What about the consequences of contract pregnancy for women? Opponents argue that the practice exploits the women who undertake pregnancy for pay and may coerce the wives of men who engage outside women to carry pregnancies for them. As discussed earlier, it is also argued, as with IVF, that the practice reinforces undesirable stereotypes of women as breeders and promotes pronatalism.

It is doubtful that the existence of contract pregnancy strongly coerces women, although it is true that women may be pressured to participate in the practice by partners eager for genetically related offspring or a nice chunk of money. Initially the worry was that the prospect of $10,000 or more would constitute an irresistible inducement for very impoverished women. As it turns out, most women who undertake contract pregnancy for pay tend to be working or lower-middle class and are poorer than those who contract for it. The going rate varies tremendously, from $10,000 to at least $75,000, with those who broker the relationships usually earning a comparable sum (Spar 2006). One would hope that most women are getting more than the now-minimal $10,000.

The fact that gestating women are poorer than the couple is unsurprising, given that contract pregnancy is a luxury good. Without a fuller critique of market transactions and/or a demonstration that there is something unusual about such transactions that makes them illegitimate even in the context of a market-based economy, this allegation fails to show that there is anything wrong with contract pregnancy.

The possibility of exploitation seems more plausible in the case of gestational contract pregnancy (Holmes 1992). First, a contracting couple might be more willing to employ a very poor woman with health problems since the quality of the egg is not at issue. Also, very poor women might be apt to find the compensation less resistible, even where poor health might put them at more risk; of course, this line of reasoning ignores the developing fetus's need for a healthy environment. Second, gestational contract pregnancy opens up the possibility of hiring a minority or third world woman who could not easily sue for custody should they change their mind about giving up the baby. However, social conditions coupled with cheap international travel probably mean that these practices would just go underground if prohibited.

There are also more general worries about women's competence to consent to contract pregnancy. Brokers now try to hire only women who already have children, but some object that each pregnancy is different and so women can never be expected to know how she will react to a new pregnancy. However, there have been relatively few cases of women changing their minds; in the notorious Baby M case, psychological tests showing that Mary Beth Whitehead would have trouble detaching herself from the baby were ignored. The conflict-of-interest inherent in such for-profit brokering suggests that only public authorities should be doing this work. Also, regulations could require a period of grace during which women can decide to keep children, returning payments by contracting individuals. Given the shameful history of belief in women's incompetence, any such claim that women can never know how they will respond to a given pregnancy should be subjected to the highest standards of evidence. In any case, the increase in gestational (as opposed to simple) contract pregnancy may render this concern less plausible.

Some object to alleged possible harm both to individual women and to women as a group. One important issue is the laissez-faire regulatory environment that allows for contracts that subject women who undertake contract pregnancy to stringent health practices or that require them to abort fetuses at the behest of the contractors. There is still much controversy about what a pregnant woman owes her fetus. It seems clear that morality requires women not to harm their fetuses, but it does not follow that there is, or ought to be, any such legal duty. Contracts that give this kind of control over a woman's body to others are morally suspect and may constitute a first step toward totalitarian control over their bodies and their lives (Spallone 1989). Also, some current practices are clearly unfair to women, especially where they deliver a stillborn child and are deprived of some portion of their fee. After all, many workers (for example, dry-cleaners, physicians) are fully paid for their services, even where their efforts are unsuccessful. There is clearly a need for a model contract that strikes a reasonable balance in favor of women's rights while taking account of the needs of fetuses and other contracting parties. Regulations of this sort would also provide reasonable protection for all from breaches of contract where the practice is unregulated or takes place despite prohibition. Additional questions about women's welfare are raised if a man can engage in contract pregnancy without the consent of his wife (especially since AID generally requires the consent of husbands). This could saddle women with children they do not want (Overall 1987). Nor is a wife's relationships with the children necessarily legally protected if the couple's relationship fails. These are serious harms to women that also require regulation.

Pre-birth Testing

Pre-birth testing is a reproductive service that falls quite naturally under the general heading of AR, even though it does not necessarily use methods other than sexual intercourse, or involve the materials or services of third parties, to reproduce. However, some forms of such testing may lead to AR, and they may also be more common after AR has been used.

Pre-birth testing can take place either before or after conception. Screening is aimed rather generally at those planning to reproduce or at pregnant women. Diagnostic testing is recommended in response to specific risk factors in individuals or couples. Participants may be seeking information about widespread risks (such as Down syndrome) or about specific genetic diseases (such as Huntington's) or about other characteristics (sex, for example). As genetic science advances, new tests for characteristics of both kinds will make it possible for parents to attempt to exert ever greater control over what their offspring will be like.

Moral evaluation of pre-birth testing varies according to its demands, responses to undesired results, and different moral perspectives.

Testing for disease or disability

Some object to the very notion of pre-birth testing, except perhaps in those cases where it is intended to provide parents with information to help them prepare for a child with special needs. The main reason is that in most cases the only way to guarantee the prevention of a disease or disability is to prevent the birth of the individual at risk.

Among the most vocal opponents are disability rights activists who argue that preventing the birth of children with disease or disability is a form of unjustifiable discrimination against the children, and against disease and disability communities more generally. They contend that individuals are harmed by not being born. Communities of those with disease or disability are also harmed because preventing such births reduces the number of those living with disease or disability (and therefore the strength and political clout of those communities); it also broadcasts the hurtful message that life with disease or disability is not worth living (Parens and Asch 2000).

Although these activists are quite vocal, the extent to which they represent those living with disease or disability is unknown. It is reasonable to believe that these attitudes might not be widely shared, as there are serious problems with the arguments. First, focusing exclusively on keeping the number of diseased and disabled up seems to violate the Kantian imperative against using others as mere means.

Secondly, these arguments often treat all diseases and disabilities as if they had the same impact on the quality of life of those who live with them; this is clearly inaccurate. Moreover, such disability activists tend to adhere to the social model of disease and disability that, for every condition, attributes most or all suffering to inadequate social supports provided by society. This is implausible. It is true that much unnecessary suffering comes from inadequate social responses to disease and disability, but it is also true that some conditions are inherently miserable in a way that could not be alleviated by any conceivable social measures. In addition, the social model self-destructs if it asserts that there is nothing intrinsically bad about disease or disability; on what grounds then is sacrifice by others to help required?

Thirdly, the motivation for wanting to prevent the births of those at risk for serious disease or disability is generally the desire to see offspring flourish, not gratuitously to insult existing persons with disease or disability. Nor is it necessarily predicated on the view that life with disease or disability is not worth living; it could merely be based on the understanding that life is better without them and that no possible child has any more right to be born than any other. It is true that attempting to prevent the birth of children with disease or disability could be (and has in the past been) motivated by prejudice or the desire to avoid the burdens associated with their care, but that fact does not render moral arguments in favor of the enterprise unsound (Purdy 1996).

Possible, potential, and future children are at the center of arguments about the permissibility of pre-birth testing. According to disability rights activists, the children who are prevented from being born are unjustly discriminated against. In the case of possible persons – those who might come to exist – this argument falls flat because of the failure to distinguish between as-yet-nonexistent individuals and those already conceived. Nonexistent individuals cannot be the objects of discrimination. But focusing solely on those already conceived assumes that it is as wrong to kill fetuses as it is to kill born persons, and conflicts with the view that abortion is morally justifiable.

Children are also at the center of arguments of some people with more moderate views. Their position is that if children are brought into existence when it is known that their afflictions will likely be so great that they would rather be dead, then they are unjustly treated. Others would lose more by being prevented from being born than by their less serious afflictions. Hence they are not treated unjustly by the failure to prevent their existence, and concern about doing so is at least misplaced, if not discriminatory (Parfit 1984: ch. 16).

Much effort has been expended to try to show why this position is unsatisfactory. Objections range from critiques of the underlying theory of personal identity to arguments that it is wrong to bring children to life in a harmed condition even if that state of affairs does not constitute any injustice to them (Brock 1995).

So far this chapter has focused on the intentions, goals, and broad consequences of pre-birth testing. However, there are also moral concerns about two aspects of its procedures and methods. First, tests may yield false positives or negatives, or simply fail to provide the certainty that would be helpful in deciding how to act in response to them; their results may also have far-reaching social consequences. Second, post-conception testing disproportionately burdens women, since fetuses are housed in their bodies (De Melo-Martin 2006).

Some genetic tests are highly reliable; others merely suggest a higher than average probability of a given condition. In the latter case, additional (and often more invasive) tests may be required. This period of uncertainty and testing is often stressful, especially where a pregnancy is strongly wanted. Moreover, some forms of testing may provide more information than is desired, as for example when the fetus is found to carry the mutations for Huntington's disease or BRCA1; in each of these cases, others may learn that they too are at risk for disease even if they would prefer not to have this knowledge. Positive results may also become grounds for discrimination on the part of employers or insurance companies unless there is legislation protecting citizens.

Post-conception testing can particularly burden women. Women may be expected to participate in testing without adequate informed consent about the nature, goals, or pitfalls of particular tests. Some tests, such as amniocentesis, may be invasive or risk the pregnancy. And, although the expressed goal of professional genetic counseling is non-directive, women may feel (or be) pressured to respond to test results in ways they feel uncertain about or disapprove of. There is also a worry that by failing to prevent the birth of children with serious disease or disability, mothers and children are vulnerable to discrimination by insurance companies refusing to insure them on the grounds that they have pre-existing conditions, or, more broadly, because their expenses could have been foreseen and prevented. Society will need to regulate these new scientific developments to insure their benefits while at the same time protecting from unnecessary harm.

Testing for other characteristics

Although pre-birth testing for disease or disability is now quite widespread in some environments, some people are concerned that rapid progress in genetics will facilitate a slippery slope to much more widespread pre-birth testing. Two prospects are considered especially worrisome. First, it may become possible to select against characteristics that some consider intrinsically undesirable, such as homosexuality or short stature. Second, it may become possible to select for other characteristics (such as strength or intelligence) considered desirable. People speculate that such testing could lead to so-called "designer babies," oppressive eugenics, and an increase in the gap between rich and poor; it could weaken parent–child relationships, pervert the proper goals of medicine, or exacerbate problems about the allocation of scarce resources (Kitcher 1996; Robertson 1994).

Although there is no immediate prospect of such testing, it is now possible to test for sex. Sex selection is most commonly done post-conception by sonogram followed by abortion of fetuses of the unwanted sex. However, recently, a quite effective pre-conception method of sex pre-selection was developed: sperm-sorting (MicroSort®) followed by AI. Sperm-sorting is about 88 percent effective in selecting for females, 74 percent in selecting for males.

Most observers believe that there are some justifiable uses of sex selection. One is selection against fetuses carrying sex-linked diseases. Another is so-called "family balancing," when parents have many children of one sex and want one of the other sex. However, relatively easy access to the low-tech approach (sonogram plus abortion) has led to widespread sex pre-selection in some countries like India and China, where males are very strongly preferred to females. Many more couples will probably consider sex pre-selection given that MicroSort® is less burdensome for women and obviates the need for abortions that some see as morally problematic.

This kind of sex pre-selection raises most of the general concerns about pre-birth testing, plus a couple of its own. First, sex pre-selection in cultures that strongly prefer males has already created serious imbalances in sex ratios. The average sex ratio at birth in human populations is 105 boys to 100 girls. Yet in China there are currently 121 boys to 100 girls; the sex ratio in India is also becoming increasingly skewed in favor of males. The consequences are to some extent unknown, except for the obvious fact that mature males will have difficulty finding mates. Some argue that this state of affairs could be beneficial for women, who would then be valued more. But others suggest that that wouldn't necessarily enhance women's autonomy but might instead lead to more stringent controls on them. Some also worry that societies with a surplus of young, unattached males might become very aggressive.

Secondly, sex pre-selection may promote and reinforce sexism. Sexism can be defined as the failure to recognize two kinds of rights for women. First, women have rights shared with men in virtue of their common humanity. Thus, for example, women have the same right to education as men. Secondly, women have rights required by their differences from men. Thus, for example, if women are not to be disadvantaged by their capacity for pregnancy, they require some distinctive rights, like maternity leave. Sexist social systems violate both these kinds of rights.

Preference for males over females is usually a manifestation of sexism. It may be based on imagined differences between the sexes, differences created by differential treatment or customs, or the unwillingness to acknowledge women's (at least) equal contribution to society. None is a legitimate base for preferring boys: they result from errors in reasoning and ethics that can and should be remedied instead. Thus, for example, the Indian view that females are so valueless that prospective husbands deserve large dowries for marrying them is morally untenable. Unfortunately, it persists despite legislation banning dowries, as does sex pre-selection; clearly, much broader measures are necessary to eradicate this deep-seated sexism.

Questions remain about some preferences for a child of one sex rather than the other. For instance, is it sexist for an Indian woman to abort a female fetus to prevent her future suffering in a sexist society? Is family-balancing (or wanting a girl) necessarily sexist and, if so, why (Steinbock 2002)?

Conclusion

AR and its related technologies are an increasingly important part of the reproductive scene. They are also a battleground where conflicting values lead to regulatory measures that may or may not prevent harm. For example, recent legislation has switched Italy from a reproductive wild west to a tightly controlled world where many procedures accepted elsewhere are prohibited. But because the limits reflect the Vatican's moral principles rather than the harm principle, participants are not necessarily better protected (*BioNews* 2005a). Elsewhere, as well, regulation tends to reflect predominant social, political, and economic influences instead of principles that protect and advance human welfare (Spar 2006). Naturally, there is also still plenty of disagreement about what the latter might require, as is shown by contradictory regulation of sex pre-selection in different countries.

References

Alpern, K. D. (ed.) (1992). *The Ethics of Reproductive Technology*. Oxford: Oxford University Press.

Arditti, R., Duelli Klein, R., and Minden, S. (eds.) (1984). *Test-tube Women: What Future for Motherhood?* London: Pandora Press.

Armour, K. L. and Callister, L. C. (2005). Prevention of triplets: trends in reproductive medicine. *Journal of Perinatal and Neonatal Nursing* 19/2: 103–11.

BioNews (2005a). Commentary: what happens to those suffering from infertility in Italy now? June 20–26.

BioNews (2005b). News digest: second frozen embryo transplant birth. June 27–July 3.

BioNews (2005c). News digest: "saviour sibling" born to Fletcher family. July 11–17.

BioNews (2007a). News digest: sixty year old woman gives birth to twins. May 21–28.

BioNews (2007b). News digest: single embryo transplant fuels multiple pregnancy debate. June 11–17.

Boston Women's Health Book Collective (1992). *The New Our Bodies, Ourselves*. New York: Simon and Schuster.

Brock, D. (1995). The non-identity problem and genetic harms. *Bioethics* 9/3–4: 269–75.

De Melo-Martin, I. (2006). Furthering injustices against women: genetic information, moral obligations, and gender. *Bioethics* 20/6: 301–7.

Holmes, H. B. (ed.) (1988). In vitro fertilization: reflections on the state of the art. *Birth* 15/3: 134–45.

Holmes, H. B. (1992). *Issues in Reproductive Technology*. New York: New York University Press.

Golombok, S., MacCallum, F., Murray, C., Lycett, E., and Jadva, V. (2006). Surrogacy families: parental functioning, parent–child relationships and children's psychological development at age 2. *Journal of Child Psychology and Psychiatry* 47/2: 213–22.

Kitcher, P. (1996). *The Lives to Come: The Genetic Revolution and Human Possibilities*. New York: Simon and Schuster.

MacCallum, F., Golombok, S., and Brinsden, P. (2007). Parenting and child development in families with a child conceived through embryo donation. *Journal of Family Psychology* 21/2: 278–87.

Mahowald, M. (1993). *Women and Children in Health Care: An Unequal Majority*. Oxford: Oxford University Press.

Nakajo, Y. et al. (2004). Physical and mental development of children after *in vitro* fertilization and embryo transfer. *Reproductive Medicine and Biology* 3: 63–7.

Narayan, U. (1995). The "gift" of a child: commercial surrogacy, gift surrogacy, and motherhood. In Patricia Boling (ed.), *Expecting Trouble: Surrogacy, Fetal Abuse and New Reproductive Technologies*. Boulder, CO: Westview Press.

Overall, C. (1987). *Ethics and Human Reproduction: A Feminist Analysis*. Boston MA: Allen and Unwin.

Overall, C. (1993). *Human Reproduction: Principles, Practices, Policies*. New York: Oxford University Press.

Parens, E. and Asch, A. (2000). The disability rights critique of prenatal genetic testing: reflections and recommendations. In Parens and Asch, *Prenatal Testing and Disability Rights*. Washington, DC: Georgetown University Press.

Parfit, D. (1984). *Reasons and Persons*. Oxford: Clarendon Press.

Purdy, L. (1996). *Reproducing Persons: Issues in Feminist Bioethics*. Ithaca, NY: Cornell University Press.

Radin, M. (1987). Market-inalienability. *Harvard Law Review* 100: 1849–937.

Reich, W. T. (ed.) (1978). *Encyclopedia of Bioethics*. New York: Free Press.

Robertson, J. (1994). *Children of Choice*. Princeton, NJ: Princeton University Press.

Sherwin, S. (1992). *No Longer Patient: Feminist Ethics and Health Care*. Philadelphia, PA: Temple University Press.

Soini, S. et al. (2006). The interface between assisted reproductive technologies and genetics: technical, social, ethical and legal issues. *European Journal of Human Genetics* 14: 588–645.

Spallone, P. (1989). *Beyond Conception: The New Politics of Reproduction*. Basingstoke: Macmillan Education.

Spallone, P. and Steinberg, D. L. (1987). *Made to Order: The Myth of Reproductive and Genetic Progress*. Oxford: Pergamon Press.

Spar, D. L. (2006). *The Baby Business: How Money, Science, and Politics Drive the Commerce of Conception*. Boston, MA: Harvard Business School Press.

Stanworth, M. (ed.) (1987). *Reproductive Technologies: Gender, Motherhood and Medicine*. Minneapolis: University of Minnesota Press.

Steinbock, B. (2002). Sex selection: not obviously wrong. *Hastings Center Report* 32/1: 23–8.

Walters, W. A. W. and Singer, P. (eds.) (1982). *Test-tube Babies: A Guide to Moral Questions, Present Techniques and Future Possibilities.* Melbourne: Oxford University Press.

Warren, M. A. (1988). IVF and women's interests: An analysis of feminist concerns. *Bioethics* 2/1: 37–57.

Further reading

Baruch, E. H., D'Adamo, A. F., and Seager, J. (eds.) (1988). *Embryos, Ethics and Women's Rights: Exploring the New Reproductive Technologies.* New York: Harrington Park Press.

Corea, G. (1985). *The Mother Machine: Reproductive Technologies from Artificial Insemination to Artificial Wombs.* New York: Harper and Row.

Coughlan, M. J. (1990). *The Vatican, the Law and the Human Embryo.* Iowa City: University of Iowa Press.

Dooley, D. et al. (2002). *The Ethics of New Reproductive Technologies: Cases and Questions.* Oxford: Berghahn Books.

Holmes, H. B., Hoskins, B. B., and Gross, M. (eds.) (1981). *The Custom-made Child?* Clifton, NJ: Humana Press.

Hull, R. T. (1990). *Ethical Issues in the New Reproductive Technologies.* Belmont, CA: Wadsworth.

Kass, L. (1979). Making babies revisited. *Public Interest* 54: 32–60.

Pretorius, D. (1994). *Surrogate Motherhood: A Worldwide View of the Issues.* Springfield, IL: C. C. Thomas.

Purdy, L. (ed.) (1989). *Ethics and Reproduction.* Special issue of *Hypatia,* 4/3.

Ramsey, P. (1970). *Fabricated Man.* New Haven: Yale University Press.

Singer, P. and Wells, D. (1985). *Making Babies: The New Science and Ethics of Conception.* New York: Scribner's.

Warren, M. A. (1985). *Gendercide: The Implications of Sex Selection.* Totowa, NJ: Rowman and Allanheld.

18

Cloning

GREGORY PENCE

Cloning and Popular Culture: A Brief History

The idea of cloning humans provokes such intense disgust that rational discussion of it often becomes an exercise in logic and resisting emotion. When there is talk of humans being cloned, commentators fume, clergy shudder, movies frighten, journalists alarm, and politicians condemn. This chapter attempts to separate superficial from real issues about cloning humans.

Long a topic of alarmist speculation in science fiction, cloning of mammals became a reality in the summer of 1996 when Scottish scientist Ian Wilmut cloned the lamb, Dolly, from her female ancestor. While waiting for patents to be granted, Wilmut announced his results on February 23, 1997, and the next day most newspapers in the world carried the story on their front page.

Over the following decade, journalists wrote more stories about cloning than any issue in the history of bioethics. Movies such as *Jurassic Park*, *The Island of Dr Moreau*, and *The Boys from Brazil* had previously primed audiences for fearful reactions. In 1998, strange characters, such as physicist Richard Seed and the Raelians, a media-seeking cult, announced intentions to clone babies (Professor Seed from his own DNA). In the early 2000s, an Italian physician, Severino Antinori, and a Greek scientist who specialized in turkey sperm, Panos Zavos, both falsely claimed to have implanted cloned embryos in women and to be on the verge of creating the first cloned human baby.

In 2005, South Korean scientist Hwang Woo Suk fraudulently claimed to have cloned 11 stem cell lines from human embryos (Kolata 2005). Newspapers covered the story as massively as they had the birth of Dolly. Carefully planned, and tipping off television cameras in advance, Hwang Woo Suk made his claim at a meeting of the American Association of Science. But he faked his results and created one of the most blatant frauds in the history of science. To avoid prosecution in Korea, he fled in 2007 to Thailand.

By making cloning appear to be something disreputable, the false claims of Hwang Woo Suk, Zavos, Antinori, and the Raelians damaged medical progress by steering young scientists and funding away from cloning. In an age of cable companies with

200 channels screaming for the public's attention each night, editors loved these stories, as they filled many evenings with sensationalistic charges. (The Raelians often claimed things when news was sparse – perfect timing!)

Combined with scary images of cloned humans in science fiction, these cases left most people feeling that cloning was disgusting, seedy, and unnatural. Cloning became synonymous with "immoral creation." As such, discussions of it encounter pre-existing bias.

Some Facts About Cloning

The word "clone" derives from the Greek word "klone" or "twig," referring to the horticultural process whereby a new plant is created asexually by planting a twig in nutrient-filled water. In modern science, "cloning" refers to reproduction of the genetic material of an ancestor-organism without sex.

This etymological and technical definition hardly does justice to the emotional weight in popular culture that rides on the word "cloning." In common thinking, "clone" connotes a subhuman, a robot, a zombie – something less valuable than humans and, because it can be controlled by others, more dangerous. Mothers worry about an army of clones escaping from laboratories to harm their children.

For ordinary purposes, three kinds of cloning merit separation: cloning of cell lines or tiny organisms (such as embryos); cloning of nonhuman animals to produce new, live litters; and human reproductive cloning, also known as cloning-to-produce-babies.

The most accurate description of cloning is somatic cell nuclear transfer, where the nucleus of an adult cell from an existing organism is taken and implanted or fused into an egg where the nucleus has been removed. Unlike twinning, in such transfers, the egg contributes a tiny amount of genetic material, called mitochondrial DNA. Presently in biology, what mitochondria does is not well understood, but some significant genetic diseases ride on mitochondrial genes, and small differences in mito-chondrial genes in embryos may produce large differences in adults.

As the early embryo develops, random inactivation of the X chromosome occurs, and this X chromosome controls some later qualities of the adult. Because of this process, "identical twins" are not exactly identical (for example, they possess different finger-prints). As a result of inactivation and mitochondrial DNA from the host egg, an embryo created by cloning will not be genetically identical to its ancestor. The two *geno-types* will differ some.

The *phenotype* of the resulting individual as an adult – in other words, how the genes are expressed in specific patterns – will also vary because, contrary to popular beliefs about genetic reductionism, how genes are expressed depends on what happens to them *in utero* and in childhood. A child with a deficiency of vitamins, or one abused by horrible parents who lock him in a closet all day, will differ greatly from his ancestor if the ancestor was brought up healthily and in a caring environment. Very small dif-ferences in environmental input at early ages can cause great differences later. Fetal-alcohol syndrome, which can occur when the mother drinks heavily while pregnant, turns normal children into retarded children. So the phenotype of the person from his ancestral genotype can vary a lot.

Exact Copies and Zombies

The previous discussion leads to this point: *a person originated by cloning from genes of an ancestor will not be an exact copy of that ancestor.* He will differ more from his ancestor than identical twins differ, because such twins at least share the same egg, mitochondrial DNA and historical era, and (usually) the same parents and culture. But a person originated by cloning will not share these similarities with his ancestor.

A second point is implied above: a being created from the human genes of a human ancestor, gestated by a human mother and raised in a human family, would be a *person, not a zombie or subhuman.* As a person, he would have free will and could make choices about his future and character, as other human persons do.

Many fears about cloning and genetics today assume *genetic fatalism*, the view that "it's all in your genes." This view is demonstrably false, at least the "all" part. Although free will may be weaker than is commonly assumed, and although some people may have less of it than others, most people have some. That is, they can change their behavior; they can make choices: they can smoke more or less, they can drink alcohol in safer rather than more dangerous ways, and they can learn to drive more carefully to reduce the probability of dying in a crash.

Some parents might try to control a child created by cloning, but some parents do that for children today and, on that topic, some children famously rebel against parental expectations. (Parental expectations are discussed below.) But someone with the genes of basketball player Michael Jordan, whose parents expected him to be a professional superstar, might be fascinated with Islam and become a scholar of the Koran; no one can predict what fascinates a young, open, human mind that possesses a range of freedom over the future.

To guard against letting the false assumption of genetic fatalism sneak into our thinking, we should be careful with our language about cloning. Already the word "clone" carries a heavy, negative connotation, as in "I may be a twin but I'm not a clone!" Indeed, use of the words "the clone" is now pejorative and to write "an army of escaping clones" differs little from using such language as "a bunch of white chicks" or "a bunch of queers."

The technical language of science refers to beings originated by somatic cell nuclear transfer, but that seems too dry for this chapter. As a compromise, I will refer to "persons originated by cloning" to emphasize that they will be *persons* and not zombies. Such language parallels new medical language: *person* with Down syndrome, *person* with spina bifida, etc.

To summarize: Two of the most common objections to human cloning are based on false premises. First, a child created by cloning and raised by different parents in another era would not be an exact copy of her ancestor, and anyone thinking or expecting such an exact copy would be disappointed. Also, secondly, the "Zombie View" is false – a child created by cloning would not be a zombie lacking free will who did the bidding of others. People originated by cloning would have free will, like other human persons.

Is Cloning Humans Unnatural?

Cloning humans is also widely believed to be unnatural, and therefore wrong. While the premise is true, there is a suppressed premise needed to get the conclusion: that everything unnatural is wrong. Is this premise true?

No. For most of human history, humans died young from communicable diseases such as malaria, yellow fever, and cholera. Before antibiotics became common in the mid-1940s, each year infections from wounds or childbirth killed millions. From one perspective, all medical progress fights natural sickness, early death, and dysfunction.

Similarly, being barren or infertile, for some people, has been natural for much of history. New techniques of assisted reproduction, such as *in vitro* fertilization and artificial insemination of sperm, allow formerly infertile couples to take home much-wanted babies. Although more radical, creation of humans by cloning is just further along this spectrum of "helping nature along."

Likewise, techniques in genetics have evolved along a spectrum from creating purebreds in pets and livestock to promulgating immortal embryonic stem cell lines. Asexual reproduction of mammals through nuclear somatic cell transfer is again just one step along a spectrum of these techniques, albeit a greater distance along than generating purebreds or cell lines.

Animal Cloning

Since creation of the lamb Dolly in 1996, scientists have successfully cloned many non-human mammals. They have cloned three generations of mice (1998), bulls (1999), five piglets (2000), goats (2000), gaurs (2001), mouflons (2001), rabbits (2002), cats ("Carbon Copy," 2002), racing mules (2003), rats (2003), African wildcats (2004), dogs ("Snuppy," 2005), water buffalo (2005), horses ("Prometa," 2005), ferrets (2006), and wolves (2007) (*Newsweek* 2007). To date, federal agencies have not allowed flesh or eggs from cloned animals in the human food supply, mainly because of alarmist fears about the safety of such food.

Does research on animal cloning waste resources? Cloned animals may save endangered species, increase the efficiency of livestock farming, and provide compatible organs for transplant to humans. Scientifically, understanding how genes, proteins, and nuclei reprogram cells during cloning at the early stages of life may yield important insights for curing diseases. Working with cloned embryos and tissue excites most cell biologists because of its great potential.

One interesting objection is that progress on such nonhuman mammalian cloning should stop, because, if successful, it will eventually lead us to safe human cloning. After all, a mammal is a mammal is a mammal.

Some critics assume that human cloning is intrinsically wrong and argue that anything leading to something intrinsically wrong is also wrong. But safe human cloning need not be intrinsically wrong and such a crucial assumption needs specific and convincing arguments.

Nevertheless, trying to originate human babies by cloning might be wrong for some other reason, and indeed, at the present time, scientific evidence indicates that neither human nor nonhuman primates can be safely and normally produced by cloning. Any scientist who could clone a monkey, gorilla, or baboon would achieve quite a feat, and many have tried. But errors in reprogramming the genetic material in the early embryo cause abnormalities that appear at birth or later.

It is likely that future research will discover a way around this problem. Remember that textbooks of mammalian physiology once claimed it to be a "law of nature" that cells could not be returned to an undifferentiated, primordial state once that had become differentiated as skin, kidney, or other specialized cells. Yet that is exactly what Ian Wilmut did in cloning Dolly. So it is likely that one day this problem will be solved.

Originating the First Cloned Baby

In the meantime, bioethics must wrestle with the issue of when human trials of reproductive cloning would be ethical. Although some consider it speciesist, a minimal condition for ethical medical experimentation is to first test a drug or procedure on nonhuman animals. In this way, heart transplants and drugs such as cyclosporin (which prevents transplanted hearts from being rejected by the immune system) were first studied in animals.

So not only would scientists need to originate some nonhuman primates by cloning, they would also need to prove the primate-babies normal and show that they could reliably, repeatedly, and safely clone these babies this way. Once that had been achieved, it would be permissible to try to originate a human baby.

The first attempt would certainly be an experiment. Because humans differ from their nonhuman primate cousins, something unforeseen could go wrong in this experiment. If physicians discovered a problem in the first or second trimester of development, the abnormal fetus could be aborted; however, the abnormality might not be discovered until birth or adolescence. Some abnormalities might not show up until mid-life. How then could such an experiment be ethical?

Two extreme views here should be noted. One holds that such experimentation could never be justified because scientists could never guarantee a perfectly normal baby. The other holds that such experimentation is justified because any child created this way would otherwise not exist at all; so provided that she has a life worth living – as she almost certainly would – how can the child complain?

If scientists followed the first view, nothing new in pediatric surgery, drugs, or care could be tried, because the same objection holds for these innovations. The morally important fact is that when researchers intend to help infants, and have good reason based on scientific theory and trials involving nonhuman animals to believe that new methods are likely to prove beneficial, trying new techniques (such as neonatal intensive care units or extracorporeal membrane oxygenation) is justified. Motives matter, too, in explaining why the second view must be rejected, because even though life with a severe defect may be better than no life at all, ethics requires that prospective parents and scientists have good motives, that they *want* to create normal babies. We cannot justify an island of Dr Moreau with abnormal children and chimeras on the grounds that, without our experiments, none of them would have existed.

Preliminary Psychological-Social Objections to Cloning

The previous sections discussed the scientific possibility of producing normal children by techniques of cloning. Some people grant that children produced this way might be genetically normal, but still claim their creation would be immoral. Such objections can be grouped into five kinds: (1) harm to the human race, (2) harm to society, (3) harm to the family, (4) evil motives of parents, and (5) psychological harm to the child. In discussions of human cloning, such as those by arch-critic Leon Kass, these objections to cloning are the most popular (President's Council on Bioethics 2002).

Harm to the human race?

The first objection fears a reduction in the diversity of the human gene pool from cloning humans. When unmasked, this objection assumes that cloned children would be produced like cookies on an assembly line, all the same.

The view is false because parents would choose many different ancestors for future children, often members of their own family. Even if everyone chose the same genotype and millions of children came from that genotype, such a change would have very little impact on the human gene pool. In 2007, more than six billion humans existed on the planet and they replace themselves every 35 years. In such vast numbers, a law of population genetics called "regression to the mean" applies. With such vast numbers of humans replacing themselves every generation, a few million cloned humans, even if quite different from the average human, would be quickly normalized over a few generations in the crush of the huge numbers, and would have precious little effect on the overall reproductive, genetic material of humanity.

Harm to society?

Some critics argue that human cloning would hurt society by exacerbating existing inequalities. How could that be? Well, assume that human cloning can be safely done. Then it could be used as a tool by the rich to create babies with superior health, intelligence, beauty, and longevity.

Now some existing inequality is wrong because it is the result of some babies getting a million-dollar trust fund at birth while other, poor babies ingest lead paint that reduces their intelligence. Already, *environmental* differences worsen hereditary inequalities, but do we want to worsen that by creating, on top of these existing inequalities, new *biological* inequalities?

And take this argument even further down the road. What if the children of cloned children also used cloning, choosing the same elite qualities and fine-tuning them? It wouldn't take too many generations to create a kind of Extraordinary Human with many advanced qualities. But would that further a just society? Such cloned, biological dynasties within families could create greater inequality across a society.

Yet with procreation, advanced societies generally leave couples broad liberty to pursue children as they want, allowing them to decide whether to have children, the number of children they want, and the risks they will take in trying to conceive them. It would take a clear and present danger to justify forbidding cloning to head off greater inequality.

Of course, procreative liberty is subject to some constraints, as parents cannot abuse their children, deprive them of education, or work them as slaves. Moreover, society discourages, but does not outlaw, women from taking risks during pregnancy, such as smoking tobacco and drinking alcohol.

The permissibility of parents taking some risks in conceiving children is important because, at some time in the future, cloning of most mammals and human-related primates, such as gorillas and chimpanzees, will probably become safe. Although not all scientists agree that cloning will ever become safe, assume for the moment that they all do and that nonhuman animal cloning has become as safe as *in vitro* fertilization. At that time, the liberty of parents to take small risks in creating children by cloning will become important.

Harm to the family?

Harm to the family is usually conceived by critics in cases where the parents clone a younger version of one of the parents and entails the worry, say, that the father will be attracted to the younger female version of his wife. This criticism overlooks the fact that many daughters already look like younger versions of their mothers and their fathers do not commit incest, and it then wrongly assumes there will be some especially strong attraction from cloning. But there is no evidence to suggest that girls who look like their mothers are now more likely to be victims of incest.

Badly motivated parents?

Critics of cloning almost always envision parents as selfish narcissists who would originate copies of themselves by cloning. This criticism assumes that people who deliberately create their children through sex aren't doing it for selfish reasons, such as having someone around in their old age to take care of them, or to see something of themselves (half their genes) continue into the future.

There is no reason to think that parents who might use cloning to originate a child would be more self-interested than ordinary parents. This is an empirical question. Some parents might use cloning to give a child the best possible genetic heritage and not assume that such a heritage would come from one of them.

Psychological damage to cloned children?

Critics of cloning sometimes claim that children created by cloning would be psycho-logically damaged. These arguments divide into two kinds: psychological trauma due to the prejudiced reactions of others, and psychological trauma due to unrealistic parental expectations.

199

The first argument can be dismissed because we do not want to count prejudice as a reason in ethics. The same reasoning wrongly justifies bans on interracial marriage. The parents will see their child as the object of prejudice by society; the child will see herself similarly, as will her friends, relatives, and hostile racists. Ergo, ban interracial marriage.

This argument reifies ignorance as reason, prejudice as justification. Just because some people react badly to something doesn't mean we should make their reactions the foundation of public policy.

Another objection of this kind is called *the argument for an open future*. This argument assumes that parents who are creating a child to replicate the characteristics of a particular person's genome will have specific expectations about this child which may harm him. Such expectations close the future of this child, unlike other human children who have an "open" future.

This objection assumes the Kantian idea that a child should be valued in itself, and hence have an open future. Children should not be created to satisfy a parent's desires or for a child's expected characteristics.

This objection mounts false ideals about creating children. When people had no control over whether to have children or over their traits, it made sense to value whatever child came along. Now that parents have choices, that ideal should be rethought.

Consider the following: Some might object to giving parents *any* choices about children's characteristics, either because they believe such choice is (a) intrinsically wrong or (b) indirectly wrong, because it will lead to bad things.

People who believe (a) often believe that God, nature, or evolution determines who is born and with what characteristics. So for humans to make such choices thwarts God's will or evolutionary biology.

People who make objections like this often confuse: (1) society or government pushing a program about desirable characteristics in children, and (2) parents making choices about such characteristics. The first, eugenics, is often associated with dictators taking away reproductive choice; the second expands reproductive liberty. Fears about the first do not support curtailing choice in the latter. Indeed, a strong right to reproduce as one chooses checks reproductive coercion.

People don't really believe that shaping characteristics of children is wrong. Based on their beliefs about what characteristics they desire in their children as adults, they send their children to one school rather than another. Some people test embryos and fetuses to avoid severe genetic disease and abort those testing positive. Mothers often avoid cigarettes and alcohol during pregnancy to help their fetuses and the children who may develop from them.

Arguments against such choices often stem from reproductive fatalism. Such fatalism also applies to pregnancy, and it is not surprising that those who oppose genetic choice usually oppose abortion and contraception. The Vatican is consistent.

From the Vatican's perspective, there is only one correct worldview, namely that humans should regard everything that happens biologically as God's will and attempt to change nothing. Each pregnancy is as it should be, and God has a sufficient reason for it. To oppose His will is sinful pride.

On the other hand, once we let people choose to take contraception and to abort because they don't want to be pregnant, it is hard to justify not letting them abort because a fetus has a genetic disease, because it will be deaf, or because it will be extremely short. Once we allow for abortion to avoid achondroplasia (a genetic condition causing short height, legs, and arms) or deafness, it is hard not to allow medical treatments at birth designed to overcome achondroplasia, such as dosages of human growth hormone. Implicit in these decisions is the judgment that being short is undesirable, being normal or tall is good. Once those judgments are made, and it becomes possible to choose children who are taller, it becomes difficult to say why it is wrong to allow parents to make these kinds of choices.

Here it will be objected that some parents will put too much weight on one characteristic, such as intelligence or the current ideal of female beauty, and then be very disappointed when the child does not measure up.

Such an expectation will often be false. Consider the infamous Baby M case of commercial surrogacy, where the Sterns chose the surrogate mother, Mary Beth Whitehead, only because she had a physique that looked like Mrs Stern. In so choosing, they disregarded Mrs Whitehead's quirky personality. Similarly, couples seeking embryos or eggs for implantation in older infertile women in American often choose on the basis of the looks of egg donors. That, of course, is a simple-minded, dangerous way to choose.

Moreover, it will often be a particular *combination* of traits that is desirable, not just a trait such as physique or skill in solving mathematical puzzles. Such a combination will very likely be the result of *both* the child's environment and his genetic endowment.

More and more, genetics teaches us that everything is complex. Because hundreds of variations exist, no simple genetic test for breast cancer exists. And if breast cancer can't be easily predicted, how much more difficult will it be to predict traits such as wit or dexterity? Many qualities of the phenotype will be multifactorial at the genomic level and multifactorial at the level of gene–environment interaction, such that how any quality gets created in a phenotype will be difficult to predict. Originating children by cloning will not in itself deprive them of an open future.

Education and experience will teach people these truths. Well-publicized cases of silly parental expectations will teach millions of people the basic lessons of Genetics 101, although it may take time for such truths to reach everyone.

Moreover, with parental expectations, it is hypocritical to pick on cloning. During the past decades, American couples adopted thousands of abandoned Chinese babies, some identified in their adoption papers by the milepost number they were found near. These couples say they feel good about adopting such babies. Many expect the adopted child as an adult to be grateful to them for being adopted. After all, without the adoption, the child likely would have died.

For Kantians, these expectations do not serve the adopted child's best interests. No parent should expect her children to see her as a saint. Nevertheless, few people criticize these parents for such expectations and no one is suggesting that, because of such expectations, adoption of such babies should be made illegal. Why, then, do people want to make human cloning illegal based on expectations associated with it?

To conclude, to the extent that the argument from parental expectations is based on false beliefs, it can be countered first by saying that we should not make public policy based on false beliefs, and, secondly, that education can counter these false beliefs and change false expectations. Even then, some psychological damage from expectations may occur, but if so, it is likely to be no greater than any other failed kind of expectation of parents about sexually created children.

Louise Brown, the first baby originated by *in vitro* fertilization, was born in 1978. Thirty years of experience with assisted reproduction counsels us to ignore alarmists who predict monstrous babies and the destruction of society, and that parents using new techniques aren't particularly selfish or narcissistic; many merely want a baby of their own. New techniques, such as *in vitro* fertilization, have created more than a million desperately wanted babies, with few problems. If and when it is proven medically safe, reproduction of humans by cloning will likely do the same.

Moral Objections Against Human Embryonic Cloning

Although most people associate cloning with the creation of live births, another kind of cloning exists: the creation of cloned lines of cells. The similarity of techniques, sharing of the same word "cloning," and the use of human embryos have made controversial the creation of cell lines by cloning from the same embryos. Religious opponents of cloning, who espouse the conceptionist view that personhood begins at human conception, link embryonic and reproductive cloning together and oppose both. Liberal thinkers may oppose reproductive cloning but allow embryonic cloning.

Although the two are distinct – one produces batches of small-celled embryos the size of the tip of a fine-point pen and one produces human babies – the two are linked in the way the human matter is initially created and in the genetic similarity of ancestor and progeny.

People who think that one kind of cloning is intrinsically wrong tend to think the other kind of cloning is also intrinsically wrong. As Senator Mary Landrieu (Republican, Louisiana) once said: "Cloning is cloning. That is why it should all be illegal" (CNN News 2003).

The above objections are conceptual, but there is also an empirical objection about the two kinds of cloning and their relations. Some critics object that, once a human embryo has been created by cloning, no one can guarantee what will be done with it. For example, if fertility clinics created such human embryos, perhaps one might end up being gestated inside a woman's uterus and, nine months later, be born as a child. If there are genuine moral reasons why such a birth at present might be harmful to a child conceived that way, then such an empirical objection might carry moral weight.

So what about the above objections? Are they overwhelming? Not at all. In a phrase, embryos aren't babies, and, more exactly, embryonic tissue in a cell line isn't a nursery full of human babies. Part of the pull of the conceptual objections is to think of these two as the same and, indeed, critics of cloning use language that reflects such thinking, speaking of the "embryo-baby."

But when someone collects 1,000 acorns outside a house and throws them away, this isn't the same as cutting down 1,000 mature oak trees. In real life, we make distinctions like this all the time, and we can do the same about embryos and babies in public policy (see chapter 14, "Abortion"). In short, we can allow embryonic cloning without immediately accepting reproductive cloning.

Conclusions

Discussion of human cloning to date shows the immaturity of ethical debate in much of the world about human reproduction. In particular, it shows the influence of sensationalistic movies, charlatans, and scientists who made fraudulent claims. If and when proved safe, human cloning may become something that could be done humanely and without the sky falling.

References

CNN News (2003). April 14.

Kolata, G. (2005). Koreans report ease in cloning for stem cells. *New York Times*, May 20: A1.

Newsweek (2007). July 9: 29.

President's Council on Bioethics (2002). *Human Cloning and Human Dignity: An Ethical Inquiry.* Washington, DC.

Part VI

The New Genetics

19

Gene Therapy

RUTH CHADWICK

Gene therapy has been defined by multiple organizations: the definition used here is that of the Human Genome Organization (HUGO) Ethics Committee (2001) as the correction or prevention of disease through the addition and expression of genetic material that reconstitutes or corrects missing or aberrant genetic functions or interferes with disease-causing processes. In a case of transfer of new genetic material into a human being, the challenges are, first, to introduce the material, using some vector such as a virus; second, to target the relevant part of the body; and, third, to succeed in producing a situation where the new material functions as it should. In the early days of discussion of gene therapy, what was envisaged was treating single gene disorders, where one gene underlies a condition, such as Huntington's disease, but there has also been considerable interest in gene therapy for multifactorial conditions, such as breast cancer. In these, a number of genes may be involved, but they are also likely to involve environmental triggers. Genes may predispose, but not predetermine, a person to develop a multifactorial condition in certain contexts. In such cases, alterations in lifestyle may be a better option than gene therapy. In the case of genetic disorders themselves, however, gene therapy offers the only hope of cure, as opposed to the alleviation of symptoms.

In the debates about gene therapy, two key distinctions have been prominent. The first of these is the distinction between somatic and germline gene therapy, and the second is the distinction between therapy and enhancement. Somatic therapy is contrasted with germline gene therapy on the basis that, while the former is directed only at the somatic cells, that is, body cells of an individual, germline therapy also targets the reproductive cells, thereby having an impact on that individual's children and ultimately on the gene pool of the species. The difference between them, however, is not entirely clear-cut. It is conceivable that cells introduced into the body in the course of somatic therapy (e.g., via a virus used to transport cells in the body) could recombine with other viruses and infect the germ cells. Further, somatic therapy, like conventional treatment of genetic disease, which may alleviate symptoms but not act at the genetic level, leads to a greater concentration of the mutant gene in the gene pool, through allowing patients who would otherwise die to survive and reproduce. Thus, while germline therapy is conceived of as changing the gene pool directly, somatic therapy could have an indirect effect. In principle, however, the consequences of germline therapy have the potential for greater control over, and impact on, the gene pool than somatic therapy.

The distinction between therapy and enhancement is also far from clear. Broadly speaking, while "therapy" refers to the treatment of disease, the term "enhancement" is used to denote the employment of therapeutic *techniques* for purposes that go beyond therapy and introduce improvement in some respect. There are difficulties, however, in explaining enhancement as "beyond therapy" (President's Council on Bioethics 2003); in principle, interventions which are intended to be therapeutic may also enhance and vice versa. Nevertheless, although both distinctions give rise to some conceptual challenges, they are both appealed to in the ethical debate.

Promise and Disappointment

The early promises of gene therapy led to disappointment, and even concern, after low success rates and setbacks, including the death of Jesse Gelsinger in a gene therapy trial in 1998. The trial concerned treatment for a condition caused by genetic deficiency of a liver enzyme. The treatment caused ammonia levels to build up in the blood with severe consequences. Gelsinger, a young man of 18 who was in tolerable health before commencing the experimental treatment, collapsed and died within 24 hours (Kelly 2007). The tragedy led to renewed debate about the ethics and regulation of gene therapy, and concerns about conflicts of interest in research (e.g., HUGO Ethics Committee 2001).

The development of other avenues of biomedical research has also challenged gene therapy's status, as traditionally understood, as the therapy of the future. RNA interference, which is a mechanism for stopping the expression of (malfunctioning) genes, stem cell research, and nanomedicine are among the new developments attracting attention, although aspects of some new technologies may themselves in fact provide more efficient delivery systems for gene therapy. The promises of gene therapy as originally conceived, have, however, continued to be discussed and researched, and in April 2008 there were reports of successful gene therapy trials for a rare form of blindness (Smith 2008).

Ethical Issues

In discussing the ethics of gene therapy, in addition to the two distinctions mentioned above (somatic versus germline and therapy versus enhancement), there are issues concerning the relationship between gene therapy and personal identity, and between individual choice and public health.

Somatic versus germline

The argument in favor of somatic gene therapy goes like this: genetic disorders cause suffering; treatment other than gene therapy can at most alleviate symptoms; somatic gene therapy offers the prospect of a cure. It is held to be analogous to other forms of medicine and thus not controversial – like an organ transplant, it is introducing functioning material into patients who lack it (cf. Davis 1990). Such a view regards somatic therapy as raising no new issues of principle and as subject to the same ethical constraints as other forms of medical intervention, such as informed consent and confidentiality.

The idea that somatic therapy should be regarded just as another form of medical treatment was considered premature, however, by the Clothier Committee set up in the United Kingdom in the early 1990s to examine the ethics of gene therapy. While accepting that somatic therapy was in principle a proper goal for medical science, the Committee took the view that it should, initially at least, be regarded as research involving human subjects, and thus subject to the regulatory requirements governing such research. They set out two principles guiding their deliberations: (1) the obligation inherent in human nature to inquire, to study, to pursue and apply research by ethical means; and (2) in the sometimes inescapable tensions between the pursuit of knowledge and the protection of patients' interests, the latter must prevail (Clothier 1992: paras 3.4, 3.6).

The course of events since that time, including the concerns about safety and conflict of interest in gene therapy trials mentioned above, may seem to support this cautious approach, but nevertheless the Committee was criticized for having an uncritical attitude toward scientific progress (Consumers for Ethics in Research 1992).

It might be thought that the arguments about potential medical benefit could be extended without too much difficulty from somatic to germline therapy. In this way, not only an existing patient but his or her descendants could benefit as well. Along with the welfare of future people argument, there are considerations of reproductive autonomy. Suppose that it becomes possible to offer gene therapy for Huntington's disease, and that somatic therapy is offered to a woman who has been found to carry the offending gene, prior to her developing symptoms of the disease. She says, however: "No, I want to make sure that my children do not have to face his: I want germline therapy on my embryos as well."

Despite some support for germline therapy at an early stage (e.g., Friedmann 1989), these arguments for it have not been widely accepted. Germline therapy is considered to raise new issues of principle, primarily *because* it will affect future generations who have not consented to it. However, if it is regarded as permissible to take decisions regarding medical treatment on behalf of children who are too young to consent for themselves, why not for future descendants? The diet provided for children may also have effects on their future reproductive capacities and thereby the children they may have.

Making decisions about what *kind* of children to have nevertheless remains controversial. Despite the advent of phenomena such as "savior siblings," where tissue typing is combined with preimplantation diagnosis to select an embryo with a view to a future transplant to help an existing child, disagreement persists as to whether we should understand reproductive autonomy to include freedom to make decisions not only about whether or not to reproduce but also about the qualities of the children in question. In particular, if people are free to choose against a disorder, should they also be allowed to choose to have children who *do* suffer from a genetic disorder, for example when deaf parents want a deaf child? This example leads some people to argue that reproductive autonomy has limits which are set by considerations relating to the interests of future children, while others accept this case as an extension of reproductive choice, and suggest that it can indeed be in someone's interests to be deaf, in some circumstances, such as where a child is born into a deaf community.

If, however, what *is* wanted is the absence of children with genetic disorders, it is not clear that germline therapy is the method of choice. The development of techniques of preimplantation diagnosis and embryo selection means that, in principle at least, most couples can produce what the British geneticist Marcus Pembrey (1992) called a "winning combination" of genes, without engaging in germline therapy. However, in the case of mitochondrial disease (where this is caused by a problem in the mitochondrial DNA rather than being due to any other cause), this would not be the case. Unlike the DNA in the nucleus, which divides and recombines with that of the other parent, mitochondrial DNA exists outside the nucleus and is passed on to all a woman's children; thus any disorder there is passed on (Lane 2005). A way of avoiding this is cell nuclear replacement, in which the nucleus is removed from the woman's egg and transferred to a donor egg from which the nucleus has been removed. The resulting genetic change (namely, the new mitochondria) would be passed on not only to the woman's children but also to the children of any daughters she might have. In effect, then, this is a case of germline therapy.

The ways in which this technique has been described, however, are significant. Opponents have been less worried about the fact that it represents a form of germline therapy than that it can be described as producing children with three parents: one father and two mothers, one of whom contributes the nucleus while the other supplies the egg with mitochondrial DNA (Lane 2008). On the other side of the debate there have been attempts to play down the role of the mitochondrial DNA, likening its input to that of a battery in a radio. However, there are also concerns about the safety of this technique, given the possibility that some of the mutant mitochondria might be transferred along with the nucleus, and cause disease generations later (Lane 2008). In the absence of this technique, for people considering reproduction in the face of worries about transmitting mitochondrial disease, the options are either avoiding reproduction altogether, or taking the risk of serious disorders in their offspring.

Therapy and enhancement

As in the case of somatic and germline therapy, the therapy/enhancement distinction has been used as an attempt to establish a moral as well as a conceptual boundary. Such boundaries may provide reassurance for those who are concerned about a slippery slope toward what they see as an unacceptable degree of genetic interference and control. There has been coverage in popular media of "designer babies" – of couples enhancing their children to suit their whims and high expectations. This is regarded as an undesirable outcome by some. For Habermas, being the result of someone else's design, an artifact, fundamentally alters one's status and self-understanding as a human being (Habermas 2003). The resulting person will regard him- or herself as, at least in part, someone else's project.

Other critics also take the view that in engaging in enhancement we might be losing something that is essentially human (cf. Fukuyama 2002). Ronald Dworkin, in *Life's Dominion* (1993), examined the question of what is sacred. He argued that the notion of human life having intrinsic value is widespread, but that there are different interpretations of what this means. One element in it is the value accorded to the outcome of evolutionary processes. He holds, therefore, that the value of a plant species that is the result of evolution is of a different kind from that of a genetically engineered plant species. If this is the case, it might explain the value accorded to the unengineered species as opposed to one that is the result of germline therapy.

However, enhancement is also increasingly attracting support, in cases where, for example, it can facilitate longer life (cf. Harris 2007), or enhance capacities for sport (Miah 2004), and indeed some have argued that it is inevitable (Baylis and Robert 2004).

Gene therapy and personal identity

The issues of identity which gene therapy, in particular germline therapy, are said to raise, have also received some attention. The implications of germline therapy for personal identity questions might be raised by either a proponent or an opponent of the technology.

In what sense might identity be at stake in thinking about germline therapy and future generations? As Ronald Dworkin has argued, in thinking about our responsibility to future generations we are normally considering "descendants whose identity is in no way fixed, but depends on what we must consider billions of accidents of genetic coupling" (1993: 77). Although we can affect, by actions taken now, who these people will be, we are not, it seems, changing the identity of specific individuals.

However, in the case of gene therapy there might be a case for thinking there are personal identity issues. While there has been much discussion in bioethics of the "non-identity problem" – where a reproduction related decision affects the identity of the child produced (Parfit 1984), what is at issue here is precisely whether a genetic change *does* constitute an identity change. It might be argued that to suggest that it does, presupposes a kind of genetic determinism and reductionism which has been undermined by the results of the Human Genome Project, which showed that there are far fewer genes in the human genome than had been predicted, leading to claims that genetic determinism had been proved false, on the grounds that the complexity of human beings could not be explained by a relatively small number (about 25,000) of genes alone: at the very least there must be other factors at work. It is difficult to see, however, why the truth or falsity of genetic determinism should be dependent upon the *number* of genes: even had there been 100,000, as originally predicted, the arguments against genetic determinism, e.g. the importance of environmental factors, need to be answered.

Even if genetic determinism were true, however, it would not settle the question whether the person who is produced as a result of germline therapy is the *same* person as the one who would have existed without the intervention. In the event that my identity resides in my genes, it might still be possible to undergo some degree of genetic change while yet remaining the same person. And there is a further question whether, or not, there is something here to be concerned about – could a future person have a legitimate grievance about having been subject to germline therapy – not on Habermasian grounds, but on the grounds that their identity had been changed?

The answer at least partly depends on when a person's life story begins. Bernard Williams, for example, put forward a zygotic principle (ZP) which holds: "A possibility in which a given human being, A, features is one that preserves the identity of the zygote from which A developed" (1990: 169). John Harris (1992), however, has argued against ZP that a person's life story begins at the gamete stage, so that a future person might have cause to express a grievance on the grounds of interventions that did or did not take place at the gamete stage. Whenever a person's life story begins, however, Zohar (1991) and Elliott (1993) assume that it is likely that some genetic alterations are identity-preserving, while others are not.

Williams (1990) has suggested that there are only two grievances that could legitimately be expressed by a future person: "I should have had a nicer time" and "It would have been better if I had never existed." There are other possibilities, however, as follows:

- I should not have had my genome altered;
- I should have been someone else;
- I should have been free of this genetic disorder;
- I should have been given genetic immunization;
- I should not have been brought into existence.

I should not have had my genome altered

The way in which this grievance is expressed, namely "I should not have had my genome altered," presupposes that identity has been preserved. In that case the source of any grievance must lie elsewhere than in an identity issue.

I should have been someone else

Unlike the first, this grievance presupposes either that an identity-changing intervention has taken place and should not have, or that an identity-changing intervention has not taken place and should have. This (as Williams says) is incoherent, because *I* could not have been someone else; what might have been the case is that I did not exist and someone else did.

I should have been free of this genetic disorder

This appears to be a coherent grievance that a future person was not given (available) treatment to relieve him or her from genetic disorder. It presupposes the possibility of sameness of person but absence of pathology.

I should have been given genetic immunization

It might be possible to produce people who have been genetically immunized against certain diseases, for example, those that might have been triggered by environmental pollutants. If it were possible to offer such genetic protection, but it was not offered in fact, the future person could coherently express a grievance, "I should have been genetically immunized." Like the previous grievance, it presupposes identity. It also, however, raises the issue of therapy versus enhancement.

I should not have been brought into existence

This is either a wrongful life claim, that a person has been harmed by being brought into life, or an impersonal claim (impersonal insofar as it is not a claim about how any persons are affected for better or worse) that it would have been better, overall, if I had not existed. It might be expressed by a person who results from an identity-changing intervention (for example, where the intervention is unsuccessful in terms of therapeutic effect). He or she might take the view that it would have been better if the original person had come into existence but that is not a claim that *his* or *her* identity has changed and that this is the source of the harm. In such a case the harm would be the effect of the change rather than the identity change itself.

On the basis of the discussion above, it seems that there is no coherent grievance that a future person can make on the grounds of having been subjected to an identity-changing intervention.

There are various possible objections to this analysis. It might be argued that whether or not it is possible for a coherent grievance to be expressed by a future person, an identity change is wrong in itself; perhaps on the grounds that there is a right not to have an identity-changing intervention or even that the situation could be described as the killing of the original person. Another potential objection is that what is important is a person's perception of their identity rather than identity per se (Chadwick 2000). Gene therapy may be opposed on the grounds that a person or group identifies with particular characteristics which they take to be genetic. We see this, for example, in arguments put forward by disability rights organizations in opposition to attempts to "cure" conditions which they do not regard as disorders. There are at least two separate strands to be disentangled here. The first is the concern that attempts to eliminate or cure genetic conditions will lead to a society less tolerant of disability. This is typically countered by an argument that what is the object of these attempts is not the *people* but the *conditions*. At this point a second strand of argument may come into play, which is that it is not possible to distinguish these two elements, because people's identity is dependent upon their genetic condition.

This discussion shows the importance of the social context in which the debate takes place – for example, whether the environment is one friendly to disability or not. The Clothier Committee, in supporting (somatic) gene therapy, was criticized for ignoring the importance of social context, such as attitudes toward disability and the link with reductionist social policies. The latter are envisaged as dangerous insofar as they have a tendency to reduce human problems to genetic causes. Where the search for genetic causes is given priority, there is the possibility that energies will be directed toward finding genetic solutions in preference to exploring what social policies can be helpful. This is regarded as undesirable both in general, insofar as opportunities to improve quality of life are overlooked and not considered, where they could make a difference in a cost-effective way, and specifically insofar as disability is regarded as at least in part socially constructed.

Private and public

Discussion of social context leads to considerations of issues of public concern, rather than the reproductive choices and personal identity concerns of individuals. Relevant issues include public health and eugenics, resource allocation and equity, and issues of collective identity. In particular, it might be argued that germ therapy, unlike somatic therapy, is a public matter, insofar as it has the greater potential to affect the gene pool.

The claim that an intervention would amount to eugenics is sometimes voiced as if it is thought to be a knock-down argument against that intervention. This cannot be assumed: what exactly is found objectionable? One aspect is the implication that some lives are more valuable than others. The attempt to reduce the incidence of genetic disorders in the population is sometimes criticized on the grounds that it embodies inappropriate attitudes toward people currently alive who suffer from those disorders. Another is that eugenics represents interference, whether openly or subtly, with personal freedoms in the area of reproduction.

Historical examples of the abuse of genetics lend credence to a view that gene therapy, especially germline therapy, could become a tool in the hands of a government with eugenic ambitions. One possible response to this is to point to the importance of controlling the use of the technology rather than avoiding it altogether, placing an emphasis on leaving decisions as much as possible to individuals to choose therapy for themselves and their descendants, rather than to government control. For some critics, however, the argument that we should concentrate on the control of abuses is naive, either because the possible harms are so great that, for example, the genetic basis of characteristics such as intelligence should not even be the subject of research (Shickle 1997), or because individual choices can be subtly influenced in certain directions, and the cumulative effect of individual choices is what is significant (Duster 2003).

Resource Allocation

Even in the (relatively uncontroversial) use of gene therapy to cure disease, there is a problem about resource allocation, related to the selection of candidates for treatment. What is envisaged and feared by some, however, is the reinforcement of differences between the wealthy and the poor, by enabling the wealthy to acquire better genes. This would be the case both within developed societies and between developed and developing countries (Holm 1994). Much depends here, of course, on what is considered to be a good, or enhancing, genetic factor and the extent to which genes, as opposed to environment, are influential in determining an individual's life chances.

Again, the outcome of the Human Genome Project and research in the post-genome era is casting these debates in a new light. Research on the extent of human variation, and the complicated nature of the interaction between genetic and environmental factors, have arguably undermined to some extent the symbolic importance of the "gene." Nevertheless, the search for gene-based therapies continues.

References

Baylis, F. and Robert, J. S. (2004). The inevitability of genetic enhancement technologies. *Bioethics* 18: 1–26.

Chadwick, R. (2000). Gene therapy and personal identity. In G. K. Becker (ed.), *The Moral Status of Persons: Perspectives on Bioethics*. Atlanta, GA: Rodopi, pp. 183–94.

Clothier, C. (1992). *Report on the Ethics of Gene Therapy.* London: HMSO.

Consumers for Ethics in Research (1992). Consumer response to Clothier. *Bulletin of Medical Ethics* 79: 13–14.

Davis, B. D. (1990). Limits to genetic intervention in humans: somatic and germline. In D. Chadwick et al. (eds.), *Human Genetic Information: Science, Law and Ethics.* Chichester: John Wiley.

Duster, T. (2003). *Backdoor to Eugenics.* London: Routledge.

Dworkin, R. (1993). *Life's Dominion: An Argument About Abortion and Euthanasia.* London: HarperCollins.

Elliott, R. (1993). Identity and the ethics of gene therapy. *Bioethics* 7: 27–40.

Friedmann, T. (1989). Progress toward human gene therapy. *Science* 244: 1275–81.

Fukuyama, F. (2002). *Our Posthuman Future: Consequences of the Biotechnology Revolution.* New York: Farrar, Straus, and Giroux.

Habermas, J. (2003). *The Future of Human Nature.* London: Polity.

Harris, J. (1992). *Wonderwoman and Superman: The Ethics of Human Biotechnology.* Oxford: Oxford University Press.

Harris, J. (2007). *Enhancing Evolution: The Ethical Case for Making Better People.* Princeton, NJ: Princeton University Press.

Holm, S. (1994). Genetic engineering and the North–South divide. In A. Dyson and J. Harris (eds.), *Ethics and Biotechnology.* London: Routledge.

HUGO Ethics Committee (2001). *Statement on Gene Therapy Research.* London: Human Genome Organization.

Kelly, E. B. (2007). *Gene Therapy.* Westport, CT: Greenwood Press.

Lane, N. (2005). *Power, Sex, Suicide: Mitochondria and the Meaning of Life.* Oxford: Oxford University Press.

Lane, N. (2008). One baby, two mums. *New Scientist* 198/2659: 38–41.

Miah, A. (2004). *Genetically Modified Athletes: Biomedical ethics, Gene Doping and Sport.* London: Routledge.

Parfit, D. (1984). *Reasons and Persons.* Oxford: Oxford University Press.

Pembrey, M. (1992). Embryo therapy: is there a clinical need? In D. Bromham et al. (eds.), *Ethics in Reproductive Medicine.* London: Springer-Verlag.

President's Council on Bioethics (2003). *Beyond Therapy: A Report by the President's Council on Bioethics.* Washington, DC: President's Council on Bioethics.

Shickle, D. (1997). Do all men desire to know? A right of society to choose not to know about the genetics of personality traits. In R. Chadwick et al. (eds.), *The Right to Know and the Right Not to Know.* Aldershot: Avebury.

Smith, K. (2008). Gene therapy treats blindness. *Naturenews.* Published online at www.nature.com/news (accessed April 28, 2008).

Williams, B. (1990). Who might I have been? In D. Chadwick et al. (eds.), *Human Genetic Information: Science, Law and Ethics.* Chichester: John Wiley, pp. 167–73.

Zohar, N. J. (1991). Prospects for genetic therapy – can a person benefit from being altered? *Bioethics* 5/4: 275–88.

20

Genetic Enhancement

JULIAN SAVULESCU

In the first part of this chapter, I examine the possibility, extent and significance of genetic enhancement. In the second part, I examine whether we should genetically enhance human beings.

Possibility, Extent and Significance of Genetic Enhancement

Possibility

Scientists at Case Western Reserve University in Cleveland, Ohio, have created a genetically engineered mouse, nicknamed Supermouse, which can run for up to six hours at a speed of 20 meters per minute before needing a rest. These special "athletic" abilities are due to the way the mice metabolize glucose in the blood. The new mouse has been genetically engineered to cause a glucose-metabolizing gene – PEPCK-C – to be over-expressed in the skeletal muscle, allowing it to avoid the muscle-cramping effects of build-up of lactic acid which normal mice, and humans, experience during prolonged exercise (Connor 2007; Hakimi et al. 2007; Sample 2007).

Although the new mice ate 60 percent more than their non-enhanced counterparts, they were fitter and leaner than normal mice and had the ability to give birth at up to 3 years old – the equivalent in human terms of an 80-year-old woman giving birth. The Supermouse had the following improvements:

- more active: 7 times more cage activity than normal mice;
- greater endurance: ran 6 kilometers on a treadmill (normal mouse: 0.2 kilometers);
- improved metabolism: ate 60 percent more but had half the body weight and only 10 percent of the body fat of a normal mouse;
- extended lifespan: "survived longer and looked healthier;"
- extended youthfulness: mice of 30 months still twice as fast as 6-month-old normal mice and reproductively active at 21 months (and up to 30 months);
- healthier: lower cholesterol levels.

This research is not unique. Anders Sandberg at the Oxford Uehiro Centre for Practical Ethics recently overviewed genetic enhancement and produced a Top 10 ranking, as shown in table 1.

Table 1: Top-10 genetic enhancements

The Doogie mouse	Better memory through overexpression of the receptor subunit NR2B.
Color vision mice	Adding human photopigment allows (at least females) to see new colors.
Methuselah Mice	By reducing growth hormone levels, long-lived dwarf mice can be produced. The current record-holder survived 4 years, 11 months and 3 weeks, while normal mice have a two-year lifespan.
Monogamous voles	Normally, polygamous voles can be turned monogamous (and made more social) by changing the vassopressin V1a receptor.
Regenerating MRL mice	These mice regenerate tissue after having holes punched in their ears as well as after sustaining some injuries to heart muscle. (Accidental breeding rather than genetic engineering.)
Schwarzenegger mice and Belgian blue cows	Increased muscle mass through myostatin knockout. Occurs naturally in some cows and humans.
Hard-working monkeys	Monkeys tend to slack off until they get close to a reward they have to work for. If injected with a DNA construct that blocks the D2 receptor, they work at an even rate. This is likely less a case of workaholism and more a case of specific memory impairment for how rewarding situations look. Still, adjusting the dopamine system is likely to enable boosts of motivation.
Anticancer mice	These mice (the result of a lucky mutation) have immune systems that kill cancer cells efficiently and can even help other mice through blood transfusions.
Antiobesity mice	These mice are protected from getting obese and diabetic from their diet by their lack of the enzyme DGAT1. Their fat tissue can even reduce obesity and glucose build-up in other mice if transplanted.
Marathon mice	These mice over-express PPARδ in their muscles, which makes them turn into slow twitch fibers that work well for long-distance running. The mice have more endurance and increased resistance to obesity.

Source: The full list, together with scientific references and a supplementary list, can be found at: www.aleph.se/andart/archives/2007/11/top_10_genetic_enhancements.html

Significance

First, this kind of research will soon change the nature of sporting competition (and everyday life). Until now, great athletes like the US cyclist Lance Armstrong have been unique because of the freakish nature of their basic metabolism, which allows them to produce more energy more efficiently. The most famous example is the Finnish skier Eero Maentyranta. In 1964, he won three Olympic gold medals. Subsequently, it was found he had a genetic mutation that meant that he "naturally" had 40–50 percent more red blood cells than average, because his genes naturally produced more of the hormone erythropoietin, EPO, which stimulates red blood cell production (Booth et al.

217

1998). But these genetic advantages will disappear as drugs are developed and, eventually, genes are engineered, which mean that these natural metabolic advantages are obliterated.

Scientists have already successfully inserted EPO genes into the cells of mice and monkeys. The amount of red blood cells in these animals was increased by as much as 80 percent (Zhou et al. 1998). However, severe anemia followed in some animals due to an autoimmune response to EPO. This illustrates that it will be some time before safe genetic enhancements will be developed in humans. Some enhancements may always carry downsides. While the NR2B "Doogie" mice (see table 1) demonstrated improved memory performance, they were also more sensitive to certain forms of pain, showing a potentially non-trivial trade-off (Wei et al. 2001).

What will sport look like in the postgenomic era? One thing seems certain: performance enhancement is inevitable and we will have to form a rational policy on doping (Foddy and Savulescu 2007; Savulescu and Foddy 2005; 2009; Savulescu et al. 2004).

But research into genetic enhancement has far more profound implications than changing the nature of sport. The creation of Supermouse and other enhanced animals represents a major step toward "biological liberation" or "genetic liberation," that is, to us being liberated from the biological and genetic constraints evolution placed on us. Until now, humans have been stuck with the biology evolution dished out. And genetic changes driven by evolution occurred very slowly, over thousands of years and many generations. The reason there are no Supermen or Superwomen, like the reason there are no naturally occurring Supermice, is that it would have been evolutionarily disadvantageous, given previous environments, to require the vast amounts of food resources to produce this advantage in speed, endurance, and reproduction (Bostrom and Sandberg 2009).

Our biochemistry is set to Pleistocene conditions. However, today we have a superabundance of food in the West – our problem is surfeit and obesity. We could easily provide the calories to run at superhuman speeds, but we have the same gene as the unenhanced mouse. Whereas evolution had her hands tied and may have had good reason not to produce superhumans, we could. This raises profound ethical issues. Our lives – when we can reproduce, whether we get cancer or heart disease, how long we live, how we perform mentally and physically – are determined in significant part by very basic biochemical cycles and biology in our bodies. As Supermouse and the other genetically enhanced animals show, we can change these basic cycles and biology with radical results. There is no reason why there could not be Supermen and Superwomen, the equivalent of Supermouse or better.

This prospect has caused concern amongst some conservatives. Hans Jonas claimed that genetic enhancement opens up:

> a Pandora's box of melioristic, unpredictable, inventive, or simply perverse-curious adventures, abandoning the conservative spirit of genetic repair for the path of creative arrogance. We are not authorized to do this, and we are not equipped for it – not with the wisdom, not with the knowledge of value, not with the self-discipline. And no longer will a tradition of reverence protect us, the demystifiers of the world, from the enchantment of thoughtless crime. Therefore, let the box remain unopened. (Cited in Wessels 1994: 239)

George Annas is even more apocalyptic, describing genetic manipulation as "genetic genocide," with "species-altering genetic engineering a potential weapon of mass destruction" that "makes the unaccountable genetic engineer a potential bioterrorist" (2001).

The market for enhancement

While writers such as Annas and Jonas articulate their worries and pronounce their judgments, genetic enhancement remains of great personal and economic interest. Enhancement is already common and will become more common.

The current market for effective enhancers is enormous. Alcohol is a mood enhancer and the World Health Organization (WHO) estimates that there are about 2 billion people worldwide who consume alcoholic beverages and 76.3 million with diagnosable alcohol-use disorders. The current market for drugs like Viagra to improve sexual performance, which normally declines with age, is estimated at US$3.8 billion, and is forecast to increase 74 percent to US$6.6 billion by 2012 (Piribo.com 2006). Worldwide, erectile dysfunction is estimated to affect more than

Table 2: Common enhancements

Cosmetic	Sport	Music	Cognitive enhancement	Mood enhancement	Sexual performance/ drive
Surgery	EPO and blood doping	Propranolol for tremor	Nicotine	Prozac	Hormonal castration of paedophiles
Botox	Anabolic steroids		Ritalin	Recreational drugs	Viagra
Beauty industry	Growth hormone		Modafenil	Alcohol	
Body art (painting and tattooing)			Caffeine		
Body modification (piercing)			Propranolol (memory modification)		
Appetite suppressants					
Gastric stapling					
Children – correction of bat ears, intersex surgery (clitoral reduction), growth hormone					

150 million men, and that number is expected to exceed 300 million men by the year 2025 (Aytaç et al. 1999). Modafinil is a new "eugeroic" drug (that is, a stimulating drug which doesn't cause the peripheral effects or addiction/tolerance/abuse of the traditional stimulants) which was initially prescribed to treat narcolepsy, obstructive sleep apnea/hypopnea, and shift work sleep disorder; but it is now prescribed off-label for ADD/ADHD, depression, and fatigue, and has also been studied for military use as an alternative to amphetamines during operations (Turner 2003). It is rapidly becoming a replacement for caffeine to improve productivity (Sahakian and Morein-Zamir 2007). The 2007 market for one version, Provigil, in the US is $1 billion. It is likely that the global market for any effective enhancer will be US$7–10 billion by 2017.

At present, enhancers are either interventions, such as surgery; devices, such as implants or computers; or pharmaceuticals. But there are good reasons to believe that genetic modifications are likely to be: (1) possible and significant (as animal research shows) and (2) highly sought after, as experience with other enhancers indicates.

The extent of genetic enhancement: plundering the kingdom of genes

It has been possible since about the 1980s to transfer genes from one species into another. One example of a genetic freak is ANDi, a rhesus monkey that has had a jellyfish gene incorporated into its DNA. This results in a unique fluorescent green glow. Alba is a genetically engineered rabbit created by French scientists for artist Eduardo Kac. Alba also has a fluorescent glow.

Most of the genetic enhancements in Sandberg's Top 10, and the example of Supermouse, involve tweaking genes which were already present in the animal. This is something natural evolution might have done, through random mutation and selection. However, transgenesis raises the possibility of much more radical genetic enhancement.

The world is full of genes in the plant and animal kingdoms which humans do not have. These genes cause these plants and animals to function in ways in which humans cannot, and probably will never be able to, through natural selection. For example, plants can photosynthesize, bats have sonar, hawks have hyperacute vision, dogs can hear sounds which humans cannot, and cats have extraordinary balance.

The existence of ANDi and Alba show that it is possible to transfer genes successfully from one species into another. There is no reason why we could not create fluorescent humans today. The science is quite basic. Indeed, there is no reason in principle why we could not create humans with the vision of a hawk, the hearing and smell of a dog, the sonar of bat, the balance and grace of a cat, the speed of a cheetah, and even the ability to photosynthesize energy from sunlight. There is no reason, in principle, why "posthumans" could not benefit from any of the genes in the living kingdom.

To conclude, genetic enhancement is possible today. There will be significant personal and economic interest in genetic enhancement. Its scope is limited only by the possibilities of manipulating genes, or by the extent of the world's gene pool. Indeed, Craig Venter has undertaken one of the most radical experiments in biology: to create an artificial bacterium, Synthia – so-called "synthetic biology" (Lartigue et al. 2007) and scientists have created new DNA base pairs (Savulescu 2009). This raises the possibility that we could create novel genetic sequences, and protein structures, which have never occurred in the kingdom of life. Posthumans could, in principle, have powers or abilities which no human, other animal, or plant has ever had before.

Should Human Genetic Enhancement Occur?

There has been considerable recent debate on the ethics of human enhancement. A number of prominent authors have been critical of the use of technology to alter or enhance human beings (Annas 2000; Elliott 2003), citing threats to human nature and dignity as one basis for these concerns (Fukuyama 2003; Habermas 2003; Kass 2002). The President's Council Report, entitled *Beyond Therapy*, was strongly critical of human enhancement (President's Council on Bioethics 2003). Michael Sandel has suggested that the problem with genetic enhancement

> lies in the hubris of the designing parents, in their drive to master the mystery of birth . . . it would disfigure the relation between parent and child, and deprive the parent of the humility and enlarged human sympathies that an openness to the unbidden can cultivate. . . . [The] promise of mastery is flawed. It threatens to banish our appreciation of life as a gift, and to leave us with nothing to affirm or behold outside our own will. (2004)

Frances Kamm (2005) has given a detailed rebuttal of Sandel's arguments, arguing that human enhancement is permissible. Nicholas Agar, in his book *Liberal Eugenics* (2003), argues that genetic selection should be permissible but not obligatory. He argues that what distinguishes liberal eugenics from the objectionable eugenic practices of the Nazis is that it is not based on a single conception of a desirable genome and that it is voluntary and not obligatory. Jonathan Glover, in his seminal work *What Sort of People Should There Be?* (1984), and more recently in *Choosing Children* (2006), gives a moderate defense of genetic selection and enhancement. In *Enhancing Evolution* (2007), John Harris gives a robust defense of enhancement.

There are five basic positions in the enhancement debate:

1 Enhancement is morally wrong and should be legally impermissible. This is the strongest negative position.
2 Enhancement is morally wrong but it should be legally permitted. People should be discouraged from employing enhancement technologies, by persuasion, taxation, etc., but they should not be prevented from enhancing.
3 Enhancement is morally neutral and should be legally permitted. This is the position of liberal eugenics.
4 Enhancement is morally right but should not be legally required. Enhancement should be encouraged and facilitated but people would be free to reject enhancements.
5 Enhancement is morally right and should be legally required. This is the strongest position in favor. It requires that people submit to enhancement like they submit to education, fluoridation, or wearing seat belts.

Definition of enhancement

What is meant by "enhancement"? Genetic enhancement refers to genetic modifications which improve the function of some system. The Doogie mice have improved memory. This is a non-normative definition of enhancement. We could have improved memory or cardiovascular function or whatever function without it being *good for the individual*. When discussing the ethics of human enhancement, we are interested not in functional enhancement, but in what is good for human beings. There are three main definitions of enhancement that parallel those of disease, impairment, and disability: naturalistic, social constructivist, and welfarist (for a more detailed discussion, see Hope et al. forthcoming [2003]).

On the welfarist view, human enhancement can be defined as any change in the biology or psychology of a person in a given set of social or environmental circumstances, C, that increases the chances of leading a good life in circumstances C.

On the welfarist account, enhancements include a family of different kinds of improvements, including:

- medical treatment of disease;
- increasing natural human potential – for example, increasing a person's own natural endowments of capabilities within the range typical of the species *Homo sapiens*, such as raising a person's IQ from 100 to 140;
- superhuman enhancements (sometimes called posthuman or transhuman) – increasing a person's capabilities beyond the range typical for the species, for example, giving humans bat sonar or an IQ above 200.

Elsewhere, I defend a welfarist account of disability (Kahane and Savulescu 2009) and enhancement (Savulescu et al. 2009). For the rest of this chapter, I will assume that some genetic enhancements not only improve function but also increase the chances of leading a good life. I will deal with the objection that genetic enhancements may improve function, but will not, or cannot be predicted to, increase well-being.

Arguments in favor of enhancement

1. Choosing not to enhance is wrong

Consider the case of the Neglectful Parents. The Neglectful Parents give birth to a child with a special genetic condition, Intellectual Sensitivity. The child has a stunning intellect but this intellect is extremely sensitive to environment. The child with Intellectual Sensitivity requires a simple, readily available, cheap dietary supplement – for example, Co-Enzyme Q – to sustain his intellect. The parents neglect the diet of this child and this results in a child with a stunning intellect becoming normal. This is clearly wrong, absent some good reason not to provide Co-Enzyme Q. Of course, it may be very expensive, or out of stock, or the parents may live in a remote place where it is not available. But absent some *good reason*, the failure to nurture this feature of the child which can predictably improve the child's life constitutes wrongful neglect.

Now consider the case of the Conservative Parents. They have a child who has a normal intellect. However, there now exists a drug which targets the genome of the child which will result in Intellectual Sensitivity. Were they to give this drug, once off very early in development, and introduce the same dietary supplement, the child's intellect would rise to the stunning level of the child of the Neglectful Parents. These parents are bioconservatives who object to genetic modification. The inaction of the Conservative Parents is as wrong as the inaction of the Neglectful Parents. It has exactly the same consequence: a child exists who could have had a stunning intellect but is instead normal.

RESPONSE

There are at least two replies to this argument. First, it might be claimed that there is a moral difference between failing to maintain a state of affairs and failing to bring about a better state of affairs.

This, however, does not cohere with normal parenting practices. We do not ask whether our children have some innate biological potential when raising them. We seek to increase their potential. What should matter to us as parents is how well our children do, not what talents they happened to be born with. It would be no objection to music practice from a very early age that it *created* the potential to be a great musician.

The second objection is that there is a difference between interventions such as diet, and genetic interventions. Sometimes, this objection is that genetic changes, if they affect the germ line, will be passed on to the next generation. But this would only be problematic if the change was not clearly a benefit. So this objection is really skepticism about whether genetic enhancements are good for people (see below). Moreover, as I argue in the next section, many environmental interventions result in permanent and heritable changes.

2. Consistency

Education, diet, and training are all used to make our children better people and increase their opportunities in life. We train children to be well behaved, cooperative, and intelligent. Indeed, researchers are looking at ways to make the environment more stimulating for young children in order to maximize their intellectual development. Blue light, simulating blue sky, has been found to set circadian rhythms and increase attention and wakefulness. These environmental manipulations do not act mysteriously. They interact with, and in some cases alter, our biology.

The work of Meaney and colleagues (Champagne et al. 2001) on the effects of different levels of mothering in rats has shown that early experience can modify the molecular interactions that regulate gene expression. Furthermore, maternal care and stress have been associated with abnormal brain (hippocampal) development, involving altered nerve growth factors and cognitive, psychological, and immune deficits later in life.

Some argue that genetic manipulations are different because they are irreversible. But environmental interventions can be equally irreversible. Once learnt, it may be impossible to unlearn the skill of playing the piano or riding a bike. These skills are not mysterious: they are permanent, coded brain changes. One may be wobbly, but one is a novice only once. The example of the mothering of rats shows that environmental interventions can cause biological changes that are not only irreversible but are

223

passed on to the next generation. To be consistent, if we believe that it is right to enhance people through education and diet, then it is right to do so through direct genetic means.

RESPONSE

Environmental enhancement *is* different from biological enhancement. Consider altering someone's political beliefs through argument compared with doing so through administration of a drug. The first, although it may be effective, still respects the person and her autonomy, and her political views remain her own. The second method is a biological form of brainwashing and fails to respect her autonomy.

This response, however, is problematic in the case of early genetic intervention. In the case of the Conservative Parents, their child will only have the Intellectual Sensitivity if given the drug early. The child has two mutually exclusive futures: one with a greater intellectual endowment and one without. There is no issue of respecting his autonomy.

In the case of a competent adult, if a person *chooses* to change her political beliefs through biological intervention, then that is an expression of her autonomy. So genetic interventions can be both good for a person and an expression of autonomy. Consider a person who has racist feelings and has tried, unsuccessfully, to alter these, which are the result of a racist upbringing. She chooses some biological means to alter these tendencies because she hates them and considers herself bad to have them. Such a use of genetic or other biological technology is an expression of humanity and an appropriate response to the limited capacity we have to change ourselves by non-biological means.

3. Enhancement is no different ethically from treating disease

If we accept the treatment and prevention of disease, we should accept enhancement. The goodness of health is what drives a moral obligation to treat or prevent disease. But health is not what ultimately matters. Health enables us to live well. Disease prevents us from doing what we want and what is good. Health is instrumentally valuable – valuable as a resource that allows us to do what really matters: lead a good life.

Disease is important because it causes pain, is not what we want, and stops us engaging in those activities that give meaning to life. Sometimes people trade health for well-being – mountain climbers take on risk to achieve, smokers sometimes believe that the pleasures outweigh the risks of smoking, and so on. Life is about managing risk to health and life to promote well-being.

It is the moral obligation to benefit people that provides the grounds for treating disease that also provides grounds to enhance people insofar as this increases their chance of having a better life.

Can biological enhancements increase people's opportunities for well-being? There are reasons to believe they might. Buchanan and colleagues (2000) have discussed the value of "all purpose goods." These are traits that are valuable regardless of which kind of life a person chooses to live. They give us greater all-round capacities to live a vast array of lives. Examples include intelligence, memory, self-discipline, patience, empathy, a sense of humor, optimism, and just having a sunny temperament. All of these characteristics may have some biological and psychological basis capable of manipulation with technology.

224

RESPONSE

Treatment and prevention of disease typically have a more significant impact on well-being than other enhancements and so should have priority.

One can accept this, while still acknowledging an obligation, based on beneficence, to enhance. The fact that some improvements in well-being are greater than others does not imply that we should ignore small or modest enhancements. Whether these should be provided turns on questions of distributive justice.

Michael Sandel (2007) argues that health is different from other enhancements because it is a "bounded good." Once healthy, one cannot be more and more healthy, unlike being more and more intelligent. We can confer health without conferring some competitive advantage, he claims. But this is a mistake. There is the concept of perfect health. While many of us are apparently healthy, we all suffer from various genetic predispositions to disease and we are all aging. If we all had the health of a 10-year-old, when aging has not commenced, we would live to over 1,000 years old, barring accidents and injury. So health is just like other goods – we can keep having more of it. The duty to make us healthier is the duty to make people's lives go better, the same duty that drives the obligation to genetically enhance.

Arguments against enhancement

1. The precautionary principle

We are unwise to assume that we can have sufficient knowledge to meddle biologically with human nature. (Sometimes this appears as the objection that we should not play God – see below.) To attempt to enhance one characteristic may have other unknown, unforeseen, and deleterious effects. Unforeseen effects are particularly likely for genetic manipulations, since genes are pleiotropic – which means they have different effects in different environments. The gene or genes which predispose to manic depression may also be responsible for heightened creativity and productivity. There is a special value in the balance and diversity that natural variation affords, and enhancement will reduce this.

RESPONSE

Such precaution is misplaced. The proper response to these concerns is to do adequate research before intervening. And because the benefits may be less than when we treat or prevent disease, we may require the standards of safety to be higher than for medical interventions. But we must weigh the risks against the benefits. If confidence is justifiably high, and benefits outweigh harms, we should enhance. Risks will always be present. We must consider whether the expected benefits outweigh the expected harms.

If one is concerned about pleiotropic genetic effects, we should limit our interventions, until our knowledge grows, to selections between different embryos, and not intervene to enhance particular embryos or people (Savulescu et al. 2006). Since we would be choosing between complete systems on the basis of their type, we would not be interfering with the internal machinery. In this way, selection is less risky than enhancement.

2. *Value of diversity*

There is a special value in the balance and diversity that natural variation affords, and enhancement will reduce this.

RESPONSE

Since natural variation is the product of evolution, we are merely random chance variations of genetic traits selected for our capacity to survive long enough to reproduce. There is no design to evolution. Medicine has changed evolution – we can now select individuals who experience less pain and disease. The next stage of human evolution will be rational evolution, where we select children who not only have the greatest chance of surviving, reproducing, and being free from disease, but who have the greatest opportunities to have the best lives. Evolution was indifferent to how well our lives went. We are not. There is therefore no special value in the balance and diversity of natural variation.

Moreover, there is no moral reason to preserve some traits – such as uncontrollable aggressiveness, a sociopathic personality, or extreme deviousness. Much of human nature could be improved (Glover 2006).

Sometimes the value of diversity argument is couched in terms of evolutionary biology: that genetic diversity increases the fitness of the species. For example, such genetic diversity allows us as a species to withstand novel infectious insults. However, we now have the technology to engineer radical genetic diversity (e.g. through the creation of gametes from stem cells) or to preserve existing genetic diversity in gene banks. There is no reason now to allow an individual to suffer, or to inflict suffering on her, for the sake of the "species."

3. *Enhancement is playing God or against nature*

We should not play God (Coady 2009). Children are a gift, of God or of Nature. We should not interfere with human nature.

RESPONSE

Most people implicitly reject this view – we screen embryos and fetuses for diseases, even mild correctible diseases. We interfere with "Nature" or "God's will" when we vaccinate, provide pain relief to women in labor, treat cancer, or give antibiotics.

Indeed, when we make decisions to improve our lives by biological and other manipulations, we express our rationality and express what is fundamentally important about our nature. Far from being against the human spirit, such improvements express what is admirable in the human spirit. To be human is, amongst other things, to choose to be better.

4. *Inequity: genetic discrimination*

These would be mere consumer decisions – but that also means that they would benefit the rich far more than the poor. They would take the gap in power, wealth, and education that currently divides both our society and the world at large, and write that division into our very biology. (McKibben 2003)

226

Enhancement will create a two-class society of the enhanced and the unenhanced, where the inferior unenhanced are discriminated against and disadvantaged all through life. This is represented in the film *Gattaca*.

RESPONSE

There is already great genetic inequality in nature. There are, for example, "gifted" children naturally. Allowing choice to change our biology could be more egalitarian – allowing the ungifted to approach the gifted.

It is *possible* to use enhancement to increase inequality, if it is made available in accordance with free market principles, but it is not a *necessary* outcome of enhancement. We have free will and a sense of responsibility; it is up to us how we choose to use and distribute this technology. We can use enhancement to increase inequality or to reduce it. We can make enhancement available in line with any theory of justice: egalitarian, prioritarian, sufficientarian, or utilitarian (Savulescu 2009).

Still more importantly, how well the lives of those who are disadvantaged go depends not on whether enhancement is permitted (natural biological inequality already exists), but on the social institutions we have in place to protect the least well off.

5. Humility, responsibility, and solidarity

Sandel argues that the problem with genetic enhancement is "hyperagency" or the modification of human nature to serve our own purposes. This will create the false belief that we are the masters of our own destiny and that we deserve what we achieve. It will reduce the sense that our lives are in part a "gift" for which we are not responsible. This in turn will reduce humility, compassion, and our sense of obligation to those who are less fortunate than ourselves:

> If bioengineering made the myth of the "self-made man" come true, it would be difficult to view our talents as gifts for which we are indebted, rather than achievements for which we are responsible. This would transform three key features of our moral landscape: humility, responsibility, and solidarity. (2007: 86)

> To appreciate children as gifts is to accept them as they come, not as objects of our design or products of our will or instruments of our ambition. Parental love is not contingent on the talents and attributes a child happens to have. We choose our friends and spouses at least partly on the basis of qualities we find attractive. But we do not choose our children. Their qualities are unpredictable, and even the most conscientious parents cannot be held wholly responsible for the kind of children they have. That is why parenthood . . . teaches . . . an "openness to the unbidden." . . . [T]he deepest moral objection to enhancement lies . . . in the hubris of the designing parents, in their drive to master the mystery of birth. Even if this disposition did not make parents tyrants to their children, it would disfigure the relation between parent and child, and deprive the parent of the humility and enlarged human sympathies that an openness to the unbidden can cultivate. (2007: 45; 46)

RESPONSE

Kamm (2005) has given a detailed critique of Sandel's arguments. Briefly, Sandel makes an empirical speculation about the reaction of children to enhancement. The opposite is possible: an increased sense of debt on the part of children who have benefited from their parents' choices rather than brute luck. It is also contestable that improving our children would make us less accepting of them. Parents love and accept their children, even though they hoped for and expected a normal healthy child, after the child is disabled in an accident. Indeed, it displays an appropriate parental virtue to improve a child's opportunities, advantages, and talents.

Being "open to the unbidden" expresses an attitude which may vary from person to person and in part be genetically determined. For example, "novelty seeking" is a trait which seems close to it, and this has a strong genetic contribution. Genetic enhancement may enhance our virtues and attitudes. Regardless, openness to the unbidden embodies willingness to see value in the other, to find what is valuable, inquisitiveness, patience, and tolerance. It is hard to see how improving memory or concentration or hedonic tone is inconsistent with, or even likely to reduce, these attitudes. And there could be no mutilation of the parent–child relationships of the kind Sandel is concerned about if enhancements were performed by third parties, and if enhancements were performed on *everyone* rather than at parental request.

6. Change society, not people

We should alter social arrangements to promote well-being, not biologically alter people.

RESPONSE

This objection claims that society should be changed to correct for our natural disabilities and disadvantages. When a genetic condition constitutes an impediment to well-being (i.e., a disability), we have a choice: to change biology, psychology, society or natural environment (Kahane and Savulescu 2009). When should we change society rather than psychology or biology?

When it comes to *existing people*, one consideration in favor of changing society is that changes to biology or psychology can endanger a person's sense of identity or psychological unity. This will be more a problem for cognitive and mood enhancements than for physical enhancements. Because how we think and feel is central to who we are, cognitive enhancement has the potential to radically change a person's sense of self. At the most extreme case, such changes may amount to a change in identity. We do not benefit a person if, in order to cure his migraine, we transplant another brain in his skull, even from a much happier person. Most cases of biological or psychological change, however, would not literally terminate one person's life and replace it with another. But such change may still threaten to disrupt the psychological unity of a person or undermine her deepest projects. However, such objections would not apply to enhancements early in life, and adults could make their own choices. We may not have an interest in radical modifications of our mind and abilities. But genetic enhancements to improve memory, especially in those with normal age-related memory decline, would remain attractive and preserve rather than reduce our sense of self-coherence and personal identity.

There are good reasons to prefer social intervention:

- it is safer or associated with fewer side effects;
- it is more likely to be successful;
- justice requires it (based on the limitations of resources);
- there are benefits to others, or less harm;
- it is identity preserving.

In some cases, we should change society. In other cases, we should change our biology. Which we should choose depends on the balance of reasons.

7. Social costs: enhancements are self-defeating

Enhancements are often self-defeating. A typical example is increase in height. If height is socially desired, then everyone will try to enhance the height of their children at some cost to themselves but no one in the end will have benefited. "If everyone stands on tiptoe no one sees any further." Economists have coined the term "positional goods" to describe goods we value principally because they are markers of our success compared with others or give us an advantage over others. Many enhancements will be for positional goods and will start a "rat race" which will end in no improvement in well-being.

RESPONSE

Many enhancements will have significant non-positional qualities. Intelligence, for example, is not only a positional good; it enables an individual to process information more rapidly in her own life, and to develop greater understanding of herself and others.

Even with regard to positional goods there is an issue of consistency. We allow individuals in society to pursue their own self-interest at some (positional) cost to others. This applies to education, access to technology, health care, and virtually all areas of life.

The claim that enhancement could have adverse social effects is an important and valid objection. But genetic enhancement is no different from other enhancements.

It is also important to realize that enhancement might have important social *benefits*. For example, improving cognitive capacities could have significant social benefits. While there is no link between higher cognitive ability and more (or less) happiness, lower cognitive ability correlates with unhappiness. It appears to be a threshold effect. (For example, one needs an IQ of 90 to complete a US tax return.) Low cognitive ability makes people vulnerable, causes accidents, hinders education, and reduces the range of jobs amongst which people can select. Higher intelligence appears to prevent a wide array of social and economic misfortunes and to promote health and educational achievement (for a full review, see Sandberg et al. (forthcoming).)

Individual cognitive capacity (imperfectly estimated by IQ scores) is positively correlated with income. There might be a less strong correlation between IQ and accumulated wealth (0.16 rather than 0.3 for income). While cognitive ability is not the only, or even largest, factor predicting income, it has a significant effect especially in white-collar work. In a very controversial book, Herrnstein and Murray (1994) argue that a 3-point increase in IQ would have the effects shown in table 3.

Table 3: Effects of a 3-point increase in IQ

Poverty rate	−25%
Males in jail	−25%
High school dropouts	−28%
Parentless children	−20%
Welfare recipiency	−18%
Out-of-wedlock births	−15%

Source: Herrnstein and Murray (1994)

These benefits are individual, but they also contribute across society by reducing overall social costs and increasing productivity. Economic models of the loss caused by small intelligence decrements due to toxins in drinking water (such as lead) predict significant individual and social effects of even a few points change, and it is plausible that a small *increment* would have positive effects of a similar magnitude. One study estimated the increase in income accruing to an individual from one additional personal IQ point to be 1.763 percent, while a later study found 2.1 percent for men and 3.6 percent for women. The annual gain per extra IQ point nationwide, for the US, would be of the order of US$55–65 billion, or 0.4–0.5 percent GDP. Even at the top end, improved IQ may have beneficial social effects. Patent production does not appear to be a competitive endeavor, but rather a sign of real creativity and wealth production. One study found that, among people with an SAT Reasoning Score in the top 1 percent, those in the top quartile produced about twice as many patented ideas as those in the bottom quartile (corresponding to about 7.5 and 3.8 times the base rate of the population respectively). This suggests that not only do the top performers do well professionally but they also add more per capita to the economy. It also indicates that even those in the top 1 percent could benefit from further enhancement.

Such data are controversial and contestable, as is the relationship between cognitive capacity and genetics, but they illustrate the point that population-wide genetic enhancement could have significant social and economic benefits.

8. The meaning of life: the perfect child, sterility, and loss of the mystery of life

Imagine a world in which we are all Supermen or Superwomen, like Supermice, running faster and faster on the treadmill of life, more aggressive, having children at the age of 80, eating more, being leaner and more productive, with ever larger and larger television screens and faster cars. There is something meaningless about such future enhancement.

Many of the deepest objections hover around vague references to the meaning of life. For example, if we engineered perfect children, the world would be a sterile, monotonous place where everyone is the same, and the mystery and surprise of life is gone. Michael Parker (2007) quotes Shakespeare's *All's Well that Ends Well*: "The web of our life is of mingled yarn, good and ill together; our virtues would be proud if our faults whipp'd them not; and our crimes would despair, if they were not cherish'd by our virtues" (Act 4: iii: 68–71). This echoes claims made by the President's Council on the value of suffering: "There appears to be a connection between the possibility of feeling deep unhappiness and the prospects for achieving genuine happiness. If one cannot grieve, one has not truly loved. To be capable of aspiration, one must know and feel lack" (President's Council on Bioethics, 2003: 299).

RESPONSE

Let us assume that the best life requires light and dark, struggle and failure, and suffering. Then we should select the right balance. Some will bask in the sun while others wither in an eternal night. The issue is whether we should accept what nature delivers up or make a choice. If we believe that it is better for people to have some weaknesses, we had better choose embryos which have some weaknesses, or even introduce embryos with enough weakness.

Of course, it is perverse to suggest that we should allow biology, psychology, or social situations to cause ill to people. It is like saying that we cannot have a happy or a good relationship without arguments. Arguments may occur, or they may be necessary to resolve disagreements, but an otherwise perfectly happy couple should not start to argue, just to have a mingled yarn.

These objections all ignore the basic fact that we live in a probabilistic world, the effects of which genetic enhancement will never eliminate. Life will be a mingled yarn because nature and life in general are unpredictable and uncontrollable. People will necessarily face adversity and difficulty. And the pursuit of self-interest will always cause harm to others. If, magically, we could remove the possibility of every natural disaster, every human conflict, every human disease and injury and make people instantly and perfectly happy, the question of how much ill they should experience might arise. But with the world as it is, and is likely to be even in the face of greater technological control, there will still remain plenty of meat of adversity, bad luck, and human suffering to get our teeth into.

Another possible interpretation of the light, dark, and mingled yarn argument is that it is constitutive of a good life to accept what nature delivers. This is like Sandel's claim that enhancement is wrong because we must be "open to the unbidden" (2007: 86). We must remain open to the mystery of life, which inevitably contains good and ill, and not seek to control every aspect of life. Again, plenty of mystery will remain even if we seek to improve our biological, psychological, and social circumstances to make our lives go well. One can choose to go to a good play rather than a poor one, and still experience the mystery of events as they unfold.

Our genes, and minds which they only in part shape, will contribute to us unraveling or inventing the meaning of life.

Conclusion

Human enhancement through the use of drugs and other biological interventions is already occurring. Radical genetic enhancement has been possible in other animals and is possible in principle in human beings.

Will the future be better or just disease-free? We need to shift our frame of reference from health to life enhancement. What matters is how we live. Genetic enhancement can now improve that. I believe one of the most admirable characteristics of humans is to be better. Or, at least, to strive to be better. We should be here for a *good* time, not just a *long* time.

Despite the widespread and numerous objections, many genetic enhancements will not merely be permissible, but may be morally required. We face the dawn of biological or genetic liberation.

References

Agar, N. (2003). *Liberal Eugenics*. Oxford: Blackwell.

Annas, G. (2000). The man on the moon, immortality and other millennial myths: the prospects and perils of human genetic engineering. *Emory Law Journal* 49/3: 753–82.

Annas, G. (2001). Genism, racism, and the prospect of genetic genocide." Retrieved January 23, 2007, from: www.thehumanfuture.org/commentaries/annas_genism.html.

Aytaç, I. A., McKinlay, J. B., and Krane, R. J. (1999). The likely worldwide increase in erectile dysfunction between 1995 and 2025 and some possible policy consequences. *BJU International* 84/1: 50–6.

Booth, F., Tseng, B., Fluck, M., and Carson, J. A. (1998). Molecular and cellular adaptation of muscle in response to physical training. *Acta Physiologica Scandinavica* 162: 343–50.

Bostrom, N. and Sandberg, A. (2009). The wisdom of nature: an evolutionary heuristic for human enhancement. In J. Savulescu and N. Bostrom (eds.), *Human Enhancement*. Oxford: Oxford University Press, pp. 375–416.

Buchanan, A., Brock, D. W., Daniels, N., and Wikler, D. (2000). *From Chance to Choice: Genetics and Justice*. Cambridge: Cambridge University Press.

Champagne, F., Diorio, J., Sharma, S., and Meaney, M. J. (2001). Naturally occurring variations in maternal behavior in the rat are associated with differences in estrogen-inducible central oxytocin receptors. *Proceedings of the National Academy of Sciences USA* 98: 12736–41.

Coady, T. (2009). Playing God. In J. Savulescu and N. Bostrom (eds.), *Human Enhancement*. Oxford: Oxford University Press, pp. 155–80.

Connor, S. (2007). The mouse that shook the world. *Independent* newspaper (London).

Elliott, C. (2003). *Better than Well: American Medicine Meets the American Dream*. New York: W. W. Norton and Company.

Foddy, B. and Savulescu, J. (2007). Performance enhancement and the spirit of sport: is there good reason to allow doping? In R. Ashcroft, H. Draper, A. Dawson, and J. McMillan (eds.), *Principles of Heathcare Ethics*, 2nd edn. Chichester: John Wiley & Sons, pp. 511–20.

Fukuyama, F. (2003). *Our Posthuman Future: Consequences of the Biotechnology Revolution*. London: Profile Books.

Glover, J. (1984). *What Sort of People Should There Be?* New York: Penguin Books.

Glover, J. (2006). *Choosing Children: Genes, Disability and Design*. Oxford: Oxford University Press.

Habermas, J. (2003). *The Future of Human Nature*. Cambridge: Polity.

Hakimi, P., Yang, J., et al. (2007). Overexpression of the cytosolic form of phosphoenolpyruvate carboxykinase (GTP) in skeletal muscle repatterns energy metabolism in the mouse. *Journal of Biological Chemistry* 282: 32844–55.

Harris, J. (2007). *Enhancing Evolution: The Ethical Case for Making Better People*. Princeton, NJ: Princeton University Press.

Herrnstein, R. J. and Murray, C. (1994). *The Bell Curve*. New York: Free Press.

Hope, T., Savulescu, J., and Hendricks, J. (forthcoming [2003]). *Medical Ethics and Law: The Core Curriculum*, 2nd edn. London: Churchill Livingstone.

Kahane, G. and Savulescu, J. (2009). The welfarist account of disability. In A. Cureton and K. Brownlee (eds.), *Disability and Disadvantage*. Oxford: Oxford University Press.

Kamm, F. M. (2005). Is there a problem with enhancement? *American Journal of Bioethics* 5/3: 5–14.

Kass, L. R. (2002). *Life, Liberty and the Defense of Dignity: The Challenge for Bioethics*. San Francisco: Encounter Books.

Lartigue, C., Glass, J. I., et al. (2007). Genome transplantation in bacteria: changing one species to another. *Science* 317: 632–8.

McKibben, B. (2003). Designer Genes. *The Orion*.

Parker, M. (2007). The best possible child. *Journal of Medical Ethics* 33/5: 279–83.

Piribo.com (2006). World market for sexual disorders, 2005–2012: traversing new frontiers in sexual chemistry. Available at: www.piribo.com/publications/diseases_conditions/world_market_sexual_disorder.html (accessed October 29).

President's Council on Bioethics (2003). *Beyond Therapy: A Report by the President's Council on Bioethics*. Washington, DC: President's Council on Bioethics.

Sahakian, B. and Morein-Zamir, S. (2007). Professor's little helper. *Nature* 450/7173: 1157–9.

Sample, I. (2007). Genetic tweak produces mighty mouse to outrun rivals. *Guardian* newspaper (London).

Sandberg, A., Bostrom, N., and Savulescu, J. (forthcoming). *The Economic and Social Impact of Enhancement*.

Sandel, M. (2004). The case against perfection. *The Atlantic* (April). Available at: www.theatlantic.com/doc/200404/sandel.

Sandel, M. (2007). *The Case Against Perfection: Ethics in the Age of Genetic Engineering*. Cambridge, MA: Harvard University Press.

Savulescu, J. (2007). In defence of procreative beneficence: response to Parker. *Journal of Medical Ethics* 33: 284–8.

Savulescu, J. (2009). Enhancement and fairness. In P. Healey (ed.), *Unnatural Selection*. London: Earthscan.

Savulescu, J. and Foddy, B. (2005). Good sport, bad sport: why we should legalise drugs in the Olympics. In *Best Australian Sportswriting 2004*. Melbourne: Black Inc.

Savulescu, J. and Foddy, B. (2009). Le tour and failure of zero tolerance: time to relax doping controls. In R. ter Meulen, J. Savulescu, and G. Kahane (eds.), *Enhancing Human Capacities*. Wiley-Blackwell.

Savulescu, J., Foddy, B., and Clayton, M. (2004). Why we should allow performance enhancing drugs in sport. *British Journal of Sports Medicine* 38: 666–70.

Savulescu, J., Hemsley, M., Newson, A., and Foddy, B. (2006). Behavioural genetics: why eugenic selection is preferable to enhancement. *Journal of Applied Philosophy* 23: 157–71.

Savulescu, J., Sandberg, A., and Kahane, G. (2009). What is enhancement and why we should enhance cognition. In R. ter Meulen, J. Savulescu, and G. Kahane (eds.), *Enhancing Human Capacities*. Wiley-Blackwell.

Turner, D. (2003). Cognitive enhancing effects of modafinil in healthy volunteers. *Psychopharmacology* 165/3: 260–9.

Wei, F., Wang, G., et al. (2001). Genetic enhancement of inflammatory pain by forebrain NR2B overexpression. *Nature Neuroscience* 4: 164–9.

Wessels, U. (1994). Genetic engineering and ethics in Germany. In A. O. Dyson and J. Harris (eds.), *Ethics and Biotechnology*. London: Routledge, pp. 230–58.

Zhou, S., Murphy, J. E., Escobedo, J. A., and Dwarki, V. J. (1998). Adeno-associated virus-mediated delivery of erythropoietin leads to sustained elevation of hematocrit in nonhuman primates. *Gene Therapy* 5: 665–70.

Further reading

Annas, G., Andrews, L. B., and Isasi, R. M. (2002). Protecting the endangered human: toward an international treaty prohibiting cloning and inheritable alterations. *American Journal of Law and Medicine* 28: 151–78.

Elliott, C. (2003). Better than well: American medicine meets the American dream. New York: W. W. Norton.

Kass, L. R. (2003). Beyond therapy: biotechnology and the pursuit of human improvement. Paper presented to The President's Council on Bioethics. Available at: http://bioethicsprint. bioethics.gov/background/kasspaper.html (accessed June 25, 2007).

Miller, P. and Wilsdon, J. (eds.) (2006). *Better Humans? The Politics of Human Enhancement and Life Extension*. London: Demos.

Parens, E. (ed.) (1998). *Enhancing Human Traits: Ethical and Social Implications*. Washington, DC: Georgetown University Press.

Savulescu, J. (2002). Deaf lesbians, "designer disability" and the future of medicine. *British Medical Journal* 325: 771–3.

Silver, L. M. (1999). *Remaking Eden*. London: Phoenix Giant.

Stock, G. (2002). *Redesigning Humans*. London: Profile Books.

21

Creating and Patenting New Life Forms

NILS HOLTUG

Introduction

Genetic engineers are able to carry out transfers of genetic material from one organism to another, even crossing species boundaries, and thus to create new kinds of beings and life forms. Amongst their more spectacular achievements is the so-called "Mighty Mouse," which is twice the size of her unmodified sisters. More importantly, they have enabled us to manufacture large amounts of therapeutic drugs, such as insulin, and a vaccine against hepatitis B, by inserting new genes into bacteria. Furthermore, efforts have been made to develop gene therapy for human diseases such as cancer, cystic fibrosis, and muscular dystrophy.

This gives rise to all sorts of ethical questions regarding whether and when it is morally permissible to genetically modify living organisms. It also raises questions regarding the moral permissibility of patenting these organisms once they are created.

In answering such questions, many ethicists have adopted a broadly consequentialist approach, according to which the moral permissibility of using the new technologies to modify biological organisms and of patenting should be assessed solely in terms of the consequences of doing so, particularly (if not exclusively) in terms of human (and animal) welfare.

Other ethicists, and a large section of the general public, have responded rather differently. Dissatisfied with the pragmatic nature of the consequentialist reasoning about genetic engineering, they have suggested that there are categorical objections to be raised against this technology or parts of it. Thus, applications of genetic engineering should be assessed in terms of whether they are wrong (or right) *in themselves*, as well as (more contingently) in terms of their ability to promote welfare.

My discussion will focus on genetic engineering, but it is also relevant for other biological technologies that may be used to create new life forms. I shall discuss genetically modified organisms quite generally, and thus set aside the notoriously complex issue of what, exactly, a "new life form" is.

Values

Essential to different approaches to ethical issues in genetic engineering are the values they invoke. One important view, "welfarism," may be defined as the claim that (1) the moral value of an act should be based exclusively on how good an outcome it brings about, and (2) the goodness of an outcome is a function only of the welfare it contains. Utilitarians are welfarists in this sense, since they believe that in order for an act to be right, it must bring about an outcome with at least as large a total of welfare as that of any alternative act. However, welfarists need not be utilitarians. They may want to take account of the way welfare is distributed. For example, given a situation in which welfare is distributed in a highly unequal way, they may prefer a situation in which there is less total welfare, but it is distributed more equally.

According to welfarists, all we have to care about when morally assessing genetic (or other) manipulations on living organisms is what the consequences will be in terms of welfare. However, since we cannot know these with certainty, the assessment will consist in weighing the expected welfare benefits against the welfare risks.

As pointed out above, many people find welfarism seriously inadequate when applied to the question of creating and patenting new life forms. Welfarism, it is claimed, does not at all accord with our intuitive responses to these issues. We are struck by a sense of unease; by the thought that scientists are playing God, or in some other way not respecting the special dignity and worth of living organisms.

The values underlying these responses are often construed as deontological constraints on when it is permissible to bring about good outcomes, for example, outcomes that are good in welfarist terms. There are certain things we must not do – for instance, violate an animal's genetic integrity – even if doing so would bring about a better outcome. This deontological approach differs from welfarism both in the choice of values and in the insistence that (some) values should be respected rather than promoted. (For example, deontologists may insist that it is always wrong to kill an innocent human life, even if killing an innocent human being were the only way in which one could stop a very large number of innocent humans being killed.) Another alternative to welfarism is the view that there are some values – for instance, biological diversity – that in themselves make outcomes better, and so should be promoted along with welfare. This view differs from welfarism only in its choice of values.

Micro-organisms and Plants

Creating new strains of micro-organisms and plants may in different ways involve substantial benefits to humans. Consider, for example, bacteria that produce life-saving medicine and new strains of plants that require less fertilizer, insecticide, and pesticide. On the other hand, there are also risks involved in creating these new strains that should be weighed against the benefits. But, at least in some cases, it seems plausible that genetic interventions are beneficial overall.

We have seen that many people do not believe that such welfarist considerations exhaust the moral realm. One objection is that genetic engineering involves playing

God, and is, for that reason, wrong. Sometimes, I suspect, the point of this objection is to remind us that, unlike God allegedly is, we are neither omniscient nor omnipotent. Therefore we should be careful not to overestimate our ability to predict and control the consequences of genetic engineering.

However, surely welfarists will agree. In order for the objection to go beyond this view, it must be interpreted differently. On one (literal) interpretation, scientists should not modify the genetic make-up of living organisms since this is God's prerogative. A key problem with this interpretation is how we can know that God does not want scientists to do so. More fundamentally, of course, we can also ask why we should believe in God. And a further question is: even on the assumption that God exists and has desires we can know about, should we necessarily do what he wants?

On another interpretation, it is claimed that genetic engineering is *unnatural* and therefore wrong. This view may seem more promising, but it faces two challenges. First, the meaning of "unnatural" must be specified in a way that satisfies three requirements: (1) it should apply to genetic engineering, (2) it should not apply to the intentional genetic modification of organisms through selective breeding (since even proponents of the "playing God" objection want to allow this technology), and (3) it should not be ad hoc. Secondly, it must be explained why, according to the favored specification, what is unnatural is also immoral. In one sense, all of medicine is "unnatural," since it seeks to prevent illnesses from taking their natural course. It is not obvious how either of these challenges could be met.

Another class of objections takes as its point of departure the claim that we should respect all living organisms. Some people argue that therefore we ought not cross (natural) species boundaries. This can be seen as an attempt to point out a relevant difference between selective breeding and (some instances of) genetic engineering. Genetic engineering often involves inserting a gene taken from one species into an organism from a different species. Therefore, (some instances of) genetic engineering will cause the distinctions between species to be blurred, thus violating the integrity of living organisms. Other people argue instead that in genetic engineering, organisms are not respected since they are treated as mere means to satisfy human desires.

There is, however, a question that needs to be addressed regarding these objections. Are micro-organisms and plants really the sort of beings that can be violated and should be respected? That is, do they have moral standing, either as individuals or as species?

The view that all biological organisms have moral standing is usually supported by the claim that even non-sentient organisms, for example, trees, have a "good of their own" (Attfield 1991) or a "will to live" (Schweitzer 1923). But as Peter Singer points out, we should be careful when assessing such claims:

> [O]nce we stop to reflect on the fact that plants are not conscious and cannot engage in any intentional behaviour, it is clear that all this language is metaphorical; one might just as well say that a river is pursuing its own good and striving to reach the sea, or that the "good" of a guided missile is to blow itself up along with its target. (1993: 279)

The difficulty is to explain why the sense in which micro-organisms and plants have a good is morally relevant. Trees, like guided missiles, do not really have a *perspective* on the world, according to which things can be good or bad for them. In other words, it cannot make a difference to them what happens to them, since they cannot desire things to go one way or the other or experience such events. Some, therefore, search for other properties on the basis of which non-sentient organisms may acquire moral standing. But to others, these considerations of interests suggest an alternative view, namely that only sentient beings have moral standing. This view, called sentientism, implies that genetic interventions cannot wrong micro-organisms and plants (or species). Obviously, such interventions can be wrong nevertheless, if they are contrary to the interests of humans or animals. But, as pointed out above, there seem to be cases in which a concern for welfare would support creating new strains of micro-organisms and plants.

Animals

A transgenic animal is a genetically modified animal. Such animals can be used as disease models for medical research, as "bioreactors" that produce proteins to be used in pharmaceuticals, or as improved livestock in agriculture. Thus, mice have been designed to develop cancer so that they can be used in cancer research, sheep have been designed to produce Factor IX in their milk, and attempts have been made to make pigs grow faster.

Unlike micro-organisms and plants, (many) animals are sentient. This means that there are clear welfarist reasons to take their interests into account, insofar as our acts (or omissions) affect them. (See chapter 41, "The Moral Status of Animals and Their Use As Experimental Subjects.") Traditionally, this moral concern has been considered only in the context of animals already in existence. However, as the case of genetic engineering brings out, we are sometimes involved in their creation. And it would seem that by creating them, we may affect their interests for better or worse. If, for instance, a transgenic animal is created such that it will experience nothing but severe pain, it seems that this animal has been harmed by being caused to exist in such a dreadful condition.

Some philosophers deny that we can harm or benefit animals (or humans for that matter) by causing them to exist. They believe that the relevant alternatives – existence and nonexistence – are evaluatively incomparable. I am skeptical about this line of argument myself (Holtug 2001), but it is worth pointing out that even if creating an animal cannot harm or benefit it, there may still be an (impersonal) welfarist concern to be taken into account when morally assessing transgenic animals. It may be claimed that it is better that there is more rather than less welfare in the world, and that it is better, other things being equal, if the animals that are created have a higher rather than a lower welfare.

Welfarists hold that there is a *pro tanto* reason not to create transgenic animals if, (a) they will experience more suffering than positive welfare, or (b) they will replace animals with better lives. (This is why the objection that welfarism does not rule out redesigning farm animals as insentient "vegetables" is misguided. Most welfarists believe that we should try to prevent animals from suffering *and* insure that they experience positive welfare.)

Perhaps, in some cases, the bad consequences referred to in (a) and (b) can be counterbalanced by benefits to humans (or other animals), for example if animal experiments are necessary to make progress in cancer research. If so, transgenesis will be acceptable from a welfarist point of view, even if the animals have lives that are worse than nothing or replace happier animals. Transgenesis will, of course, also be acceptable if it has either no impact on them, or a positive impact.

Some proponents of animal rights have argued that since sentient animals have inherent value, they should not be used as a mere means to benefit humans (Regan 1984). Therefore, it is wrong to, for example, create transgenic mice designed to develop cancer. (For related discussions, see chapter 41.)

A more sweeping objection against creating transgenic animals is to invoke the concept of "genetic integrity": "We can define the genetic integrity of an animal as the genome being left intact" (Vorstenbosch 1993: 110). Defined in this manner, "integrity is a respect- or constraint-related concept and not a 'grading' concept like welfare that suggests from an ethical point of view an 'optimizing' approach" (pp. 111–12). This objection, it should be noted, is just as much an argument against selective breeding as it is an argument against genetic engineering. Suppose, however, that we bite the bullet and accept the implication for selective breeding.

We might want to know more precisely what the value of genetic integrity is supposed to be. On the face of it, this concept seems to express a concern for animals. But does it really refer to something that is valuable from the *animal's* point of view? Suppose that an animal is genetically modified so that it will not develop a severe disease. In what way is this supposed to be of disvalue to the animal?

A different concern sometimes claimed to be important when assessing transgenic animals is respect for their telos. According to Bernard Rollin, to violate an animal's telos is to prevent it from fulfilling its natural desires or inclinations (what matters most to it). This does not make it inherently wrong to alter the telos of an animal. It is wrong only if it involves an infringement of the new telos. More precisely, "it is only wrong to change a *telos* if the individual animals of that sort are likely to be more unhappy or suffer more after the change than before" (Rollin 1986: 89). This view, then, seems to coincide with welfarism.

A different proposal, however, is that "The *telos* or 'beingness' of an animal is its intrinsic nature coupled with the environment in which it is able to develop and experience life" (Fox 1990: 32). To disrupt the harmony between the animal and its environment is to harm the animal.

Part of what motivates this view is a reaction against the claim – implied by welfarism and Rollin's view – that one way of benefiting animals is by genetically design- ing them to be happy in the environment in which we put them (e.g., on the factory farm). But it is not clear how this view avoids that claim. If the value proposed consists of a fit between the animal and its environment, then what is the problem with creating an animal that has an optimal fit with the environment in which we put it?

Maybe the point is that it is the fit between the animal and its environment that we find in nature (laid down by evolution) that must not be disrupted. This would explain why it is wrong to modify animals to fit the environment on the factory farm. But then another question emerges. How can it *harm* an animal to be created with a different fit with its environment than its ancestors had, if its new fit is a better fit than the one it would otherwise have had? Again, it is difficult to see what kind of disvalue is involved from the animal's point of view.

Humans

Most of the uses of somatic and germline gene therapy that have been discussed involve treating or preventing genetically determined diseases by inserting the normally functioning gene that healthy people have. (For further discussion, see chapter 19, "Gene Therapy.") Here, however, I want to consider gene therapy for enhancement. To clarify the difference between treatments and enhancements, let us define a "treatment" as an intervention that aims at curing or reducing the effects of a disease, where a disease is taken to be an adverse departure from species-typical functioning (Boorse 1975). An enhancement does not aim to cure or reduce the effects of a disease. Thus, enhancements may aim to affect various non-disease-related factors that have a genetic component, including intelligence, talent, strength, height, looks, and life-length. What should we think of gene therapy for enhancement?

It is a widely held view that there is a morally relevant difference between using gene therapy for treatments and for enhancements. The latter use is more questionable, if not outright impermissible. This view may seem quite plausible.

However, there are also intuitions that tell against it. Consider the following case. Jane is infected with HIV. Her immune system is starting to give in and she is about to develop AIDS. Fortunately, there is a new kind of gene therapy available – call it therapy A – that will boost her immune system, and bring it back to normal, such that she will in fact never develop AIDS. By performing the therapy, we are providing her with a *treatment*. Now consider Helen. She has not yet been infected with HIV, but she is a hemophiliac and, since blood reserves at the hospital have not been screened for HIV, we know it is only a matter of time before she is infected, unless she receives a new kind of gene therapy – call it therapy B – that will make her immune. (Unfortunately, therapy B only works on hemophiliacs, so it cannot be used on Jane.) By performing the therapy, we are *enhancing* her (or her immune system), since we are giving her a desirable property, where her present condition does not constitute an adverse departure from species-typical normal functioning.

The point is that, intuitively, it does not seem more problematic or less urgent to perform therapy B on Helen than to perform therapy A on Jane. But, according to the view that enhancing is more dubious, it must be so (since the cases are relevantly similar in other respects). Thus, the intuitive case for this view is not as clear-cut as it initially seems.

A different view is that gene therapy is only permissible insofar as it is used to treat diseases or *prevent them from developing*. This view would allow us to perform therapy B on Helen, since we would then be preventing her from developing AIDS. But why stop here? As some ethicists point out, there are more ambitious enhancements that could be claimed to substantially benefit people. For instance, though it may not be possible, John Harris argues that if we could genetically engineer better health and a disposition for a high intelligence into our children, we ought to do so. After all, we would not hesitate to send our children to a school that achieved these same ends (1992: 140–2).

It is, of course, not obvious that a scheme of, for example, genetic intelligence enhancement would be a good idea, even if it could be performed safely. Some will object that it may increase competition and the pressure on children for them to do well.

Furthermore, the risk of a slippery slope should be considered. (See chapter 28, "The Slippery Slope Argument.") Another worry is that we would experience a loss in terms of equality, since the social gaps between people who are able to pay for enhancements and those who are not so fortunate would widen. One reason for this is that the poor would be disadvantaged in the competition for jobs. Even assuming that the treatment were offered to everyone in a publicly funded health-care system, there might still be a problem of fairness, namely if it meant that resources were drawn away from people who were seriously ill and thus had a stronger claim on the health-care budget (Holtug 1999).

These reservations may all be accounted for in terms of welfarism. However, Allen Buchanan, Dan Brock, Norman Daniels, and Daniel Wikler have recently argued that genetic interventions should be assessed on the basis of a resource-egalitarian rather than a welfare-egalitarian conception of justice (Buchanan et al. 2000: chs. 3 and 4). They defend what they call a "Normal Function Model" of equality of opportunity, according to which medicine should aim to keep people as close as possible to "normal functioning," such that people may be normal competitors for advantages. Since disease and disability prevent people from developing the abilities necessary to be normal competitors in social cooperation, justice requires compensation, possibly by genetic intervention (gene therapy or genetic pharmacology).

However, the Normal Function Model does not in general require genetic *enhancements*, because such enhancements are not in general necessary to render people *normal* competitors (as opposed to *equal* competitors). Therefore, Buchanan et al. claim that this model provides a limited defense of the relevance of the treatment/enhancement distinction.

Consider a case in which two 11-year-old boys, Johnny and Billy, are predicted to have an adult height of only 160 cm (5 feet 3 inches). While Johnny's shortness is due to a growth hormone deficiency resulting from a brain tumor, Billy simply has very short parents. In this case, the Normal Function Model implies that a growth hormone treatment can be owed only to Johnny, because of the condition underlying his shortness. To provide a growth hormone "treatment" for Billy too would be to "expand our commitments to assist others beyond simply restoring normal function" (Buchanan et al. 2000: 140).

Nevertheless, it may be suggested that there is a tension in the Normal Function Model. Buchanan et al. point out that the significance of disease is that it limits people's *opportunities* by preventing them from developing the abilities necessary to become normal competitors (Buchanan et al. 2000: 74). However, with respect to *opportunities* it would seem that Johnny and Billy are in the same boat. Everything else being equal, they are equally disadvantaged by their shortness and both are disadvantaged through no fault of their own.

Another possible departure from welfarism is to raise deontological objections to enhancements. Thus, Hans Jonas argues that:

> [W]hen it comes to this core phenomenon of our humanity, which is to be preserved in its integrity at all costs, and which has not to await its perfection from the future because it is already whole in its essence as we possess it . . . then indeed the well-enough founded prognosis of doom has greater force than any concurrent prognosis of bliss. (1984: 34)

241

Jonas's view raises several questions of interpretation. These questions aside, some will find it objectionable because holding that human nature must be preserved at *all* costs implies that one must be very insensitive towards other values. Thus, a strikingly different view is taken by a somewhat ironical Jonathan Glover:

> It is easy to sympathize with opposition to the principle of changing our nature. Preserving it as it is will seem an acceptable option to all those who can watch the news on television and feel satisfied with the world. It will appeal to those who can talk to their children about the history of the twentieth century without wishing they could leave some things out. (1984: 56)

On this view, it would be unreasonable to rule out the possibility of changing human nature *as a matter of principle*. But, of course, in the light of our own fallibility and unfortunate tendency to let our own interests outweigh the interests of future generations, it is possible that the *risks* of ambitious (non-health-related) changes of human nature will always outweigh the expected benefits.

Patents

A further question is whether it is morally permissible to patent new genes and life forms. Here, it is crucial to understand what a patent is. A patent may be issued to anyone who invents or discovers any new, useful, and non-obvious process, machine, manufacture, composition of matter, or any new and useful improvement of these items (35 U.S.C. 101). The right obtained by a patent owner is to exclude others from making, using, or selling the invention. Importantly, the patent does not automatically give him or her the right to make, use, or sell it him- or herself.

Patents on life forms are often opposed partly on the basis of metaphysical views. It is argued that, if life forms are patented, life is thereby reduced to "a composition of matter," since it is only patentable as such. Obviously, this is not the place to try to resolve the dispute between materialists and their opponents. Instead, we may note that the more it is stressed that life is not just "a bag of chemicals," the harder it is to see what the moral problem is with patenting this bag of chemicals (which is all that *can* be patented), because we are then not really patenting life itself.

Another, but related, objection is that patents on life forms are incompatible with having "reverence for life." We then need an account of what the relevant difference is between patenting a life form and owning individual members of that life form. After all, having "reverence for life" is not usually thought to imply that we may not own pets, livestock, or crops.

Also, in the case of micro-organisms and plants, the sentientist challenge must be answered. Since these organisms cannot have experiences or want things to go one way or the other, in what sense can they be violated by being patented? In the case of animals, a similar question arises. Even if an animal is sentient, it has no desires regarding being patented, nor does it experience this event. So, although arguably the so-called Harvard mouse was harmed by being created, it is less clear that it was harmed or violated by being patented.

242

What, then, about welfarist concerns? For welfarists, the question of patents is quite complex. On the one hand, patents stimulate important research. On the other, patents may tend to increase prices on therapeutic drugs and other important products. And they may negatively affect the way in which we relate to life, both our own and that of animals, by increasingly commercializing it. Furthermore, they may disadvantage farmers by forcing them to pay royalty fees on the offspring of their herds, and they may disadvantage developing nations because they could not afford to buy biotechnological products once they are patented, and would experience a loss in terms of competitiveness. (These distributional consequences may seem particularly unfair in the light of the fact that more than 75 percent of the genetic resources in the world are to be found in developing nations, but are used free of cost by biotechnological companies.)

There are, of course, special concerns relating to patents on humans. Patents that would interfere with human autonomy or freedom would be quite dubious according to almost any moral view, whether they were issued on human genes, organs, or even on entire human beings.

References

Attfield, R. (1991). *The Ethics of Environmental Concern*, 2nd edn. Athens: The University of Georgia Press.

Boorse, C. (1975). On the distinction between disease and illness. *Philosophy and Public Affairs* 5/1: 49–68.

Buchanan, A., Brock, D. W., Daniels, N., and Wikler, D. (2000). *From Chance to Choice: Genetics and Justice*. Cambridge: Cambridge University Press.

Fox, M. (1990). Transgenic animals: ethical and animal welfare concerns. In P. Wheale and R. McNally (eds.), *The Bio-revolution: Cornucopia or Pandora's Box?* London: Pluto Press, pp. 31–45.

Glover, J. (1984). *What Sort of People Should There Be?* Harmondsworth: Penguin.

Harris, J. (1992). *Wonderwoman and Superman: The Ethics of Human Biotechnology*. Oxford: Oxford University Press.

Holtug, N. (1999). Does justice require genetic enhancements? *Journal of Medical Ethics* 25/2: 137–43.

Holtug, N. (2001). On the value of coming into existence. *Journal of Ethics* 5/4: 361–84.

Jonas, H. (1984). *The Imperative of Responsibility: In Search for an Ethics of the Technological Age*. Chicago: University of Chicago Press.

Regan, T. (1984). *Animal Rights*. London: Routledge.

Rollin, B. (1986). On telos and genetic manipulation. *Between the Species* 2/2: 88–9.

Schweitzer, A. (1923). *Civilization and Ethics: The Philosophy of Civilization*, trans. J. Naish. London: A. & C. Black.

Singer, P. (1993). *Practical Ethics*, 2nd edn. Cambridge: Cambridge University Press.

Vorstenbosch, J. (1993). The concept of integrity: its significance for the ethical discussion on biotechnology and animals. *Lifestock Production Science* 36: 109–12.

Further reading

Bostrom, N. and Ord, T. (2006). The reversal test. Eliminating status quo bias in applied ethics. *Ethics* 116/4: 656–79.

Brody, B. A. (1989). An evaluation of the ethical arguments commonly raised against the patenting of transgenic animals. In W. H. Lesser (ed.), *Animal Patents. The Legal, Economic and Social Issues.* New York: Stockton Press, pp. 141–53.

Donnelley, S., McCarthy, C. R., and Singleton, R. Jr (1994). The brave new world of animal biotechnology. *Hastings Center Report* 24 (special supplement): S2–S31.

Engelhardt, H. T., Jr (1990). Human nature technologically revisited. *Social Philosophy and Policy* 8: 180–91.

Hare, R. M. (1991). Moral reasoning about the environment. In B. Almond and D. Hill (eds.), *Applied Philosophy.* London: Routledge, pp. 9–20.

Holtug, N. (1997). Altering humans: the case for and against human gene therapy. *Cambridge Quarterly of Healthcare Ethics* 6: 157–74.

Kass, L. (1985). Patenting life. In Kass, *Toward a More Natural Science.* New York: Free Press, pp. 128–53.

Rifkin, J. (1983). *Algeny.* New York: Viking Press.

Rollin, B. (1995). *The Frankenstein Syndrome: Ethical and Social Issues in the Genetic Engineering of Animals.* Cambridge: Cambridge University Press.

Sandøe, P., Holtug, N., and Simonsen, H. B. (1996). Ethical limits to domestication. *Journal of Agricultural and Environmental Ethics* 9: 114–22.

Savulescu, J. and Bostrom, N. (eds.) (2007). *Enhancement of Human Beings.* Oxford: Oxford University Press.

Suzuki, D. and Knudtson, P. (1990). *Genethics: The Ethics of Engineering Life.* London: Unwin Hyman.

Wheale, P. and McNally, R. (eds.) (1990). *The Bio-revolution: Cornucopia or Pandora's Box?* London: Pluto Press.

22

Genetic Counseling, Testing, and Screening

ANGUS CLARKE

Genetic counseling can be defined in a number of ways, which emphasize different aspects of this complex activity. Perhaps the best-known definition is that of the American Society of Human Genetics (1975), which emphasizes that it is a communication process dealing with both the biological facts and the very personal, human consequences of genetic disorders. Genetic counseling aims to help individuals understand their situation and adapt to it as well as possible. Genetic counselors therefore have an educational, information-imparting role and an emotionally and practically supportive role, ensuring that, as far as possible, their clients make adjustments and decisions that accord with their beliefs, wishes and personalities but that are also firmly grounded in biological reality (McCarthy Veach et al. 2007).

While "the facts" will often appear to be much the same for different clients, the human context may be very different. The first task of the genetic counselor, therefore, is to listen to the client – to her words and to the gaps between these words – to discover the questions that need to be answered and the concerns to be addressed.

It is usually very helpful to establish the diagnosis of the condition in the family as precisely as possible. This will help to answer at least the technical, factual questions within the constraints of medical science. The conversation may then develop to explore the wider concerns of the client, including the personal meaning the disorder has for her and the likely significance for her and her family of any possible future decisions about reproduction or predictive testing.

If there is a clear genetic explanation for a child's profound handicap, then the mother may feel relieved of the anxiety that she might have caused the problems by something she did in pregnancy. On the other hand, parents or grandparents may be devastated to learn that they have transmitted "faulty genes" that have caused a serious problem in their child or grandchild. The client may wish to explore her feelings about guilt, blame, and responsibility for the problem, and the counselor may facilitate this. A mother may have sufficient scientific understanding to "know" that she is not personally at fault for the condition that affects her child, but she may still feel the burden of responsibility at an emotional level (Weil 1991). There may also be differences of perspective on the consequences of having a diagnostic label, which may help to gain access to services but may also lead to damaged self-esteem or stigmatization (Gillman et al. 2000).

Similarly, the impact on the client and on other family members of a decision to have a predictive genetic test for a neurodegenerative condition such as Huntington's disease (a dementia and movement disorder with variable age of onset, usually in middle life) may need to be discussed. How might the various family members respond if the test result is favorable, or if it is unfavorable, or unclear, or if she finally decides not to be tested? A similar process of considering the range of potential consequences may be helpful for couples who are making a decision about prenatal diagnosis and a possible termination of pregnancy, especially if other family members are affected.

For professionals, the question arises as to how challenging to be when encouraging such hypothetical reflection about possible future scenarios (Sarangi et al. 2005). How can one encourage reflection without coercing or manipulating (Wolff and Jung 1995; Clarke 1995)? The importance of client autonomy in decisions about reproduction and genetic testing is enshrined in the canons of modern bioethics, and is confirmed internationally in numerous policy documents. The importance of genetic counselors adopting a "non-directive" stance is frequently emphasized and, even if non-directiveness is unattainable in practice, the ethos of genetic counseling remains non-prescriptive. There are now several settings, however, where adherence to the doctrine of "non-directiveness" has weakened or is under challenge.

Information Management: Confidentiality, Autonomy and Non-Directiveness

Just as the core component activity of genetic counseling is the provision of information, so the principal ethical difficulties relate to how this information should be used. Information given to a client may be relevant to other members of the extended family if other individuals are at risk of developing the condition or transmitting it to their children. There may be complications of the condition that can be avoided if the individuals at risk are aware of their situation.

If the client fails to pass on the relevant information, or even just the fact that there is relevant information, then is the genetic counselor obliged to do this herself? She may not know the names or addresses of the client's relatives but, where it is possible, should she pass on the potentially important information?

It has been argued that client confidentiality can justifiably be broken in such circumstances, and that guidelines should be drawn up to clarify these circumstances. Against this position, it can be maintained that the drawing up of such guidelines will be unhelpful or even counter-productive, and may devalue the importance of confidentiality. Furthermore, passing personal information through a family network against the wishes of family members could both encounter and generate serious problems.

In almost all cases where an individual initially decides not to pass on important information to other family members, he will in practice change his mind once he has had time to consider the full implications of his decision. Furthermore, it can be argued that the legal duty of confidentiality to the primary client, and respect for the privacy of other family members, make it inappropriate to intervene in these circumstances. If guidelines for professionals are drawn up that legitimize breaches of confidentiality, then clients will know that genetic information can be passed to other family members without their consent; this may result in some being reluctant to disclose family information to professionals or to seek genetic counseling at all, although such forced disclosure is rare in practice (Clarke et al. 2005). Of course, it must also be remembered that the inadvertent disclosure of information about one person to other members of their extended family is a hazard that must always be guarded against; this can happen all too easily, especially when multiple members of a family are being seen separately but concurrently in one clinic.

To regard personal information as belonging to the whole family perhaps begs the very question at issue (Clarke 2007). One question related to this is whether the laboratory-generated mutation result should count as personal information to be controlled by the patient in the same way as knowledge about their illness and diagnosis. Should the mutation details be available for use in testing other members of the family once the diagnosis has been disclosed, without necessarily obtaining the consent of the family member in whom the mutation was first identified?

Concern for the welfare of other family members can also lead to pressure on individuals to undergo genetic testing for the benefit of their relatives rather than themselves, as when women with a family history of breast cancer may wish an affected relative to undergo testing to see if a specific gene mutation can be found. This may help family members to clarify their risk status, but the affected woman may prefer not to be tested because of the adverse prognostic implications of finding a mutation. This requires the affected person, at a difficult time, to weigh her own feelings against the interests of her relatives (Hallowell et al. 2003); but to argue that this moral tension undermines the woman's autonomy reflects a shallow, asocial notion of autonomy.

Predictive Genetic Testing

Predictive genetic testing is another context where genetic counseling has until recently maintained a thorough respect for autonomy, that is non-directiveness, but where this may now be weakening. As genetic risk comes to be assessed more frequently in the context of decisions about medical management, as with the surveillance available to those at risk of familial cancers or cardiac disease, genetics professionals are more likely to adopt a shared approach to decision-making (Elwyn et al. 2000) and to make explicit recommendations to their clients about genetic testing when it contributes to management. Non-directiveness is still the dominant ethos in reproductive decisions and the delicate context of testing for late-onset but untreatable neurodegenerative disorders, where pre-symptomatic diagnosis does not (yet) alter the clinical outcomes.

Within genetic counseling, the most intensively studied area of predictive testing has been that for Huntington's disease When predictive testing first became available for Huntington's disease, it was decided that the systematic recording of experience and the development of protocols would be needed to insure that the offer of testing did not cause more harm than good. A wide range of practical problems did arise during the first few years of testing (Morris et al. 1989). More recent experience with follow-up of those given both high-risk and low-risk results has shown that both groups can suffer social and emotional problems. Those given low risks do not always experience the anticipated sense of relief, and may suffer survivor guilt.

Before predictive testing for Huntington's disease was feasible, most at-risk individuals indicated that they would want testing. Since then, however, experience has shown that many have decided not to proceed. This serves to emphasize the importance of pre-test counseling, which gives individuals the opportunity to reflect upon the possible consequences of testing and helps them to make appropriate decisions. They can take into account the possible reactions of – among others – family members and partners, friends, employers, and insurance companies.

Predictive testing for conditions where patient management is helped by pre-symptomatic testing raises fewer ethical and psychological difficulties, although difficulties remain when the benefits claimed for prevention, early treatment, or enhanced surveillance are contested or unclear.

Childhood Genetic Testing

Special issues are raised by the genetic testing of children. When the management of a child's health problem depends upon accurate diagnosis, the use of genetic methods to establish the diagnosis is of course in the best interests of the child. Similarly, if a child is at risk of developing a late-onset disorder for which some useful intervention or surveillance is available, and which may be of particular benefit if started in childhood, then the situation is the same. But if a child is at high risk of a condition that is unlikely to develop until later in life, and if there is no health benefit to the individual from pre-symptomatic diagnosis, then the situation is different.

There are three principal grounds for concern about childhood genetic testing that may lead to a policy of caution. First, testing in childhood removes the individual's future right as an autonomous adult to make their own decision about testing. Secondly, the confidentiality that would be automatic for any adult undergoing testing will be lost. Finally, genetic testing may lead to harmful social or emotional consequences for the child. The family's expectations of the child may be altered in an unhelpful manner. This could damage the child's educational prospects and their emotional and interpersonal development, and could lead to stigmatization, discrimination, and low self-esteem. These considerations have led to recommendations that pre-symptomatic testing for Huntington's disease should *not* be performed on minors and that caution be exercised in other circumstances as well. The fact that so many at-risk adults choose not to be tested does suggest that concern about the child's loss of future autonomy is warranted.

Similar considerations apply to testing children for their carrier status, relevant especially to their future reproduction. Individuals affected by an autosomal recessive condition have a double dose of a "faulty" copy of the gene. Such carriers may have affected children if their partners are also carriers of the same faulty gene. Meanwhile, a person who carries a single faulty copy of the gene is usually perfectly healthy; their intact copy of the gene is sufficient to avoid disease. If there are harmful social and emotional effects of carrier testing in childhood, these are unlikely to relate to expectations about the child's future health. Instead, these are likely to be altered family expectations of a proven carrier's future relationships and reproduction as an adult. For example, a girl carrying (the sex-linked condition) Duchenne muscular dystrophy may be brought up in the expectation that she would have no sons, or perhaps no children.

More is at stake when testing possible carriers of chromosomal or sex-linked disorders, because such carriers are at high risk of having an affected child irrespective of the genetic constitution of their partner, and there may be implications for the health of some of these carriers.

These issues do not arise in the same way if the "child" is sufficiently mature to take the lead in requesting genetic tests – that is, if she is legally a minor but requests testing and is capable of weighing up the issues. Loss of the child's future autonomy is then not such an issue.

It may be argued that parents have a right to know the genetic status of their children, but if this is not relevant to health care during childhood, then this argument is weak; under British law, deciding what is in the best interests of the child would be the most appropriate way of coming to a decision. It might be claimed that children accept and adjust to unwelcome information more readily before adolescence than when they are older, but systematic evidence on this point is lacking. There may be more truth in the argument that those adolescents and young adults whose own decisions have not been pre-empted by parents or professionals, and who have been trusted to make the decision for themselves, will make the best adjustment to unfavorable results.

There are differences of opinion on these questions among health professionals, between professionals and parents, and also perhaps between societies and cultural groups. It is difficult to weigh the various considerations against each other – rights against rights, rights against evidence – especially when (1) research studies would require decades of follow-up, (2) the decision as to what would count as evidence (what data to collect) might be contentious, and (3) many health professionals and ethicists believe that one of the policies to be examined (a more permissive approach to testing, where parents but not professionals are allowed to be paternalistic) would be unethical.

Genetic Screening

Genetic screening can be contrasted with genetic counseling in three ways: it is proactive rather than reactive, it always involves the offer of genetic testing, and it is aimed at a whole population, or a defined subpopulation, rather than individuals and their immediate families. Screening programs therefore raise several potential ethical problems. Perhaps the most serious issue is the danger that individuals will be offered testing in a routinized manner by health professionals who clearly expect them to comply; the clients may then participate without having adequately considered the possible consequences.

Four types of genetic screening program need to be mentioned:

1 Newborn screening, usually for treatable disorders where early diagnosis greatly improves the outlook for an affected child.
2 Carrier screening – to identify carriers of recessive disorders, who will themselves usually be healthy but who may have an affected child, especially if their partner is also a carrier.
3 Prenatal screening, usually for malformations (e.g., neural tube defects) or chromosomal conditions (e.g., Down syndrome) in the fetus, but sometimes identifying

couples who are both carriers of a recessive disorder or where the woman carries an X chromosome disorder.

4 Susceptibility screening for genetic predisposition to common diseases such as common cancers, heart disease, and Alzheimer's dementia. Such population screening is feasible in terms of the technology, but the evidence of clinical utility required to justify population screening for risk of such diseases is not available, despite some commercial adventures in this area. Genetic testing for such conditions is currently applicable only within unusual, high-risk kindreds where a single gene of major effect is the predominant factor influencing whether or not an individual develops the condition; such genes of major effect are termed "Mendelian."

Informed Consent to Screening

In genetic counseling, the clients are actively seeking information about a disease of which they usually already have some knowledge and practical experience. In population screening, on the other hand, the clients may have little knowledge and no experience of the condition for which they are being screened; furthermore, they are being approached by health professionals who usually believe that the test on offer is "A Good Thing." Under these conditions, is the requirement for informed consent actually observed in practice? It is possible to debate the criteria that define informed consent, but the important question may rather be what type of consent is required in what context.

Does it matter if the consent obtained is not "fully informed," as long as the screening test *is* indeed A Good Thing? Where newborn screening is important for the sake of the child, is it really necessary for screening to depend upon fully informed (parental) consent? While we may answer "No" in that setting, similarly paternalistic arguments that downplay the need for informed consent in relation to reproduction, and that emphasize the benefits of screening for the wider society, lead directly to a new eugenics in which lip service is paid to autonomy and informed consent but in which these principles are not respected in everyday reality.

Newborn Screening

Newborn screening began nearly 40 years ago with the Guthrie test for phenylketonuria. Screening for phenylketonuria and congenital hypothyroidism is now routine in many countries. In both conditions, an early diagnosis permits effective treatment and results in essentially normal development. Without this, the affected infants would suffer profound mental handicap.

Because the benefits of screening infants for these treatable disorders are so great, programs of newborn screening have often been instituted with little explanation or information for parents. Such screening has usually been routinized, and in some states it is mandatory. Studies of parental knowledge of newborn screening have shown that few parents even know for what conditions their infants are screened; in screening for phenylketonuria and congenital hypothyroidism, is it justified to maximize compliance without insuring fully informed consent?

Newborn screening for other disorders is less widespread because the health benefits for the affected infants are less easily demonstrable, although there is a strong case for introducing tests for some other conditions in specific populations.

One newborn screening program had to be discontinued because of the adverse impact on families. This was the Swedish program identifying infants with alpha-1 antitrypsin deficiency, who are at increased risk of chronic lung disease, especially if they are exposed to smoke or dust. The screening program generated great distress in the families of affected infants; one potential benefit of such screening could have been protection of the susceptible infants from exposure to smoke, so it was particularly worrying that more fathers of affected infants smoked than did fathers of control infants (McNeil et al. 1988).

Screening is becoming available for a range of other disorders where the benefit to the identified (not necessarily affected) child may be modest, uncertain, or contentious. Newborn screening for cystic fibrosis appears likely to have some long-term benefits for the child in addition to cost savings and some improved early outcomes, although that remains uncertain. Screening for a wide range of metabolic disorders is becoming available with the introduction of tandem mass spectroscopy in many countries. Such technology-led developments in screening require careful assessment on a disease-by-disease basis rather than adoption as a package, because the advantages and disadvantages are likely to differ on the basis of the clinical picture rather than the biochemical findings.

Newborn screening for Duchenne muscular dystrophy (DMD) has been available in Wales and a few other countries for years, with the main benefits being avoidance of distress from long diagnostic delays, the early availability of genetic counseling and reproductive choice, and the opportunity for parents to plan for the future. DMD is a progressive neuromuscular condition that usually becomes apparent by the age of 5 or 6 years; it leads to the inability to walk by 8 to 12 years, and to death usually in the late teenage years or 20s. DMD is inherited as a sex-linked trait, and the mothers of many boys are healthy female carriers with a 50 percent chance of transmitting the condition to any future son. Other female relatives may also be carriers, so the diagnosis of DMD in one boy may have repercussions for the extended family. Whether or not the advantages mentioned above are sufficient to justify the program has been contentious, but improvements in treatment, based upon a precise know-ledge of the disease process at the molecular level, may resolve this. Entry to the newborn screening program is optional, on the basis of "considered parental choice," and minor modifications to the protocol for offering the test can enhance the quality of the parental decision process (Parsons et al. 2000). The principal disadvantage is the emotional trauma of such an early diagnosis. The balance between the advantages and disadvantages cannot be determined a priori; this is a clear example of the need for evidence generated by the careful evaluation of a program in operation. The social evaluation has so far found that most families with an affected child are pleased to have known early (Parsons et al. 2002), but this depends crucially on the quality of family support made available; the evidence is not yet sufficient for such a program to be generally recommended.

Carrier Screening

The frequency of carriers of recessive disorders among the general population varies, depending upon the detailed population history of a person's ancestors, but it can be high. A common recessive disorder in Britain is cystic fibrosis (CF): one in 25 Britons is a carrier and one in 2,500 children is affected. CF leads to recurrent chest infections that progressively impair lung function and to the malabsorption of food from the bowel; treatments have improved over the past 20 years, so that many affected children now survive into adult life. A common recessive disease in West Africa is sickle cell disease: one in 4 people from some areas carries sickle cell disease and one in 50 is affected. Most carriers of recessive diseases have parents, brothers, and sisters who are healthy and have no known "family history" of the disease in question.

Carrier screening may therefore generate anxieties and concerns in many people who will never "benefit" from being identified as carriers. It will never be of any significance to them because their partners are not carriers, or they are not planning any further children, or their reproductive plans would anyway not be altered by knowledge of a risk of their having an affected child. Carrier testing may be seen as burdening them with unwelcome information, and so the criteria by which to judge the informed consent procedures of carrier screening programs must be stringent. In addition, other outcomes of carrier screening – such as the recall and interpretation of test results and the impact on an individual's sense of well-being – must also be evaluated.

How can it be decided whether the modest burden of carrier testing on many people is worthwhile for the sake of a few families who will be pleased to discover their carrier status? From studies of screening programs, it is known that some couples do make use of the knowledge of their carrier status to alter their reproductive plans. But what else has been learned? Are there drawbacks to such programs?

First, it is clear that there can be disadvantages to being identified as a carrier of a recessive disease. Carriers can experience shame, social stigmatization, and institutionalized discrimination. Some carriers may have latent concerns about their own health, or may be "worried" about their carrier status even years after testing and may have concerns about their own future health. Carriers of CF have been found to have lower self-esteem than non-carriers.

Secondly, we know that many parents, aunts, and uncles of children with CF (for example) do not use – or do not intend to use – prenatal diagnosis and the selective termination of affected pregnancies. If there is no consensus among this group – those who will know much more than most about the condition – then it could be argued that it would be unwise to offer carrier screening on a wide scale to the general population. In addition, adults affected by CF – the long-term survivors – have differing views about such screening.

Thirdly, while most of those enrolled in carrier screening programs do not suffer serious distress, some carriers do regret having been tested. Furthermore, experience in Britain and elsewhere suggests that public interest in CF testing is limited. The rate of uptake of testing depends very largely on the way in which the offer is made (Bekker et al. 1993), suggesting that those accepting the test are often complying with enthusiastic health professionals but are only weakly motivated.

Those tested in such programs have a good understanding of their test results shortly after testing, but an increasing proportion of subjects have misunderstandings when asked about the significance of their result some months or years later.

Some professionals have welcomed the prospect of population carrier screening for CF with enthusiasm, seeing it as an opportunity to establish an infrastructure for community genetics which could subsequently broaden to offer screening for other diseases. However, while some professional and commercial groups do favor the promotion of population carrier screening, the financial and opportunity costs of establishing such a program for many diseases would be prohibitive if pre- and post-test counseling of high quality were to be included. The use of micro-array technology to identify the large majority of carriers of most important recessive diseases may soon transform carrier screening but will require evaluation before it could be recommended.

Prenatal Screening

The decision of a health-care system or of individual professionals to offer prenatal screening for any condition inevitably conveys a recommendation to pregnant women that accepting the test is the responsible course of action, and that a fetus identified as affected should be aborted. However much the language of reproductive choice, client autonomy, and informed consent is employed in discussions with pregnant women, the fact that the screening program exists will convey this message. This potential problem is inherent in all screening programs, but is most acute in the prenatal context. The conventional veneer of neutrality in this setting is also undermined by the outrage so widely expressed when representatives of disability rights groups call for the right to use genetic technology to select *for* a fetus affected by *their* condition, such as deafness or achondroplasia, at prenatal or pregestational (preimplantation) genetic diagnosis.

Those who fail to comply with the "standard" prenatal screening policy of their hospital may be regarded as irresponsible, and if they have a child affected by a condition that could have been "prevented" (by termination of pregnancy) they may be regarded as blameworthy. While most pregnant women explain their decision to accept screening on the grounds that they wish to make sure that the baby is alright, or simply to *see* the baby, the fear of being labeled as irresponsible may be an important, additional factor in leading those who are uncertain toward compliance. Those who accept screening, but then continue a pregnancy in which the fetus has a serious malformation or chromosome problem, often experience difficulties with professionals in their subsequent care. In some health-care systems, parents may be financially liable for the care of a sick child; if the parents declined prenatal screening then their insurance policies may exclude coverage.

In addition to the effects of prenatal screening programs on the women involved, they may also have a very negative effect on individuals within society who are affected by the condition(s) that the program is designed to "prevent." Individuals with other disabilities may also feel that prenatal screening exacerbates society's intolerance of deviations from what is seen as the ideal – being "normal."

Finally, it seems that the capacity of gene technology is on the point of shifting gear so as to generate information about the whole genome of patients, or at least about much of their genetic variation, rather than giving information about one gene at a time. This is happening just as fetal DNA comes to be more readily accessible in maternal blood; the scope of noninvasive prenatal diagnosis and prenatal screening looks set to expand at an accelerating pace. How such advances will be managed, to be made available in those circumstances where they may be helpful but not otherwise, will require very careful deliberation.

Susceptibility Screening

Great efforts are being made to identify the genetic factors that contribute to the development of the common multifactorial disorders such as colon cancer, breast cancer, diabetes, coronary artery disease, hypertension, Alzheimer's dementia and some psychiatric disorders. This could lead to the development of improved therapies but could also lead to tests that would identify those at increased risk without offering any effective interventions. At the very least, there is likely to be a lag of many years between the ability to test for risk-modifying (not predictive) genetic variants and the ability to prevent or treat the disease in question.

Predictive genetic testing is possible for single-gene disorders in known families, identifying individuals who are likely to develop uncommon conditions such as Huntington's disease or some of the familial cancers. For the common disorders being considered here, however, true predictive testing is most unlikely to be possible. Whether or not someone develops these conditions is influenced by interactions between multiple genetic factors and many environmental variables, only some of which are likely to be under the control of the individual. Genetic tests will identify the relative risk of a person developing a disease by a particular age in comparison to the average population risk, but will not be able to make firm predictions about individuals. Risk information may or may not be helpful to individuals, depending upon the availability of preventive interventions and the behavioral responses of each individual, which may prove to be medically appropriate but may also sometimes be paradoxically unhelpful. Empiric studies of how people respond to such genetic risk information will be required once it has been established as reliable.

A growing trend has been described of accounting for differences between people in relation to both disease susceptibility and non-disease traits, such as intelligence, personality, and behavior, in terms of genetic factors. This is known as geneticization. It leads society to seek solutions to its problems through scientific and technological means, often focusing on specific high-risk individuals rather than responding collectively through social, political, economic, or environmental changes (Lippman 1992). This could lead to demands for genetic susceptibility screening that may be of little health benefit to the tested individuals, but may be used by employers, insurance companies, or governments.

Genetic tests of susceptibility can generate a sense of fatalism in those at increased risk, and a sense of invulnerability in those at average risk or lower. If there is any scope for lifestyle decisions to modify disease risk, then both groups may be led to behave inappropriately by indulging in risky behaviors. To label a substantial proportion of the population as being at increased genetic risk, when there is little benefit in terms of prevention or treatment and a real risk of adverse behavioral or psychosocial consequences, would seem unwise (Clarke 1995). Despite these grounds for caution, commercially based genetic susceptibility screening tests are now being actively promoted. For the moment, the most powerful pressure seems to be the enthusiasm of venture capitalists and a few professionals to part the fool from his money, but other, more powerful, forces are likely to become increasingly important. In particular, some pharmaceutical corporations will seek to sell remedies to prevent the diseases to which individuals have been "shown" to be susceptible, linking the DNA test to a branded "remedy" that can then be purchased lifelong. Such test/drug combinations may well prove helpful in guiding the choice of drug therapies for specific diseases – let us hope for such progress – but may be less of a blessing in the indeterminate, shadowy and poorly regulated area of genetic screening to guide lifestyle choices and the purchase of branded nutritional supplements.

International cooperation may be required for the effective control of the irresponsible and inappropriate marketing of poorly validated, over-the-counter genetic tests.

Further Information Management

There are other concerns relating to the possible misuse of genetic information about individuals. Perhaps the area that has generated most debate is that of life and health insurance. It is clearly in the interests of insurance companies to know at least as much about an individual's genetic susceptibility to disease as does that individual. But the social function of insurance would be largely undermined if companies had accurate information about the disease susceptibilities of all their potential clients and used this to set differential premiums. Indeed, there are good grounds for believing this to be morally unfair; insurance would cease to be a form of collective solidarity in the face of infrequent, but potentially catastrophic, events beyond the control of individuals. Representatives of the insurance industry often reject the assertion that they should choose not to discover as much information relevant to the likely future health of their clients as possible, on the grounds that this would jeopardize the very survival of their industry. As a compromise, it has been proposed in the UK that insurance companies should not incorporate molecular genetic information into their risk calculations for modest levels of insurance cover, while they are permitted to do so for certain disorders when providing higher levels of cover.

Such problems are of greater importance in countries where the health-care system is financed through private insurance, and so health care as well as life insurance may be denied to those with unfavorable genetic constitutions. These considerations lend strong support to the organization of health care through a nationalized system, or at least through a universal and state-regulated health insurance scheme.

In addition to these concerns about the use of genetic information by insurance companies, there are other concerns about ways in which genetic information may be used to discriminate unfairly against individuals. Difficulties are faced by individuals with genetic disorders, or with a family history of such disorders, in finding access to appropriate insurance policies even in the UK, with its National Health Service, and are worse in other countries with less state provision of health and social care.

Reported cases of the misuse of genetic information strengthen calls to regulate the practice of insurance companies, and also add to the concerns about confidentiality – genetic privacy – in this area. Might employers be able to access such information about potential employees and select "the fittest"? Might those with adverse genetic test results, or even just family histories of genetic disorders, become unemployable as well as uninsurable?

Screening for susceptibility to "occupational" diseases is not yet technically feasible except in the case of A1ATD-associated chronic lung disease, but this may serve as a model disorder for considering the likely future issues. Employers might in the future attempt to impose genetic screening as a condition of employment, when a better approach might be to minimize dust exposure for all employees and monitor for early signs of the lung disorder (Lappe 1988).

How can these problems be avoided? In the USA and elsewhere, specific legislation is being developed to prevent discrimination against not only those with genetic conditions (those already affected), but also those shown to be at risk because of their genetic constitution. Fears of unfair discrimination, however, remain. If patients do not trust the health-care system to respect their privacy, they may edit the information they make available to their physicians so that adverse details are not entered in their records; this could then lead to suboptimal care being provided. Society will need to carefully define the types of genetic information that can and cannot be used by employers and insurance companies if such problems are to be avoided.

Goals of Genetic Screening: Public Health vs Individual Choice

The final ethical issue to be raised in the context of genetic counseling and screening relates to the goals and outcomes of such services. What is achieved in genetic counseling and screening? How should this be measured and justified?

There are two broad types of answer to these questions. One approach is to examine the overall impact of genetic services on the health-care system. This may be termed the "public health" approach to genetic services. The other approach is to focus on the effects of genetic services on individual clients – the "client-centered" approach. Both approaches can be applied to the long-established genetics domain of reproduction, but it is now becoming important to ask the same questions in relation to the common, complex degenerative diseases.

The public health approach to reproductive genetics assesses the outcomes of services in crude measures of the birth incidence of infants with a specific genetic disorder, or the financial costs and benefits of alternative courses of action. The cost of prenatal screening for spina bifida, Down syndrome, or cystic fibrosis and the selective termination of affected pregnancies may be weighed against the cost of caring for affected individuals. The logic of this resource-sparing approach leads to conclusions that many would regard as unjust and ethically offensive, with potential lives being terminated simply because the cost of caring for affected individuals would be greater than the cost of detecting and terminating them prenatally, whether or not their lives might be regarded as "worthwhile" and whether or not they would entail physical suffering. A system organized with this logic could lead to pressure being applied to clients to conform to the system's preferred options – insuring compliance with prenatal screening programs, and leading women to feel that they have little choice but to terminate the pregnancy whenever "medically indicated." The question, "Should society set out to prevent Down syndrome?" is answered tacitly in the affirmative by society's actions, but the question itself has never been debated comprehensively in public.

The client-centered approach to reproductive genetics can assess the effect of genetics services by measuring the information gained by individual clients, their understanding of risk information that has been supplied, their sense of personal control over their lives, and the extent to which their reproductive plans, decision-making, or behaviors have been facilitated or altered. None of these measures, however, is entirely satisfactory, and it may be that the search for readily quantifiable outcome measures for these genetic services is inappropriate. One problem is that the quality of life of affected individuals and their families is not simply an individual matter but is influenced by society's willingness to provide support for those affected and by the degree to which affected individuals feel valued or, conversely, disrespected and stigmatized in social interaction.

In relation to the common, complex disorders, a different approach may be needed. The current role of genetic services for these disorders is to tease apart the small minority of those with a family history who do have a very substantially increased risk of disease, the Mendelian subset of approximately 5 percent, from among the much larger number of those at or close to average population risk. This approach is clearly helpful to the individual and to the health-care system. The individual is offered appropriate advice about lifestyle, available preventive strategies, surveillance for early signs of disease, and gains access to early treatment; society uses its health-care resources sparingly to monitor those at definitely increased risk of disease without wasting resources on the many others who would be unlikely to develop problems (e.g., those relatives shown not to carry their family's disease-associated mutation).

Extending genetic risk assessments to the whole population is another matter. It is still the case that the application of genetic epidemiological data to generate packages of risk-modifying tests for the population would be premature, as we still do not know how to combine genotypic data from multiple loci. If we did have that knowledge, however, a major problem would still remain: we do not know how to promote the recommended, healthy behaviors most effectively. Even more seriously, we do not know whether it is the role of health professionals to effect behavior change in their patients; is it merely their role to inform and recommend? Are health professionals to be held accountable for the unhealthy behaviors of their patients? If so, what types of cynical and manipulative medical practice are we likely to encounter before long?

Conclusion

The way in which a genetics service has been structured and the way in which it operates in practice are more likely to provide accurate insight to its purpose and nature than its publicly stated objectives. If a service is promoted to the public as being client-centered, but it justifies its existence to the purchasers of health care as saving resources in a crude, reproductive cost-benefit analysis, then there is likely to be a gap between the public rhetoric and the service delivered to clients. The real goals of the service will be manifest in its practice, and they will often reveal the underlying values of those who direct it.

References

American Society of Human Genetics (1975). Genetic counseling. *American Journal of Human Genetics* 27: 240–2.

Bekker, H. et al. (1993). Uptake of cystic fibrosis testing in primary care: supply push or demand pull? *British Medical Journal* 306: 1584–6.

Clarke A. (1995). Population screening for genetic susceptibility to disease. *British Medical Journal* 311: 35–8.

Clarke A. (2007). Head to head. Should families own genetic information? No. *British Medical Journal* 335: 23.

Clarke, A. et al. (2005). Genetic professionals' reports of non-disclosure of genetic risk information within families. *European Journal of Human Genetics* 13: 556–62.

Elwyn, G., Gray, J., and Clarke, A. (2000). Shared decision-making and non-directiveness in genetic counseling. *Journal of Medical Genetics* 37: 135–8.

Gillman, M., Heyman, B., and Swain, J. (2000). What's in a name? The implications of diagnosis for people with learning difficulties and their family carers. *Disability and Society* 15: 389–409.

Hallowell, N., Foster, C., Eeles, R., Ardern-Jones, A., Murday, V., and Watson, M. (2003). Balancing autonomy and responsibility: the ethics of generating and disclosing genetic information. *Journal of Medical Ethics* 29: 74–9.

Lappe, M. (1988). Ethical issues in genetic screening for susceptibility to chronic lung disease. *Journal of Occupational Medicine* 30: 493–501.

Lippman, A. (1992). Led (astray) by genetic maps: the cartography of the human genome and health care. *Social Science and Medicine* 35: 1469–76.

McCarthy Veach, P., Bartels, D. M., and LeRoy, B. S. (2007). Coming full circle: a reciprocal engagement model of genetic counseling practice. *Journal of Genetic Counseling* 16: 713–728.

McNeil, T. F., Sveger, T., and Thelin, T. (1988). Psychosocial effects of screening for somatic risk: the Swedish alpha-1 antitrypsin experience. *Thorax* 43: 505–7.

Morris, M., Tyler, A., Lazerou, L., Meredith, L., and Harper, P. S. (1989). Problems in genetic prediction for Huntington's disease. *Lancet* ii: 601–3.

Parsons, E. P., Clarke, A. J., Hood, K., et al. (2000). Feasibility of a change in service delivery: the case of optional newborn screening for Duchenne muscular dystrophy. *Community Genetics* 3: 17–23.

Parsons, E. P., Clarke, A. J., and Bradley, D. M. (2002). Newborn screening for Duchenne muscular dystrophy: a psychosocial study. *Archives of Diseases in Childhood, Fetal Neonatal Edition* 86: F91–95.

Sarangi, S., Bennert, K., Howell, L., Clarke, A., Harper, P., and Gray, J. (2005). (Mis)alignments in counseling for Huntington's disease predictive testing: clients' responses to reflective frames. *Journal of Genetic Counseling* 14: 29–42.

Weil, J. (1991). Mothers' post-counseling beliefs about the causes of their children's genetic disorders. *American Journal of Human Genetics* 48: 145–53.

Wolff, G. and Jung, C. (1995). Nondirectiveness and genetic counseling. *Journal of Genetic Counseling* 4: 3–25.

Further reading

Clinical Genetics Society Working Party (1994). The genetic testing of children. Clinical Genetics Society, reprinted in *Journal of Medical Genetics* 31: 785–97.

Harper, P. S. and Clarke, A. (1997) *Genetics, Society and Clinical Practice*. Oxford: Bios Scientific Publications.

Lipinski, S. E., Lipinski, M. J., Biesecker, L. G., and Biesecker, B. B. (2006). Uncertainty and perceived personal control among parents of children with rare chromosome conditions. The role of genetic counseling. *American Journal of Medical Genetics* 142C: 232–40.

Marteau, T., Richards, M. (eds.) (1996). *The Troubled Helix: Social and Psychological Implications of the New Genetics*. Cambridge: Cambridge University Press.

McAllister, M., Payne, K., Nicholls, S., MacLeod, R., Donnai, D., and Davies, L. M. (2007). Improving service evaluation in clinical genetics: identifying effects of genetic diseases on individuals and families. *Journal of Genetic Counseling* 16: 71–83.

Scully, J. L., Porz, R., and Rehmann-Sutter, C. (2007). "You don't make genetic test decisions from one day to the next" – Using time to preserve moral space. *Bioethics* 21: 208–17.

Wang, C., Gonzalez, R., and Merajver, S. D. (2004). Assessment of genetic testing and related counseling services: current research and future directions. *Social Science and Medicine* 58: 1427–42.

Williams, C., Alderson, P., and Farsides, B. (2002). Is non-directiveness possible within the context of antenatal screening and testing? *Social Science and Medicine* 54: 339–47.

Part VII

Life and Death Issues

23

Medical Decisions at the End of Life

DAN W. BROCK

No other area of bioethics has captured public interest and aroused public concern more than medical decisions at the end of life. In many countries the issues have also been the subject of court cases (*Cruzan v. Director, Missouri Dept. of Health* 1990; *Airedale NHS Trust v. Bland* 1993; Blank and Merrick 2005), government commissions and studies (President's Commission 1983), professional debate and professional policy guidelines (Hastings Center 1987; British Medical Association 2001). In this chapter, I shall develop a general ethical framework for these decisions and focus on a few of the central ethical controversies about them.

An Ethical Framework for Treatment Decision-making

Medical decisions at the end of life are only a subset of medical decisions generally, though one key set of controversies is whether the ethical issues are different when life itself is at stake. Thus, in developing the decision-making framework, we can take as an initial guide the ethical values that should guide all health-care treatment decision-making – guide it in the sense of determining the proper roles of the typical parties to these decisions, as well as guiding the decision-makers in the content of their decisions. In nearly all countries, historical tradition and practice in medicine saw the physician as the principal decision-maker because of his or her superior knowledge, training, and experience regarding the patient's medical condition and prognosis, together with possible treatments that might improve that prognosis. This convention was sometimes labeled "physician paternalism." With the enormous increase in recent decades in scientific and medical knowledge and treatment capabilities, we might expect these inequalities between physicians and patients to be greater still today (though medical information is increasingly available to patients and the public, largely through the internet) and thus more firmly to support locating decision-making authority with the physician.

Yet a fundamental change in medicine over the past few decades, perhaps most advanced in the United States but present to some degree in at least most developed countries, has been the rejection of physician paternalism in favor of shared decision-making between physicians and patients, with a new, more important role for patients in decisions about their treatment. There are many reasons for this historical shift, some external to medicine itself and located in broader societal and cultural changes, some internal to medicine and changes in it. Among the external factors, perhaps the most important have been various consumer rights movements and general challenges to established authority. Within medicine, there has been an important change in the conception of medicine's fundamental goals. Traditionally, those goals were understood as the preservation and promotion of the patient's life and health – objective aims about which it was reasonable to believe that the physician, not the patient, possessed the relevant expertise.

In the newer model of shared decision-making, there are commonly perceived to be two fundamental values guiding medical practice: promoting the patient's well-being, and respecting his or her self-determination. How does well-being differ from the older conception of life and health? Health, and in turn how it is best promoted, is typically understood as an objective matter determined by biological and medical science. The alternative concept of well-being is designed to signal the respects in which the fundamental goal of medicine is in part subjectively determined by the particular patient's aims and values. What best serves the patient's well-being depends on which alternative treatment, or the option of no treatment, best furthers the patient's over-all values and plan of life; what best serves health may not always best serve well-being. The task for the physician is to use his or her medical skills to promote the patient's well-being in this sense, and to do so typically requires the patient's participation in treatment decision-making in order to bring knowledge of the patient's own values and plan of life into the decision-making process. With the increased number of alternative modes of treatment for common disease processes, with their different mixes of risks and benefits, there is often no single mode of treatment that is best for all patients with a particular medical condition. So the patient's participation in decision-making is necessary to determine which alternative will best serve his or her well-being.

The other fundamental ethical value at stake in treatment decision-making is respecting individual self-determination. Self-determination, as it bears on treatment decision-making, is the interest of ordinary persons in making significant decisions about their lives for themselves, according to their own values or conception of a good life, and in being left free by other persons, at least within limits, to act on those decisions. By the exercise of self-determination, we have substantial control over our lives and the kind of person we are and become, and thereby take responsibility for our lives. The capacity to direct our lives in this way is the central basis of the moral require-ment of respect for persons and the central source of human dignity. Patient self-determination is fundamental for health-care treatment decision-making because it is the patient, and the patient's body, that will undergo and bear the effects of any treatment; it is the principal legal and moral basis for the requirement of informed consent in health care. It grounds the increasingly broad consensus about patients' rights to decide about treatment, according to the patient's conception of the relative benefits and burdens of different treatment alternatives, and to refuse any treatment. It is important to recognize that sometimes patients may make treatment choices in the exercise of their self-determination that are bad, foolish, or irrational and that do not best serve their well-being even as determined by their own values. The importance of self-determination implies that even most bad choices of competent patients must be respected.

In medical decisions near the end of life, and in particular in decisions about life-sustaining treatment, these values, if anything, strengthen the general case for patients' rights to make treatment decisions. In the debilitated and severely compromised condition of many patients near the end of life, patients often become more concerned with maintaining their comfort, quality of life, and dignity than with extending their lives. Patients sometimes reach a point at which they decide that the best life possible for them with life-sustaining treatment is sufficiently poor that it is worse than no further life at all, and so decide to forgo any further life-sustaining treatment. But there is no objectively correct point for all persons at which further treatment and the life it sustains are no longer a benefit and wanted, but are instead a burden and without value or meaning. There are only the decisions of different competent patients about that point.

This ethical framework for treatment decision-making entitles a competent patient to weigh the benefits and burdens of alternative treatments according to his or her own values, to refuse any treatment and to select from among available alternative treatments. However, in many medical treatment decisions at the end of life, the patient is incompetent, and so a surrogate will have to decide for the patient. For several reasons, common medical practice is to turn to a close family member to act as the patient's surrogate decision-maker: first, that is usually who the patient would want to be his or her surrogate; secondly, that is usually who knows best what the patient would have wanted and who is most concerned about the patient's care; thirdly, in most societies the family is the social unit to which principal responsibility is assigned to care for dependent or incompetent members. Moreover, in many jurisdictions the law now assigns explicit legal authority to family members to serve as surrogates for incompetent patients, even in the absence of their formal appointment as surrogates by the patient or the courts.

In the case of a previously competent adult patient, there are three relevant principles to guide surrogate decision-making. (See also chapter 26, "Advance Directives.") The advance directives principle requires the surrogate to follow any instructions or preferences in the patient's advance directive, if one exists, that are relevant to the treatment choice. If there is no advance directive, the substitute judgment principle requires the surrogate to use his or her knowledge of the patient to attempt to make the decision that the patient would have made in the circumstances that then obtain, if the patient were competent. The advance directives and substitute judgment principles respect the patient's self-determination as much as possible when the patient is incompetent and unable to make decisions for him- or herself. If there is no surrogate with relevant knowledge of the patient's concerns and values, then the decision will have to be guided by the best interests principle, which looks to what most reasonable persons would want in the circumstances; this is appropriate because when the best interests principle is used, no evidence is available about how the patient might be relevantly different from most reasonable persons. In the case of a patient who has never been competent, there are no values of the patient to be respected and the surrogate will have to be guided by an assessment of the patient's best interests. Of course, in real cases the instructions in an advance directive or knowledge about a patient's wishes and values may be only partially helpful, and so reasoning based on more than one principle may have to be used.

There is a general presumption that this framework for all treatment decision-making for competent and incompetent patients applies in particular to life-sustaining treatments, but special issues arise which some persons believe place additional ethical limits on morally permissible treatment decisions when life itself is at stake. We will explore some of those issues in the rest of this chapter. But first we will take up a direct challenge to the rights of patients or their surrogates in the case of futile treatment.

Futile Treatment

Sometimes dying patients or, more commonly, the families of incompetent patients, insist on treatment that the patients' physicians believe would be futile. Probably the most common example remains insistence that an attempt be made to resuscitate the patient in the case of cardiac or respiratory arrest, but other examples include insistence that a dying patient be placed in the intensive care unit (ICU) or receive other highly aggressive interventions. Does the decision-making framework we have just sketched require physicians to provide futile treatment when families demand it? In many countries of the world, including developed countries like the United Kingdom and Japan, significant deference to physicians' recommendations still makes insistence on futile treatment uncommon. But when it occurs, it is crucial to distinguish several different senses of futile treatment. "Physiological futility" covers treatment that is known with the highest medical certainty not to produce the physiological effect in the patient for which the patient or family wants it. This is an issue on which physicians should be expert and provides the strongest case for their refusing to provide the treatment, but probably few actual cases fit physiological futility. What has been called "quantitative futility" is when there is only a very low probability, for example, no more than 1 percent, of a treatment having the hoped-for effect; for example, the possibility of patients with widely metastatic cancer surviving resuscitation to leave the hospital (Schneiderman et al. 1990). What has been called "evaluative futility" is treatment that it is agreed is likely to have a particular physiological effect in the patient, but there is disagreement about whether the effect is a benefit for, or would be wanted by, the patient; for example, ICU care for a patient in a persistent vegetative state. The crucial question for physicians refusing to provide a treatment because of quantitative or evaluative futility is why the physician's judgment of whether an outcome is sufficiently beneficial and/or likely to be worth pursuing should override the patient's or surrogate's different judgment and values, given that it is the patient who will be most affected by the decision. The policy debate about futile treatment concerns how to restrict physicians' rights to refuse to provide futile treatment to the relatively uncontroversial cases, such as physiological futility, and prevent their denial of patients' or families' right to make treatment decisions according to their own, not the physicians', values. Many health-care institutions have adopted procedural policies, typically involving ethics committees, to help resolve these conflicts.

Ordinary and Extraordinary Treatment

Traditionally, a distinction was often made between treatments that may be permissibly forgone from those that must be applied, especially in the case of a surrogate deciding for an incompetent patient. In this view, a patient need not accept extraordinary or heroic measures, but ordinary measures must be provided. One issue is how the two kinds of treatments are distinguished. Among the possible interpretations are invasive versus non-invasive, common versus unusual, high-technology versus simple, and costly versus inexpensive treatments. Since there are many possible understandings of this distinction, unless it is well defined, use of it in practice often generates confusion about which treatments are ordinary or extraordinary. However, for interpretations of the distinction like those just cited, it cannot mark a defensible distinction between obligatory and optional treatments. Why, for example, should whether a treatment employs high technology, such as renal dialysis or respirator support, or is relatively simple, such as antibiotics, make the former optional and the latter obligatory? In some circumstances, dialysis or respirator treatment will be, on balance, clearly beneficial for a patient and so would be wanted, whereas in other circumstances a patient may find the life sustained by those treatments of such poor quality and limited duration that it is without benefit and unwanted. But the same is true of antibiotics, which will usually, but not always, be of benefit for patients with treatable infections. What seems morally important, and determines whether any treatment should be employed in particular circumstances with a particular patient, is not whether the treatment employs high technology or is simple, but whether the patient judges it to be, on balance, beneficial.

The distinction between ordinary and extraordinary treatment probably originated within Roman Catholic moral theology, where extraordinary treatment is understood as treatment which is excessively burdensome or without benefit for the patient. Since whether a treatment is excessively burdensome depends on whether it produces sufficient benefits to outweigh its burdens, this interpretation of the ordinary–extraordinary distinction does mark a morally important difference between treatments – whether they are on balance beneficial to a particular patient – but adds nothing to the general benefits–burdens ethical framework we developed above. Moreover, the distinction has suggested to many that it should be possible to classify different treatments, such as nutrition and hydration or dialysis, as always either ordinary or extraordinary, and so as always either obligatory or optional. But on the beneficial–excessively burdensome interpretation, any kind of treatment like nutrition and hydration or dialysis will sometimes be ordinary, sometimes extraordinary, depending on a particular patient's condition and values. Since the ordinary–extraordinary distinction can lead to these kinds of confusions, but in its traditional and morally significant interpretation adds nothing to the general benefits–burdens framework, it has been increasingly rejected as not helpful to decisions about life-support, at least in secular contexts outside of its origins in Roman Catholicism.

Killing and Allowing to Die

It is widely accepted that physicians must respect their patients' decisions to be allowed to die, but that killing patients is morally different and rarely, if ever, to be deliberately done by physicians. The import of this issue for physician-assisted suicide and euthanasia is addressed elsewhere in this volume (see chapter 27, "Voluntary Euthanasia, Suicide and Physician-assisted Suicide"), but we shall address here the nature and moral importance of the difference between killing and allowing to die, as well as its application to decisions about life-support. The nature of the difference between killing and allowing to die is morally important if, as many believe, allowing to die can be morally justified in circumstances in which killing would not be; if there is no moral difference between the two, it is not morally important how we distinguish between them. Although I will argue briefly that killing is in itself no more seriously wrong than allowing to die, most people believe otherwise, so I shall first address the nature of the difference and then consider its moral significance. The most common way of differentiating killing from allowing to die is as the difference between acts and omissions that result in death. A person kills if he or she does an action that causes someone to die who otherwise would not have died; for example, we are in a boat, I know that you cannot swim, so I push you out of the boat, and you drown and die. A person allows someone to die if he or she has the ability and opportunity to prevent someone from dying, knows this, but does not act to prevent the death, and the person dies; for example, we are in a boat, you accidentally fall overboard, I know that you cannot swim, but I deliberately do not throw you an available lifebelt, and you drown and die.

Suppose that something close to this distinction between actions and omissions resulting in death correctly captures the difference between killing and allowing to die – is that difference morally significant? It is important to be clear about the meaning of this question, because it is easily and often misunderstood. It may be the case that most actual instances of killing, at least outside the medical context, are morally worse, all things considered, than most instances of allowing to die. For example, the motives of most who kill are probably worse than the motives of most who allow to die, and the agent's motives are usually important in our overall moral evaluation of what was done; also the cost to the potential agent in not killing is typically less than the cost or burden of not allowing anyone to die. But the moral evaluation, all things considered, of concrete cases of killing or of allowing to die is not what is at issue. Rather, the issue is whether killing is, in itself, morally worse than allowing to die; that is, whether a particular instance of killing is worse, other things being equal, than an instance of allowing to die just because it is killing and not allowing to die. Philosophers who have argued for the moral equivalence of the two have usually used an argument that compares two cases that differ in no other potentially morally relevant respect except that one is killing and the other allowing to die. Here is James Rachels's (1975) well-known example of two such cases:

> In the first, Smith stands to gain a large inheritance if anything should happen to his six-year-old cousin. One evening, while the child is taking his bath, Smith sneaks into the bathroom and drowns the child, and then arranges things so that it will look like an accident.

In the second, Jones also stands to gain if anything happens to his six-year-old cousin. Like Smith, Jones sneaks in planning to drown the child in his bath. However, just as he enters the bathroom Jones sees the child slip and hit his head, and fall face down in the water. Jones is delighted: he stands by, ready to push the child's head back under if it is necessary, but it is not necessary. With only a little thrashing about, the child drowns all by himself, "accidentally," as Jones watches and does nothing.

Rachels invites us to reflect on whether we believe that what Smith, who kills, does is any worse than what Jones, who allows to die, does. If we decide, as he believes we will, that there is no moral difference between the two cases, then the mere fact that one is killing, the other allowing to die, is not a morally important difference. Moreover, if the descriptive or empirical difference between killing or allowing to die does not contribute to any moral difference between the two, then it is not clear why it should in any other case, since the descriptive difference will be the same there. Whether killing is any worse morally than allowing to die remains controversial, but since most people believe that all decisions to forgo life-sustaining treatment are cases of allowing to die, it might seem not to matter here whether the moral equivalence thesis is true.

Consider a standard case of forgoing life-support. A clearly competent patient with ALS disease (amyotrophic lateral sclerosis, or Lou Gehrig's disease) has progressed to the point where she no longer has control over any bodily movements and is completely respirator-dependent for breathing. Her condition is progressive and irreversible; she has made a firm decision that she no longer wants to go on in this condition and asks her physician to remove the respirator and allow her to die.

It is now widely accepted that such a patient's physician may, indeed should, respect her wishes and remove her from the respirator, though it is certain that this will cause her death. Had the patient decided before she was placed on the respirator that she did not want this treatment when she could no longer breathe on her own, this too would typically have been understood as a decision to be allowed to die. Although both not starting and stopping life-support in cases such as these are commonly understood as allowing to die, not killing, I believe that is mistaken and that when the physician removes the patient from the respirator he kills the patient.

To see why this is so, consider a case exactly like the last except that the patient with ALS disease has a greedy son who mistakenly believes that his mother will never stop treatment and fears that his inheritance will be used up by her lengthy and costly hospitalization. So he slips into her room while she is sedated, extubates her, and she dies. However, the medical staff find out what he has done and, when confronted with having killed his mother, the son replies: "I didn't kill her, I merely allowed her to die. It was her ALS disease that caused her death."

I believe that we would and should reject this as transparent sophistry – the son went into his mother's room and deliberately killed her. But he performed just the same physical action that the physician did in the first case, so that if the son kills it seems the physician does so as well.

Now of course this is not to say that there are no important moral differences that make what the son does morally wrong and what the physician does morally justified. The physician acts with the patient's consent, with a good motive to respect the patient's wishes, and in a social role in which he is authorized to stop the treatment,

269

whereas the son had no such consent, a bad motive to protect his inheritance, and was not in any role that authorized his action. For these reasons the physician acts rightly and the son acts wrongly, but this does not mean that they do not both kill, only that one kills justifiably whereas the other kills wrongly, One can kill or allow to die with or without the victim's consent, with a good or bad motive, and in or not in a social role that authorizes such action; these factors determine whether what was done was morally justified, not whether it is a case of killing or allowing to die.

This argument appeals ultimately to the reader's intuitions about whether the physician kills or allows to die, as tested by the relevant similar case of the greedy son. But we can also apply the act–omission interpretation of the difference between killing and allowing to die directly to what the physician does. When the physician removes the breathing tube that is supplying oxygen to the patient and turns off the respirator, he performs an action that causes the patient to die when otherwise she would have continued to live; that is, he kills. On the other hand, suppose the physician had not intubated the patient when she initially went into respiratory distress because of the patient's prior decision to refuse that treatment; then he would have allowed her to die.

Those who construe these cases of stopping life-support as allowing to die usually have something like the following account of the cases in mind. The patient has a potentially lethal disease that is being prevented from causing the patient's death by the physician's intervention with a life-sustaining treatment, such as a respirator. When the treatment is withdrawn, even though that requires a physical action by the physician, the patient is allowed to die because the disease process is allowed to proceed unimpeded to the patient's death. We cannot pursue all the difficulties with this account except to note that it would require us to accept that the greedy son also does not kill, but only allows his mother to die.

Even when both not starting and stopping life-support are considered allowing to die, some patients, families, and physicians believe that stopping cannot be morally justified in some circumstance in which not starting would be morally justified; in this view, the difference between stopping and not starting life-support is itself morally important, even when all other circumstances are the same. The following case displays the difficulty with this position:

> A very gravely ill patient comes into a hospital emergency room from a nursing home and is sent up to the intensive care unit. The patient begins to develop respiratory failure that is likely to require intubation very soon. At that point the patient's family members and long-standing attending physician arrive at the ICU and inform the ICU staff that there had been extensive discussion about future care with the patient when he was unquestionably competent. Given his grave and terminal illness, as well as his state of debilitation, the patient had firmly rejected being placed on a respirator under any circumstances, and the family and physician produce the patient's advance directive to that effect. Most would hold that this patient should not be intubated and placed on a respirator against his will. Suppose now that the situation is exactly the same except that the attending physician and family are slightly delayed in traffic and arrive 15 minutes later – just after the patient has been intubated and placed on the respirator. Can this difference be of any moral importance? Could it possibly justify morally a refusal by the staff to remove the patient from the

respirator? Do not the very same circumstances that justified not placing the patient on the respirator now justify taking him off it? Do not factors like the patient's condition, prognosis, and firmly expressed wishes when competent morally determine what should be done, not whether we do not start, or 15 minutes later stop, the respirator? Why should the stop/not start difference matter morally at all?

Indeed, in practice, there is often an important reason to stop life-support that did not exist earlier not to start it. Often the decision to start a life-sustaining treatment like respiratory support or dialysis is made in conditions of uncertainty about whether it will provide a hoped-for benefit. If it is tried and proves not to provide the hoped-for benefit, the initial uncertainty is removed and there is then reason to stop the treatment which did not exist earlier not to start it. What is morally important are the risks and benefits of a treatment, not whether it is started or must be stopped.

Treating Pain and the Doctrine of Double Effect

With some dying patients, especially cancer patients, it can become necessary to administer increasingly large doses of analgesics to alleviate the patient's pain. Doing so is believed to carry increasingly higher risks of causing respiratory depression and hastening the patient's death. Despite intensive efforts to improve the care of dying patients, there is substantial evidence that their pain often remains inadequately treated, and one reason is the fear that doing so will cause the patient's earlier death – that is, kill the patient. Since it is widely held that it is morally wrong for physicians, or indeed anyone, deliberately or intentionally to kill a patient, is treating pain at the risk of causing the patient's death therefore wrong, or can it be morally justified? Few would hold that patients should be forced to endure great untreated pain and to die in agony in order to avoid the possibility of hastening their earlier death. In the United States, for example, the Supreme Court, in rejecting a right of individuals to physician-assisted suicide, endorsed a right of patients to receive adequate pain relief even if it may hasten death (*Washington v. Glucksberg* 1997 and *Vacco v. Quill* 1997). But there is disagreement about why it is ethically permissible for a physician to cause a patient's death in the course of treating his or her pain. Perhaps the most common line of justification focuses on the physician's intention, which is to relieve the patient's suffering, as distinguished from the unintended but foreseen possible side-effect of hastening the patient's death. This distinction invokes what is sometimes called the "doctrine of double effect," according to which an action with a bad effect (the patient's death) can be justified if that effect is not intended and is necessary to achieve a proportionately good effect (relief of the patient's suffering) (Bole 1991). There are cases in which it is difficult to determine whether a bad effect, such as hastening the patient's death, is intended or merely foreseen but unintended (e.g., the patient says that she wants to die and so asks the physician to stop life-support), but at least in the case of pain and symptom control, it seems intuitively plausible that the patient's death is not intended, whereas it would be if the physician instead performed euthanasia by deliberately giving the patient a lethal injection. According to the doctrine of double effect, the first action can be morally permissible whereas the latter is morally prohibited.

271

Critics of the appeal to double effect do not argue that we must leave a dying patient's pain inadequately treated so as to avoid the risk of hastening his or her death, but only that the distinction between whether a death is intended or foreseen but unintended cannot support the great moral difference between permissible and impermissible killing. In the case of euthanasia, just as in pain and symptom control, critics maintain that the physician's end may be the good one of relieving the patient's suffering. In neither case would death be wanted by the patient or the physician if the suffering could be avoided without it, but both patient and physician may be prepared to accept the patient's earlier death in order to relieve his or her suffering. Whereas the patient's death in the case of euthanasia is the necessary means taken in the causal path to relief of suffering, in the use of analgesics to achieve pain and symptom control it is the unavoidable side-effect following upon the relief of the patient's suffering. Together, these similarities throw into question whether the appeal to intentions in the doctrine of double effect can ground such an important moral difference between permissible and impermissible killing.

Some base the moral difference on the fact that the patient's death is certain in euthanasia, whereas in pain and symptom control it only becomes increasingly probable. A difference in the probability of the bad outcome of death is morally relevant in many circumstances, but it cannot help the defender of double effect because it is entirely independent of the distinction at the heart of double effect – whether the bad effect is intended or not. Moreover, sometimes the likelihood of hastening death from adequate pain and symptom control can become so high that the very small difference between it and the certainty of death in euthanasia could not plausibly support the very great moral difference between permissible and impermissible killing.

An alternative ethical justification for risking hastening death in order to treat pain holds that the physician is morally responsible for all the foreseen or foreseeable consequences of what he or she does, whether intended or foreseen but unintended; for example, a surgeon is responsible for his patient's unintended death in the course of a high-risk operative procedure. What justifies his or her operating is the prospect of sufficient benefit from the procedure to warrant undertaking the risk of death after securing the patient's consent to the operation when fully informed of its risks, benefits, and alternatives. Likewise, in this view what justifies the measures for pain and symptom control is not a matter of the physician's intentions, but rather the patient's request for pain-relief knowing that it risks hastening his or her death.

Conclusion

There is increasingly widespread agreement about the rights of competent patients, as well as the surrogates of incompetent patients, to decide about life-support – they can refuse any treatment and select from available alternative treatments. But substantial differences remain between different countries in the degree of consensus about these rights, as well as in the degree to which public policy (in the form of law and other professional norms) recognizes and protects them, and in the degree they are respected in medical practice. In every country, substantial work remains to be done to insure that everyday medical practice respects these rights. Even when it is accepted, the ethical framework for these decisions which we have sketched here can only guide decision-makers and decision-making; many of these decisions will remain complex, uncertain, and agonizing for those involved in them. And other debates concerning the care of dying patients, in particular the debate over physician-assisted suicide and/or euthanasia, one or both of which is legal now in the Netherlands, Belgium, Luxembourg, Switzerland, and the state of Oregon in the United States, extend beyond any ethical framework for life-sustaining treatment decisions and are only in their early stages, with their ultimate resolution far from clear.

References

Airedale NHS Trust (Respondents) v. Bland (1993). House of Lords, Judgment, February 4.

Blank, R. and Merrick, J. (2005). *End of Life Decision Making: A Cross-national Study.* Cambridge, MA: MIT Press.

Bole, T. J. (ed.) (1991). Double effect: theoretical function and bioethical implications. *Journal of Medicine and Philosophy* 16 (special issue): 467–585.

British Medical Association (2001). *Withholding and Withdrawing Life-prolonging Treatment: Guidance for Decision Making.* London: BMJ Books.

Cruzan v. Director, Missouri Dept. of Health (1990). 497 U.S. 261.

Hastings Center (1987). *Guidelines on the Termination of Treatment and Care of the Dying.* Bloomington: Indiana University Press.

President's Commission for the Study of Ethical Problems in Medicine (1983). *Deciding to Forgo Life-sustaining Treatment.* Washington, DC: US Government Printing Office.

Rachels, J. (1975). Active and passive euthanasia. *New England Journal of Medicine* 292/2: 78–80.

Schneiderman, L. J., Jecker, N. S., and Jonsen, A. R. (1990). Medical futility: its meaning and ethical implications. *Annals of Internal Medicine* 112: 949–54.

Vacco v. Quill (1997). 521 U.S. 793.

Washington v. Glucksberg (1997). 521 U.S. 702.

Further reading

Brock, D. W. (1993). *Life and Death: Philosophical Essays in Biomedical Ethics.* Cambridge: Cambridge University Press.

Buchanan, A. E. and Brock, D. W. (1989). *Deciding for Others: The Ethics of Surrogate Decision Making.* Cambridge: Cambridge University Press.

Kuhse, H. (1987). *The Sanctity of Life Doctrine in Medicine: A Critique.* Oxford: Oxford University Press.

Lynn, J. (ed.) (1986). *Forgoing Life-sustaining Food and Water.* Bloomington: Indiana University Press.

McMahan, J. (2002). *The Ethics of Killing: Problems at the Margins of Life.* Oxford: Oxford University Press.

Steinbock, B. and Norcross, A. (ed.) (1994). *Killing and Letting Die*, 2nd edn. Englewood Cliffs, NJ: Prentice-Hall.

Weir, R. F. (1989). *Abating Treatment with Critically Ill Patients.* Oxford: Oxford University Press.

24

Severely Disabled Newborns

EIKE-HENNER W. KLUGE

Introduction

The birth of a child should be a joyous event; sometimes, however, it is a tragedy. It is a tragedy when the baby suffers from such serious birth defects that it cannot live except with aggressive and sophisticated medical interventions – and even then can only survive for a short period of time. Parents and physicians must then choose between a number of options. They may elect not to intervene, but provide only palliative measures and "let nature take its course." Alternatively, they may decide to do everything to keep the child alive for as long as possible; or, finally, they may decide to end the child's suffering by actively terminating her life as quickly and painlessly as possible.

It is also tragic when the baby will live if she receives appropriate medical care but there is no reasonable expectation that she will ever grow up to enjoy an acceptable quality of life. Here, again, choices have to be made. The options include taking aggressive measures to keep the child alive and ameliorate the effects of her deficits as much as possible (usually by surgical means); taking appropriate medical measures to keep the child alive but refraining from dealing with her deficits because they are considered untreatable; providing only palliative measures and letting the child die; or, finally, terminating the child's life as quickly and painlessly as possible (Kuhse and Singer 1985; Magnet and Kluge 1985).

The decisions that have to be made in these circumstances are fraught with personal, conceptual, and ethical difficulties. The *personal* difficulties center around the psychological reactions of the parents and health-care professionals. While most prospective parents are aware of the theoretical possibility that their child may be born severely disabled, they tend not to take this possibility seriously until it actually occurs. And even when the prospective parents have reason to believe (or indeed know for certain) that their offspring may be severely disabled and have made plans for that contingency, the birth itself – and the need to make choices here and now – adds a psychological element that is absent from their previous deliberations (Kluge 2006). As for the professionals, while their training prepares them for dealing with severely disabled newborns, it is largely directed toward saving the children, not letting them die; and even when – as is increasingly the case – professional protocols allow them to withhold or withdraw treatment when the situation seems medically hopeless (American Medical

Association 2005; Arlettaz et al. 2005; Verhagen and Sauer 2005), the decision still grates on the professionals' sensibilities. As to the decision actively to terminate the newborn's suffering, this causes such psychological stress that professionals tend to hide it under such euphemisms as "appropriate palliation" and "terminal sedation" (Gevers 2006; van Delden 2007).

The *conceptual* difficulties cluster around the notions that define the situation itself. In particular, the notions of disability, suffering, and quality of life. What does it mean to say that a newborn is "severely disabled," that the child faces a "low quality of life" or a life of irremediable and incurable pain and suffering, or that the child is "better off dead"? How is "quality of life" here to be understood, and how is it to be measured? What does suffering mean in these cases, and how is it to be determined? What is meant by saying that the newborn is "better off dead" (Carr et al. 2001; Muldoon et al. 1998; Verhagen and Sauer 2005; Wilkinson 2006)?

Ethically, the following questions assume central importance: Who should make the decision about what should happen? What criteria should they use? And if it is decided that the newborn is "better off dead," what should be done after that? Should the baby be allowed to die? Should the baby be made to die? Should interventions be withheld, or should they be initiated on a trial basis and then withdrawn when continued intervention seems futile, and is there an ethically relevant difference (Cuttini, Casotto and Orzalesi 2006)? How is futility to be determined? And, finally, how should the uncertainty that attends so many medical diagnoses and prognoses be factored into the equation (Tubbs et al. 2006)?

Conceptual Issues

"Quality of life"

Beginning with quality of life, it is generally agreed that if the quality of life of a newborn baby will be exceedingly low because of its disabilities, then the infant need not be kept alive but may be either made or allowed to die (American Medical Association 2005; Doyal et al. 1994; McMillan et al. 1987; Magnet and Kluge 1985; Verhagen and Sauer 2005). It is therefore important to be clear on what the phrase "quality of life" actually means.

Unfortunately, its meaning is anything but clear. For instance, some quality-of-life measures define the notion objectively by focusing on the ability of the individual to function physically in society (Hunt et al. 1986); others use a subjective approach and focus on the experiences of the individual and her life satisfaction (Albrecht and Devlieger 1999); still others attempt to combine both subjective and objective elements in order to arrive at what is considered a more balanced scale (Shumaker and Berzon 1995). The upshot is that there is no single definition and no agreement about which quality-of-life measure is appropriate in what cases. This is true in general, but the disagreement becomes even more acute in the case of newborn children because there is no consensus on how to adjust quality-of-life measures (which have been designed for older persons) to neonates.

The situation is complicated further by the fact that most quality-of-life measures that have a subjective component focus on quality of life as it is *currently* being experienced. Arguably, this is inappropriate in the case of newborn children. At birth, newborns are only aware at a somatosensory level. Therefore, using standard subjectively based quality-of-life measures inevitably leads to the conclusion that while the baby's quality of life is very low from the perspective of the average person, it is nevertheless within acceptable limits for the baby here and now provided only that the baby's pain can be palliated sufficiently.

At the same time, if one broadens the concept of quality of life beyond the momentary and somatosensory here and now of the baby's present stage of development, and considers the case of those newborns who, despite their severe physical disabilities, have some potential for intellectual development, then the situation becomes even more difficult. One then has to take into account the fact that the newborns' awareness will grow in sophistication as the children mature. Inevitably, they will begin to understand and appreciate the nature and implications of their disabilities. If their disabilities are extreme, their increasing awareness of their situation may have such a severe impact on their psyche that they may experience extreme suffering and, at least in some cases, wish that they had never been born. No currently available quality-of-life measure takes this parameter of evolving world experience and awareness into account. However, it is arguable that to make a decision about a newborn's quality of life without taking this into account is to operate with a naive and truncated notion of quality of life. It is also to ignore the fact that the decision that is made in the neonatal intensive care unit has implications beyond the immediate medical present. The decision is not simply the decision to keep alive someone who has serious medical problems; it is a decision to keep alive someone who, in all likelihood, will experience severe suffering on a daily basis.

To generalize, the capacity to formulate life plans and expectations, and to experience the world in a cognitively significant fashion, is characteristically human (Tooley 1983; Loewy 1991). Therefore, when severely disabled newborns may survive if they are appropriately treated, the question whether they have the capacity to develop a worldview or to formulate life plans and to experience the world in a cognitively significant fashion – and above all, the question whether they will be able to fulfil these life plans consistent with standard conceptions of human dignity – should form an integral part of any quality-of-life measure that is used to decide whether the baby should live or die. Some severely disabled newborns do not have that capacity and will never be able to develop in this direction. Arguably, such lack of capacity calls into question their very status as persons, their biological humanity notwithstanding, and should be factored into the equation (Tooley 1983). However, some babies do have the capacity but will see their hopes and plans irremediably frustrated by severe, irremediable, and incurable disabilities, leading to anguish and suffering. Each of these cases presents a different aspect of the quality-of-life notion and calls for careful balancing and consideration, yet in most cases these considerations play only an ambiguous – and certainly a non-standardized – role when decision-makers make a quality-of-life based judgment about whether the baby should be kept alive (Magnet and Kluge 1985).

Disability

The notion of disability is of course integral to quality-of-life considerations, but closer consideration shows that it is also quite ambiguous. On one level, of course, the concept is fairly clear. For instance, babies who are born with severe spina bifida – an open spine with part of the spinal cord extruded – and who suffer from incontinence, lower body paralysis, hydrocephalus, and severe brain damage, are biologically compromised and require medical intervention to stay alive. Many such children can never participate in the activities in which children normally engage; and, if they survive at all, they will not be able to live the kind of life that most persons can live. They will require constant medical treatment and need assistance for all their activities of daily living. Therefore, in an intuitively obvious sense, such newborns are severely disabled as compared to other persons.

Likewise, a newborn who suffers from something like Tay-Sachs disease – which involves the progressive and irreversible deterioration of the nervous system, ultimately leading to death by age 6 – has a medically identifiable condition that is disabling in an obvious sense. The same thing is true of an infant who is born without arms and legs, or with a malformed heart and a blockage in her esophagus that prevents ingested food from reaching her stomach (esophageal atresia).

All of these are not merely cases of disability but of severe disability. On the other hand, infants who are born with a cleft palate, rudimentary intellectual capacity, or similar conditions are not quite as disabled; and children who are born blind or deaf, or with learning or attention deficits, etc., are less severely disabled still because there are interventions and services that can compensate for, cure, or ameliorate the impaired functions in question.

In other words, the question of what services are available to deal with the problems, and the degree to which they can compensate for or ameliorate the reduced ability or functioning, become relevant factors when evaluating disabilities. Using this approach, one can build up a more or less clear and graduated notion of what counts as a *disability*, what counts as a *severe* disability, and what counts as a mere inconvenience. It therefore becomes clear that the notion of disability is not an absolute concept; that it has a comparative component which, to a considerable degree, is tied to the resources of the society into which the children are born and the ability to provide remedies for dealing with the problems that the children face. Thus, spina bifida can be a severe and irremediable disability when access to modern surgery, follow-up health care, and disability services are limited or nonexistent but will be considered much less severe if appropriate treatment is readily available; being born with esophageal atresia and similar conditions can be considered an extremely severe disability that amounts to a slow death sentence if resources are limited and surgery unavailable, but when there is access to appropriate medical intervention it is usually no more than a passing disability that has no lasting effect beyond the first few weeks of life. And so on.

However, these considerations only deal with conditions that manifest themselves as soon as the baby is born. They do not deal with so-called late-onset diseases such as Huntington's disease, where the deterioration of cognitive and bodily functions will not occur until decades later in life. It is arguable that even though the deficits that are associated with late-onset diseases are not experienced immediately, the presence of such genetic determinants also constitutes a disability, and that they should be included in considerations of quality of life (Kluge 1992).

Further, some infants are born anencephalic – that is to say, they are born otherwise healthy except that they have an open skull and no brain tissue beyond a brain stem. Unless all means available to modern medicine are used to their fullest extent, this condition is incompatible with life. At first glance, therefore, anencephaly is a prime example of a severe disability. However, the situation is actually a bit more complicated. While anencephalic babies are unquestionably human beings in the sense of being members of the species *Homo sapiens*, there is the question of whether they are *persons*, and therefore *disabled persons*.

It is often accepted that a human being who has functioning brain tissue, even if only a brain stem, is a person (Doig and Burgess 2003; Joffe and Anton 2007). However, there is a growing body of opinion which argues that what makes someone a person is not the mere presence of functioning brain tissue but some capacity for sentience and cognitive awareness. This means that the so-called higher brain centers inclusive of the cerebrum (where intellection and consciousness take place) must be also present (Joffe and Anton 2006; Russell 2000; Veatch 1993). The issue of whether anencephalic babies are severely disabled *persons*, or merely severely malformed members of the species *Homo sapiens* in the purely biological sense, is important because how it is answered determines whether anencephalic babies should be the subject of the same ethical considerations that are prima facie relevant in the case of other severely disabled neonates.

"Better off dead"

Then there is the issue of life itself. Some people have argued that there are circumstances under which a severely disabled baby may be "better off dead." Among others, this is the approach that has been taken in most so-called "wrongful life" cases, where the agent for the child argues that the child has been harmed because it would have been better off dead. (*Harbeson v. Parke-Davis Inc.* 1984; Dickens 1989; *Cherryh v. Boorsman* 1990; Picard and Robertson 2007). In reply, it has been argued that such a claim is not only callous but conceptually flawed. The reasoning here is that, logically, the claim that someone is "better off dead" is based on a comparison between two states – that of being alive and that of being dead. However, in order to say that someone is better off under one set of circumstances rather than another, that person must exist in both situations in order for her life to be the subject of comparison. Someone who is dead has no life and does not exist. Therefore – so the argument goes – there can be no such a comparison and the claim that someone would be "better off dead" is an empty claim (Annas 1981; Steinbock and McClamrock 1994).

The responses to this line of reasoning have been varied. However, one particularly noteworthy reply has been to accept the argument but to reject the conclusion that we cannot say it is bad for the severely disabled person that she exists: it is not that the newborn is better off under one set of circumstances rather than another, but that human life must meet a minimal subjectively-experienced qualitative standard in order to be worth living (Steinbock and McClamrock 1994). When this is not possible, then the very fact of living constitutes a continuous injury to the newborn who is being kept alive (Engelhardt 1973). To keep the newborn alive under such circumstances is to impose on the child a life that most other persons would not want to live and which, given the chance, they would want to leave. Therefore, the decision to end such a life

– or to allow it to end – is merely to make a proxy decision on behalf of the severely disabled newborn, using quality-of-life criteria that the newborn would be likely to use if she were in a position to make a decision.

However, not even this stands unopposed. For example, others have argued that this approach devalues people who are disabled; that it introduces an instrumentalistic notion of personhood and inappropriately sets up standards that someone must meet in order to count as a person. Further, they have argued that this approach deprives society of the opportunity to develop virtues such as compassion, tolerance, and understanding, and thereby impoverishes the moral life of society in general (Ashley and O'Rourke 1982). Unless this debate is resolved, the notion of "better off dead" may face severe difficulties in application (Wilkinson 2006).

Decision Issues

Decision-makers

Then, of course, there is the whole series of questions that center around decision-making. Who should make the decisions? Using what criteria? There is general agreement that physicians are not the ultimate decision-makers, but that parents, in consultation with physicians, are the appropriate decision-makers because they have the best interests of their children at heart. However, there is also general agreement that this is a rebuttable presumption, and that when parents base their decisions on personal values that are not shared by the rest of society, and when the use of these values would disadvantage the newborn compared to other newborns, then the parents are no longer the appropriate decision-makers. In these cases, so it is argued, the courts should appoint someone else to make the relevant decisions (Gaylin and Macklin 1982).

Criteria

It is also generally agreed that the decision-makers should always make their decisions in the "best interests" of these children. Traditionally, it was assumed that "best interests" was synonymous with life itself. As we have already seen, current thinking no longer shares this assumption and no longer focuses on life itself. More generally, it is accepted that quality-of-life considerations are important, and that newborns should have some capacity for sentient cognitive awareness, for enjoyment and the like; further, that a life of unmitigated pain is generally not considered worth living, and therefore newborns who look forward only to unmitigated and protracted physical suffering need not be kept alive. In fact, it has been argued that to keep such children alive is to harm them (Arlettaz et al. 2005; Kuhse and Singer 1985; Loewy 1991; Magnet and Kluge 1985; McMillan et al. 1987; Steinbock and McClamrock 1994).

It is sometimes argued that the notion of best interests should not be approached from the perspective of the objective reasonable person but from the neonate's own point of view. More precisely, it has been argued that in the case of mentally incompetent persons – and neonates clearly fall into this group – the appropriate way to interpret the notion of best interests is to put oneself into the position of the disabled person and make the decision the way the disabled person would if the disabled person could make a decision. This is known as the "substituted judgment" approach, and it has even found legal reflection (*re S.D.* 1983). While this tends to be a minority opinion, it still plays a role in some decision-making. The question therefore remains: which sort of reasoning is appropriate?

Making vs allowing to die

There is also no universal agreement on whether there is an ethically relevant difference between withholding and withdrawing treatment, and between allowing severely disabled newborns to die and killing them as quickly and painlessly as possible. As to withholding versus withdrawing, the one side argues that to withhold is ethically questionable because it amounts to prejudging the infant's chances, whereas the other side argues that to withdraw treatment is to first treat the baby as an experimental animal, and may entail torture to life, but then simply washing one's hands of the situation when the experiment fails (Gedge et al. 2007).

On the distinction between allowing to die and actively killing, there again are two positions. One side maintains that the two actions are fundamentally distinct: to bring about the death of a person actively, deliberately, and with forethought is to commit murder, whereas to allow a person to die is simply to let nature take its course. By contrast, the other side argues that to refrain from doing something determines the eventual outcome just as much as actively doing something (Rachels 1975). The concept of negligence, so it is argued – in particular, the concept of criminal negligence – rests on this fact. Not using life-saving and/or life-prolonging measures hastens the baby's death just as surely as directly killing the newborn. The real issue is not whether the death of the neonate is brought about quickly or slowly through action or inaction, but whether attempts should be made to save the child's life.

Sometimes, the disagreement is cast in terms of causality. That is to say, sometimes it is argued that letting die and killing are morally different because the direct agent of death is different in each case. In one case, it is the disease process or the condition that brings about the newborn's death: nature is the agent and is allowed to take its course. In the other case it is the person who administers the drug or performs the intervention who is the agent of death (Ashley and O'Rourke 1982; Walton 1979). However, the other side argues that those who favour inaction and "letting nature take its course" are merely using the natural course of events – the disease process or the condition of the newborns – as the agent of their death. The moral difference – if any – lies in the intent with which the decision is made. However, the decision to "let nature take its course" is not made with the intent of saving the life of the newborn: the intent is to allow death to occur. Therefore in both cases the intent is to bring about the death of these children, no matter how artfully or strenuously the decision-maker tries to avoid this realization (Magnet and Kluge 1985; Rachels 1975). Therefore, while the difference between actively ending the baby's life and not adopting life-saving measures may be psychologically comforting to health-care professionals and parents, ethically speaking it is a non-difference.

Doctrine of double effect

In this connection, some have argued that terminal sedation is ethically acceptable and distinct from actively killing the baby by appealing to the doctrine of double effect. According to this doctrine, when an action has both a positive and a negative outcome, the action is ethically acceptable if four conditions are met: the act considered in itself is not morally blameworthy, the negative outcome is not a causally necessary precondition for achieving the positive outcome, the intent is directed solely at the positive outcome, and there is a balance between the positive and the negative effects (Cavanaugh 2006). The argument then says that palliation is not ethically reprehensible in itself, the death of the baby is not causally necessary for achieving palliation but merely an unfortunate side effect of using narcotic analgesics, the intent in palliating the baby is to alleviate its pain, and the failure to engage in palliation would amount to standing by and watching the baby suffer which would not entail an acceptable moral balance.

However, while the doctrine of double effect has a long history (Mangan 1949), it is questionable whether it amounts to more than a psychological ploy to allow parents and physicians to feel better about ending the baby's life under guise of palliation. The fact is that anyone skilled in the use of narcotic analgesics knows that using them has a depressing effect on the central nervous system of the baby and will hasten her death. That knowledge is part of the awareness of whoever intends to palliate the baby. Therefore the intent is not simply to palliate, but to palliate *despite the known deadly outcome*. This makes the claim that only the good outcome is intended highly suspect (Kuhse 1987).

Ordinary vs extraordinary means

There is a similar division of opinion over the degree to which medical intervention should be pursued in order to save the lives of severely disabled newborns. Some, like Pope Pius XII (1957), Pope John Paul II (2004), and the Sacred Congregation for the Doctrine of Faith (1980), have argued that while "ordinary" measures should always be employed to save the lives of severely disabled newborns, there is no obligation to use "extraordinary" means. Others, like Ramsey (1970) and Veatch (1976), have argued that the distinction between ordinary and extraordinary means is artificial, question-begging, and hopelessly vague. They have argued that whether an intervention is ordinary or extraordinary lies not in the nature of the intervention, but in the context in which it is employed. Still others (Kluge 1992) have argued that while the distinction between what is ordinary and what is extraordinary is meaningful, using it in this fashion commits a fundamental error. It assumes that what is morally obligatory is defined by what is usual or ordinary practice. However, the fact that something is usual or ordinary practice does not automatically render it morally defensible. It may merely reflect current social values. The example of Nazi Germany provides food for sober reflection. The real question in these cases is not what is usually done, but whether what is usually done is right in this particular case.

Conclusion

The preceding discussion has dealt with only some of the issues that arise on the birth of a severely disabled baby. There are others. For instance, what weight should be attached to the fact that, almost invariably, a severely disabled baby will place a great personal, social, and economic burden on the family into which the child is born? What weight should be attached to the burden that the birth of such a child places on the resources that society has at its disposal? On the other hand, what is the moral price that society pays if it does not protect its weakest members, and if it does not go to the limits of what it can do to assist those who cannot help themselves?

These are hard questions and, if the debate on the subject is any indication, it will be difficult to provide consistent and, above all, ethically defensible answers. That is not surprising. The birth of a child evokes our instinctive reaction to save and to protect. The added parameters of disability and need serve only to heighten the intensity of this response, whether it be at the level of family, health-care professional, or society at large. At the same time, there is also an almost irresistible urge to prevent harm, or at least to minimize its severity and extent.

The overarching challenge in all of this is to make sure that the needs of the children are not confused with the needs of the parents, of professionals, or of society, and that the values of the latter do not automatically trump the rights of the children (Kluge 2006). While many of these issues may currently be unclear, this does not mean that they should not be clarified; and while there may be competing positions on what weight to accord the different considerations, this does not mean that the issue should not be resolved, lest a tragedy become the occasion for an ethical disaster – and lest, with the best of intentions, severely disabled babies who can be saved to lead fulfilling and rewarding lives are made or allowed to die, and severely disabled newborns who face a life of irremediable suffering are tortured to life.

References

Albrecht, G. L., Devlieger, P. J. (1999). The disability paradox: high quality of life against all odds. *Social Science and Medicine* 48: 977–88.

American Medical Association (2005). *Code of Medical Ethics*. Opinion 2.215. Treatment decisions for seriously ill newborns.

Annas, G. J. (1981). Righting the wrong of "wrongful life." *Hastings Center Report* 11: 1.

Arlettaz, R., Mieth, D., Bucher, H. U., Duc G., and Fauchere J. C. (2005). End-of-life decisions in delivery room and neonatal intensive care unit. *Acta Paediatrica: Promoting Child Health* 94/11: 1626–31.

Ashley, B. M. and O'Rourke, K. D. (1982). *Health Care Ethics: A Theological Analysis*. St Louis: Catholic Health Association.

Carr, A. J., Gibson, B. A., and Robinson, P. G. (2001). Is quality of life determined by expectations or experience? *British Medical Journal* 322: 1240–3.

Cavanaugh, T. A. (2006). *Double-Effect Reasoning: Doing Good and Avoiding Evil*. Oxford: Clarendon Press.

Cherryh v. Boorsman (1990). 75 D.L.R. (4th) 608 (B.C.S.C.).

Cuttini, M., Casotto, V., and Orzalesi, M. (2006). Ethical issues in neonatal intensive care and physicians' practices: a European perspective. *Acta Paediatrica Suppl.* 95/452: 42–6.

Dickens, B. (1989). Wrongful birth and life, wrongful death before birth, and wrongful law. In S. McLean (ed.), *Legal Issues in Human.* Aldershot: Grower, p. 80.

Doig, C. J., Burgess, E. (2003). Brain death: resolving inconsistencies in the ethical declaration of death. *Can J Anesth* 50: 725–31.

Donceel, J. (1967). Mediate v. immediate animation. *Continuum* 5: 167–71.

Doyal, L. et al. (1994). Toward guidelines for withholding and withdrawal of life prolonging treatment in neonatal medicine. *Archives of Diseases of Childhood* 70 (special issue).

Engelhardt, H. T., Jr (1973). Euthanasia and children: the injury of continued existence. *Journal of Paediatrics* 83: 170–1.

Gaylin, W. and Macklin, R. (eds.) (1982). *Who Speaks for the Child?* New York and London: Plenum Press.

Gedge, E., Giacomini, M., and Cook, D. (2007). Withholding and withdrawing life support in critical care settings: ethical issues concerning consent. *Journal of Medical Ethics* 33: 215–18.

Gevers, J. K. (2006). Terminal sedation: between pain relief, withholding treatment and euthanasia. *Medicine and Law* 25/4: 747–51.

Haldane, J. and Lee, P. (2003). Aquinas on human ensoulment, abortion and the value of life. *Philosophy* 78: 255–78.

Harbeson v. Parke Davis, Inc. 746 F.2d 517 (9th Cir. 1984).

Hunt, S. M., McEwan, J., and McKenna, S. P. (1986). *Measuring Health Status.* London: Croom Helm.

Joffe, A. R. and Anton, N. (2006). Brain death: understanding of the conceptual basis by pediatric intensivists in Canada. *Arch Pediatr Adolesc Med.* 160: 747–52.

Joffe, A. R. and Anton, N. (2007). Some questions about brain death: a case report. *Pediatric Neurology* 37/4: 289–91.

John Paul II, Pope (2004). Life-sustaining treatments and vegetative state: scientific advances and ethical dilemmas. *National Catholic Bioethics Quarterly* 4: 773–82.

Kluge, E.-H. W. (1992). *Biomedical Ethics in a Canadian Context.* Scarborough, Ontario: Prentice-Hall Canada.

Kluge, E.-H. W. (2006). Hope in the neonatal intensive care nursery: value, ethics and the injury of continued existence. *Medscape General Medicine* 8/3: 74–9.

Kuhse, H. (1987). *The Sanctity-of-Life Doctrine in Medicine: A Critique.* Oxford: Clarendon Press.

Kuhse, H. and Singer, P. (1985). *Should the Baby Live? The Problem of Handicapped Infants.* Oxford, New York and Melbourne: Oxford University Press.

Loewy, E. (1991). *Suffering and the Beneficent Community: Beyond Libertarianism.* Albany, NY: State University of New York Press.

Magnet, J. E. and Kluge, E.-H. W. (1985). *Withholding Treatment from Defective Newborn Children.* Cowansville, Quebec: Brown Legal Publications.

Mangan, J. (1949). An historical analysis of the principle of double effect. *Theological Studies* 10: 41–61.

McMillan, R. C., Engelhardt, H. T., Jr, and Spicker, S. F. (eds.) (1987). *Euthanasia and the Newborn: Conflicts Regarding Saving Lives.* Dordrecht: D. Reidel Publishing Company.

Muldoon, M. F., Barger, S. D., Flory, J. D., and Manuck, S. B. (1998). What are quality of life measurements measuring? *British Medical Journal* 316: 542–5.

Picard, E. and Robertson, G. (2007). *Legal Liability of Doctors and Hospitals in Canada.* Toronto: Thomson-Carswell.

Pius XII, Pope (1957). Prolongation of life: allocution to an international congress of anaesthesiologists. *Osservatore Romano* 4.

283

President's Commission for the Study of Ethical Problems in Medicine and Biomedical and Behavioral Research (1983). *Deciding to Forego Life-sustaining Treatment: A Report on the Ethical, Medical and Legal Issues in Treatment Decisions*. Washington, DC: US Government Printing Office.

Rachels, J. (1975). Active and passive euthanasia. *New England Journal of Medicine* 292: 78–80.

Ramsey, P. (1970). *The Patient as Person*. New Haven, CT: Yale University Press.

re S.D. (1983). 3 W.W.R. 618 (B.C.S.C.).

Russell, T. (2000). *Brain Death: Philosophical Concepts and Problems*. Aldershot, UK: Ashgate.

Sacred Congregation for the Doctrine of the Faith (1974). *Declaration on Abortion*. Vatican City: Sacred Congregation for the Doctrine of the Faith.

Sacred Congregation for the Doctrine of the Faith (1980). *Declaration on Euthanasia*. Vatican City: Sacred Congregation for the Doctrine of the Faith.

Shumaker, S. A. and Berzon, R. (1995). *The International Assessment of Health-related Quality of Life: Theory, Translation, Measurement and Analysis*. Oxford and New York: Rapid Communications.

Steinbock, B. and McClamrock, R. (1994). When is birth unfair to the child? *Hastings Center Report* 24/6: 15–21.

Tooley, M. (1983). *Abortion and Infanticide*. Oxford: Clarendon Press.

Tubbs, E., Elrod, J., Flum, D. (2006). Risk taking and tolerance of uncertainty: implications for surgeons. *Journal of Surgical Research* 131/1: 1–6.

van Delden, J. J. M. (2007). Terminal sedation: source of a restless ethical debate. *Journal of Medical Ethics* 33: 187–8.

Veatch, R. (1976). *Death, Dying and the Biological Revolution: Our Last Quest for Responsibility*. New Haven and London: Yale University Press.

Veatch, R. (1993). The impending collapse of the whole-brain definition of death. *Hastings Center Report* 23/4: 18–24.

Verhagen, E. and Sauer, P. J. J. (2005). The Groningen Protocol: Euthanasia in Severely Ill Newborns. *New England Journal of Medicine* 352: 959–62.

Walton, D. N. (1979). *On Defining Death: An Analytic Study of the Concept of Death in Philosophy and Medical Ethics*. Montreal: McGill-Queen's University Press.

Weir, R. (1984). *Selective Nontreatment of Handicapped Newborns*. New York: Oxford University Press.

Wilkinson, D. (2006). Is it in the best interests of an intellectually disabled infant to die? *Journal of Medical Ethics* 32/8: 454–9.

Further reading

Botkin, J. R. (1990). Delivery room decisions for tiny infants: and ethical analysis. *Journal of Clinical Ethics* 1/4: 306–11.

Brody, H. and Bartholeme, W. G. (1988). In the best interests of . . . *Hastings Center Report* 18/6: 37–40.

Duff, A. (1982). Intention, responsibility and double effect. *The Philosophical Quarterly* 32/126: 1–16.

Hastings Center Research Project on the Care of Imperiled Newborns (1987). Imperiled newborns: a report. *Hastings Center Report* 17/6: 5–32.

Joffe, A. R. and Anton, N. (2006). Brain death: understanding of the conceptual basis by pediatric intensivists in Canada. *Archives of Pediatric and Adolescent Medicine* 160/7: 747–52.

Lantos, J. (2006). When parents request seemingly futile treatment for their children. *Mt Sinai Journal of Medicine* 73/3: 587–9.

McIntyre, A. (2001). Doing away with double effect. *Ethics* 111/2: 219–55.

Nishida, H. (1987). Future ethical issues in neonatology: a Japanese perspective. *Seminars in Perinatology* 11/3: 274–8.

Woodward, P. A. (ed.) (2001). *The Doctrine of Double Effect: Philosophers Debate a Controversial Moral Principle*. Notre Dame, IN: University of Notre Dame Press.

25

Death, Brain Death, and Persistent Vegetative State

JEFF McMAHAN

The Concept of Brain Death and its Appeal

For most of human history, there was no perceived problem in determining whether a person was alive or dead. If the person had stopped breathing and had no heartbeat, he was considered dead. During the twentieth century, however, techniques were developed that made it possible to resuscitate some people who had stopped breathing and whose heart had stopped beating. With the invention of mechanical ventilation, oxygen could be forced in and out of the lungs of people unable to breathe on their own, and in many cases this has been sufficient to stimulate the person's heart to beat and thus to maintain the functioning of the body as a whole for an indefinite period, even in the absence of any indications of consciousness. At the same time that increasing numbers of mechanically ventilated but unconscious patients began to divert medical resources away from people who could have benefited from them more, there was also a growing demand for organs for newly developed transplant surgeries. These conditions prompted a debate in medical circles about how to determine when a patient had died and could thus be removed from expensive life-support systems, thereby making both the support systems and the patient's organs available to others. This debate resulted in a surprisingly abrupt transition from universal acceptance of the traditional cardio-pulmonary criterion of death to near-universal acceptance of brain death.

Brain death is understood as the irreversible cessation of functioning in the brain as a whole. It is compatible with the presence of isolated instances of minor, residual functioning in certain areas of the brain. The practical utility of this criterion was immediately obvious: if a patient on a ventilator who appeared to be alive nevertheless tested positive for brain death, he could be declared dead, removed from the ventilator, and treated as a source of organs for transplantation. That he had appeared to be alive could be explained by the claim that the various somatic functions were being generated and sustained externally rather than being constitutive of life in the organism.

Although there is a strong consensus throughout the world in both medicine and law that brain death is death, that view has been and continues to be vigorously contested by some philosophers and a few skeptics within the medical community (Singer 1994; Shewmon 1998). Before examining the challenges that have been posed, we should try to get clear about the concept of death, so that we can understand what brain death is supposed to be the criterion *of*.

It seems a necessary truth that the only entities that can die are ones that have been alive. Since life is a biological phenomenon, it has seemed to most commentators that death must be a biological phenomenon as well. Since the late 1960s, when most of the world adopted brain death as the criterion of death, the orthodox view has been that death is necessarily a biological event that involves the cessation of integrated functioning in an organism (or, derivatively, in an organ).

Yet all these assumptions are false. Consider the way the concept of death is used in the claim attributed to Jesus that "whosoever liveth and believeth in me shall never die" (John 11:26). If our concept of death were univocal and essentially biological, we would have to understand Jesus as asserting that those organisms who believe in him will never cease to function biologically in an integrated way. Yet we all understand that what he meant is instead that the people who believe will never cease to exist. (Since we know that some people believe in Jesus and yet all human organisms cease to exist, it follows that those who believe what Jesus says in the quoted passage cannot consistently believe that we are organisms. Many such people believe we are nonphysical souls. I will return to this later.)

This shows that our concept of death allows for the possibility that death is not always a biological event, and thus that it does not always involve the cessation of integrated biological functioning. Sometimes "death" refers to a biological event, but sometimes it refers to the ceasing to exist of a person. Suppose there were a person who had survived the biological death of his body but became so tiresome in the afterlife that God finally decided to annihilate him forever. He would then die in the sense intended in the quotation from Jesus.

The ceasing to exist of a living entity is not always aptly describable as death. When a unicellular organism, such as an amoeba, undergoes binary fission, it ceases to exist but does not *die*. It does seem that there is no non-biological concept of death in the case of non-conscious organisms such as amoebas. And just as amoebas show that living beings can cease to exist and thus cease to be alive without dying, so corpses show that living beings can die, biologically, without ceasing to exist. So while all biologically living entities may cease to exist when they die and vice versa, the concepts of death and of the ceasing to exist of a living entity are distinct, though overlapping.

A Critique of Brain Death

The most important point to extract from these conceptual preliminaries is that we have two concepts of death: death as the cessation of the processes constitutive of biological life, and death as the ceasing to exist of a conscious being. One may wonder, then, for which of these brain death is supposed to be the criterion. When people have argued that, in human beings, brain death is death, have they meant that it indicates when a human organism undergoes biological death, or that it marks the ceasing to exist of the person? The answer is that they have meant both. They have assumed that when a human being dies biologically, she ceases to exist, or at least ceases to exist *here*. They have thus found brain death a compelling criterion of death not only because it has

287

the practical advantages noted earlier but also, and mainly, because it seems to capture both dimensions of death: the ceasing to exist of the person and the biological death of the human organism. Brain death, they argue, is equivalent to the ceasing to exist of the person because the brain is the seat of consciousness, so that, once it is dead, consciousness is no longer possible; and it is equivalent to the biological death of the organism because, when the brain as a whole is dead, there can no longer be any internally integrated functioning in the organism. That brain death is sufficient for the irreversible loss of both consciousness and integrated functioning is the main source of its intuitive appeal.

In fact, however, brain death is not equivalent to either the irreversible loss of the capacity for consciousness or the irreversible cessation of integrated functioning in the organism as a whole. The main part of the explanation of why this is so derives from the fact that the cerebral tissues responsible for different functions of the brain are located in different regions. Roughly speaking, consciousness is generated in the part of the brain that is spatially and figuratively higher – the cerebral hemispheres – while the regulation of somatic functions is carried out in the brain stem, the spatially and figuratively lower area of the brain. One highly important difference between these two broad regions of the brain is that the cerebral hemispheres are significantly more vulnerable to the effects of anoxia, or oxygen deprivation, than the brain stem. If the supply of oxygenated blood to the brain is disrupted, the tissues in the cerebral hemispheres die before those in the brain stem do. Because of this, when a person suffers cardiac arrest but is not revived until after five minutes have passed, it is common for the hemispheres to be damaged while the brain stem remains intact and functional.

The early literature advocating brain death as the criterion of the death of a human being emphasized the fact that brain death involves the irreversible loss of the capacity for consciousness. By highlighting this fact, the early advocates of brain death were appealing to the intuition that the capacity for consciousness is essential to our existence, so that when a person loses all possibility of consciousness or experience, she ceases to exist. The problem, however, is that while brain death is *sufficient* for the irreversible loss of the capacity for consciousness, it is not *necessary*. In some cases in which the brain is deprived of oxygen, the consciousness-generating areas of the hemispheres are wholly destroyed while the brain stem survives, leaving an individual that is permanently non-conscious but whose body may nevertheless continue to function indefinitely with no external life support other than intravenous nutrition and hydration. Such an individual is said to be in a "persistent vegetative state."

If, as some early advocates of brain death seemed to suggest, the capacity for consciousness is essential to our existence, it follows that a person who lapses into a genuine persistent vegetative state, in which there is no longer any possibility of consciousness, thereby ceases to exist. Some bioethical theorists have embraced that implication. Some have argued that because the capacity for consciousness is localized in the upper regions of the brain, the proper criterion of death is not brain death but a "higher brain" criterion, such as the death of the cerebral cortex ("cortical death"). But proposals for higher brain criteria have never been widely accepted; for they imply that a persistently vegetative patient whose body remains systematically functional with little support other than nutrition and hydration is biologically dead. And that seems obviously false.

Just as a person may irreversibly lose the capacity for consciousness without being brain dead, so in principle a human organism could suffer the irreversible cessation of integrated functioning without the person ceasing to exist. This could happen if the brain stem were to be destroyed, causing the loss of integrated functioning, while the cerebral hemispheres survived in a functional state. But this never in fact happens. If the brain stem is destroyed and external life support is not provided almost immediately, breathing and heartbeat stop, blood ceases to reach the brain, the cerebral hemispheres begin to die, and the capacity for consciousness is soon lost. If external life support *is* immediately provided so that oxygenated blood continues to reach the cortex, it is not a case involving cessation of integrated functioning. There is also an area of the brain called the "reticular formation" that is located primarily in the brain stem that functions rather like an "on–off" switch for the generation of consciousness in the cortex. If the reticular formation is destroyed, spontaneous consciousness is no longer possible. So for consciousness to be preserved, the destruction of the brain stem would have to spare the reticular formation, which is highly unlikely.

We can nevertheless imagine a case in which all of a person's brain stem except the reticular formation is destroyed and in which the only external support provided is a machine that delivers a continuous supply of oxygenated blood to the person's cortex. This could be done. Decades ago, scientists were able to maintain consciousness in the severed heads of monkeys by keeping their brains perfused with blood. The same could in principle be done, at least for a limited period, with a person's cortex and reticular formation inside his own head, even after the rest of his brain stem and indeed the rest of his body had died. This would be a case in which integrated functioning in the organism would be irreversibly lost even though brain death would not occur until later, and the person would not only not cease to exist but would even remain conscious.

Many people are reluctant to draw conclusions from examples that are merely hypothetical. But to show that brain death is not equivalent to the loss of integrated functioning in a human organism, we can appeal to real examples. These examples do not show, as the hypothetical example attempts to do, that integrated functioning can cease without brain death occurring; rather, they show that brain death can occur without the cessation of integrated functioning. There are several documented cases in which, after a pregnant woman has been reliably diagnosed as brain dead, her body has been kept systemically functional for a number of months to enable the fetus to develop and later be delivered alive (Singer 1994: 9–16). Yet the most surprising case of which I am aware is that of a 4-year-old boy who was diagnosed as brain dead but whose mother refused to accept that he was dead and insisted that he not be removed from the ventilator. When a neurologist, Alan Shewmon, examined him 15 years later, in the late 1990s, he found that there was no blood flow within the cranium and indeed that the entire brain had dissolved and "been replaced by ghost-like tissues and disorganized proteinaceous fluids." Nevertheless, during those many years in which he was officially brain dead, the boy had "grown, overcome infections and healed wounds" (Shewmon 1998: 136).

Those who hold that brain death is death are obliged to describe the examples cited above as cases in which *corpses* support fetal gestation, maintain immune functions and adjust them to the presence of a fetus, metabolize nutrients, excrete wastes, retain reproductive potential, and so on. They have to say that what appears to be integrated systemic functioning is not really integrated and so is only a simulacrum of life. Their assumption is that if these various functions are not internally regulated by the brain, they are not integrated in the way necessary for the presence of life. But this assumes that the internal integration of somatic functions has to be centralized in order for there to be life. But what the cases just cited show is that, with a minimum of external support – a ventilator, a daily hormone injection, nutrition, and hydration – the various organs and subsystems constitutive of a human organism are capable of decentralized integration. That is, they achieve effective coordination by sending, receiving, and processing signals among themselves.

Despite the evidence of these cases, many people continue to assert that regulation by the brain is necessary for functioning in the organism, however seemingly integrated it may be, to count as life. It seems that this has ceased to be an empirical claim and has instead become a *conceptual* claim, a claim about the concept of life in a human organism. Given the evidence of the cases just cited, it seems charitable to interpret recent defenses of brain death as claiming that, unless the integration of functions in a human organism is both internal and centralized in the brain, it *necessarily* cannot be constitutive of life in the organism.

This claim raises an unavoidable question – namely, *how much* of the integration of somatic functions has to be done by the brain for the organism to count as alive? The answer at one extreme is that *all* the functions normally regulated by the brain must be so regulated for the organism to be alive. But this is clearly false. A patient with a lesion to the respiratory center in the brain stem requires permanent external ventilation to survive, but no one doubts that such a person is alive. Nor can one say, at the opposite extreme, that the organism remains alive as long as *any* regulative functions continue to be carried out by the brain. For, as I noted earlier, there are various minor functions of the brain whose persistence does not exclude a diagnosis of brain death. If the continuation of those functions were incompatible with brain death, the diagnosis of brain death might in many cases have to be delayed until the patient's organs had deteriorated to the point of being unusable for transplantation. For this and other reasons, no one has ever been seriously tempted to define brain death as the cessation of *all* functions in the brain.

Yet any point along the spectrum between these two extremes would seem arbitrary as the point at which too few bodily functions are regulated by the brain for life to be present. If some functions are being regulated by machines while others are being regulated by the brain, so that the great majority of functions are occurring in a coordinated way, that would seem to be sufficient for the presence of life, especially if consciousness is among those functions. Indeed, one point on which everyone agrees is that if a human being remains conscious, he or she is not dead. But imagine a case in which the regulation of one somatic function after another is taken over from the brain by a machine. First one regulatory function of the brain is lost and taken over by a machine, then another, and another, and so on until the only brain function that remains is the one that cannot, at least not yet, be replaced by a machine: consciousness. While the brain continues to generate consciousness, the person is not dead. But now suppose that this last remaining function also ceases, and irreversibly so. When this happens, brain death occurs. Proponents of brain death claim that it is at this point, and only at this point, that the person dies, even though all the other functions of the organism continue to be carried out in an internally coordinated way, though ultimately at the prompting of machines.

Yet notice that in this case the transition from life to death with the cessation of the final brain function – consciousness – has nothing to do with the cessation of somatic regulation by the brain stem. All regulatory functions were previously taken over by machines. If some degree of regulation of somatic functions by the brain were necessary for life in an organism, this person would have been dead before he lost the capacity for consciousness. The cessation of consciousness alone is not the difference between *biological* life and death *in the organism*, as defenders of the brain death criterion themselves acknowledge when they refuse to consider a patient in a persistent vegetative state to be dead.

This scenario in which the last brain function to survive is consciousness is similar to the earlier hypothetical example in which the cerebral cortex alone outlives all the other constituent parts of the organism. As such it may be dismissed as unrealistic. But there are numerous actual cases in which the relevant features of this case are present – namely, the maintenance of consciousness in the absence of *any* regulation of somatic functions by the brain stem. Examples include cases in which the spinal cord is completely severed just below the brain stem ("high cervical transection"), and cases in which swelling and compression in the same area prevent the transmission of any signals between the brain and the rest of the body (as in some cases of Guillain-Barré syndrome). In these cases, the person is conscious but wholly "locked in," while all somatic functions normally regulated by the brain must be prompted externally. Yet because the person is conscious, no one claims that the organism is biologically dead on the ground that its manifold functions are being prompted by a ventilator and integrated in a decentralized manner as the various organs and subsystems respond to signals from one another. So the truth seems to be that *no* degree of regulation by the brain is necessary for biological life in the organism. If it were a necessary truth that some degree of regulation by the brain were necessary for life, people who are wholly locked in would be dead but conscious – not conscious in some otherworldly afterlife, but in their own dead body.

Before turning to other matters, I will conclude this critique of brain death by advancing one further argument. Recall that brain death involves the death of the brain "as a whole" but does not exclude some isolated, residual forms of functioning. The idea that brain death is death thus implies that we remain alive as long as the brain maintains a certain level of functioning but die when it loses that level of functioning. What this means is that a certain level of functioning in the brain is a necessary and sufficient condition of our remaining alive. If that is true, it seems that that level of brain function is a necessary and sufficient condition of our *being* alive. The idea that brain death is death must also, therefore, imply a certain account of when we *begin* to be alive, or "when life begins." That is, if we can *continue* to live only if we have a certain level of brain function, then we cannot *begin* to be alive until that same level of function is initially achieved. Yet I think there is literally no one who believes this. While there have been a few people who have accepted that we begin to exist when the developing human brain achieves a level of functioning sufficient to exclude a diagnosis of brain death, no one has seriously proposed that the developing human organism does not become biologically alive until that point. That is, no one claims that a human embryo in which the brain is forming but has not yet become active is an inanimate entity, or that it is not a biological individual at all but a mere aggregate of living cells or tissues. But if a human embryo one month after conception is a living human organism even though none of its functions is regulated by its brain because it has no brain, and even though it requires external life support in the form of a woman's uterus, why then is a brain-dead but fully functional human organism sustained by a ventilator not also alive?

Although the situation may have been somewhat different when the notion of brain death was first introduced, virtually all of those who now defend the notion of brain death do so because they think it indicates when a human organism is no longer biologically alive. They recognize that the death of the brain as a whole is not necessary for the irreversible loss of the capacity for consciousness. While some argue that we cannot know with complete *certainty* that that capacity has been lost until brain death occurs, that is an unstable view. For anyone who is seriously open to the possibility that consciousness may persist in the brain stem after the entire cortex has died must also be open to the possibility that it may persist in the lower parts of the central nervous system after both the cortex and the brain stem have died.

What Kind of Entity Are We?

The claim that a human organism ceases to be biologically alive only at brain death is of serious *moral* interest only if the biological death of a human organism is also the death or ceasing to exist of a person, or a person's ceasing to exist *here*. Yet the biological death of a human organism is necessarily the death of a person only if we *are* (in the sense of being identical with) human organisms. But recall that I noted earlier that those, including most Christians as well as most devotees of other major religions, who believe that we survive the biological death and decomposition of our bodies cannot consistently believe that we are biological organisms. I think it is true that we are not organisms, though not because we survive biological death. We do not need to imagine a disembodied afterlife for ourselves to see that we are not identical with our organisms, for life itself in some of its more bizarre manifestations provides sufficient evidence. There are various anomalous conditions that show that we cannot be organisms.

One such condition is dicephalus. Dicephalic twinning is a radically incomplete form of conjoined twinning in which two heads, each with its own brain and its own separate mental life, sit atop a single body. In some cases, there is very little duplication of organs below the neck; there is one circulatory system, one metabolic system, one reproductive system, and one immune system. In these cases, there are two persons but only one human organism. The two twins cannot both be the organism because that would imply that they are not distinct individuals but one and the same person. Each twin's relation to the organism is the same; therefore there can be no reason to suppose that one of them is the organism while the other is not. It seems, therefore, that *neither* of them is identical with the organism. If dicephalic twins are essentially the same kind of thing that we are, then we are not organisms either.

Some people argue that dicephalic twins are really two distinct but overlapping organisms, and in support of this contention point to the fact that in known cases there is some duplication of organs within what appears to be a single body. They must then confront a different form of conjoined twinning known as craniothoracopagus, in which there is one brain and one head, below which there appear to be two bodies, each with its own set of organs, though in one documented case the hearts and upper gastrointestinal tracts are fused. To the best of my knowledge there has never been a case of craniothoracopagus in which the twins have survived infancy, but that of course does not show that survival is physically impossible. If such twins were to survive, there would be one brain, one mind, and therefore one person. But by the criterion for individuating organisms suggested by those who claim that dicephalic twins are two organisms, it seems that there would be two organisms. For there would be two nearly complete sets of organs, either of which could in principle be separated from the other and from the head, leaving a complete living organism behind. But if there would be one person and two organisms, that person could not be identical with both organisms, and there would be no basis for claiming that he or she would be identical with one but not the other. Again, the correct conclusion seems to be that the person would not be identical with either of the two organisms. Since that person would be essentially the same kind of entity that we are, it seems that we cannot be organisms either.

There is one more form of conjoined twinning that is relevant here: craniopagus parasiticus. In cases of this sort, one conjoined twin is fully developed but the other, which is joined to the first at the head, has failed to develop a body, and is thus, as the name suggests, a second head that draws life support from an organism to which it is attached but over which it exercises no control. The second brain, in other words, has no regulative functions with respect to the organism that sustains it, so that the death of this brain might have no effect on the organism. There are only 11 recorded cases of this phenomenon, but two have occurred in the twenty-first century. In one case in Egypt, the second head was surgically removed but the remaining twin died a little more than a year later from an infection of the brain. Before the parasitic head was removed, it was observed to smile and blink, but apparently no one seriously tested for the presence of consciousness. But whatever was true in this actual case, it is clearly possible that there could be a case in which the brain in the parasitic head would be fully developed and capable of not only consciousness but self-consciousness. If that were to occur, there would then be a clear instance of a single organism supporting the existence of two persons. One might claim that the person whose head was connected directly to the organism would be identical with that organism, but that would mean that there would be at least one person – the person associated with the parasitic head – who was not identical with any human organism.

One might think that this poses no challenge to those who believe that we are organisms. For they could simply say of the person, or self-conscious being, resident in the second head that he or she is a special case. That one person is not identical with an organism is compatible with all other persons being identical with their organisms. But the problem is that any person could in principle become a parasitic head. Suppose I had an identical twin whose blood was of the same type as mine and whose immune system would treat me as self rather than other. My head could be surgically attached to my twin's body and sustained by its blood supply. This has been done in animals (Browne, 1998). The head of one monkey has been transplanted onto the body of another. The resulting creature did not survive long but when the head regained consciousness after the surgery it tried to bite the surgeon – quite reasonably in my view. If my head were similarly attached to my twin's body, I would survive but would be no more a distinct organism than the parasitic head is in actual cases of craniopagus parasiticus. But if I would not be an organism then, I cannot be identical with an organism now. For it is a matter of logic that if I am identical with something now, I cannot cease to be identical with that thing and yet continue to exist.

I think these arguments, which mostly appeal to actual phenomena, show that we cannot be human organisms. But if that is right, my death or ceasing to exist need not be the same as the biological death of my organism. I might, for example, cease to exist before my organism dies. Many religious people believe that their organism will die but that *they* will neither die nor cease to exist at that point – though they may cease to exist *here*. They are able to believe this because they also believe that they are essentially nonphysical substances – souls – that are the immediate subjects of consciousness and mental activity.

But the idea that we are souls is a highly precarious foundation for our beliefs about the nature of death. Anyone who believes that we are souls and that we begin to exist separately from the body at brain death had better have good answers to the following questions. Do animals have souls, and, if not, how can one detect the presence of the soul in a human embryo while being confident of its absence in a chimpanzee? Assuming that souls do not come in degrees, so that the possession of a soul is all-or-nothing, when in the course of evolution did our ancestors begin to be endowed with souls? Was there a detectable difference between the parent who lacked a soul and the child who had one? If the soul can survive the death of the human organism and retain its full psychological capacities in a disembodied state, why are one's psychological capacities or states affected at all by what happens to one's brain? What happens to the soul of an embryo that divides and is replaced by two new embryos? What happens to the soul when the tissues connecting a person's cerebral hemispheres are surgically severed, creating two separate centers of consciousness, each capable of experiences inaccessible to the other? And what reason is there to suppose that the soul departs from the body at brain death rather than, for example, at the onset of persistent vegetative state?

I think that there are no good answers to these questions and that there is no reason to suppose that we are souls (McMahan 2002: 7–24). What are we then? Here is one way to think about this problem. Imagine that you discover that you are in the very early stages of progressive dementia. As the dementia advances, you will gradually lose both the particular elements of your mental life – your memories, character traits, and so on – and even your basic psychological capacities, so that if your body continues to function long enough, you will eventually lose any remaining capacity for consciousness. When can you expect to cease to exist? It seems clear that you will continue to exist as long as your brain continues to generate consciousness, and indeed as long as your brain retains the capacity to generate consciousness. As long as there is a subject of experiences present, or if it is possible to revive a subject of experiences in your body, there is evidently *someone* present, and there is no reason to suppose that that would be anyone other than you. But will you still be there after your brain irreversibly loses the capacity for consciousness? What will remain at that point will be a living human organism with no capacity for consciousness or experience.

But I have argued that we are not human organisms. If that is right, that organism cannot be you. And it is hard to identify anything else that might be you. I think we should conclude that you ceased to exist along with the capacity for consciousness. That suggests that you are essentially an entity with the capacity for consciousness – a mind.

Each of us is a mind, a subject of consciousness, which is sustained by the functioning of his or her brain, which is in turn sustained by the functioning of his or her organism. But we are not identical with our organisms. Because our organisms are living biological entities, they can die. The common view, which I have no grounds for disputing, is that an organism dies with the irreversible cessation of coordinated functioning among its various parts. The best criterion for determining when this occurs is probably irreversible cardio-pulmonary failure. According to this view, a human organism can remain alive after brain death, as in the cases of the pregnant women whose bodies continued to support fetal gestation for months after they had suffered brain death. But nothing of significance hinges on this because what matters is when *we* die or cease to exist. If we are entities that essentially have the capacity for consciousness, then we cease to exist when we irreversibly lose that capacity. The best criterion for when this happens is some form of "higher brain" criterion, of the sort I mentioned earlier.

Persistent Vegetative State

In suggesting that a higher brain criterion is the correct criterion for determining when we cease to exist, I am not making the mistake of those who have proposed a higher brain criterion as *the* criterion of death. They assumed that the death or ceasing to exist of a person is equivalent to the biological death of a human organism. They were therefore forced to say that when a person loses the capacity for consciousness by lapsing into a persistent vegetative state, her organism ceases to be biologically alive, which is obviously false. By contrast, I think we must distinguish between the person and the organism and thus between the death or ceasing to exist of the person and the biological death of the organism. As I noted earlier, our language already contains the distinction between the two concepts of death – that is, between the ceasing to exist of a person and the biological death of an organism. It therefore has the conceptual resources to articulate what I think is the correct view of a patient in a persistent vegetative state – namely, that the person has ceased to exist because she has irreversibly lost the capacity for consciousness, but that her organism remains alive. Only by recognizing that the person and her organism are different entities can we properly understand both the personal and the biological dimensions of death.

If persistent vegetative state involves the ceasing to exist of the person but not the biological death of the organism, can it be permissible to remove a persistently vegetative patient's organs for transplantation? This would involve the killing of a human organism and the killing would be intentional in a familiar sense. Many people would therefore see the extraction of the patient's organs as murder. But I think this is a mistake. A human organism that does not and cannot support the existence of a person, or a subject of consciousness, does not have interests or rights. To end its life is no more objectionable morally than to kill a plant, provided that what is done does not contravene the interests or rights of the person who once animated the organism.

295

This will seem shocking to many. But consider this. The *only* difference between a genuinely persistently vegetative patient (that is, a human organism in which the capacity for consciousness has been irreversibly lost) and a fully functional but brain-dead organism sustained by a ventilator, is that some of the former's functions are regulated by the brain stem whereas those same functions in the latter are triggered by the combination of the ventilator and the decentralized action of other body parts. How can *that* be the difference between murder and permissible killing?

A living human organism in which all possibility of consciousness has been lost has much the same moral status as a human corpse. We do not think that corpses have interests or rights but we recognize that there are ways in which it would be disrespectful to treat them. Precisely the same is true of a persistently vegetative human organism: there are various forms of respect that it is owed by virtue of its association with the person who once animated it. But just as most of us have concluded that it can be permissible to use a corpse's organs for transplantation, provided that this is not done against the will of the person whose body it was, so we should conclude that it is not disrespectful of a person to take organs from his persistently vegetative organism, even though that involves killing the organism, provided that it is not done against his will. Just as people are now permitted to stipulate that their organs not be taken from their body after their death, so people should be allowed to forbid the taking of their organs for transplantation after they lapse into a persistent vegetative state. But those who would like to donate their organs for transplantation once they have ceased to exist should not be denied the opportunity to save the lives of others in that way. (It is, of course, a different question how long a patient in a persistent vegetative state must be provided with medical care, given that the resources devoted to sustaining this biological life could otherwise be devoted to the needs of persons.)

The most serious moral objection to taking organs from persistently vegetative patients, even with their advance consent, is that at present there is often uncertainty about their condition. The two most important forms of uncertainty concern the possibility of recovery and the possibility of consciousness of which external observers are unaware. Recent research has demonstrated that some people who had satisfied the clinical criteria for persistent vegetative state had not in fact lost the capacity for consciousness. In this relatively small group of patients, compelling evidence of certain forms of consciousness has been discovered, and in at least one case there has been a complete recovery of normal consciousness (Groopman 2007). These cases have made us more acutely aware both of how serious the problem of mistaken diagnosis is and of the need for more reliable diagnostic criteria. One of the problems is that the sophisticated new neuroimaging techniques that have made these discoveries possible are quite expensive, and are often not covered by medical insurance. With these advanced technologies for exploring blood flow and electrical and other activity in the brain, it is sometimes possible to be quite certain that the capacity for ordinary consciousness has been irreversibly lost. Unless such technologies are used and show that this is the case, it could be wrong to kill a patient diagnosed as persistently vegetative in order to remove her organs for transplantation, even with her advance consent. But if we as a society came to recognize that those who are *known* to have lost the capacity for consciousness have ceased to exist, and that it can be permissible to use their organs for transplantation, we might then find it more economical to deploy the expensive neuroimaging technologies more widely rather than allowing those diagnosed as persistently vegetative to lie largely ignored in nursing homes, consuming vast resources, as we tend to do now. We could then treat those who would be determined to have some chance of recovery and use the organs of those beyond the possibility of recovery to save the lives of others.

The other form of uncertainty is whether some of those diagnosed as persistently vegetative who have no prospect of improvement nevertheless experience some form of consciousness, at least intermittently. We cannot yet entirely rule out the possibility that even in patients whose cortex is wholly dead there might be some dim, flickering, primitive form of consciousness in the brain stem. (Indeed, this cannot be ruled out even in the case of some patients diagnosed as brain dead, since a diagnosis of brain death is compatible with the persistence of various forms of activity in the brain.) If the probability that some rudimentary form of consciousness might persist in the brain stem in patients in a persistent vegetative state were high, or even significant, that should prompt serious consideration of the metaphysical question whether such consciousness would be sufficient for the survival of the person. But since the probability seems very low and the metaphysical significance uncertain, the bare possibility seems insufficiently important to be a serious factor in the formulation of policy.

Some people seem to believe that even in the case of patients in a long-term persistent vegetative state, in which the prospect of recovery is statistically nil, it is nevertheless possible that the person remains robustly conscious though locked in. Many people seemed to believe this about Terri Schiavo, the persistently vegetative patient whose feeding tube was removed in 2006 after an extraordinary legal and political battle during which President Bush made the unprecedented decision to truncate his vacation by flying to Washington late at night to sign legislation prohibiting the removal of the tube (Didion 2005). The objective probability that there is any ordinary form of consciousness in patients in a long-term persistent vegetative state is negligible. But suppose it were higher. We ought not to allow notions of the sanctity of human life to deter us from imagining what such a life might be like from the inside. Even if, contrary to fact, we could be sure that it would not involve agonizing pain to which the patient could give no expression, we only have to imagine being buried alive for years or decades to get some sense of how such a life might be lived from within.

References

Browne, M. (1998). From science fiction to science: "whole body transplant." *New York Times*, May 5.

Didion, J. (2005). The case of Theresa Schiavo. *New York Review of Books* 52.

Groopman, J. (2007). Silent minds. *The New Yorker* (October 15): 38–43.

McMahan, J. (2002). *The Ethics of Killing: Problems at the Margins of Life.* New York: Oxford University Press.

Shewmon, A. (1998). "Brain-stem death," "brain death," and death: a critical re-evaluation of the purported equivalence. *Issues in Law & Medicine* 14: 125–45.

Singer, P. (1994). *Rethinking Life and Death: The Collapse of Our Traditional Ethics.* New York: St Martin's.

Further reading

Bernat, J. (1998). A defense of the whole-brain concept of death. *Hastings Center Report* 28: 14–23.

DeGrazia, D. (2005). *Human Identity and Bioethics*. Cambridge: Cambridge University Press.

Kamm, F. (2001). Brain death and spontaneous breathing. *Philosophy and Public Affairs* 30: 297–320.

Shewmon, A. Recovery from "brain death": a neurologist's apologia. *Linacre Quarterly* 64: 30–96.

26

Advance Directives

ALEXANDER MORGAN CAPRON

Advance directives for health care are the quintessential topic in bioethics. Advance directives embody the field's fundamental commitment to the principle of individual autonomy; they concern decisions about critical illness and death, the aspect of bioethics that touches more lives than any other given the inevitability of death and the prevalence of medical involvement in the dying process; and they illustrate the movement of bioethics from the bedside into the realm of the law. Yet despite the central place that they have occupied in the field of bioethics over the past several decades, and the great zeal with which they are advocated in some countries, advance directives are conceptually problematic, widely misunderstood, poorly studied, and seldom implemented.

What Are Advance Directives and Why Do We Have Them?

An advance directive is a statement made in advance of an illness about the type and extent of treatment one would want, on the assumption that one may be incapable of participating in decision-making about treatment when the need arises. Advance directives are usually written, though an oral declaration may also suffice; they may name a person to make decisions on one's behalf, give instructions on what treatments should or should not be provided under specified circumstances, or do both. In theory, advance directives provide a means to express wishes of any sort (for example, that particular treatments be used or not used, or that all possible treatment is to be provided), but they are usually thought of as a means to limit life-prolonging treatment, especially in the United States where interest in advance directives originated and has been most intense. An attempt to use a directive to insist on "all possible treatment" is an example of a fairly new phenomenon, related to the issue of "medical futility." Here, a patient – or, more commonly, family members speaking on behalf of an incapacitated patient – insists on receiving medical interventions that physicians do not want to provide because they believe the treatments are unlikely to benefit the patient or are too scarce or expensive to be justified compared to using the same treatment with other patients. The use of a directive does not alter the core substance of the ethical considerations that must be weighed in resolving disputes over "futile" treatment, though it may complicate the situation since the expression of a patient's advance wishes in the document may constrain the ability or inclination of family members to compromise with physicians who are unwilling to utilize the medical interventions the patient appears to have demanded.

Under such names as "living will," "durable (or "enduring" or "continuing") power of attorney for health care," or "health-care proxy," advance directives are a familiar part of health care today in many countries. Yet it is worth remembering that they are actually a very recent response to a modern problem, namely the worry of many people that they will become victims trapped by medicine's ever-expanding ability to sustain life indefinitely after they lose the ability to voice their wishes about how, and for how long, they want to be treated at the end of life. Of course, physicians do not set out with the purpose of inaugurating endless care of dying, unconscious patients. But treatment begun with a hope – if not necessarily an expectation – of success frequently falls short, especially when the patient has experienced a cardiac arrest, stroke, or any other injury that has cut off the circulation of oxygenated blood (even for a short period). If the damage that results to the higher centers of the brain is severe enough, consciousness is unlikely to be restored even if the vegetative functions controlled by the lower brain and brain stem persist with supportive care, ranging from mechanical ventilation and drugs to simple feeding through a tube.

In such circumstances, decisions must be made about when to provide or to forgo life-sustaining treatment for patients whose medical condition makes them unable to participate in decision-making. Some jurisdictions require very clear proof of what an incompetent patient would have wanted (at least before life-support is discontinued), in which case an advance directive may be legally necessary. And even where the law permits family members or other persons acting on behalf of an incompetent patient to decide with physicians about life-sustaining interventions based either on what they know the patient would have wanted or on what they believe would be in the patient's best interests, surrogate decision-makers and health-care professionals alike may be unwilling to act without clear documentation of the patient's wishes, in which case an advance directive may be a practical (albeit not a legal) necessity.

The Origins, and Limitations, of the "Living Will"

Indeed, advance directives arose initially as a response to the decision-making paralysis, born of guilt and uncertainty, that frequently occurs when the question is whether to forgo the medical interventions that sustain the life of someone who is no longer able to make his or her own views – if any – known. Recognizing that physicians, nurses, and other health-care providers, as well as patients' next-of-kin, often find it difficult to withhold further interventions, much less to withdraw those already being undertaken, Luis Kutner, a Chicago attorney active in a right-to-die organization, in 1967 drafted what he termed a "living will." Just as a "will" signifies a document through which a person leaves instructions for the disposition of his or her estate after death, Kutner's "living will" allows a person to give instructions for medical care in the final days of life. In particular, through a living will people, while still competent, are able to state that they do not want their dying process prolonged once they become unable to express their wishes directly.

Living wills were viewed as serving several purposes. First, by executing a living will, a person could lift the burden of decision-making off the shoulders of anxious relatives and hesitant physicians. This is particularly important when people's reasons for forgoing treatment involve not only their own physical condition but also avoiding the financial and emotional burdens that prolonged hospital or nursing home care would impose on their family. Absent a clear statement from the person, it might seem self-serving and hence illegitimate for a surrogate decision-maker to take such considerations into account. Second, if the wishes expressed in the living will are honored, a person could in effect participate in treatment decision-making even after she has lost the ability to communicate, and this at least arguably promotes her autonomy, as that term is usually used. And third, the existence of living wills – and the interest in many quarters that soon arose about them – helped to educate health-care providers about the public's sense that life-prolonging treatment is not always regarded as a good (Weir 1994).

Yet, while living wills were actively promoted by several organizations, first in the United States and then in other countries, only a tiny percentage of the population knew about them, much less signed one. Furthermore, the original form of the living will – and others that followed its language – candidly admitted its own major limitation: under the common law of agency, it lacked legal effect. The law permits one person (termed the principal) to appoint another (the agent) to carry out instructions on his or her behalf. Commitments undertaken by an agent are binding on his or her principal. If a principal is dissatisfied with an agent, the principal may discharge the agent and notify those relying on the agent that the principal will no longer be bound. Because a person who has become incapable of making his or her own decisions has also lost the ability to discharge an agent or alter his or her instructions, the common law provides that all agents are automatically discharged by operation of law when their principal becomes incompetent, lest a person be bound by the decisions of an agent whom the person was incapable of countermanding. Agents – including those who act under a formal document giving them "power of attorney" – usually have authority regarding the property, rather than the physical person, of the principal. (Such an agent is not typically an attorney-at-law but a lay person acting as an "attorney-in-fact.") Applied to the medical context, traditional agency law renders instructions in a living will non-binding at the very moment when they are intended to go into effect.

Kutner and other advocates of the living will frankly admitted that it was not legally binding because they believed that its real strength lay in the reassurance – indeed, courage – it could provide to a patient's family, spiritual advisor, and physicians to forgo life-prolonging treatment when death was near. But as medicine's powers to sustain biological functioning continued throughout the 1970s to outpace the health-care professions' ability to draw sensible limitations on the use of these powers, some advocates of the "right to die" became convinced that living wills would only be effective if they could dispel physicians' liability fears. Although the absence of adverse cases should have been enough to reassure physicians that they were at little or no risk of civil or criminal liability for following a living will, they frequently invoked such risk to justify disregarding these documents. The fear may have been genuine (though erroneous) or may have merely reflected physicians' discomfort in seeming to "give up" and admit they were unable to provide an effective cure in the case at hand. In any case, the "not

301

legally binding" excuse stood in the way of living wills becoming a truly useful and important part of patient care, and living will advocates therefore pressed for legislation that would authorize families and care providers to rely on such directives and immunize them from liability when they did. Yet, while the first "living will bill" was introduced in 1968 in Florida, the issue did not attract much public attention – and, when it did, it was often intertwined with efforts to legalize physicians taking more active steps (such as prescribing lethal drugs at a patient's request) to end the lives of dying patients.

Legislatively Authorized "Instruction Directives"

Ironically, public interest in making living wills valid legal documents was galvanized by the worldwide attention directed to a case in which the patient did not have a living will – the 1976 New Jersey Supreme Court decision regarding Karen Ann Quinlan, a young woman who had slipped into a coma after apparently taking some combination of alcohol and drugs. Her physicians refused to turn off the respirator that they said was needed to support her breathing on the ground that ceasing treatment would amount to criminal homicide. The high court disagreed and said that it would be reasonable to follow her father's request, provided that an ethics committee convened by the hospital agreed. The position – both of Ms. Quinlan and of her parents – focused attention on the unwillingness of physicians to act without clear legal authority and generated interest in moving living wills from their shadowy existence as hortatory statements to officially recognized instructions from patients expressing their wishes while they were still able to do so.

Within months of the New Jersey decision, California enacted the first statute. As explained by its author in introducing the bill: "The image of Karen Quinlan haunts our dreams. For many, the ultimate horror is not death, but the possibility of being maintained in limbo in a sterile room, by machines that are controlled by strangers." Although initially a simple attempt to give legal validity to living wills, the bill was amended dozens of times because many legislators still had severe reservations about discontinuing life-sustaining treatment. The resulting statute, the Natural Death Act, had many flaws, beginning with its name – in this era of wonder drugs and medical miracles almost no death in a health-care facility is "natural." Rather, each death reflects many human decisions about using or withholding efforts to change the course of illness and prolong life. Yet despite such limitations, the Natural Death Act stimulated legislation across the country, as states either followed the California model or drafted their own versions to overcome some of the problems in the original statute.

As a group, these statutes authorize a type of advance directive sometimes termed an "instruction directive" because the gist of the document is to instruct physicians and other care-givers about what they should do under particular circumstances. A basic problem with this type of directive is that most people are not able to predict the circumstances of their death with any precision. Therefore, instruction directives – both the original living will and the forms set forth in state statutes – are often written generically, employing either poetic language ("heroic measures") or wording that raises more questions than it answers ("means that only prolong the dying process").

Some physicians suggest using much more specific forms, in which patients indicate on a checklist precisely which interventions they would or would not want. Such specificity could prevent arguments over whether a patient intended to forgo only mechanical ventilation or also antibiotics, drugs that maintain blood pressure and the like, and tubes that supply food and fluids. Other commentators object that what is most important to patients is not the particular means used but the results produced, including the probability that some degree of recovery will be achieved and whether the treatment will cause pain or further dehumanize their dying process. Thus, they argue that a living will should be written so as to convey the person's "values history," a general orientation that would connect issues arising in the dying process with the way the person has lived his or her whole life.

A second basic issue with instruction directives is in knowing when they come into effect. Many versions of the living will are triggered when a "terminal illness" is diagnosed, but knowing what "terminal" means is often difficult. Some statutes are written in terms of an illness that would be fatal within six months, while others speak of death being imminent.

A related problem with the so-called living will statutes is that early versions encompassed only "terminal illness," while the more frightening prospect for many people is a situation that has no termination in sight, namely prolonged treatment in a permanently unconscious state when death is not imminent because their underlying condition is not a lethal one so long as basic support, such as food and fluids and comfort measures, is continued. Today, some statutes specify that an instruction directive comes into effect when a patient is unconscious (which "to a reasonable degree of medical certainty" will not be reversed), has an incurable or irreversible condition that will result in death in a relatively short time, or the "likely risks and burdens of treatment would outweigh the expected benefits"; alternatively, the person filling out such a directive may indicate the circumstances under which the instructions take effect. Likewise, the statutes – as well as judicial decisions interpreting them and determining when, if ever, an oral declaration provides a legally effective expression of a patient's wishes to forgo treatment – set forth which treatments are automatically encompassed within do-not-treat instructions and which ones (such as food and fluids by tube) need to be spelled out explicitly by the declarant in order to be valid.

Legislatively Authorized "Appointment Directives"

Limitations of this sort in instruction-type directives generated interest in finding better means to permit patients to exercise some control over medical decisions even after they lose decisional capacity. As it happened, during the latter part of the 1970s, many jurisdictions adopted statutes that allow people to execute what in the United States is called a "durable power of attorney" and in Great Britain and some other countries is termed a "continuing power of attorney." Such documents are "durable" or "continuing" in that they survive the incompetence of the principal; indeed, they may provide that the authority of the agent only comes into being when the principal loses the capacity to make decisions. These laws were enacted to enable people, especially the elderly with small estates, to appoint one of their children or another trusted person to manage their finances and other affairs if they become unable to do so, without the burden of having to seek formal court appointment of a conservator.

In one of its reports, a US presidential commission on medical ethics in 1983 recommended the adoption of statutes specifically to allow the use of durable powers for health-care decisions. Later that year, California again became the first jurisdiction to enact such a statute, the Durable Power of Attorney for Health Care law. All American states now have laws that permit the appointment of a health-care agent and all save three – Massachusetts, Michigan, and New York – also recognize a living will or other instructions concerning a patient's wishes about forgoing life-support, thereby permitting people to combine an appointment directive with a set of instructions to guide the agent's decisions. All states except for Alaska, Illinois, Montana, North Carolina, Ohio, and Washington now require a health-care provider who does not wish to implement an advance directive to aid in the transfer of the patient to a different provider who will do so. Standard forms are readily available that comply with that state's statutory requirements regarding what warnings must be provided about the actions covered by the directive (which usually exclude psychiatric treatments, sterilization, or abortion) and regarding who may serve as an agent (which usually excludes health-care providers) and as a witness to the form (which sometimes excludes those who would stand to benefit financially from a patient's death). The forms are quite simple to complete without legal assistance, though individuals who lack legal or personal agents to deal with financial or other affairs outside of health care appear to be much less likely to appoint a health-care agent in advance.

For persons who have someone they trust to serve as their health-care agent, an appointment-type directive, such as the durable power of attorney for health care, is regarded by most experts as a more useful document than a living will or other instruction-type directive. The central advantage is that the agent can step into the shoes of the patient and make decisions in light of the current medical situation and advice of the attending physician, whereas instructions may not address the situation or may be so ambiguous as to create more confusion than clarity about what the patient would actually want done under the circumstances. Experts disagree about whether it is advisable to include instructions in the document appointing an agent. Doing so may ease the burden on an agent, aiding and comforting him or her in choosing a difficult alternative. It may also increase the ability of the agent to make a decision that accurately reflects what the patient would want, especially since without such instructions neither family members nor health-care professionals turn out to be very accurate predictors of patients' preferences regarding life-sustaining treatment; the obligation that surrogates exercise "good faith" in the patients' "best interests" provides little guidance. On the other hand, to the extent that instructions are unclear or do not directly address the issues that need to be resolved, they can be mischievous, and if a dispute arises between the agent and others, such as other family members or the attending physician, the instructions may be invoked to limit the agent's ability to decide in a way that he or she is convinced best serves the patient's objectives and interests under the circumstances.

Whether or not instructions are written down, all commentators seem to agree that it is advisable for the principal and the agent to talk about what the principal hopes to get from treatment and especially about outcomes or types of treatment that the principal wants to avoid. Ideally, some of these conversations would also involve the principal's regular physician (although it appears that many people regard attorneys rather than physicians as the appropriate persons to consult regarding an advance directive). The physician can thus begin a relationship with the agent that will both facilitate good communication if it is ever necessary for the agent to become the surrogate decision-maker. Including the physician in these conversations also allows him or her to convey to the principal and agent a realistic picture of the kinds of interventions about which decisions may need to be made and the range of outcomes that is likely to flow from using or forgoing these interventions. One difficulty with the advance directive model is that physicians may lack expertise in the process of facilitating such conversations. Additionally, health insurance typically provides little or no coverage for such conversations, leaving physicians without financial incentive to engage in what may be a time-consuming communication process (Cerminara 1998). Finally, because of a 1991 federal statute requiring health-care institutions to inform patients about their rights to make decisions and to fill out advance directives, many health-care professionals associate advance directives with the admission to hospital, a moment when patients are typically in a medical crisis or anxious about imminent surgery and not the best time for "advance" planning about end-of-life decisions. Although the federal requirement has made the public more aware of advance directives, the number of people who have executed one remains quite low (by many estimates under a quarter of the population).

Advance Directives Outside the United States

Advance directives not only began as a phenomenon in the United States but to a surprising degree have remained so; by the late 1990s, advance directives had been implemented in the statute books of Denmark, Germany, the Netherlands, New Zealand, and several Australian and Canadian jurisdictions, but had not spread to the rest of the developed world. Since 2000, Great Britain and Spain have also codified laws authorizing advance directives. One reason for this delay may be that care at the end of life has been more aggressive in the US than elsewhere in the developed world, so patients in the US felt more strongly that they needed means to resist over-treatment. Moreover, legislation on advance directives often came as a response to the pleas of judges in deciding a number of high-profile cases involving physicians' insistence on continuing life-support that patients' families found inappropriate. These cases were themselves an outgrowth of litigation dating to the 1960s that, along with the writings of legal and bioethics scholars, aimed at replacing medical paternalism with patient autonomy through the development of informed consent and related doctrines.

In other countries, not only were medical heroics less likely to be employed, but judges were less inclined to diminish physicians' authority to make decisions on behalf of their patients. Thus, legislatures had less reason to develop means by which persons could extend their autonomous choice into a future in which they had lost the ability to exercise such choice. (Also, appointment-type directives were possible, through granting an agent power over one's person as well as property under a "continuing power of attorney.") In Great Britain, it was only in 1994 that a House of Lords Select Committee on Medical Ethics recommended that health-care advance directives be formulated and a code of practice be developed to guide health-care professionals in their use, though the committee did not urge legislation to give directives greater force in law (House of Lords Select Committee on Medical Ethics 1993–4). This recommendation was initially not pursued, and Great Britain waited a decade before passing the Mental Capacity Act in 2005. The Act allows for the creation of written advance directives which provide freedom from liability if a physician follows one in terminating end-of-life care. However, the Act is more limited than some of its American counterparts: a physician "does not incur liability for carrying out or continuing the treatment unless . . . he is satisfied that an advance directive exists which is valid and applicable to the treatment," and the physician may declare a directive invalid if "there are reasonable grounds for believing that circumstances exist which [the patient] did not anticipate at the time of the advance decision and which would have affected his decision had he anticipated them."

As late as 1992 in Canada, no court had addressed the validity of living wills, perhaps because physicians were willing to act on the instructions contained in such documents. The Law Revision Commission of Canada did, however, recommend that the criminal code be clarified to ensure that physicians could not be prosecuted for homicide for following the provisions of a living will and withholding all care except palliation of pain. Furthermore, during the 1990s, the provincial legislatures adopted statutes on "Natural Death" and on durable powers of attorney for health care (in some cases termed the "Medical Consent Act"), or in some provinces, such as Manitoba, providing for "health-care directives" through which a person may express his or her health-care decisions, or appoint a proxy, or both. Advance directives containing critical care instructions are specifically allowed by statute in half of Canada's 12 provinces. All jurisdictions except for Nova Scotia, New Brunswick, and Quebec include in their advance directive legislation protection from civil liability for health-care providers and substitute decision-makers for actions taken in accord with lawful treatment decisions. The Criminal Code of Canada does not currently limit the criminal liability of health-care providers or substitute decision-makers who follow an advance directive.

In Australia – under revisions to the Medical Treatment Acts (1988) adopted in 1992 in Victoria and 1994 in the Australian Capital Territory, and under the Consent to Medical Treatment and Palliative Care Act 1995 in South Australia – a person may appoint an agent to make treatment decisions, including the refusal of life-sustaining treatment, when the person loses decisional capacity. This refusal may not, however, extend to palliative care, including food and water as well as pain medication. The South Australian Act, and the Natural Death Act 1988 in the Northern Territory, also permit a person to make an advance directive regarding treatment should the person lose the ability to communicate. In South Australia, directives to forgo "life-sustaining measures" are effective if the person is terminally ill or in a persistent vegetative state; the Northern Territory legislation is narrower, allowing people to instruct against the use of "extraordinary measures" once a terminal illness has been diagnosed. It is generally accepted that advance directives are permitted under the common law of Australia, but an appropriate case has not been examined in all jurisdictions. Under regulations issued in 1996 by the Health and Disability Commissioner in New Zealand, consumers' rights to have information about services and to give or refuse consent encompass the use of a written or oral advance directive, which is defined to include choices about future health care not limited to life-sustaining interventions.

In the common law countries, the lack of formal advance directive legislation is sometimes not a true impediment to good decision-making about care at the end of life, since judicial decisions often recognize the right of next-of-kin to make decisions with physicians about the treatment of incapacitated patients, a practice which allows patients' wishes to be taken into account even if not memorialized in a formal advance directive. Elsewhere, the absence of legal authorization has posed a problem. In some countries, such as Denmark and Spain, legislation has been enacted, while in others, such as Poland and France, advance directives are not recognized.

Conceptual Problems and Practical Difficulties

The emphasis in bioethics on patient autonomy can be seen as a necessary corrective to the excesses of medical paternalism. When it results in a relationship of mutual respect and joint decision-making, it can even improve clinical outcomes not only because active patients take greater responsibility for their own health, but also because they inspire providers to measure the outcomes of medical interventions through the patient's eyes. It is less clear that trying to extend personal autonomy into a future time at which the person has lost the ability for autonomous action is clinically beneficial or even conceptually sound.

The most influential philosophical argument for the utility of advance directives stems from the work of Ronald Dworkin (1993), who distinguishes between two types of human interests: "experiential interests" and "critical interests." Experiential interests are common, everyday experiences, and they do not carry any intrinsic value of their own other than the fact that they are either painful or pleasurable. Critical interests are the kinds of values, choices, and patterns that guide our lives and how we perceive the worth of our lives. This distinction becomes extremely relevant in the case of a patient who is no longer competent. Critical interests concern difficult and sophisticated problems that cannot be examined or revised by people who are incompetent, such as a person who is minimally conscious or who suffers from advanced Alzheimer's disease. Such persons' experiences may, however, bring them either pleasure or pain. Dworkin says that if autonomy is to be respected, we must respect the critical interests of persons, because those are the important core values of a person's life; experiential interests, while certainly not irrelevant, must take a back seat.

Some commentators, such as the President's Council on Bioethics, reject the practical conclusion to which this view leads – that treatment should be ended when that was the wish expressed by a formerly competent person – on the ground that the duties of care-givers, whether physicians or family and friends, are to do what is best for a person as he or she is now, and that these duties must trump our concerns for the autonomy of others (The President's Council on Bioethics 2005). Other critics raise several conceptual objections to Dworkin's formulation of the problem. First, some have argued that it is inappropriate to rely on an advance directive in making decisions about

307

patients who have suffered severe and permanent injuries, such as those in a persistent vegetative state, because these patients are no longer the persons they were at the
time the directive was executed. This shift in personal identity makes it wrong to
dictate the treatment of the patient in the bed by the wishes of the person that formerly
occupied this body; rather, treatment should be guided by an assessment of what would
be in the best interests of the present patient. The lack of continuity makes autonomy
concerns inapplicable. Legislators and judges seem largely unmoved by such philosophical
objections and adhere instead to the commonsense notion that finds a continuity
between a formerly competent person and his or her present being even following a
brain injury that obliterates consciousness, memory, and self-awareness.

Other commentators argue that as both a practical and conceptual matter, individuals are ill-equipped to make informed decisions about what they would in fact want
if they became incompetent to make medical decisions: not only are people usually
unaware of what their future medical conditions may be; they are often incapable of
fully understanding the medical choices (Schneider 2006). Indeed, it is difficult really
to imagine oneself as incompetent. Practically, for example, a patient who says "no
mechanical respiration" may be concerned that the use of such devices always leads
to a long period of dependence, when, in certain circumstances, a ventilator would only
be needed for a short period while the person recovers from an injury or from surgery.
It would be hard to argue that people's true autonomy has been advanced by giving
effect to choices that originate in insufficient information or that would require impossible mental feats. Additionally, as the House of Lords Select Committee on Medical Ethics
(1993–4) concluded: "A patient who has made an advance directive could unwittingly
be depriving himself or herself of professional medical expertise or of beneficial
advances in treatment."

Finally, critics simply challenge the centrality of critical interests and contend that
as a patient slips further into dementia experiential interests become more important
(Dresser 1995). This view rejects the notion that incompetent, dying patients
retain an interest in having their treatment accord with the overall arc of their life,
as Dworkin argues. It is not clear why this division of values could not be left to
each individual, that is, by each person executing a directive being asked to recognize
the trade-off between the interests and incorporating their preference into their
advance instructions. A further complication concerns whether permanently unconscious patients retain any interests beyond being protected from inhumane or degrading treatment. Since such patients lack conscious sensations, it is impossible to
prioritize their experiential interests, yet they are also unaware whether their treatment
wishes have been followed or not, rendering critical interests essentially prospective
concerns of competent persons rather than current interests of permanently unconscious persons.

Supporters of advance directives contend that, particularly when an appointment-
type advance directive is used, the health-care agent is usually able to take changed
medical circumstances and a current assessment of the patient's best interests into account
when participating with physicians and nurses in deciding about the patient's care,
rather than being bound in an ironclad fashion by instructions given at a time before
those circumstances were known. At the same time, executing an advance directive
provides comfort to people based on the sense that their family and physician will not

put them through endless treatment because these surrogate decision-makers are unsure whether stopping treatment would accord with the patient's wishes.

A further complication involves the relationship between loss of decision-making capacity and the implementation of an advance directive. Although health-care directives were developed specifically to respond to the barriers in existing law for agents to act on behalf of incompetent persons, the standards by which, and the processes through which, this "trigger" is found to exist are not well developed. It is frequently the case that decisions need to be made with some urgency in a hospital, nursing home, or other health-care institution in light of a patient's ever-changing medical condition, yet the patient may never have been declared "incompetent" by a court. The assumption is that physicians and others involved in treating the patient can determine (perhaps after consultation with an ethics committee) that the patient lacks decision-making capacity. But there are certainly cases where such a determination is debatable, particularly when it rests on a finding that the patient has disordered thinking rather than being unconscious or similarly impaired. If a patient attempts to revoke an earlier advance directive or countermand a surrogate's decisions, it may seem wrong to ignore the patient's objections, though some experts believe that the law would require the surrogate and the treatment team to do so were they convinced that the person, while still competent, had explicitly considered the very decision in question and had been clear about what should be done (Hornett 1995).

Barriers Remaining to the Effective Use of Advance Directives

However such conceptual issues are resolved – some of which underlie serious practical problems – advance directives remain an unfulfilled dream in many ways. First, advance directives are not yet a routine part of medical care. Few people want to think about their own demise, and many physicians have also been reticent about raising the subject and helping patients to think concretely about how their deaths may occur and the choices that will need to be made along the way. Second, even when an advance directive has been executed, it may not be available when needed. Sometimes, people file their advance directive away with other valuable papers (perhaps even in a safety deposit box in a bank) and the directive is only found after their death; this is another reason why appointment-type directives usually work better, since it is likely that a copy will have been given to the person named as the patient's agent. Even when the paper is accessible in the person's home or a copy has been given to the primary physician, the person may be hospitalized while traveling. To overcome such problems, Denmark has a computer registry for advance directives, which can be accessed by health-care providers treating patients who are unable to communicate their wishes regarding treatment, provided of course that the patient has both executed a directive and submitted it to the registry. Similar computerized services are provided for a fee by several organizations in the United States, though they have not been extensively used because they are not well known either among people who fill out directives or among hospital personnel. In 2005, Montana created a secure, free, online database of health-care instructional documents, but this has not been duplicated in other states. Even if health-care providers are able to obtain a copy of a patient's advance directive,

309

there is a real possibility that the physician will not honor it, either under pressure from family members or because they do not think the directive is in the patient's best interest. It has been estimated that perhaps as many as 25 percent of known advance directives are ignored by service providers (Winick 1998).

Third, the underlying premise of advance directives – that people should have a means to extend their individual autonomy into the future when they would otherwise be unable to control what happens to them – does not correspond to what some people regard as appropriate medical decision-making. Some people feel more comfortable relying on their physician's judgment; issuing any sort of a "directive" seems totally inappropriate to them. For others, social norms may dictate that decisions about treatment do not reside with the individual but with his or her family (which may be the patriarch or matriarch of an extended family, or the eldest child in a nuclear family, or the entire family through consensus) or community (as embodied in a tribal or religious leader); even if such a person could articulate personal wishes about, for example, limiting death-delaying interventions at the end of life, the person may still want to defer to custom and allow decisions to be made by a spouse or adult offspring, who in turn may feel the need to manifest his or her own love and respect by insisting on maximal treatment (Blackhall et al. 1995).

The controversy surrounding the 2005 termination of care of Terri Schiavo, a Florida woman in a persistent vegetative state, also provided a reminder that significant numbers of people, particularly in the United States, categorically believe that human life should never be cut short if the possibility exists for medical extension. To these thinkers and activists, autonomy interests are not sufficient to allow for individuals to end life prematurely and betray what they see as a moral duty to themselves and to God. Despite the enthusiasm in the bioethical community about advance directives, the Schiavo debate – which was at one point being officially examined simultaneously in the federal courts, the Florida state courts, the federal legislature, the state legislature, and the state Department of Children and Families – should highlight that other views retain considerable political clout. Even when statutes legitimize the use of directives, they may – as is the case in a number of jurisdictions in the United States – create the presumption that the person executing a directive wants tube-feeding unless the person affirmatively states otherwise; or they may – as in England – allow physicians to override a directive that they believe does not accord with the choice a well-informed patient would have made.

On a deeper level, advance directive statutes remain only partially effective because, while they furnish means for people to express their wishes, they provide no help in thinking about what those wishes should be. They are neither informative about the clinical realities of the dying process for various diseases nor do they offer spiritual assistance in understanding how one's values could or should shape the arc of one's final days. For such matters, people must continue to rely on the health-care professionals who take care of them and on the family members and others who care for them. While the long-term worth and effectiveness of advance directives remains more an article of faith for many bioethicists and public policy-makers, rather than a matter of empirical proof, it is likely that they will become a more common, albeit still imperfect, part of the medical landscape in the coming years.

References

Blackhall, L. J., Murphy, S. T., Frank, G., Michel, V., and Azen, S. (1995). Ethnicity and attitudes toward patient autonomy. *Journal of the American Medical Association* 274/10: 820–5.

Cerminara, K. (1998). Eliciting patient preferences in today's health care system. *Psychology, Public Policy and Law* 4: 688–702.

Dresser, R. (1995). Dworkin on dementia: elegant theory, questionable policy. *Hastings Center Report* 25/6: 32–8.

Dworkin, R. (1993). *Life's Dominion*. New York: Alfred A. Knopf.

Hornett, S. (1995). Advance directives: a legal and ethical advance. In J. Keown (ed.), *Euthanasia Examined: Ethical, Clinical and Legal Perspectives*. Cambridge: Cambridge University Press, pp. 297–314.

House of Lords Select Committee on Medical Ethics (1993–4). *Report*. London: House of Lords 21-L.

Law Commission of Great Britain (1995). *Report No. 231. Mental Incapacity*. London: February 28.

The President's Council on Bioethics (2005). *Taking Care: Ethical Caregiving in our Aging Society*. Washington, DC: US Government Printing Office.

Schneider, C. (2006). Rethinking health law: after autonomy, *Wake Forest Law Review* 41: 422–3.

Weir, R. F. (1994). Advance directives as instruments of moral persuasion. In R. H. Blank and A. L. Bonnicksen (eds.), *Medicine Unbound: The Human Body and the Limits of Medical Intervention*. New York: Columbia University Press, pp. 171–87.

Winick, B. (1998). Foreword planning for the future through advance directive instruments, *Psychology, Public Policy and Law* 4: 579–609.

Further reading

Advance Care Planning (1994). *Hastings Center Report* 24/6 (special supplement).

Beltran, J. E. (1994). *The Living Will*. Nashville, TN: Thomas Nelson Publishers.

Cantor, N. L. (1993). *Advance Directives and the Pursuit of Death with Dignity*. Bloomington and Indianapolis: Indiana University Press.

Hackler, C., Moseley, R., and Vawter, D. E. (eds.) (1989). *Advance Directives in Medicine*. New York: Praeger.

Hoefler, J. M. (1997). *Managing Death*. Boulder, CO: Westview Press.

King, N. M. P. (1996). *Making Sense of Advance Directives*. Washington, DC: Georgetown University Press.

Olick, R. S. (2001). *Taking Advance Directives Seriously: Prospective Autonomy and Decisions Near the End of Life*. Washington, DC: Georgetown University Press.

Sass, H.-M., Veatch, R. M., and Kimura, R. (eds.) (1998). *Advance Directives and Surrogate Decision Making in Health Care: United States, Germany, and Japan*. Baltimore, MD: Johns Hopkins University Press.

27

Voluntary Euthanasia, Suicide, and Physician-assisted Suicide

BRIAN STOFFELL

Legally approved medical practice in Belgium, Luxembourg, the Netherlands, and the USA, the activities of death rights activists like Dr Jack Kevorkian, the short-lived legislation in Australia's Northern Territory, and some highly publicized individual cases in Canada, England, France, Italy, and Spain have put voluntary euthanasia and assisted suicide firmly on the public agenda. Yet there is no bioethical issue with a longer philosophical lineage. The place of suicide in a rational life plan drew attention from classical antiquity's major thinkers and schools. Diogenes Laertius' discussion of Zeno's death is typical in its straightforward identification of honorable reasons for a voluntary death (*voluntaria mors*): "The sage leads himself rationally (*eulogos*) out of life, namely on behalf of fatherland or friends, also when he suffers from pain which is too fierce, mutilations or incurable diseases" (7.130).

Pain, mutilations, or incurable disease still form the basis for modern requests for euthanasia and assisted suicide, although there is less discussion these days about self-deliverance from such conditions. This is unfortunate, since the classical discussion of grounds for suicide correctly identifies it as the paradigm case of voluntary death; euthanasia and assisted suicide are morally derivative. Mature reflection on illness, death, and choice of exit should begin from suicide as the central case, then move on to requests for help in quitting life. In this chapter, all cases will be taken as motivated by suffering during terminal illness, and all references to euthanasia will be to active voluntary euthanasia. So the primary topic is suicide in the face of impending death.

If modern discussion of self-deliverance has been sporadic, the events of September 11, 2001 changed that. Unparalleled real-time, worldwide television coverage was given to the destruction of the World Trade Center. A part of that catastrophe was the choice of death by suicide for some 200 people who leapt from the Towers. Many, faced with the horror of being consumed in an inferno, chose an end considered less awful. I have heard no voices raised in condemnation of those who jumped, but the usual chorus of pious outrage still attends the death of many stricken individuals in our society. Political prudence has always been a strong suit for religion, so their silence is no surprise, but the inevitable question is, "Is there any significant moral difference between the two sets of voluntary deaths?" Those who jumped, along with the terminally ill who have committed suicide, faced the reality that there is more to dying than death. Death, being dead, is our common lot, but dying has different forms: our fates are not the same.

So although you cannot escape death by embracing death, as Martial quipped, you certainly can escape one form of dying by choosing another, although you may need Papinian's "intrepid virtue" (Gibbon 1906 [1776]: vol. I, ch. 6) to act. The issue here is control of one's death in the face of anxiety about how the dying process will unfold. The kind of anxiety or dread that attaches for some to mortality itself – alluded to by Philip Larkin in the lines from *Aubade*: "The sure extinction that we travel to / And shall be lost in always. Not to be here, / Not to be anywhere" – is not part of my concern here (see Levi 1998; Ewin 2002).

That bioethical discussion of voluntary death does not normally begin in this way is a function of the period separating us from Greek and Roman debate about *auto-thanasia* (Daube 1972; Griffin 1994; van Hooff 1990) Since Josephus in the first century and Augustine in the fifth, the treatment of suicide has been largely negative. Both writers drew on much older traditions of folklore and philosophy in exhibiting an attitude of abhorrence, buttressed by arguments designed to show that suicide is inherently wrong. Despite the largely religious provenance of their arguments – covering the sinful and the impious rather than the immoral – their attitude has had a dramatic impact on our thinking, mediated in the main through religious authorities and law.

This chapter is concerned with the three modes of voluntary death as they arise in bioethical cases, but concentrates on suicide as the key concept. There are three stages involved. The first identifies the source of some traditional attitudes, investigating how certain construals are responsible for distorting the structural relationship between the main concepts. The second deploys an argument sketch to show how to approach the issues once the distortions affecting suicide and killing are removed. The third is more positive, suggesting how voluntary deaths can be assessed, thereby providing a moral basis for discussing public policy on assisted suicide and euthanasia. Establishing the moral status of an act and the moral motivation for policy change is one thing, but it is quite another to evaluate the status of any policy that legitimates the act in law. In the present case I consider only the structure of the public policy debate and indicate where I believe emphasis should be placed.

The Traditional Prejudice

All societies have strong prohibitions against certain forms of killing, but it is often mistakenly thought that the Hebrew and Christian traditions enshrine a blanket social prohibition against killing, backed by a fervent religious reverence for human life. The way people view the tribal code of the Hebrews is a prime example, commonly assuming it to contain the commandment, "Thou shall not kill." The mitzvah at Exodus 20:13 and Deuteronomy 5:17 is, "Thou shall do no murder," not "Thou shall not kill." The Hebrew term for murder is transliterated as *râtsach*. Hebrew is rich in terms for species of killing. When their god Yahweh orders killings to be done, the term used is sometimes *mûwth*, which means both to be made dead, but also worthily so, and sometimes the same term is found in Psalms 10:8, which has "in the secret places (of the villages) doth he murder the innocent." Here the murderer is *hârag*, one who makes slaughter (see also Numbers 31:17–18). There is no term in Hebrew for suicide. The acts of suicide reported are described in terms of the means employed. For example,

Achitophel, in II Samuel 17–23: "[He] put his household in order, and hanged (*chânaq*) himself, and died, and was buried in the sepulcher of his father." No pejorative taint attaches to the act either here or at any other place in the Hebrew Bible where suicide is described. Being realistic, how could the Hebrew Bible ever be seriously thought to proscribe killing when its main character, Yahweh, demands genocide. A similar account holds for the Christian scriptures (Daube 1972).

The negative tradition has always been eclectic in its assemblage of arguments, perhaps in part because its basic texts – Hebrew and Christian – do not support a prohibition on voluntary death (Schopenhauer 1970). Equally, how "sanctity," a word first used to denote the ostentatious ascetic qualities of particular religious lives, became a property of the abstract noun "life" needs explanation (Hume 1762: vol. I, ch. 1, sec. 2; Hobbes 1845, vol. III: 273; Kuhse 1987). What is beyond doubt is that prejudicial attitudes toward suicide indelibly mark our intellectual history (Alvarez 1974; Daube 1972).

Killing

Nothing of moral significance can be gleaned from the words "suicide" or "killing." But particular acts are amenable to moral evaluation undertaken within the general category of suicide, where "suicide," like the even broader "killing," is a morally neutral term awaiting specification of detail (Kovesi 1967). The answer to the question, "What is wrong with killing per se?" is, strictly speaking, "Nothing," although it might be charitable to expect that the thrust of the question is really, "Why is murder wrong?" or, perhaps, "Are all killings wrong or only some?" To either question, a substantial response is required (Ewin 1972).

Unhappily, discussions of suicide often start from the assumption that this type of killing needs special justification simply because it is a form of killing, all killing being wrong. This is false. If some suicides – the ones whose grounds connect logically with assisted suicide and euthanasia – are evaluated as either manifesting moral excellences or as morally neutral, then they are clearly not wrong. If they are not wrong, then it follows that the common assertion that because killing is wrong it follows that suicide is wrong is simply false, because these suicides are undoubtedly killings.

A second line of approach supports the conclusion that suicide cannot, for conceptual reasons, be included among the cases of killings that count as murders and are wrong. This is not to be confused with the weak claim that suicides are bad insofar as they are killings, but excusable: suicide lacks the essential element which allows us to include it among the subset of killings that are wrong.

There is no plausible secular argument to show that suicide is a subset of murder. There cannot be, since there is convincing argument to suggest that "self-murder" is an oxymoron: injustice to oneself is an incoherent idea, as Hobbes, who explained murder as a species of injustice, demonstrated:

> Whatever is done to man, conformable to his own Will signified to the doer, is no Injury to him. For if he that doeth it, hath not passed away his original right to do what he pleases, by some Antecedent Covenant, there is not breach of Covenant; and therefore no injury done him. (1845: 137)

Considerations of justice are sufficient to show that suicide cannot be murder, and so cannot figure among the class of morally prohibited killings. We cannot have a blanket moral prohibition against suicide as such, but considerations of justice do not exhaust moral evaluation of suicide. Analysis of individual suicides results in the conclusion that some are tragically misguided – for reasons to do with impulsiveness, irrationality, drugs, depression, or, in some cases, spite (some of these being causes addressed in suicide prevention programs) – while others are not.

Suicide

If reasons for action can be divided into those that are largely self-related and those that are mainly social or other-related, then a planned suicide will normally encompass reasons of both kinds. The solitary person who chooses a quick end to terminal pain may be obliged to consider only reasons of the first sort, but most of us face death accompanied part of the way by family or professional carers. Establishing the reasonableness or otherwise of a particular suicide will normally be a function of assaying both sorts of reasons, but it is plain that choosing to reject unbearable suffering is about as good as reasons for action can possibly get. Whether others are so moved in similar situations is neither here nor there as far as reasonableness is concerned; what matters is that we can appreciate the weight of the reasons for the person. Someone might reasonably see horrific personal suffering as worthy (how else can martyrs be understood?), whereas another may equally reasonably reject great suffering outright and act to subvert it.

The key issue is not suffering per se, but its place in a personal scheme of things. This scheme of things might be understood in terms of conscientious commitments that allow a person to express values intrinsic to their understanding of an authentic way of life (Wollheim 1986). Too fixed a concentration on the role of pain in terminal illness can obscure this, resulting in a form of moral blindness. We see only the patient's pain, rather than the significance of their pain and anguish within their personal scheme of things. This is why the issue of palliative care and its adequate provision is not central to discussion of assisted suicide and euthanasia, nor relevant to the case for their legalization. At its very best, adequate provision of services simply reduces the number of those who may choose death. A consideration of what was perceived to be important for the patients aided by Dr Jack Kevorkian supports this point.

There are a number of other reasons that motivate people to suicide, but they do not connect with bioethics in quite the same straightforward way that pain, suffering, and debilitation do. When a spy swallows cyanide rather than submit to torture that would result in confession and the subsequent capture and death of comrades, her courageous decisiveness is exemplary; but her reasons derive from loyalty rather than amelioration of her situation. A much closer parallel to the bioethical case is provided by the prisoner who suicides by hanging rather than go through some ghastly form of public mutilation and execution. His action exhibits great courage as well as eminent good sense in avoiding a much greater evil. Similarly, wounded soldiers who kill themselves rather than submit to being live bayonet practice for their advancing enemies manifest the same prudence and courage. We are accustomed to admire

315

altruistic suicides but seriously underestimate the moral worth of those carried out for purely self-regarding reasons. The reluctant suicides of September 11 can be looked at in the same way: extreme courage exhibited by people faced with shocking adversity. Bravery, after all, has never been the sole prerogative of warriors.

I have suggested that there is nothing morally complex about suicide as such, because it is at best an incomplete moral notion awaiting further specification (Kovesi 1967). But there is real moral complexity within suicides, and in particular where there are personal reasons for choosing death, but socially related reasons for persevering with life under great difficulty. I have outlined some cases where suicide is morally admirable because both prudent and extremely courageous. There will also no doubt be cases where suicide might show resolve and courage, but be cowardly or shameful for reasons to do with the abandonment of others. However, even in these cases the negative evaluation of the action is in terms of its dereliction or abandonment of those in our care; the fact that this occurs via suicide rather than flight is incidental and morally irrelevant. The moral evaluation of particular acts is all the evaluation that we have available to us here, but it may be difficult to venture very far. Let me explain.

The terminally ill who see suicide as a means of exercising sovereign control over the timing of their death may do so for different reasons. Access to those reasons could only come through a deeper knowledge of their life project and how it was conscientiously shaped. There is no guarantee that their aspirations are easily accessed by those who see them professionally, and it is not uncommon for members of the same family to be in dispute about choices near death. Consider the following case. A woman's resolve to die before all semblance of personality is obliterated by disease, pain, or drugs might be flatly at odds with her partner's desire to care for her despite profound dependence and disability. To judge the dying woman at fault for denying her partner's wishes is an impertinence of a particularly deep and nasty kind. We have reached a point where two reasonable conceptions of what morality requires – one purely social and the other more existential – part company, and where there is no obvious candidate to arbitrate (Falk 1965). Sensitivity requires a non-judgmental silence. Sadly, this silence is often impossible for those whose conception of a *right to life* manifests as the claimed right to meddle in others' lives.

Assisted Suicide and Euthanasia

Both these modes of voluntary death are morally derivative from suicide, because if there is compelling reason to provide aid in dying, either indirectly or directly, it stems from the sovereign role of the dying patient in determining that their life project is to be completed. The strength of the person's reasons for terminating life through suicide provides whatever reasons there are for helping. Respect for the patient's authentic desires and compassion for their suffering provide the moral case for assisted suicide and euthanasia: they establish a claim – usually stated as a moral right – to aid-in-dying, and provide the basis for a charge that any legal structure which impedes access to aid is cruel because it perpetuates pointless unwanted suffering.

Significantly, this moral claim has long been protected in law for a small subset of the dying, namely those who require life-support to stay alive. In many countries, there is either a statutory or a common law right that allows a patient to direct that medical treatments be withdrawn. A person suffering from motor neurone disease who requires intermittent ventilation may determine their time of death by deciding when they will have ventilation withdrawn. This statutory right divides the dying into two classes: those who may achieve their aim of a swift death by refusing further mechanical aid, and those who are at the same stage with their illness but need no mechanical procedures to stay alive. The suffering and anguish may be the same in both cases, but only one group has a death option medically catered for. This form of discrimination is patently unjust.

To avoid the charge of unjust discrimination it would be necessary to argue that the partition among the dying is morally neutral or morally required. This move is implausible if the plight of the patients and their desires are to all intents and purposes the same. Precisely this argument of parity has proven decisive in two rulings in the United States. On March 6, 1996, the Ninth Circuit Court of Appeals, sitting in San Francisco, (covering nine western states) found that liberty interests based on the 14th Amendment made American law forbidding physician-assisted suicide unconstitutional. Of the 11 judges, 8 concurred in the judgment that there is a constitutionally protected liberty in determining the time and manner of one's death. On April 2, 1996, the Second Circuit Court of Appeals, sitting in New York, (covering three eastern states) came to the same conclusion for slightly different reasons. Relying on the equal protection clause of the 14th Amendment, the court argued that there was no difference between withdrawal of life-support systems and the prescription of drugs to cause death. This was a unanimous decision of the three judges. Referring specifically to the fact that patients who are machine-dependent have the right to dictate their time of death, two of the judges said that terminally ill patients "should be free to do so by requesting appropriate treatment to terminate life during the final stages of terminal illness." These judgments were subsequently overturned by the US Supreme Court, but there were many who thought that the Second and Ninth Circuit Court decisions were more convincingly reasoned.

Quite predictably, there will be the dying who are physically or psychologically unable to enact a suicide, even if the means are legally prescribed for them. It follows from the justice argument outlined above that, if it is unjust to discriminate against those who are terminally ill but not machine-dependent, then it is equally unjust to discriminate against a subset of them, namely those who are disabled to a point where suicide is not a realizable option but who nonetheless strongly desire a swift death.

Australia's Northern Territory was the first legislature in the world to carry this justice argument to its required conclusion, through the passage of its Rights of the Terminally Ill Act (1995). This Act briefly legalized both physician-assisted suicide and euthanasia, and in so doing closed the last remaining moral loophole. While the Northern Territory legislation has since been overturned by the Australian Federal Parliament, both the Netherlands and Belgium have since enacted laws that allow both practices, while the US State of Oregon's 1997 legislation is restricted to physician-assisted suicide. (In Switzerland, assisted suicide in general – not merely when carried out by physicians – has, under certain circumstances, been tolerated for many years, but euthanasia remains a crime.)

317

From Morality to Public Policy

It is conventional and correct to point out that our Western liberal polities are plural-ist, encompassing a wide variety of value assumptions, some of which are incompat-ible (Engelhardt 1986). Perhaps the most glaring example of incompatibility can be found in differing evaluations of the fundamental value of life. This contested territory can be described in different ways, but in terms of my remarks about the moral evaluation of killing, the locus is sovereignty with respect to one's own life and its termination. The tradition that I have taken, in Zeno, as an emblem for this discussion treats the ceding of such control as base: abject slavery. Its opposition, in communitarian or religious guise, asserts that control of personal destiny should be strictly limited in the question of timing of death.

The primary public policy question addresses what is to be done in the light of pluralism, and the liberal democratic answer is normally in terms of a harm principle identified by Mill in the line, "the only purpose for which power can be rightfully exer-cised over any member of a civilised community, against his will, is to prevent harm to others" (1960 [1859]). It would seem that both sides in the public policy debate are therefore obliged to conduct their case in consequentialist mode with societal outcomes as their *lingua franca*. This must cause some discomfort for people whose primary moral evaluations are often voiced as a rejection of consequentialism: do they see public policy argument as a moral-free zone, or as a necessary but grubby trading in the immoral? Pious fraud perhaps?

The argument sketched through earlier sections is the standard prima facie case for assisted suicide and euthanasia; whatever weight it has rests on beliefs about the role of compassion and sovereignty in life. Both sides arrive at the public policy debate with opposed beliefs about what morality requires firmly in hand, so it would seem that if morality alone should dictate public policy then no policy can be stated in any area where unanimity is missing. This is clearly not the case, because the process of public policy-making merely starts from a consideration of moral values and argumentation. In the current case, evaluating courses of action must start from an obvious moral fact: there are many people in our communities who are terminally ill, anguished, and suffering, and seeking deliverance via medical help. This fact is not a mere belief, unlike positions based on scriptural interpretation, dogma, or hypotheses about the fabric of our communities.

The fact of real, present, and unremitting misery must inevitably shape the policy debate, delivering the following structure: the prima facie case to legalize assisted suicide and euthanasia is established on facts about suffering; it is then commonly confronted with causal arguments that outline unacceptable scenarios (see chapter 28, "The Slippery Slope Argument"). The structure of such arguments from social engineering needs to be clear. If the arguments against the prima facie position prove unconvincing as causal arguments, then the case against legalization dies there, allowing the prima facie moral case to shape appropriate public policy through legal change.

In all the political contexts where this policy issue has been debated, the role of the negative causal arguments has appeared to be critical in the formation of views. I say "appeared," because the role of basic moral views cannot be easily evaluated in this arena, especially when politicians vote on conscience and where causally shaped arguments about public safety can be cynically aired as a rationale for defending one's idiosyncratic religious values. However, all these arguments against legalization rest on hypotheses about future states-of-affairs, against which the real and present plight of many is being balanced and usually discounted at an alarming rate. Joel Feinberg (1992) has argued that these arguments about social dangers and abuse overestimate the risks and seriously underestimate the burden of suffering actually borne by the terminally ill.

Conclusion

Suicide is the key concept in any broadly philosophical discussion of voluntary death, whereas bioethics, because of its narrower concerns, concentrates on responses to suffering and anguish in terminal illness. I have suggested that a component part of our tradition makes moral evaluation of particular suicides either very difficult or impossible, whereas the grounds for such evaluation were well understood and investigated in Greek and Roman philosophy. Conceptual confusion surrounding the morality of voluntary death, derived in the main from traditional religious attitudes, thwarts mature evaluation of suicide, assisted suicide, and euthanasia. I have also acknowledged that whereas we can easily recognize some voluntary deaths as morally excellent, because prudent and courageous, it is likely that in other cases morality counsels its own silence.

When we make the step from moral evaluation to social policy and legislation, it is still going to be a moral stance that directs our line of endeavor. I have suggested that considerations of justice are sufficient to move us from our current protection of a patient's right to refuse therapy all the way through to legalizing voluntary euthanasia, with appropriate safeguards on the model of the short-lived, but pioneering, Northern Territory legislation. Finally, I have sketched the outlines of the public policy debate, claiming that the role of suffering initiates a presumption for change that is so strong only a clear and compelling causal argument to social harm could rebut it.

References

Alvarez, A. (1974). *The Savage God*. Harmondsworth: Penguin.

Daube, D. (1972). The linguistics of suicide. *Philosophy and Public Affairs* 1/4: 387–437.

Engelhardt, H. T. (1986). *The Foundations of Bioethics*. New York: Oxford University Press.

Ewin, R. E. (1972). What is wrong with killing people? *Philosophical Quarterly* 22: 126–39.

Ewin, R. E. (2002). *Reasons and Fear of Death*. Lanham, MD: Rowan & Littlefield.

Falk, W. D. (1965). Morality, self, and others. In H.-N. Castaneda and G. Nakhnikian (eds.), *Morality and the Language of Conduct*. Detroit, MI: Wayne State University Press.

Feinberg, J. (1992). *Freedom and Fulfillment*. Princeton, NJ: Princeton University Press.

Gibbon, E. (1906 [1776]). *The History of the Decline and Fall of the Roman Empire*. New York: Fred de Fau and Co.

Griffin, M. (1994). Roman suicide. In K. W. M. Fulford, G. Gillett, and J. M. Soskice (eds.), *Medicine and Moral Reasoning*. Cambridge: Cambridge University Press.

Hobbes, T. (1839–45). *The English Works of Thomas Hobbes of Malmesbury*, ed. Sir William Molesworth. London: John Bohn.

Hume, D. *The History of England.* (1754–62). London: Andrew Millar.

Kovesi, J. (1967). *Moral Notions.* London: Routledge & Kegan Paul.

Kuhse, H. (1987). *The Sanctity-of-Life Doctrine in Medicine.* Oxford: Oxford University Press.

Levi, D. (1998). Is death a bad thing? *Mortality* 3/3: 229–49.

Mill, J. S. (1960 [1859]). *On Liberty.* London: J. M. Dent.

Schopenhauer, A. (1970). On suicide. In *Essays and Aphorisms.* Harmondsworth: Penguin.

van Hooff, A. J. L. (1990). *From Autothanasia to Suicide.* London: Routledge.

Wollheim, R. (1986). *The Thread of Life.* Cambridge: Cambridge University Press.

Further reading

Brandt, R. (1975). The rationality of suicide. In S. Perlin (ed.), *A Handbook for the Study of Suicide.* Oxford: Oxford University Press.

28

The Slippery Slope Argument

GOVERT DEN HARTOGH

An Example

Slippery slope arguments can be used in the context of any discussion whatsoever, but if you are asked to give an example, the odds are that the example which first comes to your mind will be one from a bioethical discussion. In such discussions the argument is used very commonly, mostly in order to object to proposed changes in moral thinking or legislation. To give but one example, compiled from various sources:

> Prenatal diagnostics is wrong in principle, if abortion is the only thing we can do when a genetic defect is found. First a suspicion of Huntington's disease or cystic fibrosis will be counted as a good reason for abortion. Then it will be diabetes, sickle cell anemia, Down syndrome, then a club-foot, a harelip, myopia, color blindness, an extra Y chromosome, left-handedness, and finally skin color. It will be argued that it is in the interest of the future child itself not to be born. But how can we decide that someone's life will not be worth living? People have no right to decide that the life of a handicapped person has no value. To do so is a violation of the basic principle of equality. If we allow ourselves any exceptions to that principle, handicapped people will come to be seen as the products of parental negligence. People will say to them: "Why are you here? You should have been aborted." And if these people are consistent, they will in the end believe that the lives of these people should still, in their own interest, be terminated.

The Paradigmatic Form of the Argument

The term "slippery slope argument" is often used loosely: it is sometimes used for the appeal to a dangerous precedent (see the next section); it is also applied to all kinds of arguments pointing to negative consequences of a proposed action, especially, but by no means exclusively, when the causal chain leading to these consequences consists of several links. So loose is present usage, in fact, that it does not refer to any distinctive form of argument meriting a separate discussion. Instead, I will present a characterization of what I take to be the paradigmatic form of the argument, noting along the way some possible deviations from this standard form, but without deciding which of these deviations should be called slippery slope arguments:

1   The discussion in which the argument is used concerns whether a certain class of actions – call them A – should be considered morally acceptable or be legally permitted.
2   The discussion presupposes a status quo position, in which people hold each other, or are held by legal authority, to certain norms of behavior, prohibiting A.
3   It is proposed to move from the status quo position to a new one, which I will call the top of the slope, in which A will be considered acceptable or be permitted. (There is no logical reason why the proposal should not be to prohibit an action which has up to now been accepted, but, remarkably, slippery slope arguments very rarely take this form.)
4   The opponents of the proposal do not question the acceptability of the top position directly. They neither assume that actions of type A are offensive as such, nor suggest that such actions are to be avoided because of their negative consequences (though, as a matter of fact, they will usually hold one or both of these positions).
5   Instead, the opponents argue that a movement will not stop before we have reached the bottom of the slope; unpacking the metaphor, it is alleged that a causal mechanism exists which, once we accept actions of type A, will cause us to accept actions of type N as well. Note that in the paradigmatic form of the slippery slope argument it is not the A-type action itself which is supposed to have negative consequences, but rather the decision to consider such actions acceptable.
6   The causal mechanism referred to has the character of a chain reaction: once we accept A, we will predictably accept B as well, this will cause us to accept C, and so on, until eventually we come to accept N. If such intermediate steps are lacking, we have a "cliff or a wall rather than a slope" (Lode 1999). What is the nature of the links of the chain? We should consider one possibility in particular. Once we accept A, we have no reason to reject B, and, being reasonable people, we may be expected to realize this fact in due time.

Discussions of the slippery slope argument usually distinguish a logical form of the argument from a causal one. The logical form would simply consist of pointing out that, once we accept A, we are rationally committed to accepting B, C, and eventually N. But in practice this logical form is almost always incorporated into a prediction. The opponents assume that even the supporters of the proposal agree that actions of type N are beyond the pale, either for intrinsic reasons, or because of their bad consequences, or both. Most of the time it is silently presupposed that actions of type N, once they are accepted, will be done more often. However, even if this is not the case, it may be alleged that the fact that these bad actions are not only done, but also tolerated, is a bad thing in itself. On the other hand, the opponents may also argue that, whether or not actions of type N will be accepted, they will in any case be done more often than they are done at present, and that is what should deter us from accepting A in the first place.

The Appeal to a Pernicious Precedent

I will start my discussion by considering a form of argument which deviates from the paradigmatic one on two points. This is the appeal to a pernicious precedent. It is again conceded that A, on the face of it, has an innocent look. However, it is argued that, once we accept A, we have no reason to reject B, which in all relevant respects resembles A. But B is clearly unacceptable. This is not a paradigmatic slippery slope argument, because it does not make any predictions about whether, once we accept A, we will in fact accept B. The claim is the more limited one that, if we accept A, we are rationally committed to accepting B.

This is a form of argument which is not deductively valid but has real force nevertheless: the considerations presented, if true, really give us good, if not decisive, reasons to accept the conclusion. The force of the argument depends on a well-known characteristic of normative predicates: their *supervenience*. If an action is acceptable, it is always because it has certain other characteristics which make it acceptable. A supervenient predicate is necessarily also a universalizable one, at least in this sense: if, of two action types, one is acceptable and the other is not, it has to be true that they differ in at least one other characteristic. It doesn't follow, however, that if one action-type has a number of characteristics which, taken together, make actions of this type acceptable, all actions which share the characteristics are acceptable as well. They may have other characteristics that make them unacceptable. For this reason, moral as well as legal argument is *defeasible*. Even good arguments need not be decisive ones.

This explains how the appeal to a pernicious precedent can be withstood: not only by pointing to a right-making characteristic of A which B doesn't share, but also by pointing to a wrong-making characteristic of B which A doesn't share. The value of the argument is that it lays down the burden of arguing either of these two points (or the acceptability of B) squarely on the shoulders of the defendants.

Slopes of Reason

I said above that the purely logical slippery slope argument can seldom be found in actual use. Nevertheless it is worth discussing, because it can be integrated into a causal argument.

The best-known use of this argument is in the context of abortion. If one considers the killing of a zygote to be acceptable, there is no reason to prohibit the killing of an embryo 14 days after conception. If that is acceptable, there is no reason to be concerned about the killing of a fetus of three months – and so on. As the development from zygote to child occurs without any sudden jumps, once you have denied protection to the zygote, there is no point at which you can reasonably think it imperative to protect the developing human being. Viability will not do, because it depends on the skills of doctors; nor will birth, which after all doesn't involve any change in the child, but only in its environment.

This argument is similar in form to the one discussed in the previous section: it simply repeats the appeal to a precedent, until a clearly pernicious one is reached. If you permit A, you are committed to permitting B; if you permit B, you are committed to permitting C, etc. Therefore, if you permit A, you are committed to permitting N, which clearly is wrong. If the appeal to a pernicious precedent is a valid form of argument – in the weak sense of validity which allows for the possibility of defeat – then the logical slippery slope argument, it seems, cannot be an invalid one. We could say that each step offers the defendants new chances of pointing out relevant differences, but the point of the argument is precisely to minimize the differences between the cases compared in each step. That is the snag. If the accomplishment of the argument is seen as a shift in the burden of proof, the burden it imposes on the defendants is to identify exactly the point at which they dig in their heels. And that is what they often cannot do.

However, the requirement itself rests on a fallacy, known from ancient times as the Sophism of the Heap (Sorites). Consider any person with normal hair growth. Take away one of her hairs. That wouldn't make her bald, would it? Take away another hair. How can one hair make the difference between a bald person and a non-bald person? It cannot. So we take away another hair, and another one, etc. At the end of the process she has no hair left. Still, we are not allowed to call her bald, for we couldn't meet the requirement of pinpointing the exact moment at which she joined the class of bald persons. (It may be objected that only a person with no hair at all is a bald person, strictly speaking, but that is not how we normally use the word.)

It is difficult to explain exactly why this is a fallacy. Logicians still disagree about it. The argument uses three premises:

1   This person has a certain determinate number of hairs.
2   This person isn't bald.
3   If a person with a certain determinate number of hairs isn't bald, a person with one hair less isn't bald either.

The problem is that premises 1 and 2 may be true, premise 3 seems indisputable, and the form of argument which we use in deriving the absurd conclusion that a person with no hairs left isn't bald is clearly a valid one. Perhaps we should hold that the argument form isn't applicable in all cases, in particular not when the relevant predicate ("bald") is a vague term, i.e., a term referring to an indeterminate section of a continuum.

It is difficult to explain why Sorites is a fallacy, but it is beyond doubt that it is a fallacy, and that is the important thing. That there is a gray area, and that its boundaries are indeterminate themselves, doesn't imply that we cannot identify points which are definitely at one or the other side of the gray area. For that reason the logical slippery slope argument doesn't succeed in shifting the burden of proof. The requirement to locate the exact stopping-place on the slope should simply be rejected. If you are able to point to a relevant difference between a zygote and a newborn child, it doesn't matter that you are unable to tie the emergence of the difference to an exact point in time. If you are in doubt whether a genetic predisposition for retinitis pigmentosa (an illness which reveals itself in the gradual, but eventually complete, loss of sight between the ages of 20 and 40) is a good reason for abortion, you are not barred from being sure that Huntington's disease is a good reason for abortion, and color-blindness is not.

It is true that we are in need of conventional or legal norms locating such a point. For if we allow embryo experimentation or abortion in the first trimester, and forbid infanticide and the use of babies in life-endangering medical experiments, then we have to identify a point at which protection starts, or a series of points at which it gradually increases. If there is no principled way of making this identification, the only reasonable thing to do is to fasten upon an arbitrary point lying safely within the core zone of the gray area. This point will tend to be a "salient" one, like viability or birth, but, as far as this argument goes, even these points don't have any intrinsic importance. It is sometimes argued that we should aim at "erring on the safe side," and therefore stay squarely on one side of the gray area. But that suggestion rests on the mistaken idea that, after all, there really exists a clear dividing line between the bald and the non-bald, and the problem is just that we don't know where it is.

In the case of the discussion about abortion, we can illustrate the fatal weakness of the logical slippery slope argument in another way. The proponent of the argument obviously presupposes that the status quo position isn't indeterminate at all: the protection of human life begins at conception. However, fertilization is a continuous process, just like fetal development, only involving a smaller being and a shorter time span. So where exactly do we draw the line? When the sperm contacts the plasma membrane of the oocyte? When it penetrates its zona pellucida? When the second meiotic division is completed? When the male and female pro-nuclei have formed, each with its own membrane or when these membranes break, allowing the chromosomes to mingle? If there is no non-arbitrary answer to this question, does it follow that conception cannot be a morally relevant boundary line?

You will only be able to reject a logical slippery slope argument in this way if you are able to point to a relevant difference between the top and the bottom of the slope. Some liberals on abortion have a problem here, because the characteristics they believe to be the real basis for protecting the human being (and other animals) are such that they cannot be ascribed to babies. These are the characteristics of persons, most basically an awareness of the self as continuous through time, which in its turn is presupposed in the abilities of having a memory, of making plans, of identifying others and communicating with them. However, that doesn't mean that the logical slippery slope argument is rehabilitated. As I suggested, it can be seen as an elaboration of the appeal to a dangerous precedent, presupposing that, wherever we can draw a continuous line between A and N, such that it is impossible for anybody to identify a clear boundary on the line, A really is a precedent for N. This presupposition is false. But, of course, that doesn't mean that we cannot appeal to the wrongness of N directly in order to argue against the acceptance of A. That argument really succeeds in shifting the burden of proof. Liberals can respond in either of two ways: they can try to find a relevant difference between zygotes and babies after all (for instance, the role of the being in human relations and social conventions), or they can bite the bullet and accept that there are no intrinsic reasons for protecting the life of a baby more than the life of a zygote. Birth is then, they may say, at most a convenient point for drawing the arbitrary dividing line we have to draw anyway.

Slopes of Unreason

In describing the paradigmatic form of the slippery slope argument, I said that the causal mechanism it relies upon for its prediction of dire consequences sometimes relies on human rationality. In this section I will discuss cases in which the causal mechanism isn't assumed to involve any form of rational commitment.

More specifically, I said that in the first class of cases the causal mechanism relied on human rationality in the following way: once we accept A, we have no reason not to accept B, and, being reasonable people, we may be expected to realize this fact. So we will accept B. Then for the same reason we will accept C, and so on until we reach N. We now see that reasoning in this way is not rational at all, but fallacious. The interesting thing, however, is that this need not impair the force of the prediction. Perhaps this is a kind of fallacy people are particularly prone to commit, as their tendency to be impressed by the logical slippery slope argument itself testifies. In other words: the only moral boundaries which have any chance of being respected are determinate ones. Morality should eschew the continuum. Very often the use of a slippery slope argument depends on this assumption. (It is, for example, basic to the defense of the rational respectability of the argument in Lamb 1988.)

From the point of view of moral psychology, determinacy has its advantages; so much seems true. But we should not exaggerate these advantages. It is hard to decide in any general way what kind of line will tend to be more respected: a hard and fast but (assumingly) irrelevant one, or a rather indeterminate one which at least has clear instances of morally different cases at both sides of the line. What we know of the development of moral sensibility suggests that people will start their career as moral agents pretty close to the first position, but gradually move away from it. The question then becomes: to what extent should we trust our fellows to be moral adults?

In judging the importance of determinacy, it matters whether we are discussing a change in moral view or in legal status. We usually suppose our judgments of moral acceptability to be matters of belief: considering A to be acceptable means believing that it is. The slippery slope argument amounts to saying: once you believe this, you will end up believing N to be acceptable as well, and this is clearly and catastrophically false. But even if that were true, it is no reason at all for not believing A to be acceptable. A proposition isn't any the less true if believing it has undesirable consequences. It isn't any the less true, either, if believing it leads people to believe some false things as well, as long as this is not a matter of rational commitment.

In order to make any sense of the argument, we have to move in one of two directions. The first option, which most proponents of a slippery slope argument will hate to take, is to assume that what we are discussing is not a matter of basic moral truth but a matter of human convention. The proposal which the slippery slope argument is meant to refute would then be that we have good reason to change our conventions, from the status quo to the new position.

Even if we conceive it in this way, the argument has a strong smell of paradox. Someone proposes to a certain audience, possibly involving anyone sufficiently interested to read about these matters, that it would be a good thing if people generally allowed each other to do A. The slippery slope argument presents an objection to this proposal to the same audience. The objection is that implementing the proposal would lead people, irrationally, to allow each other to do some really nasty things as well. It is hard to believe that any audience will be convinced by this objection, if the audience consists of a random selection of the very same people who are supposed to be irredeemably subject to the relevant causal mechanism. If they can understand the argument, why can't they correct their reasoning? The slippery slope argument, it has been said, urges people to forgo making a sound decision today for fear of having to draw a sound distinction tomorrow (attributed in Volokh 2003 to Sir Fredrick Maitland).

So it seems that we have to move in the other direction: suppose that the argument is addressed to a moral elite. The true morality can only be a secret doctrine, revealed to a chosen few. We, the enlightened, know that to enlightened people A would be fully acceptable. However, we shouldn't tell the mob, for they will immediately start to steal the silver from the table.

If the new position we are discussing is a matter of legal provision rather than of moral acceptance, however, our judgment of the value of determinacy can and should be different. It can be different, for a legal enactment, even if it should be justified to a large extent by moral belief, is not an expression of that belief. It is really a matter of decision. For that reason, it isn't improper to argue that A should not be permitted because it will lead to N being permitted, either by a different authority or by the same one (presumably when staffed by different people). Or, the argument may go, permitting A will lead at least to N being done more often by those subject to the law (Schauer 1985; Van der Burg 1991).

Furthermore, the value in law of determinacy is indisputable. To give one example: doctors occasionally use morphine to give a little "push" to dying patients who are no longer able to communicate but seem still to be suffering severely from refractory symptoms. One could sensibly hold that such an action is morally permissible in itself because it benefits the patient, but still believe that the law should forbid it. In the first place because "dying" and "severe suffering" are vague terms, it is to be expected that doctors will interpret it in more or less strict ways, creating some inequality and legal uncertainty, with some doctors going beyond what the law intends to allow. In the second place, the question in such cases is not only what kind of boundaries command respect, but also which forms of respect can be intersubjectively verified, for example, by police officers or judges, but also by fellow citizens. Lastly, it is relevant that it will almost always be possible to relieve the patient's suffering by deep sedation.

Even if we accept that a legal regulation may be preferable to alternatives because it avoids creating gray areas, the boundaries it stipulates will be most acceptable if they draw a line within a recognizably gray area which has to be drawn anyway. If an arbitrary boundary is chosen for the only reason that it is determinate, even if it prohibits morally innocent behavior which is important to the people involved, it is questionable whether this boundary should (or will) be respected. So even in this case the effective use of the slippery slope argument presupposes that the status quo position has other moral credentials besides determinacy. Perhaps we may expect a slippery slope argument to have an independent force in this area, in particular in those cases in which it is used to tip the scale in favor of the status quo, when people disagree about whether the status quo or the new position is intrinsically morally superior. Arguments against delimiting the domain of free speech often take this form.

It has been argued (Lode 1999) that the fact that people are prone to commit the Sorites fallacy should lead legislators and judges to avoid arbitrary boundaries rather than indeterminate ones. To take our illustration again from the abortion debate, it is not difficult at all to identify some more or less determinate point in human development after conception; the problem is that no such point is more compelling than others. Avoiding arbitrariness would be particularly pressing for courts, because they have a duty to respect precedents and, in any case in which they decide not to follow it, to identify a relevant difference between the case at hand and the precedent case. However, a court *could* present as its *ratio decidendi* that it has to draw a line somewhere. Moreover, the wish to avoid arbitrariness can only be a reason to stay at the status quo point, for example conception as the beginning of full protectability, if that is a morally defensible position to begin with. The use of a slippery slope argument of this kind on its own will therefore hardly convince the unconverted.

Factual and Moral Plausibility

So far I have established two main points:

1   Of those slippery slope arguments that refer to a slope of reason, the only valid form is that which avoids relying on the construction of a continuum of intermediate cases (if it can properly be called a slippery slope argument at all).
2   In the domain of moral argument the slippery slope argument cannot be applied to matters of basic moral truth, but at most to matters of convention.

Which other general conditions, if any, can we state for constructing a sound slippery slope argument? One obvious point is that the causal mechanism supposed to be responsible for the slippage should be a plausible one. This means that such a causal mechanism should be specified in the first place and that some evidence should be marshaled to confirm the prediction that it will be operative under conditions similar to the present ones. To show that this is not an impossible task, some authors point to past slides down slippery slopes (e.g., the sexual revolution). Some of these examples are more convincing than others. The basic problem with this kind of argument, however, is that while we may be able confidently to explain afterwards why things went wrong, that doesn't mean we could confidently have predicted this beforehand. We can only conclude that we should be rather modest in our estimation of the probability of bad consequences, if we can give any weight at all to the prediction.

Some possible mechanisms have been suggested in the literature (see, in particular, Volokh 2003). The position people take after deliberation often depends on the spectrum of positions they see as the feasible ones, and their view of this spectrum may change when the status quo position is left and the new position adopted. This may, for example, determine what, in a situation of intense controversy, they see as the fairest compromise. The adoption of the new position may also be celebrated as a first victory by a party campaigning for more large-scale social change, and give that party political momentum. "A ban is broken." And even when an organized interest group has fully realized its aims, it may look around for a new cause in order to avoid losing its *raison d'être*.

The causal mechanism most often referred to in slippery slope arguments is probably desensitization. Perhaps, it has often been claimed, it is morally defensible to make an exception to the absolute prohibition of killing when the remainder of a dying patient's life will be one of unremitting suffering and her only wish is to be spared that last part. But if we start allowing doctors to end the life of such patients, we will begin a process of erosion of their and our deep-rooted feelings of the inviolability of life. We will next allow suffering patients who cannot make such requests to be killed, and then patients who are only expected to suffer in the future, and finally people whose life is a burden to society. The absolute prohibition of the law expresses and reinforces our basic commitment to the inviolability of life, and we should not surrender that bulwark.

It is true that moral change tends to be cumulative and incremental. Dominant views and prevailing policies are important elements of the context which shapes moral debates and decision-making, hence changes of these views and these policies also tend to change this shape. In 1995 it was discovered that a nurse in a Dutch hospital for elderly people had killed four patients in advanced states of Alzheimer's disease, by giving them overdoses of insulin. She claimed, probably honestly, that she acted from a motive of mercy. According to the psychiatric report she was a very unbalanced person prone to project her own mental sufferings onto others. It is clear that in terms of the moral consensus and the legal regime concerning mercy killing accepted in the Netherlands, her actions were wrong: she did not conform to any clearly expressed will of those patients, there was probably no unbearable suffering, she was not a physician, and she acted in a way designed to escape accountability for her actions. Nevertheless, it could be argued, and it has been argued, that she could only have acted in this way because the Dutch moral consensus and legal regime does allow euthanasia in some cases. Believing that mercy could be a good reason for killing, she could come to think, however mistakenly, that it was a good ground in those cases. It is obviously difficult to substantiate a claim like this. It would probably not pass a court of law. Nevertheless, it is not wholly implausible.

This was a rare incident, but by similar processes people's collective moral outlook could change over time. However, it is hard to predict the direction of this collective learning process, and the suggestion that it always will proceed in one direction (whether downward or upward) is plainly false. In 1989 a doctor who had allowed a newborn child with Down syndrome to die from duodenum atresia (a condition which is routinely and easily removed by operation) was acquitted by the Dutch Supreme Court. This was widely perceived as another downward move on the slippery slope that was supposed to have been initiated by the recognition of the possible permissibility of euthanasia by the same court. As a matter of fact, however, the response of the Dutch medical community to the court's verdict was such that a similar medical decision would by now be unthinkable. Similarly, it has often been predicted that the sexual revolution would eventually lead to the widespread acceptance of pedophilia, but the contrary seems to have been the case.

Moreover, even when we can predict the direction of moral change, our present understanding of this change as a form of desensitization rather than sensitization may be fallible. When Mary Wollstonecraft had published her *Vindication of the Rights of Woman*, one Thomas Taylor replied with a *Vindication of the Rights of Brutes*. Taken as a prediction of slippage, this response may not have been mistaken. But the very idea that he could use it to ridicule Wollstonecraft's proposal seems itself ridiculous from our present perspective (LaFollette 2005). Perhaps we should use some restraint in pressing our present moral views on posterity.

I do not mean to reject desensitization arguments as a class: as with other proposed mechanisms, we have to consider each claim on its own merits. Speaking more generally, new conventions and laws almost always open up new possibilities of abuse and mistakes, even if abuse and mistakes are to be identified in terms of the new conventional or legal standard. Whether or not these consequences belong to the area of the slippery slope argument proper (they don't always involve a causal chain, or actions of acceptance as links of the chain), these possibilities have to be taken seriously (see Battin 1994 on legalizing euthanasia and physician-assisted suicide).

But even if it is reasonable to give quite a lot of weight to such considerations, it will not automatically be a decisive weight. In this context, the metaphor of the slippery slope is somewhat misleading: slopes incline to one side only. But in discussing actual moral problems, we will mostly find that staying at the status quo has its moral costs as well. For example, people who find their predictions concerning the Dutch experiment with euthanasia confirmed by the actions of the nursing-home nurse are mostly rather selective in their accounting of the moral costs. They don't attach any weight at all to the fact that, if the option of euthanasia is not available, some people who strongly want to avoid any further suffering will have to go through a prolonged period of severe suffering before they die.

This selectivity in taking account of negative consequences points to another way in which the use of a slippery slope argument usually presupposes the full moral acceptance of the status quo position. Only if taking a life is always wrong, even if it is done to prevent unbearable and hopeless suffering, are we justified in neglecting that side of the balance.

The appeal to new possibilities of mistake and abuse may by now be the most prominent one used by opponents of the legalization of physician-assisted suicide and euthanasia. It is often selective in another, equally telling, way. One form it takes is to suggest that it would be dangerous to allow doctors to make such decisions in a country like the US, in which health care is highly commercialized and large sections of the population lack adequate health-care insurance. This is a quite proper concern. But the odd thing is that the authors who point this out rarely show any similar concern about the ways in which doctors make decisions to abstain from treatment or use medicine with possibly life-shortening effects for (ostensibly) palliative reasons, although the power to make such decisions seems at least as dangerous. This second kind of selectivity, like the first, may show that the authors who press such arguments are still basically moved by sanctity-of-life considerations.

If we take the slippery slope argument as an independent argument, even in cases in which the prediction it makes is not implausible, it will mostly fail to be decisive. That is not in itself a weakness of the argument. But it often has a more important weakness which can again be illustrated by the euthanasia debate. We assume that the bad consequences the argument predicts follow from people making mistakes in reasoning, as the Dutch nurse did. (In other words, we are assuming that the bad consequences are not the result of people deriving the right consequences from their acceptance of the new position.) This means that when we use a slippery slope argument in order to argue against the conventional or legal acceptance of voluntary euthanasia, we deny some people their wish to avoid any more of the suffering which for them is necessarily involved in living; and we do so not because there is anything improper in granting their wish, but because other people will erroneously do unacceptable things if such wishes are granted. But is it fair to require those who urgently want voluntary euthanasia to sacrifice their most vital interests, in order to prevent other people from sinning?

This is a general weakness of all forms of consequentialism which do not systematically distinguish between direct and indirect responsibility. (Indirect responsibility is my responsibility for states of affairs occurring by other people responding in predictable ways to my actions.) It is ironic that this weakness can be found in an argument which is such a favorite with people who generally strongly oppose consequentialist views and insist (e.g., in their support of the doctrine of double effect) on the importance of the distinction between what I directly intend, and what I merely foresee will happen, as a result of my action.

Appearance and Reality

This shows once again that the slippery slope argument cannot stand on its own feet. So far I have taken the argumentative claims of the slippery slope argument at face value. I have found that, in its usual causal form, it has no formal defect and can have some, occasionally considerable, force, but only when it is accompanied with an informed and balanced assessment of the probability of its predictions. The proper conclusion of such assessments of relevant risks will often not be that we should not take them, but rather that we should look for ways of limiting them. The most prominent aspect of the appeal to slippery slopes in actual discussion, however, is that these requirements are seldom met: predictions of slippage are usually not supported by any evidence at all, yet they are put forward as certainties, unreservedly deciding the matter in favor of the status quo position.

It is seldom worthwhile to address such arguments directly. They should rather be taken as expressions of allegiance to the moral superiority of the status quo position, and should be addressed as such. What they mean is this: the one important moral boundary is the boundary between the status quo and the new position. The boundary the defendants suggest exists between the top and the bottom, on the other hand, is not a morally important one at all. Therefore, if we move to the top position, we have crossed the Rubicon, we have entered into a sphere in which the bottom position is really, whatever the defendants believe, no longer a moral impossibility. The prediction – that we will eventually accept the bottom position as well – is only a way of dramatizing this claim. It doesn't add anything substantial to it.

Reconstructed this way, the argument amounts to an appeal to a pernicious precedent. The prediction doesn't matter, the intermediate cases don't matter, and the suggestion of detachability from the primary moral controversy is misleading. To return to the example I started with: the real question about prenatal diagnostics is whether the decision to prevent the birth of a handicapped child really is equivalent to saying that handicapped people have no life worth protecting. If it is, then the procedure stands condemned, and the "consequences" pointed out in the argument I quoted at the beginning don't add to the grounds for this condemnation. They only express it.

The best course for defendants to take in such cases is to ask their opponents squarely whether they believe the slippery slope argument to be independent from their loyalty to the status quo. If they answer that they don't, we can discuss the intrinsic moral merits of the status quo and the new position. If they answer that they do, the defendants most of the time will be able to show that this claim is untenable. Only if it isn't does it make sense to enter into a discussion of the plausibility and force of the argument.

References

Battin, M. P. (1994). *The Least Worst Death*. New York: Oxford University Press.

Govier, T. (1999). *The Philosophy of Argument*. Newport, VA: Vale Press.

LaFollette, H. (2005). Living on a slippery slope. *Journal of Ethics* 9: 475–99.

Lamb, D. (1988). *Down the Slippery Slope*. London: Croom Helm.

Lode, E. (1999). Slippery slope arguments and legal reasoning. *California Law Review* 87: 1469–544.

Schauer, F. (1985). Slippery slopes. *Harvard Law Review* 99: 361–83.

Van der Burg, W. (1991). The slippery slope argument. *Ethics* 102: 42–65.

Volokh, E. (2003). The mechanisms of the slippery slope. *Harvard Law Review* 116: 1026–134.

Walton, D. (1992). *Slippery Slope Arguments*. Oxford: Oxford University Press.

Part VIII

Resource Allocation

29

Deciding Between Patients

JOHN HARRIS

That men would die was a matter of necessity; which men would die, though, was
a matter of circumstance, and Yossarian was willing to be the victim of anything
but circumstance. (Joseph Heller, *Catch 22*)

The necessity for choosing between patients presupposes scarcity of resources. The scarcity
may be radical, where there are not enough resources to treat all in need, and the result
is that some will be left untreated or die before their turn arrives. Scarcity may, on the
other hand, be comparative, where patients have to be prioritized but the intention is
that all will eventually be treated. However, in either case some will inevitably die or
their condition irrevocably worsen before their turn comes round.

That scarcity of resources for health care is a permanent and inescapable condition
is usually taken to be axiomatic. Resources, so it is claimed, are, after all, not infinite,
therefore they must be finite, and, if finite, then assuming expanding demand, scarcity
is inevitable. Two things need to be said about such a claim. The first is that, while
resources are not infinite, they are not finite either: they are indefinite and can be
expanded. Any given budget may be increased if other budgets are traded off against
it, or, in the case of public funding, if taxes are increased. And within any budget – the
health budget, say – different things may be funded if others are not. Priorities can always
be reassessed. There are also good grounds for denying the other part of the catechism,
namely that demand is potentially infinite and that this is shown by the increasing problems experienced in public health-care systems. The claim that "demand for a zero-priced
service is bound to be infinite" is, as Peter Oppenheimer, an Oxford economist, has shown,
simply "wild talk."

The amount demanded of a free service is determined at the point where customers see
no additional benefits to be gained from additional recourse to the service in question. This
occurs at modest demand levels for most forms of medical care (as for most public libraries
and public lavatories). (1988b)

However, for the rest of this chapter I will assume the necessity to choose between
patients and examine the ethics of some of the ways that are usually proposed for
coping with scarcity.

What Is "Greater Need" for Health Care?

A common way of prioritizing patients is in terms of their need for treatment. There are a number of things that might be meant by "need" when people argue that priority should be given to those in the greatest need. We might think that the person with the greatest need will be the person who is suffering most, or the person in the worst health state, or the person who will be left in the worst state of health after treatment, or the person who will benefit most from health care, or the person who feels her need for health care most desperately. Here of course we must be careful to distinguish the need for health from the need for health care. Where health care cannot ensure that health is better than it would have been without health care, while there may well be a need for health, there can hardly be an argument for delivering useless and wasteful health care.

Need is often defined in terms of the capacity of the patient to benefit, with the implication being that the greater the capacity to benefit, the greater the need. On this view, the degree of need is the same as the degree of capacity to benefit measured in life years or quality-adjusted life years (QALYs) to be gained from treatment. The greater the number of years of good-quality life that can be gained from treatment, so the argument goes, the greater the need (Williams 1985).

Is the degree of need for health care equated in any way to the capacity to benefit from it, where capacity to benefit is measured in terms of quality and quantity of life?

The degree of need for health care has at least three dimensions:

- the urgency, intensity, or importance of the need;
- the amount of whatever it is that is needed; and
- the capacity of the individual to benefit from what she needs.

If Tom says, "I badly need a drink," and Dick says, "I wouldn't mind a drink," they are expressing (probably) different degrees of need in the first sense. If Tom says, "My thirst won't be satisfied till I've downed ten pints," and Dick says, "I'll be happy with a couple of pints," then they are expressing different degrees of need in the second sense. If Tom says, "I'll want another ten pints tomorrow and every day thereafter," and Dick says, "Those two pints will satisfy me for a week," they are again recording differences in the amount of what they (claim they) need. And, finally, if Tom says, having downed his allocation, "My thirst is satisfied but I still feel terrible," whereas Dick says, "Not only has my thirst gone but I feel great," they are expressing different degrees of benefit from need satisfaction.

It is not clear that it is plausible to say that Dick has a greater need for beer than Tom because his capacity to benefit is greater, or to say that Tom has a greater need because his need is more urgent, intense, or important, or because he needs a greater amount. It is not obvious which of the following is the best measure of need: urgency, intensity, or importance of need; amount needed; length of satisfaction once the amount needed is supplied; or capacity to benefit from the provision of what is needed. Indeed, none of these measures alone should be deemed to capture what is meant by "need."

It should be noted that I have chosen here an example which uses a subjective notion of need, but this is only to make clear the differences between the different dimensions of need. Those same differences, of course, are also equally present in so-called "objective" needs, believed to be common for everyone, like the need for food and shelter or health care.

To return to health care, there is a distinction between the need for health and the need for health care, which is relevant only where health care cannot deliver health. If I am ill but there is nothing that medicine can do for me, then, though I need health, I can't be said to need health care. Where medicine can help, then the need for health care cannot legitimately be equated exclusively with *one* measure of the degree to which health care can benefit an individual.

Economists and some utilitarians tend to equate need with capacity to benefit, rather than with other conceptions of need, because they believe they know how to measure capacity to benefit. But they cannot be permitted to hijack the English (or any other) language in order to claim to have provided a way of measuring need. What they may have done is provide a way of measuring one of a sizeable number of *dimensions of need.*

I am not, of course, suggesting that we should not use need as one of the most important criteria for prioritizing people for health care. But what we need to do is decide which dimensions of need plausibly indicate greater necessity for treatment, or a more compelling claim on the resources available for health care.

One plausible candidate for such a dimension is the scale of what the patient stands to lose if she is not treated. On such a view, loss of life itself would almost always be a greater loss than diminution in quality of life. But, in the case of loss of life, is the loss greater the more years of life that are lost? Is the claim weaker, the fewer the life years that may be gained by treatment? It is a fallacy to suppose an affirmative answer to such a question is necessarily the right one, though many think it is. Indeed, since no one knows how long she would have lived had she not died at a particular moment, the scale of the loss measured in this way is always speculative.

If the millionaire and his lowly employee both lose all they have in the stock-market crash, on one way of thinking about the loss, each has suffered the same degree of loss, each has lost everything. On another, each has suffered a different quantity of loss measured by the total sum lost. There is no straightforward way of reconciling these different approaches to the assessment of loss. If we are searching for an equitable approach to loss, it is not obvious that we should devote resources allocated to loss minimization to ensuring that the millionaire is protected rather than his less well-off employee. Even if it is agreed that resources devoted to health care are resources devoted to minimizing the loss of health or maximizing the health gain, it could not be demonstrated that the person who stands to lose more life years if they die prematurely stands to suffer a greater loss than the person who has a shorter life expectancy. Nor can it be shown that the measure of health gain must be equated with the number of life years, quality adjusted or not, which flow from treatment. Arguments can (and have) been made on both sides, but to define need in terms of capacity to benefit and then argue that the greater the number of life years deliverable by health care, the greater the need for treatment (or the greater is the patient's interest in receiving treatment), is just to beg the crucial question of how to characterize "need."

Longevity

Advances in stem cell research and gerontology, and the emergence of regenerative medicine, have resulted in a considerable body of research which anticipates substantial further increases in life expectancy (Harris 2000). If these were to be achieved, it might be possible to create or modify humans so that they would have their life expectancy increased by scores, possibly by hundreds, of years. Any metric of the value of life which made value a function of years lived or of life expectancy would automatically favor such enhanced individuals, as would metrics like the QALY to which we are about to turn, which accord value to life years rather than to lives. It is not obvious that a principle which says the equivalent of "to those that have shall be given, and to those who contrive to have more will be given even more" is either the most just or the most appropriate principle for the allocation of scarce public resources.

Should the Health-care System Maximize QALYs?

We have seen that, among others, the life-years approach to defining health gain (whether or not those life years are adjusted for quality of life or other considerations), and hence to defining what is to be delivered by health-care systems, is not the obvious answer to the question of which patient is in most need of health care. However, it remains *an answer* to that question. Part of its attraction as an answer is that it dictates a policy of maximizing QALYs which says: "Choose the patient and the treatment which will deliver more Quality Adjusted Life Years per currency unit." How good an answer is it? There is much literature on this question (Williams 1985; Harris 1987), and justice cannot be done to the complexities of the discussion in this brief space. I will simply summarize some of the problems the QALY-style answer has to overcome and leave the judgment as to how successfully it is possible to overcome these problems to the reader. The use of a QALY approach to micro-allocation tends to bias the health-care system in favor of the young and against the old, because, other things being equal, the young have more life years to gain from treatment than the old. This approach might be thought to amount to ageism, and will be discussed in more detail presently. It also tends to favor patients who have conditions which are at present cheaper to treat. This may prevent research and development achieving economies in the treatment of conditions that are at present expensive to treat, and hence not only discriminate against conditions which are initially expensive to treat, but also against groups of citizens identified by their condition, for example, AIDS patients or cancer patients (Claxton and Culyer 2006; 2007; Harris 2005a; 2005b; 2006; 2007a; Holm 2006; Rawlins and Dillon 2005). Finally it discriminates against those with disability.

The impact of disability on what is sometimes called "the global burden of disease" prompted a "refinement" to the QALY. The use of the disability-adjusted life year (DALY) approach is favored by the World Health Organization (WHO 2008) and other bodies, but the DALY fares no better than the QALY for the same or related reasons. While DALYs can indeed say something about the burden of disease globally, the moment they are used in priority-setting, their disastrous effect on human rights and human-istic values is revealed. As Arneson and Nord (1999) have observed:

338

[The DALY approach] seems to be that the healthier the person, the more valuable their life is to themselves and to society and the greater their claim on restricted healthcare resources to have their life extended. . . . A valuation of human beings according to their functional capacity is in sharp contrast to the humanistic values laid down in the Declaration of Human Rights "recognition of the inherent dignity and of the equal and inalienable rights of all members of the human family is the foundation."

Arneson and Nord conclude that "The DALY approach . . . presupposes that life years of disabled people are worth less than life years of people without disabilities."

A further injustice in the use of both QALYs and DALYs arises from the possibility of "double jeopardy," an idea first introduced into the resource allocation debate in 1987 (Harris 1987) but often misunderstood. Hofstetter and Hammitt (2002), for example, mention the *double jeopardy argument*, which they correctly identify as showing that people with disabilities are disadvantaged twice by QALY- and DALY-based approaches: "First they suffer the disability, maybe for their whole life, and second they are disadvantaged because a year of life saved counts less [for them]." Hofstetter and Hammitt seem not to notice that arguments against health metrics, like the argument from double jeopardy, which they list but do not discuss, raise serious doubts about the overall utility and justice of such measures. Moreover, they wrongly credit the double jeopardy argument to those who reject it, which perhaps accounts for their failure to take it seriously.

QALYs and Equality

QALYs, DALYs, and other metrics of health care often extrapolate moral conclusions about how the health-care system should treat claimants for health care from questions put to individuals about what they would want for themselves. People are invited to say whether they would prefer long life over shorter life, for example, and then the conclusion is drawn that it is legitimate to allocate resources so that they go to people who will gain the most life years from treatment. Suppose, as is likely, my own life would be better and of even more value to me if I were healthier, fitter, had more money, more friends, more lovers, more children, more life expectancy, more everything I want; it does not follow that others are entitled to decide that because I lack some or all of these things I am less entitled to health-care resources, or less worthy to receive those resources, than are others, who by hypothesis have more of those things – or that those resources would somehow be wasted on me.

Imagine twin sisters: Jackie was born paralyzed from the waist down and Jill was born healthy. Now in their 30s, Jackie has established a life for herself that she finds worthwhile and satisfying. So has her twin. Both agree, however, and all the evidence indicates, that Jackie's quality of life is objectively substantially lower, and both agree that Jackie's life expectancy is substantially less. Both, we will suppose, are now involved in an accident and resources available can only treat one before death strikes them both. It seems to me that not only is it unethical to choose between them, but that there is no rational basis for so doing. Both want to live; both have lives they find worthwhile.

Both sisters agree that if they had to choose, they would prefer Jill's life to Jackie's. It does not follow that either of them is committed to the view that health resources should be devoted to Jill rather than to Jackie. When it is said, "People not only prefer good quality life to poor quality life but also more life of a given quality to less" (Claxton and Culyer 2006), this is right, but if policies that condemn Jackie to death and rescue Jill are implemented, it is fraudulent to imply that this somehow has the endorsement of both sisters and of all people who want longer and healthier lives.

If we believe that we should prefer to rescue those for whom treatment makes more of an improvement in quality of life, then we should surely rescue Jill. Suppose, however irrational it might seem, that quality of life is measurable numerically, and suppose it is agreed that Jackie's quality score before illness or accident was 6 and Jill's was 10. Then to rescue Jill makes a difference of 10, while saving Jackie yields only a score of 6. It is surely the treatment and the rescue that makes this difference, because without them Jackie and Jill would score zero. They would be dead. This shows that the QALY scores of the treatment are not meaningfully separable from the QALY scores of the individual treated, if what matters is the QALY expectations of the individual after treatment. Indeed, how could it be otherwise, for the point of high QALY scores of *treatments* is to deliver high QALY scores to *individuals*. The same is of course true of life expectancy.

Once we grant that part of the justification for using QALYs as a prioritizing principle is that we ought to maximize quality as well as quantity of life, then it clearly defeats the object to draw a distinction between quality or quantity which is *independent of* treatment and quality *delivered by* treatment, where both affect the outcome. The effects, whether measured in QALYs or not, of treating someone successfully for lethal illness x, when he will die a week later of y, are the same as a treatment for x which will only yield one week of remission.

The whole plausibility of QALYs depends upon our accepting that they simply involve the generalization of the "truth" that "given the choice a person would prefer a shorter healthier life to a longer period of survival in a state of severe discomfort." On this view, giving priority to treatments which produce more QALYS, or for which the cost per QALY is low, is both efficient and is also what the community as a whole, and those at risk in particular, actually want. But whereas it follows logically from the fact that, given the choice, a person would prefer a shorter healthier life to a longer one of severe discomfort, that the best treatment for that person is the one yielding the most QALYS, it does not follow, and logic does not dictate, that treatments yielding more QALYs are preferable to treatments yielding fewer where different people are to receive the treatments.

Surely the principle governing any distribution of public resources must be equality: that each is entitled to the same concern, respect, and protection as is accorded to any. People are equal and equally worth treating or saving, and equality is not health-status dependent. When we say all are equal, we exclude discrimination on the basis of all the usual suspects: race, gender, religion, and so on. The moral principle outlawing discrimination protects (or should protect) all persons equally. People's lives and fundamental interests should be given equal weight regardless of race, creed, color, gender, age, life expectancy, or quality of life, so long as that quality of life is worth having for the person whose life it is. As the judge, Mars-Jones J, said in a famous English judgment:

> However gravely ill a man may be . . . he is entitled in our law to every hour . . . that God has granted him. That hour or hours may be the most precious and most important hours of a man's life. There may be business to transact, gifts to be given, forgiveness to be made, 101 bits of unfinished business which have to be concluded. (*R v. Carr* 1996)

The point is that, while it may be true that QALYs are of equal value no matter who gets them, we treat people as equals only when they have an equal opportunity with any one else to receive the QALYs they need to survive.

The Evidence Base for QALY-informed Decisions

It is usually claimed that, whatever else may be true of them, QALYs represent the most cost-effective use of medical resources. A therapy or procedure is not cost-effective if "the health benefits that it is estimated could be gained from the technology are less than those estimated to be forgone by other patients as other procedures are necessarily curtailed or not undertaken. It is this comparison of health gained and health forgone that is at the heart of the rationale of cost-effectiveness analysis" (Claxton and Culyer 2007). To estimate whether the gains made are less than the gains forgone, a health provider or funder must therefore know which gains would have to be forgone if the procedure or technology is approved, or there can be no data for the required calculation. If they don't know this, they cannot know whether the gains might have been less or more than the benefits forgone in any particular case. In the United Kingdom, the body charged with determining which treatments should be funded, the National Institute for Health and Clinical Excellence (NICE), has admitted that:

> neither NICE nor any other decision making entity . . . can know precisely which . . . activities will be displaced by their guidance or prescribing decisions nor exactly who will forgo which specific health benefits. However we do know there will be health forgone to real, albeit unidentified, patients and we maintain the value judgement that the consequences for those unidentified individuals ought to be valued in the same way as the consequences for others who gain from the technology under consideration. (Claxton and Culyer 2007)

Of course they should, but unless it is known which consequences for unidentified individuals we are talking about, it cannot be known whether or not they outweigh the gains. From this it follows inexorably that NICE is not, and cannot be, doing cost-benefit analysis – they simply don't and cannot know what the alternative uses are. The issue is not whether the health forgone is to identified or unidentified individuals; the point is whether it is health that is forgone or something else, and if it is health is it health that is more or less important or urgent than the health that might have been funded? In a complex health-care system, the money saved by not funding a new but expensive cancer treatment might go on white-lining the hospital car-park rather than be devoted to patient care. But the justification for not funding a treatment because it is not cost-effective implies, and is justified by, the assumption that the money will go on something we would agree to be more important or more urgent. Without that assurance, the moral justification for withholding funding to any particular

341

treatment is absent, except as a general claim that there is not enough money for every-thing. But that raises, but does not solve, the question of an appropriate basis for any proposed rationing.

We need now to review the other major considerations which are often used to justify selection between claimants for care. I will first try to identify many of the major sorts of consideration and then say something about how we should try to move forward in the face of so many diverse and conflicting considerations.

Choosing Between Claimants

We have looked briefly at the concept of a needs-based approach and noted that needs are often cashed out in terms of *quantity of life* and *quality of life*. An idea strongly related to quality-of-life considerations is that of *the value of someone's life*. When this appears in justifications for treating one person rather than another, three different sorts of appeal are often made. Sometimes the *value to the community* of someone's life is invoked; others lay stress upon a patient's *value to others* nearer to her (children or family perhaps); finally, some believe that the strength of the value an individual attaches to their own life, *value to oneself*, should be taken into account.

Those who equate need with capacity to benefit are often inclined to look at a patient's *prognosis* and argue that those with the best chance of successful treatment should be given priority. Related appeals are often made in terms of someone's *past contribution* to society, or to the health-care system itself in terms of service to it, or payment for it via national insurance contributions. *Future or expected contribution* is sometimes thought relevant, and someone's potential for contribution, in all the above ways, and also perhaps via exceptional skills, to possible medical or scientific advance, is often thought to establish a strong claim.

Issues concerning *personal responsibility for health* have been the occasion of much debate about priorities in health care (Higgs 1993; McLachlan 1995; Underwood and Bailey 1993). An individual's lifestyle, his eating habits, whether or not he smokes, the dangerous pastimes or sports he indulges in, the danger of not indulging in dangerous sports and becoming unfit and obese, the sexual preferences he has and the frequency with which he indulges them, and with whom and with what care, are all arguably reasonable bases for claims to priority or lack of it in the allocation of health-care resources. Then there are issues that arise from such factors as where people live, the occupational hazards they have to face, how and on or in what they travel: all of these contribute to a person's responsibility for ill health and all have been cited in arguments about priority for care.

Moral character and *fault* are also very popular candidates. Should the drunken driver be given the same priority as his victim? If the prison and the hospital are on fire, where should the ambulance go first?

Then there are what we might call *impersonal features*. An individual's illness or treat-ment may have significance for research purposes, for example; or perhaps, because there is a useful byproduct of their treatment (such as oocytes for donation or cell lines for development), there may be powerful arguments to prioritize their treatment. Where someone is prioritized because they happen to be part of a larger group and they

342

become part of a strategy of maximizing numbers treated, we might also think of this as an impersonal feature.

I have not tried to be exhaustive. I have failed to mention *triage, compliance,* cases where someone poses an *innocent threat to others,* and a number of other considerations. To what extent can we or should we take account of all or any of these things?

Allocation and Liberation

It is a truism that individuals are individual. People are different from one another in a myriad of ways. Among these are, of course, ways that make some people better than others, morally, spiritually, existentially. Some are more valuable to society, others make better parents, some are healthier and have better life expectancy, others have a quality of life that is enviable and even perhaps envied by the man on the Clapham omnibus. Some people are simply nicer than others and some are even fundamentally nasty.

Of the ways in which it is sometimes thought appropriate to distinguish between candidates for care, many of which we have just reviewed, a substantial number identify moral differences. When we ask whether priority for treatment should be given to the productive executive or to the chronically unemployed, or when we compare the claims of the young mother of four with that of the friendless loner, or when we consider whether the drunken driver or his victim should be treated first, or when we allocate a low priority to smokers, we are making moral assessments. Although these may also have a clinical component, they can never be purely matters of clinical judgment. To concentrate on one dimension of this problem: of all the ways in which people may be said to have contributed to their own adverse health state, it is usually only the most clearly unpopular candidates that are singled out. Thus, although sports injuries, occupational hazards, and lifestyle-related illness are all examples of personal responsibility for an adverse health state, anecdotal evidence suggests that discrimination in the allocation of medical resources has tended to concentrate on those who smoke, those who drink excess alcohol, and those who are HIV-positive.

Moreover, medical needs are seldom simply that. They are often also opportunities to go on living or to be free: free of pain, free or freer in the sense of being mobile or more mobile, more able effectively to operate in the world. Health care is important not simply because we all value health and all want long and healthy lives. It is important also because good health is liberating and poor health is confining.

Since choices between patients as to which will receive the resources required for health care are often choices as to who will be offered the chance to have their life saved, or their pain relieved, or their mobility – their freedom – restored, three pressing questions arise. They are:

1 Given that we cannot avoid choosing between patients, do we want that choice made in a way that has the ethical evaluation of the patient or contested value judgments as a large component of the decision procedure?
2 Where other non-clinical factors are in play, such as the issue of what weight is to be given to the fact that a patient has dependents, the same question arises: do we want evaluation of these factors to determine treatment outcomes?

343

3   If we are content that we must or should choose between candidates for care in a way that involves the moral evaluation of those candidates or of other non-clinical features of their situation, are we content to leave that evaluation to doctors or health administrators to make on the basis of whatever information just happens to be available at the time?

There are a number of issues here. I think we have good reason to be concerned to avoid making choices that may be life-or-death decisions on the basis of moral evaluation of persons. But even if we were satisfied that this was a proper thing to do, we should under no circumstances leave such evaluation to untrained medical staff or other health professionals, nor permit such decisions to be made on the basis of necessarily sketchy information. When I talk of "untrained" medical staff, I mean that, although they are medically trained, they are not trained to make the moral evaluations of which we are speaking. Indeed, it is doubtful whether such training exists.

Moral Evaluation of Persons

Where decisions about eligibility for treatment or prioritization are made by medical staff or other health-care purchasers or providers, and where evaluation of the person plays some part in that decision, two immediate problems arise. The first concerns the adequacy of the information on which the judgment is based and the opportunities for fair assessment of all relevant facts. The second concerns problems of measuring degrees of responsibility. In terms of decisions based on the moral evaluation of persons, as we have seen, most of the circumstances in which people are tempted to use moral evaluation as a determinant of the allocation of medical resources turn on cases where the individual is apparently herself wholly or partially responsible for her predicament, for the fact that she needs health care.

For the sake of brevity we will concentrate on the question of whether the person who needs health care because she has over-indulged in alcohol should be given lower priority than candidates who are not apparently responsible for their own adverse health state. There are two good reasons for doing so. The good reasons are that excessive drinking is seen as both voluntary and unnecessary; moreover, its harmful effects are well established and have been long known and well publicized.

One consideration often adduced in favor of discriminating against alcohol abusers, which is of some immediate intuitive force, is the suggestion that when faced with a choice between treating someone whose condition is alcohol-related and someone who has diligently attempted to protect her own health by avoiding intoxicating beverages, it would be unfair to prefer the drinker. The argument behind this judgment may be that the drinker should not be "rewarded" for her recklessness, while the prudent individual is "punished" for her care of her own health. A related thought may be that it seems unfair that the non-drinker should be denied the benefit that she has a reasonable expectation would be the just reward for her virtue.

We should remember that it is not entirely true that a non-drinker who is given a lower priority for treatment than a drinker has had the benefit of her virtue negated in some way. Non-drinkers do, other things being equal, get benefit from their virtue;

they are less likely to need health care. They do have an advantage over drinkers. They have already been rewarded for their virtue. This is not at issue. The question that must be asked is, should they be rewarded *again* by the public health-care system? Does their virtue increase their entitlement to benefit from public health care?

Then there is the suggestion that the drinker should not be *preferred* to the non-drinker, that such a preference would be unfair in that it rewarded vice at the expense of virtue. No one is, I think, suggesting that drinkers should be preferred to non-drinkers; but should they have an *equal* chance of access to health care?

If they are given an equal chance of care and treatment, then, of course, drinkers will sometimes be treated while non-drinkers are not. It may be unfair in some cosmic sense when the virtuous suffer and the less virtuous prosper. But should we use public resources and even legislation to try to ensure that this does not happen? And if we do so, are we in danger effectively of punishing people for their choice of lifestyle and doing so in a way which not only violates principles of natural justice, as we shall see, but which creates additional and gratuitous injustice.

It is sometimes said that giving a low priority to drinkers in the allocation of resources for health care is justified, not as a punishment for them or a reward for the virtue of abstainers, but because to fail to do so would encourage dangerous and anti-social habits in the community and fail to give a much-needed incentive to people to give up alcohol. However, if the prospect of better health and a longer life on the one hand, and, on the other, fear of premature death from alcohol-related diseases or injuries do not act as an incentive, it is surely unlikely that the further fear of failure to get priority in medical care will add much to the incentives and disincentives already in place. If it is right that refusals to treat, or low positions on waiting lists, are unlikely to have much impact on behavior, then discrimination against drinkers in the allocation of health-care resources will effectively function as a punishment and should be seen as such.

This raises a large issue which we have no space here to tackle adequately. It is the question of the appropriateness of allowing doctors, or indeed the health-care system, to hand out punishments and rewards for behavior that is quite legal. If this is effectively a form of punishment, and insofar as it is, it would be punishment without a hearing or trial, by individuals who were effectively judge, jury, and executioner rolled into one. Moreover, there would be little prospect of appeal or remission of sentence. Not only is there a problem of double jeopardy here, of people being effectively "punished" twice for the same offence (once by their contracting a condition caused by alcohol and a second time by the refusal to treat that condition), but there is also an insurmountable problem of natural justice.

Moreover, a health-care system which penalized people on the basis of information about their general health state and life expectancy would almost certainly discourage the divulging of information relevant to health and would therefore tend to undermine the public health considerations which are often thought to be part of its attraction.

It can scarcely be necessary to argue the point, but decisions which may involve life or death are as consequential as any decisions can be. Such decisions should clearly only be taken at all under the pressure of overriding necessity. I have suggested at the start of this chapter that such claims may be rather more difficult to sustain than many believe. However, even if it is granted that there is overriding necessity in the form of radical scarcity of resources, clearly some just and impartial procedure must be established for making such decisions. In particular, there must be appropriate mechanisms for establishing the facts on which such decisions are based and an appropriate appeals procedure. Where such "facts" include judgments as to moral worth, there must at the very least be agreement about, and acceptance of, the appropriate bases for such judgments.

Natural Justice

I believe that the ways that most life or death decisions involving choices between patients which are currently taken within public health-care systems, where the result is that a patient who could have had his life sustained dies as a consequence of adverse selection, involve violation of the principles of natural justice. This is equally true where the decisions are not matters of life or death but which simply confer benefits or relieve burdens.

It is worthwhile reminding ourselves just what these principles are and what they involve. I will quote from one of the standard texts and most authoritative sources on the question of natural justice:

> The rules of natural justice are minimum standards of fair decision-making, imposed by the common law on persons or bodies who are under a duty to "act judicially." They were applied originally to courts of justice and now extend to any person or body deciding issues affecting the right or interest of individuals where a reasonable citizen would have a legitimate expectation that the decision-making process would be subject to some rules of fair procedure. . . . All that is fundamentally required of the decision-maker is that his decision . . . be made with due regard for the affected parties' interests and accordingly be reached without bias and after giving the party or parties a chance to put his or their case. (De Smith and Brazier 1994: 602)

In the absence of agreement about, and acceptance of, the appropriate bases for judgments based on, or with a component of, moral worth and with no evidence-gathering or checking mechanisms in place, it is surely doubtful whether the first rule of natural justice could be satisfied in micro-allocation decisions. This rule requires *nemo judex in sua causa*, that no one be a judge in his own cause. This means that an adjudicator "must not be reasonably suspected, or show a real likelihood, of bias." Equally, without affording patients the opportunity of knowing that they have been selected against, and a chance to argue their corner with, perhaps, access to an appeals procedure, it is doubtful whether the second rule of natural justice could be complied with. This involves *audi alteram partem*, the right to a fair hearing.

Finally, one other consideration should be mentioned. Even if we could solve the problems of complying with the principles of natural justice, many of the bases for selection involve information. Determining responsibility for one's own health state, utility to society or level of past or future contribution, numbers of dependents or friends, membership of some larger group, and so on, all involve comprehensive information-gathering and information access and retrieval of a high order. Whenever priorities between patients are set, the appropriate decision-maker would need to have immediate access to a wealth of personal information about all the individuals involved which would include their family details, sexual habits, lifestyle choices, diet, domicile, work, genetic constitution, income levels, and much besides. A real question is: would we want to live in a society that routinely gathered, stored, and had instant access to such comprehensive personal information? Moreover, this society would have to license officials (medical staff?) to act on such information instantly, sometimes with life-or-death consequences. Would we be happy that the information was accurate, had been appropriately assessed, and that something crucial was not missing?

Utility to Society

Much the same could of course be said about an individual's utility to society. There are the immense problems of agreeing the appropriate bases for judgments about utility (is a postman more useful than a refuse collector?) and the problems of gathering and having readily available the relevant information which we have noted. Of course there will be cases where fairly complete information on a particular individual may just happen to be to hand. The justice of acting upon it in these cases would share the justice of a tax system which taxed only those on whom tax-relevant information happened to be available, but which had no systematic gathering of information (tax returns, etc.) and no investigative, checking, or appeals procedures.

Numbers of Dependents

Many people believe that we should favor those with dependents in the allocation of resources for health care and that the objection that this is unfair "loses a lot of its force when the preference is justified by citing the interests of dependents rather than the merits of the person selected" (Glover 1977). There are two major problems with such an approach. The first is that it is not clear why, where someone's survival or treatment is dependent on the interests of third parties, the interests of third parties who are dependents should take preference over the interests of third parties who are not. Moreover, it is unclear why only interests *in favor* of treatment should count. Third parties, dependent or not, may have as strong an interest that someone should not be treated and perhaps should not survive as that they should receive treatment. Third parties might stand to benefit financially from someone's death, for example, or might object to treatments such as abortions or fertility treatments.

The second problem is that the feeling that it is somehow more important to treat those with relatives, when elevated to the level of policy, amounts to a systematic preference for those with families over those without. It is not clear how such a policy would avoid the offensive division of people into grades, some more worth saving than others.

Age and Life Expectancy

Implicit in this discussion has been an argument against ageism in the distribution of resources for health care. This argument can be stated thus:

> All of us who wish to go on living have something that each of us values equally although for each it is different in character, for some a much richer prize than for others, and we none of us know its true extent. This thing is of course "the rest of our lives." So long as we do not know the date of our deaths then for each of us the "rest of our lives" is of indefinite duration. Whether we are 17 or 70, in perfect health or suffering from a terminal disease, we each have the rest of our lives to lead. So long as we each wish to live out the rest of our lives, however long that turns out to be, then if we do not deserve to die, we each suffer the same injustice if our wishes are deliberately frustrated and we are cut off prematurely. (Harris 1985: 89)

An important element of anti-ageism expressed in this way is that it links opposition to discrimination on the basis of chronological age to discrimination on the basis of life expectancy. These are not of course necessarily linked. Some people have formulated what might be termed a "fair innings argument" (Harris 1985; Callahan 1990). This suggests that people are entitled to every opportunity to live a fair lifespan (60 or 70 years?). Up to that point they have equal entitlement to health care; beyond the fair innings, they are given very low priority. This argument is tempting because it explains the strong intuition people have that there is something wrong with treating the claims of an octogenarian and those of a 20-year-old as equal. However, the fair innings argument has a number of defects and ultimately fails (Harris 1985). It assumes that the value of a life is to be measured in units of lifetime, the more the better up to a certain point but thereafter extreme discounting begins. This results in the problems created by QALYs and DALYs noted above.

The problem is that people value particular events within their life disproportionately to the time required to experience those events. Although the fair innings argument gives great importance to a life having shape and structure, these things are again not necessarily only achieved within a particular time span. On the fair innings argument, Nelson Mandela's entitlement to life-sustaining treatment was exhausted before he left Victor Verster prison. And it is not only for such as Mandela that the most important part of their life might well begin after a so-called "fair innings" had been achieved.

Without the vast detail of each person's life and their hopes and aspirations within that detail, we cannot hope to do justice between lives. I believe the only sensible alternative is to count each life for one and none for more than one, whatever the differences in age and in other quality considerations.

It is this outlook that explains why murder is always wrong, and wrong to the same degree. When you rob someone of life, you take from them not only all they have, but all they will ever have; taking life is an act so different in degree to any other, so radical, that it makes for a difference in the quality of the act. However, the wrongness consists in taking from them something that they want. That explains why it is coherent to claim that voluntary euthanasia is not wrong and murder is.

Those who believe in discriminating in favor of the young or against the old must believe that, insofar as murder is an injustice, it is less of an injustice to murder the old than the young, and since they also believe that life years are a commodity like any other, it is clear that in robbing people of life you take less from them the shorter their life expectancy is.

Fairness and Quality of Life

The same ideas which underpin discrimination against the old on the grounds of fairness would also entail trying to equalize quality as well as quantity of life. The argument here would be that resources required for survival should be distributed not only so as to favor the young, but also so as to favor those whose quality of life has been relatively poor. Suppose two patients, both about 40 years old, need a liver transplant but only one suitable liver is available. One of the patients (the first) has had a much worse life than the other. In this case it might be argued that it seems most fair to give the liver to the first person. Again, such a view has some appeal, but it has the same problems concerning information-gathering that we have already noted. We could never make decisions as to how to allocate life-saving, or indeed other, scarce resources between people until we had their whole (and very complete and detailed) life history. It is surely better to treat each person as counting for one, and none for more than one, than even to embark on the massively invasive (of privacy) data collection which it would be necessary to hold and have instantly available on each and every citizen, and which could never be complete, accurate, or proof against abuse.

If it is right to attempt to even out quality of life between people, then we should do so as a matter of public policy throughout society, not simply in the rare cases where resource-allocation decisions in health care arise. This might have to include making sure that no one lived longer than the person who has the shortest lifespan and no one was happier than the most miserable. This is likely to be dysfunctional in terms of species survival, but we will ignore this problem for obvious reasons.

Ultimately we will be comparing different moral priorities. However, there seems much to be said for taking individual persons and their preferences and fundamental interests as what matters from the point of view of morality. This means that we must recognize that although their lives will all differ in length, happiness, and success, in short, in the degree to which their fundamental interests are satisfied, people matter morally despite these differences not because of them, and each person's wish to have the treatment that will offer him the chance of continued flourishing to the extent that his personal health status permits is as urgent and important as that of any other person.

Conclusion

Where consensus about degree of need for health care can be achieved, this should be the basis of choice. Where, as in many cases, this is unlikely to be possible, the alternatives are unattractive indeed. The alternatives of either complying with the principles of natural justice where decisions between patients are taken, or taking such decisions in a way that shows no preference (by lot, for example), may be equally daunting. In the light of this, the option of finding a higher level of resources for health care might not seem so unattractive or so onerous.

References

Arneson, T. and Nord, E. (1999). The value of DALY life: problems with ethics and validity of disability adjusted life years. *British Medical Journal* 319: 1423–5.

Callahan, D. (1990). *What Kind of Life: The Limits of Medical Progress.* New York: Simon and Schuster.

Claxton, K. and Culyer, A. J. (2006). Wickedness or folly? The ethics of NICE's decisions. *Journal of Medical Ethics* 32/7 (July): 373–7.

Claxton, K. and Culyer, A. J. (2007). Rights, responsibilities and NICE: a rejoinder to Harris. *Journal of Medical Ethics* 33 (August): 462–4.

de Beaufort, I. (1998). Individual responsibility for health: some thoughts on drinkers, drunken drivers, champagne drinkers and health freaks. In C. Erin and R. Bennett (eds.), *HIV/AIDS: Who Should Know?* Oxford: Oxford University Press.

De Smith, S. and Brazier, R. (1994). *Constitutional and Administrative Law,* 7th edn. Harmondsworth: Penguin.

Glover, J. (1977). Causing Death and Saving Lives. Harmondsworth: Penguin.

Harris, J. (1985). *The Value of Life: An Introduction to Medical Ethics.* London: Routledge & Kegan Paul.

Harris, J. (1987). QALYfying the value of life. Journal *of Medical Ethics* 13/3: 117–23.

Harris, J. (1996a). What is the good of health care? *Bioethics* 10/4: 269–92.

Harris, J. (1996b). Could we hold people responsible for their own adverse health? *Journal of Contemporary Health Law and Policy* 1: 147–55.

Harris, J. (2000). Intimations of Immortality. *Science* 288/5463: 59.

Harris, J. (2005a). It's not NICE to discriminate. *Journal of Medical Ethics* 31 (July): 373–5.

Harris, J. (2005b). Nice and not so nice. *Journal of Medical Ethics* 31: 685–8.

Harris, J. (2006). NICE is not cost effective. *Journal of Medical Ethics* 32 (July): 378–80.

Harris, J. (2007a). *Enhancing Evolution.* Princeton and Oxford: Princeton University Press, ch. 4.

Harris, J. (2007b). NICE rejoinder. *Journal of Medical Ethics* 33 (August): 467.

Higgs, R. (1993). Controversies in treatment: Should smokers be offered coronary bypass surgery? Human frailty should not be penalised. *British Medical Journal* 306 (April 17): 1049–50.

Hofstetter, P. and Hammitt, J. (2002). Selecting human health metrics for environmental decision support tools. *Risk Analysis* 22: 5.

Holm, S. (2006). Self inflicted harm – NICE in ethical self destruct mode? *Journal of Medical Ethics* 32: 125–6.

McLachlan, H. V. (1995). Drinkers, virgins, equity and health care costs. *Journal of Medical Ethics* 21: 209–13.

Oppenheimer, P. (1988a). Economics and the health service. *Independent,* March 7, p. 17.

Oppenheimer, P. (1988b). Economic health and NHS decline. *Health Service Journal* May 19.

R v. Carr (1996). *Sunday Times,* November 30.

Rawlins, M. and Dillon, A. (2005). NICE discrimination. *Journal of Medical Ethics* 31 (December): 683–4.

Underwood, M. J. and Bailey, J. S. (1993). Controversies in treatment: Should smokers be offered coronary bypass surgery? Coronary bypass surgery should not be offered to smokers. *British Medical Journal* 306 (April 17): 1047–8.

WHO (2008). www.who.int/healthinfo/boddaly/en/index.html. Accessed April 10, 2008.

Williams, A. (1985). Economics of coronary artery bypass grafting. *British Medical Journal* 291: 326–9.

350

30

Society's Allocation of Resources for Health

DANIEL WIKLER AND SARAH MARCHAND

Each society must decide what share of its resources it should devote to health care, and must also decide, within that budget, the relative priority of alternative uses of resources. In addition, funds spent on education, transportation, and other goods may be guided in part by their effects on health, even if these effects are not their primary aim. There is rarely enough money to meet all existing needs, and all these decisions pose difficult ethical dilemmas. Decisions to meet some needs are simultaneously decisions not to meet others, and the latter, in particular, must be justified both to those who lose out and to the broader society.

Determinants of Health

Health status is determined only in part by health care. Longevity and morbidity vary with a range of social conditions, including education, economic development, class, and race. European men live decades longer than men in Bangladesh – and in Harlem, the African American district of New York City (Marmot 2001; McCord and Freeman 1990). While advances in medical care have extended lives and reduced the burden of illness, the health impact of social changes is often greater. Economic development is usually accompanied by better health, while the health of middle-aged and elderly citizens of the former Soviet Union deteriorated alarmingly during the transition to a market economy (Stuckler et al. 2008).

The scope of a comprehensive and global treatment of allocation of resources for health would transcend the health sector and also national boundaries. Within countries, inequalities in health status correlated with social position persist even where everyone has access to health care. The sources of these gaps in health lie outside the health sector, as do some of the remedies. Inequalities in health among nations reflect national differences in economic and social development, among other factors. Most of this chapter, however, will focus on resources within the health sector of individual countries.

Who, If Anyone, Allocates Health Resources?

Health resource allocation can be carried out with varying degrees of detailed planning. A centralized national health service may assign responsibility for nearly all allocation to a single executive office; a fully privatized system relying on fee-for-service payment leaves these decisions to buyers and sellers. In actual practice, most allocation schemes mix these approaches. Even the most detailed central plan for health care must leave many decisions to the clinician at the bedside. (See chapter 29, "Deciding Between Patients.") And pure markets are rare in medicine apart from in the poorest countries. Because health-care costs can be catastrophic and unexpected, modern medicine delivered in markets requires health insurance and, in bargaining over the limits of coverage, sellers and buyers of insurance jointly make allocation decisions.

Determining the Share of the Overall Budget
To Be Devoted to Health

Countries differ widely in the share of their resources that are devoted to health care. Developing countries often allocate less than 3 percent of a relatively tiny gross domestic product (GDP). Among the richest countries, the share of GDP falls between 6 and 17 percent (OECD 2008). The relative share of GDP devoted to health care tends to mirror a nation's overall relative wealth, reflecting the fact that non-basic health care is an expensive luxury. The wide variation in the share of GDP spent on health care in advanced countries reflects, among other factors, the considerable variability in efficiency among national health systems.

Decisions to allocate funds to health care rather than to other ends may reflect formal or informal cost-benefit analyses. Cost-benefit analysis (CBA) attempts to weigh gains in health against other ways of increasing welfare. CBA computes the benefits and costs using a common denominator (usually money), allowing the comparison of health benefits with other kinds of benefits, such as education and highways, to permit a reasoned decision on where funds should be spent.

CBA, an art as well as a science, is open to several important ethical challenges. It does not necessarily measure the moral importance of health care, which may be based on factors other than its desirability to individuals – particularly when this is measured by their willingness to pay for it. Moreover, the question that CBA is designed to answer – whether the overall benefit of health care is worth its overall cost – is not the only concern of a health policy. The United States, for example, maintains a separate hospital system for its war veterans, an allocation of resources which attempts to repay a debt.

Allocation Within the Budget for Health

No consensus exists on which principle or principles should govern the allocation of resources within the health-care budget. The most widely espoused principle is that of maximization of health benefit, or "value for money." From a moral point of view, this principle is a good starting point, but it does not resolve many of the ethical dilemmas facing those who must allocate health resources. One reason is that the principle, on close examination, incorporates or presupposes a number of ethical judgments, each of which deserves independent consideration. Another is that the principle can conflict with other moral principles which also seem applicable. These dilemmas cannot be resolved by the principle itself, but, again, require ethical judgment.

Health Needs and Benefits

The most widely used method for determining which interventions permit the achievement of maximum health benefits with available resources is cost-effectiveness analysis (CEA). CEA, unlike CBA, is designed to permit prioritization among health-related benefits only. Like CBA, it requires that diverse goods be quantified in comparable units; but in CEA they are units of health benefit. A comparison of treatments for a specific condition, such as hypertension, can use units specific to that condition (in this case, decrease in millimeters of mercury). Treatments for different conditions, if they are to be ranked in priority, must use a more general measure, such as net loss or gain in years of life. More fine-grained comparisons take into account not only the quantity of life saved by a health-care intervention, but also its quality. Highest priority is thus assigned to health-care interventions which involve the lowest cost per unit of health-related quality of life gained (Gold et al. 1996).

The most widely used general unit of measure of medical benefit, the quality-adjusted life year (QALY), discounts life years compromised by symptoms and functional limitations, as does the disability-adjusted life year (DALY), a measure used by the World Health Organization (WHO) in its Global Burden of Disease surveys. Health problems are a heterogeneous category: sterility, stunting, hallucinations, paraplegia, chest pain, and cancer all detract from perfect health, but their impact varies in degree and in kind. QALYs and DALYs are constructed through a variety of techniques for assigning relative weights to these conditions. For example, respondents might be asked how many years of life in a wheelchair would be as valuable to them as 10 years of perfect health. This ratio can then be compared to that offered in response to similar questions about other limitations, yielding a scale that can be used in assigning a number representing the decrement in a healthy life year due to a particular health problem. The several techniques used to assign these weights rest on somewhat different assumptions and yield different results; the goal of achieving a standard overall measure of health for these purposes remains elusive (Brazier et al. 2007; Salomon et al. 2003).

QALYs are usually understood as permitting the measurement of the impact of medical interventions on overall well-being ("utility"). As such, they are not, strictly speaking, measures of *health*. Health and well-being may not be fully separable: the value of a given health benefit, such as restoration of mobility, may depend on the individual's wealth and other circumstances (Broom [In preparation]).

Ethical Issues in Measuring Health Benefits:
Quantity and Quality of Life

Any attempt to measure health-related quality of life requires that assumptions be made on a host of ethically sensitive issues. At the most abstract level, a decision must be made whether to measure the benefits of longevity and quality of life in terms of objective features, such as living an additional year, or maintaining the ability to live independently or to hold a job. Alternatively, we might rely on measures of personal satisfaction with the course of one's life as a whole. Extending a 75-year-old's life by five years, in this view, might represent a smaller benefit to her than the benefit an additional five years represents to someone aged 35, even if quality of life in the two cases is the same (and regardless of any differences in consequent benefits to others). For example, the older person might already have achieved her life goals, whereas the younger could come closer to doing so if given five more years.

The QALY measure counts years as equal in value, so long as the quality of those years is the same. QALY arithmetic assumes that, when the quality of each year is identical, two years of life are twice as valuable as one, and that two years of life for one person have the same value to that individual as one year for each of two other people has in total. An alternative, whole-life understanding of what counts as a health benefit would not necessarily permit a summing of numbers of years to represent the value of quantity of life. For example, someone given two extra years might not judge her life as a whole to have been made better by twice the amount by which someone else judges his life to have been made better by being given one extra year (Griffin 1989).

Measurement of the *quality* of life involves further challenges along these lines. The value assigned to a state of health such as mild arthritis or blindness varies according to whether the respondent has experienced these conditions. Healthy people may not be able to imagine what it is like to live with a given disability or symptom. Healthy people consistently rate conditions such as blindness as imposing greater burdens than do the blind themselves. In part, this is because they do not understand how successful people can be in coping with their disability, and how little effect the disability may have on their ability to enjoy life. The problem is not fully solved, however, by relying solely on the responses of those who have had experience with the conditions in question. To make the best of their bad situation, they may have changed their life goals and reduced their expectations of what they might hope to achieve, do, and enjoy. While this kind of adjustment to one's real limitations typically enhances the value of life as a whole, having to give up worthwhile pursuits and activities which a disability makes difficult or impossible should count as lowering the objective quality of life, regardless of subjective satisfaction. A satisfactory measure of the relative value of health states for individuals may require combining objective and subjective evaluations, a task which has not yet been successfully undertaken in health measurement.

Ethical Issues in the Distribution of Health Benefits

How should measures of health-related quality of life be used in allocating health-care resources? One option, as mentioned above, is maximization of the total sum of units of health-related quality of life; indeed, it is widely assumed that this is the point of the measurement. There are, however, alternative principles of allocation which use these same measures, and defenders of maximization must answer some important ethical challenges.

If we are concerned only about the highest total amount of health benefits, rather than about their distribution among individuals, a patient in severe distress might lose out in competition for health funds to a number of patients in much better condition, providing that the aggregate gain in health-related quality of life of the latter group was greater. In the extreme case, a person with a life-threatening, treatable condition would be allowed to die so that others could enjoy relief from mild discomfort. The total maximizing strategy assumes, controversially, that the latter should outweigh the benefit of saving a life simply provided that the total gain per dollar from helping the many is larger, but in common moral intuition rescuing people from calamities, or averting them altogether, ought to have some priority over lesser forms of aid.

One apparent virtue of QALYs and other measures of health-related quality of life is their inherent equality. As with utilitarianism, one unit of benefit counts the same no matter who enjoys it. But from a different point of view, maximization of the sum total of benefits does not treat people on equal terms. Those who can be cheaply cured, for example, would always take priority over those whose cure would cost more per unit of benefit. Maximization of health benefits treats patients the same if they stand to gain by the same amount per dollar of expenditure; but in the other view of equality, health-care resources are allocated equally only if patients are treated the same who have the same health-care needs.

Maximization of health benefits measured in QALYs favors the young, since in general they will enjoy the benefits of a particular health service for more years. To some critics, this is unjust on its face. But others hold that under maximization the young are not favored enough: a 20-year-old person who might be given 10 extra QALYs would lose out to a 65-year-old who might live another 11 QALYs using the same resources. As mentioned above, an alternative measure of benefit which focuses on the value to lives as a whole might not count the years of these two patients as offering the same benefits. Even if we adjusted the measure accordingly, however, distributional considerations might prompt us to favor the younger patient on the grounds that each person should be given an opportunity for "fair innings," the chance to live at least a good part of the prime of life (Williams 1997).

Critics of the maximizing principle have urged a number of alternatives. For example, some priority might be given to the most critically ill, or to other groups whose well-being is of greatest concern. In the most elaborate program yet undertaken of explicit rationing in health care, the American state of Oregon retreated from an initial maximizing strategy to one which used categories of health-care services ranked by moral importance, with acute life-saving care given highest priority (Strosberg et al. 1992). Another alternative would provide weighted lotteries, with patients given chances for resources in proportion to the amount of benefit they would receive per dollar of treatment. In the view of its proponents, this procedure would recognize that patients who would benefit less still have some claim on resources, one that a pure maximization strategy counts for nothing (Goodwin 1992).

355

Defenders of total maximization have argued that all these objections can be accommodated within that strategy. One suggestion is that the worst health outcomes be given weights which distinguish them from less bad outcomes. In some cases, the result would be that interventions that would avert very bad outcomes would not be given higher priority than interventions that prevented milder but much more numerous outcomes; this mode of measurement would block at least some of the trade-offs that seem, intuitively, to slight those in the greatest need, while still allowing useful comparisons between treatments offering the lesser benefits. A different strategy for blocking these trade-offs involves measuring and counting the strength of preferences of fellow citizens that their compatriots in need be rescued, even at the cost of forgoing a greater quantity of benefit distributed in small amounts over large numbers of people. In effect, their distress at standing by while those with severe health needs go untreated would be added to the suffering of the afflicted person, and the resulting sum might then be larger than the total of small benefits which would otherwise command the scarce resources in question. This adjustment, however, seems to mix health-related benefits with other benefits, which strays from the domain of CEA; it would, in effect, allocate on the basis of popularity. In any case, it seems to offer the wrong reason to favor priority for the worst off, which we view as important not because others care but because those in greatest need are entitled to our help.

Even if we accept the thesis that macro-allocation of health-care resources should aim to maximize QALYs (weighted or otherwise), further ethical choices are unavoidable. For example, some insist that future QALYs be given the same value as present QALYs, on the grounds that the moral importance of a healthy life year is independent of when it is realized. Discounting the value of future health benefits merely because they occur in the future, in this view, is nonsensical. But the allocation of health resources is in large part an economic decision, and it is standard practice to discount future expenditures. In CEA, health consequences are usually discounted as well. One reason is that, in their actual spending and budgeting decisions, the public seems to give future health benefits a lower present-day value. Another is that a practice of discounting costs but not benefits arguably leads to paradoxical results: if future benefits can be bought with discounted expenditures, health-care interventions should very often be postponed. The debate over discounting health benefits within CEA is partly over logic and partly over empirical issues, but its bearing on the allocation of health-care resources charges the controversy with ethical significance (Brock and Wikler 2006).

Other Principles of Allocation

Thus far we have considered allocation principles which are based, in one way or another, on the individual's need for treatment and potential benefit from treatment. Health-care allocations have served other goals, however. In the nineteenth century, advocates of social medicine, which sought to improve health by social and environmental reforms as well as by access to health-care services, argued that the national investment required was justified because it would provide a healthier workforce. The practice of triage in military medicine puts a premium on a wounded soldier's fighting potential. Those deciding whom to treat in the poorest sub-Saharan African countries with expensive antiretroviral therapy for AIDS have been urged to give priority to skilled workers and to parents of young children, to avoid a general collapse of the country's social structure. In times of rapidly spreading infectious diseases, such as SARS or pandemic avian influenza, benefits to treated individuals may take a back seat to the overwhelming necessity of containing the spread of the disease.

According to some theorists, the degree of one's responsibility for one's own state of health should sometimes be a factor in deciding how health-care resources ought to be allocated. By adopting healthy habits of living, many people can help themselves more than their doctors can help them. Those who fail to take the steps necessary to stay healthy, in this view, thereby forfeit some of their entitlement to care. This conclusion is based on the premise that those who take risks should be made to bear part of the cost themselves, and also on the argument that the basis for entitlement to health care is ordinarily that patients become ill through no fault of their own. When the illness *is* the patient's fault, in this view, there is a reduced entitlement (Cappelen and Norheim 2005; Wikler 2006).

Though the theme of personal responsibility for health has been sounded period-ically in health policy debates, it has not been much used as the basis for alloca-tion of resources. One reason is that it is often uncertain whether changes in habits, be these losing weight, quitting smoking, moderating alcohol intake, or reducing stress, were within the power of the individual in question. Another objection to setting priorities in health care according to the degree of personal responsibility for illness is that those who adopt unhealthy lifestyles can be made to pay their own way by imposing fees that reflect risks and costs. In some jurisdictions cigarette taxes are high enough to ensure that smokers, as a group, present no net cost to non-smokers. Finally, it has not escaped notice that the "bad habits" for which individuals are held responsible are largely their sins – gluttony, sloth, lust, and the rest – whereas other risks to health, such as child-bearing, are subsidized without complaint. A rare instance of what seems to be allocation according to degree of responsibility for illness is the refusal of some transplant surgeons to provide alcoholics with healthy livers (when non-alcoholics are competing for the same life-saving resource). Even here, however, the explanation given by the surgeons tends to be that alcoholics would enjoy fewer QALYs rather than that these patients have not earned the care (McCallum and Masterton 2006).

Allocation and Social Justice

How should ethical judgments in health resource allocation take into account broader issues of social justice? Much of the literature on the subject focuses, understandably, on how best to weigh competing needs of individuals needing care or protection. We expect people to be treated according to what they need and what can be done for them, and not according to who they are or how well they have done in life. In practice, devi-ations from these precepts nearly always favor the better-off (Tudor Hart's "Inverse Care Law" – see Hart 1971), and are generally viewed as moral flaws in health systems.

But might a "bias" (i.e., priority) in favor of the less well-off be justifiable, or even requisite? Our societies are imperfectly just: all are hierarchical, and the pecking order in actual societies never coincides with such inequalities that theorists of justice might condone. The universal social gradient in health – the association between wealth (and socioeconomic status) and health – reflects a complex and incompletely understood web of causes, including the impact of poverty and inequality on health, the effect of poor health on earnings, and other factors that affect both health and earnings. For some, any significant disparities in health between rich and poor (and those coinciding with other social boundaries, such as race and ethnicity) are an offense to justice, and narrowing these gaps should be accepted as a national priority (Marchand et al. 1998). What actions this would entail depends on our understanding of the sources of the social gradient. Outside the health sector, some of the contributing factors are obvious, such as inadequate control of vermin in public housing projects. It is less clear, given evidence currently available, whether reductions in overall socioeconomic inequality are necessary for, or would effect, substantial reductions in health gaps.

Within the health sector, we would expect disparities in health to narrow if we were to steer resources for health toward those occupying the lower rungs of the socioeconomic and social ladder. This is a different policy from giving priority to the sickest or most vulnerable patients, though it is true that the latter are overrepresented among the poor and marginalized. It would direct us to give priority to people who are in similar health states, so long as they are less fortunate overall.

Setting priorities in health resource allocation to promote equity among the more and the less fortunate requires a choice between "egalitarian" and "prioritarian" goals. Egalitarians want equality; "prioritarians" merely favor giving some degree of priority to the worst-off. The former aim at narrowing health gaps; the latter seek to improve the lot of those closer to the bottom (Parfit 1991). In practice, these may recommend similar (or even identical) policies, but they could diverge; and criteria for judging success might be quite different. Public health measures that are effective in improving the health of the poor and marginalized may prove to be as beneficial to the better-off, or even more so, and existing gaps in prospects for long life and good health may persist or even widen. For prioritarians, but not for egalitarians, the fact that the benefit of these measures is not confined to the low end of the socioeconomic spectrum would not only be acceptable, but would be a strong point in their favor.

Democratic Choice

To what extent should macro-allocation of health-care resources be the result of democratic decision-making? Two lines of argument point to a key role.

One argument offered in favor of resolving disagreements over macro-allocation through democratic choice is the alleged want of a reasoned alternative. In this view, there is little hope of reaching consensus on principles or patterns of allocation of health-care resources. Intercultural and interpersonal variation in views of justice, and of what justice requires in health care, point to very different macro-allocation policies, and there is as little chance of agreement on the latter as there is of agreement on politics and morality. Since no argument or data will convince everyone to adopt the same position, there is no way to proceed to an acceptable policy of macro-allocation other than to vote (Daniels 1993).

A second reason to look to democratic participation and decision-making in the macro-allocation of health resources is that these processes might provide a kind of procedural justice. Whether the results of such a process conformed to what any philosophers or health planners considered just, they would still represent the combined preferences of the very population whose care would be governed by the priorities arrived at through democratic choice.

As demands increase for finite resources, the concept of democratic decisions on the allocation of health-care resources is increasingly attractive in the absence of any agreement on principles of allocation. Governments find rationing unpopular, regardless of how it is carried out, and democratic procedures promise to shift responsibility away from officials. Some priority-setting initiatives, such as that of the American state of Oregon, have encouraged public participation on a mass scale to provide advice to a Health Services Commission. Other governments, including one in New Zealand, have commissioned studies of how individuals from diverse demographic and ethnic groups respond to a series of fictionalized allocation dilemmas. Skeptics have faulted these programs on the grounds that the citizens participating in these hypothetical choices are often ill-informed, that, in any case, the degree of democratic involvement is small, and, more sweepingly, that these measures are actually subtle marketing campaigns to get the public to accept less provision of health care. Moreover, procedural approaches to health resource priority setting do not eliminate the need to think these questions through on their merits, for participants are expected to promote not their personal interests but, rather, their vision of what fairness requires (Ashcroft 2008).

Conclusion

The need for principles of macro-allocation is becoming ever more apparent as costs of health care rise, populations age (in the countries with the costliest health-care systems), and the growth of resources fails to keep step. Physicians have not in general received training for, or been accustomed to, tailoring their practices to these principles, and those who pay and regulate the physicians turn more frequently to economists and others who offer a rational basis for allocation decisions. Cost-effectiveness (value for money) is an important objective, but if the allocation is to be ethically defensible it cannot be the only one. The ethical assumptions and theories of those who allocate health resources will come under increasing scrutiny and analysis in bioethics in the years ahead.

References

Ashcroft, R. (2008). Fair process and the redundancy of bioethics: a polemic. *Public Health Ethics* 1: 3–9.

Brazier, J., Ratcliffe, J., Tsuchiya, A., and Salomon, J. (2007). *Measuring and Valuing Health Benefits for Economic Evaluation*. Oxford: Oxford University Press.

Brock, D. and Wikler, D. (2006). Ethical issues in resource allocation, research, and new product development. In D. Jamison et al. (eds.), *Disease Control Priorities in Developing Countries*. Oxford: Oxford University Press.

Broom, J. (In preparation) Measuring the burden of disease. In D. Wikler and C. Murray (eds.), *Health, Well Being, Justice: Ethical Issues in Health Resource Allocation.* Geneva: World Health Organization.

Cappelen, A. W. and Norheim, O. (2005). Responsibility in health care: a liberal egalitarian approach. *Journal of Medical Ethics* 31: 476–80.

Daniels, N. (1993). Rationing fairly: programmatic considerations. *Bioethics* 7: 224–33.

Gold, M., Siegel, J., Russell, L., and Weinstein, M. (eds.) (1996). *Cost-effectiveness in Health and Medicine.* Oxford: Oxford University Press.

Goodwin, B. (1992). *Justice by Lottery.* Chicago: University of Chicago Press.

Griffin, J. (1989). *Well-Being: Its Meaning, Measurement, and Moral Importance.* Oxford: Oxford University Press.

Hart, J. T. (1971). The inverse care law. *The Lancet* (February 27): 405–12.

Marchand, S., Wikler, D., and Landesman, B. (1998). Class, health, and justice. *Milbank Quarterly* 76/3: 449–68.

McCallum, S. and Masterton, G. (2006). Liver transplantation for alcoholic liver disease: a systematic review of psychosocial selection criteria. *Alcohol and Alcoholism* 41/4: 358–63.

McCord, C. and Freeman, H. P. (1990). Excess mortality in Harlem. *N Engl J Med* 322: 173–7.

Marmot, M. (2001). Inequalities in health. *N Engl J Med* 345: 134–6.

OECD (2008). *OECD Health Data 2008.* Paris: OECD, Organization for Economic Cooperation and Development.

Parfit, D. (1991). Equality or priority? *The Lindley Lecture.* Lawrence: University of Kansas Press.

Salomon, J. A., Murray, C. J. L., Ustun, T. B., and Chatterji, S. (2003). Health state valuations in summary measures of population health. In C. J. L. Murray and D. Evans (eds.), *Health Systems Performance Assessment: Debate, Methods, and Empiricism.* Geneva: World Health Organization, pp. 409–36.

Strosberg, M. A. et al. (1992). *Rationing America's Medical Care: The Oregon Plan and Beyond.* Washington, DC: Brookings Institution.

Stuckler, D., King, L., and Coutts, A. (2008). Understanding privatisation's impacts on health: lessons from the Soviet experience. *J Epidemiol Community Health* 62/7: 664.

Wikler, D. (2006). Personal and social responsibility for health. In S. Anand, F. Peter, and A. K. Sen (eds.), *Public Health, Ethics, and Equity.* Oxford: Oxford University Press, pp. 107–31.

Williams, A. (1997). Intergenerational equity: an exploration of the "fair innings" argument. *Health Economics* 6: 117–32.

Further reading

Anand, S., Peter, F., and Sen, A. K. (2006). *Public Health, Ethics, and Equity.* Oxford: Oxford University Press.

Bell, J. M. and Mendus, S. (1988). *Philosophy and Medical Welfare.* Cambridge: Cambridge University Press.

Brock, D. (1993). Quality of life measures in health care and medical ethics. In M. Nussbaum and A. Sen, *The Quality of Life.* Oxford: Oxford University Press.

Daniels, N. (2007). *Just Health.* Cambridge: Cambridge University Press.

Kamm, F. M. (1993). *Mortality, Morality,* vol. I. Oxford: Oxford University Press.

Kamm, F. M. (2007). *Intricate Ethics.* Oxford: Oxford University Press.

McKeown, T. R. (1976). *The Role of Medicine: Dream, Mirage, or Nemesis.* London: Nuffield Provincial Hospitals Trust.

Marmot, M. (2005). *The Status Syndrome: How Social Standing Affects Our Health and Longevity*. New York: Times Books.

Menzel, P. (1990). *Strong Medicine*. Oxford: Oxford University Press.

Murray, C. J. L. and Lopez, A. D. (1996). *The Global Burden of Disease*. Cambridge, MA: Harvard University Press.

Wilkinson, R. (1996). *Unhealthy Societies: The Afflictions of Inequality*. London: Routledge.

31

Is There a Right to Health Care and, If So, What Does It Encompass?

NORMAN DANIELS

Is There a Right to Health Care?

Legal vs moral rights to health care

One way to answer this question is to adopt the stance of legal positivists, who claim there are no rights except those embodied in actual institutions through law. We would then be able to reply that, in nearly every advanced industrial democracy, there is a right to health care, since public health protections are provided to whole populations, reducing the risk of disease and injury, and institutions exist in them that also assure everyone access to needed personal medical services regardless of ability to pay. A notable exception among developed countries is the United States, where many poor and near poor people have no insurance coverage for, and thus no assured access to, medically necessary services, although by law they cannot be denied emergency services. In some developing countries, there is a constitutional right to health care, though the assertion of this legal right is often not matched by health care adequate to meet population needs.

Internationally, there is a legal framework that recognizes a human right to health and health care as the result of covenants and treaties signed by many countries. This international legal framework assigns primary responsibility for assuring the "progressive realization" of a right to health and health care to signatory governments. It also affirms a duty of signatory countries to assist other states in realizing such a right. The claim that persons have a (legal or moral) right to health (as opposed to health care) is contained in international human rights treaties, but it is considered to be conceptually confused by some. After all, if everything humanly possible is done to protect health, but it fails anyway, then no right is violated. A more charitable gloss on the claim to a right to health would understand it as a right to the fair distribution of the socially controllable factors that affect health and its distribution. These factors include personal medical services, public health protections, and the fair distribution of the social determinants of health, including various other rights, opportunities, education, income, and wealth (Daniels et al. 2000). In what follows, we shall restrict the discussion to a right to health care, understanding health care broadly to include both public health protections and personal medical services.

362

At the national level, the legal right to health care, in particular to personal medical services, is embodied in a wide variety of types of health-care systems. These range from national health services, where the government is the provider of services – as in Great Britain – to public insurance schemes, where the government finances services – as in Canada – to mixed public and private insurance schemes – as in Germany and the Netherlands. Despite these differences in the design of systems, there is a broad overlap in the scope or content of the legal right to health care in these countries. Most cover "medically necessary" services, including a broad range of preventive, curative, rehabilitative, and long-term care for physical and mental diseases, disorders, and disabilities. Most exclude uses of medical technologies that enhance otherwise normal functioning or appearance, such as purely cosmetic surgery. The legal rights vary in significant ways, however, for example in the degree to which they cover new reproductive technologies, or in the types of mental health and long-term care services that are offered.

In the context of rising costs and the rapid dissemination of new technologies, there is growing debate in many countries about how to set limits on the scope of a right to health care. This debate about the scope of a right to health care pushes moral deliberation about such a right into the forefront, even where a legal right is recognized. Legal entitlements, most people believe, should reflect what society is morally obliged to provide by way of medical services. What, then, is the basis and scope of a moral right to health care?

Positive vs negative rights

A right to health care is a *positive* as opposed to a *negative* right. Put quite simply, a positive right requires others to do something beneficial or enabling for right-bearers, whereas a negative right requires others to refrain from doing something, usually harmful or restrictive, to right-bearers. To say that others are required to do something or to refrain from doing something is to say they must so act or refrain even if they could produce more good or improve the world by not doing so (Thomson 1990). For example, a negative right to free expression requires others to refrain from censuring the expression of the right-bearer even if censuring this speech would make a better world. Some public health measures that protect people against interference with their health, such as environmental protections that protect people against polluters of air, water, and food sources, might be construed as requirements of a negative right. More generally, however, a right to health care imposes an obligation on others to assist the right-bearers in obtaining needed and appropriate services. Specifically, claiming a right to health care includes these other claims: society has the duty to its members to allocate an adequate share of its total resources to health-related needs; society has the duty to provide a just allocation of different types of health-care services, taking into account the competing claims of different types of health-care needs, ranging from protections against certain kinds of risks to treatment for disease, injury, and other kinds of health impairments; each person is entitled to a fair share of such services, where a "fair share" includes an answer to the question, "Who should pay for the services?" (Daniels 1985). Health-care rights thus form a part of a broader family of positive "welfare" rights that includes rights to education and income support. Because

363

positive rights require other people to contribute their resources or skills to benefit right-bearers, rather than merely refraining from interfering with them, they have often been thought more difficult to justify than negative rights, and their scope and limits have been harder to characterize.

Theories of justice and rights to health care

If we are to think of a right to health care as a requirement of justice, then we should look to more general theories of justice as a way to specify the scope and limits of that right. On some theories of justice, however, there is little basis for requiring people to assist others by meeting their health care or other needs. Libertarians, for example, believe that fundamental rights to property, including rights to personal assets such as talents and skills, are violated if society coerces individuals into providing "needed" resources or skills (Nozick 1974). Some libertarians recognize an "imperfect" duty to act beneficently or charitably, but this duty involves discretion. It can be discharged in different ways that are matters of choice. People denied charity have no right to it and have no complaint against people who act charitably in other ways. Though some have argued that the difficulty of coordinating the delivery of charitable assistance might justify coercive measures (Buchanan 1984), and others have tried to show that even libertarians must recognize some forms of welfare rights (Sterba 1985), most libertarians resist any weakening of the property rights at the core of their view (Brennan and Friedman 1981).

A specter sometimes raised by libertarians against the idea of a right to health care is that such a right is a "bottomless pit." Since new technologies continuously expand the scope of "medical needs," a right to health care would give rise to unlimited claims on the resources of others (Engelhardt 1986; Fried 1969). Protecting such an expansive right to health care would not be compatible with the function of a libertarian "minimal state" to assure the non-violation of rights to liberty and property.

Though there remains controversy about whether utilitarians can provide a basis for recognizing true moral rights, there are strong utilitarian arguments in favor of governments assuring access to at least some broad range of effective medical services. Preventing or curing disease or disability reduces suffering and enables people to function in ways that contribute to aggregate welfare. In addition, knowing that health-care services are available increases personal security and strengthens the ties of community. Utilitarians can also justify redistributing the burden of delivering these benefits to society as a whole, citing the decreasing marginal utility of money to support progressive financing of health-care services (Brandt 1979).

Beneath these quite general arguments, however, there lies a more specific controversy about the scope of utilitarian entitlements to health care. There seems to be little utilitarian justification for investing resources in health care if those resources would produce more net welfare when invested in other things, yet many people believe they have moral obligations to assist others with their health-care needs even at a net cost in utility. For example, some highly expensive and effective medical treatments that most people believe should be offered to people might not be "cost beneficial" and thus not defensible on utilitarian grounds. Similarly, many forms of long-term care, especially for those who cannot be restored to productive social activity, are also difficult to defend on utilitarian grounds, yet we insist our health-care systems are obliged to provide such services.

Lack of moral acceptance of the distributive implications of utilitarianism makes many uncomfortable with the use of methods, such as cost-effectiveness analysis (CEA), that are intended to guide decisions about resource allocation in health care. For example, an assumption of CEA is that a unit of health benefit, such as a quality-adjusted life year (QALY), is of equal value or importance regardless of where it is distributed. But this assumption does not capture the concerns many people have about the degree of priority we should give to the sickest patients, or the view that it is more important to deliver a greater benefit to fewer people than it is to maximize the aggregate benefit by giving a more modest benefit to a larger number of people (Daniels 1993; Nord 1993).

Two points about a utilitarian framework for a right to health care are worth noting. Recognizing a right to health care is compatible with recognizing limits on entitlements that result from resource scarcity and the fact that there are competing uses of those resources. Consequently, recognizing a right to health care need not open a bottomless pit. Second, just what entitlements to services follow from a right to health care cannot be specified outside the context of a *system* properly designed to deliver health care in a way that promotes aggregate utility. For the utilitarian, entitlements are *system-relative*. The same two points apply to other accounts of the foundations and limits of a right to health care.

Because many people reject the utilitarian rationales for health care (and other welfare) rights, theorists have explored other ways to ground such rights. Some claim that these rights are presupposed as enabling conditions for the exercise of other rights or liberties, or as practical presuppositions of all views of justice (Braybrooke 1987) or as a way of avoiding vulnerability and exploitation (Goodin 1988). One approach that has been developed in some detail views a right to health care as a special case of a right to equality of opportunity (Daniels 1985). This approach shows how the most important contractarian theory of justice, Rawls's (1971) account of justice as fairness, can be extended to the problem of health care, since that theory gives prominence to a principle protecting equality of opportunity (Rawls 1993). Without endorsing that account here, we shall use it to illustrate further the complexity surrounding the concept of a right to health care.

Equal opportunity and a right to health care

The central observation underlying this account of a right to health care is that disease and disability restrict the range of opportunities that would otherwise be open to individuals – that is, that it would be reasonable for people to incorporate within their plans of life. This is true whether they shorten our lives or impair our ability to function, including through pain and suffering. Health care in all its forms, whether public health protections or medical, preventive, acute, or chronic care, aims to keep people functioning as close to normally as possible. Since we are complex social creatures, our normal functional capabilities include our capabilities for emotional and cognitive functioning, not just our physical capabilities. Health care thus preserves for us the range of exercisable opportunities we would have, were we not ill or disabled, given our talents and skills.

The significant contribution health care makes to protecting the range of opportunities open to individuals is nevertheless *limited* in two important ways. It is limited because other things, such as the distribution of wealth, income, and education, also profoundly affect equality of opportunity. It is also limited because health care, by restricting its aim to protecting normal functioning, leaves the normal distribution of talents and skills unmodified. It aims to help us function as "normal" competitors and cooperators, not strictly equal ones.

It might seem that other recent work on egalitarian approaches to distributive justice would abandon the limit involved in the appeal to normal functioning. For example, early formulations of the view that the target of justice is equality of opportunity for welfare or advantage (Arneson 1988; G. A. Cohen 1989) or equality of capabilities (Sen 1980; 1992) might seem to require us to use health-care technologies whenever doing so would equalize opportunity for welfare or advantage or equalize capabilities. For example, if through medical intervention we can "enhance" the otherwise normal capabilities of those who are at a competitive disadvantage, then our commitment to equality of opportunity requires us to do so. Obviously, this version of an equal opportunity account would vastly expand the moral requirements on medicine, yielding a right to health care much more expansive than any now embodied in actual systems and, arguably, one that would make administration of a health-care system unwieldy (Sabin and Daniels 1994).

The challenge from such views to a limit set by normal functioning is more apparent than real (Daniels 2008). The equal opportunity for welfare or advantage view was originally developed in order to avoid the "expensive taste" problem that confronted the theory that happiness (welfare) should be the object of egalitarian concerns (Dworkin 1981), but expensive preferences for non-pathological but medically correctable deficits in traits pose an analogous problem. Sen (1999) also moves away from an egalitarian view of capabilities to one that says we owe each other only sufficient sets of capabilities, which may imply that his view converges significantly with the normal functioning view. In any case, our concern for equality must be reconciled with considerations of liberty and efficiency in arriving at the overall requirements of justice (Cohen 1995; Daniels 1996; Sen 1992). Such a reconciliation seems to underlie the limits we commonly accept when we appeal to equality of opportunity. We generally believe that rights to equal opportunity are violated only if unfair social practices or preventable or curable diseases or disabilities interfere with the pursuit of reasonable plans of life within our society by making us lose competitive advantage. We accept, however, the fact that the natural distribution of talents and skills, working in an efficient market for them, will both enhance the social product and lead to inequalities in social outcomes. A just society will try to mitigate the effects of these inequalities in competitive advantage in other ways than by eliminating all eliminable differences in capabilities. For example, on Rawls's account, transfers that make the worst off as well off as they can be mitigate the effects on equality of allowing the natural distribution of talents and skills to enhance productivity. In what follows, the account of a right to health care rests on a more limited appeal to equal opportunity, one that takes the maintenance of normal functioning as a reasonable limit.

What Does a Right to Health Care Include?

System-relative entitlements

By making the right to health care a special case of rights to equality of opportunity, we arrive at a reasonable, albeit incomplete and imperfect, way of restricting its scope while still recognizing its importance. The account does not give individuals a basic right to have all their health-care needs met. At the same time, there are social obligations to design a health-care system that protects opportunity through an appropriate set of health-care services. If social obligations to provide appropriate health care are not met, then individuals are definitely wronged. For example, if people are denied access – because of discrimination or inability to pay – to a basic tier of services adequate to protect normal functioning, injustice is done to them. If the basic tier available to people omits important categories of services (for example, whole categories of mental health or long-term care or preventive services), without consideration of their effects on normal functioning, their rights are violated.

Still, not every medical need gives rise to an entitlement to services. The scope and limits of rights to health care – that is, the entitlements they actually carry with them – will be relative to certain facts about a given system. For example, a health-care system can protect opportunity only within the limits imposed by resource scarcity and technological development within a society. We cannot make a direct inference from the fact that an individual has a right to health care to the conclusion that this person is entitled to some specific health-care service, even if the service would meet a health-care need. Rather, the individual is entitled to a specific service only if, in the light of facts about a society's technological capabilities and resource limitations, it should be a part of a system that appropriately protects fair equality of opportunity. As we shall see shortly, reasonable people will disagree about what to include among these entitlements, and resolution of those disagreements will require a fair deliberative process. The equal opportunity account of a right to health care not only makes entitlements to health care system-relative, like the utilitarian account, but it must be supplemented with a fair process that ultimately determines the specifics of those entitlements.

Effective treatment of disease and disability

The health care we have strongest claim to is care that effectively promotes normal functioning by reducing the impact of disease and disability, thus protecting the range of opportunities that would otherwise be open to us. Just what counts as "effective," however? And what should we do about hard cases on the boundary between treatment of disease or disability and enhancement of capabilities?

It is a common feature of public and private insurance systems to limit care to treatments that are not "experimental" and have some "proven effectiveness." Unfortunately, many services that count as standard treatment have little direct evidence about outcomes to support their use (Hadorn 1992). They are often just customary treatment. Furthermore, it is often controversial just when new treatments or technologies should count as "safe and efficacious." What counts as "reasonably effective" is then a matter of judgment and depends on the kind of condition and the consequences of not correcting it. We might, for example, want to lower our standards for effectiveness when we face a treatment of last resort, or raise them if resource scarcity is very great. On the other hand, we do not owe people a chance to obtain miracles through whatever unproven procedures they prefer to try.

By focusing a right to health care on the maintenance of normal functioning, a line is drawn between uses of medical technologies that count as legitimate "treatments" and those that we may want but which do not meet our "health-care needs." Although we may want medical services that can enhance our appearance, like cosmetic (as opposed to reconstructive) plastic surgery, or that can optimize our otherwise normal functioning, like some forms of counseling or some uses of Prozac, we do not truly need these services to maintain normal functioning. We are obliged to help others achieve normal functioning, but we do not "owe" each other whatever it takes to make us more beautiful or strong or completely happy (Daniels 1985).

Though this line is widely used in both public and private insurance practices, it leaves us with hard cases. Some of the hardest issues involve reproductive technologies. Abortion, where there is no preventive or therapeutic need, does not count as "treatment" because an unwanted pregnancy is not a disease or disability. Some people nevertheless insist that requirements of justice, including a right to control one's body, mean that non-therapeutic abortion should be included as an entitlement in a health-care system. Some national health insurance schemes do not cover infertility services. Yet infertility is a departure from normal functioning, even if some people never want to bear children. Controversy may remain about how much social obligation we have to correct this form of impaired opportunity, especially where the costs of some interventions, such as *in vitro* fertilization, are high and their effectiveness is modest. Different societies will judge this question differently, in part because they may place different values on the rearing of biologically related children or on the experience of childbearing.

Hard cases involve non-reproductive technologies as well. In the United States, for example, many insurers will cover growth-hormone treatment only for children deficient in growth hormone, not for those who are equally short but without any pathology. Yet the children denied therapy will suffer just as much as those who are eligible. Similar difficulties are involved in drawing a line between covered and non-covered uses of mental health services (Sabin and Daniels 1994). As in the cases of reproductive technologies, there is room for different societies to "construct" the concept of mental disorder somewhat differently, with resulting variation in decisions about insurance coverage.

Rights and limits on effective treatments

Even when some health-care service is reasonably effective at meeting a medical need, not all such needs are equally important. When a disease or disability has little impact on the range of opportunities open to someone, it is not as morally important to treat as other conditions that more seriously impair opportunity. The effect on opportunity thus gives us some guidance in thinking about resource allocation priorities.

Unfortunately, the impact on our range of opportunities gives only a crude and incomplete measure of the importance or priority we should give to a need or service.

In making decisions about priorities for purposes of resource allocation in health care, we face difficult questions about distributive fairness that are not answered by this measure of importance. For example, we must sometimes make a choice between investing in a technology that delivers a significant benefit to few people or one that delivers a more modest benefit to a larger number of people. Sometimes we must make a choice between investing in a service that helps the sickest, most impaired patients, or one that helps those whose functioning is less impaired. Sometimes we must decide between the fairness of giving a scarce resource to those who derive the largest benefit, or giving a broader range of people some chance at getting a benefit. In all these cases, we lack clear principles for deciding how to make our choices, and the account of a right to health care we are discussing does not provide those principles either (Daniels 1993). Some methodologies, like cost-effectiveness analysis, are intended to help us make appropriate resource allocation decisions in these kinds of cases. But these methodologies may themselves embody controversial moral assumptions about distributive fairness. This means they cannot serve as decision procedures for making these choices and can at best serve as aids to decision-makers who must be explicit about the moral reasoning that determines the distributive choices they make (Gold et al. 1996; IOM 2006).

In any health-care system, then, some choices will have to be made by a fair, publicly accountable, decision-making process. Just what constitutes a fair decision-making procedure for resolving moral disputes about health-care entitlements is itself a matter of controversy. It is a problem that has rarely been addressed in the literature. Our rights are not violated, however, if the choices that are made through fair decision-making procedures turn out to be ones that do not happen to meet our personal needs, but instead meet needs of others that are judged more important (Daniels and Sabin 2007).

Choice or Consent and the Exercise of our Right to Health Care

Our entitlements to personal medical services are mediated by individual choice in the following sense: we can, if competent and informed, refuse to accept what we are owed in the way of medical treatments. For example, we may consent to a "do not resuscitate" order and then providers no longer owe us efforts at resuscitation if our hearts stop. In the context of preventive, public health interventions, such choice or consent does not generally mediate the delivery of what is owed. Workers, for example, cannot insist on working in places where an airborne toxin exceeds some imposed safety standard; they cannot refuse the protection in the way they might a medical service. Choice thus plays different roles in our exercise of our right to medical services and our right to certain public health protections.

How equal must our rights to health care be?

How equal must our rights to health care be? Specifically, must everyone receive exactly the same kinds of health-care services and coverage, or is fairness in health care compatible with a "tiered" system? Around the world, even countries that offer universal health insurance differ in their answers to this question. In Canada and Norway,

369

for example, no supplementary insurance is permitted. Everyone is served solely by the national health insurance schemes, though people who seek additional services or more rapid service may go elsewhere, as some Canadians do by crossing the border. In Britain, supplementary private insurance results in about 10 percent of the population gaining quicker access to services for which there is extensive queuing in the public system. Basing a right to health care on an obligation to protect equality of opportunity is compatible with the sort of tiering the British have, but it does not require it, and it imposes some constraints on the kind of tiering allowed.

The primary social obligation is to assure everyone access to a tier of services that effectively promotes normal functioning and thus protects equality of opportunity. Since health care is not the only important good, resources to be invested in the basic tier are appropriately and reasonably limited – for example, by democratic decisions about how much to invest in education or job training as opposed to health care. Because of their very high "opportunity costs," there will be some beneficial medical services that it will be reasonable not to provide in the basic tier, or to provide only on a limited basis – for example, with queuing. To say that these services have "high opportunity costs" means that providing them consumes resources that would produce greater health or other benefits, and protect opportunity more, if used in alternative ways.

In a society that permits significant income and wealth inequalities, some people will want to buy coverage for these additional services. Why not let them? After all, we allow people to use their after-tax income and wealth as they see fit to pursue the "quality of life" and opportunities they prefer. The rich can buy special security systems for their homes. They can buy safer cars. They can buy private schooling for their children. Why not allow them to buy supplementary health care for their families?

One objection to allowing a supplementary tier is that its existence might undermine the basic tier either economically or politically. It might attract better-quality providers away from the basic tier, or raise costs in the basic tier, reducing the ability of society to meet its social obligations. The supplementary tier might undermine political support for the basic tier – for example, by undercutting the social solidarity needed if people are to remain committed to protecting opportunity for all. These objections are serious, and where a supplementary tier undermines the basic tier in either way, economically or politically, priority must be given to protecting the basic tier. In principle, however, it seems possible to design a system in which the supplementary tier does not undermine the basic one. If that can be done, then a system that permits tiering avoids restricting liberty in ways that some find seriously objectionable.

A second objection is not to tiering itself, but to the structure of inequality that results. Compare two scenarios. In one, most people are adequately served by the basic tier and only the best-off groups in society have the means to, and see the need to, purchase supplementary insurance. That is the case in Great Britain. In another, the basic tier serves only the poorest groups in society and most other people buy supplementary insurance. The Oregon plan to expand Medicaid eligibility partly through rationing the services it covers has aspects of this structure of inequality, since most people are covered by plans that avoid these restrictions (Daniels 1991). The first scenario seems preferable to the second on grounds of fairness. In the second, the poorest groups can complain that they are left behind by most others in society even in the protection of their health. In the first, the majority have fewer grounds for reasonable resentment or regret.

If the basic tier is not undermined by higher tiers, and if the structure of the inequality that results is not objectionable, then it is difficult to see why some tiering should not be allowed. There is a basic conflict here between concerns about equality and concerns about liberty, between wanting to make sure everyone is treated properly with regard to health care and wanting to give people the liberty to use their resources (after tax) to improve their lives as they see fit. In practice, the crucial constraint on the liberty we allow people seems to depend on the magnitude of the benefit available in the supplementary tier and unavailable in the basic tier. Highly visible forms of saving lives and improving function would be difficult to exclude from the basic tier while we make them available in a supplementary tier. In principle, however, some forms of tiering will not be unfair even when they involve medical benefits not available to everyone.

References

Arneson, R. (1988). Equality and equal opportunity for welfare. *Philosophical Studies* 54: 79–95.

Brandt, R. (1979). *A Theory of the Good and the Right*. Oxford: Oxford University Press.

Braybrooke, D. (1987). *Meeting Needs*. Princeton, NJ: Princeton University Press.

Brennan, G. and Friedman, D. (1981). A libertarian perspective on welfare. In P. G. Brown, C. Johnson, and P. Vernier (eds.), *Income Support: Conceptual and Policy Issues*. Totowa, NJ: Rowman & Littlefield.

Buchanan, A. (1984). The right to a decent minimum of health care. *Philosophy and Public Affairs* 13: 55–78.

Cohen, G. A. (1989). On the currency of egalitarian justice. *Ethics* 99: 906–44.

Cohen, J. (1995). Amartya Sen: *Inequality Reexamined. Journal of Philosophy* 92/5: 275–88.

Daniels, N. (1985). *Just Health Care*. Cambridge: Cambridge University Press.

Daniels, N. (1991). Is the Oregon rationing plan fair? *Journal of the American Medical Association* 265: 2232–5.

Daniels, N. (1993). Rationing fairly: programmatic considerations. *Bioethics* 7: 224–33.

Daniels, N. (1996). *Justice and Justification: Reflective Equilibrium in Theory and Practice*. Cambridge: Cambridge University Press.

Daniels, N. (2008). *Just Health: Meeting Health Needs Fairly*. New York: Cambridge University Press.

Daniels, N. and Sabin, J. (2007). *Setting Limits Fairly: Can We Learn to Share Medical Resources?* 2nd edn. New York: Oxford University Press.

Daniels, N., Kennedy, B., and Kawachi, I. (2000). *Is Inequality Bad For Our Health?* Boston, MA: Beacon Press.

Dworkin, R. (1981). What is equality? Part 1: equality of welfare. *Philosophy and Public Affairs* 10: 185–246.

Engelhardt, H. T. (1986). *The Foundations of Bioethics*. Oxford: Oxford University Press.

Fried, C. (1969). *An Anatomy of Value*. Cambridge, MA: Harvard University Press.

Gold, M., Siegel, J., Russell, L., and Weinstein, M. (eds.) (1996). *Cost-Effectiveness in Health and Medicine: Recommendations of the Panel on Cost-effectiveness in Health and Medicine*. New York: Oxford University Press.

Goodin, R. (1988). *Reasons for Welfare*. Princeton, NJ: Princeton University Press.

Hadorn, D. (ed.) (1992). *Basic Benefits and Clinical Guidelines*. Boulder, CO: Westview Press.

IOM (Institute of Medicine) (2006). *Valuing Health: Cost-effectiveness in Regulatory Settings*. Washington, DC: National Academies Press.

Nord, E. (1993). The relevance of health state after treatment in prioritizing between different patients. *Journal of Medical Ethics* 19: 37–42.

Nozick, R. (1974). *Anarchy, State, and Utopia*. New York: Basic Books.

Rawls, J. (1971). *A Theory of Justice*. Cambridge, MA: Harvard University Press.

Rawls, J. (1993). *Political Liberalism*. New York: Columbia University Press.

Sabin, J. and Daniels, N. (1994). Determining "medical necessity" in mental health practice. *Hastings Center Report* 24/6: 5–13.

Sen, A. K. (1980). Equality of what? In S. McMurrin (ed.), *The Tanner Lectures on Human Values*. Salt Lake City: University of Utah Press.

Sen, A. (1992). *Inequality Reexamined*. Cambridge, MA: Harvard University Press.

Sen, A. (1999). *Development as Freedom*. New York: Alfred Knopf.

Sterba, J. (1985). From liberty to welfare. *Social Theory and Practice* 11: 285–305.

Thomson, J. (1990). *The Realm of Rights*. Cambridge, MA: Harvard University Press.

Part IX

Organ Donations

32

A World of Transferable Parts

JANET RADCLIFFE RICHARDS

Introduction

Many of the moral problems raised by transplantation are familiar from other areas of medicine. There are all the usual clinical issues of risk, autonomy, and consent, for instance, as well as all the wider questions about distributive justice. There are also, as in other areas, special problems about treatment of children and non-competent adults. But there is one set of problems distinctive to transplantation, in that any organ given to one person must first be taken from another. For every recipient there must be a donor, and the moral problems peculiar to transplantation are nearly all, in one way or another, concerned with procurement.

From the point of view of potential recipients, transplantation appears as a straightforward good, offering the chance of life, or at least of freedom from the crushing constraints of chronic illness or dialysis. But even to the extent that expertise and facilities are available and affordable, the possibilities for transplantation are limited by the fact that there are nowhere near enough donated organs to go round (Abouna 2008). Increased efforts are being made to train transplant coordinators and make both professionals and the public more sympathetic to donation (Kemp et al. 2008), but although these efforts are all to the good, and have some success (Smith and Murphy 2008), they leave the fundamentals untouched. All these campaigns, and all individual decisions, take place against a social framework of laws, conventions, and institutions that themselves constrain procurement.

It is hardly surprising that the framework should have such a tendency. Our rules about the treatment of people and bodies, both living and dead, long predate much possibility of using parts of one person to remedy the defects of another, and therefore naturally tend to concentrate on the interests of the people we now see as potential donors in ways that impede procurement. Some of these constraints may, however, turn out to be rooted in ideas no longer accepted as the basis of our moral and political thinking. Others, although reflecting justifiable concerns, may not be important enough to outweigh the benefits the new technology can bring. Given that people are dying every day because of the shortage of organs, there is at the very least a case for rethinking all legal and institutional impediments to procurement.

The starting point of this chapter is that anyone who regards the preservation of life by transplantation as intrinsically desirable must recognize an a priori *presumption* in favor of removing any policy that restricts, or probably restricts, the acquisition of organs for that purpose. Any presumption is, of course, potentially defeasible, and sometimes the objections seem so obvious that it may be difficult to recognize even that the presumption exists. As John Harris pointed out some years ago (Harris 1986), we could guarantee the availability of organs by agreeing to enter a lottery that, whenever needed, selected a random victim whose organs would be used as spare parts for half a dozen others; but although such an arrangement would increase the life expectancy of all participants, it seems to be something nobody would want to enter. However, the fact that some existing constraints on procurement seem beyond question does not imply that all must be, and starting with the presumption in favor of procurement is methodologically invaluable. It shifts the usual dynamics of the argument by emphasizing the costs of keeping to currently accepted legal and ethical standards, and demonstrating the case for rethinking them.

Policies and attitudes that constrain procurement vary considerably between societies, and no attempt will be made here to describe those variations. This chapter must be understood as presenting only a series of conditionals: *if* anyone defends this or that transplantation-obstructing law or convention, *then* these are the challenges they need to meet. The arguments give some suggestion of the problems that need to be thought through.

Procurement From the Dead

Variation between societies shows particularly strongly in laws and customs for treatment of the dead, but, in most countries today, cadaveric donation of organs is regarded as a matter for personal decision by individuals and families. Even if this starting-point is taken for granted, however, there is still considerable scope for different opinions about how such choices should be made, and different arrangements are bound to affect the number of organs available.

Opting in and out

If it is accepted that you should have the right to decide for or against posthumous donation, the next question is whether your organs should be used only if you have expressed a positive wish to donate (opted in to the donor register), or merely failed to refuse (not opted out).

From the point of view of maximizing procurement, the opting-out system must be presumptively better, since even the well intentioned may simply not get round to opting in. But the converse of this claim is precisely the objection brought by the opposition. You may not get round to opting out either, or even know about the need to do so, and then your organs would be used in contravention of your right to determine what happened to your own body (Verheijde et al. 2008).

However, the issue here is not the right to determine whether your body is used or not, since both options allow that right. The question is only about the direction of default if you fail to express a preference. It is now generally taken for granted that positive consent is required for any medical intervention in the living body of a competent adult, and the opting-in system amounts to extending this presumption to the dead. But even if seems clear that the living should be presumptively inviolable, it is not at all obvious that the same should apply to the dead, whose interests, if they have any, are very different. The question at least needs separate consideration.

The issue is probably best understood as calling for a risk analysis. In cases where no preference has been expressed, is it better to take the organs or not? Either course risks a bad outcome, since if we do not take them, we risk letting someone die (or suffer) for want of an organ to whose use its source would not have objected, and if we take them to prevent that death or suffering, we risk using an organ whose source would have objected. Which risk is it better to take? This depends on two matters: the relative badness of the two bad outcomes, and the probability that each will occur.

From the point of view of the enquirer, the first question is a matter of fundamental values. Do you think it more important to ensure that no life is lost unnecessarily or that no organ is used against the former wishes of its source? (Note that this question is not about your personal preferences for yourself, since if you were thinking about the matter at all you could arrange to opt out. The issue is the treatment of people in general.)

Perhaps some people may conclude that wishes of the now-dead source are more important than the interests of the living. But equally significant, from the point of view of risk, is the likelihood that each harm will occur. Who are more likely not to get round to making their preferences known: the opters out or the opters in? This is an empirical question (see, e.g., Johnson and Goldstein 2003), but even without direct evidence, it seems likely that people would be far more likely to take the trouble to opt out, if that were necessary, than to opt in. Most people are much more likely to get round to protecting their own interests than those of unknown others, and people with the strongest objections are likely to belong to cultural or religious groups which would be anxious to make sure their members got round to it. And even among the most altruistic would-be donors, the ones with the most valuable organs are precisely the ones who are young and well enough to think there is plenty of time to plan for death.

If this is so, then it seems that to recommend opting in rather than out, you need to claim that it is overwhelmingly more important to protect the possible posthumous interests of people who are unaware of the need to opt out (and therefore will never know anything of the matter) than to save the lives of living people. This does seem a surprising position for anyone to hold, and certainly hard to justify in societies whose laws have a secular basis.

Family veto

The next obstacle to increased rates of cadaveric procurement is allowing veto by relatives. Even in countries where families have no legal right of veto, it is nevertheless almost universally allowed in practice, and since many families do refuse, it must be presumed that disallowing their veto would significantly increase donation rates (Downie et al. 2008).

In some countries, traditions of family relationships may be so deep that any such change would be unthinkable (Lock 2002), but the question can be asked about places where individuals' rights to self-determination generally prevail over family en-titlements. In such places, what objection could be raised to a removal of veto?

The most obvious objection is that such an arrangement would cause suffering to an already grieving family. But to assess the force of that objection, it is again necessary to raise two questions: how much suffering would the removal of family veto actually cause, and is preventing such suffering worth the cost of preventable death in patients waiting for transplants? The first question is empirical, and it may seem obvious that, since so many families do object, a change would indeed cause significant suffering (Eckenrod 2008). But this is not necessarily true: the distress may lie less in the procurement itself than in the idea of giving permission for it. The very fact of families' being asked implies that the responsibility is theirs, and as the recently bereaved still often feel a strong duty of care to the deceased, it is not surprising that many find it difficult to consent to what seems like an assault. But if it were taken for granted that the wishes of the deceased would be implemented automatically – as in the case of wills – and that everything went ahead routinely behind the scenes, it is not obvious that families would suffer any more than they now do from legally required post-mortems, or indeed from what goes on in the handling of bodies by under-takers. There is also the question of how likely it is that the situation would arise, since, if you knew your family would feel strongly about the matter, you could either opt out of donation or specify that the family should make the decision. This suggests that nearly all the cases where the family would suffer would be ones where the would-be donor's views were significantly at odds with those of the family.

If so, the conclusion is this. To justify the continuing of the family veto, you need to claim not only that the suffering and death of the living – and the distress of their own families – are less important than the sensibilities of the bereaved, but also that they are more important than the wishes of the deceased themselves. If it is, in addition, true that such suffering would be considerably diminished by the removal of the feeling of responsibility that comes with the present requesting of permission, it is difficult to see how the continuing of family veto can be justified in countries that generally give individuals the right to determine their own interests. At the very least, it must be worth experimenting with a change in arrangements.

Directed donation

At present, deceased donation is typically anonymous, with donors having no say in the destination of their organs, and recipients not knowing who the donors were. But many people with a disinclination to donate might be much more willing if they felt some affinity with the eventual recipient. Many transplant coordinators, worried about low donation rates among minority groups, think the supply might increase if potential donors thought their organs would go to people they particularly cared about, rather than being taken by an anonymous establishment for use by strangers (Volk and Ubel 2008). Some potential donors already try to impose conditions on the destination of their organs. We could almost certainly increase the donation rate by allowing some kinds of directed donation.

The first objection usually raised to this suggestion – and presented as if it were decisive – is that it would allow for racism. This is one of the contexts in which it is necessary to ask many background questions. Is it clear, for instance, where commendable community-mindedness ends and objectionable racism begins? Is it obviously better to allow potential recipients to die than save them with the (corrupt?) organs of racists? We do not normally assess the moral character of donors and families before accepting their donations. More fundamentally, however, no objection based on the unacceptability of particular kinds of specification can work as a justification for rejecting directed donation as such, because we could, if we wanted to, easily rule out any specifications regarded as objectionable while still allowing others. There are many forms a system of directed donation might take, and we might reasonably expect to experiment until we found the one that produced the greatest increase in donations with the fewest drawbacks. Objections to racist specifications in particular cannot justify an outright rejection of directed donation of any kind.

A wider objection, that would indeed rule out directed donation altogether, is "the fundamental principle that organs are donated altruistically and should go to patients in the greatest need" (Department of Health 2000: 25). But attractive as this may sound, with its invocation of altruism and its concern with needs, it runs into serious difficulties. The most fundamental of these is that the application of any general principle of distribution – distribution on the basis of need, or merit, or age, or anything else – *presupposes* that the goods being distributed are to be regarded as public goods. This must be true, because the essence of private goods is that they are not available for general distribution, and it means that the first thing that advocates of the "fundamental principle" need to establish is that donated organs should indeed be regarded as public goods.

Some bioethicists do argue that all usable parts of the dead should be regarded in this way, and taken over automatically by the state for distribution on the basis of need. This, however, is not the claim being made by opponents of directed donation within the present system, because that depends on altruistic willingness to donate rather than compulsory requisition. This means, in effect, that your organs are being treated as private goods to the extent that you can choose whether to donate them or not, but that if you do choose to donate them, your only option is to offer them as public goods for general distribution. This is like saying that although you can choose whether to offer your spare time for voluntary work, you cannot choose to offer it (altruistically) to the local Oxfam shop, but must make yourself available to some public agency that will send you to wherever it decides needs you most. Or – a closer analogy with posthumous organ donation – it is like saying that you may not bequeath your worldly wealth to the Methodist Homes for the Aged: you can have it buried with you, if you like, but must otherwise hand it over to the government for impartial distribution. Nobody, presumably, would recommend either of these curious mixtures of choice and conscription.

There are endless controversies about which of the goods individuals like to regard as their own should be taken for public use and which left as private, and about the allowable uses of either, but in no other context does anyone seem to recommend that the only option for private goods is to make them public or waste them altogether. In the absence of considerable further argument, the so-called "fundamental principle" ruling out directed donation must be recognized as arbitrary, anomalous, at odds with all our other ideas about altruistic giving, and difficult to defend in any terms whatever. More specifically, it is totally incompatible with our procedures for living donation, which

379

is almost always directed. Nobody suggests that if your sister desperately needs a kidney, all you can do is offer yours to whoever is at the top of the waiting list.

The claim that directed donation would increase the overall supply is an empirical one that needs testing. The confused inadequacy of the objections suggests that it certainly should be tested, at least as long as anything like current systems of distribution persist. The suggestion might become irrelevant, however, in the light of the next point.

Compulsion and reciprocity

If the aim is to get as many organs as possible for life-saving transplants, the most obvious way to improve the situation is to give individuals no choice at all about donation. Perhaps the state should just impound all dead bodies, as a kind of death duty, taking any usable parts for the benefit of the living.

This has often been suggested (e.g. Spital 2005); and, as we know that attitudes to the proper treatment of the dead can change, it is perhaps something to be aimed for in the long run. At present, however, it does not seem to be on the political map; and of course if people think it more important to preserve their veto over the use of their dead body than to increase their life expectancy by a change of rules that would make transplants more available, that is up to them.

At the moment, however, this is not the situation. People who are unwilling to donate do not at present lessen their own chances of receiving a transplant, because the organs available are distributed impartially among those who need them, and this suggests a quite different possible remedy for the shortfall. As well as trying to increase supply, we could lessen demand by making ineligible for transplantation any adult who had opted out of the transplantation register. And since presumably – in the long run, at least – such a provision would provide a considerable disincentive to opting out, the effect would eventually be to lessen the discrepancy between supply and demand by the more desirable means of increasing supply (Jarvis 1995; see also the discussion between Murphy and Veatch 2006 and Tabarrok and Undis 2006).

This is such an obvious idea – maximizing freedom of choice at the same time as providing incentives to donate – that it is curious to consider why it has not been taken for granted from an early stage. The intuitive objection seems to be that of injustice: the idea that medical treatment should be given strictly on the basis of need. That is of course an attractive idea in itself, but, when it comes to the point, hardly anyone will find they hold views about access on the basis of need in such an unqualified way. If people are to have a right to public goods, someone must have the duty to supply them, and for that reason rights of access (as opposed to charitable donations) always have implied boundaries. There are two main ways in which we organize entitlement on the basis of need. One is by specifying a group, such as the nationals or inhabitants of a country, and giving all of them access to goods such as health care on the basis of need, while at the same time requiring appropriate contribution through taxation ("from each according to his means"). The other is to form a group of people who choose to contribute and in return have access to benefits, as in the case of private insurance. Both these methods have their defenders, but no one seems to defend the hybrid version – that you can choose not to contribute, while retaining equal access to benefits – which is just the situation we have in the case of organ donation.

Reciprocity is positively demanded by all our normal principles about the distribution of common goods on the basis of need. If at the same time we want to allow freedom of choice about contribution, it is difficult to see what principled objection anyone could have to trying to devise a policy that restricted benefits to potential contributors.

Procurement From the Living

There are some ways in which procurement from the living raises fewer problems than procurement from the dead, because the living are still there to give or refuse consent. But there are contexts in which even when competent consent is apparently offered, procurement may still not be allowed. There are several of these. For instance, there are legal limits to the extent to which harm to others is allowable, even with consent: a surgeon is not allowed to go along with your wish to donate your heart (e.g. Human Tissue Act 2004). There are also many obstacles placed in the way of donation by so-called "altruistic" living donors – ones who offer to donate to anyone in need – and to potential donors in particular situations, such as prisoners. However, theoretically interesting as all these areas are, they are at present of relatively little practical importance. By far the most significant issue in this area is the widespread, almost universal, prohibition of payment for kidney donation. This has far-reaching practical effects, and also illustrates particularly well the way arguments can be distorted by strong feelings (Radcliffe Richards 1996).

Paid donation

Once again, the discussion needs to begin with the recognition that transplantation saves lives, and that many people will offer otherwise unavailable organs in return for payment. It must be presumed that the prohibition of organ-selling results in many deaths.

The most familiar objections to allowing sales are based on horror stories about the fates of vendors. Campaigners and journalists bring reports of exploitation, cheating, shoddy operations, lack of counseling and follow up, and a train of vendors with damaged health and no lasting benefit to compensate. Inevitably, there are questions about the extent to which these stories are either true or representative, but, even on the assumption that they are both, that does not mean that they justify the current prohibition on selling.

It must be remembered that living donation is now in itself so safe that many surgeons encourage it. The only obvious difference between paid and unpaid donation, from the point of view of the donor, is that the vendor receives something in return – and that, to all appearances, is a positive advantage. This means that if vendors are in practice disproportionately harmed, it must be because of something to do with the surrounding circumstances rather than the removal of the organ itself. The reasons may be complex, but it is striking that the kinds of harm reported are exactly what is to be expected of a black market – and as long as prohibition continues, the market is inevitably black. People who are desperate for life on the one hand and money on the other will get together somehow, and the only way to protect them is to legalize paid donation so that some control is possible (Wilkinson 2003). We may never be able to

381

protect everyone, but at the moment we can protect no one. The current horror stories are therefore part of the case for ending prohibition, not for continuing it.

Another set of objections is that the consent of the vendors is not genuine. The first version of this line of argument is that the donors come from populations too poor and ignorant to give informed consent (Sells 1993). One problem with this idea is that these same populations seem to be regarded as competent to consent to all other medical procedures, including unpaid organ donation. But, quite apart from that, you cannot rule out particular *procedures* on the grounds that some – or even many – of the people who may present themselves are not competent to consent, because competence is about individuals. If the argument seems to work, it is probably because of the question-begging assumption that anyone inclined to consent must *ipso facto* be non-competent. Such an idea undoubtedly does lurk in the background of incompetence claims, but there is nothing irrational – by any normal standards – about consenting to a minimally risky procedure for a significant reward. And, indeed, the worse off the person involved, the smaller the reward need be to provide a rational justification of the risk.

Another version of the argument is that the consent is invalidated by coercion. The vendors, it is said, are coerced by poverty, and coerced consent is not genuine (Dossetor and Kjellstrand 1992). This objection conflates several issues, which take some unraveling (Radcliffe Richards 1996), but the essence of the matter is this. The coercion referred to is a matter of having so few options that people make choices they would rather not make. But if organ-selling is the best option the poor have open to them, you cannot help them by reducing the range of options still further and forcing them into something they regard as even worse. The only way you can help is to give them *more* options, ideally by lessening their poverty.

To this it is replied that of course that is just what we should be doing: lifting the poor out of poverty (Dossetor and Kjellstrand 1992). No one could reasonably dispute that, but, as so often with arguments in this area, the benevolent premise does not support the required conclusion. If we could make everyone so well off that no one wanted to sell, prohibition would be pointless because it would have nothing to do. Conversely, as long as anyone does want to sell, there must be some people for whom selling is the best option, and who are made worse off by prohibition.

An even more familiar defense of prohibition is the already mentioned, and frequently invoked, principle that organ donation must be altruistic, but this also runs into confusion. To start with, altruism in its normal sense cannot make a systematic distinction between giving and selling, since you may have altruistic reasons – such as paying for your children's education or medical treatment – for wanting to sell organs or anything else. Conversely, you may have thoroughly non-altruistic reasons – fears of rejection or resentment, hopes of reward – for giving anything. This means that a principle of altruism can be used to justify a conclusion against selling only if altruism is defined in the first place in terms of non-selling, in which case the argument is question begging. Second, the supposed requirement of altruism in either of these senses – selflessness or non payment – is anyway totally arbitrary, completely out of line with our ideas in other contexts. We may encourage and praise selflessness and gift-giving, but there is no other context in which we say that unless you can get someone to give what you need as a gift, purely out of the goodness of their hearts, you must do without whatever it is entirely – let alone die – rather than pay for it. The idea is manifestly absurd, and no reason is offered for thinking it any less so in the context of organ procurement.

A similar set of problems faces another familiar claim: that allowing sales is a contravention of human dignity (Cohen 2002). Unless there is an independent account of human dignity, this argument is also question-begging, and any account of human dignity compatible with the ideas of autonomy used as the basis of most modern law-making will not support the conclusion.

These arguments (and many others not mentioned here) all try to justify the prohibition of organ-selling by invoking principles from which it is alleged to follow, and they all run into difficulties either because the principles are themselves not accepted by their proponents in other contexts, or because the principles do not support the conclusions, or both. But a quite different kind of argument – widespread in all parts of the transplantation debate, and in ethics controversies in general – is that if policies were changed there would be adverse consequences so great as to outweigh any anticipated benefit. In the organ-selling controversy, for instance, it is often claimed that the effect of allowing sales would be to reduce the rate of voluntary donation (Dougherty 1987).

Claims of this kind cannot be rejected a priori, since any policy may turn out to have unintended and unexpected consequences. However, much can be said about the methodology of the approach. Once again, if transplants are an intrinsically good thing, there is a presumption in favor of any policy that will increase their availability. To defeat that presumption, it is not enough to raise *possible* harms: there needs to be strong enough evidence (not just the intuitions of the opponent) that such harms will actually occur, and will be greater than the corresponding good. Furthermore, even if there is such evidence, anyone who recognizes the good will try to devise ways of keeping as much as possible of it while lessening the bad. There are potential harms in all areas of buying and selling, but it does not usually occur to us to try to prevent buying and selling altogether: we try to contain the harm with safeguards of various kinds, while allowing as much scope as possible for the good. Arguments of this form need to be watched with care, as they are often last-ditch attempts to rationalize preconceptions that seem to be defying other attempts at justification.

This list nowhere near exhausts the range of arguments in support of prohibition – ingenuity is infinite when there are strong feelings to defend (Radcliffe Richards 1996; Radcliffe Richards et al. 1998). But these illustrations should at least show that the case for prohibition of organ-selling is nothing like as clear as it may seem, and give some indication of where to look in assessing other candidate arguments as they appear.

The Transition from Life to Death

A quite different set of problems about procurement from the dead arises from the fact that successful transplantation depends critically on the freshness of the organs, and there are several legal obstacles to preservation of organs in the best possible state. The underlying issues have far-reaching implications in many parts of medicine, but they arise with particular acuteness in the transplantation context.

The interests of the donor

A competent patient may consent to any treatment that does not exceed legally acceptable limits of harm. But near the end of life, patients often become non-competent, and under those circumstances there is a widespread legal requirement that treatment must be solely in the interests of the patient (DeVita and Caplan 2007). This means that work to preserve the organs cannot begin until after death, and that many organs are lost or at least damaged as a result.

The justification for these restrictions is presumably that living people should not be treated, without their consent, as means to other people's ends. There are, however, various ways of countering this as an objection to pre-mortem organ preparation. The simplest is to claim – strongly in line with current trends in mental capacity law – that if you become non-competent your interests should be understood in terms of what you would have wanted when you were competent, and willing donors would want their organs kept in a usable state (see Human Tissue Authority 2006).

A more radical proposal would be that once patients became permanently non-competent, it should be allowable to give any treatment that did not actually harm them. This is more controversial, and a first step on to the tricky ground of the next section.

The dead donor rule

The better the condition of the organs, the better the prospects for success in transplantation. But for cadaveric donation, the donor must be dead, and the dying process necessarily involves the deterioration of organs – since that, of course, is what dying is. The earlier organs can be collected the better, which is why living kidney donation is preferred by so many surgeons, but you cannot take most major organs from the living without actually killing them.

On the other hand, it is arguable that there are circumstances when you might take even vital organs from the living without *harming* them. If someone has lost all interest in being alive – through permanent unconsciousness, for example – it can be argued that it would not be against their interests to remove vital organs before they were dead, or – which amounts to the same thing – hasten death to get the organs. If we could do this, we might considerably increase the number of available organs and the success rate of transplants.

The proposal that we should abandon the so-called "dead donor rule" has been made, but not widely pressed (Taylor 1997; Truog 1997). In most countries, the active, intentional ending of life by another is not allowed even when it is positively desired by dying people for their own sakes, and any breath of suggestion that surgeons might plunder living bodies for organs leads to horrified headlines and sharp declines in donation rates. Still, even if it is accepted that hastening death through organ removal is out of the question, the same problem is nevertheless forcing itself on us from a different direction. Transplantation has confronted us with a particularly acute version of the ancient problem of how we can really be sure that someone is dead.

To whatever extent that there was any room for doubt about whether someone was really dead, the traditional solution was to wait for absolute certainty. It was better to err on the safe side: better to leave the dead unburied than risk burying the living. But the essence of the transplantation problem is that the question of what counts as being on the safe side is not so clear, because (as it were) the more safety there is for the donor (making sure he is actually dead), the less there is for the recipient (whose life or health is at stake). So transplantation puts us under pressure to declare death at the earliest possible point.

The point at which death can be declared with confidence depends to a large extent on the state of scientific understanding. Once the cardio-pulmonary criterion for recognizing death had been established, for instance, safety no longer required waiting for putrefaction. You might expect, therefore, that as science and technology advanced, and monitors were developed to show the slightest flicker of anything, it would become easier to tell when anyone was really dead. But the development of techno-logy has also brought another problem. We may be able to judge with certainty when some physical function has finally closed down; but which functions, precisely, must close down in order for the dying process to be complete? Different parts of the system close down at different rates, and we can now not only extend the closing down period for many of them, but also, crucially, stagger the various elements. Artificial nutrition and hydration, for instance, mean that people with irretrievably damaged upper brains, who will never again regain consciousness and who not long ago would have died within a couple of weeks, can now be kept going for years. And, of much more pressing importance, ventilators can now maintain heartbeat and circulation once consciousness and spontaneous breathing and circulation have finally stopped. It was proposed in 1967, and has since been widely accepted, that brain death should be accepted as a criterion for death as such; but by the original cardio-pulmonary criterion, venti-lated brain-dead bodies should still count as alive – as in many parts of the world, and to a considerable extent, in both popular and medical intuition, they still do (Singer 1995; Shewmon 1998).

Which of these views, and the variations on them, is right? What these developments are making clear is that the problem is not one that can be solved by science or tech-nology. Those can tell us, with increasing accuracy, what state any body is in and what chance there is for reversal of any declining function, but that does not amount to telling us which of those states is really death. This is true whatever you think death actually is. If, as many people believe, the essence of life is the presence of an immaterial soul, death occurs when that soul finally leaves the body; but as science cannot detect souls, it cannot determine when that is. If, on the other hand, life is a complex organization of physical parts and nothing more, then when you know everything there is to know about the physical state of the body there simply is no further, objective question of whether the person is really dead. Either way, the question of when death occurs is not a scientific one.

This means the problem needs to be understood in a different way. The reason why the diagnosis of death has always mattered so much is that the difference between life and death is traditionally of enormous *moral* importance, and the problem we are faced with now must be recognized as a moral one. Rather than a decision about the true moment of death, we need a decision about the *morally appropriate treatment* of people at the different stages of the closing-down process that constitutes dying. To people who think there is an objective point of death, even though we cannot be sure when it occurs, it may seem that the only acceptable course is the traditional one of waiting until there can be no possible doubt. To others, the problem is to determine which aspects of the individual are the ones that *matter*, and the proposal of the brain death criterion depended on the idea that what mattered was *personhood*. The idea was that when brain function had finally gone, along with consciousness and all that went with it, the ventilator was pumping blood around an empty shell rather than a person. But although the brain death criterion is now widely accepted, the personhood idea makes the life/death distinction very uncomfortable around the margins, because by that standard people should probably be declared dead when their upper brains are so damaged as to preclude any possibility of consciousness or its return, even though the brain stem is still intact and spontaneous breathing continues.

When all this is fully understood, it raises serious doubts about whether we should recognize a sudden change of moral status between life and death at all. Perhaps there needs to be a penumbral morality, to go with the penumbral states between the clearly alive and the clearly dead: before what is clearly death, but after the individual's interests have finally gone. It might be possible, even without much change in the existing law, to allow individuals to determine their own treatment in these states through advance directives.

The implications of these questions go far beyond transplantation, but since transplantation presents in a particularly clear way the possibilities of doing great good to one group without harm to another, it also emphasizes the need for rethinking.

Conclusion

The foregoing arguments all suggest that we are at present too conservative in our approach to the procurement of organs for transplantation. And since conservatism is (no doubt for good evolutionary reasons) a deeply rooted aspect of the human condition, and difficult to dislodge, it is important to stress that none of the arguments has appealed to any new and radical moral theory. The only appeal has been to principles that most people involved in the transplantation debate would themselves profess in other contexts.

Nevertheless, there often persists a deep feeling that there must be something wrong with the whole approach implied by these arguments, because – as is often said as a last resort – bodies and body parts are simply not like other things. They are not like ordinary possessions; they must be regarded in a quite different way.

There are two things to be said about this kind of objection. First, if this is intended as a morally serious claim, not just an all-purpose block to genuine debate, objectors need to explain exactly what moral status is being claimed for bodies and parts of them. Until this is done it is impossible either to assess the claim or to see whether it entails the conclusions it is supposed to entail.

But second, and more fundamentally, the new transferability of body parts has in many ways made bodies and body parts much more like other possessions. For most of history few body parts were of any use to anyone else. There was not much you could do with a dead body except dispose of it, or preserve it, in a way that expressed your attitude to the deceased, and removing parts of living bodies was in general painful and extremely dangerous. The situation now is radically different. Body parts are in many ways more like other things: valuable to others – and therefore worth giving, bequeathing, selling, and stealing – and, to an ever increasing extent, detachable from living bodies with limited harm to the source.

Not surprisingly, people adjust their feelings to the new situation at different rates. Many people have come to feel that once the *person* has gone, the body matters only to the extent that it is useful to the living, and that while people are alive they alone should decide the limits of what can be done to them. Others are a long way from such ideas, still feeling it far more important to show traditional respect to the dead than to use bodies to benefit others, and thinking that there should be limits to what can be done to living bodies even with their owners' consent.

If people do prefer such traditional attitudes, even when they have thought matters through and fully recognized the costs of their preferences, that must be regarded as a simple fact about them – like the (interesting) fact about the rest of us that we would apparently prefer to keep our current life expectancy than lengthen it by entering the Harris survival lottery. The question then is how to take account of these differences in our laws and institutions – and there are innumerable possibilities. Dogmatists of various kinds might think that everyone should be made to go along with the arrangements specified by their dogma; some kinds of democrat might think the preferences of the majority should be binding on everyone. But most people involved in this debate probably take the general view that, as far as possible – as far as can be done without harm to others – people should be allowed to follow their own preferences.

If so, it suggests that we need to take very seriously the idea of arrangements that will allow people to decide whether or not they want to be part of a system in which they agree to the use of their deceased organs in return for access to transplants should they need them. Perhaps, too, people with the attitudes that made them willing to do this might also be willing to make advance directives agreeing to treatment for preservation of their organs before death, and even specifying when organ procurement could begin.

The complexities are enormous, but at the moment traditional habits of mind are making it difficult even to recognize the necessary questions. People are suffering and dying every day while the procurement issues remain in a quagmire of intellectual, and therefore moral, confusion.

References

Abouna, G. M. (2008). Organ shortage crisis: problems and possible solutions. *Transplantation Proceedings* 40/1: 34–8.

Archer, M. (2008). Presumed consent again: proactive opt-in already exists. *British Medical Journal* 336/7642 (March 1): 464.

Cohen, C. B. (2002). Public policy and the sale of human organs. *Kennedy Institute of Ethics Journal* 12/1: 47–64.

Department of Health (2000). *An Investigation Into Conditional Organ Donation.* London: UK Department of Health, Crown Copyright.

DeVita, M. A. and Caplan, A. L. (2007). Caring for organs or for patients? Ethical concerns about the Uniform Anatomical Gift Act (2006). *Annals of Internal Medicine* 147/12: 876–9.

Dossetor, J. B. and Kjellstrand, C. M. (1992). Commercialization: the buying and selling of kidneys. In J. B. Dossetor and C. M. Kjellstrand (eds.), *Ethical Problems in Dialysis and Transplantation*. Dordrecht: Kluwer, pp. 61–71.

Dougherty, C. J. (1987). Body futures: the case against marketing human organs. *Health Progress* 68/5: 51–5.

Downie, J., Shea, A., and Rajotte, C. (2008). Family override of valid donor consent to postmortem donation: issues in law and practice. *Transplantation Proceedings* 40/5: 1255–63.

Eckenrod, E. L. (2008). Psychological/emotional trauma of donor families. *Transplantation Proceedings* 40/4: 1061–3.

Hanto, D. W. (2007). Ethical challenges posed by the solicitation of deceased and living organ donors. *New England Journal of Medicine* 356/10: 1062–6.

Harris, J. (1986). The survival lottery. In P. Singer (ed.), *Applied Ethics*. Oxford: Oxford University Press, pp. 87–97.

Human Tissue Act (2004). Available at: www.opsi.gov.uk/acts/acts2004/20040030.htm (accessed September 1, 2008).

Human Tissue Authority (2006). Code of Practice 2 – Donation of organs, tissue and cells for transplantation. July. Available at: www.hta.gov.uk/_db/_documents/2006-07-04_Approved_by_Parliament_-_Code_of_Practice_2_-_Donation_of_Solid_Organs_200607133233.pdf (accessed September 1, 2008).

Jarvis, R. (1995). Join the club: a modest proposal to increase availability of donor organs. *Journal of Medical Ethics* 21/4: 199–204.

Johnson, E. J. and Goldstein, D. (2003). Do defaults save lives? *Science* 302/5649 (November 21): 1338–9.

Kemp, C. D., Cotton, B. A., Johnson, J. C., Ellzey, M., and Pinson, C. W. (2008). Donor conversion and organ yield in traumatic brain injury patients: missed opportunities and missed organs, *Journal of Trauma* 64/6: 1573–80.

Lamb, D. (2005). *Death, Brain Death and Ethics*. Albany, NY: State University of New York Press.

Lock, M. M. (2002). *Twice Dead: Organ Transplants and the Reinvention of Death*. Berkeley: University of California Press.

Murphy, T. F. and Veatch, R. M. (2006). Members first: the ethics of donating organs and tissues to groups. *Cambridge Quarterly of Healthcare Ethics* 15/1: 50–9.

Radcliffe Richards, J. (1996). Nepharious goings on. Kidney sales and moral arguments. *Journal of Medical Philosophy* 21/4: 375–416.

Radcliffe Richards, J., Daar, A. S., et al. (1998). The case for allowing kidney sales. International forum for transplant ethics. *Lancet* 351/9120: 1950–2.

Sells, R. A. (1993). Resolving the conflict in traditional ethics which arises from our demand for organs. *Transplantation Proceedings* 25/6: 2983–4.

Shewmon, D. A. (1998). "Brainstem death," "brain death" and death: a critical re-evaluation of the purported equivalence. *Issues in Law and Medicine* 14/2: 125–45.

Singer, P. (1995). *Rethinking Life and Death: The Collapse of our Traditional Ethics*. New York: St Martin's Press.

Smith, M. and Murphy, P. (2008). A historic opportunity to improve organ donation rates in the UK. *British Journal of Anaesthesia* 100/6: 735–7.

Spital, A. (2005). Conscription of cadaveric organs: we need to start talking about it. *American Journal of Transplantation* 5/5: 1170–1.

Tabarrok, A. and Undis, D. J. (2006). Response to "Members first: the ethics of donating organs and tissues to groups" by Timothy F. Murphy and Robert M. Veatch (*CQ* vol. 15, no 1). Missing the mark. *Cambridge Quarterly of Healthcare Ethics* 15/4: 450–6.

Taylor, R. M. (1997). Reexamining the definition and criteria of death. *Seminars in Neurology* 17/3: 265–70.

Truog, R. D. (1997). Is it time to abandon brain death? *Hastings Center Report* 27/1: 29–37.

Verheijde J., Mohamed R., McGregor J., and Murray C. (2008). Legislation of presumed consent for end-of-life organ donation in the United Kingdom (UK): undermining values in a multi-cultural society. *Clinics* 63/3.

Volk, M. L. and Ubel, P. A. (2008). A gift of life: ethical and practical problems with conditional and directed donation. *Transplantation* 85/11: 1542–4.

Wilkinson, S. (2003). *Bodies for Sale: Ethics and Exploitation in the Human Body Trade.* Routledge: London.

Part X

Global Health-care Issues

33

Global Health Responsibilities

CHRISTOPHER LOWRY AND UDO SCHÜKLENK

Introduction

We all get sick at one time or another, and for the vast majority of us, disease will play a (usually large) causal role in our deaths. This is – at least given foreseeable technological advances – a permanent condition of the human species. So, the mere fact that people suffer and die from disease is not as such ethically objectionable. What is objectionable, however, is that much of the world's suffering and premature death could be prevented but is not. The current global extent of disease-related suffering and death is, in an ethically significant way, *unnecessary*. Global health refers to health issues and problems that are most efficiently addressed by transnational collaborative actions and solutions.

The overall global trends have been quite remarkable over the past half-century. Average life expectancy at birth rose nearly 40 percent, increasing from 46.5 years during 1950–5 to 65.2 in 2002 (WHO 2003: 3); and during that same time under-5 mortality dropped nearly 60 percent (Moser et al. 2005: 203). Additionally, international health aid is up, especially recently, nearly doubling between 2002 and 2005 to US$11.2 billion (Lane and Glassman 2007). However, 11 million children still die every year, and 6 million of those deaths are considered easily preventable (Kruse and Høgh 2007: 40; cf. Bryce et al. 2005). The global gains in health have not been uniform across all countries. Improvements in child mortality have been slowest in the countries with the highest rates.

Global health is not only a matter of comparing the different statuses of public health of different countries. It is also worthwhile to consider the differences in the distribution of significant health indicators *within* one country compared with others. Although national averages in health continue to improve among developed countries, there is a trend since at least the early 1990s of increases in health disparities by social class (Spencer 2004). At the same time, health-care costs are rising, especially in countries whose health-care systems are more market-driven (Bean 2005). The increasing health disparities between socioeconomic groups, for instance in the US, have been vigorously discussed, as well as the connection between these disparities and race/ethnicity (Harper et al. 2007; Singh and Kogan 2007; Tomashek et al. 2006).

Merely citing these facts is not in its own right making an ethical case one way or another. What is needed is a rationale for why the cases of suffering and the deaths spoken to by these facts are preventable, and why they ought to be prevented. The ethical urgency of the needlessness of much of today's suffering and death is most apparent from a global perspective. In order to explain how unethical the health-care delivery shortfalls in, for instance, sub-Saharan Africa are, we need to investigate the resources (financial and otherwise) that richer countries could reasonably marshal in response – and explain why they ethically ought to do so. This analysis needs to demonstrate that such health-care shortfalls are not merely personal tragedies as well as health policy failures by explaining why this status quo is unethical. Global health-care shortfalls are not exclusively a matter of rich versus poor countries, but also a matter of how large a portion of a country's population has effective and reliable access to high-quality health services. There are examples, such as the oft-cited Indian state of Kerala, where the achievement of very wide access has yielded remarkable results even in the stark absence of funding increases (Sen 1999: 21–4). A key desideratum of an ethical analysis of global health is that it can be usefully deployed both across and within national borders.

A good way to begin thinking about the ethics of health care is to ask why health is important. One of the reasons why we can get considerable convergence on practical health policy issues among different ethical frameworks is that the reasons why health matters are so broad. First, health is arguably a necessary condition for happiness (or utility), whether conceived in terms of mental states or as preference satisfaction. We should be careful not to overstate this correlation; there are plenty of miserable people in perfect health, and plenty of people with chronic illness or disability who enjoy immensely satisfying lives. All other things being equal, however, it is undoubtedly better to be healthy than to be sick. Health contributes in significant ways to happy lives. This provides sufficient reason for utilitarians to defend pro-health policies. Health is also defended on the basis of its importance for the opportunity people have to choose different kinds of lives (or conceptions of the good), as well as its importance in facilitating democratic participation, both of which appeal to Kantian contractualists as well as liberal egalitarians. And moving beyond strictly individualistic reasons, the economic importance of a healthy workforce for the prosperity of any given society should not be overlooked.

This array of reasons for health's importance *can* yield considerable convergence among ethical frameworks on policy implications for health; but that is not to say that it always *does*. There continues to be real debate on a host of vital questions: On what basis do people deserve access to health-care services? Are health-care needs on a par with the other factors that affect utility/opportunity/autonomy, or are they special in some ethically relevant way? If there are moral duties to promote health, whose duties are these, and to whom are they owed? More specifically, what do governments owe their citizens in terms of health care? What do rich countries owe to poor ones? What do citizens of rich countries owe? Or companies, especially multinational ones? And, increasingly, is the answer to be found in strategies proclaiming a "human right to health"? This human rights claim is frequently defended in deontological cosmopolitan approaches to international justice (Pogge 2007). Political philosophers have turned their attention to the question of whether some kind of global citizenship and global governance are required to deal effectively with the moral challenges faced (Attfield 1999; Falk 1994).

We do not aim to achieve the impossible in this chapter, namely to provide definitive resolutions to all these questions. Our aim is to highlight the key issues and, where feasible, to defend some plausible ways forward. Our initial discussion is focused on responding to what we refer to as the "libertarian objection to global health ethics." In the first section, the objection is raised, and ethical reasons in favor of internationally applicable moral duties to prevent unnecessary disease-related suffering and death are presented. Next, the question of who it is that bears or owes these duties is discussed. Finally, we conclude with some applications of those duties.

Doubts About Libertarianism

The libertarian objection to global health ethics is essentially the view that (1) so long as a country abstains from harmfully interfering with other countries, its citizens have no collective moral duty to treat the citizens of those other countries with equal moral concern, or indeed with any moral concern at all; and (2) so long as a person similarly abstains, she has no such individual moral duty – with the exception of paying to support the minimal or "nightwatchman" state (Nozick 1974). The upshot of this position is that the redistribution of health resources across and within national borders becomes only a matter of supererogatory charity or economic efficiency, rather than also a demand of distributive justice. (Not all libertarian theories fit this description; in particular, "left-libertarians" argue for some global redistribution measures as rectification for the inequitable distribution of natural resources among countries (Vallentyne et al. 2005).)

This position seems to rule out any global health ethics. There are good reasons to reject such an approach. This stark form of libertarianism relies upon the claim that people come to have positive moral duties (i.e., duties beyond not violating others' rights) only in virtue of being under a common state authority, and it limits those duties severely. Many theories reject the idea that equal moral concern is contingent upon an account of our institutional relations, and instead defend some version of the claim that people deserve equal moral concern because of the kind of beings they are. Utilitarians attribute moral standing to sentient beings (Sidgwick 1907). Utilitarian writers proceed from the assumption that preventable deaths, usually accompanied by preventable suffering, are a bad thing that we ought to avoid if we are able to do so without excessive cost to ourselves or others. Social or physical proximity are irrelevant factors in determining our moral obligations (Singer 1972; Unger 1996). Kantians emphasize our rational faculties (O'Neill 2000). "Comprehensive" liberals argue that what gives a person equal moral standing is the fact that she has a good of her own, such that her life can go better or worse (Kymlicka 1990). What is common to these approaches is that because their criteria for equal moral concern do not involve any social or political relations, their responses are, at least in principle, not limited by geographic or other divisions.

Other global justice theorists, especially those who are sympathetic to "political" liberalism, agree with libertarians that political claims about equal moral concern need to be grounded in our institutional relations. Global political liberals respond to the libertarian objection by seeking to extend the reach and scope of relationally grounded moral concern. They argue that the relevant kinds of institutional relations extend beyond national borders (Tan 2004). Pogge (2002), for instance, maintains that there is a world economic order that is imposed by the world's rich nations upon the world's poor nations. This economic world order harms the world's poor. His contention is that the world's affluent nations are harming the global poor by maintaining an unjust economic world order. His theory can support a global moral duty to prevent unnecessary disease-related suffering on the basis of his claim that rich countries are responsible for causing that suffering.

A more serious objection is to question whether the grounds of moral obligations toward those in need should be based on libertarian grounds. Arguably, the continuing preventable loss of human lives is comparable to other types of emergencies where human lives are at immediate risk. We would not normally accept the argument that we have no obligations toward someone about to drown or burn to death in an accident if we are capable of rescuing her without unreasonable risk to our own well-being. Indeed, this commonly accepted obligation seems not only one directed at individuals capable of assisting, but also to states. Disaster assistance is routinely rendered from one state government to another, and so from the citizens of one country to the citizens of another country.

Obligations

The general global moral duty that we briefly argued for in the previous section requires further specification if it is to be of any practical use. To whom are these duties owed (i.e., which countries should receive health aid)? Who are the primary duty-bearers (i.e., which countries and/or corporations should fund this aid)? And, what, in practical terms, is the content of these duties (i.e., what specifically is the health aid for)? We will begin with the "what" question.

Disease-related suffering and death can be unnecessary for at least three reasons: (1) easily preventable diseases are not prevented; (2) easily treatable diseases are not treated; and (3) other diseases still lack an effective treatment or cure because of a failure to allocate health research funding in adequately health needs-sensitive ways. This third reason brings out the importance of distinguishing between health aid whose primary goal is improving health-care delivery and health aid that funds drug R&D for diseases that disproportionately affect the global poor and have usually been neglected by profit-driven pharmaceutical companies.

A disease can be considered easily preventable if there is a known cure or vaccine that could be provided to all, or very nearly all, those afflicted (or at risk in case of a preventive vaccine) at a cost that would leave the donor countries still well-off (in absolute terms by any reasonable standard) or leave the donor corporations still commercially competitive. Furthermore, diseases that currently lack a cure or vaccine can also be considered easily preventable (in the slightly longer term) if the combined cost of developing and delivering a cure would similarly not impose an unreasonable sacrifice on donor countries and/or corporations. This definition covers most tropical diseases, for instance. The global moral duty under discussion requires providing health aid sufficient to prevent all such diseases that significantly affect utility, opportunity, and autonomy.

Likewise, a disease can be considered easily treatable if there exists an effective medical procedure or drug that could be provided to all those afflicted at a cost that would leave the donor countries still well-off and the donor corporations still commercially competitive, or if an effective treatment could be developed and delivered meeting the same conditions. Specifying what counts as an *effective* treatment will vary a bit among ethical frameworks because of the various reasons for valuing health. For example, utilitarianism measures effectiveness by how well a treatment removes barriers to utility, whereas political liberalism is concerned with how well a treatment enables political and economic participation. However, typically a disease that seriously affects one value – say, a person's opportunity to be an active citizen – will also affect the other values (i.e., utility, autonomy, economic productivity, etc.). This allows for convergence on the importance of at least those treatments that address the central effects of serious diseases. For now, that is enough to push for considerable increases of health aid.

Who is owed?

To whom are these duties owed? Since these duties won't be met for everyone overnight, we need to know how to decide which countries should get priority. This will affect allocation decisions for both delivery-oriented aid and R&D aid, in that R&D for diseases that are concentrated in high-priority countries will be favored, provided that such R&D meets reasonable requirements regarding scientific promise. For the utilitarian, the priority question is entirely a matter of efficiency: the aid should go to wherever it will have the greatest benefit for aggregate utility. Assessments of need and responsibility are considered relevant only insofar as they help us more accurately predict expected utility gains. Global political liberals like Pogge are instead concerned about which countries have been, and continue to be, most disadvantaged by the world economic order (and often also by historical colonialism). Pogge's view holds back from giving priority to relieving a country's plight insofar as that plight is attributable to natural disasters or the country's own poor choices. Autonomy-oriented comprehensive liberals give importance to the extent to which countries in need meet, or are working toward, standards of human rights and basic civil and political liberties. This is because comprehensive liberals seek to secure for everyone the liberal social conditions that they defend as most conducive to people's ability to pursue a good life. One upshot common to all three frameworks is that, except for emergency aid for urgent health crises, countries suffering from corruption, volatile politics, or military conflict are not ideal recipients, despite their often high levels of need. (However, utilitarians are careful to take seriously the possibility of a country plagued by such difficulties being, nonetheless, very efficient in making use of health aid, which would give that country priority from the utilitarian perspective.) This underscores the interdependence of health aid and other forms of development, political and economic (Anand et al. 2006).

Who owes?

Who are the primary duty-bearers? There are excellent arguments emphasizing the aid-giving responsibilities of affluent individuals, who from a global perspective include most citizens of developed countries (O'Neill 2004; Singer 2002; Unger 1996).

397

In terms of efficacy, the question remains, of course, why target individual actors as opposed to their representative governments? Our discussion here focuses on the duties of countries and, for reasons given later, to a lesser extent on the proposed duties of corporations. On that question, causal responsibility and ability to provide aid are regularly appealed to. We will also discuss the ethical relevance of economic relationships.

Concerning causal responsibility, ex-colonizers have a special moral duty to aid countries whose continued plight is significantly attributable to their shared colonial past (Miles 2006). Also, the countries that can claim most of the causal responsibility for having given the world economic order the shape it now has – with respect to its features that impose disadvantage on badly-off countries – have a special moral duty to aid the countries that are disadvantaged in this way. This raises practical difficulties, however, since there may well be distrust between an ex-colonizer and an ex-colonized country, as well as between a powerful country and a country disadvantaged by the world economic order. Moreover, an ex-colonizer and especially a powerful country can have a state interest in maintaining the inferior economic or political position of the disadvantaged countries in question, or at least an interest in designing and carrying out aid projects in ways that maintain or strengthen their power over them. One way around this conflict of interest could be to separate the provision of aid funding from management and executive tasks by, for example, pooling the funding in an independent globally accountable health aid agency of the sort that the WHO strives to be.

With the numbers the way they are, even non-consequentialist theories can and should agree that a country's level of affluence increases its moral duty to provide health aid. The cost of providing an immense benefit can amount to an almost negligible sacrifice when placed against other national expenditures of affluent countries. For example, the US$5.1 billion that experts estimate it would cost to save the lives of 6 million of the 11 million children dying of easily preventable disease (Bryce et al. 2005) is slightly more than 1 percent of the 2008 US defence budget of US$481.4 billion (OMB 2008) and less than 0.25 percent of the total health spending in the US in 2005 of US$2 trillion (Kaiser Family Foundation 2007). One objection to saddling the most health aid duty on the richest countries is that doing so does not necessarily reflect the patterns of causal responsibility discussed above. Two responses are in order. First, although health aid can and should be part of the reparations that countries make for past injustices, the ethical considerations that ground health aid are not exhausted by reparative ones. And, secondly, it needn't be claimed that in order to assign an ethical obligation to provide health aid we must decide between these two factors (i.e., causal responsibility and ability to pay). They are best treated as complementary, such that either is sufficient to ground an obligation, and when both are present the obligation is strengthened accordingly.

A third, less frequently discussed factor is the presence of economic ties between a country in need and an affluent country or a wealthy corporation. Concerning corporations, when the affluence of its owners or shareholders is made possible by its economic partnership with a country in need that, for example, houses one of its factories or service centers, there are ethical (as well as pragmatic) reasons for the corporation to give back to the relevant community, with health aid being a key part of that. However, it is worth pointing out that there is in principle no difference then between, say a pharmaceutical company, a car manufacturer, or a mining company.

This is typically discussed as a matter of corporate social responsibility and sustainable development. For example, DaimlerChrysler in South Africa has established clinics and community-based facilities to provide comprehensive HIV/AIDS treatments to its employees, their families and the community (UNAIDS 2003: 21). A similar kind of relationship can occur between an affluent and a developing country, as in the case of Japan and China, whose strong economic ties largely explain Japan's considerable development aid, including health aid (Takamine 2006).

From within a liberal framework, the idea of reciprocity can be used to explain the ethical reasoning behind these types of obligation (Rawls 2001). There is considerable debate about how best to specify the idea of reciprocity and the related idea of fairness. The core notion, however, is that in cases of cooperation that yields unequal benefits (where typically the already advantaged party to the business contract receives the greater share), this inequality is morally acceptable so long as the terms of cooperation are such that they can be affirmed by the less advantaged party *when that party conceives of itself as the moral equal of the other*. Because that affirmation may not be possible immediately, it is important for the advantaged party to contribute to fostering the social conditions that would make it possible as well as reasonable. We can thus assign an ethical obligation to provide health aid as a matter of enabling fair terms of economic cooperation between advantaged countries or corporations and disadvantaged countries or communities.

Lastly, there are good consequentialist reasons to think that for-profit operators in the health industry have a limited moral duty to provide health aid, especially pharmaceutical companies (Schüklenk and Ashcroft 2001). The poor accessibility (financial and otherwise) of many life-saving drugs in developing countries is caused in large part by the needs-insensitivity of these companies' business strategies. Pharmaceutical companies are capable of acting morally in aid of those affected by health emergencies. Indeed, many companies accept that they have such responsibilities (Schüklenk and Gallagher 2007). Myriads of schemes, ranging from drug donations to large financial contributions and differential pricing to public–private partnerships, have been on the international agenda. However, none of them has come anywhere near to what is required to resolve the health emergencies faced by the world's poor. So, while there is nothing in principle wrong with such activities – after all, some very badly-off people will be better off as a result of any one of these strategies – they certainly are not the last word on this debate. This is so because, ultimately, developing countries cannot reasonably be expected to rely in their health planning on voluntary, time-limited donations or discounts from pharmaceutical multinationals. This is certainly true in the case of HIV/AIDS, for instance, where many more people than ever before receive life-preserving medication. If they were ever cut off from this medication because companies stopped discounting their prices or stopped donating what is needed, they would die fairly quickly, while in the process developing drug-resistant mutations of the virus. This could easily result in a global health disaster of unprecedented proportions. We have reason to be concerned about voluntary solutions, which are not underwritten by the state, to challenges such as this. After all, listed companies, as most pharmaceutical companies are, have a fiduciary responsibility to their owners to maximize returns on their investments. The world's markets follow their progress pretty much on an hourly basis. Companies failing on this count will quickly see their stock market value collapse. They will either close down or be taken over by a more successful rival. For this reason alone, we can only expect fairly limited delivery of non-profitable drug R&D by pharmaceutical multinationals. It is for this reason that the regulatory tool of compulsory licensing offers some help with regard to existing drugs, but no solution at all with regards to neglected-disease drug R&D. One possible response to this challenge could be that global equity requirements be imposed by states across at least all listed companies, not just those operating in the health-care sector, alongside the safety requirements that the health industry must already meet.

Currently proposed drug research and development financing mechanisms

One kind of proposal with considerable support from international political leaders is an Advanced Marketing Commitment (AMC) or Advanced Purchase Commitment (APC) instrument, through which donor countries pledge to reward innovations concerning vaccines for diseases that disproportionately affect developing countries, such as HIV/AIDS, malaria, tuberculosis, cervical cancer, pneumococcal diseases, and rotavirus diarrhea (IFPMA 2006). However, serious ethical and policy concerns have been raised against this idea. Donald Light points out that "the appeal of APCs seems based on its future benefits that cost national leaders nothing to promise, [and] its design that favours the multinational drug companies. . . . Yet if a modified APC were applied to existing vaccines for diseases of the poor, it could rapidly begin to eradicate many of these diseases" (2006: 140). In the United States, a bill suggesting a Medical Innovation Prize Fund to reward innovations that target medical needs not addressed by the market was introduced in Congress but not passed (OLPA 2006). A third proposal is a global medical R&D treaty, according to which signing countries would collectively recognize an obligation to contribute to globally beneficial health R&D (Hubbard and Love 2004).

Conclusions

Far too many, mostly poor, people suffer from curable or preventable diseases, and die preventable deaths – they suffer unnecessarily in today's world. The reasons for this have much to do with their inability to purchase the health care that affluent citizens in wealthier nations can take for granted. Libertarian justifications for a continuation of the current status quo are unconvincing. Ethical frameworks encompassing as diverse theories as contractarianism and utilitarianism converge on the view that reasonably well-off people have moral obligations aimed at reducing unnecessary disease-related suffering and reasonably preventable deaths toward the poor. These obligations include the reduction of the developing world's disease burden. A moral case can be made in support of the view that citizens of wealthy nations, and, as a corollary the states representing them, and to a limited extent companies, should assist in providing health care to the world's poor.

The need to ensure the reasonable long-term sustainability of health-care research, as well as delivery programs, suggests that the proper agent responsible for the delivery must be states, possibly bound by international treaties and monitoring regimes. Different competing models have been suggested as best suited to deliver on those objectives, some entirely public, others based on public–private partnerships. It seems to us that whatever regime is likely to generate best possible outcomes for the largest number of people in need is preferable to any alternative program.

References

Anand, S., Peter, F., and Sen, A. K. (2006). *Public Health, Ethics, and Equity.* Oxford: Oxford University Press.

Attfield, R. (1999). *The Ethics of the Global Environment.* Edinburgh: Edinburgh University Press.

Bean, J. R. (2005). National healthcare spending in the US and Japan: national economic policy and implications for neurosurgery. *Neurologia Medico-Chirurgica (Tokyo)* 45: 18–24.

Bryce, J., Black, R. E., Walker, N., Bhutta, Z. A., Lawn, J. E., and Steketee, R. W. (2005). Can the world afford to save the lives of 6 million children each year? *Lancet* 365: 2193–200.

Falk, R. (1994). The making of global citizenship. In Bart van Steenbergen (ed.), *The Condition of Citizenship.* London: Sage, pp. 127–140.

Harper, S., Lynch, J., Burris, S., and Davey Smith, G. (2007). Trends in the black–white life expectancy gap in the United States, 1983–2003. *Journal of the American Medical Association* 297: 1224–32.

Hubbard, T. and Love, J. (2004). A new trade framework for global healthcare R&D. *PLoS Biology* 2: 147–50.

IFPMA (International Federation of Pharmaceutical Manufacturers and Associations) (2006). Advanced market commitment (AMC) proposal an important step in right direction to develop and provide access to new vaccines: New release. Geneva, Switzerland, April 24. Available at: www.ifpma.org/News/NewsReleaseDetail.aspx?nID=4762 (accessed October 9, 2007).

Kaiser Family Foundation (2007). *Health Care Costs: A Primer.* Menlo Park, CA: Kaiser Family Foundation. Available at: www.kff.org/insurance/upload/7670.pdf (accessed October 8, 2007).

Kruse, A. Y. and Høgh, B. (2007). International child health. *Danish Medical Bulletin* 54: 39–41.

Kymlicka, W. (1990). Two theories of justice. *Inquiry* 33: 99–119.

Kymlicka, W. (2002). *Contemporary Political Philosophy: An Introduction,* 2nd edn. Oxford: Oxford University Press.

Lane, C. and Glassman, A. (2007). Bigger and better? Scaling up and innovation in health aid. *Health Affairs* 26: 935–48.

Light, D. (2006). Advanced purchase commitments: moral and practical problems. In J. C. Cohen, P. Illingworth, and U. Schüklenk (eds.), *The Power of Pills: Social, Ethical and Legal Issues in Drug Development, Marketing and Pricing.* London: Pluto, pp. 134–40.

Mathers, C., Iburg, K. M., Salomon, J. A., Tandon, A., Chatterji, S., Ustün, B., and Murray, C. J. L. (2004). Global patterns of healthy life expectancy in the year 2002. *BMC Public Health* 4: 66.

Miles, S. (2006). Human genomic research ethics: changing the rules. In J. C. Cohen, P. Illingworth, and U. Schüklenk (eds.), *The Power of Pills: Social, Ethical and Legal Issues in Drug Development, Marketing and Pricing.* London: Pluto, pp. 203–14.

Moser, K., Shkolnikov, V., and Leon, D. A. (2005). World mortality, 1950–2000: divergence replaces convergence from the late 1980s. *Bulletin of the World Health Organization* 83: 202–9.

Nozick, R. (1974). *Anarchy, State and Utopia*. New York: Basic Books.

OLPA (Office of Legislative Policy and Analysis) (2006). Legislative Update: Medical Innovation Prize Act of 2005. Available at: http://olpa.od.nih.gov/legislation/109/pendinglegislation/medicalinnovation.asp (accessed October 9, 2007).

OMB (2008). Office of Management and Budget, US Department of Defense. Available at: www.whitehouse.gov/omb/budget/fy2008/defense.html (accessed March 26, 2009).

O'Neill, O. (2000). *Bounds of Justice*. Cambridge: Cambridge University Press.

O'Neill, O. (2004). Global justice: Whose obligations? In D. K. Chatterjee (ed.), *The Ethics of Assistance: Morality and the Distant Needy*. Cambridge: Cambridge University Press, pp. 242–59.

Pogge, T. (2002). *World Poverty and Human Rights*. Cambridge: Polity.

Pogge, T. (ed.) (2007). *Freedom from Poverty as a Human Right: Who Owes What to the Global Poor?* Oxford: Oxford University Press; Paris: UNESCO.

Rawls, J. (2001). *Justice as Fairness: A Restatement*, ed. E. Kelly. Cambridge, MA: Harvard University Press.

Schüklenk, U. and Ashcroft, R. E. (2001). Affordable access to essential medication in developing countries: conflicts between ethical and economic imperatives. *Journal of Medicine and Philosophy* 27: 179–95.

Schüklenk, U. and Gallagher, J. (2007). Obligations of the pharmaceutical industry. In R. E. Ashcroft, A. Dawson, H. Draper, and J. McMillan (eds.), *Principles of Health Care Ethics*, 2nd edn. Chichester: Wiley, pp. 743–60.

Sen, A. (1999). *Development as Freedom*. New York: Anchor Books.

Sidgwick, H. (1907). *The Methods of Ethics*, 7th edn. Indianapolis, IN: Hackett.

Singer, P. (1972). Famine, affluence, and morality. *Philosophy and Public Affairs* 1: 229–41.

Singer, P. (2002). *One World: The Ethics of Globalization*. New Haven, CT: Yale University Press.

Singh, G. K. and Kogan, M. D. (2007). Widening socioeconomic disparities in US childhood mortality, 1969–2000. *American Journal of Public Health* 97: 1658–65.

Spencer, N. (2004). The effect of income inequality and macro-level social policy on infant mortality and low birthweight in developed countries: a preliminary systematic review. *Child: Care, Health and Development* 30: 699–709.

Takamine, T. (2006). *Japan's Development Aid to China: The Long-running Foreign Policy of Engagement*. London: Routledge.

Tan, K.-C. (2004). *Justice Without Borders: Cosmopolitanism, Nationalism, and Patriotism*. Cambridge: Cambridge University Press.

Tomashek, K. M., Qin, C., Hsia, J., Iyasu, S., Barfield, W. D., and Flowers, L. M. (2006). Infant mortality trends and differences between American Indian/Alaska Native infants and white infants in the United States, 1989–1991 and 1998–2000. *American Journal of Public Health* 96: 2222–7.

UNAIDS (2003). HIV/AIDS: It's your business. Geneva: UNAIDS. Available at: http://data.unaids.org/Publications/IRC-pub06/JC1008-Business_en.pdf (accessed October 9, 2007).

Unger, P. (1996). *Living High and Letting Die: Our Illusion of Innocence*. New York: Oxford University Press.

Vallentyne, P., Steiner, H., and Otsuka, M. (2005). Why libertarianism is not incoherent, indeterminate, or irrelevant: a reply to Fried. *Philosophy and Public Affairs* 33: 201–15.

WHO (1978). Declaration of Alma Ata. Alma Ata: World Health Organization. Available at: www.who.int/hpr/NPH/docs/declaration_almaata.pdf (accessed October 14, 2007).

WHO (2003). *The World Health Report 2003: Shaping the Future*. Geneva: World Health Organization.

Further reading

Bennett, B. and Tomossy, G. (eds.) (2006). *Globalization and Health*. Dordrecht: Springer.

Daniels, N. (2008). *Just Health Care*. New York: Cambridge University Press.

Dworkin, D. (2000). *Sovereign Virtue: The Theory and Practice of Equality*. Cambridge, MA: Harvard University Press.

Petryna, A., Lakoff, A., and Kleinman, A. (eds.) (2006). *Global Pharmaceuticals*. Durham, NC: Duke University Press.

Rhodes, R., Battin, M. P., and Silvers, A. (eds.). *Medicine and Social Justice*. New York: Oxford University Press.

34

Developing World Challenges

UDO SCHÜKLENK, MICHAEL KOTTOW, AND PETER A. SY

Introduction

> People living in poor countries not only face lower life expectancies than those in richer countries but also live a higher proportion of their lives in poor health.
> (Mathers et al. 2004)

This is the verdict of WHO officials working in the unit for Evidence and Information Policy. In this chapter, we will provide an overview of selected bioethical issues that are particularly pressing in developing countries. Unsurprisingly perhaps, most of these issues are linked in one way or another to the question of what a just distribution of resources between wealthier and poorer nations would be like (Lowry and Schüklenk 2008). We cannot do justice to this overarching question in this chapter. Our objective is more limited. We shall discuss the following issues: the migration of health-care professionals; international loans with conditions relevant to health care; the impact of culture and religion; and research using subjects from developing countries.

Extreme societal poverty is directly linked to higher child (infant) mortality, female illiteracy, lower per capita expenditure on health care, and unreliable access to clean water, sanitation, and immunization (Ruger and Kim 2006). Once differences in cost of living and population size are accounted for, high-income countries spend approximately 30 times more on health than do low-income countries (Schieber et al. 2007). In low- and middle-income countries, 50–90 percent of citizens are denied access to medicine when they are unable to pay for it. This renders life-preserving drugs unaffordable for many (Mendis et al. 2007). The recent debate on neglected-disease research has focused on infectious diseases such as HIV/AIDS, malaria, and TB. Millions of human lives are lost prematurely because of the failure to treat or prevent infectious diseases. However, today, roughly 70 percent of the United States' overseas aid budget for health is dedicated to HIV/AIDS, while US health funding in areas such as child mortality and women's reproductive health has decreased (Schieber et al. 2007: 927). Kenyan HIV specialist Ibrahim Mohammed argues that the refusal of donor programs to provide funding for health workers in areas other than HIV/AIDS is in part responsible for the country's loss, between 1994 and 2001, of about 15 percent of its health workers. The result is a continuing deterioration of other health-delivery programs. The Malawian Health Minister reports that, during the last five years, the country lost most of its health-care administrators, nurses, and doctors, primarily to foreign NGOs offering better salaries and working conditions. Reportedly, "nothing is being done to replace the workers who once dealt with malaria, dysentery, vaccination programs, maternal health, and other issues that lack activist constituencies" (Garrett 2007: 14).

Only about 18 percent of the world's doctors and nurses reside in developing countries. Developed world countries continue to recruit health-care professionals who were initially trained in the developing world. About one out of every five African-born medical doctors works today in the developed world (Clemens and Pettersson 2008). The rich, in other words, are free-riders depending to some extend on a continuing transfer of health-care professionals from the developing to the developed world.

While it seems easy to point our fingers towards the world's rich and argue for more and more assistance to the poor, it is perhaps worth noting that African nations' military spending increased between 1997 and 2006 by 51 percent, with Central Asia's rising by a whopping 73 percent (Stålenheim et al. 2007). This indicates that resource allocation decisions by some of the developing world's governments do not necessarily prioritize their people's health needs. Essential drugs are still being taxed in many developing countries, thereby reducing these medicines' affordability for many of their citizens, compounding the challenges posed by pharmaceutical multinationals' pricing policies. When local leaders thus fail to do the best by their citizens, there may be a moral obligation for well-placed others to take over the relevant responsibilities.

Developing world bioethics mimics to a large extent the debates of developed countries, discussing popular textbooks' bioethical principles, the details of informed consent, and the mechanics of bioethics committees. These issues are important, as they have direct consequences for individuals caught in clinical or research quandaries. However, the central ethical issue of underdevelopment is social inequity.

Medical Migration and Moral Responsibility

The effects of health workers' migration from the developing world to developed countries are serious. The lack of access even to the most basic health care for at least 1.3 billion people worldwide is partly due to medical migration (WHO 2006). Ghana lost half its locally educated doctors to the US, UK, Canada, and Australia, leaving it with only three doctors for every 100,000 citizens (Hagopian et al. 2004). Hosting 11 percent of the world's population, and carrying 24 percent of the global burden of disease, sub-Saharan Africa only has 3 percent of the world's health workers to deal with the enormous health problems in its region, yet it is far from being a no-recruitment zone for medical institutions in the developed world (WHO 2006). In the developing world, the mere availability of medicine, or of sufficient international financial aid focused on ameliorating the lack of available health-care facilities and medicines, is inadequate to address health problems there, due to the lack of health workers (Editor 2007: 63). Medical migration has rendered many peoples in the developing world "vulnerable" – that is, "less able than others to safeguard their own needs and interests adequately" (AHRC 1998).

405

To address this issue, we identify the *loci* of moral responsibility in three distinct groups of moral agents – namely, recruiters and policy-makers from developed countries, international medical aid organizations, and medical practitioners from the developing world. We can take at least two complementary approaches in establishing moral responsibility with regard to this problem: philosophical and practical. Philosophically, moral responsibility can be assigned if we can specify the necessary and sufficient conditions under which the moral agents mentioned can be demonstrated (a) to have brought about some of the harmful consequences of medical migration, and (b) to have done so voluntarily. This approach takes "responsibility" broadly to include deliberate collective actions (or omissions to act when one could and should have acted) of governments and groups of moral agents. Thus, policy-makers and governments in the developing world would be morally blameworthy on consequentialist accounts of ethics if they failed to institute appropriate measures to address the severe lack of health-care workers in their home countries when it would have been within their powers to do so, and provided that doing this would not have caused more serious problems elsewhere in their societies. Responsibility is a relevant consideration not only in terms of assigning liability or punishment (legal or otherwise), but also in terms of social treatments in general including praise, reward, blame, and forms of sanction. Even though there are few legal sanctions against recruiters from rich countries who target medical graduates from the developing world, their actions are arguably morally blameworthy. Wealthy developed nations have the financial and human resources to train their own health-care staff in sufficient numbers. To essentially free-ride on the investment developing nations make in the education and training of health-care workers is wrong.

On a practical level this is being acknowledged by relevant actors in this area, which indicates a recognition of their own moral responsibility. Responding to criticism that the UK was poaching skilled nurses from developing countries, the UK government issued guidelines to regulate its international recruitment of nurses in order to "have no adverse effects upon the recruit's home healthcare system" (Department of Health 1999). By committing to exercise restraint, and regulate a practice that otherwise would benefit its citizens, the UK government acknowledges its moral obligation not to aggravate the health-care delivery situation in the developing world.

Recruiters and policy-makers from developed countries

Recruiters and policy-makers from developed countries arguably have the moral obligation, at a minimum, not to worsen the damage caused by medical migration, especially from countries where certain types of health professionals are in critically low supply. This means halting the recruitment of doctors from countries like Ghana. In other less extreme cases, it might instead require highly regulated, selective, or focused recruitment of medical personnel where there is a relative abundance. The restraint should not be seen as a purely altruistic action of the developed world; rather, it is partly a reasonably responsible moral move vis-à-vis the developing world's effective and substantial subsidy on medical education of migrating health professionals that is already benefiting developed countries. In South Africa, for instance, the cost of training a general practice doctor is approximately US$60,000. According to an estimate by the African Union, roughly US$500 million a year is spent by low-income countries as a quasi-subsidy of their health-care workers who are bound for the developed world (Kirigia et al. 2006).

In no way should this argument be construed as a proposal to discriminate against developing world professionals who apply for jobs in developed countries after serving their own nations. However, establishing an international health-care workers' migration regime that balances the right of free movement of workers *and* the protection of vulnerable populations seems a reasonable and morally responsible act that the international community should consider. This could be achieved by, for instance, compensating the developing countries from which health-care workers originated. Compensation could come in the form of training for medical educators, access to international medical textbooks and journal databases, provision of critical medical equipment for training in the developing world, and support for research addressing the diseases mostly affecting developing countries.

International medical aid organizations

International medical aid organizations aim to respond to medical emergencies in regions of the developing world where health infrastructures barely exist (Editor 2007). But like other aid organizations, medical aid organizations may be tempted to overstate particular medical situations, creating further dependencies through their own ecosystems of lobbyists, fundraisers, and intermediaries without at the same time producing efficient and sustainable results. It is a well-documented phenomenon that aid flows and aid organizations' disaster marketing efforts are not always proportionate to the actual impact of the problem at hand (Christie et al. 2007). Frequently, NGOs and aid-providing governments have overlapping or competing agendas. The fate of the poor in need of help depends to a large extent on the priority-setting decisions of individuals who are not directly accountable to them in agencies such as Doctors without Borders (Fuller 2006). Problems associated with this have led Ghanaian-born Kwame Ampomah of the United Nations Joint Program on HIV/AIDS to suggest: "You need a clear health care system with equity that is not donor driven" (Garrett 2007). The ethical rationale for this is fairly straightforward. If we accept that equal health problems ought to be treated equally, it cannot be just that patients suffering from some (life-threatening) diseases are treated differently from patients suffering from other (life-threatening) diseases that are less popular with Western funding agencies, NGOs, and the like. The main point we wish to make here is that objective health needs should drive resource allocation decisions by international medical aid organizations. There is sufficient evidence to suggest that that is not always occurring now. International medical NGOs should also be required to inform their donors (and those they wish to help) about the decision-making criteria that they apply when they decide where to deploy their resources, and for how long. Accountability both to their donors and to those they aim to assist is an important consideration in this context.

The moral significance of this matter becomes apparent when we take a closer look at how some aid organizations operate in developing countries. They fly in presumably well-meaning "experts" who often do not understand the local conditions and language and therefore must hire local support staff. These organizations thereby become highly sought-after employers of local professionals. This carries a cost. Many of the best-educated local workers are thus lured away from jobs in government or other public services, including health services, that are vital to the successful long-term functioning of the society. Such unintended, though perhaps not unforeseen, harmful consequences could be minimized if international aid agencies became self-critical of their actions, and if resources were focused on addressing barriers to the self-sufficiency of developing countries.

The responsibilities of medical practitioners from the developing world

While no argument (except perhaps in rare cases of national emergencies and epidemics) is strong enough to justify a complete ban on medical migration, medical professionals need to recognize that they have at least some limited responsibility to offer services to their communities for an appropriate period of time in return for the societally subsidized training that they received. While health-care workers are no more required to act in a supererogatory manner than anyone else, we do think they are bound to live up to commonly accepted standards of medical professionalism. We understand professionalism here in the historical sense of serving the public good, partially in return for support received by the professional during her training from the public. Health-care professionals are, for instance, obliged to be where their medical skills are most needed, at least for a reasonable time after graduation. Indeed, this kind of community service has become government regulation in South Africa, for instance.

Possible counter-arguments

It could be argued that the prospect of well-paying jobs in developed countries might motivate more people to train for the health-care professions in developing countries. This could possibly compensate for the loss due to migration and prevent a net loss of medical personnel in the long run. So far, there is no empirical evidence to suggest that this argument is correct. Furthermore, this vague "long run" could be too long for a developing country that faces a medical crisis that is as time-sensitive as an infectious disease outbreak, or a natural disaster such as the 2004 tsunami in Southeast Asia. The price in human suffering to be paid waiting for a desirable outcome – which is not certain to come anyway – might be too high. Even if one accepted the speculative "long run" argument, how long should we ask a developing country to wait until its job market is able to equilibrate and address its own peoples' critical health-care needs?

Another argument suggests that the remittances sent to families back home by health-care workers in developed countries reduces poverty and boosts the economies of those countries. There is some truth in that argument, but it is still unclear whether the resulting economic gains are available quickly enough, and in sufficient quantity, to address critical medical crises in the developing world (not to mention other significant social costs of medical migration on concerned families and communities). Given the severity of medical crises in some developing countries, it seems reasonable for policy-makers to implement measures that mitigate the ill-effects of medical migration.

Lending Money to Developing Countries

In the 1970s and '80s, Latin America and the Caribbean received substantial loans from international institutions, foremost the World Bank, conditional on the introduction of a number of policy reforms designed to implement neoliberal economics and privatize many social services, including health care (Almeida 2002). The ensuing decentralization and weakening of state responsibilities in public health and health-care policies have reduced funds for epidemiological campaigns, which in Brazil, for example, has led to a marked upsurge of endemic diseases that had previously been brought under control, such as malaria, yellow fever, dengue, and Chagas disease. This raises challenging ethical questions about the moral responsibilities of international lending institutions for the detrimental side effects of their policies.

As part of international loan arrangements, many developing countries were required to introduce the practice of managed health care, producing a major influx of usually well-paid international consultants and institutions. The consequence in Latin America has been a distinctly two-tiered system, in which the underfunded and purportedly mismanaged public health system services 75 percent of the population, while the wealthier segments of the population are cared for in well-resourced private facilities (Iriart et al. 2000). Mexico, for instance, was subject to complex institutional interactions at the economic and health-care levels. The World Bank and the International Development Bank played major roles in redirecting public health policies. They persuaded the Mexican government to implement a so-called mixed health-care system that, arguably, is more accurately described as private (Abrantes Pêgo and Almeida 2002). The World Bank's official mission is to lend money to "fight poverty with passion," with its goal being "the elimination of poverty" (World Bank 2007; cf. Buse and Walt 2000a; 2000b). International banks now refer to "poverty reduction" instead of the previously used term "structural adjustment," but continue to prioritize private health insurance and care in developing countries.

A number of claims have been presented to justify the World Bank's loan and privatization policies:

1   The poor should pay a user fee to help finance the system.
2   Public–private partnerships are a more efficient means to deliver health services.
3   "It seems beneficial in absolute terms for the poor if the better-off benefit substantially from a programme or a technology" (Wagstaff 2001).

These programs have not contributed toward resolving the problem of how to provide equitable and efficient health care to the poor. The view taken by the World Bank is essentially that public health delivery systems in many developing countries are irredeemably bad. The strategic decision made was to aim for a privatization of health service delivery. Patients were expected to pay for service in order to finance the system. The obvious difficulty, and arguably the reason for the failure of this strategy, is that far too many patients who are most in need of health services are unable to pay for them. The third point made above seems to be a typical example of "trickle-down" economics, assuming that even if the small wealthy segments of a given society benefit disproportionately, some measurable benefits will eventually trickle down to the rest of the population, so that eventually (nearly) everyone will be better off. We doubt that it can be demonstrated that this claim is correct for many Latin American or African countries.

In nine African nations, it was observed that investments tend to go to hospital facilities used by the more affluent few, whereas primary care centers that service the poor receive substantially fewer resources (Castro-Leal et al. 2000). World Bank policies continue to support market-oriented health-care services, strong private financing, reduction in fiscal spending, universal user fees, and decentralization of public health programs, even though social inequality is increasing and health-care conditions continue to deteriorate (Labonté and Schrecker 2007).

Current international money-lending conditions raise various ethical concerns insofar as market-driven economic policies are often required of developing countries facing an economic crisis. The governments of these nations may well prefer to buttress state responsibility regarding social services and citizen protection, instead of privileging market-based strategies, but it would be extremely difficult for them to refuse the offered loans, even with the conditions attached to them. Impoverished patients, who make up the majority of public sector patients in developing countries, have predictably lost out from this situation – at a minimum, their waiting lists grew longer while those of their richer fellow citizens decreased (Almeida 2002).

Culture and Religion

The Roman Catholic Church is undoubtedly the major religious force in Latin American countries. In other underdeveloped regions like Africa, Roman Catholicism constitutes only about one third of all confessional affiliations. This fact, combined with the importance of other cultural traditions, distinguishes these countries to some extent from Latin American countries, which helps to explain the lesser impact of Catholicism on public policies. A strong sense of community is a constitutive feature of African culture. Religious practices are less institutional and often related to social customs, including the worship of elders and the experience of god through ancestors (Kasenene 2000). In countries dominated by Catholicism, on the other hand, public policies and politicians tend to adhere to the Church's teachings. In practical terms, this has meant, for instance, opposition to the promotion and distribution of condoms, which has, in effect, produced a social divide between those who can buy them and those who depend upon free distribution, as recently reported from Colombia (Viveros-Vigoya and Hernández 2006). The Church's rationale is that only abstinence is 100 percent effective, but undoubtedly its stance is also motivated by a strong inter-est in controlling sexual behavior. As a harm minimization strategy, abstinence undoubtedly works for some people, but not for most. It is one thing, then, for the Church to issue moral appeals to its adherents, admonishing them to abstain. The Church should not, however, employ its political influence to use state power to enforce its moral views, on this and other issues, across whole countries. The Roman Catholic Church is opposed to any kind of contraception. It is this view more than anything else that determines the Church's stance on the matter of condoms as a means of AIDS prevention.

This uncompromising view on contraception has serious consequences in a range of reproductive health areas. We chose here to look at the opposition to condoms as just one example where religious views that are enforced by governments result in harmful public health outcomes.

In Latin America, the separation of Church and State has often been only *pro forma* or non-existent. In nations with deep social inequities, Catholic and upper-class politicians have tended to agree on conservative policies (Diniz et al. 2007). They strongly opposed reforms that would eventually become the concern of bioethics, by taking stances that were impervious to social needs and deprivation. Contraceptives, for example, were strongly rejected and for long periods of time were unavailable in public health-care facilities. Levonorgestrel, the morning-after pill, has been bitterly opposed in some nations, and voluntary sterilization remains for the most part illegal (Díaz et al. 2003a; 2003b). Abortion is either absolutely forbidden, or restricted to therapeutic indications and cases of rape. A recent report from Costa Rica shows how the prohibition of abortion is upheld by the medical community, whereas the illegality of sterilization is easily circumvented by willing physicians who follow their own ethical norms and are perceptive to social values that consider sterilization morally acceptable (Díaz et al. 2003a; 2003b). In some countries, governments have made sterilization more acceptable than abortion (Carranza 2007). Statistics from Brazil reveal the influence of economic factors: surgical sterilization has been performed on 40 percent of fertile women in that country, but is offered in less than half of public medical facilities, so that, as a recent survey shows, more than 60 percent paid for the intervention (Guilhem and Azevedo 2007; Vieira and Ford 2004).

Such policies consolidate high fertility and mortality rates that are demographic characteristics of poor populations, perpetuating and increasing socioeconomic contrasts with wealthier social segments whose members have low fertility and mortality rates. In some countries where liberal governments had made abortion more readily available, military regimes or conservative rulers reversed such tendencies. Whereas Cuba freely permits abortion, Nicaragua (which at present has a left-wing government, but a dictatorial past and a strong Church) has issued an absolute ban on abortion, much as Chilean dictator Pinochet abolished therapeutic indications as the one remaining legal indication for abortion. Brazil permits abortion for rape or therapeutic reasons, yet health-care providers have repeatedly been observed to treat women consulting for complications of abortion induced illegally in ways that were cruel, violent, and degrading. The same phenomenon can be witnessed today in post-apartheid South Africa. Arguably, this constitutes unprofessional conduct by health-care staff insofar as they prioritize their personal religious views over the well-being of their patients (Soares 2003).

Most of the universities established in the former Spanish colonies were created and run by the Church. Schools were also to a great extent confessional. At present, most Latin American countries show a strong proliferation of new, private universities, many of which are also strongly confessional: Roman Catholic, Episcopalian, Legionnaires of Christ, and Opus Dei. These institutions aim to ensure that their graduates, as future professionals, scientists, and scholars, will represent and defend the values of the relevant faith. Funding constraints mean that secular bioethics is seriously underrepresented.

411

UDO SCHÜKLENK, MICHAEL KOTTOW, PETER A. SY

Health Research and Resources

Developing treatment

An ongoing discussion in international research ethics is focused on the question of whether or not the standard of care that ought to be provided in clinical research should be of the same standard everywhere or whether a local standard of care should apply. This could, for instance, mean that patients in a multicenter, multination trial will be offered the gold standard of care in the control arm, while others might be offered only a placebo. Is this just? Health-care policies and programs in developing nations are constrained by scarce resources and access difficulties, especially affecting geographically isolated and socially marginalized populations. Most of these countries would not have the boldness to refer to their efforts as "a standard of health care," for general policies to provide specific levels of health care are hard to come by and mostly succumb to contextual problems. Rather, standards of care are established by outside observers or interested parties, and are frequently conflated with whatever is available to the poorest patients relying on public sector health-care delivery (Lie et al. 2004). This has led to the introduction of double standards in research ethics, suggesting ethical excellence – frequently labeled "aspirational" – for developed countries, and economics-driven ethics – frequently labeled "contextual" – for poorer nations (Macklin 2004). The idea here is, basically, to deploy a rhetorical tool that implies that those aiming at the gold standard of care are somehow naively aspirational in their aims, while those aiming for lower standards of care are more appreciative of the socio-economic local context, and, therefore, more realistic. Much of this rhetoric is arguably begging the question (Schüklenk 2004).

The most recent version of the World Medical Association's Declaration of Helsinki (WMA 2004), explicitly requires that research participants receive the best proven diagnostic and therapeutic methods of care – a requirement that some developed world researchers and sponsors have chosen to interpret as the "standard that prevails in the country in which the clinical trial is carried out" (Levine 1998: 6). By choosing a country too poor to have any standard of medical care, or a very low standard of care, investigators consider suboptimal care (or none at all) justified for control groups in randomized trials. This provides them with the sought-after justification to use placebo controls in developing countries that would be considered unethical (indeed, illegal) in developed countries. The acceptance of use of placebos in the Declaration of Helsinki was confirmed by means of a note of clarification added to §29. It grants ethical acceptance if "compelling and scientifically sound methodological reasons" make placebos necessary (WMA 2004). The question of what is ethical or not is here reduced to a mere question of scientific method.

It has been suggested, in defense of the low(er) standard of care position, that developing world trial participants are not being exploited because they are no worse off than before entering the trial. Those who see no exploitation under such circumstances argue that the participants recruited had no medical care in the first place, so there was no reason to put them on the active medication arm during the investigation or to secure post-investigational improvements of their pre-trial condition. It is argued here that biomedical researchers have no binding reason to help people in need, even if they have benefited from these participants' participation. This would be unacceptable in their home countries. Accepting the argument that no one was any worse off would also offer an incentive to pharmaceutical companies to ensure, by means of prudent drug-pricing regimes, that there are always enough patients priced out of the market. This would guarantee a continuing supply of patients on whom the use of placebo controls would become "ethical."

Post-trial access to medicines

In §30, the Declaration of Helsinki states that after the conclusion of a trial, participants should continue to receive the therapeutic benefits that their participation helped develop, especially in cases where it is vitally essential that the medication should not be interrupted. Initially rejected by some developed world scholars, the article was finally watered down to a "note of clarification," added in 2004, requiring post-trial arrangements to be "described in the study protocol" (Glantz et al. 1998; WMA 2004).

Proposed post-trial benefits are at the heart of other heated international discussions. It has been argued that trial participants should remain on medication found to be effective in the study that they took part in, and that the host community should receive some kind of compensation. There are several possible ethical rationales for this. One such argument is based on a reason put forward to justify trials in the *developed* world. Subject to conditions such as voluntary and informed consent being met, clinical research's implicit ethical rationale is that the people who made the trial possible would personally benefit from any successful trial medication as it would eventually be provided to them (and people like them in their societies) through their societies' healthcare systems. The same cannot be said for developing countries' trial participants, as more often than not they are unable to afford the innovative drug or procedure that their personal risk-taking helped to develop. Some bioethicists have joined researchers and other interested parties in decrying such post-trial provision of medical care as being unaffordable. They point out that much needed important research would be prevented if this level of post-trial care became obligatory. This claim is an empirical claim, yet its nature is such that it is difficult to test or disprove. There is at least one prominent counterexample: initially, the sponsors of AIDS vaccine trials insisted that providing care to trial participants who become infected during trials would render these vital trials unaffordable. When South African ethical review committees refused to budge and insisted that care be provided, it took the sponsors of these trials only a few months to purchase private health insurance that covered the trial participants. Clinical AIDS care is expensive and, given the chronic nature of the infection, must be provided life-long. Arguably, if under such difficult circumstances post-trial care can be ensured, it should be possible to achieve the same for most, if not all, other conditions (Schüklenk 2008).

Conclusions

We have chosen for this chapter a number of issues that are currently considered important in developing countries, even though different issues command different levels of relevance in different geographical regions of the developing world. The specific socioeconomic and cultural conditions that form the framework in which health care is delivered and health policy is created in developing countries lead more often than not to a different perspective on these issues when compared with analyses delivered by developed world-based bioethicists. For instance, organized religion does not any longer feature as a prominent concern in much of developed world bioethics writings. This is not so in Latin America, as this chapter demonstrates. Standards of care in clinical trials, an issue that barely registers as an ethical concern in developed world research ethics, remains firmly center stage in developing world contributions on the same topic. This is not to suggest, of course, that there is one consensus of opinion on any of the issues discussed herein, either among developed or developing world-based bioethicists. However, if anything, this chapter demonstrates that context matters.

References

Abrantes Pêgo, R. and Almeida, C. (2002). Theory and practice in health systems reform in Brazil and Mexico. *Cadernos de Saúde Pública* 18/4: 971–89.

AHRC (Agency for Healthcare Research and Quality) (1998). *Request for Applications on Measures of Quality of Care for Vulnerable Populations* (RFA: HS-99-001, released December 22, 1998). Available at: http://grants.nih.gov/grants/guide/rfa-files/RFA-HS-99-001.html (accessed December 11, 2007).

Almeida, C. (2002). Health system reform and equity in Latin America and the Caribbean: lessons from the 1980s and 1990s. *Cadernos de Saúde Pública* 18: 905–25.

Braga, C., Albuquerque, M. de F. P. M., and Morais, H. M. de (2004). Scientific knowledge and public health policies: reflections on the occurrence of filariasis in Recife, Pernambuco, Brazil. *Cadernos de Saúde Pública* 20/2: 351–61.

Buse, K. and Walt, G. (2000a). Global public–private health partnerships. Part I: A new development in health? *Bulletin of the World Health Organization* 78/3: 549–61.

Buse, K. and Walt, G. (2000b). Global public–private health partnerships. Part II: What are the health issues for global governance? *Bulletin of the World Health Organization* 78/5: 699–709.

Carranza, M. (2007). The therapeutic exception: abortion, sterilization and medical necessity in Costa Rica. *Developing World Bioethics* 7: 55–63.

Castro-Leal, F., Dayton, J., Demery, L., and Mehra, K. (2000). Public social spending in Africa: do the poor benefit? *Bulletin of the World Health Organization* 78/1: 66–74.

Christie, T., Asrat, G. A., Jiwani, B., Maddix, T., and Montaner, J. S. G. (2007). Exploring disparities between global HIV/AIDS funding and recent tsunami relief efforts: an ethical analysis. *Developing World Bioethics* 7/1: 1–7.

Clemens, M. A. and Pettersson, G. (2008). New data on African health professionals abroad. *Human Resources for Health* 6: 1.

Department of Health (1999). *Guidance on International Nursing Recruitment.* Available at: www.dh.gov.uk/prod_consum_dh/groups/dh_digitalassets/@dh/@en/documents/digitalasset/dh_4034794.pdf (accessed November 24, 2007).

Díaz, S., Hardy, E., Alvarado, G., and Ezcurra, E. (2003a). Acceptability of emergency contraception in Brazil, Chile, and Mexico. 1: Perceptions of emergency oral contraceptives. *Cadernos de Saúde Pública* 19/5: 1507–17.

Díaz, S., Hardy, E., Alvarado, G., and Ezcurra, E. (2003b). Acceptability of emergency contraception in Brazil, Chile, and Mexico. 2: Facilitating factors versus obstacles. *Cadernos de Saúde Pública* 19/6: 1729–37.

Diniz, D., Perea, J.-G. F., and Luna, F. (2007). Reproductive health ethics: Latin American perspectives. *Developing World Bioethics* 7/2: ii–iv.

Editor (2007). International: more money than sense; global public health. *The Economist* (July 7).

Fuller, L. (2006). Justified commitments? Considering resource allocation and fairness in Médecins Sans Frontières – Holland. *Developing World Bioethics* 6: 59–70.

Garrett, L. (2007). The challenge of global health. *Foreign Affairs* 86/1: January/February.

Glantz, L. H., Annas, G. J., Grodin, M. A., and Mariner, W. K. (1998). Research in developing countries: taking "benefit" seriously. *Hastings Center Report* 28: 38–42.

Guilhem, D. and Azevedo, A. F. (2007). Brazilian public policies for reproductive health: family planning, abortion and prenatal care. *Developing World Bioethics* 7/2: 68–77.

Hagopian, A., Thompson, M. J., Fordyce, M., Johnson, K. E., and Hart, L. G. (2004). The migration of physicians from sub-Saharan Africa to the United States of America: measures of the African brain drain. *Human Resources for Health* 2 (December): 17.

Iriart, C., Merhy, E. E., and Waitzkin, H. (2000). Managed care in Latin America: transnationalization of the health sector in a context of reform. *Cadernos de Saúde Pública* 16/1: 95–105.

Kasenene, P. (2000). African ethical theory and the four principles. In Robert M. Veatch (ed.), *Cross Cultural Perspectives in Medical Ethics*. Sudbury, MA: Jones and Bartlett.

Kirigia, J. M., Gbary, A. R., Muthuri, L. K., Nyoni, J., and Seddoh, A. (2006). The cost of health professionals' brain drain in Kenya. *BMC Health Services Research* 6: 89.

Labonté, R. and Schrecker, T. (2007). Globalization and social determinants of health: the role of the global marketplace (part 2 of 3). *Globalization and Health* 3: 6. Available at: www.globalizationandhealth.com/content/3/1/6 (accessed August 7, 2007).

Levine, R. J. (1998). The "best proven therapeutic method" standard in clinical trials in technologically developing countries. *IRB: Ethics and Human Research* 20/1: 5–9.

Lie, R. K., Emanuel, E., Grady, C., and Wendler, D. (2004). The standard of care debate: The Declaration of Helsinki versus the international consensus opinion. *Journal of Medical Ethics* 30: 190–3.

López-Arellano, O. and Blanco-Gil, J. (2001). Health policy polarisation in Mexico. *Cadernos de Saúde Pública* 17/1: 43–54.

Lowry, C. and Schüklenk, U. (2008). Global health responsibilities. *This volume*, ch. 33.

Macklin, R. (2004). *Double Standards in Medical Research in Developing Countries*. Cambridge: Cambridge University Press.

Mathers, C. D., Iburg, K. M., Salomon, J. A., Tandon, A., Chatterji, S., Usntün, B., and Murray, C. J. L. (2004). Global patterns of health life expectancy in the year 2002. *BMC Public Health* 4: 66.

Mendis, S., Fukino, K., Cameron, A., Laing, R., Filipe, Jr, A., Kathib, O., Leowski, J., and Ewen, M. (2007). The availability and affordability of selected essential medicines for chronic diseases in six low- and middle-income countries. *Bulletin of the World Health Organization* 85/4: 279–88.

Penna, M. L. F. (2003). Dengue control: a challenge for the public health system in Brazil. *Cadernos de Saúde Pública* 19/1: 305–9.

Ruger, J. P. and Kim, H.-J. (2006). Global health inequalities: an international comparison. *Journal of Epidemiology and Community Health* 60: 928–36.

Schieber, G. J., Gottret, P., Fleisher, L. K., and Leive, A. A. (2007). Financing global health: mission unaccomplished. *Health Affairs* 26/4: 921–34.

Schüklenk, U. (2004). The standard of care debate: against the myth of an "international consensus opinion." *Journal of Medical Ethics* 30: 194–7.

Schüklenk, U. (2008). AIDS as a global health emergency. *This volume*, ch. 37.

Soares, G. S. (2003). Health professionals and legal abortion in Brazil: challenges, conflicts, and meanings. *Cadernos de Saúde Pública* 19/suppl. 2: S399–S406.

Stålenheim, P., Perdomo, C., and Sköns, E. (2007). Military expenditure. In *SIPRI Yearbook 2007*. Oxford: Oxford University Press, pp. 267–97.

Vieira, E. M. and Ford, N. J. (2004). Provision of female sterilization in Ribeirão Preto, São Paulo, Brazil. *Cadernos de Saúde Pública* 20/5: 1201–10.

Viveros-Vigoya, M. and Hernández, F. G. (2006). Educators, advisors, therapists? Youth, sexuality, and social intervention. *Cadernos de Saúde Pública* 22/1: 201–8.

Wagstaff, A. (2001). Economics, health and development: some ethical dilemmas facing the World Bank and the international community. *Journal of Medical Ethics* 27: 262–7.

WHO (2006). *The World Health Report*. Geneva: World Health Organization. Available at: www.who.int/whr/2006/en/index.html (accessed December 11, 2007).

WMA (World Medical Association) (2004). *Declaration of Helsinki: Ethical Principles for Medical Research Involving Human Subjects*. Available at: www.wma.net/e/policy/pdf/17c.pdf (accessed December 11, 2007).

World Bank (2007). *About Us – Challenge*. Available at: http://go.worldbank.org/Dm4A38OWJ0 (accessed August 6, 2007).

35

Global Pharmaceutical Markets

KEVIN OUTTERSON AND DONALD W. LIGHT

Introduction

We live in a world of both abundance and scarcity. Global pharmaceutical markets share this pattern. Abundance and wealth deliver numerous medicines that prolong and enhance life for the billion people who enjoy high incomes. Scarcity and poverty, however, plague most of the rest of humanity, with devastating effect on health. The high price of patented drugs lies at the heart of a major global public health crisis: the global poor are often denied access to life-saving drugs due to high cost. Paul Hunt, the United Nations Special Rapporteur on the right to health, clearly describes the problem:

> Almost 2 billion people lack access to essential medicines. Improving access to existing medicines could save 10 million lives each year, 4 million of them in Africa and South-East Asia. Access to medicines is characterised by profound global inequity. 15% of the world's population consumes over 90% of the world's pharmaceuticals. (Hunt 2007: 1)

Pricing policies are a major contributor to this situation. Oxfam (2007) estimates that 85 percent of the world is effectively excluded from the market for medicines due to price and the World Health Organization (WHO 2004) estimates that 10 million people die each year because of a lack of access to existing medicines and vaccines. The human and economic costs of inadequate access are staggering (DFID 2004; WHO 2006).

Global access to essential medicines involves both ethical and legal issues. This chapter uses the language and forms of the law in order to make ethical observations on the structure and functioning of the intellectual property system for global pharmaceutical markets. Law is a socially created institution, with local and global effects. We need an accurate picture of the impact of global intellectual property law in order to evaluate the choices we have made and the alternatives that are available.

For better or for worse, the WTO's Agreement on Trade-Related Aspects of Intellectual Property Rights (TRIPS) is the global legal nexus for access to medicine. In TRIPS-related discussions, two sets of arguments are usually forwarded. Some argue that pharmaceutical prices are necessarily high because innovation requires it.

417

Pharmaceutical companies demand patents as an incentive for future innovation. They posit that the research and development enterprise must be nurtured by high prices in order to yield the next generation of breakthrough therapies. Patent-based drug companies have steadfastly opposed involuntary access initiatives and claim that market-based pricing is generally both legal and ethical (Bale 2002: 100–12; Dr Bale is the Director-General of the International Federation of Pharmaceutical Manufacturers Association).

Others counter that many of the profits going to pharmaceutical companies are used for marketing and other expenses rather than for R&D (Angell 2004; Avorn 2004; Goozner 2004) and that, without affordable access, innovation is a cruel taunt for the poor. New wonder drugs will not improve health unless patients are actually able to use them. A pill you cannot afford isn't effective. Medicines, according to this argument, are not normal market goods to be distributed primarily to the wealthy. Health and human rights activists, among others, seek to reduce financial barriers to access to patented medications. Some argue that it is ethical to intervene in public health emergencies, even if patent laws must be modified (Hunt 2007; MSF 2005; Oxfam 2007; 't Hoen 2002); indeed it may be unethical to stand by and not act (Singer 1972; Unger 1996).

Some scholars look for ways to provide low-cost generic medicines without significantly undermining innovation incentives (Finkelstein and Temin 2008; Fisher and Syed 2007; Hollis 2005; Love and Hubbard 2007; Outterson 2005; Outterson and Kesselheim 2008; Pogge 2005b; 2005c). One such proposal is differential or equity pricing. A prominent example relates to the AIDS-treatment crisis. Differential pricing permits antiretroviral drugs for AIDS to be sold cheaply, or donated, to low- and medium-income populations, while maintaining high prices in high-income markets like the United States. In theory, high prices in high-income markets support innovation, while lower prices in low- and medium-income markets improve access (WHO 2001). Actual implementation of differential pricing has been disappointingly limited, with companies unwilling to undertake it on a sufficient scale (Oxfam 2007).

Patent law also provides a safety valve for access while supporting innovation. Under the laws of many countries, patent rights may be modified to support other important goals, such as public health and competition, and for government use. *Compulsory licenses* are one important way of modulating patent rights in light of these other objectives. Compulsory licenses are an internationally recognized flexibility built into patent law, particularly for public health or government use. Several countries have used compulsory licenses for public health purposes, most notably the United States, Thailand, and Brazil, including for drugs other than AIDS antiretroviral. The patent-based drug companies have vigorously opposed these efforts, despite unequivocal support for the practice in the TRIPS Agreement (Outterson and Kesselheim 2008).

One of the most innovative ideas in this field is generally attributed to James Love and Tim Hubbard. They propose decoupling markets for medicine from markets for innovation, using huge prize funds to stimulate innovation. The patent system remains untouched, but the prize funds purchase drug patents according to their health impact. These drugs essentially become generic or join patent pools immediately after the patent is purchased. Global and local coordination functions are supported through a global research and development treaty and patent pools (KEI 2007; Love and Hubbard 2007). Three other research groups have subsequently proposed other decoupling mechanisms. Aidan Hollis (2005) and Thomas Pogge (2005b) are working on a health-care innovation prize fund project to link the market for medicines more efficiently to health needs. Two Harvard researchers propose a global credit-trading system based on actual health needs rather than merely ability to pay (Fisher and Syed 2007) and two MIT researchers propose separating drug-discovery from drug-marketing, with public funding of the R&D phase (Finkelstein and Temin 2008). These major reforms are the subject of intense discussion at the present time in various international organizations such as the WHO and WTO.

One important normative assumption in these approaches is that if we can promote access without harming innovation, then we should do so. In the language of a legal analogy, it assumes that we have an ethical duty to rescue people who need essential medicines, especially when the rescue can be accomplished with minimal risk and cost. In the next section, we examine a modest duty to rescue in the context of global intellectual property rights in medicines.

The Shipwreck of the *Richmond* and the Duty to Rescue

On August 2, 1849, the whaling vessel *Richmond* ran aground in the Bering Straits, near present-day Alaska. The *Richmond* was hunting whales during the brief weeks that those waters were navigable in the mid-nineteenth century. The crew could not repair the ship. The advancing polar ice was expected to arrive before the end of August. If the ship became icebound, both the crew and the valuable cargo would be lost. (With today's global warming, the *Richmond* would not be in immediate danger, as the Bering Straits no longer become icebound in late August.)

Two days later, other whaling ships found the *Richmond* and rescued the crew. The masters of the *Panama* and the *Elizabeth Firth* purchased the oil and whalebone at a very low price, and then the two surviving ships began the long voyage home to New York City via Cape Horn. Upon arrival in New York, the owners of the *Richmond* sued to set aside the sales contracts. They argued that the situation was one of extreme duress – stranded in the Artic while the sea-ice closed in – and they should not be held to the "unreasonable bargain" struck in such dire circumstances. Eventually, the US Supreme Court agreed (*Richmond v. Jones* 1856).

The facts of this case raise interesting ethical questions that can shed light on the debate over access to essential medicines. Did the masters of the *Panama* and the *Elizabeth Firth* have any duty to come to the aid of the *Richmond*? Can a rescuer take advantage of very desperate circumstances to negotiate a tough contract? Put another way, does a rescuer have some duty to act fairly during an emergency (Lifshitz 2008)?

The Supreme Court noted that the salvage "was effected in a couple of days, with some trouble and labor, but little or no risk or danger." In such circumstances, the Court did not permit the rescuer to "take the advantage of his situation, and avail himself of the calamities of others to drive a bargain; nor will they permit the performance of a public duty to be turned into a traffic of profit."

In the *Richmond*, the risk to cargo and crew was grave and immediate; the whaling vessels *Panama* and *Elizabeth Firth* were well positioned to salvage; the risks and costs

419

of salvage were modest, but there was no suggestion that either ship had contributed to the *Richmond*'s accident. Some of the facts were peculiar, to be sure. The masters of the *Richmond* and the *Elizabeth Firth* were brothers. The owners of the *Richmond* argued that the brothers may have colluded in the bargain sale, but the Supreme Court did not decide this issue, relying instead on the "public duty" of ships to avoid hard bargains in desperate circumstances. According to the Court, the *Panama* and the *Elizabeth Firth* should be content with generous, but not extortionate, payment for their services (Lifshitz 2008).

It should be noted that the common law of the United States does not recognize a general legal duty to rescue. In most circumstances, the law will permit an innocent bystander to remain aloof and refuse to offer life-saving aid. This case focuses on the compensation due for a voluntary salvage operation: neither ship was obliged to attempt a rescue. This principle is well established in US common law. One classic problem for first-year law students involves the person on a bridge who could save a drowning child by simply throwing a rope. The common law is clear: a duty to rescue is not imposed, even if the rescue could be done easily with no risk (Heyman 1994; Hyman 2006; Lifshitz 2008; Romohr 2006; Volokh 1999; Weinrib 1980).

Two exceptions to this rule are worth mentioning. First, if the bystander has some special relationship to a person in need or to a person who poses a danger, then a legal duty to rescue or reduce the danger might be imposed. Examples include a shopkeeper who must protect a customer in her store from dangerous conditions, and a therapist who must warn foreseen victims that her client plans a violent act. In both cases, the special relationship entails a modest legal duty. Secondly, if the bystander was in some way responsible for the situation, or was impeding rescue by others, then a court might categorize the incident as misfeasance rather than nonfeasance, even absent any fault on the part of the bystander. For example, if your car breaks down on a dark road – through no fault of your own – the law may impose a duty to take steps to minimize the dangers created for other drivers. You cannot just leave the unlit car on the dark road, and claim innocent bystander status when an accident occurs. You must take some steps to minimize the risk you created: pull the car off the road, light a warning flare, call the police, etc. Likewise, you may be liable if you volunteer to rescue and do so negligently, or actively prevent others from undertaking a rescue. These exceptions are important analogies for the ethical case for global access to vital medicines, as we describe in the next section.

The Ethics of Global Access to Essential Medicines

Suppose we examine global intellectual property law and the access to medicines crisis through the lens of the *Richmond* and the duty to rescue. Global pharmaceutical companies resist the notion that they are ethically compelled to rescue others by providing their drugs equitably to the poor. If they have no global corporate social responsibility in this area, the companies are free to remain disinterested bystanders, and sell their products at high prices in hard bargains with the world's poor. We seem untroubled that the poor cannot afford Rolex watches or fly first class. If medicines are an ordinary market good, then perhaps the same attitude should hold here.

420

In 1972, Peter Singer wrote a seminal essay on our utilitarian obligations to the distant poor and victims of tragedies, such as the millions destitute in East Bengal in 1971. If we walk by a shallow pond, see a child drowning, and believe we should wade in and rescue her, even though we will get wet and muddy, Singer argued, then "[i]t makes no moral difference whether the person I can help is a neighbor's child ten yards from me or a Bengali whose name I shall never know, ten thousand miles away" (Singer 1972: 231–2). Secondly, Singer's principle makes no distinction between cases in which I am the only person who could possibly do anything and cases in which I am just one among millions in the same position. The principle is that "if it is in our power to prevent something bad happening, without thereby sacrificing anything of comparable moral importance, we ought, morally, to do it." This principle "requires us only to prevent what is bad, and not promote what is good" (p. 231). In the global access to medicines crisis, some individuals have acted with charity in order to provide needed medicines to the poor. These piecemeal efforts, while individually significant, do not recognize the institutional issues relating to health-care systems in general and global pharmaceutical markets in particular. Significant change requires something beyond individual responses. Institutions, policies, laws, and markets must be revised if patented medicines are to be provided on a globally equitable basis.

In *Living High and Letting Die*, Peter Unger (1996) extends and refines Singer's original work through a series of test cases, like the man with a very nice car who sees a person lying by the road with a gash in his leg, waving for help as he bleeds profusely. Should the car owner take the time and trouble to drive the bleeding man to the hospital and get the inside of his nice car soaked with blood? Even more disturbing is the man who has left his priceless vintage Bugatti on a railroad siding and who sees a runaway empty train barreling toward a child playing on the main track. The man could run and throw the switch so the train would miss the child but destroy his Bugatti. Should he save the child? Most people think he should. Leaving aside fine points, responses indicate that people should be ready not only to help those in need, but also to make material sacrifices.

Approaches not grounded in utilitarianism also describe a duty to rescue. In telling the parable of the Good Samaritan, Jesus of Nazareth didn't make the rescue effortless. The Good Samaritan expended time, effort, and money in a potentially risky situation to care for a stranger in need. Jesus blessed this example, telling his listeners to "Go and do likewise" (Luke 10:25–37, NIV).

Some, however, remain unconvinced. Responding to Singer, Jan Narveson writes: "I have seen no plausible argument that we *owe* something, as a matter of general duty, to those to whom we have done nothing wrong" (2003: 419). Others, including libertarians, will have more difficulty defending this position in the context of global intellectual property rights, since those rights are state-created positive law.

Thomas Pogge (2002; 2005c) argues for a special moral imperative to rescue those who are dying or seriously suffering when we have participated in creating the situation through legal, institutional, or economic practices. A prominent proposal with similar aims is the draft *Human Rights Guidelines for Pharmaceutical Companies in Relation to Access to Medicines*, prepared by Paul Hunt (2007), the United Nations Special Rapporteur on the right of everyone to the enjoyment of the highest attainable standard of physical and mental health. The *Human Rights Guidelines* articulate principles

421

Table 1: Five elements of the duty to rescue

Element of duty to rescue	Application
Importance of the rescue	WHO estimates 10 million lives are lost annually from lack of access to essential medications.
Capacity of the bystander to rescue	The relevant medicines are already invented.
Role of the bystander in contributing to the risk	Patent-based drug companies helped create the global intellectual property regime that delays low-cost generics and they have encouraged poor countries to raise higher barriers to low-cost drugs. These companies both contributed to the creation of the institutional system and also actively prevent rescue by others through their control of the relevant drug patents.
Special relationship of the bystander	Patent-based drug companies receive billions of dollars in tax subsidies. For most products, important early research was performed in government laboratories or in university laboratories with government funding.
Risk or cost to the bystander	Some access proposals do not impose any significant risk or cost on patent-based pharmaceutical companies.

of ethical corporate social responsibility in the realm of access to medicines. Oxfam's briefing paper, *Investing For Life: Meeting Poor People's Needs for Access to Medicines Through Responsible Business Practices* (2007) reaches broadly similar conclusions. Our project complements these projects by exploring the ethical justifications for requiring corporate action and institutional reform. At the core, all of them claim a special status for medicines, calling for ethical responses above and beyond the way we handle ordinary market goods.

In the following sections, we apply five elements of the duty to rescue to the global access to medicines problem. In short, we develop the ethical justifications for proposals to provide generic-priced drugs to the world's poorest people. Singer and Unger find positive moral duties on the rich to care for the needy. Our aim is much narrower: we argue that global intellectual property law should be modified to *permit rescue by others*, especially when the patent-based drug companies are not significantly disadvantaged thereby.

Importance of the rescue

Pharmaceutical companies tout the power of their products to prolong life and transform human health. Denying these drugs to the poor on the basis of patent-based and market-based pricing is a major public health disaster, leading to perhaps 10 million deaths per year. While many factors disadvantage the global poor, lack of access to medicines is clearly among the important ones that we can modify (WHO 2004).

People living with AIDS in resource-poor settings have waited for a long time for access to life-saving antiretrovirals. Almost six million people in low- and middle-income populations are dying for want of antiretrovirals today; despite a multitude of programs, access remains inadequate (PEPFAR 2008; WHO 2004). Just as treatment in low-income countries is scaling up, so biological resistance to first-line AIDS therapy is increasing. Second-line antiretrovirals, including protease inhibitors, are not generally available at generic prices. Manufacturers of patented second-line therapies are pricing them at US levels in low-income countries. Even with voluntary discount programs, second-line therapies cost much more than the first-line drugs (Chase 2008; MSF 2005).

We should also not make the mistake of assuming that only AIDS, malaria, and tuberculosis plague the developing world. The diseases of the rich and poor are converging, and include cardiovascular disease, stroke, mental illness, diabetes, cancer, and arthritis. Equitable access to medicines should include all medicines that can improve the health of the world's poor (Outterson 2008).

Capacity of the bystander to rescue

For the most significant diseases in the developing world, good therapies are already at hand, invented to serve markets in high-income countries. While additional research is always desired for neglected diseases, the pharmaceutical tools required to treat significant global diseases are already invented and in production.

The WHO sorts diseases into three categories (WHO 2006). The first category includes diseases that occur throughout the world – for example, cancer, heart disease, diabetes, depression, and other familiar conditions. Wealthy country markets stimulate innovation for Type I diseases. Type II diseases are endemic primarily in low- and medium-income countries, but enough cases are still present in wealthy countries (or in tourists or soldiers from wealthy countries who are temporarily located in low- and middle-income nations) to create an attractive market. AIDS and malaria could be considered Type II diseases. The third category includes the truly neglected diseases of the tropics, including those that lack any viable commercial market, such as leishmaniasis, lymphatic filariasis, onchocerciasis, and schistosomiasis.

Type I and Type II cause most of the disease burden in the world, including in developing countries. Markets in wealthy countries will continue to stimulate innovation in treatments for these diseases. As a result, the most straightforward solution is simply to make the medicines for these diseases available to the world's poor at competitive generic prices. These drugs are already discovered and, in the absence of intellectual property rights in these markets, generic firms could produce the drugs for low- and medium-income country populations. For example, relatively modest numbers of cervical cancer deaths in high-income countries were sufficient incentive to prompt the creation of novel HPV vaccines to prevent most cases of cervical cancer. But HPV vaccines are one of the most expensive vaccines in history, and are not affordable by 93 percent of the women who die from cervical cancer (Outterson and Kesselheim 2008).

Type III diseases require different solutions. Most neglected-disease conditions lack a market not because of allegedly inadequate intellectual property rights in low-income countries, but because of the poverty of the afflicted. Perhaps the best description of a neglected-disease drug is one where market-based innovation is unlikely because the target population will require the drug or vaccine to be distributed at or below the lowest possible marginal cost of production. Any such drug will require non-market funding for innovation and distribution, with or without US-style intellectual property regimes. Many public–private product-development partnerships have been founded in recent years to address the need for neglected-disease innovation. These are important and high-profile projects, but we do not have to wait decades for success in neglected-disease research: the heaviest burdens of disease in the developing world are Type I and II, and drugs for those diseases are already discovered. In short, it is the poor themselves who are being neglected, not just their diseases.

Role of the bystander in contributing to the risk

A small number of global companies crafted the TRIPS Agreement, ending a long tradition around the world of exempting medicines from patent laws. Among the companies were Bristol-Meyer-Squibb, Johnson and Johnson, Merck, and Pfizer, but all the patent-based drug companies benefit from the system thus created. The explicit goal was to prohibit free trade of low-priced generics from the emerging pharmaceutical industries in developing countries. The TRIPS Agreement globalized intellectual property law on the US model, and bilateral trade agreements included additional provisions (Correa 2000; Drahos and Braithwaite 2002; Helfer 2004; Sell 2003).

Therefore, the patent-based drug companies are not strangers to the global access to medicines problem; nor are they innocent bystanders who happen upon a tragedy by chance. They cannot rely on libertarian arguments to absolve themselves of responsibility. They helped create the global system of intellectual property law that stands as a barrier to generic production for the poor. They applied for the patents in developing country markets to block generic production. In the past decade they have pressed hard on the US government to include additional provisions in their bilateral free trade agreements. These agreements apply to trading partners of various income levels and extend prohibitions against free trade of patented or copyrighted products in many contexts. At the behest of industry leaders, the US Trade Representative's Office has vigorously opposed compulsory licensure and pressured poorer countries not to use TRIPS flexibilities in order to get affordable medicines to their patients (GAO 2007). The patent-based drug companies are among the chief architects and beneficiaries of this global system, and thus bear enhanced responsibility for its effects on the poor (Pogge 2005a), even in the absence of fault or negligence. They are active participants in the creation of the problem rather than innocent bystanders (Weinrib 1980).

The patent-based drug companies actively work to prevent rescue by others. Generic production and distribution of patented drugs for low- and medium-income country populations is possible, as demonstrated by the actions of generic drug companies such as Cipla Ltd of India and charities such as Médecins Sans Frontières. But the drug companies can use patent law to block generic production of the best available medicines and to drive "unreasonable bargains" on pricing. The Supreme Court found the latter practice objectionable in the *Richmond* case. Patent law gives companies the right to block generic production for poor countries during the patent period, but exercising it transforms the companies from innocent bystanders into entities claiming the legal right to prevent rescue.

424

Special relationship of the bystander

Approximately half of effective global R&D for medicines is supported by public funds, and 84 percent of all global funds to discover new medicines comes directly or indirectly from public sources (Light 2006; Outterson 2008). Much of this research occurs in government and nonprofit university laboratories, which profess allegiance to a broader social mission. The duty to rescue is more salient when the bystander has received public support for the task at hand. A hospital receiving US public funds is obligated to offer emergency treatment to anyone who comes through its doors, without regard for ability to pay. A captain of a ship can no longer ignore the passenger who falls off the ship, even when the accident occurs through no fault of the captain (Weinrib 1980). Pharmaceutical research programs that receive public support should be under a similar duty. Billions of dollars of public funds have been expended to create these drugs; some duty is appropriate in these circumstances (Chaifetz et al. 2007).

The drug company's status is also unique because of the patent law's ability to block the activities of others. Return to the paradigm case of the bystander on the bridge as the child drowns. The common law does not impose a legal duty to throw the rope. But what if the bystander actively prevented others from throwing the rope? The legal result would be quite different; vigorous actions to prevent or block a rescue may violate both tort and criminal law. As Ernest Weinrib has stated: "Although it may be nonfeasance to refuse to rescue a drowning person whose predicament arose independently, it is misfeasance to hide the rope that others might toss out to him" (1980: 258).

Risk or cost to the bystander

Peter Singer (2002) argues on behalf of the poor for an ethical duty to provide assistance. This duty entails obligations upon the wealthy to divert some of their resources to help improve conditions for the poor. Paul Farmer (1999) reaches similar conclusions when he advocates for a preferential option for the poor, particularly in health. While some find their accounts persuasive, the wealthy have not adequately responded to the pressing need (Pogge 2005a). One major stumbling block is pharmaceutical companies' perception of their economic self-interest: companies are not in the business of giving away their products as charity, and vigorously defend their intellectual property rights.

Economic theory seems to support these companies in their perceptions. Consider the economic concept of rivalry. A service or good is *rivalrous* in an economic sense if one or more users degrade the resource. If I eat an apple, I have denied it to all others. Even looking at an apple is rivalrous at some point: a million people cannot admire it in person; neither can thousands share a house, or a car, or a farm at the same moment. Most forms of property are therefore rivalrous, and this makes donations of property rivalrous as well. If a pharmaceutical company donates drugs that cost millions to produce, then the pills become the property of the recipients and are lost to the donor. We should not expect pharmaceutical company donations to meet the medical needs of the world's poor in this way. These pills are not costless to produce and their consumption is rivalrous. Any involuntary mandate would operate as a tax on these firms and their shareholders. The companies are conducting a business, not a charity.

425

But perhaps this account of rivalry is mistaken. What if you could give a gift that didn't cost anything? Imagine if pharmaceutical companies could make a donation for the world's poor that didn't diminish their wealth in any way. If some property was *non-rivalrous*, then something of great benefit to the world's poor could be made available without consuming the property. While this might sound almost magical, in fact most pharmaceutical knowledge is non-rivalrous and can be shared without diminishing anyone else's knowledge (Outterson 2005).

The primary reason drug companies don't openly share pharmaceutical knowledge is to safeguard their profits in the marketplace. The global system of intellectual property law creates an artificial scarcity in knowledge, making knowledge rivalrous by law rather than by necessity. Public policy accedes to this unnatural scarcity in order to promote future innovation. But we don't have to be forced into an unfortunate choice between access and innovation. Some equitable access proposals aim to capture the benefits of sharing non-rivalrous knowledge while retaining optimal innovation incentives. All such proposals share a common insight: poor populations constitute very modest markets for global patent-based drug companies; so forgoing these markets will not harm innovation to a significant degree. Diversion of equitably priced medicines into wealthy country markets is the primary concern generally expressed, but the threat of diversion has been overstated in the past, and simply hasn't materialized. Donors have distributed billions of dollars of AIDS drugs in very poor countries without observable diversion in commercial quantities to wealthy country markets (Outterson and Kesselheim 2008). Free-riding by the world's poorest citizens is not only possible, but may be entirely appropriate for essential medicines (Scherer 2004).

One proposal is a patent buy-out for the developing world. Generic companies would be permitted to purchase particular pharmaceutical patent rights for low- and medium-income countries. Generic competition would stimulate production at the lowest sustainable cost, which would maximize equitable access. Optimal innovation would be supported by the combination of buy-out royalties and continuing rent extraction (patent profits) in high-income markets. This is the voluntary "patent buy-out" model (Ganslandt et al. 2001; Outterson 2006; Outterson and Kesselheim 2008; Stein and Valery 2004). Involuntary versions of this proposal would utilize compulsory licenses, as permitted under TRIPS. Other variants utilize prize funds, as discussed earlier in this chapter.

These proposals are made more plausible by a realistic account of the net costs to companies of R&D to innovate. While the industry claims that it costs more than $1 billion on average to develop a new drug, it issues little verifiable and transparent data on this issue, and independent sources suggest the actual costs are much lower. A recent review points out that corporate tax returns have itemized the costs for clinical trials as a fraction of the costs used to generate high estimates (Light 2007; Love 2003). The size and length of trials are both reported as much smaller by the Food and Drug Administrations (FDA) and the National Institutes of Health (NIH) than by corporations. About half of industry estimates consist of a built-in high estimate for profits not made on the money invested in research. Figures from the National Science Foundation survey of basic and applied research have led one policy research team to conclude that only 1.3 percent of pharmaceutical revenues, after taking into account tax subsidies, are devoted to discovering new molecules (Light and Lexchin 2005). Thus a fair price for patent rights for lower- and middle-income countries should be relatively modest. More importantly, if access proposals impose a very modest or perhaps zero risk or cost on the patent-based drug companies, then modifications are indicated to global intellectual property law to permit rescue by others.

Conclusion

Global pharmaceutical markets distribute medicines based on ability to pay rather than medical need. As a result, billions of people are inappropriately priced out of the market through a global system of intellectual property rules that pharmaceutical companies helped create and which plainly benefits them. Many other people are locked into "hard bargains," paying inappropriately high prices akin to the shipwreck of the *Richmond*. As contributors to the creation of, and active participants in, global pharmaceutical markets, the patent-based drug companies may be subject to an ethical duty to permit an easy rescue, which in this case includes allowing opportunities to expand equitable access while preserving optimal innovation. At the very least, they should not actively hinder the rescue efforts of others and should permit generic licensing for those unable to pay wealthy country market prices.

References

Angell, M. (2004). *The Truth About Drug Companies: How They Deceive Us and What to Do About It*. New York: Random House.

Avorn, J. (2004). *Powerful Medicines: The Benefits, Risks, and Costs of Prescription Drugs*. New York: Alfred A. Knopf.

Bale, Jr, H. E. (2002). Patents, patients and developing countries: access, innovation and the political dimensions of trade policy. In Brigitte Granville (ed.), *The Economics of Essential Medicines*. London: Royal Institute of International Affairs, International Economics Programme, pp. 100, 102–4.

Chaifetz, S., Chokshi, D. A., Rajkumar, R., Scales, D., and Benkler, Y. (2007). Closing the access gap for health innovations: an open licensing proposal for universities. *Globalization and Health* 3/1. Available at www.globalizationandhealth.com/content/3/1/1 (Accessed 21 June, 2008).

Chase, M. (2008). Clinton Foundation, Unitaid strike deals on price cuts for AIDS drugs. *Wall Street Journal* (April 29): D3.

Congressional Budget Office (1998). *How Increased Competition from Generic Drugs Has Affected Prices and Returns in the Pharmaceutical Industry*. Washington, DC: Congressional Budget Office, pp. 45–8.

Correa, C. M. (2000). *Intellectual Property Rights, the WTO and Developing Countries: The TRIPS Agreement and Policy Options*. London: Zed Books Ltd.

DFID (2004). *Increasing Access to Essential Medicines in the Developing World: UK Government Policy and Plans*. London: Department for International Development.

Drahos, P. with Braithwaite, J. (2002). *Information Feudalism: Who Owns the Knowledge Economy?* New York: The New Press.

Farmer, P. (1999). *Infections and Inequalities: The Modern Plagues*. Berkeley: University of California Press.

Finkelstein, S. and Temin, P. (2008). *Reasonable Rx: Solving the Drug Price Crisis*. New Jersey: FT Press.

Fisher, W. W. and Syed, T. (2007). Global justice in healthcare: developing drugs for the developing world. *University of California Davis Law Review* 40 (March): 581–678.

Ganslandt, M., Maskus, K. E., and Wong, E. V. (2001). Developing and distributing essential medicines to poor countries: the DEFEND proposal. *World Economy* 24: 779–95.

GAO (2007). *Intellectual Property: US Trade Policy Guidance on WTO Declaration on Access to Medicines May Need Clarification*. Report 07-1198. Washington, DC: Government Accountability Office, pp. 15, 19, 23.

Goozner, M. (2004). *The $800 Million Pill: The Truth Behind the Cost of New Drugs*. Berkeley: University of California Press.

Helfer, L. R. (2004). Regime shifting: the TRIPS agreement and new dynamics of international intellectual property lawmaking. *Yale Journal of International Law* 29/1: 1–83.

Heyman, S. J. (1994). Foundations of the duty to rescue. *Vanderbilt Law Review* 47: 673–755.

Hollis, A. (2005). An efficient reward system for pharmaceutical innovation. Available at http://econ.ucalgary.ca/fac-files/ah/drugprizes.pdf (accessed June 21, 2008).

Hunt, P. (2007). Human rights guidelines for pharmaceutical companies in relation to access to medicines (draft for consultation).

Hyman, David A. (2006). Rescue without law: an empirical perspective on the duty to rescue. *Texas Law Review* 84: 653–737.

KEI (2007). Collective management of intellectual property. The use of patent pools to expand access to essential medical technologies. Knowledge Ecology International Research Note 3/1. Available at www.keionline.org/index.php?option=com_content&task=view&id=65&Itemid=44 (accessed June 21, 2008).

Kesselheim, A. S. and Avorn, J. (2006). Biomedical patents and the public's health: is there a role for eminent domain? *Journal of the American Medical Association* 295/4: 434–7.

Lifshitz, S. (2008). Distress exploitation contracts in the shadow of no duty to rescue. *North Carolina Law Review* 86: 315–78.

Light, D. W. (2006). Basic research funds to discover important new drugs: who contributes how much? In M. A. Burke (ed.), *Monitoring the Financial Flows for Health Research 2005: Behind the Global Numbers*. Geneva: Global Forum for Health Research, pp. 27–43.

Light, D. W. (2007). Misleading Congress about drug development. *Journal of Health Politics, Policy and Law* 32: 895–913.

Light, D. W. and Lexchin, J. (2005). Foreign free riders and the high price of US medicines. *British Medical Journal* 331: 958–60.

Love, J. (2003). *Evidence Regarding Research and Development Investments in Innovative and Non-Innovative Medicines*. Washington DC: Consumer Project on Technology.

Love, J. and Hubbard, T. (2007). The big idea: prizes to stimulate R&D for new medicines. *Chicago-Kent Law Review* 82/3: 1519–54.

MSF (Médecins Sans Frontières) (2005). Campaign for access to essential medicines: European parliament committee on international trade hearing on TRIPS and access to medicines. Available at http://europapoort.eerstekamer.nl/9345000/1/j9vvgy6i0ydh7th/vgbwr4k8ocw2/f=/vgz6mnudecs3.pdf (accessed June 21, 2008).

Narveson, J. (2003). We don't owe them a thing! *The Monist* 86: 419–33.

Outterson, K. (2005). Pharmaceutical arbitrage: balancing access and innovation in international prescription drug markets. *Yale Journal of Health Policy, Law and Ethics* 5: 193–286.

Outterson, K. (2006). Patent buy-outs for global disease innovations for low- and middle-income countries. *American Journal of Law and Medicine* 32: 159–73.

Outterson, K. (2008). Should access to medicines and TRIPS flexibilities be limited to specific diseases? American Journal of Law and Medicine, 34.

428

Outterson, K. and Kesselheim, A. (2008). Market-based licensing for HPV vaccines in developing countries. *Health Affairs*, 27/1: 130–9.

Oxfam (2002). Fatal side effects: medicine patents under the microscope. In Brigitte Granville (ed.), *The Economics of Essential Medicines*. London: Royal Institute of International Affairs, International Economics Programme, pp. 81, 88.

Oxfam (2007). *Investing for Life: Meeting Poor People's Needs for Access to Medicines Through Responsible Business Practices*. Oxfam Briefing Paper 109 (November). Oxford: Oxfam.

PEPFAR (2008). *The Power of Partnerships: Fourth Annual Report to Congress on PEPFAR*. Washington, DC: The United States President's Emergency Program for AIDS Relief.

Pogge, T. W. (2002). *World Poverty and Human Rights: Cosmopolitan Responsibilities and Reforms*. Malden, MA: Polity.

Pogge, T. W. (2005a). World poverty and human rights. *Ethics and International Affairs* 19/1: 1–7.

Pogge, T. W. (2005b). Human rights and global health. *Metaphilosophy* 36: 182–209.

Pogge, T. W. (2005c). Human rights and global health: A research program. In C. Barry and T. W. Pogge (eds.), *Global Institutions and Responsibilities: Achieving Global Justice*. Oxford: Blackwell.

Richmond v. Jones (1856). 60 U.S. 150 (19 How. 150).

Romohr, P. W. (2006). A right/duty perspective on the legal and philosophical foundations of the no-duty-to-rescue rule. *Duke Law Journal* 55: 1025–57.

Scherer, F. M. (2004). A note on global welfare in pharmaceutical patenting. *World Economy* 27, pp. 1127, 1141.

Sell, S. K. (2003). *Private Power, Public Law: The Globalization of Intellectual Property Rights*. Cambridge: Cambridge University Press.

Singer, P. (1972). Famine, affluence, and morality. *Philosophy and Public Affairs* 1/3: 229–43.

Singer, P. (2002). *One World: The Ethics of Globalization*. New Haven: Yale University Press.

Stein, P. and Valery, E. (2004). Competition: an antidote to the high price of prescription drugs. *Health Affairs* 23/4: 151–8.

't Hoen, E. (2002). TRIPS, pharmaceutical patents, and access to essential medicines: a long way from Seattle to Doha. *Chicago Journal of International Law* 3/27: 29–30.

TRIPS Agreement (1994). *Agreement on Trade-Related Aspects of Intellectual Property Rights*, April 15, 1994. Marrakesh Agreement Establishing the World Trade Organization, Annex 1C, art. 27.1, Legal Instruments – Results of the Uruguay Round vol. 31, 33 I.L.M. 81 (1994). The United States implemented the WTO agreements in the Uruguay Round Agreements Act, Pub. L. No. 103-465, 108 Stat. 4809 (1994).

Unger, P. (1996). *Living High and Letting Die: Our Illusion of Innocence*. New York: Oxford University Press.

Volokh, E. (1999). Duties to rescue and the anticooperative effects of law. *Georgetown Law Journal* 88: 105–14.

Weinrib, E. J. (1980). The case for a duty to rescue. *Yale Law Journal* 90: 247–93.

WHO (World Health Organization) (2001). Report of the workshop on differential pricing and financing of essential drugs: A WHO/WTO secretariat workshop. Available at http://whqlibdoc.who.int/hq/2001/a73725.pdf (accessed June 21, 2008).

WHO (2004). Equitable access to essential medicines: a framework for collective action. In WHO, *Policy Perspectives on Medicines*. Geneva: World Health Organization.

WHO (2006). *Public Health, Innovation and Intellectual Property Rights: Report of the Commission on Intellectual Property Rights, Innovation and Public Health*. Geneva: World Health Organization.

36

Infectious Disease

MICHAEL J. SELGELID

The Ethical Importance of Infectious Disease

The ethical importance of infectious diseases partly relates to the fact that their consequences are almost unrivalled. Historically they have caused more morbidity and mortality than any other cause, including war (Price-Smith 2001). The Black Death eliminated one-third of the European population in just a few years during the mid-fourteenth century; the 1918 flu epidemic killed between 20 and 100 million people; and smallpox killed between 300 and 500 million people during the twentieth century alone – i.e., three times more than were killed by all the wars of that period (Oldstone 1998).

Secondly, because the public health measures used to control them sometimes involve infringement of widely accepted individual rights and liberties, infectious diseases raise difficult philosophical questions about how to strike a balance between the goal of protecting the greater good of public health and the goal of protecting individual rights and liberties. Quarantine and travel restrictions, for example, violate the right to freedom of movement. Other public health measures – such as contact tracing, the notification of third parties, and the reporting of the health status of individuals to authorities – can interfere with the right to privacy. Mandatory treatment and vaccination, finally, conflict with the right to informed consent. Though measures such as these may sometimes be necessary to avert public health disasters, how great must a public health threat be for such measures to be justified? Most would deny that either the goal of promoting the greater good of society in the way of public health or the goal of protecting individual rights and liberties should always take priority over the other.

Thirdly, because infectious diseases primarily affect the poor and disempowered, the topic of infectious disease is closely connected to the topic of justice (Selgelid 2005). Malnutrition, dirty water, crowded living conditions, bad working conditions, poor education, lack of sanitation and hygiene, and lack of decent health-care provision all increase chances that those who suffer from poverty will also suffer from infectious disease. Malnutrition weakens immune systems, for example, and this increases chances of infection. Dirty water harbors infectious pathogens. Crowded living and working conditions facilitate the spread of disease from person to person. Those who are poorly educated fail to take sufficient disease-avoidance measures. And poor communities often lack adequate resources to improve sanitation and hygiene. Finally, when the poor do become infected, they suffer worse consequences than would otherwise be the case because health-care systems are weak in poor countries and because impoverished individuals cannot afford to pay for the (often expensive) medicines they need. Factors like these explain why the vast majority of infectious disease morbidity and mortality occurs in developing countries.

Infectious diseases raise additional issues of global ethics because they fail to respect national borders. An epidemic in one country or region can quickly spread to others. The international spread of infectious diseases is facilitated by the dramatic increase in trade and travel associated with globalization. The mobility of infectious diseases is illustrated by the spread of AIDS from Africa to the rest of the world during the 1980s, and by the rapid spread of SARS from Asia to Canada in 2003. Many are currently worried that H5N1 avian influenza or H1N1 swine influenza may lead to a global pandemic rivaling that of 1918.

One implication of infectious disease mobility is that the poverty and poor health-care conditions in developing countries have negative implications for health in rich countries. In order to protect their own populations, rich countries should thus take greater interest in both poverty reduction and health-care improvement in poor countries.

The Global Infectious Disease Status Quo: AIDS and TB

Infectious diseases cause approximately 15 million deaths worldwide yearly, and they cause almost one in two deaths in developing countries. AIDS, tuberculosis (TB), and malaria are the biggest killers. Together they account for approximately 6 million deaths each year; 40 million people are currently infected with HIV. During each of the past few years, 5 million people became newly infected with HIV and 3 million people died from AIDS. Two-thirds of cases occur in sub-Saharan Africa, where adult HIV prevalence rates commonly reach (and sometimes exceed) 30 percent; 95 percent of AIDS deaths occur in developing countries. Although prices for antiretroviral medications have dropped considerably (to as low as US$100 for a year of treatment), they are still relatively expensive and thus unaffordable to the very poor. At the beginning of the twenty-first century, only 5 percent of those in need received antiretroviral medication. Though coverage improved as a result of the WHO/UNAIDS "3 by 5" program that aimed to provide treatment to three (i.e., half) of the 6 million people who needed it by the end of 2005, only 24 percent of those in need were receiving treatment at the end of 2006. AIDS has killed more than 30 million people since the disease was first recognized in 1981.

TB kills almost 2 million people each year. Though considered eradicable during the 1950s, TB "is now more prevalent than in any previous period in human history" (Gandy and Zumla 2002: 385). One-third of the human population is infected with the latent form of the disease; and, a tenth of these are expected to develop active illness. The WHO declared TB a global health emergency in 1993, and in 2002 estimated "that between [then] and 2020, approximately 1,000 million people will be newly infected, over

150 million people will get sick, and 36 million will die of TB – if control is not further strengthened" (WHO 2002). It further found that 95 percent of TB cases and 98 percent of TB deaths occur in developing countries (WHO 2007).

There are numerous reasons why it is especially tragic that TB kills nearly as many people as AIDS each year. Curative TB drugs have existed for more than 50 years, and they are much less expensive that AIDS medications (which are not themselves curative). A standard course of TB medication costs only US$10–$20. From an economic standpoint, therefore, the morbidity and mortality resulting from TB should have been more easily avoidable. Another reason for concern is that TB, being airborne, is contractible via casual contact and is much more contagious than AIDS. While behavior modification (with respect to intravenous (IV) drug-use and sexual practice) can essentially eliminate the risk of infection with AIDS, TB can be passed from one individual to another via coughing, sneezing, and even talking. In some ways, then, the threat to "innocent individuals" – and public health in general – is greater in the case of TB.

Though the consequences of TB rival those of AIDS – and though TB seems especially problematic for reasons mentioned immediately above – it is worth noting that bioethics discussion of AIDS has, to date, dwarfed that of TB. The comparative lack of attention to ethical issues associated with TB is revealed via searches on the internet. A *Pubmed* search of titles and abstracts (conducted in 2004) for the terms "ethics" and "AIDS" yielded 2,617 entries; while a similar search for the terms "ethics" and "tuberculosis" yielded only 130. TB and AIDS are, in any case, mutually reinforcing. Those with TB are more likely to contract AIDS, and vice versa.

Infectious diseases like these are driven by poverty (for the reasons noted above); but such diseases themselves in turn promote poverty. A vicious cycle exists between poverty and infectious disease. AIDS and TB have brought numerous communities in sub-Saharan Africa to the verge of economic collapse. Economies suffer when those who are sick or die cannot work, when employers need to hire and train new personnel, when consumers shift spending away from durable goods to things like funerals and health care, and for numerous other complex reasons.

Poverty alleviation would be one way to reduce disease; and disease reduction would be one way to alleviate poverty. There are numerous implications from the standpoint of justice. If international justice requires poverty reduction – and thus provision of means for poverty reduction – then international justice requires the reduction of major infectious diseases like TB and AIDS.

Many of the social, political, and economic conditions (including poverty) that promote infectious diseases like AIDS and TB are themselves products of past injustices and human rights abuses. Examination of the social, political, and economic causes of AIDS and TB reveals that current prevalence rates in southern Africa are partly a legacy of slavery, colonialism, cold war manipulation (by superpowers), racist oppression, and (in the case of South Africa) apartheid (Barnett and Whiteside 2002). Rather than being a product of mere bad luck, the health-care status quo in southern Africa is rooted in historical injustice. Some would argue that reparations are therefore called for. If this is correct, then rich countries that have caused or been complicit in the exploitation of African countries have responsibilities to help improve the situation (Pogge 2002; Singer 2002).

Drug Resistance

The increase in drug-resistant disease is a paramount growing global concern. A 2002 WHO report claimed:

> Drug resistance is the most telling sign that we have failed to take the threat of infectious diseases seriously. It suggests that we have mishandled our precious arsenal of disease-fighting drugs, both by overusing them in developing nations and, paradoxically, both misusing and underusing them in developing nations. In all cases, half-hearted use of powerful antibiotics now will eventually result in less effective drugs later. . . . [O]nce life-saving medicines are increasingly having as little effect as a sugar pill. Microbial resistance to treatment could bring the world back to a pre-antibiotic age. . . . The potential of drug resistance to catapult us all back into a world of premature death and chronic illness is all too real.

WHO considers drug resistance to be one of the three most important issues in global health. The personal opinion of Karl Ekdahl, Strategic Advisor to the Director of the European Centre for Disease Prevention and Control (ECDC), is that "drug resistance is the greatest threat to health over the next 25 years"; and he agrees that "the antibiotic era may soon be a thing of the past" (Ekdahl 2006).

A major cause of drug resistance is that patients do not always complete a full course of therapy. When a patient starts but does not complete a course of antimicrobial therapy, this selects for drug-resistant strains of disease: germs most vulnerable to the drugs are killed, allowing mutant resistant strains (that might have been killed if therapy had been completed) to thrive in the absence of microbial competitors in the environment of the patient's body.

Though "noncompliant" patients are often blamed for the problem of drug resistance, it is often impossible for patients in poor countries to complete a course of medication when drug supplies run out at local clinics because of a lack of resources and the general weakness of local health-care infrastructure (both of which make it difficult to maintain a steady supply of medication). Poor patients are also often unable to complete treatment because they cannot continue to pay for medications they have started, or because they cannot afford (often difficult) transportation to (often faraway) medical facilities (Farmer 1999).

When a drug-resistant strain of disease emerges in one person's body, this has implications for others – because drug-resistant diseases, like infectious diseases in general, are usually contagious. There are also implications for global health because contagious drug-resistant diseases, like contagious infectious diseases in general, show no respect for international borders. Lack of access to medicine in poor countries thus has adverse affects for health in rich countries.

One way of addressing the problem of drug resistance would be to make medicines more accessible – via price reduction or drug donations – to poor populations in developing countries, as this would help stall the emergence of drug resistance. In the meantime, however, new antibiotics (and other antimicrobials) are desperately needed, because the power of our existing supply has increasingly declined. Vaccine development is also important, because vaccination prevents infection to begin with.

433

There has been a dearth of vaccine and antibiotic drug development for decades, however. Almost no new classes of antibiotics have been developed since 1970. Lack of antimicrobial research and development reflects the fact that these are unattractive areas of investment for the profit-driven pharmaceutical industry. Because infectious diseases primarily affect the poor, the potential for recouping antimicrobial drug-development costs is low. This explains "the 10/90 divide," a phenomenon whereby less than 10 percent of medical research resources is spent on diseases accounting for 90 percent of the global burden of disease. Rather than addressing the world's most important health-care needs, a majority of funds is spent on research aimed at meeting the wants and needs of a minority of the world's population – those who are relatively wealthy.

This unjust distribution of research resources may come back to haunt us all, rich and poor alike, if we do in fact return to a situation analogous to the pre-antibiotic era (Selgelid 2007).

The reality of the threat is well illustrated by the case of TB, for which "there has been a 40 year standstill in . . . drug development" (WHO 2004) – and for which no new drugs can realistically be expected before 2015. Multi-drug-resistant TB (MDRTB) is defined as TB resistant to at least two of the four "first-line" TB medications. While ordinary TB can be cured with an inexpensive six-month course of treatment, MDRTB takes two years to treat, and treatment can be 100 times more expensive. The "second-line" medications used to treat MDRTB are, furthermore, both more toxic and less effective than "first-line" drugs.

More alarming still is the emergence and spread of virtually untreatable "extreme" or "extensively" drug-resistant TB (XDR-TB), as announced by the US Centers for Disease Control and Prevention (CDC) and WHO in 2006 (CDC 2006; WHO 2006). XDR-TB is defined as TB resistant not only to first-line but also to several second-line medications (CDC 2006; WHO 2006). The most dramatic epidemic of XDR-TB is currently under way in South Africa, where a recent study showed that 41 percent of suspected patients were infected with MDRTB and that 24 percent of these had XDR-TB. Of the 53 patients with the latter, 52 died within 25 days (MSF 2006). Implications of XDR-TB for the international community are starkly revealed by the CDC's statement (2006) that XDR-TB "has emerged worldwide as a threat to public health and TB control, raising concerns of a future epidemic of virtually untreatable TB." In the meantime, a suspected case of XDR-TB in 2007 has already led to the first imposition of a federal quarantine restriction in the US since 1963.

Limiting Liberty in Contexts of Contagion

Quarantine was also called for in Asia and Canada during the SARS crisis of 2003, and the imposition of quarantine can similarly be expected in the event of a major flu pandemic. As noted above, however, quarantine conflicts with the right to freedom of movement. Quarantine can also violate the right to life. If an airplane carrying a passenger infected with a deadly strain of flu is quarantined, for example, then other previously uninfected passengers held in close confinement may become infected and die as a result. Does this mean that the coercive imposition of quarantine would be unethical or wrong? Not necessarily. Individual rights and liberties matter, and we should not ride roughshod over individuals in the name of public health, but the goal of promoting utility in the way of public health matters greatly too.

If a disastrous epidemic would result from the maximal protection of individual rights and liberties, then individual rights and liberties must be compromised. Even arch-libertarian Robert Nozick hints that we might need to violate "side-constraints" (i.e., human rights as he perceives them) when this is necessary to avoid "catastrophic moral horror" (Nozick 1974: 30n). Though it should be considered an extreme or exceptional measure, there is no reason in principle to rule out quarantine altogether, even if it sometimes ends up killing innocent people, just as there is no ethical reason to rule out participation in just war, which also inevitably involves compromise of innocent individuals' rights, including the right to life.

Ethical principles regarding quarantine should arguably include the following. First, an extreme measure such as this should not be employed unless there are compelling reasons to believe that it would be an effective means of controlling disease in the circumstances under consideration. While authors such as George Annas (2005) deny that quarantine actually works, this is of course an empirical question. We should avoid making and/or accepting sweeping empirical claims in the absence of empirical evidence. There are historical cases – such as that of American Samoa during the 1918–19 flu pandemic – where long-term coercive social distancing measures appear to have been highly effective (Crosby 2003). This important case reveals that we should, in addition to rejecting the sweeping claims of Annas, perhaps be skeptical about the often-heard claim that measures like quarantine could only have an early and minor role in the event of a major flu pandemic. That might be true for most places on large continents, but demographic context matters here – and islands, at least, are a different story.

The evidence for or against the effectiveness of quarantine warrants further study. Given the difficulty of conducting controlled studies in the context of quarantine, however, it will not be easy to conclusively demonstrate whether or not quarantine would be effective in any given circumstance, and greater uncertainty will arise in the case of unknown novel pathogens. There is an ethical imperative, in any case, that researchers with relevant expertise further examine this issue as best they can; relevant data is required for solving ethical/policy questions as well as questions more purely concerned with public health science.

Second, mandatory quarantine should not be employed unless it is actually required. If alternative, less restrictive means are available to achieve the same ends regarding public health protection, then these should be employed instead. If voluntary quarantine, for example, would likely be just as effective as mandatory quarantine, then the latter should not be imposed. Mandatory quarantine should only be used as a last resort (Gostin 2006).

Third, an extreme measure such as quarantine should not be imposed unless the consequences of failing to do so would be great. It would be wrong to think that rights violations and the imposition of harms on individuals are justified whenever this would lead to a net pay-off for society as a whole. The maximal promotion of public health should not be the sole goal of ethical public health policy. The stakes would need to be high in order for liberty-infringing measures to be permissible.

Fourth, for quarantine to be ethically acceptable, it must be implemented in an equitable manner. It would be unjust, that is, if quarantine were used (as it often has been in the past) in a discriminatory fashion against those who are already socially marginalized or disempowered. One could argue that the grounds for imposing quarantine must be strongest when those being considered for confinement are members of the worst-off groups in society. Just as research ethics guidelines give special protection to those who are vulnerable, so quarantine guidelines should arguably do the same. If justice requires improving the situation of the worst-off groups of society (Rawls 1971), then we should be especially reluctant to infringe upon the rights and liberties of such groups' members.

Fifth, quarantine, if implemented, should be made as minimally burdensome as possible. Those confined should be provided with basic necessities such as food, water, comfort, and health care. A sixth, and related, point is that those who endure quarantine for the benefit of society should be compensated in return. If there are limited amounts of medicine and vaccine available, for example, then those who have been quarantined deserve special priority when allocation decisions about medical resources are made. If the overall benefits of quarantine outweigh the costs – as would have to be the case for quarantine to be justified in the first place – then a net social dividend results from liberty infringement. Part of this should be returned to the victims of coercion. It would be wrong if confined individuals are expected to shoulder the burdens required for the protection of society, and then receive nothing in return. The burdens associated with epidemic disease are shared more fairly if those who make sacrifices by succumbing to quarantine are provided with compensation for doing so. This is a matter of reciprocity (University of Toronto Joint Centre for Bioethics 2005). A final benefit of putting a compensation/reward scheme into place is that this would likely enhance trust in – and thus cooperation with – public health systems (Ly et al. 2007). It is well known that trust is important for public health systems to succeed.

Improving Global Health

The section above presents a conflict between social values: the aim to promote utility in the way of public health conflicts with the aim to protect individual rights and liberties in situations where quarantine or other intrusive public health-care measures are called for. We then ask what balance to strike between these goals. In a way, however, this is a false dilemma. If global health were better, the conflict (requiring sacrifice of either utility or human rights/liberties) would arise less often. Infectious diseases, recall, primarily affect the poor; and infectious disease contributes to the poverty of the poor. If the health of those who are now poor were better to begin with, then the global infectious disease threat would diminish; and we would not so often be forced to choose between promoting utility in the way of public health, on the one hand, and protecting human rights and liberties, on the other. Improvement of global health (and thus poverty reduction) would promote multiple important social goals: equality, human rights/liberty, and utility.

From a global perspective, one of the most important questions is whether or not – or why – wealthy developed nations should be motivated to do more to help improve the health-care situation in developing countries (given that the latter lack sufficient resources to do so adequately on their own). In what follows, we see that cumulative ethical and self-interested reasons justify wealthy world funding of disease reduction in poor countries (Selgelid 2008).

There are numerous ways in which health-care improvement in developing countries would promote equality. One of the best-developed arguments for treating health care as a special kind of good is that provided by Norman Daniels in *Just Health Care* (1985). Disease interferes with species-typical functioning and thus detracts from equality of opportunity – and equality of opportunity is a requirement of justice. We should thus guarantee equal access to a basic minimum package of health care for all members of society. Daniels appeals to Rawls's theory of justice for domestic society, however; and Rawls resists application of domestic principles of justice to the global scene. Several have rightly argued, on the other hand, that Rawls's weaker requirements for international justice are inconsistent with what he says elsewhere (Moellendorf 2002; Pogge 2002). Theory aside, Daniels's argument that health is crucial to equality of opportunity holds; and the idea that equality of opportunity matters in other countries, just as it matters in our own, will be accepted by many as a common sense precept.

Another egalitarian reason for improving the health of the poor is that this would make the worst-off better off. The sick and poor in southern Africa are, by any measure, clearly among the worst-off members of global society; and increased provision of health care is one of the things most needed to improve their situation. Improvement of health in developing countries would also reduce *undeserved inequalities* in well-being. Despite the fact that some suffer from AIDS as a result of their own (informed) careless sexual or drug-injecting behavior, most who suffer from AIDS, TB, and other infectious diseases in developing countries are in no way responsible for, nor do they deserve, the illnesses from which they suffer.

It can also be argued that many of those who suffer from these diseases are, directly or indirectly, victims of injustice. Insofar as rich countries have benefited and contributed to the exploitation of developing countries – while this in turn has promoted poverty and disease in the latter – rich countries should recognize obligations to amend inequalities that they are partly responsible for.

In addition to promoting equality in these ways, health improvement in poor countries would promote human rights. It is commonly believed that human beings have rights to have their most basic needs (for things like shelter, clothing, housing, food, and clean water) met. The idea that there is a human right to health care is reflected by the existence of universal health-care systems in every industrialized nation except the US. Such rights are, furthermore, enshrined by authoritative international documents such as the Universal Declaration of Human Rights, which claims in Article 25:

> Everyone has the right to a standard of living adequate for the health and well-being of himself and his family, including food, clothing, and medical care . . . [and that] every individual and every organ of society . . . shall strive . . . by progressive measures, national and international, to secure [its] universal and effective recognition. (UN 1999)

Because human rights are supposedly taken seriously in other contexts of foreign policy-making – as grounds for waging war to prevent their violation, for example – it is inconsistent to ignore their violation in the context of health care.

437

Utilitarian reasons strengthen the case for health-care improvement in developing countries. Given that a $20 course of TB medication or even a $100 yearly course of AIDS medication can each make all the difference between life and death – and enable prevention of enormous suffering – these are among the very best uses that can be made of such sums of money in terms of positive impact on human lives, especially when compared to the frivolous way such sums are routinely spent in wealthy countries. Promotion of the greater good in terms of human well-being provides *a* reason for taking one action rather than another, even if other potentially overriding legitimate social aims must also be taken into consideration. One need not subscribe to utilitarianism to think that the greater good of humanity is (one of the things that is) morally important and should thus be taken into consideration by policy-makers in rich countries. Only a minor sacrifice by wealthy developed nations would be required to achieve tremendous benefits in terms of reduced suffering and saved lives in poor countries. According to Jeffrey Sachs (2005):

> The [Commission on Macroeconomics and Health] concluded that donor aid [to invest in global health] ought to rise from around [US]$6 billion per year [in 2001] to $27 billion per year (by 2007). With combined GNP of the donor countries equal to around $25 trillion dollars as of 2001, the commission was advocating an annual investment of around one thousandth of rich-world income. The commission showed, on the best epidemiological evidence, that such an investment could avert eight million deaths per year.

Improvement of health care in developing countries is thus justified on numerous ethical grounds. This would promote equality, the human right to health care, and utility – and only a minor sacrifice would be required for wealthy developed nations to achieve enormous benefits. As noted above, it would also promote liberty, because the reduction of infectious diseases in poor countries would diminish their prevalence worldwide, and so the need for liberty restricting public health-care measures would arise less often.

In addition to these moral reasons that should motivate wealthy nations to do more to improve health care in developing countries, there are straightforward self-interested reasons as well. When infectious diseases thrive in poor countries, this has negative implications for health in rich countries. One implication of poverty and the lack of health care in poor countries is that everyone everywhere is subject to greater risk of infection than would otherwise be the case. This was well illustrated in the above discussion of drug resistance. When the poor lack adequate health care, drug-resistant strains of disease emerge and threaten global health. The idea that we might soon return to a situation analogous to the pre-antibiotic era – and the *fact* that we already again live in a world with untreatable TB – should not be taken lightly.

References

Annas, G. J. (2005). *American Bioethics: Crossing Human Rights and Health Law Boundaries.* New York: Oxford University Press.

Barnett, T. and Whiteside, A. (2002). *AIDS in the Twenty-First Century: Disease and Globalization*. New York: W.W. Norton.

CDC (2006). Emergence of *Mycobacterium tuberculosis* with extensive resistance to second-line drugs – worldwide, 2000–2004. *Morbidity and Mortality Weekly Report* 55/11: 301–5.

Crosby, A. W. (2003). *America's Forgotten Pandemic: The Influenza of 1918*, 2nd edn. Cambridge: Cambridge University Press.

Daniels, N. (1985). *Just Health Care*. New York: Cambridge University Press.

Ekdahl, K. (2006). *Ethical Issues from the ECDC Perspective. Bioethical Implications of Globalisation Processes (BIG) Workshop on Globalisation and New Epidemics: Ethics, Security and Policy Making*. Brussels: The European Commission.

Farmer, P. (1999). *Infections and Inequalities*. Berkeley, CA: University of California Press.

Gandy, M. and Zumla, A. (2002). The resurgence of disease: social and historical perspectives on the "new" tuberculosis. *Social Science and Medicine* 55: 385–96.

Gostin, L. O. (2006). Public health strategies for pandemic influenza. *JAMA* 295: 1700–4.

Ly, T., Selgelid, M. J., and Kerridge, I. (2007). Pandemic and public health controls: toward an equitable compensation system. *Journal of Law and Medicine* 15/2: 318–24.

Moellendorf, D. (2002). *Cosmopolitan Justice*. Cambridge, MA: Westview.

MSF (2006). Extensive drug resistant tuberculosis (XDR-TB), October 27, 2006. Available at: www.accessmed-msf.org (accessed February 2007).

Nozick, R. (1974). *Anarchy, State, and Utopia*. New York: Basic Books.

Oldstone, M. B. A. (1998). *Viruses, Plagues, and History*. New York: Oxford University Press.

Pogge, T. W. (2002). *World Poverty and Human Rights*. Cambridge: Polity.

Price-Smith, A. T. (2001). *The Health of Nations: Infectious Disease, Environmental Change, and Their Effects on National Security and Development*. Cambridge, MA: MIT Press.

Rawls, J. (1971). *A Theory of Justice*. Cambridge, MA: Harvard University Press.

Sachs, J. (2005). *The End of Poverty*. London: Penguin.

Selgelid, M. J. (2005). Ethics and infectious disease. *Bioethics* 19/3: 272–89.

Selgelid, M. J. (2007). Ethics and drug resistance. *Bioethics* 21/4: 218–29.

Selgelid, M. J. (2008). Improving global health: counting reasons why. *Developing World Bioethics* 8/2: 115–25.

Singer, P. (2002). *One World: The Ethics of Globalization*. Melbourne: The Text Publishing Company.

UN (1999). *Universal Declaration of Human Rights*. First adopted and proclaimed in 1948. New York: United Nations: Resolution 217 A (III). Available at: www.un.org/Overview/rights.html (accessed February 8, 2006).

University of Toronto Joint Centre for Bioethics, Pandemic Influenza Working Group (2005). Stand on guard for thee: ethical considerations in preparedness planning for pandemic influenza. Available at: www.utoronto.ca/jcb/home/documents/pandemic.pdf (accessed January 6, 2006).

WHO (2000). *Report on Infectious Diseases 2000 – Overcoming Antimicrobial Resistance*. Available at: www.who.int/infectious-disease-report/2000/ (accessed August 30, 2006).

WHO (2002). *Fact Sheet No 104. Tuberculosis*. Available at: www.who.int/mediacentre/factsheets/fs104/en/print.html (accessed June 2004).

WHO (2004). Drug resistant tuberculosis ten times higher in Eastern Europe and Central Asia. Press release, available at: www.who.int/mediacentre/releases/2004/prl17/en/print.thml (accessed March 7, 2004).

WHO (2006). *Weekly Epidemiological Record, September 2006*. Available at: www.who.int/wer (accessed February 2007).

WHO (2007). *Global Tuberculosis Control: Surveillance, Planning, Financing*. WHO Report. Geneva, World Health Organization. WHO/HTM/TB/2007.376.

439

Further reading

Balint, J., Philpott, S., Baker, R., and Strosberg, M. (eds.) (2006). *Ethics and Epidemics*. Amsterdam: JAI Press.

Cohen, J. C., Illingworth, P., and Schüklenk, U. (eds.) (2006). *The Power of Pills: Social Ethical and Legal Issues in Drug Development, Marketing and Pricing*. London: Pluto Press.

Coughlin, S. S. and Beauchamp T. L. (eds.) (1996). *Ethics and Epidemiology*. New York: Oxford University Press.

Lemon, S. M., Hamburg, M. A., Sparling, P. F., Choffnes, E. R., and Mack, A. (Rapporteurs, Forum on microbial threats) (2007). *Ethical and Legal Considerations in Mitigating Pandemic Disease: Workshops Summary*. Washington, DC: The National Academies Press.

Selgelid, M. J., Battin, M. P., and Smith, C. (eds.) *Ethics and Infectious Disease*. Oxford: Blackwell Publishing.

Van Niekerk, A. A. and Kopelman, L. M. (eds.) (2005). *Ethics and AIDS in Africa: The Challenge to Our Thinking*. South Africa: David Philips Publishers.

37

AIDS as a Global Health Emergency

UDO SCHÜKLENK

AIDS is an acquired immunodeficiency syndrome, the first cases of which were reported in the USA by the Centers for Disease Control in 1981. People with AIDS suffer from a progressive decline in the functioning of their immune system, a consequence of which is a greater likelihood of developing opportunistic infections. These infections (either alone or in combination) prove fatal to patients who are denied life-preserving AIDS drugs. People's increasingly global mobility, combined with the fact that AIDS is a primarily sexually transmitted illness, have made it possible for AIDS to travel the globe in a very short time, earning its classification by the medical profession as a pandemic. Moreover, its impact is so great in the most affected areas, such as sub-Saharan Africa, that it has there become one of the main causes of death (Shisana and Simbayi 2002).

There has been enormous interest in AIDS from the media, scientists, health-care professionals, and bioethicists. There were many reasons for this, among them the fact that HIV is sexually transmissible and has the potential to kill an infected person many years after infection. The fascination surrounding AIDS is also related to fact that the majority of people infected in developed countries are gay men and intravenous (IV) drug-users (UNAIDS/WHO 2006).

Bioethicists have been concerned predominantly with the following issues:

- HIV testing;
- whether an HIV infection acquired during voluntary unsafe sexual encounters should be considered a case of harm to others or harm to self;
- AIDS clinical research and access to experimental drugs;
- access to affordable life-preserving medication; and
- the problems surrounding HIV-infected health-care professionals and the duty to treat people with HIV and AIDS.

HIV Testing

In the early years of the bioethical debate over AIDS-related matters, the issue of voluntary or compulsory HIV testing was prominent. The point of testing lies in the subsequent use of knowledge of the test's outcome. Compulsory testing and subsequent isolation of those found positive for antibodies to the cause of AIDS has been suggested and even enacted, for instance, in Cuba. The general consensus among bioethicists at the time was that mandatory testing is, all other things being equal, only acceptable when there is a successful therapy for the disease available. In an early paper Ronald Bayer and colleagues argued that "there is no demonstrable public health benefit that justifies universal mandatory screening, given the invasion of privacy involved" (Bayer et al. 1986: 1770). This line of argument, which is based in part on the importance of respect for individual autonomy, has been accepted by those health officials responsible for the AIDS policies of most Western countries. It accepts essentially that until there is a clear benefit to the infected individual from knowing about her infection, there is no paternalistic reason to implement mandatory testing. If there is no benefit for the society at large in knowing that certain individuals are infected, there is no good public health reason for mandatory testing. On this argument, the rejection of mandatory HIV testing is conditional upon having no efficient drugs that could either prevent the outbreak of AIDS, prolong the disease-free period, or improve the quality of life of a person at risk for AIDS. This condition no longer holds true; there are now treatment regimes that are capable of substantially improving the quality of life of people with AIDS, and preserving their lives.

Once the panic of the early years of the epidemic had disappeared, the issue of voluntary testing of selected risk populations was on the agenda. The approval of the chemotherapeutic AZT (azidothymidine) as an AIDS treatment in 1987 led a number of bioethicists to argue for broad-scale educational campaigns in favor of voluntary testing. For instance, James F. Childress argued in favor of selective voluntary screening by pointing to the possible benefits to HIV-positive individuals which "include closer medical follow-up, earlier use of AZT (and other treatments), prophylaxis or other care for associated diseases, protection of loved ones, and clearer plans for the future" (Childress 1991: 58).

These arguments paid special attention to pregnant women, because of medical advances in mother-to-child transmission prevention. Without such treatments, HIV is passed from mother to newborn in approximately 35 percent of cases. By 2004 the number of children worldwide infected with HIV in this manner reached between 2.1 and 2.8 million, and more than 600,000 new cases were added in 2005, along with a matching death toll attributed to AIDS that year (UNAIDS/WHO 2005). The current treatment employing zidovudine provides a 67.5 percent relative reduction in mother-to-child transmission prevention, provided that the patient receives antenatal care and screening for HIV, and consents to medical intervention. This efficacy was conclusively demonstrated by Connor et al. (1994). The persistence of high mother-to-child transmission rates can only be explained by failures on a number of fronts, producing for the communities in question a heavy burden of personal tragedies and a formidable public health threat.

This raises a variety of ethical concerns. Does the goal of achieving the best possible treatments for the fetuses justify mandatory HIV testing for pregnant women? There is no way to test the HIV status of the fetus without also uncovering the mother's status. Does the mother's interest in privacy outweigh the fetus's interest in optimal treatment (assuming we can even defensibly attribute interests to fetuses; see chapter

15, "Mother–Fetus Conflict")? In addition, once HIV status is known, it is a further issue whether mother-to-child transmission prevention should be mandatory as well.

Access to confidential HIV tests and free or affordable mother-to-child transmission prevention drugs is increasing in developing countries. When pregnant women decline these opportunities, they risk very serious consequences for their child-to-be. Without state-of-the-art medical care, HIV-infected newborns live on average for just two years, during which their quality of life is low (UNFPA 2003: 11).

In response Peter Clark argues that, "the prevention of perinatal HIV transmission in Botswana, because of the availability of antiretroviral therapy for infected mothers and their children, greatly outweighs the burdens of the possible violation of the pregnant woman's privacy" (2006: 17). This argument appears to be part of the beginning of a long-awaited shift toward the mandatory approach. We now find mandatory testing of newborns in several US states, as well as indications of more legislation to come mandating HIV testing for pregnant women (Zivi 2005: 315).

This has met with opposition from some feminist thinkers and activists in developed countries, who criticized the allegedly "maternal ideology [according to which] good mothers engage in acts of self-sacrifice and self-abnegation, always putting the interests of their children before their own" (Zivi 2005: 349). Yet testing and treatment need not be seen as self-sacrificing, since they also preserve the mothers' lives. Furthermore, this particular feminist argument takes this issue to be an instance of the traditional conflict between fetal and maternal interests. However, this interpretation is misguided. The concern surely is directed at the interests of the future child rather than the fetus. The decision to bring a child into being carries with it a moral obligation to improve the newborn's chances of having a life worth living. Declining abortion and then refusing HIV testing and treatment counts as harm to others. The claim that when the cost to oneself is not unreasonably high there is no serious moral difference between deliberately refraining from preventing harm and actively causing harm is supported by arguments from various ethical frameworks (Glover 1977; Rachels 1986).

The other reason for mandatory testing has classically been seen in cases where unprotected sexual intercourse takes place and HIV infection is considered as harm to others. This issue will be discussed at greater length in the next section.

HIV Infection: Harm to Self or Harm to Others

Interfering with individual choices by means of the criminal law is traditionally defended on moral grounds only when there is a need to prevent and/or punish harm to others. The use of the criminal law to prevent consenting adults from harming themselves has been seen as much more problematic. In many countries legislators have had to decide whether an HIV infection that is acquired during unsafe sexual encounters between consenting competent adults should be considered harm to self, or whether it should be seen as harm to others. At issue is the fact that most infections that are the result of sexual encounters occur as a consequence of voluntary consensual acts among adults. Libertarians such as Richard Mohr and liberals such as Patricia Illingworth have argued that under such circumstances there is no room for the criminal law. Mohr suggested that AIDS' "mode of contagion assures that those at risk are those whose actions contribute to their risk of infection, chiefly through intimate sexual contact and shared hypodermic needles" (Mohr 1987: 38). Mohr's argument for non-intervention in cases of unsafe sexual encounters among autonomously acting consenting adults is this:

> If independence – the ability to guide one's life by one's own lights to an extent compatible with the like ability on the part of others – is, as it is, a major value, one cannot respect that value while preventing people from putting themselves at risk through voluntary association. (1987: 39)

Arguments for the claim that HIV infections constitute harm to others or to the wider public are taken up in more detail in the second part of this section. Obviously, even if one agrees with Mohr's interpretation, the option of justifying interventions by health authorities through *paternalistic* strategies remains, and does not look prima facie unreasonable. After all, society often interferes to prevent harm to self (legislation to enforce the use of seat-belts in cars is a good example of this). Why should AIDS be treated differently? Why should we allow people who wish to have unprotected sexual intercourse (in particular when they belong to high-risk groups) to do so? But there are good liberal grounds for rejecting both laws to require people to wear seat-belts and laws allowing paternalistic intervention by health-care authorities. At least within a liberal framework, "it would be wrong to adopt policies which would interfere with individual liberty" (Illingworth 1990a: 11). The classical principle of *to the one who consents no injustice is done* can be utilized to support this point of view.

A few commentators have argued that HIV-positive gay men have a duty to disclose their antibody status to their prospective sexual partners in impersonal sexual encounters. Empirical research has demonstrated that "the majority of communication in sex is non-verbal," hence a duty to disclose could not mean that it is a duty on the side of the HIV-positive person to *say* explicitly that he is infected because this would violate the basic "rule of conduct" in many situations which lead to sexual encounters (Davies et al. 1993: 49). Illingworth pointed out that a policy of disclosure may have the consequence that uninfected people take fewer precautions to avoid infection. A fictitious example of hers is quite compelling: "If Sam believes that it is Bob's moral responsibility to inform him of his antibody status, he may construe Bob's silence as an invitation not to practice safe sex" (1990a: 42). A duty of this sort clearly requires everyone to be aware of his or her antibody status *as well as* to comply with the rules of this alleged moral duty to disclose.

It is doubtful, however, that the harm-to-self argument could succeed when applied to people in long-term relationships, be they married or otherwise. Such relationships are usually based on the unspoken premise of trust that your partner will not put your life at risk, certainly not for reasons as trivial as having unsafe sexual relations outside the relationship. This trust-based relationship is violated by a partner who engages in unsafe sexual relations outside the relationship and puts his or her partner's health at risk by not informing him or her of this. It is important to keep in mind that, like any freedom, the freedom of women to refuse to have unprotected intercourse with their sexual partners requires, if it is to be a genuinely exercisable freedom, a variety of social conditions that are frequently lacking outside the developed world.

444

As virtually always in pluralistic societies, there is no general consensus that HIV infection primarily constitutes harm to self, not even in those cases where the individuals are autonomous people who are perfectly aware of the risks they take and where these individuals have voluntarily agreed to engage in unsafe sexual encounters with other individuals whose antibody status is unknown to them. Ronald Bayer concedes that HIV infections in voluntary sexual encounters are a matter of "private choices, choices that will be made in the most intimate of settings beyond the observation of even the most thoroughgoing surveillance" (1989: 11). He maintains, however, that any interpretation which would assume that the transmission of AIDS "between consenting adults [is] belonging to the private realm alone and therefore beyond the legitimate concern of the state would make a serious mistake" (1989: 12). The argument continues that HIV infection must always be considered as harm to others and should be interpreted as a "public health" matter. The reasoning behind this interpretation is that the chances of keeping the disease under control are good when only a few responsibly acting individuals are infected and the odds turn against societal interests when the level of infection reaches certain saturation levels. It is problematic to ignore the collective harmful impact of individual acts which lead to HIV infections. This view asserts that the health of the public is somehow threatened by consensual unsafe sexual encounters, yet its proponents fail to explain exactly what they mean when they talk about "public health." Libertarians hold against this that all known interpretations of "public health" are either meaningless or totalitarian in their nature (Mohr 1987: 46–50). Nevertheless, the ethicists invoking a "public health" obligation to intervene go to great lengths in criticizing the alleged failure of public health authorities to close gay bathhouses, in order to enforce the exercise of restraint and responsibility that they request. Liberals have responded to such ideas by pointing out that they violate basic liberal principles on which Western societies are based, and that the interventionists have failed to provide a theoretical defense of such violations.

On a very practical level it won't be possible to prevent such alleged harms to others from occurring, no matter how much we would like to do so. It is surprising that proponents of such policies seem not to have considered this. Sex-on-venue premises continue to exist, though perhaps no longer in the *form* of gay bathhouses. It was naive to assume otherwise. In practice, in this sense the ideology of "public health" has failed.

Access to Experimental Drugs and the Ethics of Research Clinical Trials

Terminally ill people, by definition, have no successful standard treatment available to them. Until recently, AIDS was such a terminal illness. Certain drugs might have extended patients' survival time, but ultimately the patients would succumb to a disease that was life-threatening and incurable. In contrast to some other life-threatening diseases, such as certain cancers, for instance, people with AIDS tended to be fairly young and were more likely to put up a fight to preserve their lives. Highly sophisticated and creative activist groups such as ACT UP have not only raised public awareness for AIDS with a number of publicity-gaining acts, but have also vehemently criticized the initially slow response of research agencies to the crisis (Nussbaum 1990). On ethical

445

grounds, they questioned the status quo in the two different areas of the testing and availability of drugs. These arguments remain relevant even today. In the US there is currently debate about whether Congress should pass legislation permitting terminally ill patients to access experimental agents. The contributions of bioethicists mirror what was put forth in the early years of the AIDS epidemic and, unfortunately, display little awareness of this history (Bender et al. 2007). AIDS activists argued that, given the time involved in the AIDS research establishment's drug-testing and approval process, they wanted access to experimental drugs. Their point was that in the case of terminal illness no government has a moral right to prevent patients from taking their chances with experimental agents of their liking. As Martin Delaney, at the time director of the AIDS activist group Project Inform, pointed out in an address to an annual meeting of the US Infectious Diseases Society:

> It is as if I am in a disabled airplane, speeding downward out of control. I see a parachute hanging on the cabin wall, one small moment of hope. I try to strap it on when a government employee reaches out and tears it off my back, admonishing, "You cannot use that! It does not have the Federal Aviation Administration Sticker on it. We do not know if it will work." (1989: 416)

This view claims that autonomous terminally ill individuals have a right to take charge of their own lives. The objections are twofold. The first is strongly paternalistic. It concedes that patients are actually aware of the risk they are running when they take unapproved drugs, but maintains that it is not in their best interest and that these patients very probably will harm themselves or will be subject to exploitation by ruthless quacks. As Walters (1988: 601) pointed out: "Unnecessary suffering would be visited on people with HIV infection if they were provided immediate access to ineffective 'therapies' or treatments with toxic effects that far outweigh their therapeutic benefits." This argument assumes the point that is in dispute. If patients knew that a certain unapproved drug did not work, they surely would not use it. The point is that they do not know, but that they are willing to accept certain risks, given that their very survival is at stake and furthermore that the health-care profession has no successful therapy to offer. The second major argument against patient access to experimental drugs has been advanced on the grounds that this constitutes harm to others. Cooper suggested:

> The more devastating the disease and less satisfactory the existing therapy, the stronger the disincentive for a patient to enroll in a randomized controlled trial, if the drug can be obtained in some other way. Consequently, a national policy of early widespread availability of unproved experimental agents would slow or even halt the completion of controlled clinical trials through which therapeutic advances are established and then improved on. (1989: 2445)

This stance makes it obvious that there is a conflict between the interests of current patients and those of future patients. At this point the connection between access to experimental agents and the ethics of research clinical trials becomes apparent. Conflicts between participating patients' survival interests and broader research interests seem to be inevitable and are well documented in the literature (e.g., Nussbaum 1990: 123). Some ethicists have suggested that under such circumstances the recruitment of terminally ill patients as participants in clinical trials exploits these patients' vulnerability in an unethical way. Patients do not really give voluntary consent to a trial protocol that to some degree neglects their survival interests. They do so only because they are left with no other choice if they want access to an experimental agent they are interested in (Minogue et al. 1995). The basic question seems to be this: for terminally ill patients who choose to join a research clinical trial in order to have access to otherwise unavailable experimental therapies, can we expect them to take on the risk of an even earlier death for the sake of altruism (Schüklenk 1998)? For liberals and libertarians, the answer has to be a clear "no," because the infringements of civil liberties of dying people would be unacceptably high. It seems, however, that even consequentialists would ultimately not try to coerce such people into clinical trials for pragmatic reasons. They would not expect a level of altruism that is superhuman. This seems true even if we accept Harris's (2005) view that we have a moral obligation to participate in clinical research as research participants.

A substantial number of people with AIDS did just about everything they could to join clinical trials. Some used other drugs despite their denials, and some even secretly shared the experimental agent with other patients who ended up in the placebo arm of the trial. The predictive value of the results of such trials remains in doubt. In the US, reports from AIDS researchers confirmed that people with AIDS often used concurrent treatments, shared drugs with other trial participants, and even bribed researchers to get into a certain trial or into a certain trial arm. Those who had been randomized to a placebo dropped out quickly and in large numbers (Delaney 1989). Some bioethicists have criticized this patient survival strategy as unethical, and suggested that those patients have a moral obligation toward the principal investigator to keep their part of the bargain – that is, to stick to the trial protocol. This claim rests on the assumption that these patients are *real* volunteers. A terminally ill patient who has been robbed of the option to access the drugs he believes might save his life is not acting voluntarily if he joins a clinical trial which offers him only a 50:50 chance to get this drug (or an even smaller chance in trials with multiple arms) (Minogue et al. 1995). Hence, it does seem at least arguable that it is not necessarily unethical for such patients to join trials under false pretences.

Developing Preventive Vaccines

Bioethicists and AIDS activists, the latter mostly in developing countries, have focused their attention on another issue related to research ethics. A serious ethical challenge arises with regard to the question of what is owed to participants of HIV vaccine trials who happen to become infected during the course of the trial. By necessity, in prevention trials the participants are not infected when the trial begins. Not surprisingly, given the prominence of HIV/AIDS in many parts of the developing world, HIV vaccine trials became the focal point of this debate. It is worth noting at the outset, however, that the same arguments that apply to HIV vaccine would apply to any number of microbicide trials aimed at protecting women against a large variety of sexually transmitted illnesses (Tarantola et al. 2007). One of the controversial questions in this debate has been the issue of whether or not an infection acquired by vaccine trial participants during the course of the trial can reasonably be considered a trial-related injury that ought to be subject to compensation (in the form of access to good-quality AIDS treatments, including antiretrovirals).

Weijer and LeBlanc (2006) reject the argument that trial sponsors have good reason to accept such an infection as a trial-related injury that should be subject to compensation (Schüklenk and Ashcroft 2000: 168). Proponents of the criticized view argued that *some* trial participants would become infected during the course of such trials because of a phenomenon known as the therapeutic misconception – that is, the mistaken idea that they have received a working HIV vaccine offering some or complete protection. Arguably, such infections should be treated as trial-related injuries, and should trigger at a minimum the provision of life-preserving AIDS medication while it confers a clinical benefit to such individuals. Weijer and LeBlanc point toward a meta-analysis (Slack et al. 2005) of studies investigating the comprehension of vaccine trials among (actual and prospective) trial participants. One of the results of this meta-analysis was that risk behavior among trial participants decreased when compared to the rest of the populations from which they were recruited. This fact does not invalidate the argument it seeks to set aside.

The argument that *some* participants will become HIV infected during HIV vaccine trials as a result of a therapeutic misconception cannot be discarded by admitting that such infections could occur, but likely in only a small number of participants. This is so even if, as some of the studies mentioned by Slack et al. report, overall risk behavior in the trial cohort decreased. Different trial participants behave in different ways. Many (even most) trial participants could display reductions in risk behavior and, at the same time, some (a few) participants show increases in risk behavior. Both such behavioral changes could be a result of trial participation.

If such behavioral patterns were confirmed for the majority of participants in HIV vaccine trials, this would provide us with powerful ethical, and public health, reasons to conduct such studies. The studies in question are not only designed to develop medicines assisting us in reducing the number of future AIDS patients by preventing infections; they even seem to reduce the number of infections in the participating cohorts regardless of the efficacy of the experimental agent.

However, ethical review committees must have the foreseeable "losers" in mind when they determine what obligations trial sponsors have with regard to trial participants. It seems perfectly reasonable to request that sponsors provide life-preserving AIDS medication to seroconverting trial participants. It is unsurprising that ethical review committees refused to approve of such trials unless such post-trial care was guaranteed. Usually this was put into effect by simply taking out a health insurance covering relevant clinical care for those who become infected during the course of the trial. The reason for this stance is clearly that these review committees, while rightly approving the trials based on the ethical argument just provided, also realized that they had an ethical obligation toward seroconverting trial participants. Nobody denies that some (even many) of these participants might have become infected anyway, and nobody denies that it is possible that fewer people would have seroconverted in such a trial than would have in the same cohort of people in the absence of the trial. The pro-care argument acknowledges that among those people who become infected will be some who would not have become infected had they not had a misconception of the trial (with

448

higher risk-taking activities triggered by this misconception). It is no good for them to know that, overall, the trial meant that fewer people (like them) became infected during the trial than otherwise would have. They still suffer a substantial worsening of their health outlook as a result of their trial participation. Some of those who became infected might have understood the risk and took it anyway. The point is that it is virtually impossible to know. Under these circumstances, as in the legal tradition, the principle of *in dubio pro reo*, or, in the case under consideration, *in dubio pro patiente*, should guide research policy-making.

This debate is not of a purely academic nature for at least two reasons. One is that vaccine trial participants in the developing world would not by default enjoy the levels of care that their counterparts in the developed world would enjoy. It has been suggested that access to care for such trial participants is either not necessarily required or a matter of individual negotiating success for particular trial participants. We ought to reject such proceduralism in favor of a substantive ethical stance. The second reason is that while it was relatively easy to achieve a reasonable level of consensus on this issue with regard to well-resourced HIV vaccine trials, the same cannot be said for microbicide trials that are less well resourced and, for that reason, less likely to ensure infected trial participants' access to clinical care post-trial.

Affordable Access to Life-preserving Medication

The relationship between access to essential drugs for the poor in developing countries and intellectual property rights, patent protection, and drug prices is a matter of international debate, including contributions by bioethicists and political philosophers (see chapter 35, "Global Pharmaceutical Markets"). A focal point in this debate is the fact that the overwhelming majority of people in developing countries are cut off from essential drugs because of the pricing policies of the patent-owning pharmaceutical multinationals. This seems to be pretty clearly at odds with the public interest-based argument that provides the main justification of intellectual property rights and patents. The claim is that the desirable public objective of private investment in significant research and the production of new drugs is commercially feasible only if companies are able to reap or anticipate a sufficiently high return. Yet this very rationale warrants overriding some patents in some countries – namely, those countries where patent laws effectively cut off, rather than secure, access to privately developed drugs. The protection of those patents in those circumstances is no longer defensible (Schüklenk and Ashcroft 2002). Of course, that's oversimplifying a bit. In developed countries, expensive, patented drugs are within the reach of most people who need them. But since this is not so in developing countries, the argument has some bite there. Indeed, the World Trade Organization's TRIPS Agreement expressly states that in public health emergencies such as HIV and AIDS developing countries are permitted to override patents for necessary drugs. Furthermore, when assessing the strength of the public interest argument, we should keep in mind that the high profits in question have never been generated in the developing world.

It is worth emphasizing that in this debate, although bioethicists' arguments began with demands for donations from pharmaceutical multinationals, they are now engaging more demandingly in policy reform. This is progress beyond the usual ethical fare of encouraging particular actions in line with moral principles, to proactive policy development (Cohen and Illingworth 2003).

HIV Infection in Health-care Professionals and Patients

Ethical analyses focused on the issues of whether health-care professionals should be tested mandatorily for HIV infection and/or whether their patients should be tested. I cannot see that there is an ethically relevant difference between these situations. Patients of HIV-infected health-care professionals who are having invasive procedures run a *remote* risk of infection and so do health-care professionals from HIV-infected patients. The debate about HIV-infected health-care professionals focuses primarily on whether all health-care personnel should be mandatorily tested for HIV antibodies and, if so, whether those who test HIV-positive should be allowed to continue working as health-care professionals. The heat in the public debate over this issue was turned up significantly after newspaper reports of the first cases of patients who were allegedly infected by health-care professionals – in one case a dentist and in another a physician. So far, mandatory testing of health-care personnel has not been recommended by professional medical bodies. The amount written about this issue clearly exceeds its real significance. One meta-analysis reports that unpublished studies looking back at thousands of patients of infected health-care workers have not documented HIV transmission from such professionals to their patients (Weiss 1992). Some ethicists have nevertheless suggested that there is a significant risk of infection for patients of health-care professionals who perform invasive procedures and that these professionals should refrain from performing such procedures (Gostin 1990: 308). Gostin believes that such professionals should be required to report their HIV status to their employers (but not to their patients) and "should be carefully monitored in their performance of their functions," but he leaves it open whether they should refrain voluntarily from performing invasive procedures, or whether they should be forced to do so. Positions such as this were subsequently criticized for suggesting a restriction on the involvement of infected personnel in invasive procedures and for exaggerating the real risk faced by patients. Feldblum points out that the "ramifications of his [Gostin's] policy statement for the overall system of health care delivery are so significant that the lack of sufficient data is compelling" (1991: 136). Indeed, cases of alleged HIV infection in patients caused by infected health-care workers which were reported around the world by the news media turned out to be unsubstantiated (Dickinson et al. 1993).

With regard to patients, the question was whether they should be mandatorily tested for HIV and, if so, were they to test HIV-positive, whether there is an obligation for a physician to treat them. Professional medical associations were quick to point out that physicians have a professional obligation to treat AIDS patients.

Let us now examine the relevant ethical arguments. A conversation reported by Daniels (1991) phrased the risk assessment-based argument permitting discrimination against HIV-infected patients by doctors in the following way: "Lots of surgeons carry antibodies for hepatitis B. That's a risk we all have taken, but I won't take the chance of bringing AIDS into my bed and killing my wife."

This has been discussed in sophisticated ways by both contractarians (e.g., Daniels 1991) and consequentialists (e.g., Smolkin 1997). Historically, the medical profession was a high-risk profession, certainly before the introduction of antibiotics. The physician as hero was made a common literary theme by Albert Camus and others. But that history does not necessarily provide a moral prescription for heroism among health-care professionals, either then or now. Independent argument is needed to establish a moral obligation for them to accept unusually high occupational risks.

The leading example of a contractarian argument on this issue is provided by Daniels (1991), who argues that a moral obligation to, for example, treat HIV-infected patients can be attributed to doctors only if it can be established that they voluntarily agreed or consented to do so as part of their decision and commitment to pursue a career in medicine. Morally (and often legally) binding professional codes of conduct can indeed impose considerable risk to the parties involved, even including loss of life, as in the fire-fighters who responded to the attack on the World Trade Center on September 11, 2001. With respect to the code of conduct for health-care professionals, Daniels's arguments have not yet made clear whether agreeing to it includes specifically agreeing to treat patients with a life-threatening virus. But what is clear is that the choice to enter the health-care profession was voluntary, and it was a choice that typically involved a public declaration to uphold that profession's code of conduct. Zuger and Miles (1987) develop a virtue ethics approach that draws on the religious etymology of "professionalism," meaning to profess to serve the public good; and they argue that refusal to treat HIV-infected patients is in violation of that understanding. Their approach is probably most in line with the traditional ethos of the medical profession.

The contractarian approach, advanced by Daniels and others, denies the need to argue for a supererogatory obligation rooted in professionalism, on the grounds that the infection risk is not great enough. The empirical evidence provided by Daniels in the early 1990s for this stance has since then been confirmed and strengthened. Though other epidemics (e.g., the plague) have had infection risks great enough to consider the efforts of physicians supererogatory, this is not normally the case for HIV and AIDS.

In contrast, consequentialists focus their concern on the outcomes of various possible policies. Comparing the consequences of a volunteerist policy versus a mandatory treatment of patients policy, and adopting similar empirical assumptions about risks as Daniels's proposal, Smolkin argues that the implementation of a policy of volunteerism would bring about a number of harms, namely: (1) the infection risk for the doctors who do volunteer would be greater than if treatments were evenly dispersed; (2) the unavoidable public knowledge of the policy would give HIV-infected patients incentives to conceal their HIV status, undermining the trust that is meant to be the foundation of the doctor–patient relationship; and (3) that same incentive might impede the effective treatment of HIV, which requires prompt and full disclosure of relevant information and timely and reliable access to health-care services. This, along with broader social ill-effects of discrimination against people with HIV by the medical profession, could cause significant physical and psychological harm.

> From the point of view of an HIV-infected patient who is trying to get in to see a physician and who is unable to do so, or who finds out that she has to wait long periods of

451

time to be seen, while other non-HIV-infected patients can be seen by a doctor almost immediately, the painful feelings of being "second class citizens," or being "marginalized," or being "and undesirable," must be profoundly wounding. (Smolkin 1997)

Moreover, beyond being wounding, the consequences of delayed treatment can be fatal.

Against this position, a policy requiring doctors to treat HIV-infected patients might be thought to carry some significant costs. Such a policy is in tension with the professional autonomy of health-care workers. Also, reluctant physicians might provide a substandard quality of care to the patients that such a policy forces them to treat. Finally, perhaps medical colleges would see enrolment numbers drop if mandatory treatment were required. In the literature, these last two worries have been discredited. The quality-of-care argument attributes an unfair and unwarranted degree of pettiness to health-care professionals. And, despite the rulings of most countries' medical bodies to mandate treatment, global enrolment in the medical training continues to increase steadily.

The history of HIV treatment and policy responses is substantially responsible for resolving this particular debate. And it is a resolution that can provide lessons for the development of policies guiding health-care professionals' responses to future public health emergencies involving infectious agents. Moreover, it importantly demonstrates that the traditional values of the medical profession have a continued and strong role to play.

Final Remarks

AIDS has become *the* paradigmatic infectious disease used by bioethicists in order to analyze ethical problems surrounding conflicts involving individual versus public interests. It is paradigmatic for particular types of disease, namely those that require, in most cases, that those who become infected have participated actively, and usually voluntarily, in risk-taking that eventually translated into an infection. In that crucial sense, AIDS is different from other illnesses such as, for instance, drug-resistant tuberculosis, which is on the rise again worldwide.

AIDS is also *the* paradigmatic disease for discussions surrounding the entitlement or otherwise of terminally ill patients to access (experimental) drugs. The pandemic disease has also been the initial rallying point of international efforts to address global health problems, whether on the level of infection control or on the level of questions to do with just financing mechanisms for drug research and development involving diseases suffered by the global poor. Many of current bioethics discussions to do with AIDS have changed their focus from developed world settings and anticipated huge AIDS case-loads there to real-world case-loads on an overwhelming scale in parts of the developing world.

References

Ayanian, J. Z. (1994). Race, class, and the quality of medical care. *Journal of the American Medical Association* 271: 1207–8.

Bayer, R. (1989). *Private Acts, Social Consequences*. New York: Free Press.

Bayer, R., Levine, C., and Wolf, S. M. (1986). HIV antibody screening: an ethical framework for evaluating proposed programs. *Journal of the American Medical Association* 256: 1768–74.

Bender, S., Flicker, L., and Rhodes, R. (2007). Access for the terminally ill to experimental medical innovations: a three-pronged threat. *American Journal of Bioethics* 7/10: 3–10.

Childress, J. F. (1991). Mandatory HIV screening and testing. In F. G. Reamer (ed.), *AIDS and Ethics*. New York: Columbia University Press, pp. 50–76.

Clark, P. A. (2006). Mother-to-child transmission of HIV in Botswana: an ethical perspective on mandatory testing. *Developing World Bioethics* 6: 1–12.

Cohen, J. C. and Illingworth, P. (2003). The dilemma of intellectual property rights for pharmaceuticals: the tension between ensuring access of the poor to medicines and committing to international agreements. *Developing World Bioethics* 3: 27–48.

Connor, E. M., Sealing R. S., Gelber R., et al. (1994). Reduction of maternal infant transmission of human immunodeficiency virus type 1 with zidovudine treatment. *New England Journal of Medicine* 331: 1173–80.

Cooper, E. (1989). Controlled clinical trials of AIDS drugs: the best hope. *Journal of the American Medical Association* 261: 24–45.

Daniels, N. (1991). Duty to treat or right to refuse? *Hastings Center Report* (March/April): 36–46.

Davies, P. M., Hickson, F. C. I., Weatherburn, P., and Hunt, A. J. (1993). *Sex, Gay Men and AIDS*. London: Falmer Press.

Delaney, M. (1989). The case for patient access to experimental therapy. *Journal of Infectious Diseases* 159: 416–19.

Dickinson, G. M., Morhart, R. E., and Klimas, N. G., et al. (1993). Absence of HIV transmission from an HIV-infected dentist to his patients. *Journal of the American Medical Association* 269: 1802–6.

Feldblum, C. R. (1991). A response to Gostin, "The HIV-infected health care professional: public policy, discrimination, and patient safety." *Law, Medicine and Health Care* 19: 134–9.

Glover, J. (1977). *Causing Death and Saving Lives*. Penguin: Harmondsworth, pp. 92–116.

Gostin, L. O. (1990). The HIV-infected health care professional: public policy, discrimination, and patient safety. *Law, Medicine and Health Care* 18: 303–10.

Harris, J. (2005). Scientific research is a moral duty. *Journal of Medical Ethics* 31: 242–8.

Illingworth, P. (1990a). *AIDS and the Good Society*. London: Routledge.

Illingworth, P. (1990b). Review essay. *Bioethics* 4: 340–50.

Minogue, B. P., Palmer-Fernandez, G., Udell, L., and Waller, B. N. (1995). Individual autonomy and the double-blind controlled experiment: the case of desperate volunteers. *Journal of Medicine and Philosophy* 20: 43–55.

Mohr, R. D. (1987). Gays, AIDS and state coercion. *Bioethics* 1: 35–50.

Nussbaum, B. (1990). *Good Intentions: How big Business and the Medical Establishment Are Corrupting the Fight Against AIDS, Alzheimer's, Cancer and More*. New York: Penguin.

Rachels, J. (1986). *The End of Life*. Oxford: Oxford University Press, pp. 106–17.

Schüklenk, U. (1998). *Access to Experimental Drugs in Terminal Illness: Ethical Issues*. New York: Pharmaceutical Products Press.

Schüklenk, U. and Ashcroft, R. E. (2000). International Research Ethics. *Bioethics* 14: 158–72.

Schüklenk, U. and Ashcroft, R. E. (2002). Affordable access to essential medication in developing countries: conflicts between ethical and economic imperatives. *Journal of Medicine and Philosophy* 27: 179–95.

Shisana, O. and Simbayi, L. (2002). *Nelson Mandela/HSRC Study of HIV/AIDS*. Cape Town: Human Sciences Research Council.

Slack, C., Stobie, M., Milford, C., Lindegger, G., Wassenaar, D., Strode, A., and Ijsselmuiden, C. (2005). Provision of HIV treatment in HIV preventive vaccine trials: a developing country perspective. *Social Science and Medicine* 60: 1197–208.

Smolkin, D. (1997). HIV infection, risk taking, and the duty to treat. *Journal of Medicine and Philosophy* 22: 55–74.

Tarantola, D., Macklin, R., Reed, Z. H., Kieny, M. P., Osmanov, S., Stobie, M., and Hankins, C. (2007). Ethical considerations related to the provision of care and treatment in vaccine trials. *Vaccine* 25: 4863–74.

UNAIDS/WHO (2005). *AIDS Epidemic Update 2005*. Geneva: UNAIDS/WHO.

UNAIDS/WHO (2006). *2006 Report on the Global AIDS Epidemic*. Geneva: UNAIDS/WHO.

UNFPA (2003). *The Impact of HIV/AIDS: A Population and Development Perspective*. New York: UNFPA.

Walters, L. (1988). Ethical issues in the prevention and treatment of HIV infection and AIDS. *Science* 239: 597–603.

Weijer, C. and LeBlanc, G. J. (2006). The balm of Gilead: is the provision of treatment to those who seroconvert in HIV prevention trials a matter of moral obligation or moral negotiation? *Journal of Law, Medicine and Ethics* 36: 793–808.

Weiss, S. (1992). HIV infection in healthcare workers. *Medical Clinics of North America* 76: 269–80.

Zivi, K. (2005). Contesting motherhood in the age of AIDS: maternal ideology in the debate over HIV testing. *Feminist Studies* 31: 347–74.

Zuger, A. and Miles, S. H. (1987). Physicians, AIDS, and occupational risk. *Journal of the American Medical Association* 258: 1924–8.

Further reading

Capron, A. M. (1974/5). Informed consent in catastrophic disease research and treatment. *University of Pennsylvania Law Review* 123: 340–438.

Clark, M. E. (1990). AIDS prevention: legislative options. *American Journal of Law and Medicine* 16: 107–53.

Gostin, L. O. (2004). *The AIDS Pandemic: Complacency, Injustice, and Unfulfilled Expectations*. Chapel Hill: University of North Carolina Press.

Gray, J. N., Lyons, P. M. Jr, and Melton, G. B. (1995). *Ethical and Legal Issues in AIDS Research*. Baltimore, MD: Johns Hopkins University Press.

Hunter, N. D. and Rubenstein, B. (eds.) (1992). *AIDS Agenda: Emerging Issues in Civil Rights*. New York: Free Press.

Van Niekerk, A. and Kopelman, L. (eds.) (2006). *Ethics and AIDS in Africa: The Challenge to Our Thinking*. Claremont: David Philip.

Weait, M. (2007). *Intimacy and Responsibility: The Criminalisation of HIV Infection*. London: Routledge-Cavendish.

Part XI

Experimentation With Humans and Animals

38

Research Involving Human Beings

FLORENCIA LUNA AND RUTH MACKLIN

Introduction

Why is ethics important in research? People can be harmed and people can be wronged, even if they are not harmed. In addition, groups and populations can be exploited when they are taken advantage of by powerful agents seeking their own ends. While most of the ethical concerns addressed in this chapter can apply to research in any setting, the increase in multinational research conducted in developing countries poses some special concerns, some of which remain unresolved.

Leading historical examples of abuses in research illustrate the ways in which people have been harmed or wronged. Each example violates one or more fundamental ethical principles, which will be elucidated further below.

The Nazi experiments

The most significant cases that revealed the need for establishing guidelines in research ethics were the abuses during World War II. Physicians conducting experiments under the Nazis forced people to drink seawater to find out how long a person could survive without fresh water. In the concentration camp, Dachau, Russian prisoners were immersed in icy waters to see how long a pilot might live when shot down over the English Channel and to find out what kinds of protective gear or warming techniques were most effective. In another experiment, 52 prisoners were exposed to phosgene gas, a biological warfare agent, to test possible antidotes. Also in Dachau, inmates were infected with a broad range of pathogens to test homeopathic preparations. Nazi military authorities were worried about exotic diseases that German troops might contract in Africa or Eastern Europe, and physicians in the camps reasoned that the "human materials" at their disposal could be used to develop remedies. Hundreds of people died in these experiments, and many of those who survived were forced to live with painful physical or psychological scars (Annas and Grodin 1992). The celebrated Nuremberg Code, a consequence of the trial of the doctors who conducted these experiments, broke new ground. Its requirement for informed consent in the first article stated: "The voluntary consent of the human subject is absolutely essential" (Nuremberg Code 1949). A later influential document that again embodies this requirement is the *Declaration of Helsinki* issued by the World Medical Association.

The Tuskegee syphilis study

From the mid-1930s into the early 1970s, the US Public Health Service conducted observations of African American men in a rural setting who were suffering from secondary syphilis. At the time, no efficacious treatment existed. However, after 1945, penicillin became available and was routinely used successfully to treat patients with syphilis. That treatment was withheld from these men, without their knowledge or consent. The Public Health Service officials used the ethically unsound defense, claiming that now that antibiotics could successfully treat syphilis, it would impossible to study its long-term effects.

Jewish Chronic Disease Hospital

In 1964, in the Jewish Chronic Disease Hospital in Brooklyn New York, 22 elderly patients were approached by a researcher who wished to study the body's immune mechanisms. The material actually injected into these patients was tissue consisting of live cancer cells. The subjects were told only that some tissue would be injected, that a lump would form, and would disappear in a few days. The researcher was certain that injecting cancer cells into the subjects would not cause cancer, but he wanted to determine how quickly and in what manner the patients' immune systems would reject the cancer cells. He defended withholding the information that the tissue consisted of cancer cells, noting that the fear that the word "cancer" strikes in people is very great. Although these elderly patients, some of whom were debilitated or senile, were not physically harmed, they were wronged.

Fundamental Ethical Principles for Research

Three principles, *respect for persons*, *beneficence*, and *justice*, are widely accepted as stipulating the requirements of ethics in research involving human beings. Although the principles and their elaboration are derived from sources in Western philosophy, they have become acknowledged as governing research designed and conducted throughout the world, as noted in the CIOMS *International Ethical Guidelines for Biomedical Research Involving Human Subjects* (2002).

Respect for persons is described as incorporating at least two fundamental ethical considerations (CIOMS 2002):

• respect for autonomy, which requires that those who are capable of deliberation about their personal choices should be treated with respect for their capacity for self-determination;
• protection of persons with impaired or diminished autonomy, which requires that those who are dependent or vulnerable be afforded security against harm or abuse.

458

The second ethical principle, *beneficence*, refers to the ethical obligation to maximize benefit and minimize harm; this requires that risks be reasonable in light of expected benefits.

The third principle, *justice*, can embody several different conceptions. The most common application to research is known as *distributive justice*. Distributive justice requires a fair distribution of the benefits and burdens of research:

- risks of research should not be borne by groups or populations that will not receive the benefits of the research;
- those who share in the benefits of research should also share in the risks;
- differences in distribution of burdens and benefits are justifiable only if they are based on morally relevant distinctions, such as vulnerability. (CIOMS 2002)

Another conception of justice is *compensatory justice*, which requires that subjects who are injured in the course of their participation deserve appropriate medical treatment and possibly also monetary compensation. A third conception is *justice as reciprocity*. According to this conception, something is owed to research subjects who may still need treatment when their participation is ended in a trial that results in successful products.

The informed consent requirement of the Nuremberg Code illustrates the need to comply with the first ethical principle, *respect for persons*. The participation of the concentration camp inmates was coerced; there was no respect for them as autonomous human beings. The episode in the Jewish Chronic Disease Hospital was a clear violation of this same principle, since the elderly subjects were not truthfully informed about the research procedures. The Tuskegee syphilis study violated all three fundamental principles. The men in the study were uninformed, so their autonomy was not respected; they were harmed when they could have been benefited by not being treated once penicillin became available; and, as they were poor and members of a racial minority, selecting them was unjust because they were doubly disadvantaged and, therefore, vulnerable.

The following sections address the three fundamental principles, their application to the research setting, and some of the ethical problems they confront.

Respect for Persons: Informed Consent

Empirical studies and anecdotal evidence make it abundantly clear that a large gap exists between the ideal of informed consent to research and the reality. Prospective research participants must be provided with information sufficient to make an informed choice of whether or not to enroll in a study. The information must be conveyed either in writing (the preferred method) or orally (when it does not make sense to have written documents) in terms that potential subjects can understand: in their mother tongue, obviously; free of medical jargon; at a level of language comprehensible to people whose schooling has not gone beyond the elementary level. Consent must also be voluntary, that is, obtained without pressuring potential subjects and without exerting "undue influence." Despite the reasonableness of these requirements, informed consent documents remain overly long, filled with technical information, and far from "user friendly."

The therapeutic misconception

A major problem that exists in industrialized countries as well as in developing countries has come to be known as "the therapeutic misconception" (Appelbaum et al. 1982; King 1995). Empirical studies of informed consent practices have revealed that subjects often do not read the consent documents they are given to sign, because they trust their doctors to act in their best interest (Advisory Committee on Human Radiation Experiments 1996). This illustrates the widespread confusion between participating in research investigating new, unproven therapies, on the one hand, and receiving an established, effective treatment for a health-related condition, on the other. The trust that patients have in their own physicians in the clinical setting relies on the important feature of the physician–patient relationship that physicians should choose the most appropriate treatment for the individual patient. To think that that same obligation applies in the research setting is to fall prey to the confusion between the aims of research and the aim of individualized treatment of patients. The features that characterize the physician–patient relationship should not be assumed to be present in the researcher–subject relationship.

Informed consent in developing countries

A frequent assumption is that the quality of informed consent in clinical research in developing countries is deficient or worse than in developed countries. Part of the rationale has to do with beliefs that may often be true: Participants are illiterate, lack familiarity with biomedical research and informed consent, and have limited access to health-care services (Alvarez Castillo 2002; Levine 1998; Resnick 1998). However, the assumption that the quality of informed consent is worse in developing countries was shown to be unwarranted. As Pace et al. (2003) wrote: "There are indeed warning signs about participants' comprehension and whether they are acting voluntarily, but in contrast to some claims, these warnings seem to apply to both developed and developing countries."

Although informed consent requirements have been introduced in the research setting in many developing countries, it is much less common for physicians to obtain consent from patients for medical treatment in those parts of the world. Some of the same problems persist in industrialized countries, despite their long experience with human subjects research. Still, particular problems pertaining to the process and documentation of informed consent appear especially difficult to resolve in countries where cultural features differ considerably from those common to most Western nations.

One example of this problem is a breast cancer study conducted in Vietnam in the 1990s. A researcher from the United States encountered problems surrounding informed consent in a randomized clinical trial of adjuvant treatment for breast cancer conducted in Vietnam; the investigator reported that he "found himself uncertain about the application of American standards of informed consent in the Vietnamese setting." After consultation with Vietnamese persons and cultural experts, he concluded: "American standards would not be acceptable to Vietnamese physicians, political leaders in Vietnam, or the vast majority of Vietnamese patients" (Love and Fost 1997: 424).

A key reason for this unacceptability is the paternalistic practice of medicine in Vietnam, in which patients do not participate in medical decision-making, but look to their physicians to tell them the appropriate treatment. As a result, the researcher contended that it was necessary to withhold from potential subjects any elements of the consent process that would convey uncertainty by the treating doctor. Specific items that were to be left undisclosed were alternative therapies and an explanation that the subject's proposed treatment had been determined by randomization. The investigator requested that the research ethics committee in his American medical school that reviewed the proposal "waive the requirement for informed consent, at least with respect to the subject of randomization"(Love and Fost 1997: 429). After many months of deliberation and considerable negotiation, the final version of the consent form did include the key elements of informed consent, "though with somewhat less detail than is typical in a US consent form" (Love and Fost 1997: 430). Yet the authors acknowledge that it is unclear whether the women in the study understood that their treatment was determined by chance.

How to deal with cultural practices that depart from the requirements of informed consent embodied in international ethical guidelines and many national laws and regulations remains a challenge for researchers who conduct clinical trials in developing countries. Ethical relativists have defended at least the following situations that constitute departures from widely accepted ethical standards for informed consent; that is, the perceived need to withhold key information from potential research subjects. Supporters cite three different considerations in defense of such departures.

The first is that the departures are justified by the cultural context in the country or community where the research is carried out. This relies on the widely accepted view that researchers should be culturally sensitive. Second, researchers contend that it would be impossible to conduct research without these deviations from what they call "Western" requirements of informed consent. This is the pragmatic defense. The third consideration follows from the second: requiring adherence would result in a loss of contributions to medical science and lack of consequent benefits to the population in those countries or communities. This is an appeal to justice, citing the consequences of not conducting the research in the developing country.

Cultural differences are challenging for research in the international arena and conducted in multicultural settings because of the tension between the ethical requirements of informed consent and the need to remain culturally sensitive, both of which are stated in international guidelines.

Beneficence

Beneficence is best understood as a variant of the philosophical principle of utility, which stipulates that right actions are those that have a preponderance of good consequences over bad. Beneficence therefore requires that research projects maximize potential benefits and minimize the risk of harm. However, if harms do occur, they are borne by the research participants, whereas the benefits may accrue to the participants themselves, to future patients, or may even constitute contributions to

461

knowledge. In designing and carrying out their projects, researchers have an obligation to comply with the principle of beneficence. In addition, committees that conduct prior review of research proposals are similarly bound by the obligation of beneficence (see below).

Applying the principle of beneficence to research studies is easier to describe than to implement in practice. For one thing, although it is common to speak of "balancing risks and benefits," or "assessing the risk–benefit ratio," no objective methodology exists for doing this. In addition, even experienced researchers may assign different levels of risk to the same procedure used in a research study. Moreover, the benefits may be largely unknown and difficult to anticipate, especially in an early phase of research. Finally, research that provides no direct benefits to subjects (such as base-line physiological measurements in healthy individuals) is permissible, as long as it holds the prospect of benefits to future patients or contributions to scientific knowledge. This makes it all the more difficult to determine that the risks to subjects are reasonable in light of the anticipated benefits.

"Gold standard" methodology and ethics

The requirements of beneficence cannot be met unless research projects are well designed and comply with rigorous methodological standards. Poorly designed research can yield no benefits, either to the participants or to others. One major concern is the long-standing controversy over the appropriate use of placebos, or inert substances, to compare with an active experimental medication in a clinical trial.

There are several methodological reasons why it is sometimes desirable to compare an experimental medication with a placebo. The least problematic, from an ethical point of view, is the situation in which there simply is no known treatment for a medical condition. In that case, the purpose of the trial is to see whether the experimental medication is better than nothing. Since good scientific methodology dictates that neither the researcher nor the participant should know which product is being administered, the placebo is manufactured to resemble the experimental drug. The ethical problem arises, however, when a placebo is proposed to compare with an experimental drug even if there exists a proven treatment for the condition under study. Proponents argue that some illnesses have a fluctuating course, others spontaneously get better, and still others are affected by patients' beliefs that they are receiving a medication that will make them better (the so-called "placebo effect"). Drug regulatory authorities generally require, or strongly prefer, placebo-controlled design of trials for the above reasons. Drug companies prefer placebo-controlled trials because they can be conducted more quickly and cheaply than a study that compares an experimental medication with a standard treatment.

Critics argue that it is unethical to withhold proven, effective medications from trial participants. The argument is that it is unethical deliberately to make people worse off in research than they would be outside a clinical trial. Withholding from research subjects an existing treatment that they could obtain from their own physicians if they were not in the trial violates the obligation to minimize harm and maximize benefits to research subjects.

Azidothymidine (AZT) trial in developing countries

A clinical trial that came to light in 1997 sparked new, worldwide attention to international research. That episode was a controversy that surrounded a set of studies of mother-to-child HIV transmission carried out in several developing countries, in which some of the women were given a placebo even though a proven, effective treatment was available in industrialized countries.

The international collaborative studies were carried out in Thailand and other developing countries that could not afford the expensive, high-dose AZT regimen routinely used in the US and European countries. These clinical trials were testing a lower dose of AZT, which was much cheaper and therefore presumed to be affordable to the poorer countries that would make it available to pregnant women. The developing country studies also began the cheaper AZT treatment much later in pregnancy, since women in those parts of the world do not routinely receive early prenatal care. And the AZT was administered by mouth rather than through a vein, which was more in line with the medical facilities used in these developing countries. These departures from the proven treatment available in industrialized countries were intended to adapt the treatment to the medical realities in the developing countries where it could be introduced.

Critics of this research argued that women in the trials should have been given the treatment used in industrialized countries and proven to reduce the incidence of HIV infection in their infants, and many lives could have been saved. The rebuttal by defenders of the research included the following main points (not all defenders invoked all of these justifications). The first defense was that the "standard of care" for HIV-positive women in these developing countries is no treatment at all, so they are not being made worse off by being in the study. A second point was that a placebo-controlled trial can be carried out with many fewer subjects and completed in a much shorter time than could a study with a control arm containing an active treatment, so benefits to this population could be available much sooner. A third justification was that the expensive AZT treatment that has become standard in the West is not, and will never be, available to this population, so its use in a research study cannot be justified. A final point was that the actual rate of transmission of HIV from mother to child was not precisely known. That meant there would be no way to tell if the new, experimental treatment would be better than no treatment, or sufficiently better to justify the expense of providing the new treatment.

The chief ethical problem identified by the critics was that these studies used a placebo to compare with the experimental treatment when they could have used the treatment available in the industrialized world. In that case, none of the women in these studies would have been denied a proven or potentially effective treatment. However, this trial raises another ethical concern about research conducted in developing countries. These AZT trials could not have been conducted in the North, since they would have denied participants an effective preventive method available outside the study. Those who defended the study agreed that it could not ethically have been conducted in industrialized countries, yet argued that the situation in developing countries is different. That argument defends the use of "double standards": one for poor countries and another for wealthier nations. Critics of double standards in research contend that the standards are not merely different, but lower in the developing country, and therefore violate a principle of global justice.

The above controversy was not limited to a discussion of the AZT trials themselves. The debate gave rise to an examination of the *Declaration of Helsinki* and a call to revise some of its key provisions. That process was itself fraught with controversy, and ended with the current substantially revised version issued in 2000, which was amended twice since then.

Justice

The original concerns of ensuring justice in research focused on the fair selection of subjects. If the pool of research subjects was mainly a poor population in a country, but those who would receive the eventual benefits were the middle and upper classes, that situation was perceived as unjust. More recently, however, failure to share in the benefits of research when successful products or contributions to knowledge result has been acknowledged as a major shortcoming in research sponsored by industrialized countries or industry and conducted in resource-poor countries. This poses the question, "What, if anything, does justice require when industrialized countries sponsor or conduct research in resource-poor countries?"

Although not universally accepted, current thinking about justice in international collaborative research accepts the following premises:

- research should be responsive to the health needs and priorities of the population where the research is conducted;
- it is unjust for research subjects to be made worse off afterwards than they were during the research – that is, by not providing them with a treatment they still need when their participation ends;
- it is ethically unacceptable for external sponsors to conduct research in developing countries and leave nothing behind when the research is over, that is, failure to provide some post-trial benefits to the community.

Evidence of an evolution of thought in this regard is that earlier versions of the *Declaration of Helsinki* did not include any statement expressing a general requirement for making successful products available to research subjects or to others. The 2000 revision of Helsinki, however, addresses the point in two separate paragraphs. Paragraph 19 says: "Medical research is only justified if there is a reasonable likelihood that the populations in which the research is carried out stand to benefit from the results of the research." The brevity of this statement, and the absence of any commentary or explication in the *Declaration of Helsinki*, leave crucial questions wide open. For example, what are the criteria by which "likelihood of benefit" is to be determined? And what degree of likelihood is necessary?

Helsinki also addresses the question of benefits to the research participants in a strong requirement in paragraph 30: "At the conclusion of the study, every patient entered into the study should be assured of access to the best proven prophylactic, diagnostic and therapeutic methods identified by the study." Although some commentators objected to this strong requirement, others argued that failure to provide post-trial benefits would be to exploit the individuals who volunteered to participate, without whom there could be no proven results of clinical trials.

Vulnerability and Exploitation

What makes individuals, groups, or even entire countries vulnerable? And why is vulnerability a concern in research ethics? A simple answer to both questions is that vulnerable individuals and groups are subject to exploitation, and exploitation is morally wrong. Although there is virtually universal agreement that exploitation is wrong, there are sharp disagreements on what constitutes exploitation. The answer is too simple also because not all wrongful actions can properly be considered exploitation. Some situations may be unjust without being exploitative, and some may involve harm inflicted on vulnerable people without having exploited them. Moreover, actions seeking to protect vulnerable individuals or groups might be construed as paternalistic, and therefore questioned by the very groups for whom protection is sought.

An interesting example is the view that women are potentially vulnerable as research participants. What characteristics of women would make them more vulnerable than their male counterparts of the same age and circumstances? Is it that women are less capable of protecting their own interests? That they lack autonomy? Or is it, rather, that women are capable of becoming pregnant so that it is the fetus – not the woman herself – that stands in need of protection? The latter is the likely explanation. However, given that women do not lack capacity to protect their own interests, the question remains whether those who are capable of becoming pregnant are the ones who should determine the best interest of their fetus or future child, and therefore decide whether to be participants in biomedical research. But if not the woman, then who is the most appropriate decision-maker in this context? The woman's husband? The state? There is no reason to believe that the alleged father of a child or the government cares more or is a more appropriate decision-maker than the woman who will be the mother of the future child.

When it comes to enrolling children in research, the parents are the legally and ethically appropriate decision-makers. The historical and still prevailing view is that research should not be conducted on children for conditions that affect both adults and children. Or at least, that adults should be participants in these studies first. The result is that much research has not been conducted on children, with the result that data is lacking about safety and efficacy for this group. Not only must the appropriate dose for children be tested, but also some medications that are effective in adults are not similarly effective in children.

Moreover, a paradox arises from two opposing perceptions of research. One – the standard view – construes research involving human beings as a risky enterprise, one that can harm or exploit people. At the same time, research can provide direct benefits to participants, giving rise to a positive view of the research enterprise. This may especially be true of individuals who lack adequate medical care outside clinical trials. This shift in the perception of research as beneficial came to light especially at the outset of the HIV/AIDS epidemic, a fatal disease for which there was no treatment or

465

cure. As a result, HIV-infected individuals were eager to enter the few clinical trials in which new potential treatments were being tested. It is true that participants in clinical trials often receive better care and treatment than they would receive outside a trial. This can be because of the expertise of the research personnel, the diagnostic tests that have to be performed that could reveal an undiscovered medical problem, and the possibility that illnesses other than the one being studied will be treated. Given these opposing perceptions and the reality underlying both, the question arises whether conducting multinational research in resource-poor countries benefits or exploits the population in those countries.

Drug companies are especially eager to conduct their clinical trials in developing countries. The research can be done more cheaply, more quickly, and possibly with less rigorous ethical review. One of the major concerns regarding these forays by the pharmaceutical industry is that the population in developing countries may be exploited. Exploitation occurs when wealthy or powerful individuals or agencies take advantage of the poverty, or powerlessness, or dependency of others by using the latter to serve their own ends (those of the wealthy or powerful), without any compensating benefit for the less advantaged individuals or group. This charge has been leveled at some industry-sponsored research.

One viewpoint considers populations in developing countries to be vulnerable, and therefore inappropriate to involve in research when the same studies could be done in an industrialized country. An opposing view maintains that requiring research to be conducted in industrialized countries before initiating a similar study in a developing country is an unacceptable form of paternalism. It treats developing country decision-makers, researchers, and research subjects like children, incapable of knowing their own interests and protecting those interests in the way the rights and welfare of research subjects are protected in industrialized countries.

A great deal of research is conducted in both industrialized and developing countries when the same health problem exists in both places. Some people from developing countries are among those who encourage this trend, arguing that their countries are capable of protecting their own citizens from harm or exploitation at the hands of local and foreign researchers alike. If the population in these countries has to wait for drug trials to be completed in industrialized countries before the medications can be tested and approved by their own regulatory authorities, the delay can result in untreated diseases and loss of lives. Others remain concerned about exploitation, and point out that in the absence of routinely available medical treatment, the population is likely to accept whatever is offered in the context of research.

Research Ethics Committees

How can human subjects of research be adequately protected against harm or exploitation? What mechanisms exist to protect the rights and welfare of research subjects? The two main safeguards are the requirement of voluntary, informed consent of each individual research subject (discussed earlier), and prior review of proposed research by an independent ethical review committee. Despite the universally acknowledged need for these two safeguards, ample evidence exists that they are at times flawed, often inadequate, and sometimes even nonexistent.

The two main charges to research ethics committees are to assess the risks and benefits of proposed research, and to review and approve the informed consent documents for the study. Research ethics committees conduct prior review of research proposals to ensure fulfillment of fundamental ethical principles. Multidisciplinary committees may be established within a research institution, on a regional level, or sometimes at the national level. An increasing number of commercial or "for profit" committees have been established. Critics argue, however, that these private boards operate with very limited government oversight and, because they are being paid by the drug company sponsoring the research, they have a direct financial interest in keeping their drug company clients happy (Elliott and Lemmens 2005).

All research ethics committees face many obstacles. A frequent concern is the gap between what laws or regulations stipulate and what actually occurs in practice. Another problem focuses on the constitution of these committees, which are made up mostly of researchers and physicians who can be biased in favor of research.

Many developing countries face these and other problems. One is the poor training of some of the members, as well as the lack of resources for infrastructure (for example, subscriptions to journals, photocopies, and books) and administrative backup, which undermines the efficacy of the committee. Part of the problem lies in the lack of a system that can assess the performance of the ethics committees and the accuracy of their work. In contrast to the strong responsibility and demands implied in approving a research protocol, there is a lack of institutional support (for example, committee members may not be given time off work to sit on the committees; physicians or hospital staff may have to attend patients at the same time; or there may be a lack of secretarial support). This is closely related to the status of these committees, but it also has to do with the scarce resources and revenue to finance some of their tasks. Finally, unlike the model in Northern Europe, which has a high percentage of lay members of the community, many committees in developing countries experience serious difficulties in incorporating representatives of the community.

Conclusion

Research involving human beings is continually evolving in many ways. Despite the existence of settled issues, such as the need for individual, voluntary informed consent, new problems continue to arise. One of the most salient is the increase in international collaborative research, raising, among other problems, the issue of whether double standards are acceptable. Perhaps surprisingly, debates in this connection have challenged the long-standing provision in the Declaration of Helsinki: "In medical research on human subjects, considerations related to the well-being of the human subject should take precedence over the interests of science and society" (WMA 2000: para. 5). Research continues to bring new complexities and subtleties, requiring ethical resolutions and when possible, consensus among all stakeholders. Nevertheless, the need exists to maintain universal ethical standards that protect the rights and welfare of all human participants in research.

Acknowledgments

Portions of this chapter are excerpted from the following previously published works:

F. Luna, *Bioethics and Vulnerability: A Latin American View*, Value Inquiry Book Series (Amsterdam, NY: RODOPI, 2006); F. Luna, "Research ethics committees in Argentina and South America," *Notizie di Politeia (Revista di Etica e Scelte Pubbliche)*, Anno XVIII, n. 67 (2002): 95–100; F. Luna, "Research in developing countries," in B. Steinbock (ed.), The Oxford Handbook of Bioethics (Oxford: Oxford University Press, 2007), pp. 621–47.

R. Macklin, "Bioethics, vulnerability, and protection," *Bioethics* 17/5–6 (2003): 472–8; R. Macklin, *Double Standards in Medical Research in Developing Countries* (Cambridge: Cambridge University Press, 2004).

References

Advisory Committee on Human Radiation Experiments (1996). *The Human Radiation Experiments: Final Report*. New York: Oxford University Press, pp. 459–81.

Alvarez Castillo, F. (2002). Limiting factors impacting on voluntary first person informed consent in the Philippines. *Developing World Bioethics* 2/1: 21–7.

Annas, G. J. and Grodin, M. A. (eds.) (1992). *The Nazi Doctors and the Nuremberg Code: Human Rights in Human Experiments*. New York and Oxford: Oxford University Press.

Appelbaum, P., Roth, L. H., and Lidz, C. W. (1982). The therapeutic misconception: informed consent in psychiatric research. *International Journal of Law and Psychiatry* 5: 319–29.

CIOMS (2002). *International Ethical Guidelines for Biomedical Research Involving Human Subjects*. Geneva: Council for International Organizations of Medical Sciences.

Elliott, C. and Lemmens, T. (2005). Ethics for sale: for-profit ethical review, coming to a clinical trial near you. *Slate*. Available at: www.slate.com/id/2132187/.

King, N. M. P. (1995). Experimental treatment: oxymoron or aspiration? *Hastings Center Report* 25: 6–15.

Levine, C. (1998). Placebos and HIV: lessons learned. *Hastings Center Report* 28: 43–8.

Love, R. R. and Fost, N. C. (1997). Ethical and regulatory challenges in a randomized control trial of adjuvant treatment for breast cancer in Vietnam. *Journal of Investigative Medicine* 45: 423–31.

Nuremberg Code (1949). *Trials of War Criminals before the Nuremberg Military Tribunals under Control Council Law No. 10*, vol. 2. Washington, DC: US Government Printing Office, pp. 181–2.

Resnick, D. B. (1998). The ethics of HIV research in developing nations. *Bioethics* 12: 286–306.

Pace, C., Grady, C., and Emanuel, E. (2003). What we don't know about informed consent. *Science and Development Network* (28 August). Available at: www.scidev.net/content/opinions/eng/what-we-don't-know-about-informed-consent.cfm.

WMA (World Medical Association) (1964). Declaration of Helsinki, Adopted by the 18th WMA General Assembly, Helsinki, Finland, June 1964, and amended by the 29th WMA General Assembly, Tokyo, Japan, October 1975, 35th WMA General Assembly, Venice, Italy, October 1983, 41st WMA General Assembly, Hong Kong, September 1989, 48th WMA General Assembly, Somerset West, Republic of South Africa, October 1996, and the 52nd WMA General Assembly, Edinburgh, Scotland, October 2000.

39

Regulating Experimentation in Research and Medical Practice

PAUL ULHAS MACNEILL

Introduction

The previous chapter discussed *research* involving human beings; in this chapter I consider *experimentation* on human beings. Both activities are expressions of an inclination that is quintessentially human and something we humans derive satisfaction and benefit from. The inclination to explore and experiment is evident from an early age. Without that drive – and discoveries made through exploration, experimentation, and research – life would not be as rich and rewarding as it is. Yet there is an obvious downside. When we experiment on ourselves, on other human beings, on animals, or on the environment, there is a risk of harm. That risk is inherent, by definition, in an activity that is initiated without knowing what the outcome will be. Human experimentation becomes a difficult *moral* issue when the experiment is conducted by one person, who stands to gain from the experiment, on another person, who bears the risks of the experiment.

Although a great deal of experimentation is conducted internationally, there are few reports of adverse events. Yet experimentation on human subjects has caused harm and death. In 1999, Jesse Gelsinger, who was 18 years old, died in an experiment that aimed to correct a genetic deficiency he suffered from. Inquiries into his death, at the University of Pennsylvania Institute of Human Gene Therapy, revealed failures in protective mechanisms that may have avoided his death (Thompson 2000). Ellen Roche died, aged 24, after ingesting a chemical agent that suppressed the action of nerves that are normally active in breathing. She was a healthy technician who had volunteered for a number of experiments at the Johns Hopkins Asthma Research Center where she worked. Inquiries into her death also identified breakdowns in protective mechanisms. Yet, as the Dean of Johns Hopkins University School of Medicine acknowledged openly in responding to Roche's death: "At a certain point some patient is going to die in clinical trials. . . . There is no question about it" (Steinbrook 2002).

How then can we respond to this difficult ethical quandary: that some people stand to gain from conducting experiments that subject other people to real and sometimes unforeseen risks of harm (Capron 2006: 431)?

Experimentation and research

The Cambridge dictionary defines an experiment as a "test done in order to learn something or to discover whether something works or is true." In this sense, ordinary medical treatment *may* be experimental, and innovative treatments certainly are. The courts, however, have distinguished experimentation from treatment by the extent of risk to the patients (or human subjects of the experiment) and the relative lack of any therapeutic benefit for them (McNeill 1993: 119). It is experimentation in this latter and more confined sense that I am referring to: the kind of experimentation that offers little or no established benefit to the subject and carries with it some risk of harm.

Research, however, is defined by the intention to collect and publish data. Without that intention, the work may be considered innovative treatment but not research (Glatstein 2001). In other words, an experimental treatment would only be regarded as research if the physician had the intention to collect data and publish the results. Yet an intention to publish is only one of the factors (and not the major factor) relating to the risk of harm. From the patient's perspective, the critical issue relates to *experimentation* rather than *research*. Furthermore, not all research carries any substantial risk, whereas an experiment (defined as above) may well do so, especially when it has a direct bearing on the physical, emotional, mental, or social well-being of a patient. For this reason the focus of this chapter is on *experimentation* rather than *research*.

The question therefore is whether or not it is reasonable to *experiment*, and what circumstances justify *experimentation*. Yet the question most often asked is whether it is reasonable to conduct *research* on human beings. As a result, research has been closely regulated, whereas experimentation (other than experimentation conducted as a part of a formal research program) has been comparatively free of scrutiny and regulation. Consequently, surgeons and other medical practitioners have, until recently, been relatively at liberty to innovate and experiment in the course of their practice.

Distinction between experimentation and innovative treatment

The reasons for this liberty are in part historical, and partly they derive from assumptions made about the intention of professionals in serving their clients or patients. In medicine, "clinical freedom" is a further justification for experimentation. While it is assumed that medical practitioners are motivated by a desire to benefit their patients when they treat them, that assumption may be misplaced when it comes to experimentation, and especially when an experiment has no possible therapeutic benefit. It is accepted that researchers are committed to successful outcomes from their research; and are motivated by the desire for knowledge, and the benefits that may come from participating in research and publishing their findings. This constitutes a bias that may lead to underestimates when assessing risks to the welfare of subjects of experiments. As a consequence, it has been recognized, at least since the 1960s, that the well-being of subjects may be compromised because it is secondary to the researcher's major preoccupations.

There is a blurred area, however, when it comes to experiments in the course of therapeutic treatment. Doctors who experiment with innovative procedures in the diagnosis, treatment, and management of their patients are assumed to be acting in the best interest of their patients. The tendency is to regard innovative therapeutic treatment as an extension of therapy, rather than as experimentation, and to leave the decision about whether it is appropriate to experiment or not to the treating doctor's discretion. The assumption is that doctors, in attempting new approaches, are doing the best for their patients and should be free to exercise their clinical judgment. However, a doctor's intention is not sufficient to protect patients who volunteer for medical experiments. When people test their ideas, whether it is in surgical practice or within "non-therapeutic" research programs, they tend to overestimate the benefits and underestimate the risks that may flow from the new procedure. Furthermore, benefits accrue to medical practitioners when they pioneer a new approach in medicine. These factors can, and do, lead to bias in assessing the potential for harm in innovative medical treatment, and put the volunteer, who is suffering from a medical condition, at risk – as the Gelsinger case demonstrated.

The fundamental issue however, and the central *moral* concern, is the same as in any experiment: when a new procedure is tested on people for the first time, there are inherent risks in that the outcome *cannot* be known in advance. In practice, one group of people carries the risks and, until that experimental procedure is better understood and the practical issues resolved, others are the likely beneficiaries. This distinction, between experiments done as a part of medical treatment and experiments in the course of non-beneficial research, has blurred the focus on this central moral dilemma.

History of Experimentation on Human Beings

It is apparent that experimentation has been a part of medical practice for as far back as there are historical records. Hippocrates took advantage of the exposed cortex of an injured boy to scratch its surface and to observe corresponding movements in the boy's body. In early Egypt and Persia, doctors were permitted to use prisoners for medical experiments. In 1721, condemned prisoners at Newgate Prison in England were offered a pardon if they took part in experimental smallpox vaccinations. Plague experiments were conducted on 900 condemned prisoners in the Philippines in the early 1900s. During World War II, in the Stateville Penitentiary experiments, "volunteer" prisoners were infected with malaria by mosquito bites and anti-malarial drugs were tested to find an effective prophylaxis for American combatants in the Pacific. Even after the war, prisoners in US jails were routinely used to trial new pharmaceutical agents in an ongoing "war on disease" (Pappworth 1967; Annas et al. 1977; McNeill 1993). In the United States in the 1800s, slaves were put into pit ovens so that heat stroke could be studied, and scalding water was poured over them as an experimental "treatment" for typhoid fever. Crawford Long (an American dentist) tested the effectiveness of ether as an anesthetic agent in the amputation of a boy's fingers. In his own words, he "amputated two fingers of a negro boy: the boy was etherized during one amputation, and not during the other; he suffered from one operation, and was insensible during the other" (Wall 2006).

Throughout history, it has been marginalized people in society, including racial minorities, prisoners, and slaves, who have been most experimented on. These experiments attracted little criticism within "educated" society because of prevailing attitudes.

Large-scale experimentation

With changes in predominant theories and methods in the late eighteenth and early nineteenth centuries, disease came to be seen (especially in the hospitals of Paris) as the effect of pathological entities within specific organs and tissues of the body (Ackerknecht 1982: 146). Doctors through Europe, impressed with this new scientific approach, deliberately infected healthy human beings with material taken from sick patients to test theories about the transmission of disease. There was no apparent regard for the victims who were harmed by these experiments. There are horrific reports (from Germany, Russia, and Britain) of people having pus, and other body matter from infected people, applied to cuts, injected into them, or placed in body orifices.

For example, in the early 1800s, Dublin physician William Wallace deliberately cut two boys (aged 12 and 15 years respectively) on their thighs and introduced pus or blood from syphilitic patients into the fresh wounds. Within two months, both boys showed the unmistakable symptoms of syphilis (Katz 1972: 286–7). This was not an isolated incident. In the late nineteenth century, German doctor Ernst Bumm introduced a culture of gonococcal material directly into the urethra of two women, which led to gonorrheal infection in both of them. Another German doctor, E. Fraenkel, introduced the secretions of gonorrheal patients into the eyes of newborn babies, who were suffering from other medical conditions from which they were likely to die. One of these babies contracted the disease and died 10 days later, exuding pus from a gonorrheal infection of the eyes. Another German, Dr Tischendorff, performed similar experiments with young children. In 1875, Dr Voss, a Russian physician, injected breast milk from a woman suffering with syphilis into three relatively healthy girls (of ages 13, 15, and 16), two of whom subsequently contracted syphilis. The doctor claimed that the girls were prostitutes and that they had given their consent, yet from any moral perspective, neither their consent nor their social status justified his cruelty (Katz 1972: 285–90).

Fortunately, not all doctors at the time were as callous and uncaring of the plight of the people experimented on. French virologist Viday de Cassi, who himself deliberately infected patients with syphilis (apparently with no qualms), complained that some of his peers refrained from this "greatest service to science" on the ground that they regarded these experiments as immoral (Katz 1972: 289).

A major change in attitude worldwide came as a result of revelations about experiments that had been conducted on human beings in Nazi concentration camps.

German experimentation in World War II

In the aftermath of World War II it became apparent that German doctors had conducted experiments with callous disregard for any suffering, harm, or death they inflicted on their human subjects.

The "Allied Control Council" (comprising the United States, Soviet Union, United Kingdom, and France) held trials of Germans accused of war crimes, and empowered the US military to conduct "subsequent Nuremberg Trials." In the first of these (known as the "Doctors' Trial"), 20 medical doctors and 3 non-medical personnel were accused of war crimes and crimes against humanity (as defined in Article 11 of Allied Control Council Law No. 10). Most of the 23 had held positions in various medical services within the Third Reich. Of the defendants, 16 were found guilty, 7 of whom (including Karl Brandt, Hitler's personal physician) were hanged.

The defendants were accused of conducting medical experiments predominantly on Jews, but also on Gypsies, Slavs, the mentally insane, and captured members of the Allied armed forces. They were accused of murder, brutality, cruelty, and atrocities in the course of those experiments. Telford Taylor, the chief prosecutor for the United States, stated in his opening address that the defendants had treated their fellow human beings as "less than beasts" and produced ample evidence to support this charge (Annas and Grodin 1992: 67–93).

Many of the experiments conducted within the Nazi program had a military objective, including "high-altitude" experiments that were designed to test the limits of human endurance and human existence in low-pressure chambers. In other experiments, humans were held in tanks of iced water for up to three hours as a means of testing various methods for resuscitating pilots who had been severely chilled or frozen after falling into the sea. Experiments with typhus, malaria, jaundice, spotted fever, and wounds (deliberately inflicted and infected) were designed to find cures to combat diseases troubling German occupation forces. Experiments in the removal of bone, muscle, and nerves from one group of prisoners, and the transplantation of this material into others, were conducted with the ultimate aim of assisting injured soldiers (Katz 1972: 292–306).

There is an even uglier side. Some of the experiments were part of the Third Reich's program for "racial hygiene" that aimed to "purify" the German people by exterminating and sterilizing unwanted groups. Tests on prisoners were made of various methods for sterilizing men and women. Other prisoners were given poison in their food and observed as they died; or they were murdered, after ingesting poisoned food, and their bodies dissected. Others were shot with poisoned bullets.

The accused argued in their defense that they had acted on superior orders, that the sacrifice of a few lives was necessary to save the lives of many, and that experimentation was necessary to support the war effort. They also argued that much of the experimentation on human subjects throughout history had been conducted in an ethically questionable manner (including experiments conducted in the United States); and that "volunteers" in these medical experiments had seldom given proper consent to take part. While none of these defenses could justify the horrors committed in the name of science, it has to be acknowledged that their claims about the unethical conduct of experimentation on human subjects through history were justifiable.

The Nuremberg Code

Neuro-psychiatrist Leo Alexander, physiologist Andrew Ivy (both from the USA), and German medical historian Werner Leibbrand advised the Nuremberg Tribunal on relevant codes of ethics, including the Oath of Hippocrates, German Codes (of 1900 and 1931), and principles formulated by the American Medical Association for the Nuremberg Doctor's Trial (Annas and Grodin 1992; Shuster 1997). In their judgment, the American judges enumerated 10 "basic principles" that must be observed in conducting medical experiments on human beings, "in order to satisfy moral, ethical and legal concepts." These principles adopted much of what had been recommended by Alexander and Ivy but gave added emphasis to an absolute right of a subject to consent to an experiment before it could be conducted. Consent included the right to be fully informed and free of any coercion. The judges went further than the recommendations put to them by adding a right for subjects to bring an experiment to an end (Shuster 1997). Their principles put an onus on experimenters to be scientifically qualified; to justify experiments in terms of potential "fruitful results"; to design their experiments properly and base them on previous animal experiments; to avoid unnecessary physical and mental suffering and injury; and to terminate an experiment if it becomes clear that harm will result. These principles subsequently became known as the "Nuremberg Code."

In historical terms, this was a formulation that went beyond most previous medical codes in recognizing a difference between patients, within a doctor–patient relationship, and subjects of experimentation, in that the primary goal of an experiment is not treatment but the acquisition of knowledge, regardless of the subject's best interest. The Nuremberg principles were unique in giving subjects themselves the right actively to protect themselves. All previous codes were based on doctors' responsibility to protect subjects in their experiments.

Japanese medical experiments

The Germans were not alone in conducting cruel and inhumane experiments on human subjects. From 1932 until the end of World War II, Japanese doctors and bioscientists conducted horrific experiments, largely on Chinese residents and prisoners and also on some prisoners of war, in a number of heavily guarded installations throughout Manchuria in China. Among other horrors, the experimenters performed live vivisections on men, women, and children with no anesthesia. Some victims had limbs successively frozen and removed until only their heads and torsos remained. Even then they were subjected to experiments with plague and other pathogens. Others were burned, shot with shrapnel, exposed to lethal doses of X-rays, or spun to death in centrifuge machines (Byrd 2005; Harris 2002).

The Japanese experimenters displayed a similar attitude to their victims as the German doctors had to victims in German concentration camps. They were regarded as less than human. For example, staff in Unit 731 referred to the people they experimented on as "Maruta" – a Japanese word meaning "log of wood."

The Japanese atrocities had little influence on subsequent developments however. This was because they were kept secret for many years after the war to keep from public view an agreement between the American government (at the behest of the American Occupation Forces Command in Japan) and the Japanese experimenters, which gave the experimenters immunity from prosecution if they provided the results of their experiments on human beings. The US Command considered the information was relevant to biological warfare. Most of the information about Japanese experiments only became public as the result of freedom of information actions in the United States in the 1980s (Harris 2002; Williams and Wallace 1989).

Political dimension

The stark contrast between the action of the United States against the principal German experimenters and their lack of response to the Japanese counterparts illustrates the important role that politics has played in the development of codes of ethics for the conduct of experimentation on human subjects. Secrecy denied the public an opportunity to react to Japanese atrocities (and US complicity in concealing them) and helped to maintain a belief that atrocities of this sort were an aberration that could be confined to the peculiar circumstances of Nazi Germany. This diverted world attention from the extent of inhumane experimentation worldwide, and the need to give attention to humane standards for experimenting on human subjects in all countries.

Regulation of Human Experimentation

Although the Nuremberg Court condemned, in the strongest possible way, inhumane experiments on human beings, it was not itself very influential. The attitude of the medical profession was that the circumstances of experimentation in German concentration camps during the war bore little relation to normal medical practice and research in peacetime, and that the Code threatened medical progress (Howard-Jones 1982). The major difficulty the profession had was that an absolute requirement for consent, prior to any experimentation on human subjects, ruled out experiments with children, those mentally incompetent to consent, and unconscious patients. The Nuremberg Code was perceived as a "rigid set of legalistic demands" that challenged the right of doctors to conduct research (Beecher 1970: 279).

Subsequently, in Rome in 1954, the World Medical Association (WMA) adopted "Principles for those in Research and Experimentation" that allowed for proxy consent for experiments on patients who lacked the capacity to consent for themselves. The predominant thrust of the WMA principles was to give primary importance to the responsibility of the researcher rather than the willingness of the subject. It was also to emphasize "therapeutic research" and distinguish that from "non-therapeutic research" (McNeill 1993: 44). A further effect was to give emphasis to *research* rather than *experimentation*.

Unethical experimentation in the USA

Ivy, the American College of Surgeons' expert witness, had testified in the Nuremberg trial that the "principles" he advocated reflected common research practice within the United States (Shuster 1997). Subsequent revelations of American unethical experimentation undermined that assertion.

It was revealed that in 1963 doctors had injected live cancer cells into elderly debilitated patients in the Jewish Chronic Disease Hospital. In 1966, an article by Henry Beecher in the *New England Journal of Medicine* drew attention to 22 unethical experiments that had endangered the lives of human subjects (Beecher 1966). In one of these, intellectually disabled children at the Willowbrook State School were intentionally infected with hepatitis. Also in the late 1960s, publicity was given to the Tuskegee syphilis case in which 400 poor black men from rural areas in the South, diagnosed with syphilis, were left untreated as a part of a study that began in 1932 to chart the development ("natural history") of the disease in those men. Even after penicillin, which is an effective treatment for syphilis, became available (in the 1940s), these men were offered no treatment and were simply observed as their condition deteriorated. They had not been informed of their diagnosis (only that they had "bad blood"), nor had they been asked for their consent to take part in the study (Jones 1981).

Development of committee review in the USA

One of the early responses was a requirement in 1966, by the US Surgeon-General, for a committee review of applications for Public Health Service grants. Each applicant was required to state that a committee had considered the risks of the research for any human subjects and had satisfied itself of the adequacy of protection of their rights.

Subsequently, the US Senate established a national commission on human experimentation that published reports, including the Belmont Report (outlining basic ethical principles) and the Institutional Review Board Report with a survey of the Institutional Review Boards (IRBs). The Senate also insisted on the promulgation of regulations covering research on human beings and those regulations incorporated and strengthened the National Institutes of Health policy requiring all publicly funded research to be approved by a committee.

Committee review in other countries

In 1966, Canada followed the United States' lead and adopted a requirement for review by committee, and the following year the Royal College of Physicians of London recommended committee review of research proposals within its guidelines for research with human subjects. New Zealand introduced a requirement for committee review in 1972 and a policy of committee review was adopted by the National Health and Medical Research Council in Australia in 1973. Other countries also followed this lead, and international codes, such as the Council for International Organizations of Medical Science Guidelines, adopted committee review of research proposals as a major protection for human subjects of experimentation.

Within Scandinavia, Sweden has required ethics committee review from the late 1960s, Denmark since the late 1970s and Finland since the early 1980s. In 1984 the Swiss Academy of Sciences recommended advisory bodies on experimentation and, in the same year, both the Netherlands and Belgian governments issued decrees requiring ethics committee review (McNeill 1993).

Guidelines, Regulations and Directives to Regulate Human Experimentation

The rules applying to research in most countries have been issued as guidelines (variously called "codes," "guidelines," "statements," or "standards"). These guidelines have been issued by funding bodies such as the Canadian Medical Research Council, the Australian National Health and Medical Research Council, and governmental departments such as the Departments of Health in New Zealand and the UK and professional bodies such as the Royal College of Physicians of London. Internationally there is very little legislation specifically addressing experimentation on human subjects. The US was exceptional in issuing governmental regulations covering human experimentation. As indicated above, both the Netherlands and Belgian governments have issued decrees. Since that time, the European Parliament has issued directives (Capron 2006: 433).

Common features of guidelines to regulate research

There are a number of common features in all these guidelines, standards, and regulations. They all rely on prior review by a committee of proposals for research on human subjects; the committees are required to consider whether proposals are ethical; they can approve a proposal, request modifications, or reject it; membership of the committees is specified to include some members with expertise in research as well as one or two community (or lay) members. There are some differences between countries about other members of the committees. Typically, the guidelines state the matters that the committee should take into account in deciding whether or not to approve the proposal: for example, the requirement to consider whether the potential benefits of the research justify any risks of harm to the human participants. Although there are few explicit sanctions against researchers, or their institutions, for failure to comply, rejection by an ethics committee, or failure to present a proposal for approval by a committee, will often have implications for funding and may lead to refusal by a journal to publish any results from the research program.

Critique of research regulation

Committee review of research has come in for considerable criticism, particularly from researchers, who argue that it adds considerably to the burden and cost of research administration, slows research down, and deters some research altogether. The claim is that an enormous effort is expended by many people in reviewing research proposals, most of which entails very little risk of harm, and there is little or no gain for all this effort in terms of actually avoiding harm.

Capron's (2006) more telling criticism is that those "elaborate rules and processes" have had the effect of normalizing human experimentation and avoiding the "moral dilemma that lies at the heart of every research encounter": that a person is asked to volunteer for research and accept unforeseen risks of harm in order that others might benefit. He suggests that researchers have a vested interest in enrolling human subjects into research programs and may be unwilling or incapable of a frank conversation that adequately presents this central issue.

Therapeutic misconception

There is a particular problem with clinical research in that desperately ill patients who volunteer may be motivated more by a desire to survive than by altruism (Horrobin

2003). Even when told explicitly that a procedure is experimental and that they may not benefit from it, these patients tend to receive an invitation to enroll in a study as grounds for hope of a cure or remission. This phenomenon has been termed the "therapeutic misconception," and its ethical significance has continued to be debated in the literature since the term was coined in 1982 (Appelbaum and Lidz 2006; Appelbaum et al. 1982; Miller and Joffe 2006). However, the difficulty is not only on the patients' side. Medical practitioners find it difficult to adequately inform patients that clinical trials are experiments (Brown, Butow, Butt, et al. 2004; Brown, Butow, Ellis, et al. 2004; Capron 2006). It is claimed that researchers exploit the therapeutic misconception. This is one of the reasons given for arguing that large clinical trials of drugs for people with rapidly advancing diseases are usually unethical (Horrobin 2003).

Regulation of Experimentation in Surgery and Clinical Medicine

At the outset of this chapter, it was claimed that the important ethical issue relates to *experimentation* on human subjects. However, review by committees is of *research*. The language has shifted to the "ethics of research with human participants" and away from "human experimentation."

Distinction between "therapeutic" and "non-therapeutic research"

The right to experiment within medicine has been staunchly defended by the medical profession on the ground that "desperate" measures could be taken with seriously ill patients if they offer hope of recovery. The 1954 WMA principles allowed that "operations of a daring nature" could be conducted on sick patients in rare and "desperate cases" if the conscience of the doctor would allow it. In the subsequent WMA Helsinki Declaration of 1964 this was spelt out as a fundamental distinction between "clinical research combined with professional care" and "non-therapeutic clinical research."

Although this distinction has been challenged, it remains in the current Helsinki Declaration. Doctors are permitted to experiment with new procedures in the care of their patients, especially where "proven prophylactic, diagnostic and therapeutic methods do not exist or have been ineffective." The Declaration provides that a physician is "free to use unproven or new prophylactic, diagnostic and therapeutic measures, if in the physician's judgment it offers hope of saving life, re-establishing health or alleviating suffering" (Declaration of Helsinki 2000: Principle 32). This is a continuation of a longstanding practice whereby doctors have offered experimental treatment when it "offers hope" with no requirement that the hope be grounded on anything more substantial than "the physician's judgment." This is very different from requirements for the ethical approval of research.

This distinction, between experiments done as a part of medical treatment and those done in the course of non-beneficial research, blurs the focus on a central moral dilemma (as was claimed above). The issue is that patients who are experimented on carry the risks of, and are unlikely to benefit from, new procedures. If the procedure is shown to be effective, it has usually been others who have benefited, when it has become better understood and the practical issues have been resolved (Horrobin

2003). Furthermore, when the assessment of potential benefit is left entirely to the "physician's judgment," and the sole criterion is that it "offers hope," then any procedure, even one that has only a remote possibility of success, can be justified.

Similar latitude to that of the Helsinki Declaration is extended in some national guidelines. For example, Australian ethical guidelines provide that the decision on whether a change in treatment is an innovation or clinical research is "generally a matter for the responsible clinician's judgment" (Australian National Statement 2007). This sidesteps the important moral consideration of whether or not the proposed change is an *experiment*, and what safeguards are in place to reduce any risks of harm to the patient. It also maintains a culture in which doctors have felt free to experiment on their patients.

Nineteenth-century operations on slave women for vesico-vaginal fistula

There are many historical accounts of experimental surgical procedures that were performed on people suffering from appalling diseases because an experimental procedure offered some hope, however slim. For example, US surgeon Dr J Marion Sims conducted experimental surgery between 1845 and 1849 on seven black slave women, without anesthesia, in an operation to correct vesico-vaginal fistula. This is a painful condition in which a narrow, often ulcerated, channel extends from the bladder to the vagina and allows a continuous discharge of urine. In the course of perfecting an operation to correct this condition, Sims practiced on these women (up to 30 times on one of them) and subsequently offered the operation to white women in the North. He has been accused of performing "unethical experimentation" on "African-American women [who] were enslaved as his experimental subjects" (Ojanuga 1993). A counter-claim is that Sims was motivated by a genuine desire to help black women who had pleaded with him to relieve their symptoms (Wall 2006).

Twentieth-century hemodialysis, heart, and transplant surgery

The twentieth century witnessed many advances in surgery and medicine. Hemodialysis, which now saves the lives of many, was developed in the 1940s. Operations on "blue babies" for heart defects, open-heart surgery, heart and heart-lung transplants, and kidney, liver, and bone marrow transplants all became "success stories" and are now practiced almost routinely. However, many of the people who were first operated on died and, in the course of their treatment, endured enormous suffering.

Thorwald, a German journalist, recounted the experiences of men, women, and children who "submitted to pioneering operations on failing vital organs." He gave a graphic description of Dutch surgeon Willem J. Kolff's experiments in the 1940s, in which the blood of patients with diseased kidneys was passed through 20 meters of cellophane tubing in an artificial kidney machine to extract urea. One of the many problems was that the cellophane tore easily, allowing blood to mix with the saline solution in the apparatus. Thorwald described a macabre scene of bloody foam spilling over the side of the apparatus and onto the floor around Kolff and his assistants, who stood in watertight shoes on bricks to avoid getting their feet wet. In the early days of this experiment, 16 patients died, before Kolff's machine successfully treated a 67- year-old woman suffering with extreme kidney failure (Thorwald 1971: 73–91).

There are similar stories in the development of pioneering operations on congenital heart disease in children, and open-heart surgery. In the 1950s and 1960s, operations performed by Dr Harken to assist faulty heart valves with various artificial devices led to 22 or more deaths, although 10 patients survived with "some improvement." The first patient to receive a complete mechanical heart valve-replacement died, as did a further 10 patients. However 5 patients did survive this operation. One of the early recipients, Mary Richardson, lived for many years, although she needed two further valve-replacement operations, and suffered a stroke at age 41 that paralyzed the left side of her body. Since those pioneering operations, replacement valve surgery has become a reliable and a relatively safe operation. (Thorwald 1971: 51–70).

Following early lung and heart transplants, most patients survived the initial transplant and lived for a short period, before dying from various complications. In 1963, surgeon James D. Hardy conducted the first lung transplant into a convicted murderer, 58-year-old John Russell, in the Mississippi Medical Center Hospital. Russell survived the operation but died 18 days later from kidney failure. In the following year, Dr Hardy transplanted a chimpanzee's heart into Boyd Rush, a deaf-mute man, who died on the operating table. In 1967, South African surgeon Christiaan Barnard replaced the diseased heart of 55-year-old grocer, Louis Washkansky, with the healthy heart of a young woman who had been struck by a car and suffered fatal brain injuries. Prior to the operation, Barnard gave Washkansky an unfounded and misleading assurance that he had an "80-per-cent chance." Washkansky survived in very poor condition and, in spite of persistent efforts by Barnard, including massive doses of anti-rejection drugs, his new heart failed 18 days after the surgery (Thorwald 1971: 217–89).

Barnard was criticized by colleagues for embarking on a human heart transplant even though dogs he had experimented on had only stayed alive for a few days after heart transplants. In justifying himself, he said that the patient with an irreversible disease "will beg you for it. He'll beg for the chance. Because that's what it means to him – a chance" (Barnard and Pepper 1970).

Criticism of "dying" justification for experimental treatment

George Annas has maintained a consistent criticism of poorly substantiated surgery and medical treatment that is offered to a dying person who has "nothing to lose" because it exposes terminally ill patients to a "special risk for exploitation." The patient's "dying status itself" is used "as an excuse to justify otherwise unjustifiable research" (Annas 1985). In a more recent article (2007), he wrote that, "for seriously ill patients, fear of death will predictably overcome fear of unknown risks." Yet there is an obligation to protect these patients "because terminally ill patients can be harmed and exploited" and because "there are better and worse ways to die." Annas had previously described the "horrible and prolonged" deaths of Barney Clark and William Schroder following their artificial heart transplants (1992: 130).

Annas claims that it is an abdication of professional responsibility to rely solely on patient autonomy to justify risky and unsubstantiated experimental treatment. As he puts it, "respecting patient autonomy does *not* require that we accept demands for mistreatment, experimentation, torture, or whatever the dying might want" (1992: 130). On the other hand, surgeons and physicians experience "extreme difficulty" in responding to desperately ill patients who want any innovative procedure, whatever the risk. Refusal, in the face of repeated demands, is difficult to justify in that the surgeon may be deciding for the patient that it is "better to die" (Little 2008).

What is needed is independent assessment of the proposed innovative treatment. Annas states that "choices can and should be limited to reasonable medical alternatives, which themselves are based on evidence" (2007: 413). However, what counts as a "reasonable medical alternative" and as "evidence" is not easy to specify. Is evidence of successful trials of innovative treatments in animals a sufficient basis for their use in humans? For example, the results of animal trials are taken as evidence of the viability of innovative surgery, and as a basis for approving trials of new drugs with healthy volunteers. Yet animal trials can at best be indicative of the risks of harm and potential for benefit in humans. This is a point that will be expanded in the "Discussion" section below.

Cardiothoracic surgeon Elliot Shinebourne (1984) deemed "haphazard experimentation by many different surgical teams" as unethical. He argued for control over the exercise of clinical freedom by surgeons and proposed that "new operations" should be "subject to the same ethical review as other research procedures." Plastic surgeon C. M. Ward (1994) criticized the "haphazard and cavalier fashion in which new surgical techniques are allowed to be introduced" and compared the lack of regulation of innovative surgery unfavorably with the "rigorous control demanded of a new drug."

Bristol Royal Infirmary case and Kennedy Report

Shinebourne's paper had specifically criticized the "arterial switch procedure in children" in the hands of inexperienced surgeons and the willingness of experienced surgeons to attempt variations. He claimed that these practices led to mortality rates of 52 percent. This was eerily suggestive of the later Bristol Royal Infirmary Case in which 29 out of 53 children (55 percent) who were given arterial switch operations and other procedures died, and another four sustained severe brain damage. Two cardiac surgeons and the Chief Executive of the Royal Infirmary were subsequently found guilty of serious professional misconduct and were struck off the medical register. This case has been described as bringing about a "sea change in medical and wider British societal attitudes to professional self-regulation, clinical competence" (Walshe and Offen 2001). The final report of a public inquiry into this case, conducted by Ian Kennedy, recommended inter alia that:

- any clinician carrying out an established procedure for the first time must be directly supervised by colleagues who have the necessary skill, competence and experience;
- any new invasive clinical procedure undertaken for the first time should be shown to be in the patient's interests and approved by the local research ethics committee;
- patients are entitled to know the extent to which a procedure is innovative or experimental and to be informed about the experience of the clinician who is to carry out the procedure;
- there should be training of surgeons, particularly in new techniques. (Final Report 2001: Recommendations 99–103)

The UK Department of Health responded comprehensively and positively to the Kennedy Report recommendations (Learning from Bristol 2002). It committed itself to "minimising the number of adverse events occurring . . . when a clinician undertakes a procedure for the first time or when new interventional procedures are introduced" and to establishing a National Institute for Clinical Excellence (NICE), independent of the Department of Health, to give effect to these measures.

Registration and investigation of new interventional procedures

Amongst other activities, NICE established a Safety and Efficacy Register of New Interventional Procedures (SERNIP) and assumed responsibility for registering new interventional procedures according to their safety and efficacy. This program prompted the Royal Australasian College of Surgeons (RACS) to develop the Australian Safety and Efficacy Register for New Interventional Procedures – Surgical (ASERNIP-S) (Boult et al. 2002). There are regular reports of the procedures registered within both SERNIP and ASERNIP-S (ASERNIP-S/RACS 2002). In addition, the Royal College of Surgeons of England has published standards for surgeons that require innovations to be approved by an ethics committee and registered with SERNIP (Good Surgical Practice 2002).

In Australia there have also been measures taken at a governmental level. For example, the New South Wales (state) government Department of Health issued a Model Policy for the Safe Introduction of New Interventional Procedures into Clinical Practice to provide a standard process for assessing new interventional procedures (NSW Health 2003). There are also restrictions on new services that operate through the process of accreditation of hospitals in Australia (Minister for Health for NSW 2004). These measures have resulted in changes in practice in some hospitals (at least). For example, the Royal Prince Alfred Hospital in Sydney now requires that the hospital's ethics committee approve proposed innovative surgical procedures and new services.

In the United States, however, surgeons continue to test new surgical procedures without prior review or ethics approval and without properly informing their patients (Capron 2006: 441). The American College of Surgeons is said to be considering a registration scheme for new interventional procedures (Campbell 2003).

Discussion

The chapter has focused on *experimentation* rather than *research* on the ground that the primary moral concern relates to unforeseen risks of harm in an experiment, whether or not that experiment is a part of a research program. At the outset, experimentation was defined as procedures that pose a risk of harm to patients, or to human subjects of research, with a relative lack of any benefit offered to them. Most of the critical attention, however, has been given to *research*, including research where there is little apparent risk of harm (such as qualitative research and studies based on questionnaires). Innovative surgery, and experimental treatment within clinical medicine, have had little scrutiny.

The distinction drawn in the Helsinki Declaration between non-therapeutic research and therapeutic research was one factor in this. Doctors were much freer to experiment when research was combined with therapy. Another factor was the response of the US Congress to research scandals within the United States and the emphasis that the subsequent regulations gave to research. Another factor has been the robust resistance, evident for example in the World Medical Association, to any restriction of doctors' clinical freedom.

Regulation of human experimentation has developed in response to atrocities and scandals, most notably the Nazi experimentation on humans during World War II and research scandals in the United States following the war. While there was growing criticism of surgeons' freedom to experiment on patients, it took another scandal to bring about change. The Bristol Royal Infirmary case, and the subsequent Kennedy Report, have led to a recognition that new and untested medical interventions need to have been properly assessed, both in terms of their efficacy and their potential for harm, and that doctors need training to perform innovative procedures safely. Whereas scandals in the United States led to changes in the review of research, the United Kingdom, prompted by the Bristol case, has driven changes in practice in (and attitudes toward) experimental surgery and medicine. Australian surgeons, and some health authorities, have rapidly followed this lead. Other countries have yet to adopt comparable measures.

What is at stake, as has been recognized by critics both within and outside the medical profession, is that any experimental procedure should be considered in terms of the "reasonable medical alternatives" and be "based on evidence" (Annas 2007). Yet these may be exceedingly difficult to determine. What evidence is sufficient when a procedure is to be tried for the first time in a human being? Animal studies may provide some indication but can never amount to conclusive evidence. Furthermore, what *kind* of evidence is sufficient? Quantitative studies may give some basis for deciding on the likelihood of a successful outcome, but give no indication of a particular individual's experience, or the extent of possible suffering, in undergoing the procedure.

I suggest that independent assessment of the evidence, taking account of the limits of that evidence and a review of all the circumstances in each particular case, is required to substantiate whether the proposed treatment is a "reasonable medical alternative." Those circumstances should include a report of both the doctor's and the patient's expectations and goals, the nature and extent of the patient's understanding of the experiment and possible consequences (including the risks of harm), and the limits of any evidence suggesting a procedure's efficacy (Kerridge 2008). An independent assessment may also alleviate, although not remove, the difficulty for a surgeon or physician in refusing a patient's request for an unsubstantiated procedure. Yet any innovative procedure, even one that has been thoroughly investigated and appears to offer beneficial outcomes, may carry unforeseen risks of harm.

More is required. The communication between a treating doctor and a desperately ill patient is critical. When the best that can be offered is an experimental procedure, there is a need for frank discussion that goes beyond "the facts." Capron refers to physicians finding a "vocabulary of relationships to fill the gaps, the moral silences . . . a language not solely of duties but of hopes and fears, of uncertainties and magical thinking" (Capron 2006: 435). It takes an ethical commitment, and special skill, to present an option in an open and unbiased manner to a person who is desperate to find a cure or remission from a serious disease, without leaving her with the illusion that an experimental procedure can be offered as therapy. Both doctor and patient need time to discuss their hopes and fears, and time for silence. It may be that a patient's desperation to try anything masks a deep sadness and resistance to accepting her impending death. The opportunity to talk openly with her treating doctor may allow her to move from this position. Equally, a patient may have reached a calm assessment of her situation and choose, nevertheless, to undergo a procedure that offers no substantial (or substantiated) basis for hope. Many standard and accepted medical procedures began in just this way.

References

Ackerknecht, E. H. (1982). *A Short History of Medicine*, Rev. edn. Baltimore, MD: Johns Hopkins University Press.

Annas, G. J. (1985). Baby Fae: and the "anything goes" school of human experimentation. *Hastings Center Report* 15/1 (February): 15–17.

Annas, G. J. (1992). The changing landscape of human experimentation: Nuremberg, Helsinki, and beyond. *Health Matrix: The Journal of Law-Medicine* 2/2: 119–40.

Annas, G. J. (2007). Cancer and the constitution – choice at life's end. *New England Journal of Medicine* 357/4: 408–13.

Annas, G. J. and Grodin, M. A. (eds.) (1992). *The Nazi Doctors and the Nuremberg Code: Human rights in human experimentation.* New York and Oxford: Oxford University Press.

Annas, G. J., Glanz, L. H., and Katz, B. F. (1977). *Informed Consent to Human Experimentation: The Subject's Dilemma.* Cambridge, MA: Balinger.

Appelbaum, P. S. and Lidz, C. W. (2006). Re-evaluating the therapeutic misconception: response to Miller and Joffe. *Kennedy Institute of Ethics Journal* 16/4: 367–73.

Appelbaum, P. S., Roth, L. H., and Lidz, C. W. (1982). The therapeutic misconception: informed consent in psychiatric research. *International Journal of Law and Psychiatry* 5: 319–29.

ASERNIP-S/RACS (2002). Available at: www.surgeons.orghttp://www.surgeons.org/Content/NavigationMenu/Research/ASERNIPS/default.htm (accessed October 2007).

Australian National Statement on Ethical Conduct in Human Research (2007). Available at: www.nhmrc.gov.au/publications/synopses/_files/e72.pdf (accessed October 2007).

Barnard, C. and Pepper, C. B. (1970). *One Life.* Sydney: Australasian Publishing Co.

Beecher, H. K. (1966). Ethics and clinical research. *New England Journal of Medicine* 274/2: 1354–60.

Beecher, H. K. (1970). *Research and the Individual.* Boston, MA: Little, Brown and Co.

Boult, M., Babidge, W., Roder, D., and Maddern, G. (2002). Issues of consent and privacy affecting the functioning of ASERNIP-S. *ANZ Journal of Surgery* 72: 580–82.

Brown, R. F., Butow, P. N., Butt, D. G., Moore, A. R., and Tattersall, M. H. N. (2004). Developing ethical strategies to assist oncologists in seeking informed consent to cancer clinical trials. *Social Science and Medicine* 58/2: 379–90.

Brown, R. F., Butow, P. N., Ellis, P., Boyle, F., and Tattersall, M. H. N. (2004). Seeking informed consent to cancer clinical trials: describing current practice. *Social Science and Medicine* 58/12: 2445–57.

Byrd, G. D. (2005). General Ishii Shiro: his legacy is that of genius and madman. MA thesis, Department of History, East Tennessee State University.

Campbell, B. (2003). Interventional Procedures Safety and Efficacy. Available at: www.nice.org.uk/page.aspx?o=38300 (accessed October 2007).

Capron, A. M. (2006). Experimentation with human beings: light or only shadows symposium. In: A world less silent: celebrating Jay Katz's contributions to law, medicine, and ethics. *Yale Journal of Health Policy, Law, and Ethics* 6: 431–64.

Declaration of Helsinki (2000). As amended in the 52nd WMA General Assembly, Edinburgh, Scotland. Available at: www.wma.net/e/policy/b3.htm (accessed October 2007).

Final Report (2001). Learning from Bristol: the report of the public inquiry into children's heart surgery at the Bristol Royal Infirmary 1984–1995. Bristol Royal Infirmary Inquiry (July). Available at: www.bristol-inquiry.org.uk/ (accessed October 2007).

Glatstein, E. (2001). What is research? *International Journal of Radiation Oncology, Biology, Physics* 51/2: 288–90.

Good Surgical Practice (2002). Royal College of Surgeons of England (September). Available at: www.rcseng.ac.uk/standards/good.html/?searchterm=Good%20Surgical%20Practice (accessed October 2007).

Harris, S. S. (2002). *Factories of Death: Japan's Biological Warfare 1932–45 and the American Cover-up*, rev. edn. New York and London: Routledge.

Horrobin, D. F. (2003). Are large clinical trials in rapidly lethal diseases usually unethical? *Lancet* 361/9358: 695–97.

Howard-Jones, N. (1982). Human experimentation in historical and ethical perspectives. *Social Science and Medicine* 16: 1429–48.

Jones, J. H. (1981). *Bad Blood: The Tuskegee Syphilis Experiment*. New York: Free Press.

Katz, J. (1972). *Experimentation with Human Beings: The Authority of the Investigator, Subject, Professions, and State in the Human Experimentation Process*. New York: Russell Sage Foundation.

Kerridge, I. H. (hematologist and Director of Centre for Values, Ethics and the Law in Medicine, University of Sydney) (2008). Personal communication.

Learning from Bristol (2002). The DH response to the report of the public inquiry into children's heart surgery at the Bristol Royal Infirmary 1984–1995. Available at: www.dh.gov.uk/prod_consum_dh/idcplg?IdcService=GET_FILE&dID=19383&Rendition=Web (accessed October 2007).

Little, M. (Emeritus Professor of Surgery, University of Sydney) (2008). Personal communication.

McNeill, P. M. (1993). *The Ethics and Politics of Human Experimentation*. Cambridge, New York, and Melbourne: Cambridge University Press.

Miller, F. G. and Joffe, S. (2006). Evaluating the therapeutic misconception. *Kennedy Institute of Ethics Journal* 16: 353–66.

Minister for Health for NSW (2004). Answer to question from Mr Barry O'Farrell to Minister for Health, 1381–Public Hospital Accreditation; Questions and Answers Paper No. 53. NSW Government Information Bookshop: Hansard and House Papers. Available at: www.parliament.nsw.gov.au/prod/la/qala.nsf/ad22cc96ba50555dca257051007aa5c8/ca25708400173f67ca25704a0009926b!OpenDocument (accessed October 2007).

NSW Health (2003). New South Wales Department of Health: Clinical practice – model policy for safe introduction of new interventional procedures. Available at: www.health.nsw.gov.au/policies/PD/2005/PD2005_333.html (accessed October 2007).

Ojanuga, D. (1993). The medical ethics of the "Father of Gynaecology," Dr J Marion Sims. *Journal of Medical Ethics* 19/1: 28–31.

Pappworth, M. H. (1967). *Human Guinea Pigs: Experimentation on Man*. Boston, MA: Beacon Press.

Shinebourne, E. A. (1984). Ethics of innovative cardiac surgery. *British Heart Journal* 52/6 (December): 597–601.

Shuster, E. (1997). Fifty years later: the significance of the Nuremberg Code. *New England Journal of Medicine* 337/20: 1436–40.

Steinbrook, R. (2002). Protecting research subjects – the crisis at Johns Hopkins. *New England Journal of Medicine* 346/9: 716–20.

Thompson, L. (2000). Human gene therapy: harsh lessons, high hopes. *FDA Consumer: The magazine of the US Food and Drug Administration* 34/5 (September–October). Available at: www.fda.gov/fdac/features/2000/500_gene.html (accessed November 2007).

Thorwald, J. (1971). *The Patients*, trans. R. and C. Winston. New York: Harcourt Brace Jovanovich.

Wall, L. L. (2006). The medical ethics of Dr J Marion Sims: a fresh look at the historical record. *Journal of Medical Ethics* 32: 346–50.

Walshe, K. and Offen, N. (2001). A very public failure: lessons for quality improvement in health-care organisations from the Bristol Royal Infirmary. *Quality in Health Care* 10: 250–56.

Ward, C. M. (1994). Surgical research, experimentation and innovation. *British Journal of Plastic Surgery* 47/2 (March): 90–4.

Williams, P. and Wallace, D. (1989). *Unit 731: Japan's Secret Biological Warfare in World War II*. New York: Free Press.

40

Research Using Preimplantation Human Embryos

MARY WARNOCK AND PETER BRAUDE

The ethical issues arising specifically out of research using human embryos are somewhat different from those discussed in the other chapters in this book concerned with experimentation on human beings (see chapters 38 and 39). In considering these issues there will inevitably be some overlap with some of the ideas in chapter 14 on abortion, since the problems arise not from matters of autonomy or consent, but from the status that ought to be accorded to the embryo.

In the report of the Committee of Inquiry into Human Fertilisation and Embryology (Warnock 1985; Warnock et al. 1984), the committee attempted to distinguish between pure and applied research, and to separate both from the use of new and untried treatment, though it was admitted that the categories overlapped. It was probably a mistake even to attempt to separate them. In a relatively new science such as embryology and its practical applications, the "pure" motive for research, curiosity, or the desire to seek further knowledge of the subject, will always exist alongside the motive of new applications of knowledge. New potential clinical applications must inevitably be experimental to some extent, and thus themselves be part of a research program. In any case, there is probably a general consensus that no research using human beings should be undertaken frivolously and without good medical reasons. In discussing issues in bioethics, one must not forget that, although people hold different moral views on many topics, there exists a number of shared values, common to most human beings, binding them, however loosely, in a moral community to which other living creatures do not belong. It is when these basic values seem to be threatened that a sense of outrage arises. Indeed, the starting point of any debate about the use of human embryos for research is the common assumption that to use other human beings for research purposes is something that must not be undertaken lightly.

The question of justification, then, has always been in the foreground of discussions about research using live human embryos, with debate about the moral relevance of the embryo's degree of development figuring prominently. We have to remind ourselves how comparatively recently this discussion began. For the general public, at least, it began with the birth in the UK of the first IVF baby, Louise Brown, in 1978 (Edwards et al. 1980). Until that time, most people did not appreciate that experiments to fertilize human eggs in the laboratory had been taking place since the mid-1960s (Edwards 1965), nor that embryos had been grown *in vitro* since 1969 (Edwards et al. 1970;

Steptoe et al. 1971); but when the experiment succeeded, and not only was the egg fertilized, but implantation in the mother's uterus was achieved, a pregnancy established, and a healthy baby born, public debate began in earnest. Despite the concept being around since at least the early 1930s (Editorial 1937), and some debate following the first clinical success with an ectopic pregnancy in 1976 (Steptoe and Edwards 1976), this was the first time that most of the public became aware that IVF offered a real possibility of alleviating some kinds of infertility. It was the remedying of the misery brought about by infertility in those who wanted children that was the justification of the original, and indeed much of the subsequent, research.

The likelihood of success had seemed remote, and indeed the success rate of the procedure at the beginning was very low. There was still considerable public ignorance of the early stages of the development of the embryo, but at least it became clear that if IVF was to be offered as a practical remedy for infertility, then its success had to be increased and this entailed research into the nature of fertilization, early cleavage, and successful implantation. The then Archbishop of York, John Habgood, speaking in the House of Lords in 1989, put it thus:

> I believe that research must continue if *in vitro* fertilization is to continue. One cannot separate them, and I regard as totally unrealistic, and indeed immoral, any proposal to continue *in vitro* fertilization without a proper backing in research. This for the simple and basic reason that imperfect techniques without a backing in research are bad practice medically and, I believe, wrong morally.

To use parents desperate to have children as experimental material, while pretending to offer them therapy would have amounted to exploitation, and would indeed have been morally wrong (and this is so even though no hard line can be drawn between new treatment and research).

In considering why research was needed, we must first try to clarify the early stages of fertilization and embryonic development. Normally, an egg released from a woman's ovary encounters sperm traveling along the fallopian tube and is fertilized there. If the tubes are blocked, or if sperm are few or weak, egg and sperm cannot meet, and the couple is infertile. It was to meet this kind of case that, in the UK, Patrick Steptoe and Robert Edwards, after years of research using eggs retrieved from donated ovaries, devised a way of removing an egg from a woman's ovary at the appropriate time of their menstrual cycle and placing them with her partner's sperm in a dish outside the body in a specially prepared fluid. When fertilization had occurred and the first stages of early development had taken place, the cleaving embryo was replaced in the woman's uterus, in the hope that it would implant in its wall. This was *in vitro* fertilization.

The egg, once fertilized, undergoes cleavage: regular divisions of cells without much growth (Braude and Johnson 1990). Following the first division, it cleaves to 4, 16, and so on, until, by day four, there are around 64 cells. Further cleavage over the next four days is accompanied by differentiation: the allocation of some cells toward tissues that will give rise to the embryo proper, the rest to the formation of the placenta, the amnion, the umbilical cord, and the other membranes that will be the support system of the embryo when it is fully formed. Further development and differentiation of the embryo occurs over the next week with the formation of the three germ layers:

the primitive precursors that will give rise to the main tissue types in the body. At this stage, a line called the primitive streak can be discerned, from which the middle of the three germ layers stream, and along which will develop the rudiments of the spinal cord and the central nervous system of the embryo. Up until this stage the embryo can still twin; how the embryos share their placenta and membranes will depend on precisely when this process happens. If the twinning process occurs early, say prior to the formation of the blastocyst stage, then generally the embryos will develop in separate sacs although sharing a placenta; if later, they will tend to develop within one amniotic sac. (The issues surrounding research into the differentiation of these embryonic cells is discussed later in this chapter.) By eight weeks from fertilization, the placenta and all the protective membranes have separated from the embryo proper, and the main organs of the body and all the limbs have been formed.

The areas in which research was needed were various (Braude et al. 1986). Little was known about the actual process of fertilization in humans, or about the structure of the human preimplantation embryo. Secondly, it was necessary to experiment with the composition of culture media within which egg and sperm would be brought together, and the environment (temperature and oxygen and carbon dioxide concentrations) in which the preimplantation embryo would be grown. There was a need to examine the factors that would promote successful implantation once the embryo had been transferred to the uterus.

The ethical issues that arose from the use of embryos in this research were a matter of public rather than private morality. The question was not so much whether individual scientists might be tempted to carry out such research, but whether people wished to be members of a society that permitted it to occur; that was a matter of public policy and the law. But the law had to be made. There was no existing law that could be stretched to cover such a wholly novel situation; any new law would have to reflect as far as possible the moral views not merely of Parliament, but of the country as a whole. Here lay the greatest difficulty. There was no received wisdom about the moral status of living human embryos in the laboratory and how, if at all, they might be used (Warnock 1987). There could be none, since the first such embryo *in vitro* had come into existence only a few years before.

There is a presumption that legislation which forms public policy should be based on a broadly utilitarian weighing-up of harms and benefits, a kind of cost-benefit analysis. From the outset, most people were prepared to accept that the alleviation of infertility was a major benefit; but as the debate progressed, other benefits that might flow from embryo research began to emerge. More might be discovered about the causes of miscarriage and new methods of contraception might be developed. Above all, the possibility of detecting faulty genes in very early embryos opened new possibilities of healthy babies being born to couples who were at significant risk of passing monogenic diseases such as Duchenne muscular dystrophy or cystic fibrosis to their children. With the help of IVF, embryos could be examined in the laboratory and only those found to be free of the defective gene would be implanted (McLaren 1987). In the British Parliament, by the time that the Embryology Bill came to be debated at the end of 1989, those in favor of permitting research using human embryos placed as much weight on the possibility of eliminating monogenic diseases as on remedying infertility, and some rested their arguments on this entirely. In order to make IVF not only theoretically accepted, but also a routine procedure applicable to the infertile as well as, where necessary, to the fertile, the research must continue. And all these good things seemed to be promised with no harm or pain to anyone to weigh against them; because the early embryo, which had no central nervous system, could not suffer pain whatever was done to it in the course of research. The justification for research seemed overwhelmingly strong on utilitarian grounds.

However, simple utilitarian arguments were not enough to convince all opponents. It was argued that human embryos were different from other research material, simply because they were human; and there were those who thought that this was the end of the matter. There could be no justification for research that would bring about the destruction of the embryo. Other human subjects, it was argued, may be used for research (with their consent) if and only if there is some chance that the research may benefit them personally. Not only can embryos not give consent, but it was agreed generally that any embryo which had been the subject of research must be destroyed and not implanted in a woman's uterus, for fear that it might have suffered damage from the research procedures and develop into a disabled child. Therefore these embryos were doomed to destruction from the start. The benefit that would come from research would be for others, not for the embryos themselves. There were those who argued that it was particularly wrong to fertilize eggs specifically for research; there were others who, perhaps more consistently, claimed that it made no difference to the prohibitionist argument whether the embryo had been created for the sake of research or for the sake of intended implantation but was then surplus to the needs of the woman undergoing treatment. In either case, a human embryo would be destroyed as an outcome of the research – which was unacceptable however good the intentions of the research.

Such moralists were, and still are, implacably opposed to any embryo research. Some of them, retaining the utilitarian framework of argument, held that the weighing up of benefits and harms must include the harm done to the embryos that would be used. Though these embryos could not suffer pain, they could and did suffer death, which was worse. In their calculus of gains and losses, human beings who had been born were to be given no priority over those who had just been conceived, whether implanted or not. All were equal; to kill some human beings to benefit others was not something to be morally condoned, and this was what embryo research amounted to. This attitude often did not recognize the practicalities of IVF procedures to alleviate infertility, wherein embryos are created by fertilization of a number of eggs, but relatively few of them have any potential to develop in the womb even after replacement there; many cleaving embryos in culture are of such poor morphology that they are discarded without transfer as part of the normal IVF therapeutic procedure. Those opposed to any embryo destruction would therefore be consistent in opposing all IVF therapy.

Other prohibitionists were not inclined to adopt utilitarian arguments, nor any argument that depended on the consequences of a given act. They simply asserted that deliberately to take the life of another human being was wrong, whatever its stage of development. If it were agreed, as it must be, that embryos used for research were both human (they belong to no other species of animal) and alive, then it must be wrong to destroy them. Human life is sacred.

There was another argument often used by itself, but sometimes as an extra to reinforce those outlined above; the slippery slope argument. This argument, used in

490

many different contexts, has an immense appeal to the imagination. Unlike the argument from the sanctity of human life, it is not an absolutist or an a priori argument, but empirical, supposedly based on facts, albeit facts about the future. The argument is that even if research using human embryos might be justified by its results, it was nevertheless the kind of activity that would inevitably lead to even worse activities which nearly everyone would agree were wrong. A law allowing research that used human embryos would inevitably be abused. An example of a slippery slope argument is this: there might be little harm in using pre-14-day embryos as research subjects, but soon it would be live fetuses that would be used, and then premature babies, then all babies and eventually we would arrive at the Holocaust. In this argument there is no suggestion that one of these steps followed by logical necessity from another. It is an argument based on a supposed truth about human nature rather than on logical consistency. People being what they are, it suggested, "given an inch will take a mile." (See chapter 28 for a more detailed discussion of the slippery slope argument.)

It is in the attempt to counter this kind of argument that legislative regulation of embryonic research has been fairly generally accepted. In those countries and states where such research is not prohibited, a legislative barrier backed by mandatory penalties has been erected to block descent down the slope. As in the UK, it would require primary legislation to permit research using human embryos more than 14 days from fertilization.

The law demands certainty; and this was why a specific number of days was proposed in the committee's report, and incorporated into the Act, beyond which embryo research would become a criminal offence. In a way, it did not very much matter where the block was placed on the slope as long as it was unambiguous. The 14-day rule was not entirely arbitrary (McLaren 1984). As we have already seen, there are relevant changes in the embryo that begin at about 14 days after fertilization. The primitive cell planes that will develop into all the various tissues of the body are discernible; it cannot any longer be thought of as just a collection of cells in a loose bundle. Since twinning does not occur after this time, in one sense each embryo has become an individual, albeit incompletely formed. Before that, though the increasingly numerous collection of cells had genetic identity, that was all it had. Many people are now reasonably satisfied with this line of thought, and are prepared to accept the continuation of research until this time, subject to regulation, and with the criminal law in the background.

Most people, however sensitive to moral issues, are probably biological gradualists. They grieve less over an early than over a late miscarriage; they do not regard it as a moral outrage that at the very beginning of a pregnancy a miscarriage may occur and pass unnoticed, or that an intrauterine contraceptive device prevents implantation of the fertilized egg. Most people no longer believe that there is one single identifiable moment when a human being comes into existence and must be separately valued and protected. Aristotle, without the benefit of microscopes or the concept of the human ovum, relying mostly on guesswork, held that male sperm conveyed something called *pneuma* to female menstrual blood and that this *pneuma*, which had no permanent life of its own, caused the embryo to come into being. It gave the embryo life (or soul): first merely vegetative as shared by all living things, then such as all living animals have, and finally rational, unique to the human species. The rational soul began in the male embryo at about 40 days from the entry of the *pneuma* into the uterus, in females at about 90 days. From then on the fetus must be protected, as potentially human (De Generatione Animalium 729a). This doctrine was taken over almost in its entirety by Aquinas, nearly 15 centuries later. Even Aristotle and Aquinas were gradualists of a kind, in that they held that the early embryo (however they thought it came into existence) was to be valued less highly than the later fetus, to say nothing of the baby who has been born. We, knowing incomparably more, have all the more reason to believe that all biology is a matter of gradual change. Just as in evolution there was no single instant when a hominid became a human, though the differences between them are now profound, so, in the case of individual development, there need be no instant when a zygote becomes an embryo, an embryo a fetus or a fetus a baby. And as the development goes on, so we accord more moral importance to that which is developing. We know that more than a fifth of conceptions (implanted embryos) are lost through early miscarriage. We do not think they should be mourned as so many people who have died. Even the Roman Catholic Church did not explicitly insist that, from the moment of fusion of sperm with egg, human life must not be deliberately destroyed until 1987 (Sacred Congregation for the Doctrine of the Faith 1987). Indeed, unless one is blinkered by a dogmatic belief that all human life is equally valuable, it would be hard to deny that we think of the developing embryo as more valuable the further it has developed.

The controversy over the moral status of the embryo broke out again, perhaps with even more violence, over the question of the use of embryos for the generation of stem cells for research, and hoped-for therapy. It has been understood from mouse embryology since the early 1980s (Evans and Kaufman 1981) that some cells within the early preimplantation embryo remain undifferentiated and thus still retain the potential to form every cell in the body (apart from placenta). Such pluripotent cells might therefore be useful in replacing damaged or aging cells in an individual. It was not until 1998 that experiments demonstrated that these pluripotent stem cells could be isolated from human embryos growing *in vitro*, and heralded the potential for a new field of medical science: regenerative medicine (Thomson et al. 1998). Derivation of stem cells requires the isolation of a portion of the blastocyst, an embryo on day five or six of *in vitro* development, and its culture in the laboratory with layers of feeder cells to retain them in this pluripotent state. Deliberate changes in the culture environment can be used to drive these cells into particular tissues: nerve cells, beating cardiac muscle cells, insulin-producing cells, bone, and cartilage, all of which might be useful in tissue replacement. Naturally, the debate about sources of embryos and the various arguments about use of embryos for such purposes once more fueled acrimonious debate and political wrangling.

If, one day, embryonic cells can be used in regenerative medicine, a wide range of people could benefit. This situation contrasts with *in vitro* technology which can only help those suffering from infertility, and ensured that a large audience of possible beneficiaries took an interest in the debate. Some staunch opponents of embryo research in the 1990s now began to waver in the face of their own loved ones potentially benefiting from such research; President Reagan's wife was one such in the face of her husband's progressive Alzheimer's disease. The arguments against use of embryos for research or therapy, by those who believe the fertilized egg sacred as an individual from the moment of sperm penetration, continued in many countries, but this time with a movement toward permissiveness in some – for example, Switzerland – perhaps because of the ubiquity of the therapeutic promises. However in the US, despite the potential of huge resources for research, President George W. Bush and his supporters remained intransigently opposed to embryos being employed in this pursuit using federal funds.

Although the moral arguments based on the embryo are no different from those that underpinned debate about embryo research using surplus embryos following IVF, the pressure to find sources of eggs that can be fertilized to create embryos for stem cell research has renewed ethical concerns about payment of "donors." In addition, because of the scarcity of human eggs for stem cell derivation, possibilities of transferring human somatic cell nuclei to cow or rabbit eggs to create human/ animal hybrids from which stem cells could be isolated for research (and possible therapy) has brought new moral dilemmas about the status of such "embryos" when compared to purely human/human embryos *in vitro* (Academy of Medical Sciences 2007). Reproductive science continues to push our moral boundaries, and with no precedent to fall back upon, legislation and regulation have been made even more complicated.

In the question of the ethics and regulation of research using human embryos, as in the case of embryonic stem cell research, we are essentially concerned with public morality, or public policy. Such policy will generally be translated into law. But legislators cannot disregard the spontaneous, often unargued reactions of members of the public. One cannot take away the right of people to express their moral opinions. Nevertheless, education, information, discussion, and time for thought all help in turning what may be a gut reaction into a considered moral position. Such a position will probably contain the proviso that human research material should not be used without serious beneficial purpose that otherwise cannot be achieved. In the end a kind of consensus has to come into being, or the laws, where they exist, will be unenforceable, and scientists will have to turn to other fields of research, for fear that their laboratories will be vandalized and even their lives put at risk. Consensus, though despised by individualists and fundamentalists of every persuasion, is in fact the foundation of law, and the rule of law. If consensus entails compromise, in the highly emotionally charged field of medical ethics, legally enforced regulation of research is probably the best compromise that can be achieved.

References

Academy of Medical Sciences (2007). *Inter-species Embryos*. Available at: www.acmedsci.ac.uk/p47prid51.html (accessed January 10, 2008).

Braude, P. R. and Johnson, M. H. (1990). The embryo in contemporary medical science. In G. R. Dunstan (ed.), *The Human Embryo*. Exeter: University of Exeter Press, pp. 208–21.

Braude, P. R., Bolton, V., and Johnson, M. H. (1986). The use of human pre-embryos for infertility research. In G. Bock and M. O'Connor (eds.), *Human Embryo Research: Yes or No*. London: CIBA Foundation Tavistock Press, pp. 63–82.

Editorial (1937). Conception in a watch glass. *The New England Journal of Medicine* 217: 678–9.

Edwards, R. G. (1965). Maturation in vitro of human ovarian oocytes. *Lancet* 286: 926–9.

Edwards, R. G., Steptoe, P. C., and Purdy, J. M. (1970). Fertilization and cleavage in vitro of pre-ovulatory human oocytes. *Nature* 227: 1307–9.

Edwards, R. G., Steptoe, P. C., and Purdy, J. M. (1980). Establishing full-term human pregnancies using cleaving embryos grown in vitro. *British Journal of Obstetric Gynaecology* 87: 737–56.

Evans, M. J. and Kaufman, M. H. (1981). Establishment in culture of pluripotential cells from mouse embryos. *Nature* 292: 154–6.

McLaren, A. (1984). Where to draw the line? *Proceedings of the Royal Institute* 56: 101–21.

McLaren, A. (1987). Can we diagnose genetic disease in pre-embryos? *New Scientist* 116 (Decemmber): 42–7.

Sacred Congregation for the Doctrine of the Faith (1987). *Instruction on Respect for Human Life in its Origin and on the Dignity of Procreation*. Vatican City.

Steptoe, P. C. and Edwards, R. G. (1976). Reimplantation of a human embryo with subsequent tubal pregnancy. *Lancet* (April 24): 880–2.

Steptoe, P. C., Edwards, R. G., and Purdy, J. M. (1971). Human blastocysts grown in culture. *Nature* 229: 132–3.

Thomson, J. A., Itskovitz-Eldor, J., Shapiro, S. S., Waknitz, M. A., Swiergiel, J. J., Marshall, V. S., and Jones, J. M. (1998). Embryonic stem cell lines derived from human blastocysts. *Science* 282: 1145–7.

Warnock, M. (ed.) (1985). A question of life. In *The Warnock Report on Human Fertilisation and Embryology*. Oxford: Basil Blackwell Ltd.

Warnock, M. (1987). Do human cells have rights? *Bioethics* 1: 1–14.

Warnock, M. et al. (1984). *Report of the Committee of Inquiry into Human Fertilisation and Embryology*. London: HMSO.

Further reading

Warnock, M. (1998). *An Intelligent Person's Guide to Ethics*. London: Duckworth.

41

The Moral Status of Animals and Their Use As Experimental Subjects

BERNARD E. ROLLIN

For most of human history, society has been satisfied with a very minimalistic ethic for animal treatment. This ethic, which prohibits the deliberate, useless, willful, sadistic, intentional infliction of pain and suffering on, or outrageous neglect of, animals, reflects both the commonsense empathetic awareness that animals could suffer, and a realization that those who cruelly abuse animals are likely to go on to abuse people. The latter insight has been confirmed by contemporary research (Arkow 1994; Kellert and Felthous 1985).

The major reason that such a minimal ethic was socially adequate is that the overwhelming use of animals was agricultural (food, fiber, locomotion, and power) and the essence of agriculture was husbandry. Husbandry (etymologically, "bonded to the house") entailed care of the animals, specifically placing them in environments for which they were biologically suited, and augmenting their natural coping attributes with additional food, shelter, protection from predation, etc. The relationship with animals was symbiotic, in that humans in turn benefited from using the animals' products, labor, or lives. So powerful was this caring relationship with the animals that the psalmist in the 23rd Psalm uses it as a model for God's relationship to humans: "The Lord is my shepherd . . ."

This sort of symbiotic agriculture required that the farmer maximize the satisfaction of the animals' basic interests, and not cause the animals harm. Harming the animals meant diminishing the animals' production: if you hurt the animal you hurt yourself – the strongest possible sanction for a self-interested rational person. Thus a minimalistic ethic forbidding cruelty was socially sufficient to deal with those who were sadistic or irrational – the carter who in a rage beats his horse, the sadist who tortures animals for pleasure, the deviant farmer who does not feed or water the animals.

The development of high-technology intensive agriculture – "factory farming" – destroyed symbiotic husbandry-based agriculture. Technological "sanders" such as antibiotics and vaccines allowed us to put animals into environments which harmed the animals while still promoting efficiency and productivity. This new kind of agriculture, coupled with the rise of significant and highly visible research on animals, in essence destroyed symbiotic animal use and forced society out of its longstanding satisfaction with the traditional, minimalistic ethic.

It is patently obvious that research on animals is radically different from husbandry agriculture. Whereas traditional agriculture necessitated inflicting minimal harm on animals, the infliction of pain, suffering, disease, deprivation, fear, injury, and various other noxious physical and psychological states upon animals in order to study their effects was essential to research. However, neither factory farming nor research on animals fitted the traditional notion of cruelty, since neither activity was sadistic, purposeless, or useless. Although many animal advocates opposed animal research as "cruel," it was difficult and implausible for society as a whole to equate medical researchers, whose intention was to advance knowledge and cure disease, with the sadists and psychopaths to whom the anti-cruelty ethic was addressed and whose intention was simply to achieve pleasure at another being in pain. (In conjunction with this view of research, virtually all anti-cruelty laws in the United States exempted animal research from their purview, either by statute or by judicial interpretation.) The conceptual limits of the traditional simplistic understanding of our treatment of animals as either husbandry, "kindness," or cruelty was exposed, and the need for more sophisticated moral evaluation of the burgeoning field of animal research and testing made manifest.

The Moral Critique of Research on Animals

Both Plato and Hegel argued that at least part of a moral philosopher's job is to help draw out and articulate nascent and inchoate thought patterns in individuals and society. In keeping with this notion, several philosophers, beginning in the 1970s, made explicit a number of moral reservations about human uses of animals in general, including invasive animal use in research and testing, and thereby helped draw out the moral queasiness at such use that had gradually developed in society in general. This task was first engaged by Peter Singer in 1975 as a chapter in his book *Animal Liberation*, wherein he challenged the moral justification for a great deal of animal use, including the moral permissibility of harming animals to advance scientific knowledge. Singer's discussion of research on animals elegantly articulated widespread social reservations about such *use* of animals, and is still in print. In 1982, Bernard Rollin's *Animal Rights and Human Morality* again challenged the morality of hurting animals in research, and also pointed out the inadequacy of the *care and husbandry* provided to such animals, leading to additional suffering which was not only not part of the research, but also, in many cases, inimical to its purposes. Additional work by Tom Regan, Steve Saportzis, Evelyn Pluhar, and numerous other philosophers, aided by scientists such as Jane Goodall, who have come to see the moral issues with clarity, has continued to give prominence to the moral questions of research on animals.

Although different philosophers have approached the issue from different philosophical traditions and viewpoints, it is possible to find a common thread in their arguments questioning the moral acceptability of invasive animal use. Drawing succor from society's tendency during the past 50 years to question the exclusion of disenfranchised humans such as women and minorities from the scope of moral concern, and the correlative lack of full protection of their interests, these philosophers applied a similar logic to the treatment of animals.

In the first place, there appears to be no morally relevant difference between humans and at least vertebrate animals, which allows us to include all humans within the full scope of moral concern and yet deny such moral status to the animals. A morally relevant difference between two beings is a difference that rationally justifies treating them differently in some way that bears moral weight. If two of my students have the same grades on exams and papers, and have identical attendance and class participation, I am morally obliged to give them the same final grade. That one is blue-eyed and the other is brown-eyed may be a difference between them, but it is not morally relevant to grading them.

Philosophers have shown that the standard reasons offered to exclude animals from the moral circle, and to justify not assessing our treatment of them by the same moral categories and machinery we use for assessing the treatment of humans, do not meet the test of moral relevance. Such historically sanctified reasons as "animals lack a soul," "animals do not reason," "humans are more powerful than animals," "animals do not have language," "God said we could do as we wish to animals" have been demonstrated to provide no rational basis for failing to reckon with animal interests in our moral deliberations. For one thing, while the above statements may mark differences between humans and animals, they do not mark *morally relevant differences* that justify harming animals when we would not similarly harm people. For example, if we justify harming animals on the grounds that we are more powerful than they are, we are essentially affirming "might makes right," a principle that morality is in large measure created to overcome. By the same token, if we are permitted to harm animals for our benefit because they lack reason, there are no grounds for not extending the same logic to non-rational humans, as we shall shortly see. And while animals may not have the same interests as people, it is evident to commonsense that they certainly do have interests, the fulfillment and thwarting of which matter to them.

The interests of animals that are violated by research are patent. Invasive research such as surgical research, toxicological research, and disease research certainly harm the animals and cause pain and suffering. But even non-invasive research on captive animals leads to pain, suffering, and deprivation arising out of the manner in which research animals are kept. Social animals are often kept in isolation; burrowing animals are kept in stainless steel or polycarbonate cages; and, in general, animals' normal repertoire of powers and coping abilities – what I have elsewhere called their *teloi* or natures (Rollin 1982) – are thwarted. Indeed, Dr Tom Wolfle, a leading laboratory animal veterinarian and animal behaviorist at the US National Academy of Science, has persuasively argued that animals used in research probably suffer more from the ways in which they are kept for research than from the invasive manipulation they are exposed to within research.

The common moral machinery that society has developed for adjudicating and assessing our treatment of people would not allow people to be used in invasive research without informed consent, even if great benefit were to accrue to the remainder of society from such use. This is the case even if the people being used were so-called "marginal humans" – infants, the insane, the senile, the retarded, the comatose, etc. A grasp of this component of our ethic has led many philosophers to argue that one should not subject an animal to any experimental protocol that society would not be morally prepared to accept if performed on a retarded or otherwise intellectually disabled human.

There appears in fact to be no morally relevant difference between intellectually disabled humans and many animals – in both cases, what we do to the being in question matters to them, as they are capable of pain, suffering, and distress. Indeed, a normal, conscious, adult non-human mammal would seem to have a far greater range of interests than a comatose or severely retarded human, or even than a human baby.

While we do indeed perform some research on marginal humans, we do not do so without as far as possible garnering their consent and, if they are incapable of giving consent, obtaining consent from guardians specifically mandated with protecting their basic interests. Applying such a policy to animals would forestall the vast majority of current research on captive animals, even if the bulk of such research is non-invasive, given the considerations detailed above concerning the violations of animals' basic interests as a consequence of how we keep them. Steve Sapontzis has further pointed out that we do have a method for determining whether an animal is consenting to a piece of research – open the cages! (Note that an animal's failure to leave the cage would not necessarily assure consent; it might merely demonstrate that a condition like learned helplessness has been induced in the animal.)

The above argument, extrapolated from ordinary moral consciousness, applies even more strongly to the case of animals used in psychological research, where one is using animals as a model to study noxious psychological or psychophysical states that appear in humans – pain, fear, anxiety, addiction, aggression, etc. For here one can generate what has been called the psychologist's dilemma: if the relevant state being produced in the animal is analogous to the same state in humans, why are we morally entitled to produce that state in animals when we would not be so entitled to produce it in humans? And if the animal state is not analogous to the human state, why create it in the animal?

The Uses of Animals in Research

Before examining the response of the animal-using research community to the moral critique presented, it is worth pausing to examine the various ways in which animals are used in research. The different usages are fairly well accounted for by the following seven categories:

1 Basic biological, behavioral, or psychological research – that is, the formulation and testing of hypotheses about fundamental theoretical questions, such as the nature of DNA replication, mitochondrial activity, brain functions, or learning, with little concern for the practical effect of that research.
2 Applied basic biomedical and psychological research – the formulation and testing of hypotheses about diseases, dysfunctions, genetic defects, etc., which, while not necessarily having immediate consequences for treatment of disease, are at least seen as directly related to such consequences. Included in this category is the testing of new therapies: surgical, gene therapy, radiation treatment, treatment of burns, etc. Clearly there will be a spectrum, rather than a clear-cut cleavage, between categories 1 and 2.
3 The development of drugs and therapeutic chemicals. Again, this differs from the earlier categories (especially category 2) by degree, but is primarily distinguished by what might be called a "shotgun" approach; that is, the research is guided not

so much by well-formulated theories that suggest that a certain compound might have a certain effect but, rather, by hit-and-miss, exploratory, inductive "shooting in the dark." The primary difference between this category and the others is that here one is aiming at discovering specific substances for specific purposes, rather than at knowledge per se.

4   Food and fiber research, aimed at increasing the productivity and efficiency of agricultural animals. This includes feed trials, metabolism studies, some reproductive work, and the development of agents like BST to increase milk production.

5   The testing of various consumer goods for safety, toxicity, irritation, and degree of toxicity. Such testing includes the testing of cosmetics, food additives, herbicides, pesticides, and industrial chemicals, as well as the testing of drugs for toxicity, carcinogenesis (production of cancer), mutagenesis (production of mutations in living bodies), and teratogenesis (production of monsters and abnormalities in embryo development). To some extent, this category will overlap with category 3, but it should be distinguished in virtue of the fact that (3) refers to the discovery of new drugs, and (4) to their testing for human – and, in the case of veterinary drugs, animal – safety.

6   The use of animals in educational institutions and elsewhere for demonstration, dissection, surgery practice, induction of disease for demonstrative purposes, high-school science projects, etc.

7   The use of animals for extraction of drugs and biological products – vaccines, blood, serum, monoclonal antibodies, TPA from animals genetically engineered to produce it in their milk, etc.

Approximately three million animals are used in experiments in Britain each year. In the US, no precise figures are available, as no records are kept of rats, mice, and birds, all of which are exempt from the Animal Welfare Act, even though rats and mice constitute the majority of animals used in research. US estimates range from 20 million up.

The Response of the Research Community to the Moral Critique of Animal Research

Unfortunately for rational moral progress, the research community has had a historical tendency not to engage the moral challenge to animal research, but to sidestep it. Until the mid-1980s, it was not uncommon to hear scientists affirm that "animal use is not a moral issue, it is a scientific necessity."

The primary reason for researchers taking such a position, a view that in fact flew in the face of social morality, lies in what I have elsewhere called scientific ideology, or the commonsense of science, which is to scientific activity what ordinary commonsense is to everyday life (Rollin 1989; 2006a). Scientific ideology is the set of assumptions and presuppositions taught to nascent scientists as indisputable fact rather than debatable assumptions, along with the data germane to their particular disciplines.

The origin of this ideology lies in the understandable desire to separate science from speculative philosophy and unverifiable notions like "life force," "entelechies," absolute space, and time and ether, which were plentiful in science at the end of the nineteenth century. Fueled by the advent of a philosophical movement known as logical positivism, scientific ideology stressed an aspect of modern science prominent since Newton – namely, that only claims that can be directly verified by experience or experiment can be legitimately admitted into science.

The effect of this approach on the issue of animal research was profound. In the first place, scientific ideology banished ethical and other value issues from the legitimate purview of science, as moral judgments could not be proven empirically. The result was an almost universal adherence among scientists to the dogma that science was "value-free" and could not and did not deal with ethical issues in science. Under the influence of positivism, ethical judgments were perceived as exclusively emotive and, as such, they could not be rationally engaged. The fact that many if not most animal advocates couched their opposition to animal research in highly emotional terms further convinced researchers that ethics was simply emotion, and that opposition to animal research on moral grounds needed to be met with emotional appeals based in vivid accounts of human suffering from disease, and the threat to human health that would be occasioned by even regulating animal research, let alone abolishing it.

A second component of scientific ideology strongly buttressed the denial of ethics in science. This involved agnosticism about the ability of science to study or even know the existence of consciousness in humans or animals. Rooted in the positivistic commitment to allowing only the observable and testable into science, this component expressed itself in the United States and Britain as behaviorism, the movement in psychology which eschewed talk of mental states, and allowed as scientifically legitimate only the study of overt behavior. The logic of this position can be reconstructed as follows: one should allow into science only what is intersubjectively observable. Mental states are not intersubjectively observable. Therefore mental states are not scientifically able to be studied. Therefore mental states are not scientifically real. Therefore mental states are not of concern to scientists. Felt pain in animals (as opposed to the physiological substratum or machinery of pain) is a mental state. Therefore felt pain in animals is neither scientifically real nor of concern to scientists. (Although this same logic would naturally apply to humans, and behaviorists in fact denied the cogency of talking about consciousness in people, they were clearly unable to act on this ideology in their dealings with humans, since people would hardly accept the claim that their pain was not real.)

It is probably for the above set of reasons that there are fewer works defending the use of animals in research than criticizing it. One book, *The Case for Animal Experimentation* by Michael A. Fox, which did attempt to provide a systematic justification for animal use in research, was repudiated by its author within months of publication. Nonetheless, there are certain arguments that are frequently deployed by defenders of animal research.

The argument from benefits

Research on animals has been intimately connected with new understanding of disease, new drugs, and new operative procedures, all of which have produced significant benefits for humans and for animals. These significant results and their attendant benefits would have been unobtainable without animal use. Therefore animal research is justified.

Critics of animal research might (and do) attack the argument above in two ways. First of all, one may question the link between premises and conclusion. Even if significant benefits have been garnered from invasive animal use, and even if these benefits could not have been achieved in other ways, it does not follow that such use is justified. Suppose that Nazi research on unwilling humans produced considerable benefits, for example, as some have argued, in the areas of hypothermia and high-altitude medicine. It does not follow that we would consider such use of human subjects morally justifiable. In fact, of course, we do not. Indeed, there are significant numbers of people in the research community who argue that the data from such experiments should never be used or even cited, *regardless of how much benefit flows from its use*.

The only way for defenders of animal research to defeat this counter-argument is to find a morally relevant difference between humans and animals that stops our extending our consensus ethic's moral concern for human individuals to animals.

Second, one can attack the argument from benefits in its second premise, namely that the benefits in question could not have been achieved in other ways. This is extremely difficult to prove one way or the other, for the same reasons that it is difficult to conjecture what the world would have been like if the Nazis had won World War II. We do know that, as social concern regarding the morality of animal research mounts, other ways are being found to achieve many of the ends listed in our discussion of the uses of animals in research.

The argument that moral concerns of the sort required to question animal research apply only to humans

This approach is, in essence, an attempt to provide what we indicated was necessary to buttress the argument from benefits. Such an attempt was made by Carl Cohen in a *New England Journal of Medicine* article (1986) generally considered by the research community to be the best articulation of their position.

One of Cohen's chief arguments can be reconstructed as follows (the argument is specifically directed against those who would base condemnation of animal research on the claim that animals have rights, but can be viewed as applying to our earlier version of the general argument against invasive animal use). Only beings who have rights can be said to have sufficient moral status to be protected from invasive use in research. Animals cannot reason, respond to moral claims, etc. – necessary conditions for being rights-bearers. Therefore they cannot morally be said to be protected from invasive use.

The problems with this argument are multiple. In the first place, even if the concept of a right (or of sufficient moral status to protect one from being used cavalierly for others' benefit) arises only among rational beings, it does not follow that its use is limited to such beings. Consider an analogy. Chess may have been invented solely for the purpose of being played by Persian royalty. But given that the rules have a life of their own, anyone can play it, regardless of the intention of those who created the rules. Similarly, rights may have arisen in a circle of rational beings. But it doesn't follow that such rational beings cannot reasonably extend the concept to beings with other

501

morally relevant features. In fact, that is precisely what has occurred in the extension of rights to marginal humans.

To this, Cohen replies that such extension is legitimate since marginal humans belong to a kind that is rational, while extension to animals is not. The obvious response to this, however, is that, by his own argument, it is being rational that is relevant, not belonging to a certain kind. Further, if his argument is viable, and one can cavalierly ignore what is by hypothesis the morally relevant feature, one can turn it around on Cohen. One could argue in the same vein that, since humans are animals, albeit rational ones, and other animals are animals, albeit non-rational ones, we can ignore rationality merely because both humans and animals belong to the same kind (i.e., animal). In short, his making an exception for non-rational humans fails the test of moral relevance and makes arbitrary inclusion of animals as rights-bearers as reasonable as arbitrary inclusion of non-rational humans.

Another attempt to provide a morally relevant difference to undercut the argument against invasive animal use is provided by those who argue that scientific ideology is correct and that animals are incapable of pain, suffering, and other morally relevant mental states. Such a neo-Cartesian stance has recently been revived by Peter Carruthers and Peter Harrison, and in essence questions the claim that what we do to animals matters to them.

A detailed exposition of and response to such a strategy is impossible to undertake here. (Evelyn Pluhar (1995) has engaged this task in *Beyond Prejudice*.) However, the following points can be sketched. First, a heavy burden of proof exists for those who would convince commonsense and common morality that animals are merely machines. Even the anti-cruelty ethic took animal pain for granted. Second, such a position would make the appearance of pain and other modes of awareness in humans an evolutionary miracle. Third, the neurophysiological, neurochemical, and behavior evidence militates in favor of numerous similar morally relevant mental states such as pain in humans and animals. Fourth, if animals are truly just machines, devoid of awareness, much scientific research would be vitiated, for example, pain research conducted on animals and extrapolated to people.

One possible way to exclude animals from direct moral status, and thereby justify invasive research on them, is a philosophically sophisticated exposition of the claim we discussed above by Cohen that morality applies only to rational beings. This position, which has its modern roots in Hobbes but in fact was articulated even in antiquity, was more recently thrust into prominence by the work of John Rawls. It has been directly applied to the question of animals' moral status by Peter Carruthers, who was mentioned above as advancing the neo-Cartesian argument, in his book *The Animals Issue* (1992). Interestingly enough, Carruthers's contractual argument is independent of his denial of consciousness to animals. Even if animals are conscious and feel pain, Carruthers believes that the contractual basis for morality excludes animals from the moral status necessary to question the moral legitimacy of experimentation on them.

According to Carruthers, morality is a set of rules derived from what rational beings would rationally choose to govern their interactions with one another in a social environment, if given a chance to do so. Only rational beings can be governed by such rules, and adjust their behaviors toward one another according to them. Thus, only rational beings, of which humans are the only example, can "play the game of morality," so only they are protected by morality. Animals thus fall outside the scope of moral concern. The only reasons for worrying about animal treatment are contingent ones, namely that some people care about what happens to animals, or that bad treatment of animals leads to bad treatment of people (as Thomas Aquinas argued), but nothing about animals in themselves is worthy of moral status. Further, the above contingent reasons for concern about animal suffering do not weigh heavily enough to eliminate research on animals.

There is a variety of responses to Carruthers. In the first place, even if one concedes the notion that morality arises by hypothetical contract among rational beings, it is by no means clear that the only choices of rules such beings would make would be to cover only rational beings. They might also decide that any rules should cover any beings capable of having negative or positive experiences, whether or not they are rational. Second, even if rational beings intend the rules to cover only rational beings, it does not follow that the rules do not have a logic and life of their own that lead to adding other beings to the circle of moral concern, as indeed seems to be happening in social morality today. Third, Carruthers seems to assume that according moral status to animals entails that the status be equal to that of humans, "yet," he says, "we find it intuitively abhorrent that the lives and suffering of animals should be weighed against the lives or suffering of human beings" (1992: 195). But it is not at all clear that contractualism, even if true, could not accord animals sufficient moral status to prohibit experimenting on them, yet not say they were of equal moral value to normal humans. Further, as Sapontzis (1993) has pointed out, Carruthers's argument is circular. He justifies such uses as research on animals by appeal to contractualism, and justifies contractualism on the grounds that it renders morally permissible such uses as research on animals.

The argument from experimenting on marginal humans

The final defense of research on animals that we shall consider is the utilitarian one advanced by R. G. Frey (1983). Unlike the previous arguments, it is a tentative one, offered up in a spirit of uneasiness.

Frey's argument essentially rests upon standing the argument from marginal humans on its head. Recall that this argument says that animals are analogous to such marginal humans as the retarded, the comatose, the senile, the insane, etc. Since we find experimenting on such humans morally repugnant, we should find experimentation on animals equally repugnant.

Frey's argument reaffirms the analogy, but points out that, in actual fact, many normal animals have richer and more complex lives, and thus have *higher-quality* lives, than many marginal humans do. The logic of justifying research on animals for human benefit (which assumes that humans have more complex lives than animals, and thus more valuable lives) would surely justify doing such research on marginal humans who both have lower qualities of life than some animals do and who are more similar physiologically to normal humans, and are thus better research "models." If we are willing to perform such research on marginal humans, we are closer to justifying similar research on animals.

Obviously, the force of Frey's argument as a defense of research depends upon our willingness relentlessly to pursue the logic by which we (implicitly) justify animal research and apply the same justification to using humans not different from those animals in any morally relevant way. As Frey himself affirms, there are some "contingent" (i.e., not logically necessary) effects of deciding to do research on marginal humans as well as on animals that would work against such a decision. He cites the emotional (rather than rationally based) uproar and outrage that would arise (because people have not worked through the logic of the issue), and presumably such other responses as the knee-jerk fear of a slippery slope leading to research on normal humans. But, in the end, such psychological rather than moral/logical revulsion could conceivably be overcome by education in and explanation of the underlying moral logic.

I believe that Frey's argument fails as a defense of research and ends up serving those who originally adduced the argument from marginal humans as a *reductio against* research on animals. If people do see clearly and truly believe that doing research on animals is (theology aside) exactly morally analogous to doing research on marginal humans, they are, in our current state of moral evolution, likelier to question the former than accept the latter. In fact, in my 30 years of working with scientists and animal researchers of all sorts, I have found that the overwhelming majority of them do not, if pressed, feel morally justified in doing research on animals, but tend to focus on the benefits produced and simply ignore the moral perspective, a tack much aided by the scientific ideology described above.

The only argument in defense of animal research that seems at all cogent is the argument from benefits discussed above. A utilitarian thinker might argue that with regard to animal subjects or human subjects utilized in research, even invasive research, such research is justified if the benefits to sentient beings, humans or animals, outweighs the cost to the subjects. Peter Singer, for example, a consistent utilitarian, has, in a televised interview, agreed that certain invasive neurological research on non-human primates might be justified if it is the case that, as the researchers allege, the health of a large number of humans has markedly improved as a result of that research, and that outcome could be attained in no other way.

Our societal ethic, embedded in our laws, does not of course accept such an argument, and checks a purely utilitarian ethic by use of the deontological notion of rights, protecting individual humans from having their basic interests infringed upon even for the sake of the general welfare. Hence, as we said earlier, society roundly condemned Nazi research that was scientifically and medically valuable, such as hypothermia and high altitude medical research along with the patently useless research performed by Josef Mengele.

For the sake of argument, in order to illustrate another moral problem in animal research, let us assume that invasive animal research is justified only by the benefit produced. It would then seem to follow that the only morally justifiable research would be research that benefits humans and/or animals. But there is in fact a vast amount of research that does not demonstrably benefit humans or animals. Much behavioral research, weapons research, and toxicity testing as a legal requirement are obvious examples, as is much of basic research which is invasive but has no clear benefit. Obviously a certain amount of research meets that test, but a great deal does not. Someone might respond that "we never know what benefits might emerge in the future," and appeal to serendipity or unknowns. But if that were a legitimate point, we could not discriminate in funding between research likely to produce benefit and that unlikely to do so; yet we do. If we appeal to unknown but possible benefits, we are literally forced to fund everything – which we do not. We do in fact weigh expected cost versus benefit in human and animal research; why not weigh cost to the animal subject as a relevant parameter?

Thus we find a second major moral issue in animal research (which, along with the first issue, is discussed more fully in Rollin 2007). To recapitulate: the first issue arises from the suggestion that any invasive research on an object of moral concern is morally problematic. In response, researchers invoke the benefits of research. Even assuming this is a good argument in principle, it gives rise to another moral issue: why do we not do only animal research that clearly produces more benefit than cost, allowing for the cost to the animals? So even if we disregard the general point about the morality of invasive animal research, we are still left with the fact that much animal research does not fit researchers' own moral justification for it. I have referred in other writings to this moral claim about justifying invasive research by appeal to benefits as the "Utilitarian Principle" – if one accepts the benefit argument, we are left with the conclusion that the only justifiable animal research is that which is expected to produce results yielding more benefit than harm (however this is measured).

Thus, even if we retreat to the utilitarian argument in moral defense of invasive animal research, we find that a good deal of such research fails to meet that criterion. But this is not all; yet another ethical issue arises. Suppose we ignore the cost-benefit criterion discussion, as well as the first argument questioning the morality of all invasive animal research, which is, of course, what we do in practice. Would it not then at least be morally required that we treat the animals in the best possible manner commensurate with their use in research? To put the question another way, are research animals given the best possible treatment they could get while being used in research? Regrettably, the answer is "no," as one can easily demonstrate, both historically and in the present.

The demand that if we do use animals in invasive research, we at least do our best to meet their interests and needs, minimize their suffering as much as possible, and respect their *telos* seems to be a requirement of common decency, particularly if we are using them in a way that ignores the moral problems recounted thus far. Sadly, this is not the case.

Historically, in the US at least, basic animal care was a very low priority in animal research, ironically harming the science by failing to control pain, stress, and other variables, and very much failing to meet the ideal set forth in the third set of moral issues just enumerated. Ordinary commonsense would dictate that one of the worst things one can do to a research animal is to cause unrelieved pain to it. Since animals do not understand sources of pain, particularly the sort of pain inflicted in experiments, they cannot rationalize "this will end soon"; they cannot anticipate its cessation, so their whole life becomes the pain. This insight has led veterinary pain specialist Ralph Kitchell to surmise that animal pain may be worse than human pain (Kitchell and Guinan 1989); as I have put it, humans have *hope*. Further, pain is a stressor, and can skew the results of experiments in numerous ways. Thus, for both moral and scientific reasons, one would expect pain control to be a major emphasis when scientists undertook

505

painful experiments. If someone were conducting fracture research, for example, one would thus expect liberal use of pre-emptive and post-surgical or post-traumatic analgesia, since the pain is not the point of the experiment, and unmitigated pain actually retards healing. Yet a literature search conducted in 1982 revealed that only two papers existed on animal analgesia, and none specifically devoted to laboratory animal analgesia. Fortunately the 1985 laws mandated control of pain and distress, and the literature on, and practice of, pain control have proliferated since.

As important as the infliction of pain and suffering, which only sometimes arises in research, is the fact that 100 percent of the animals utilized in research have the basic needs and interests flowing from the biological and psychological needs constituting their natures thwarted by how we keep them.

Practical Resolution

Whatever the ultimate socio-ethical resolution to the question of the moral legitimacy of research on animals turns out to be, it is clear that the arguments against such use have captured a significant moment in social thought, and have helped accelerate the development of an ethic in society that goes well beyond concern about cruelty to concern about all animal suffering, regardless of source. This has in turn resulted in the passage of major legislation in the United States, Britain, and elsewhere regulating animal research. In my view, law is, in Plato's phrase, social ethics "writ large." While Britain has had a 100-year history of such regulation, the passage of the US laws in 1985 is especially significant, both because research there had essentially hitherto enjoyed a laissez-faire status and because the legislation was vigorously opposed by the research community, which warned of significant danger to human health if it were passed.

The US laws of 1985 can be summarized as follows: The amendment to the Animal Welfare Act specifies:

1 Establishment of an institutional animal care committee to review prospective research proposals, monitor animal care and use, and to inspect facilities. Members must include a veterinarian and a person not affiliated with the research facility.
2 Standards for exercise of dogs are to be promulgated by the Secretary of Agriculture.
3 Standards for a physical environment, which promotes "the psychological well-being of primates," are to be promulgated.
4 Standards for adequate veterinary care, including use of anesthetics, analgesics, and tranquilizers, are to be promulgated. The control and minimization of pain and suffering is emphasized.
5 No paralytics are to be used without anesthetics.
6 Alternatives to painful procedures must be considered by the investigator.
7 Multiple surgery is prohibited except in cases of "scientific necessity."
8 The Animal Care Committee must inspect all facilities semi-annually, review practices involving pain, review the conditions of animals, and file an inspection report detailing violations and deficiencies. Minority reports must also be filed.

9   The Secretary of Agriculture is directed to establish an information service at the National Agricultural Library, which provides information aimed at eliminating duplication of animal experiments, reducing or replacing animal use, minimizing animal pain and suffering, and aiding in training animal users.

10   The facility must provide for training for all animal users and caretakers.

The second bill passed was called the NIH Reauthorization Act, or the Health Research Extension Act, and basically made NIH Guidelines, hitherto cavalierly ignored, into law. This law, which complemented the Animal Welfare Act amendment, covered all vertebrate animals, while the former exempted rats, mice, and birds from coverage. Violation of the second law can result in seizure of all federal research funding to an institution, and this was the major sanction for these new policies.

New laws and policies have been forthcoming in numerous other countries based on the increased societal concern for the treatment of laboratory animals. Many are variations on the Animal Care and Use Committee protocol review concept; such laws obtain in Australia and New Zealand. Canada has not legislated, but adherence to such principles is presuppositional to government research funding. In Europe, 19 countries utilize the ethical review system: Austria, Belgium, the Czech Republic, Denmark, Estonia, Finland, France, Germany, Greece, Ireland, Italy, Latvia, Lithuania, the Netherlands, Norway, Poland, Spain, Sweden, and Switzerland (Smith et al. 2007). The UK also deploys institutional review, but it is a recent superimposition upon a complex system of licensure and inspectors that goes back to 1876 and was considerably revised in 1986.

In addition to generating law, the emerging ethic has led to the abandonment of some frivolous research animal use, for example, some of the uses of animals in cosmetic testing; the elimination of many invasive and brutalizing laboratory exercises in undergraduate, graduate, medical, and veterinary curricula; and the development of new ways to teach surgery, for example, by way of spay-neuter clinics, cadavers, and models for teaching manual skills. Increasing numbers of scientific journals are refusing to publish manuscripts detailing research where severe pain and suffering were involved. And there is far more serious effort than ever before across the scientific community to consider alternatives to animal use, be these a *reduction* of numbers of animals, *refinement* of painful procedures (e.g., substituting a terminal procedure for a painful one), or *replacement* of animals by various modalities (e.g., cell culture, tissue culture, or epidemiology).

In my view, there is a new and serious moral issue associated with animal research that has not received sufficient attention. This arises from the advent of genetic engineering technology. By use of this technology, one can create animal "models" for the thousands of gruesome human genetic diseases hitherto not able to be studied in animals. Since many of these diseases involve symptoms of great severity, yet the research community is embracing the creation of such models, a new and significant source of chronic animal suffering is developing. The issue is worsened by virtue of the fact that few modalities exist for controlling chronic pain and suffering. Unfortunately, this issue has hitherto occasioned little discussion.

In my view, new laws and, more importantly, the growing societal concern for animals that drove their passage have had salubrious consequences for the moral status of animals in research. For one thing, they vividly underscore the fact that society sees invasive animal research as a significant moral issue. For another, they explode the scientific ideology which we have seen precludes ethical engagement by animal research scientists with the issues their activities engender. Finally, they have led to what I call the "reappropriation of commonsense" with regard to the reality and knowability of animal suffering, and the need for its control. One can be guardedly optimistic that animal research will evolve into what it should have been all along – a moral science.

References

Arkow, P. (1994). Child abuse, animal abuse, and the veterinarian. *Journal of the American Veterinary Medical Association* 204: 1004–6.

Carruthers, P. (1992). *The Animals Issue: Moral Theory in Practice.* New York: Cambridge University Press.

Cohen, C. (1986). The case for the use of animals in biomedical research. *New England Journal of Medicine* 315: 865–9.

Fox, M. A. (1986). *The Case for Animal Experimentation.* Berkeley: University of California Press.

Frey, R. G. (1983). Vivisection, morals and medicine. *Journal of Medical Ethics* 9: 94–7.

Harrison, P. (1989). Theodicy and animal pain. *Philosophy* 64 (January): 79–92.

Kellert, S. and Felthous, A. (1985). Childhood cruelty toward animals among criminals and non-criminals. *Human Relations* 38: 1113–29.

Kitchell, R. and Guinan, M. (1989). The nature of pain in animals. In B. E. Rollin and M. L. Kesel (eds.), *The Experimental Animal in Biomedical Research*, vol. I. Boca Raton, FL: CRC Press, pp. 185–205.

Pluhar, E. B. (1995). *Beyond Prejudice.* Durham, NC: Duke University Press.

Regan, T. (1983). *The Case for Animal Rights.* Berkeley: University of California Press.

Rollin, B. E. (1982). *Animal Rights and Human Morality.* Buffalo, NY: Prometheus Books (rev. edns. 1992 and 2006).

Rollin, B. E. (1989). *The Unheeded Cry: Animal Consciousness, Animal Pain and Science.* Oxford: Oxford University Press.

Rollin, B. E. (1995). *The Frankenstein Syndrome: Ethical and Social Issues in the Genetic Engineering of Animals.* New York: Cambridge University Press.

Rollin, B. E. (2006a). *Science and Ethics.* New York: Cambridge University Press.

Rollin, B. E. (2006b). The regulation of animal research and the emergence of animal ethics: a conceptual history. *Theoretical Medicine and Bioethics* 27/4: 285–304.

Rollin, B. E. (2007). Animal research: a moral science. *EMBO Reports* 8/6: 521–5.

Sapontzis, S. (1987). *Morals, Reason and Animals.* Philadelphia: Temple University Press.

Sapontzis, S. (1990). The case against invasive research with animals. In B. E. Rollin and M. L. Kesel (eds.), *The Experimental Animal in Biomedical Research*, vol. I. Boca Raton, FL: CRC Press, pp. 3–19.

Sapontzis, S. (1993). Review of *The Animals Issue. Canadian Philosophical Reviews* 13/4: 40–2.

Singer, P. (1975). *Animal Liberation.* New York: Avon Books.

Smith, J. A. et al. (2007). Principles and practice in ethical review of animal experiments across Europe: Summary of the report of a FELASA working group on ethical evaluations of animal experiments. *Laboratory Animals* 41/2: 143–60.

Further reading

Baird, R. M. and Rosenbaum, S. E. (eds.) (1991). *Animal Experimentation: The Moral Issues*. Buffalo, NY: Prometheus Books.

Rollin, B. E. (1985). The moral status of research animals in psychology. *American Psychologist* (August): 920–6.

Rollin, B. E. (1990). Ethics and research animals – theory and practice. In B. E. Rollin and M. L. Kesel (eds.), *The Experimental Animal in Biomedical Research*, vol. I. Boca Raton, FL: CRC Press, pp. 19–37.

Rollin, B. E. (1995). Laws relevant to animal research in the United States. In A. A. Tuffery (ed.), *Laboratory Animals*, 2nd edn. London: John Wiley, pp. 67–87.

Rowan, A. N. (1984). *Of Mice, Models, and Men*. Albany, NY: SUNY Press.

Russell, W. M. S. and Burch, R. L. (1959). *Principles of Humane Experimental Technique*. London: Methuen.

Smyth, D. H. (1978). *Alternatives to Animal Experiments*. London: Scholar Press.

Part XII

Ethical Issues in the Practice of Health Care

42

Confidentiality

RAANAN GILLON AND DANIEL K. SOKOL

The obligation to maintain patients' confidentiality is one of the oldest codified moral commitments in health care. The Hippocratic Oath, believed to have been written by Hippocrates *circa* 425 BC, required doctors to swear that, "Whatever, in connection with my professional practice, or not in connection with it, I see or hear, in the life of men, which ought not to be spoken of abroad, I will not divulge, as reckoning that all such should be kept secret" (Wootton 2006: 5; BMA 2004). This requirement remains in modern codes of medical ethics, such as those of the World Medical Association (WMA), the British Medical Association (BMA), the French *Ordre National des Médecins* (the French Medical Council) and the American Medical Association (AMA).

While modern codes of medical ethics stress the fundamental importance of respecting patient confidentiality, it is rarely considered to be an absolute obligation, and exceptions are recognized both professionally and legally. The General Medical Council, the medical profession's ruling professional body in the UK, while instructing doctors that "patients have a right to expect that you will not pass on any personal information which you have learned in the course of your professional duties, unless they agree" (GMC 1995a), also describes a wide variety of exceptional circumstances in which doctors may break medical confidentiality (GMC 1995b). These include circumstances in which the patient's agreement can be assumed (emergencies, for example); where disclosure is deemed to be in the patient's best interests, even if consent cannot be obtained (for example, if a patient is believed to be victim of serious abuse); where disclosure is for the purposes of medical teaching, research, or audit (for example, in teaching medical students and doctors-in-training, in medical research in which patient records need to be consulted, and in self-monitoring of the quality of their medical performance by groups of doctors); where disclosure even without consent is required to prevent significant harm to others (for example, where failure to disclose would expose others to risk of death or serious injury or illness – instances include driving when medically unfit and when a patient refuses to inform a sexual partner that he or she is infected with the HIV virus – or where disclosure is necessary to prevent or detect serious crime); and where doctors are legally obliged to break confidentiality (for example, when ordered by a judge to do so, or where under a statutory obligation to do so, as in notification of abortions, certain sorts of drug addiction, and information that would prevent terrorism or materially help police to apprehend terrorists) (Brazier 1992).

Small wonder, with so many derogations to what is widely considered a central tenet of medical ethics, that in the early 1980s an American physician and ethicist, after finding that between 25 and 100 people at his university hospital would have legitimate access to a patient's *confidential* hospital notes, called medical confidentiality "a decrepit concept" (Siegler 1982); and that in the 1990s a UK medical lawyer was still calling the ethics and law of medical confidentiality "fuzzy and unpredictable" (Brazier 1992). French law, for example, declares the duty to respect patient confidentiality to be *absolute*, but then goes on to list several exceptions (Ordre National des Médecins 2003).

So what moral sense can be made of the issue? One approach might be to abolish the commitment altogether. Patients would simply come to the doctor and doctors would pass on information about them as and when they saw fit – they "would give no pretence to the keeping of any secrets," and it would be up to patients to decide whether their privacy or their health were more important. Sometimes people's health would suffer, but it would be "in a good cause – that of their individual autonomy" (Warwick 1989).

While this sort of approach to confidentiality is adopted in many spheres of ordinary life, the problem with it in medical practice – and much other health-care practice – is that, in order to do a good job for their patients, doctors often need to have information of a sort that people generally regard as private, even secret. Indeed, so intimately linked are secrets and confidentiality that the French refer to confidentiality as the *secret médical*. Some of the information is embarrassing to discuss, and some may be positively harmful to the patient or others if it is divulged. Doctors routinely ask a series of questions about bodily functions that people would not dream of discussing with anyone else. When a patient's medical problems relate to genito-urinary functions, a doctor may need to know about that patient's sexual activities, sometimes in detail. When a patient's problems are psychological, a doctor may need to know in great detail about the patient's experiences, ideas and feelings, past and present relationships, even in some contexts about the person's imaginings and fantasies. In the field of genetics, investigations may reveal non-paternity – i.e., that the putative father of a patient's child is not the biological father.

Such intrusive medical inquiries are not based on prurience or mere inquisitiveness, but on the pursuit of information that may assist the doctor in treating and helping the patient. Nonetheless, many patients are unlikely to pass on this information unless they have some assurances of confidentiality. A recent UK study, for example, showed that 55 percent of young people aged 13 and 14 would not attend sexual health services if these were not confidential (Thomas et al. 2006).

Quite apart from the medical benefits to the patient, maintenance of confidentiality may in some circumstances benefit the health of others. In the context of transmissible diseases, especially sexually-transmissible diseases, so long as the patient continues to trust his or her doctor, the doctor is left in a position to educate and influence the patient in ways that can reduce the likelihood of the disease being passed on. As soon as confidentiality is broken, the trusting relationship is likely to be undermined and, with it, the opportunity to help reduce the spread of the disease lost (Boyd 1992).

Thus, the primary moral justification of medical confidentiality seems to be that it produces better medical consequences. It is in order to encourage their patients to talk freely about private matters, and thus obtain information necessary to practice better medicine, that doctors have for so long assured their patients of confidentiality. Their

514

fundamental Hippocratic moral commitment is to provide medical benefits to their patients with minimal harm. To do so properly, they require relevant private and sensitive information about their patients. To overcome people's natural reluctance to reveal such information, doctors must establish their patients' trust. A strict professional obligation of confidentiality, known to be enforced on pain of severe professional and sometimes legal sanctions, helps to achieve these ends.

This consequentialist defense of medical confidentiality could be generalized further if, as seems likely, the achievement of optimal health benefit for patients is likely to contribute to optimizing general welfare, both in the actual provision of medical care and in the prospect of such provision (for we are all potential patients and most of us would wish our medical care to be optimal). A prima facie moral case can therefore be made for claiming that a professional commitment by doctors to maintain their patients' confidences is likely not only to be beneficial to those patients and their health care, but also to maximize the general welfare.

Medical confidentiality can also be defended from a variety of other moral perspectives. Respect for autonomy, the fundamental value in Kantian ethics, would also seem to support a commitment to confidentiality, at least if autonomy is understood in its contemporary sense of self-determination, or deliberated or thought-out choice for oneself. For, given the imbalance in power between a sick patient and a well and knowledgeable doctor, it seems coercive to say to a patient, as Warwick (1989) puts it: "I need information about your private life and if you don't give it to me you are likely to suffer because my ability to help you overcome your disease may well be impaired – but I am not prepared to offer you any assurances of confidentiality."

Assuming that the patient's autonomous preferences would typically be for optimal treatment (including disclosure of necessary private information) in a context of confidentiality, the above approach may offer medical aid but does not benefit the patient in an autonomy-respecting, empowering way. The doctor who refuses to agree to confidentiality in providing treatment is somewhat like the surgeon who will operate but refuses to provide an anesthetic. As Warwick says, the treatment can be given if the patient so chooses, but the treatment is both less beneficial and fails to respect a patient's autonomous preferences, generally for no good moral reason (though more about this below).

Once the doctor has accepted the patient's desire for confidentiality and has promised, implicitly or explicitly, to maintain a patient's confidences, respect for the patient's autonomy becomes an even stronger justification for maintaining confidentiality – for the doctor has promised, and the patient is justified in running his or her life on the assumption that the doctor will keep that promise (autonomy literally means self-rule – i.e., running one's own life); to break the promise is to infringe the patient's autonomy.

Another common moral perspective is that of justice, and from the perspective of rights-based justice it is widely claimed that patients have a right to have their confidences respected by their doctors. Certainly from the perspective of legal justice such rights to confidentiality are widely entrenched in law, more or less firmly according to the jurisdiction involved. Article 8 of the European Convention on Human Rights, for example, guarantees that "everyone has the right to respect for his private and family life." and captures the disclosure of confidential medical information (McClelland and Thomas, 2002).

In addition, preservation of confidentiality may be supported by moral perspectives that emphasize the importance of relationships based on trust, and virtues such as caring, loyalty and faithfulness ("confidentiality" is derived from Latin roots meaning "with trust" and "with faithfulness").

Thus, to do away with the norm of medical confidentiality is likely to undermine medical care and the general welfare, offend against moral norms of respect for autonomy and respect for patients' rights, and undermine moral concerns to preserve and enhance trusting relationships and virtues such as faithfulness, loyalty, and care.

Given such strong moral justifications for confidentiality in health care, perhaps we should move to the other end of the spectrum of attitudes and accept medical confidentiality as an absolute obligation. Approximating to this was the position favored by the AMA in its Principles of Medical Ethics from 1903 to 1912 ("none of the privacies of individual or domestic life, no infirmity of disposition or flaw of character observed during medical attendance should ever be divulged by physicians, except when imperatively required by laws of the state"), and absolute confidentiality was required by the WMA in its original 1949 International Code of Medical Ethics ("A doctor shall preserve absolute secrecy on all he knows about his patient because of the confidence entrusted in him"). When acting as confessors, Roman Catholic priests commit themselves to such absolute confidentiality; and lawyers in the United Kingdom not only consider their communications with clients when preparing for judicial proceedings absolutely privileged, but such privilege is legally protected, unlike the qualified privilege of doctors and priests. Certain types of general moral obligation are sometimes regarded as absolute. Emperor Ferdinand's dictum about justice is often quoted as an example: "*fiat justicia, et pereat mundus*" ("let justice be done though the heavens fall").

One of the strongest defenses of absolute medical confidentiality is presented by Kottow (1986), who argues powerfully that it has to be "an all or none proposition," "an intransigent and absolute obligation," and "a guarantee of fairness in medical actions." The entire basis of trust between doctors and patients is undermined by any breach of confidentiality; it is a deceit to patients to assure them of confidentiality and then retrospectively disown that assurance; and the putative benefits to society of building in exceptions to medical confidentiality are outweighed by the undoubted harms of breaking it.

More recently, Kipnis (2006a) has called for a near-absolute obligation to respect patient confidentiality. He argues that since a qualified duty of confidentiality will lead some patients to withhold potentially important information, or indeed dissuade them from consulting their doctor, a virtually absolute duty is morally preferable since it will encourage patients to seek medical help while still allowing doctors to persuade patients to divulge whatever information might benefit third parties (a non-existent opportunity if the patient is absent for fear of having his or her secrets revealed), and will maintain the all-important trust in the medical profession. "Paradoxically," he concludes, "ethical and legal duties to report make it less likely that endangered parties will be protected."

Desirable though it may seem to be to maintain an absolute principle of medical confidentiality, unless it is the only absolute moral obligation it runs up against the general problem for plural absolute moral obligations: assuming that, by definition, it must be morally unacceptable to transgress an absolute moral obligation, if two or more absolute moral obligations conflict, then people confronted with such a conflict are logically unable to act in a morally acceptable way, even where the conflict is in no way their responsibility, let alone their fault. If the obligation of medical confidentiality were absolute, it could never be morally justified to transgress it. Yet in some cases the justification for overriding medical confidentiality seems morally overwhelming.

If a doctor learns in the course of a medical consultation that his patient intends to murder someone – or, to make the example even clearer, that the patient is a terrorist, has already murdered at random in the pursuit of his political stance, and has now planted a bomb in a busy city center (imagine the patient saying, "I'm only telling you this, Doc, because obviously I can trust you never to reveal it, but this evening there's going to be mayhem in one of the city squares"), few people, even after the most thorough reflection, would believe that the doctor's professional obligation to maintain medical confidentiality should override his or her obligation as a citizen to help protect members of the community from murder, and to obey (morally acceptable) laws, and so inform the police.

At a more day-to-day level, what if a patient reveals that he or she is dangerously abusing a child, physically, mentally, or sexually? While protecting the child may in practice be achievable without breaking confidentiality, suppose it is not? Or suppose that it is legally required, as in the UK, to report such abuse to the social services, which themselves are in certain cases required to inform the police. Are all such putative counter-examples to be overridden by absolute confidentiality? All in all, it seems that maintenance of confidentiality would in some circumstances be wrong, and thus that an absolute obligation to maintain medical confidentiality in all cases, without exception, is morally untenable. In a later paper, Kottow came to accept this, while maintaining the need for "stringent and predictable" medical confidentiality which has moral priority "over many, perhaps most but not all other considerations" (1994: 472–8). Kipnis (2006b), in response to various critics who interpreted his argument as defending absolute confidentiality, clarifies his position by stating that confidentiality "should be taken as unqualified in *virtually all* . . . cases," while adding that confidentiality is "far closer to an absolute obligation than it has generally been taken to be."

It seems, then, that neither discarding medical confidentiality, nor making it an absolute moral obligation, are morally acceptable alternatives. The obvious fallback position is the one that has in practice been widely accepted and is described above – notably, that while the obligation is stringent, it is not absolute, and exceptions are justified where maintenance of confidentiality would be too harmful. The problems with this position are equally obvious, for once it is known that confidentiality may be breached by doctors and other health-care workers, patients' trust is undermined, and with it respect for patients' autonomy, their rights, and the doctors' loyalty and fidelity to their patients.

So even if it is accepted that there must be some exceptions to the maintenance of confidentiality, there will remain a tension between the desire for an absolute or near-absolute rule of confidentiality that maximizes patients' trust in doctors, and thus facilitates good medical practice, and a prima facie rule of confidentiality that allows exceptions when these clearly promote the public welfare, even when the damage that results from undermining trust in doctors is taken into account.

How to maintain this difficult compromise position in practice is far less clear. Some pointers are apparent. It seems highly desirable for doctors and all health-care workers to commit themselves to, and be committed to (for example, by their terms and conditions of service), a strong though not absolute moral obligation of confidentiality to their patients which should be overridden only where there is a clear moral justification for doing so. Even then, thoughtful efforts to avoid the need to break confidentiality should always be made. As Boyd and his working party (1992) point out, sometimes, even when breaking confidentiality would be helpful, it is possible to achieve the desired beneficial effects for others without having to do so. They also warn that doctors considering the possibility of breaching confidentiality should assess carefully the likelihood of achieving the protection of others that they are seeking – not only may this fail in the long term, it may also fail in the short term (if, for example, the patient has given the doctor a false name and address, and simply disappears when he or she suspects that the doctor is about to break confidentiality).

Failure in the long term to protect public health and welfare, even if individuals may be protected in the short term, is an important consideration. In this context, the maintenance of a strict standard of confidentiality by doctors specializing in the treatment of HIV and AIDS seems particularly important. Porter (1986) gives an important "warning from history" about the dangers of using heavy-handed coercive legal measures to try to control the spread of sexually transmitted disease. While such measures have undoubtedly been effective in controlling infectious diseases such as plague, cholera, and typhoid, they were totally ineffective when applied to syphilis in Victorian times. In the case of AIDS, the lesson of history, he argues, is not to make it a compulsorily notifiable disease, but to rely on confidentiality and voluntary cooperation between patients and health workers.

The final pointer to dealing with the dilemmas of confidentiality is the need for openness; for the dilemmas are relevant to anyone considering the questions of medical confidentiality, be they patients, potential patients, or health-care workers. There seems no plausible way to evade them, but at least let us acknowledge them openly and indicate the sorts of ways we aim to respond to them. This transparency, by forcing us to articulate our own position and its rationale and inviting others to comment, is likely to lead to improved moral judgments when deliberating about which of the two dilemmatic horns to embrace: respecting patient autonomy by maintaining confidentiality or preventing significant harm by breaching confidentiality. One of the authors of this chapter (RG), when practicing as a doctor, aimed to maintain confidentiality to the maximum extent possible while respecting the (morally acceptable) laws of the country, refusing to evade opportunities to avert major harms, and exercising commonsense both in assessing what his patient would want him to do when he was unable to consult the patient or a proper proxy directly, and in relatively trivial cases where such consultation is likely to appear – and be – simply foolish (Gillon 1985: 106–12). But we do not pretend that such an approach would be acceptable to all, or that other approaches may not be morally acceptable – such, alas, is the nature of genuine moral dilemmas.

References

AMA (American Medical Association). *Principles of Medical Ethics 1903*. Available online at: www.ama-assn.org/ama1/pub/upload/mm/43/1903principalsofethi.pdf.

BMA (British Medical Association) (2004). *Medical Ethics Today*, 2nd edn. London: BMJ Publishing Group.

Boyd, K. (1992). HIV infection and AIDS: the ethics of medical confidentiality. *Journal of Medical Ethics* 18: 173–9.

Brazier, M. (1992). *Medicine, Patients and the Law*, 2nd edn. Harmondsworth: Penguin.

Gillon, R. (1985 and subsequent reprints). *Philosophical Medical Ethics*. Chichester: John Wiley.

GMC (1995a). *Good Medical Practice*. London: General Medical Council.

GMC (1995b). *Confidentiality*. London: General Medical Council.

Kipnis, K. (2006a). A defense of unqualified medical confidentiality. *American Journal of Bioethics* 6: 7–18.

Kipnis, K. (2006b). A defense defended. *American Journal of Bioethics* 6: W32–W34.

Kottow, M. (1986). Medical confidentiality: an intransigent and absolute obligation. *Journal of Medical Ethics* 12: 117–22.

Kottow, M. (1994). Stringent and predictable medical confidentiality. In R. Gillon and A. Lloyd (eds.), *Principles of Health Care Ethics*. Chichester: John Wiley.

McClelland, R. and Thomas, V. (2002). Confidentiality and security of clinical information in mental health practice. *Advances in Psychiatric Treatment* 8: 291–6.

Ordre National des Médecins (2003). Code de déontologie médicale. Available online at: www.web.ordre.medecin.fr/deonto/decret/codedeont.pdf (accessed April 2, 2007).

Porter, R. (1986). History says no to the policeman's response to AIDS. *British Medical Journal* 293: 1589–90.

Siegler, M. (1982). Confidentiality in medicine: a decrepit concept. *New England Journal of Medicine* 307: 1518–21.

Thomas, N., Murray, E., and Rogstad, K. (2006). Confidentiality is essential if young people are to access sexual health services. *International Journal of STD and AIDS* 17/8: 525–9.

Warwick, S. J. (1989). A vote for no confidence. *Journal of Medical Ethics* 15: 183–5.

WMA (World Medical Association) (1949). International code of medical ethics. *World Medical Association Bulletin* 1/3: 109, 111. Available online at: www.wma.net/e/policy/c8.htm (accessed April 2, 2007).

Wootton, D. (2006). *Bad Medicine: Doctors Doing Harm Since Hippocrates*. Oxford: Oxford University Press.

43

Truth-telling

ROGER HIGGS

Trusting someone to look after you usually means you do not expect them to tell you lies. Yet the problem of telling the truth in health care continues to engage us. Most patients have wondered at one time or other whether their own medical advisors are being completely open with them. Anxiety can create frightening shadows. But a policy of openness is a recent innovation in the long history of Western medicine, and in some quarters the revolution has yet to happen. The phrase "doctor knows best" enshrines a tradition of paternalism which may extend throughout a health service. Some cultures expect that their doctors may not be telling the truth: some doctors feel that proper patient care may sometimes require untruths. Whatever the rhetoric of the modern mission statement or user information sheet, health-care systems still leave ultimate control of decision-making, and much of the information flow which underpins these decisions, firmly in professional hands. In view of this, we need to examine both the traditional approach and the modern insistence on patients' rights to be told about the circumstances of their own case. Should health-care professionals always tell the truth, and, if not, what exceptions should there be and with what moral justification? What are the implications of our modern expectation and where might they lead us?

The Clinical Encounter

Those who work in hospitals or primary care or who have experience as patients will immediately see that this is a field of concern, but others may need to be reminded of the reality. Many will remember lies told to them as children by older children or adults (to "kid" them), but in clinical medicine the paradigm situation is where the news has to be given to someone that he is suffering from a serious condition from which he will shortly die, in which suffering will be intense, or for which there is no cure. This is associated in the modern mind so closely with the diagnosis of cancer that this word has become a metaphor for the hopeless case. Even if many cancers are now curable (and there are many other threats to life), in some way we all dread such a diagnosis. New diseases like AIDS have added further dimensions to the fear. For out-siders, a window to this misery is offered by published accounts, like that by Quill and

Townsend (1991) of an interview with a woman who had recently been infected by her partner with HIV disease. But whatever the condition, similar encounters can be found daily in every health service in every country. To be told this sort of news must be the ultimate horror; to have to tell it as part of one's job falls not far short. "Breaking bad news" seems like a euphemism: no wonder professionals are tempted not to tell the truth. As one of my young colleagues muttered as he walked away from a crying patient, after a long and thoughtful interview: "I'm sure I didn't sign up for this dreadful sort of job."

The dramatic should not demean the everyday. Many ordinary decisions may be as difficult. A clinician often has to ask herself when the possibility of some serious but unlikely diagnosis should be shared with the patient. Screening may unearth something abnormal that may not affect the patient's life, but in a system where patients have access to their notes, even recording possible concerns or incidental findings could cause distress. Consulting with children or families raises a further set of questions. The illness of a colleague or the discovery of an unacknowledged clinical error immediately pose dilemmas for health-care staff: what should be said to whom, and when? Advocacy also has its problems: a professional may want to help, and may be asked to add medical weight to a situation where medicine has no expertise. The patient, uncertain about the professional's response, may himself chose to tell a lie to gain such backing. Such questions probe deeply not only into veracity in health care but also into views of the role, goals, and boundaries of clinical work. In a multicultural society, it is more than likely that the patient or relatives may have expectations or perceptions that are different from those entertained by the professional. Such complexity may mean that the ideal response is hard to define; at the end of a frantic working day, "the good enough" approach may be all that anyone can expect of herself. Clinical care of acute or terminal illness is where much of the concern has been focused, but community care, public health, teaching, research, and management will all offer us examples where we may need not only appropriate guidelines, rules or principles, but also fine judgment to bring together the different requirements of moral action.

Medical Paternalism Re-examined

In the face of such issues, it is not surprising that there has been a tradition within most societies that a doctor may, or indeed should, withhold the truth from the patient in some circumstances. Although the reasoning behind this may be less convincing to modern eyes, some of the ideas here are too important to be abandoned without careful thought.

The most common confusion is the appeal to *uncertainty.* Because the living body cannot be taken apart, there is always an element of uncertainty about a medical diagnosis. Prognosis too may be based at best on statistics, at worst on well-informed guesswork, while the treatment plan can be judged only by reference to the assessment of others similarly afflicted and treated. Bringing such information together around one patient, when not only that person's future but also their detailed physical and psychological make-up, together with their precise social circumstances and their likely reaction to the illness, are largely unknown, means that a clinical encounter is really a "trial of one." In such circumstances, recordings of clinical interviews often seem like the blind leading the blind. There are so many questions unasked, in both directions. Lawrence Henderson's (1955) response encapsulates the confusion this causes, and may appear to offer an escape clause from the whole issue: "It is meaningless to speak of telling the truth, the whole truth and nothing but the truth to a patient . . . because it is . . . a sheer impossibility. Since telling the truth is impossible, there can be no sharp distinction between what is true and what is false."

Tempting as this appeal is, however, it will not serve the purpose here, because this uncertainty could perfectly well be shared with a patient without destroying confidence in the clinician's skill and judgment. Henderson's statement elides *truth*, the realities of what exists, or may turn out to happen, with *truthfulness or veracity*. We are concerned with a truthful exchange between people, not with abstract issues of metaphysics or epistemology. It is not our state of knowledge but *our intention* that is crucial. Sissela Bok sets this out incisively: "The moral question of whether you are lying or not is not settled by establishing the truth or falsity of what you say. In order to settle the question, we must know whether you intend your statement to mislead" (1978: 6). Bringing together all forms of deception under one head, as it were, may be too stern a standard for some people, but it has the huge virtue of making it crystal clear to deceivers of all kinds not to deceive themselves. Whatever we may decide to call them, "lesser" forms of intended deception will not, in this view, automatically contain their own justification.

Linked to the problem of uncertainty is the concern that, in discussions between professional and lay people, *putting across a technical issue may be too difficult.* A patient, untrained in medicine or bioscience, simply cannot understand the issues; so, goes the argument, it's best not to try. The arrogance (or laziness) that lies behind this attitude undermines professional endeavor. Any skilled person who is at the interface with the public must be able to explain what they are up to. Those who cannot must learn how to do so. Medicine is a good deal less complex than many activities. As science advances, things may appear to become more complicated, but professionals have a duty all the time to bring their public up to date. To dress up simple ideas or uncertainties as mysteries is the mark of the charlatan.

Medical ethics became publicly important at least in part because of the power gradient between knowledgeable, confident, and healthy professionals and unin-formed, anxious, and ill people seeking their help. There are risks of all sorts in that situation, from the temptation for the busy professional to take the quicker route, through to the frank manipulation or abuse of someone who is trusting but helpless. Thinkers since the Enlightenment have been concerned that the individual should be sovereign over her own affairs. Illness threatens a person's autonomy in a number of ways: by restricting her ability to take action, by preventing her from being able to think clearly through what is facing her, and perhaps by reducing her willpower and energy. The infantilizing effects of illness and health care are additional threats, allied to the temptation for a helper to take over inappropriately. In procedural terms, simply allowing a doctor to touch another normally requires that person to give consent, and proper consent requires appropriate information. In this line of thinking, enshrined in law in most countries, respecting the autonomy of competent patients requires that they be informed, and that means that the professional be honest with them in a way that they can understand – about what is wrong, what they are advised should be done, and what the risks and prospects are.

It is interesting to reflect how the ethics of personal health care derives from those political concerns of the eighteenth and nineteenth centuries to protect the personal sphere of individuals from public intrusion, usually from those in power as rulers. It is of course precisely because health care crosses and recrosses the boundary between public and private that clear thinking and proper safeguards are in order. It is possible for debates about rising budgets and fears for the health of the next generation to press thinkers on both the welfarist left and the libertarian right to redraw these boundaries: and the arguments about preserving these boundaries need to be rehearsed (Shklar 1989: 21–38). But it is also possible for a thoroughly respectful physician to take the view that, having crossed that boundary, in some sense she now can see what is best for a patient and the patient is "better off not knowing." It is easy to imagine how in some circumstances a person's life would not be enhanced, and might be ruined, by knowing that something bad lay round the corner which they did not expect. If respect for autonomy is important, so also are the duties to care and to avoid harming the patient. Although disease and illness may be major harms, so too may be anxiety: the person disabled not by disease, but by fear of it, is sadly common.

But the argument that deception is justified to prevent anxiety carries its own rebuttal. The usual antidote to fear is not silence but open discussion. Sometimes in incurable illness, for instance, sharing of problems in this way is the only therapy on offer. Were trust to decline so that patients did not believe what was being said to them, not only reassurance but also genuine support during an illness would become impossible. I recorded (Higgs 1982) a case of a woman lied to who wasted what remained of her life waiting for a recovery that could never come. This returns us to the crucial insights of the last paragraph. Competent people must be allowed to choose for themselves. If they do not have the information on which to base a choice, or even a realization that a choice is necessary at all, it seems hard not to see this in itself as a major harm. Of course, balancing harm versus benefit is neither simple nor easy. Particular benefits and particular harms are in the balance: Campbell and Higgs (1982: 83–97) showed how, for different people, apparently similar harms (or benefits) may have very different values. But in whatever respect the professional has crossed the boundary, however well she has understood the patient's point of view, proper respect for a person's autonomy dictates that, unless circumstances make this impossible, the person who should judge the patient's best interest should be the patient.

Examples of the pitfalls lying in wait abound in clinical decisions at the end of life (Higgs 1997), but may be even more important at the beginning of an illness. For instance, a very bright but chronically anxious young woman in her last year at school developed symptoms which her doctor thought most likely to be early indications of multiple sclerosis. He decided to share this with her parents, not the patient, because of her personality and the uncertainty of the diagnosis. The parents, although very upset, had high ambitions for their daughter, and postponed any discussion with her so that she would not be distressed during her university entrance exams. The young woman, turned down shortly afterwards for life insurance, confronted the doctor, who now felt unable to withhold the reason for the insurance company's attitude and the now probable diagnosis. Intensely angry with him and with her parents, the woman left home to live with a boyfriend and, in the confusion, became pregnant. Her neurological condition worsened dramatically; she was unable to start her course. However difficult decisions might be in such tragic situations, the doctor's (almost literally) paternalistic initial action had set in train events which deprived the young patient of some of the only effective management strategies in an incurable medical condition – developing confidence in her own abilities to make wise choices about herself, and trust in those around her who could help.

Ethical Frameworks

The justification for dismissing medical secrecy derives its strength from the framework of biomedical principles (as laid out by Beauchamp and Childress 2009 [1979] and Gillon 1994: xxi–xxxi), which in turn have their roots both in the duty-based thinking of Kant and in consequentialism, particularly J. S. Mill's utilitarianism. But naturally these two philosophical approaches differ in detail, since a strict deontologist would see being truthful as a primary duty, not to be negotiated, whereas consequentialists might well see other issues impinging on the decision. The same debate might well occur in the clinic or on the wards: is telling the truth an *absolute* duty, or are there occasions when deception may be justified? As soon as we acknowledge the possibility of other issues of equal importance bearing on any particular case, such as, say, those of confidentiality or of kindness, it becomes untenable to suggest that the claims of truthfulness are absolute. Given the prime importance of good communication between doctor and patient, it seems to place veracity at an inhumanely high level if *no* other considerations can ever be taken into account. Indeed, some have noted that a thoughtless "dumping" of information on an unprepared person could become a harm in itself: certainly in a medical crisis where life hung in the balance (say, treating the sole survivor of a family just after an accident), there might well be an argument against adding the further stress of receiving tragic news, at least until the patient's condition had been stabilized and other support was at hand. Even when the person being approached is not ill, this is the sort of thinking that leads clinicians to avoid breaking bad news to relatives over the phone. An absolutist approach does not seem to allow the nuances or necessities required in clinical practice to be expressed.

The Temptation to Deceive

A clear rule, however, does at least help to deal with the opposing problem: that in our lives in general as individuals there is a strong temptation to avoid telling the truth, especially when we might appear in a bad light or are trying to do something difficult. The mere acquisition of a medical degree doesn't make this any easier. Individuals and cultures obviously differ in the circumstances when the sanctions against lying are lifted; but that lying is one of the strategies human beings need to use is not in doubt. Nyberg (1993: 219) suggests that in ordinary life we need deception to "survive as a species and to flourish as persons." Lying may be used by those in power to maintain their position; but it may also be the only way the powerless can defend themselves in times of political or religious persecution (Oborne 2005: 116–19). Certainly, interest in the language that others are using, especially whether it is being used to misinform or mislead, is considered by ethnographers to be a human universal (Pinker 2003). The same author uses examples from social psychology experiments to show that the people we may most often deceive are ourselves. So the possibilities are thus raised for self-deception about whether we are actually being deceptive, setting the scene for the sort of examination that could become troublingly recursive. With this in prospect, we either have to find a regular way of reflecting on what we are saying, or fall back on an invariable rule.

Bernard Williams (2002), by distinguishing between sincerity and accuracy, may help the professional out of this trap. Any clinician or scientist who was deliberately inaccurate would normally be considered to be acting unprofessionally, but, although someone with real integrity is always a pleasure to meet, the requirement of a clinician to attend to *anyone* who presents as a patient, whether that person is likeable or not, means that sincerity may not always be possible. For instance, if a patient has no need or right (in the general sense) for information about a professional's private life, there can be no requirement for the professional to be open and transparent about her own thoughts or feelings unless they are inextricably part of her clinical role. But in the public and accountable roles of medical care, whether as doctor, teacher, researcher, or manager, she would be expected to be honest. What does that word imply?

Different Forms of Deception

Honesty can easily appear to have a two-dimensional, "open and shut" feel to it; the "tell or not tell" approach has a seductive simplicity but it actually collapses together unhelpfully (and untruthfully?) the different forms of deception. There are situations in medicine, just as in other walks of life, where information may be withheld for good reasons. In clinical trials, for instance, an informed patient agrees to be kept in the dark. Withholding information in other circumstances might be considered justified through arguments about acts and omissions, such as where the information arises as a side issue from other work, as when an isolated and unexpected abnormal test result that makes no immediate sense is found when a patient is being checked for something quite different. Here the need for professional competence suggests at the very least that the clinician should have checked and have some explanation of the result before sharing it with the patient: until that point, the information may be best withheld. The philosopher Jennifer Jackson in her critique (1991) of my article (Higgs 1985), concludes that while clinicians have a prima facie duty not to lie, since there are also other forms of intentional deception which should not count as lies, professionals are not duty-bound to avoid these other forms. Further, she notes that by making an inviolable rule, we may be setting our sights too high. Doubting whether "aiming for the best" is necessary or even intelligible, Jackson suggests that in life in general we need the rule against lying "just so as to get by – whatever particular further aims we happen to have in life. If the rule would still allow us to get by if certain departures were generally allowed,

525

then the departures *can* be allowed. If the rule would only allow us to get by if certain departures were allowed, then the departures *must* be allowed" (1991: 8).

Communicating Outside Medicine

If courage to face up to unpleasant truths is required, it is needed more from patients than from professionals. We need to be reminded that outside medicine it would be a normal (and accepted) human reaction initially to avoid facing up to difficult questions. "Human kind cannot bear very much reality," was T. S. Eliot's comment (1969: 172). A common argument against telling the truth is that it may destroy hope. For many of us, the hope is that we shall not need to be reminded of our mortality, rather than that we shall be able to make momentous decisions about our continuing lives. "Getting by" may involve avoiding the big questions, rather than looking for truthful answers. Socrates thought that the unexamined life was not worth living, but he was by all accounts a remarkable man in every respect. Only the fortunate and gifted minority will have had opportunities to rehearse before it is their life itself that is really examined. It is a brave person who decides to look into the abyss, confronting the reality of their impending death. "Bad news choosers" often choose to narrow the field of their choice. Self-deception here may be an important mechanism for maintaining mental health in the face of stress. Any professional attempting to set the record straight must also be prepared to offer time and support while someone comes to terms with cold reality.

In all forms of communication, whether with our inner self or with other people, there are verbal and non-verbal processes at work. People have feelings as well as thoughts, and these feelings may be mixed: ambiguity, the force behind so much great poetry, is also the currency of everyday conversation. Hints, euphemisms, inflexion, "telling" silences, are all part of this form of human intercourse. In the abstract, a truth is a hard-edged, clear thing; it is either communicated or not (and certainly, once stated, it may be very difficult to withdraw). With this perspective, honesty may almost feel like a measurable virtue, unlike, say, courage or prudence. But luckily, in practice, a truth, even if clearly delivered, is taken on by the hearer little by little, as Kübler-Ross (1970) points out: sometimes at first apparently not heard, or not fully understood, or initially denied.

All these things suggest that, in health care at least, *how* a truth is told may be as important as *what* is conveyed. It is important not to put unreal requirements on communications between doctors and patients, or to create so stringent or exacting rules that these become self-defeating. Like most things that need to be done well, it may initially need time and not a little practice. It is worth reminding ourselves at this point that although the studies of what patients (and would-be patients) wanted to know from their physicians indicate that the majority do wish to hear the truth about their condition, there is usually a minority, albeit a small one, who do not. A clinician does not know which group the patient is in until some form of inquiry is made. So she may preface her comments to the patient with words such as these: "It is my usual practice to share with a patient what the situation is as soon as I can be reasonably sure. Is that what you would like, and if so is there someone else who you would like to be with you to hear this too?"

Character, Context, and Care

Bioethics came into being because the decisions were hard, and there are few harder things than negotiating the moral pitfalls of truth-telling in actual clinical practice. Sokol (2007) has proposed a helpful checklist approach to deciding whether it is morally acceptable to deceive a patient. Whatever intellectual system is used to think through the options, however, there is a feeling that something else is required. Iris Murdoch's call (1970) for further study of "concerned responsiveness" or "loving attention" to particular individuals as the basic moral coinage certainly seems to have heralded an increasing interest in what sort of *character* the clinician should try to develop. As patients, we want the clinicians we meet to be competent and honest, certainly, but we also usually want them to be kind and, perhaps rather desperately, to deal with us as individuals, as the persons we are. So kindness and attentiveness climb up beside honesty in the list of key virtues. Martha Nussbaum (1990: 66–75) has taken Aristotelian practical reasoning to imply that the *particular*, in the sense of context and/or relationship, should have priority, especially in reasserting the importance of a "finely tuned concreteness in ethical attention and judgment." Elsewhere (1986: 316), she talks about a "flexible movement back and forth between particular and general." Contextualizing decisions about honesty – talking to *this* person about *this* issue, *now* – will require attention to detail and may alter the balance of the decision. Nel Noddings (1984), in putting forward an ethics based on *care* rather than rule or principle, has developed an approach influential in nursing: as an educationalist, she gives as an example an account of a lie from the "one-caring" (the parent) to enable the "cared-for," in this case a child, to stay away from school. The context and the particular relationship indicate that the cardinal virtue at this point should be care for that individual, not a disassociated honesty.

From a *cultural* perspective, human groups set priorities that move their members toward a resolution of these conflicts in a similar way. In some groups, for instance, kindness or loyalty may be much more important than truthfulness. But moral relativism sometimes seems to say more about power distribution and fear than about human freedom: so arguments derived from relativism in support of deception may tell us more about the critical problems of a particular society than the legitimate moral concerns of an individual within it. Nevertheless, these cultural effects are encountered in clinical context and have to be properly managed. But if that clinical context is seen in any sense as having a (generally accepted) culture *of its own*, we need to think how sense can be made for everyone within it of the need to respect people by telling the truth, while considering the undoubted importance of the critiques noted above.

One of Alastair MacIntyre's reminders (1967) is that we should put our thinking into historical perspective. Certainly, at this time we are seeing great changes in the practice of scientific medicine, in the organization of health care, and thus in the doctor–patient relationship too. When little could be done for a patient, in the modern curative sense, perhaps a powerful, mysterious, and alien healer was important. Now the position is changing. Clinical relationships are becoming more equal, personal, and potentially deeper. Not only does traditional paternalism reduce a person's autonomy,

527

but it may also trap someone in a patient role and threaten his recovery: in this way it may be, in Illich's phrase, a "sickening" process (Illich 1975). So procedures that insure that the truth be fully told may be as important a step in clinical care now as the development of asepsis was in surgery. Where a question is asked, it must be answered truthfully. But just as asepsis is not the overriding factor in, say, trauma at the roadside, in critical issues in truth-telling other issues may be of crucial importance and may justify exceptions. Medical encounters should be conducted under the rubric of honesty. As health care changes, there is a hope that clinicians and patients may be developing a more open relationship, in which truthfulness may be part of something deeper.

References

Beauchamp, T. J. and Childress, J. F. (2009 [1979]). *Principles of Biomedical Ethics*, 6th edn. New York: Oxford University Press.

Bok, S. (1978). *Lying: Moral Choice in Public and Private Life*. New York: Pantheon Books.

Campbell, A. V. and Higgs, R. (1982). *In That Case: Medical Ethics in Everyday Practice*. London: Darton Longman and Todd.

Eliot, T. S. (1969). Four Quartets: Burnt Norton. In *The Complete Poems and Plays*. London: Faber and Faber.

Gillon, R. (1994). *Principles of Health Care Ethics*. Chichester: John Wiley.

Henderson, L. J. (1955). Physician and patient as social system. *New England Journal of Medicine* 212: 819–23.

Higgs, R. (1982). Truth at the last – a case of obstructed death? *Journal of Medical Ethics* 8: 152–6.

Higgs, R. (1985). On telling patients the truth. In M. Lockwood (ed.), *Moral Dilemmas in Modern Medicine*. Oxford: Oxford University Press, pp. 187–202.

Higgs, R. (1997). Shaping our ends: the ethics of respect in a well led NHS. *British Journal of General Practice* 47: 245–49.

Illich, I. (1975). *Medical Nemesis: The Expropriation of Health*. London: Calder and Boyars.

Jackson, J. (1991). Telling the truth. *Journal of Medical Ethics* 17: 5–9.

Kübler-Ross, E. (1970). *On Death and Dying*. London: Tavistock.

MacIntyre, A. (1967). *A Short History of Ethics*. London: Routledge & Kegan Paul.

Murdoch, I. (1970). *The Sovereignty of Good*. London: Routledge & Kegan Paul.

Noddings, N. (1984). *Caring: A Feminine Approach to Ethics and Moral Education*. Berkeley and Los Angeles: University of California Press.

Nussbaum, M. C. (1986). *The Fragility of Goodness: Luck and Ethics in Greek Tragedy and Philosophy*. Cambridge: Cambridge University Press.

Nussbaum, M. C. (1990). *Love's Knowledge: Essays on Philosophy and Literature*. New York: Oxford University Press.

Nyberg, D. (1993). *The Varnished Truth: Truth Telling and Deceiving in Ordinary Life*. Chicago: University of Chicago Press.

Oborne, P. (2005). *The Rise of Political Lying*. London: Free Press.

Quill, T. E. and Townsend, P. (1991). Bad news: delivery, dialogue and dilemmas. *Archives of Internal Medicine* 151: 463–68.

Pinker, S. (2003). *The Blank Slate: The Modern Denial of Human Nature*. London: Penguin Press.

Shklar, N. (1989). The liberalism of fear. In N. L. Rosenblum (ed.), *Liberalism and the Moral Life*. Cambridge, MA: Harvard University Press.

Sokol, D. (2007). Can deceiving patients be morally acceptable? *British Medical Journal* 334: 984–6.

Williams, B. (2002). *Truth and Truthfulness: An Essay in Genealogy*. Princeton: Princeton University Press.

Further reading

Brody, H. (1992). *The Healer's Power*. New Haven, CT: Yale University Press.
Hattori, H. et al. (1991). The patient's right to information in Japan – legal rules and doctors opinions. *Social Science and Medicine* 32: 1007–16.
Kerr, P. (ed.) (1990). *The Penguin Book of Lies*. London: Viking Penguin.
MacIntyre, A. (1981). *After Virtue*. London: Duckworth.
Reich, W. T. (ed.) (1978). *Encyclopedia of Bioethics*. New York: Free Press.
Zeldin, T. (1994). *An Intimate History of Humanity*. London: Minerva.

44

Informed Consent and Patient Autonomy

ROBERT YOUNG

Though the doctrine of informed consent is largely a creation of various court judgments about the health care provided to specific patients, and of the establishment of regulatory standards in connection with medical experimentation, it ultimately rests on a moral foundation. I will, first, set out that moral foundation; second, highlight some of the landmarks in the development of the legal form of the doctrine; and, third, note some exceptions to the doctrine. (For discussion of the giving of informed consent by patients who are at the same time subjects of medical research see chapter 38, "Research Involving Human Beings.")

The Moral Foundation

An autonomous, or self-determining, person chooses or devises a plan for her life, rather than having one imposed on her by others or allowing circumstances to dictate one for her, and lives in accordance with that plan. It should be noted that, in using the term "plan," I do not have in mind anything like a blueprint. People's life plans can be, and indeed are, subject to revision over time, and occasionally far-reaching revision at that. What is certainly implied by my characterization is that an autonomous person does not merely make choices and decisions about major concerns such as career, lifestyle, and fundamental values, but is actively involved in shaping and directing her life so as to realize those choices and decisions (Brock 1987; Dworkin 1988; Young 1986). The following oft-cited remarks of Isaiah Berlin convey very clearly the way in which champions of autonomy consider it to be foundational to our moral agency:

> I wish my life and decisions to depend on myself, not on external forces of whatever kind. I wish to be the instrument of my own, not of other men's, acts of will. I wish to be a subject, not an object; to be moved by reasons, by conscious purposes, which are my own, not by causes which affect me, as it were, from outside. I wish to be somebody, not nobody; a doer – deciding, not being decided for, self-directed and not acted upon by external nature or by other men as if I were a thing, or an animal, or a slave. . . . I wish, above all, to be conscious of myself as a thinking, willing, active being, bearing responsibility for my choices and able to explain them by references to my own ideas and purposes. (1969: 131)

In a health-care setting, a patient exercises her autonomy when she decides which of the options for dealing with her health-care problem (including having no treatment at all) will be best for her given her particular values, concerns, and goals. A patient who makes autonomous choices about her health care is able to opt for what she considers will be best for her, *all things considered*. To obtain a patient's informed consent to health care is thus to recognize the value of her autonomy. The seriousness of that recognition is tested, however, whenever a patient autonomously decides on a course of action which runs counter to the judgment made by her health-care advisors about what would be *medically best* for her. For most of the time during which there has been a clinical approach to health care, the idea has prevailed that health-care practitioners should act with the intention of doing the best they can for their patients, and this has, in turn, been understood to mean doing what is medically best. So, when achieving this aim made it necessary to deny the patient the information she needed to make an informed choice, it was considered to be in her interests that the information be withheld. Paternalistic health-care practices effectively placed a person's health-care interests ahead of her interest as an autonomous agent in deciding for herself what would be best for her, *all things considered*.

Autonomy is, of course, not the only thing of value, so other values, including those of a person's health and well-being, may, and indeed should, sometimes take precedence over autonomy. But if, following Berlin, the interest a person has in being self-determining is seen to reflect the importance to her of making decisions about her life that accord with her own aims and values, paternalism in health care will be inappropriate whenever a patient is able to give (or withhold) her informed consent to a health-care procedure.

For a patient to be capable of giving informed consent, she must be competent, must understand the information disclosed to her and appreciate its significance, and must give (or withhold) her consent freely. I shall elaborate on each of these features in turn. First, it is a working assumption that a normal adult is competent to make judgments about her health care in that she is able to make decisions that reflect her concern for her own well-being (Brock 1987: 110ff; Buchanan and Brock 1989: ch. 1; Dworkin 1988: 112f; Young 2007: ch. 8). When a person proposes to pursue a course of action that seems likely to have an adverse effect on her well-being, the question will arise as to whether she should be (paternalistically) prevented from pursuing such a course. The effects of injury, illness, and medication can increase the probability that a patient will make choices that appear unbalanced and so call into question her competence to make decisions about her health care. This will be more likely to occur if a patient's choice about how to proceed is at odds with that of her health-care practitioner. But disagreement as such cannot be taken to signify that a patient is incompetent.

Suppose, for example, that, against medical advice, an active sportswoman requests that analgesics be given intravenously after an operation, rather than by means of an epidural, because she wishes to avoid the remote risk of being left paralyzed. Suppose, further, that the epidural would not only be medically more efficacious, but would reduce discomfort. If there is no reason to doubt her competence, it is her judgment as to what, all things considered, will be best that should prevail, given the significance she attaches to her sporting aspirations. Even cases where life-sustaining treatment is refused do not show that a patient lacks competence. An adult Jehovah's Witness, for example, may competently refuse a life-preserving blood transfusion even though such a refusal is tantamount to accepting death (cf. *Malette v. Shulman* [1990] 67 Dominion Law Reports (4th) 321; [1991] 2 Medical Law Review 162 (Ontario, Canada)).

The second element in informed consent, the patient's capacity to understand and appreciate the information with which she is provided, has perhaps been the most contentious of the three elements. Oftentimes, health-care practitioners have wished to put the emphasis on what has been *disclosed* to a patient rather than on what she has *understood*, the latter obviously being harder to determine. Such a stance makes greatest sense if the concern is to maximize patient sovereignty. However, if obtaining informed consent is of importance, it is the patient's understanding that should occupy center stage since, at the extreme, failure on the part of the patient to understand the information she has been given effectively vitiates any claim that she is able to make an informed choice. For that reason alone, the practitioner has an obligation to strive to promote understanding. (For a more comprehensive discussion of the criteria that need to be satisfied for understanding, and some suggestions on ways of satisfying those criteria, see Faden and Beauchamp 1986: ch. 9.)

Some health-care practitioners who declare themselves to be opposed to paternalism in health care are nevertheless keen to resist the position that I have just outlined. Sometimes the resistance is grounded in a conviction that health-care professionals, just because they are health-care professionals, bring certain values to their practice that necessarily influence the way in which information is provided to patients. At its crudest, this may amount to a presupposition that, for instance, more of life is better than less, and result in informing patients only about procedures likely to lengthen life. What makes this so crude is that it is simply not unqualifiedly true that more of life is better than less – for some patients the converse is true.

There is, however, a more subtle idea that grounds the resistance of some health-care professionals to thinking they are obligated to insure that competent patients understand such information as is material to their health and its management. Consider the fact that the way in which information is "framed," as psychologists say, determines its significance for those (e.g. patients) to whom it is provided. Thus, for example, if procedures are spelled out in terms of the probability of their resulting in death, rather than the probability of their extending life, there is a marked difference in the way people evaluate the alternatives. (For references to the psychological literature and discussion, see Savulescu 1995: 328f; see also Wear 1998: ch. 6, for a sensitive treatment of related issues.) From this it might be thought that since the values of health-care practitioners will influence the ways in which they frame information to patients, it is unrealistic to think that they can at the same time meet an obligation to promote understanding on the part of patients who do not share similar values. This is perhaps most dramatically illustrated when a competent patient refuses recommended life-sustaining therapy, or (in those jurisdictions where it is legal to do so) requests her doctor's assistance to help bring about death, but similar issues are likely to arise if a doctor thinks that it would be futile to provide the kind of medical treatment sought by a patient. If the obligation to promote the understanding needed for informed consent is to be taken seriously, the practitioner should alert her to the values underpinning the way in which information has been framed. If, having endeavored to do so, the practitioner cannot rationally dissuade the patient from her preferred course of action, the practitioner should (as mentioned previously) either withdraw from the case or agree to respect the patient's choice, despite thinking it mistaken.

To satisfy the third requirement for informed consent, consent must be given freely. If "consent" results from coercion, manipulation, or undue influence, it cannot be considered a genuine authorization even if the patient is given full information and understands and appreciates that information. This will be true even if the motive for the manipulation is a desire to serve the patient's best interests. However, now that paternalism in health care is out of favor (officially, at least), patients are less likely to be coerced or subjected to undue influence than was once the case. Nonetheless, the possibility remains of information being provided to patients in ways that increase the likelihood that they will choose as practitioners would wish (cf. Brock 1987: 119). Coercion, or undue influence, by third parties, is another matter altogether. A patient's family, in particular, may pressure a patient into deciding on a course of action she does not favor. Be this as it may, it is likely that it is only when the actions of a health-care practitioner undermine the voluntariness of a patient's choice that a legal remedy will be sought.

On the assumption that the three requirements I have just detailed are satisfied, the following principle should be honored: in the absence of a sufficient reason (and the fact that a patient holds a different view from her health-care advisors on the management of her case is not on its own a sufficient reason) for thinking that injury, illness, or medication has robbed her of her competence, a patient's decisions about her health care shall be binding. Though this principle may seem very strong it merely restates the moral requirement to respect a competent person's autonomous decisions and does not preclude care-givers from making reasonable attempts to persuade a patient about alternative measures, or even of facilitating a referral or transfer of a patient to another practitioner if acceding to the patient's wishes would necessitate a violation of the care-giver's professional integrity. (For more on issues of referral and transfer, see Young 2007: ch. 7.) What the principle does preclude is the paternalistic overruling of a competent patient's wishes (e.g. via the use of deception to engineer a change of mind by the patient).

My focus to date has been on the moral foundation for requiring informed consent, but it is important to realize that the requirement is one of relatively recent origin (not only in the context of interest to us – i.e. health care – but also in others, like consumer protection) *and* that the most important contributions to its formulation have come from legal determinations. In particular, it is to developments in the law of torts that we must look if we are to understand the process by which we have reached the present requirement in various jurisdictions for obtaining informed consent from patients. That is not to suggest there is a single and settled legal position which holds wherever the requirement has come to be recognized. But there have been a number of landmark cases, especially in the English-speaking world, which have contributed greatly to the way the doctrine is presently conceived. So, while it has to be acknowledged that the following discussion is narrowly based, at least as regards the social, political, and legal settings from which the cases I refer to are drawn, it will provide us with insight into why informed consent has come to be a moral and legal requirement in much of the English-speaking world, and why there is agitation for it to be introduced elsewhere.

(For some brief reflections on the bearing of cultural considerations on the significance of obtaining informed consent, see Berg et al. 2001: 311ff.)

The Legal Requirement for Consent in Therapeutic Settings

The right of individual self-determination has been the basis for court findings in favor of requiring the informed consent of competent patients to health-care procedures. If competent people have the right of self-determination, then, at the very least, they must be able to claim protection against interference with their bodies, including within the health-care practitioner (especially, doctor)–patient relationship. Once that is acknowledged, medical judgment and practice cannot be viewed simply in terms of the practitioner acting beneficently for the good of the patient. For the practitioner not to acknowledge and respect the autonomy of the patient constitutes "assault and battery." Such a view was eloquently stated in the judgment of Justice Cardozo in the 1914 American case of *Schloendorff v. Society of New York Hospitals* when finding that surgery ought not to have been performed on a patient who had agreed to an abdominal examination under anesthesia, but had specifically refused an operation. Cardozo declared that: "Every human being of adult years and sound mind has a right to determine what shall be done with his own body; and a surgeon who performs an operation without his patient's consent commits an assault, for which he is liable in damages" (211 N.Y. 125, 105 N.E. 92).

Because it so clearly articulated the central importance of patient self-determination, the judgment in *Schloendorff* has been seen as critical to the development of the legal doctrine of informed consent. But, in truth, there were quite a few judgments in the early part of the twentieth century in which appeal was made to a patient's right not to be touched without prior consent. In some there was also recognition of the fact that, in order to exercise self-determination, a patient has to weigh the dangers and risks of surgery and other medical interventions against the anticipated benefits. That being so, subsequent case law can be seen as having made more explicit the need not only for consent to be given, but for information to be disclosed to the patient so as to enable the patient's consent to be informed. Hence, the development of the legal doctrine of informed consent went hand in hand with the establishment of a duty of disclosure for health-care professionals (though, as will emerge, not one of ensuring understanding).

Even though the American case, *Salgo v. Leland Stanford Jr. University Board of Trustees*, is perhaps best known for coining the phrase "informed consent," it can also be called into service to highlight a problem about just what the legal duty of disclosure requires. Mr Salgo underwent a treatment (which is no longer used) involving puncturing the aorta through the back in order to inject a radio-opaque dye, and was left with permanent paralysis of the legs. According to the direction given to the jury: "The physician has . . . discretion [to withhold alarming information from the patient] consistent, of course, with the full disclosure of facts necessary to an informed consent" ([1957] 317 P.2d 170 (Cal. Ct. App.) at 181).

It is obvious that the direction given to the jury was confused. There simply cannot be any discretion to withhold alarming information if *full* disclosure of the facts necessary for informed consent is required (Katz 1984: 60ff). But *Salgo* did at least highlight the issue of the extent and nature of disclosure required to facilitate informed patient consent even granted that, for reasons of practicality, disclosure can never be entire and complete. Various subsequent cases were resolved by courts requiring only that disclosure conform to the "professional practice standard," namely, what a reasonable health-care practitioner would do under similar circumstances. To do any less, it was held, would be tantamount to negligence. However, it quite quickly became apparent that the professional practice standard set the bar too low, a point forcefully brought home in another landmark American case, *Canterbury v. Spence* ([1972] 464 F.2d 772 (D.C. Cir.)), in which the patient fell out of his hospital bed after undergoing a laminectomy and suffered major paralysis. No warning had been given about the possibility of this rare outcome. The professional practice standard was held to be inadequate because it failed to respect patient self-determination. Given this role for patient self-determination, the professional practice standard had to give way to a patient-centered "reasonable person standard" – in effect, what any reasonable patient would consider it material to know, as against what it might be customary for professionals to disclose (Faden and Beauchamp 1986: 133ff). This single move served to overcome three main weaknesses of the professional practice standard: first, that agreed professional standards of disclosure were typically set too low to satisfy patient demand for information; second, that there were no agreed standards for new procedures; and, third, that patients were put at a significant disadvantage in having to rely upon expert witnesses (usually other health-care practitioners) in disputes about standards of care (Berg et al. 2001: 46f).

The adoption of a reasonable person standard signaled that, as far as the law was concerned, health-care practitioners had to make a greater effort to get patients to participate in decision-making about their own health care, something we have already seen to be morally required. But until quite recently, courts have never imposed the yet stronger requirement that practitioners must disclose (without qualification or restriction) *whatever* the patient might consider material. Thus, for example, in *Canterbury* it was made explicit (at 787) that to require such a standard would be unreasonable on the ground that only the patient's word could settle a dispute as to whether she would have consented had she been adequately informed about the risks of a procedure. However, as will be mentioned below when I consider which risks ought to be disclosed, the judgment in a recent Australian case raised the bar in relation to disclosure of risks far higher than in any previous case and has begun to have an influence in other jurisdictions.

I have been considering the evolutionary development of legal protection for the autonomy of patients through health-care professionals being required to satisfy specific standards for disclosure of health-care information. It is important to remember the context for these developments – namely, they have stemmed from legal determinations of whether particular health-care practitioners (the defendants) have adequately informed their patients (the plaintiffs). Tort law is about obtaining redress, so the decisions were not motivated by a desire to provide advice for practitioners on what to tell their patients. But some legislation has been introduced in the last couple of decades aimed at insuring that practitioners provide better information to their patients. By putting the judicial opinions and legislative enactments together, it is possible to provide guidelines on what practitioners should disclose. Four *elements* of disclosure have come to be considered necessary for informed patient consent: the nature of the proposed procedure; its risks; whether there are alternatives to it (including that of not treating); and, its benefits (Berg et al. 2001: 53–65).

The nature of the procedure

Patients should be advised whether a procedure is merely diagnostic, or is intended to be therapeutic, given that ordinarily their reason for seeking help is the relief of suffering. Among other aspects of the procedure that should be disclosed are whether it is invasive (i.e. involves physically entering some part of the body), and, if so, what part of the body will be entered and how; what effect, if any, there will be on that bodily part; whether an anesthetic, a blood transfusion, or an X-ray or scan will be needed; how long the procedure will take; where the procedure will be carried out; and whether the procedure is experimental.

The risks of the procedure

The element that has been most emphasized in the courts has been the nature of the risks associated with a health-care procedure, but within bioethics, too, there has been significant discussion, as is exemplified in the debate about the risks to patients occasioned by variability in the performance of surgeons (Clarke and Oakley 2007). While it has to be borne in mind that disclosure of risks is only a necessary, not a sufficient, condition for obtaining informed consent, patients do need to know about the kind of risks they face, how likely it is that those risks will eventuate, and, if they do, what the effects will be and when they will occur. Of course, these features won't matter equally for all patients in all circumstances – age, life expectancy, and occupation are three obvious considerations that can bear directly on how material a risk is to a particular patient – but it is the patient who should decide how much they matter.

The likelihood of a risk eventuating is clearly of importance to patients. But many practitioners appear to believe that if something (even something serious) is very unlikely to occur, there is no need to disclose the possibility. The finding in a recent court case in Australia (where, as in many other places outside America, there had been a notable reluctance to override a reasonable professional standard in favor of a reasonable person standard), shows that such a belief is out of step with contemporary ideas about patient autonomy. In *Rogers v. Whitaker* ([1992] 175 CLR 479, [1993] 4 Med LR 79 (High Court of Australia)), the plaintiff, who went to the defendant ophthalmic surgeon for a routine procedure on her bad right eye (in which she had little sight because of a childhood accident), ended up losing the sight in her good left eye as well, as a result of a condition known as sympathetic ophthalmia. Evidence was given that there was a 1 in 14,000 chance of such a result. The plaintiff, unaware of this risk, did not ask about it (although she was insistent about knowing of any risks to her good eye), and the defendant did not inform her of it (though he was aware it was a remote risk). The High Court of Australia, in finding for the plaintiff, held that when even a fairly remote risk is considered by a patient to be material to her decision about whether to agree to a procedure, she should be advised of that risk to enable her to make an autonomous decision. (Subsequent court judgments in, for example,

Castell v. de Greef [1994] (4) SA 408 (Cape Provincial Division of the Supreme Court of South Africa), and *Smith v. Tunbridge Wells Health Authority* [1994] 5 Med LR 334, have shown the influence of the judgment in *Rogers v. Whitaker.*)

In addition to knowing about the likelihood of a risk eventuating, it is important, too, for a patient to know when the risk might materialize. The patient is then in a better position to decide how much weight to put on its possible occurrence. Finally, it is not just the more serious of the risks to which a patient is likely to be exposed that a health-care practitioner needs to disclose, but also risks that are generally considered less serious and even risks that are considered common knowledge. As regards the former, it is very important that lesser risks be disclosed if only because some outcomes represent "a fate worse than death" for particular patients despite others considering them of far less significance. As regards the latter, if a reasonable person standard is to apply, health-care practitioners ought to be able to assume that a competent patient knows what a reasonable person could be expected to know.

The alternatives, if any, to the procedure

Where there are other procedures that might be offered to a patient than the one preferred by the health-care practitioner, it is important that those alternatives be disclosed. As was seen earlier, once it is acknowledged that patients have other interests than their health interests, health-care practitioners are obligated not simply to decide (beneficently) what would be best for a patient. A surgeon's preferred strategy might not coincide with a patient's simply because the patient may wish to give weight to non-medical considerations. (Consider, famously, the way that women have not always been advised of alternative, less disfiguring approaches to breast cancer than radical mastectomy.) It is particularly important that alternatives be discussed when the practitioner's preferred strategy comes down to personal taste (cf. the significance of this consideration in relation to, for example, some procedures in obstetrics like episiotomies and Cesarean sections), or where the professional is not able to offer or perform an alternative procedure.

Benefits of the procedure

If the first three elements have been properly dealt with, it will usually be unnecessary to spell out the benefits of the proposed procedure, such as that it will relieve suffering. However, when a procedure is experimental, or when there is reason to think that their suffering will not be fully relieved, patients need to know of these things in order to assess how worthwhile it will be for them to undergo the proposed procedure.

These, then, are the four elements in which adequate disclosure consists. But, though many practitioners have wished to focus on disclosure, and the courts have frequently appeared content to grant that wish, adequacy of disclosure is only a necessary condition for obtaining informed consent. There can be no truly informed consent without an accurate understanding of what has been disclosed. The need both for disclosure by the practitioner and understanding on the part of the patient shows that informed consent involves the participation of both, even if it is the patient's understanding that is ultimately the more critical. The clear implication is that there should be an insistence on health-care practitioners making a good faith effort to ensure that their patients understand the nature, risks, and benefits of procedures they are to undergo; this, in turn, will have implications both for institutional practices for obtaining informed consent and for the sort of evidence which might be tendered in a civil court to support a health-care practitioner's belief that a patient did understand information material to her treatment.

The Exceptions

I turn now to the final matter I flagged for discussion, namely, exceptions to the requirement of obtaining informed consent from competent patients. These exceptions have been well set out elsewhere (e.g. Meisel 1979; Berg et al. 2001: 75–91), so I can be brief. There are three kinds of exception to which I shall draw attention: waiver, therapeutic privilege, and emergency.

I have insisted that disclosure of information does not exhaust the idea of informed consent. It is also necessary that patients understand the information with which they are provided and then freely give their consent to any proposed procedure. Both of these are required if there is to be autonomous participation by patients in decision-making about their health care. These requirements are, however, prone to come apart in exceptional circumstances. Consider the situation with waivers. Let it be granted that a patient has a right to waive disclosure of information. Nevertheless, she should not be put in a position where she thinks she should exercise that right because it is what her health-care practitioner would prefer. I mentioned previously that patients may be manipulated into adopting views that have that effect. So, while it can be a legitimate exercise of a patient's autonomy for her to waive her right to disclosure, and advice should, therefore, be given to that effect, health-care practitioners should not initiate discussions about waivers if they wish to avoid it being suggested that they manipulated a patient into waiving her right to make her own decision. Even though waivers are compatible with respect for patient autonomy, their use should, nonetheless, be regarded with some skepticism. A patient who is frightened by, or in denial about, her illness may need to be encouraged by her health-care practitioner to reflect openly and fully on her illness rather than resort to waiving her right to participate in the determination of suitable treatment. Patients sometimes waive their right to be informed because of a mistaken belief that the practitioner is the one with the relevant expertise who should, therefore, make the treatment decisions. However, if those decisions cannot properly be made without reference to the patient's own values and aspirations, the exercise of a waiver will be inappropriate. I do not deny that there will be some patients who are made anxious, depressed, or even confused by having to make decisions about their health care, and for whom it will, therefore, be quite appropriate to exercise their right to a waiver. But, in order to limit the risk of well-intentioned misuses of this right, it seems advisable, at least initially, for health-care practitioners to treat waivers skeptically (cf. Wear 1998: 162ff).

Larger issues arise with the idea of therapeutic privilege. According to this idea, a health-care practitioner may withhold information that would otherwise have to be disclosed if it is judged that disclosure would be likely to lead to harm to a patient. There is a risk that when a practitioner thinks it is possible that a patient's refusal of treatment will prove harmful, therapeutic privilege may be invoked. This would jeopardize the autonomy of the patient. Again, at least initially, it seems best to set the boundaries for the invocation of therapeutic privilege by reference to whether a patient has competently decided on a course of action, not by reference to whether such a course would possibly be harmful. (Related issues are treated in chapters 26 and 27 in this volume.) Some of those who advocate securing a place for therapeutic privilege urge it in a relatively weak form – namely, as the position that is defensible whenever disclosure of *risks* would be likely to lead to harmful consequences (e.g. triggering an independent health risk, or exacerbating the one being treated) that would undermine competent decision-making. Indeed, such a view was put in the case of *Canterbury v. Spence* mentioned previously. There, it was claimed (in relation to disclosure of risks) that "it is recognized that patients occasionally become so ill or emotionally distraught on disclosure as to foreclose a rational decision" ([1972] 464 F.2d 772 (D.C. Cir.) at 789). Since patients may already be in a vulnerable state because of illness or injury, to entertain a stronger version of therapeutic privilege would be likely not only to jeopardize their autonomy, but their trust in their health-care practitioners too (cf. Dworkin 1988: 120).

Finally, there is an issue concerning how to proceed in an emergency. In some emergencies, patients will lack competence to consent to any procedure; in others, there will be no time to determine whether the patient has sufficient understanding of her options for care-givers to be confident of her competence to consent. In consequence, in the absence of an advance directive that provides clear guidance as to how a patient would prefer to be treated, it will often be necessary in an emergency to make an exception to the requirement to obtain informed consent before giving medical treatment. However, it is plausible to believe that, in general, reasonable patients want to be provided with effective treatments if they are available, including in emergencies, and especially if they face a serious risk of mortality or morbidity. Accordingly, when a patient's views about treatment are not known, it is no violation of the reasonable person standard to provide treatment in an emergency without first obtaining informed consent.

But matters are much less clear in two other sorts of circumstance (cf. Wear 1998: 159ff). Consider the use of aggressive life-prolonging treatment in emergency situations involving patients whose death is known to be imminent. In emergencies of this sort, to proceed to give such treatment will often be inappropriate. These cases serve to highlight the importance of holding discussions beforehand with patients receiving end-of-life care with a view to avoiding the administration of unwanted life-prolonging treatment. A second troublesome sort of circumstance arises when it is possible to disclose just enough information to an apparently competent patient to obtain consent to the emergency procedures, but the consent will be less informed than would normally be required. While it might seem that to endeavor to obtain consent in such a circumstance has the merit of honoring the idea of a patient having the maximum feasible say in what happens to her body, it is doubtful that it is a wise way to proceed. To begin with, though the patient may appear to be competent (despite, perhaps, suffering from shock or loss of blood), her choice will *ex hypothesi* be based on incomplete information. Furthermore, because the patient has not been provided with all relevant information, the chance that she may refuse the emergency procedure has to be taken seriously. If she were to refuse, treatment would have to be withheld until further discussion, and perhaps even counseling, had taken place (which would hardly be feasible in an emergency). On the other hand, to ignore her refusal would make a mockery of the process of seeking her consent. On the assumption that a clear advance directive has not been issued, the wiser part in an emergency would, again, therefore, seem to be to make an exception to the requirement to obtain informed consent *unless* the patient's competence is not at issue *and* the opportunity exists to provide her with all relevant information.

References

Berg, J. W., Appelbaum, P. S., Lidz, C. W., and Parker, L. S. (2001). *Informed Consent: Legal Theory and Clinical Practice*, 2nd edn. New York: Oxford University Press.

Berlin, I. (1969). *Four Essays on Liberty*. Oxford: Clarendon Press.

Brock, D. (1987). Informed consent. In T. Regan and D. Van De Veer (eds.), *Health Care Ethics*. Philadelphia: Temple University Press, pp. 98–126.

Buchanan, A. and Brock, D. (1989). *Deciding for Others: The Ethics of Surrogate Decision Making*. New York: Cambridge University Press.

Clarke, S. and Oakley, J. (eds.) (2007). *Informed Consent and Clinician Accountability: The Ethics of Report Cards on Surgeon Performance*. Cambridge: Cambridge University Press.

Dworkin, G. (1988). *The Theory and Practice of Autonomy*. New York: Cambridge University Press.

Faden, R. and Beauchamp, T. L., in collaboration with King, N. M. P. (1986). *A History and Theory of Informed Consent*. New York: Oxford University Press.

Katz, J. (1984). *The Silent World of Doctor and Patient*. New York: The Free Press.

Meisel, A. (1979). The "exceptions" to the informed consent doctrine: striking a balance between competing values in medical decision-making. *Wisconsin Law Review* 79: 413–88.

Savulescu, J. (1995). Rational non-interventional paternalism: why doctors ought to make judgments of what is best for their patients. *Journal of Medical Ethics* 21: 327–31.

Wear, S. (1998). *Informed Consent: Patient Autonomy and Physician Beneficence Within Clinical Medicine*, 2nd edn. Washington, DC: Georgetown University Press.

Young, R. (1986). *Personal Autonomy: Beyond Negative and Positive Liberty*. London: Croom Helm.

Young, R. (2007). *Medically Assisted Death*. Cambridge: Cambridge University Press.

45

Patients Doubtfully Capable or Incapable of Consent

CARL ELLIOTT

If the concept of autonomy has played the starring role in the development of bioethics, then the problems of non-autonomous patients have been its supporting cast. For better or worse, the way bioethics has come to see the problems of incompetent and marginally competent patients has been colored by the way it has seen the problems of competent, autonomous adults. The rights of competent adults were the focus of a considerable amount of the earliest work in bioethics – issues surrounding informed consent, for example, or the patient's right to refuse life-sustaining medical treatment. Moreover, quite a lot of this work got its start in the individualistic, rights-conscious United States. Given this background, it should be no surprise that incompetent patients have presented bioethics with some of its most troubling ethical problems, and that the field is still struggling to find a conceptual framework in which to consider them.

Indeed, the very fact that all incompetent and marginally competent patients are often lumped together in the same category says something about the way the field has evolved. It is only in contrast to more commonly agreed-upon attitudes toward competent patients that incompetence comes to be identified as a morally distinctive feature. Yet identifying it as the most morally relevant feature about a patient downplays the fact that incompetent and marginally competent patients comprise a vastly diverse range of human beings who present very different ethical problems. From an ethical point of view, an anencephalic infant, a 65-year-old woman with Alzheimer's disease, a violent man with schizophrenia, and a 6-year-old with incurable lymphoma are probably divided by more than they share. Not only do different incompetent patients present different ethical problems, they also occupy radically different places in our moral and emotional lives. We generally think of children, for example, in ways very different from the ways we think of incompetent adults. While our attitudes toward adults are often centered on respect for the patient's previous values and the narrative of her past life, our moral attitudes toward children are commonly located within notions of dependence, protection, growth, and the child's relationship to her parents.

Many of the ethical problems associated with pediatrics have developed in situations where there is a divergence between the attitudes of parents and health-care workers toward the care of a child. For example, parents of religious faiths such as the Jehovah's Witnesses or Christian Scientists often have moral and religious objections to certain medical treatments for their children in situations where health-care workers (in agreement with broader Western society) generally regard the treatments as medically necessary for a child's well-being. More generally, conflicts between parents and health-care workers arise over the use of life-sustaining medical interventions such as cardio-pulmonary resuscitation, mechanical ventilation, or artificial nutrition. Physicians sometimes undertake interventions on a severely ill or disabled child, for example, that the child's parents see as excessively burdensome. On the other hand, parents sometimes demand interventions that physicians see as futile. Some of the starkest conflicts have come with anencephalic infants or children in a persistent vegetative state whose parents want treatment pursued, regardless of the poor prognosis, out of a belief that even unconscious life should be protected and preserved. In neonatology, such conflicts between parents and health-care workers are complicated still further, because aggressive medical interventions on premature, severely ill, or disabled newborns must often be undertaken under conditions of grave uncertainty (Arras 1984). The outcomes for such newborns often span a great range, from a full cure and normal development, to life with severe mental and physical disability, to death after prolonged and burdensome treatment.

Problems surrounding aggressive or life-sustaining medical treatment also arise for incompetent adults, and often center around conflicts between the opinions of health-care workers, the patient's previously expressed wishes about treatment and the wishes of various members of the patient's family. Yet the care of incompetent and marginally competent adults has also raised a much broader range of questions. Psychiatrists deal with a number of relatively specialized ethical questions about the care of mentally ill persons, many of which intersect with legal issues: questions about the conditions under which a psychiatric patient accused of wrongdoing is competent to stand trial, or when a psychiatrist is justified in breaching confidentiality, and when he has a duty to warn the victims of a potentially violent patient. Psychiatrists must also consider the question of when it is justifiable to confine or treat an incompetent or marginally competent patient against his (incompetent) expressed wishes – for instance, with antipsychotic drugs or, less commonly, with electroconvulsive therapy. The fact that many mentally ill and disabled patients live in long-term care institutions raises many questions of its own, such as the effects of institutionalization on the quality of informed consent.

While there is still fierce debate on many of these issues, over the past decade or two a fairly broad consensus has emerged in the bioethics literature about two questions that are relevant to many incompetent patients: how competence should be assessed, and how decisions should be made for patients who are incompetent. What I will do here is outline the standard approaches to these questions, and then point out several of the problems that they leave unanswered or unasked.

The Standard Models of Decision-making Capacity and Surrogate Decision-making

Decision-making capacity or competence (the legal term) is conventionally defined as the ability to perform a task – here, to make decisions about one's medical care, or about taking part in biomedical research (Faden and Beauchamp 1986: 290). Patients with decision-making capacity, it is widely agreed, generally have the right to make their own health-care decisions, even decisions that others believe are contrary to the patient's interests. However, as a result of illness, disability, or immaturity, some patients do not have the mental abilities required to make these decisions. If given the opportunity, many of these patients would make decisions that are risky, dangerous, or which they simply would not otherwise make if they were thinking soundly. Assessments of competence (or capacity) protect incompetent patients from the consequences of such decisions, while also protecting the rights of competent patients to make decisions for themselves.

Most writers agree that what is most important for judging competence is how patients reach their decisions, rather than what they decide. Merely because a patient reaches a conclusion that his physician regards as unreasonable – say, refusing effective treatment for a life-threatening illness, or deciding to enroll in a risky research protocol – does not mean that the patient is incompetent. Since different patients have different values and needs, they may reach different conclusions even when presented with the same choice. While it is a matter of debate exactly what mental abilities are necessary for competence, many standards require that a patient have a relatively stable set of goals and values; be capable of understanding the consequences of the decision, including its risks and benefits; be able to reason about the relevant information and communicate a choice; and be able to appreciate how the decision will affect them personally (Dunn et al. 2006; Grisso and Appelbaum 1995; President's Commission 1982).

Often patients are clearly not competent, but their families and physicians must still make decisions for them (Buchanan and Brock 1989). For these patients, a hierarchy of decision-making standards has evolved, based largely on commonly held notions of respect for persons. First, when patients have expressed any wishes about the treatment in question while competent (through an advance directive, for example), their surrogate decision-makers should abide by those wishes. Second, when incompetent persons have not expressed any such wishes, surrogates should rely on the "substituted judgment" standard, according to which decisions are reached according to what patients would have decided if they were able, based on the patients' values, goals, and desires. Finally, in the event that a patient has never been competent – a small child, for example – the surrogate must make decisions based on the "best interests standard." What the interests of a patient are is often unclear or controversial, but they are generally understood to include, at a minimum, certain basic interests such as avoiding pain and disability and having conscious life extended.

The problem of competent irrationality

Some patients understand all the important aspects of their decision, including its risks and benefits, yet still make decisions that seem irrational (Brock and Wartman 1990). Sometimes these decisions are irrational even from the perspective of the patient's own goals and desires. For example, an apparently competent diabetic patient being asked to consent to the amputation of a gangrenous toe might refuse, even if avoiding death is more important to him than avoiding the amputation, and even if he realizes that his refusal is threatening his life. What are we to make of such a choice? Doctors and nurses, not to mention family members, are understandably reluctant to abide by a patient's decision when that decision is irrational, especially if it is also self-destructive. Yet irrationality is a part of ordinary life. At times we all deceive ourselves, take poor risks, make impulsive decisions, act out of fear or anxiety, downplay future risks or benefits in favor of present ones, and otherwise behave in ways that seem unreasonable, idiosyncratic, or odd. Should an irrational decision be given the same degree of respect as a rational decision?

A related problem revolves around the question of which mental abilities are relevant to competence. Severely depressed patients may be capable of reasoning and deliberating about a decision, yet make very poor decisions, at least partly because of their depression (Elliott 1997). They may understand the risks of their decision, for instance, yet simply not care about them. Is a severely depressed person who wishes to die competent to refuse life-saving treatment? Similarly, people with addictions may want to resist a desire and understand that giving in to the desire is contrary to their own self-interest, yet still find the desire extraordinarily difficult to resist (Charland 2002). Is a heroin addict competent to consent to a research study involving the administration of heroin?

The decisions of children raise similar problems. The decision of a child may be influenced by the views of his or her parents or by other factors to such an extent that a clinician might reasonably question whether that decision is truly the child's own. A 12-year-old child of parents who are Jehovah's Witnesses may refuse a life-saving blood transfusion and, further, may appear capable of understanding both the religious reasons why Jehovah's Witnesses regard blood transfusions as morally wrong and the brute medical facts relevant to that decision. Yet it may still be unclear whether the child's refusal is competent. This is partly because it is unclear where the point lies at which a child's decision becomes truly authentic and autonomous, and partly because it is unclear what sort of factors should cause one to question a child's competence. Some clinicians might see fear, guilt, and the influence of the child's parents as reasons to question a child's competence, while others would see them as parts of ordinary decision-making.

The problem of personal identity

The standard way of making decisions for incompetent but previously competent patients has come to be the patient's previously expressed wishes. Yet many neurologically damaged or demented patients are not, in some sense, the same persons they were before the damage or dementia. This is especially obvious for patients who are permanently vegetative, where the patient's higher brain functions are absent, but it is also true for patients with other types of cerebral damage, such as stroke or trauma. The patient's personality and values may have changed dramatically; his memory of his past life may be impaired; his intellectual and other mental abilities may be severely damaged. When this broad gap in identity separates the patient's current and past selves, it becomes a matter for debate how much weight should be given to the wishes, values or desires of the patient as he was in the past. Should the patient's previously expressed wishes prevail even when they seem to run squarely against his current interests?

Sometimes we may have reason to think that the person would have changed his mind if he could be made aware of subsequent events and developments – for example, a man in a persistent vegetative state from traumatic injury who, before his injury, had never been sick in his life, who had expressed a lifelong wish to have his life extended as long as possible regardless of the circumstances, but whose family feels would have changed his mind if he had ever been in a hospital intensive care unit. At other times the patient's wishes and values in the past may directly contradict his present wishes and values (Dresser 1995; Nelson 1995). Take, for example, a writer who has devoted her life to matters of the mind, and for whom the mental deterioration associated with Alzheimer's disease has always seemed the cruelest way for a life to end. She has told her son that if her mental faculties were to deteriorate, she would rather have euthanasia. What she regards as most humiliating of all is the lack of awareness of one's condition that dementia brings. Yet when her mental faculties eventually deteriorate, she seems perfectly content with her life. She has no memory of her earlier wishes, and as far as anyone can determine, she would not now want her life to end. What value should we place on the wishes and values of a patient's previous self, and what should we place on those of the current self?

The problem of involuntary "altruism"

It is an article of faith in pediatric hospitals that medical decisions for a child should serve that child's best interests. Yet some medical interventions are clearly not in the child's interests, and in fact are designed for other purposes. For example, surgeons often transplant kidneys or bone marrow from children too young to consent, usually matched siblings of the transplant recipient. Unlike the conventional medical interventions for which parents are asked to consent on behalf of a child, transplantation from child donors exposes children to risks that are not balanced by commensurate benefits – or at least not benefits to them personally (Dwyer and Vig 1995). This problem parallels a problem in certain types of clinical research, where children undergo risks or discomforts not for their own benefit, but to generate scientific knowledge that may eventually benefit others. For example, Phase 1 cancer trials are designed to test the safety and toxicity of new regimens for the treatment of cancer. The subjects in Phase 1 pediatric cancer trials are usually children whose cancer has a very poor prognosis and for whom standard therapy has not been effective. These trials are not designed to test the effectiveness of the new therapy, and the chance that children enrolled in the trials will experience any therapeutic benefit is relatively small. As with parents of living organ donors, parents of potential subjects in clinical research that has a poor risk–benefit ratio are asked to expose their child to risks, harms, or discomforts for the sake of someone (or something) other than themselves.

When competent adults take risks or undergo harms for the sake of others, we ordinarily consider their actions not morally obligatory, but altruistic or supererogatory – beyond the call of duty. Certainly they are not things that an adult should be forced to do. Yet if this is true, on what grounds can we justify such interventions on young children? Many of the justifications given in the past have a notably ad hoc feel about them. For example, some writers have argued for organ transplantation from living siblings by appealing to the psychological benefit that the sibling would gain from donating. On these grounds, a case is made for donation as an intervention that is in the best interests of the donor. Yet while there is no doubt some sense in which a child, at least an older child, might benefit by being volunteered to help his or her brother or sister, it is precisely because undergoing such risks are ordinarily not regarded as being in an adult's interests that they are seen as altruistic (Crouch and Elliott 1999).

Other writers have appealed to a sort of hypothetical autonomy, suggesting that a child can be "volunteered" if at a later point she would come to see the intervention as ethically justifiable, or if the intervention is something for which she would have a moral obligation to volunteer if she were able (McCormick 1974). Yet what a child will come to see as morally acceptable will depend on the interests and character he or she develops, and often these things cannot easily be predicted (Ackerman 1979). Moreover, at least some of the interventions in question, such as Phase 1 trials, are not generally regarded as something in which adults have a moral duty to take part. If taking part is not obligatory for adults, the argument that it is justifiable for children is radically weakened. If we admit that an adult stands on solid moral ground in refusing to take part, then the ground for "volunteering" a child unable to consent seems much less firm.

The problem of the moral imagination

Deciding what kinds of medical care an incompetent patient ought to receive often means trying to decide what kind of care would be in the patient's interests. How aggressively one should treat a newborn with severe spina bifida; whether a mentally retarded adolescent with cancer should undergo a burdensome course of chemotherapy with uncertain efficacy; determining the point at which a patient with schizophrenia should be treated against his will; deciding whether to treat pneumonia in a child with cerebral palsy and profound neurological impairment: understanding the interests of such patients requires a kind of imaginative leap. Like anthropologists who must try to understand cultures vastly different from their own, health-care workers must try to understand patients whose lives differ dramatically from theirs by virtue of illness or disability.

Imaginatively sharing another person's particular, subjective point of view, however, requires imagining a logical impossibility. It asks the question: what would it be like for me, if I were someone else? The most problematic cases arise when we must imagine what life is like for a person whose mental life appears radically different from our own, as a result of mental retardation, mental disability, or mental illness. This kind of imaginative leap requires us to imagine what it would be like not to have the mental abilities that we have, including those by virtue of which we are able to imagine. Adam Smith thought that in imagining what the experience of the mentally impaired is like, a person is tempted to "imagine what he himself would feel if he were reduced to the same unhappy situation, and what is perhaps impossible, regard it with his present reason and judgment" (Smith 1982: 12). There are at least two serious dangers to this sort of exercise. One danger comes with trying to imagine the experience of the permanently unconscious, such as anencephalic children or permanently vegetative persons. This is the danger of imagining, in Nagel's words, that "there is something that it is like" to be permanently unconscious, and making a misguided judgment as to the permanently unconscious person's quality of life.

The other serious danger is that of underestimating the quality of a mentally impaired or disabled person's life. The fact that I would not want to live such a life, or the fact that I would not regard my life as worthwhile if I were to lose my mental faculties, says little about the quality of that person's life. For Hauerwas, the "crucial point is that the retarded do not feel or understand their retardation as we do, or imagine we would, but as they do. We have no right or basis to attribute our assumed unhappiness or suffering to them" (1986: 67). The reality of these dangers has been made evident by the willingness of physicians and hospitals to deny treatments to patients on the basis of their mental disabilities, such as the often mild mental handicap associated with Down syndrome.

The problem of asymmetrical relationships

One serious criticism of the "best interests" standard of decision-making for children is that by focusing solely on the child it overlooks the role of the family (Nelson and Nelson 1995). This can leave us with a kind of misplaced individualism, as if the only ethically important considerations are those that have to do with the child himself – intrinsic abilities like his intellect, his awareness, his physical abilities, and so on. But this is an odd way to look at children, since what is most striking about children is not their intrinsic abilities but their dependence. Children exist in relationships of dependence on their families, and with time those relationships become deeper and richer and more complex. It seems ungainly to try to consider children's interests apart from the interests of their families because their interests are bound up together. This is more than simply saying that parents are best placed to judge the interests of their child; it is saying that very often their interests are the same. It would not be exaggerating to say that very often the worst thing that could happen to parents would be for something to happen to their children.

Because of these kinds of questions, bioethics has begun to pay more attention to families, and has tried to locate our ethical thinking about children within the parent–child relationship. Some writers have argued that what is morally important about children cannot be reduced solely to their intrinsic capacities, but instead needs also to take account somehow of their relationships with others. What matters morally about children is connected to the fact that they are loved by their parents, and what we value about human beings is not just their intellect but also their capacity for these deep human relationships.

But with some children – for example, those who are left with profound neurological damage from traumatic and anoxic brain injury – these relationships are often completely asymmetrical. Many of these children will never be able to experience the kind of love that they are given, and they will never be able to give it back. Many will never even be able to recognize their parents. What sort of respect and value should we place on these kinds of relationships? Many families seem to have made a place in their lives for such profoundly damaged children, and when it comes to questions about medical care, they want the child treated very aggressively, even when the treatment is very burdensome or painful. Here health-care workers are often torn between a desire to respect the parent–child relationship and the realization that the child is not really a participant in that relationship. Often parents of such children make such tremendous emotional sacrifices for the child, and labor under such guilt about their responsibility for the child's care, that physicians wonder whether it is ethically justifiable to place all the burden of decision-making on the parents.

The problem of meaning and the profoundly damaged child

Human activities and discourse are played out against a backdrop of understandings – some widely shared, some rather more fragmented – about what counts as a good life. These are not necessarily a matter of choice for us, or not entirely: they are the framework of tradition and culture within which our choices are made. Part of this framework concerns understandings about what might be called the meaning and significance of life: questions about the way in which we make sense of our lives, what gives our lives significance, beliefs about how one ought to live, stories that we tell ourselves about successful lives and failed ones (Taylor 1989). Different cultures and eras have answered these kinds of questions in different ways, of course, and many individuals will answer them differently even within contemporary Western culture. Yet some widely shared Western views may call into question the meaning of the life of a person with profound neurological damage. These questions present deep problems for decisions about the conditions under which such lives should be prolonged.

For example, when we in the West talk about what gives our lives meaning, and the reasons we have chosen to do what we have done with our lives, we often find common ground between us. Many of us talk about the people we love, such as our families, and we also talk about our work – about a calling or a sense of mission, the satisfaction of artistic creativity or taking part in a broader social or political movement. Charles Taylor (1989) calls this emphasis on family and work the "affirmation of ordinary life." Moreover, this view locates meaning at least in part within the individual himself. That is, we ordinarily think that the meaning of our lives has something to do with us as individuals and the choices we make – with discovering and following a calling, with looking inward and finding one's own special character or talents, with developing a relationship with God and so on.

What is important to realize, however, is that this kind of life is inaccessible to many people with profound neurological damage. If a person is incapable of appreciating and sustaining the emotional bonds of family, and incapable of finding meaning through work, she will not be able to live the kind of life that is widely regarded in our culture as meaningful. It could be otherwise, of course – for example, in a culture in which meaning is found through occupying one's place in the natural order of things, or in which all life is seen as glorifying God, or in any number of other cosmologies. But these are not our Western cosmologies. This may help to explain why such profoundly damaged lives seem so tragic to us, even when we realize that the disabled child is not actually in pain. There is a gap between the kind of life through which the rest of us achieve those goods that make it worthwhile, and what we see as the trajectory that this child's life will inevitably take.

This struggle to find meaning in such profoundly damaged lives places us in a difficult position when it comes to clinical decisions. On the one hand there are extremely powerful moral ideals in our culture that make us very reluctant to deny these children beneficial medical treatment. Our tradition of rights and equality makes us wary of withholding treatment from a person because of her intelligence. Moreover, we realize that these are the most vulnerable and dependent of human lives, and that they may have deep significance for other people, such as the child's family. Yet these ideals lead us into a kind of ethical double-talk. We feel as if these lives deserve respect, yet, at the same time, they fail to meet the criteria by which we count our own lives as meaningful. We want to protect vulnerable lives, yet our own measure of the good life for ourselves does not include a life like this.

This is not to say that we can simply decide to discard or change the broader framework of culture and tradition within which such choices are made. It is only to suggest that we are unlikely to achieve a lasting or ethically satisfying resolution to these choices unless we take these broader questions seriously.

References

Ackerman, T. F. (1979). Fooling ourselves with child autonomy and assent in nontherapeutic clinical research. *Clinical Research* 27/5: 345–8.

Arras, J. D. (1984). Toward an ethic of ambiguity. *Hastings Center Report* 14/2: 25–33.

Brock, D. W. and Wartman, S. A. (1990). When competent patients make irrational choices. *New England Journal of Medicine* 322: 1595–9.

Buchanan, A. E. and Brock, D. W. (1989). *Deciding for Others: The Ethics of Surrogate Decision Making.* Cambridge: Cambridge University Press.

Charland, L. (2002). Cynthia's dilemma: consenting to heroin prescription. *American Journal of Bioethics* 2/2: 37–47.

Crouch, R. and Elliott, C. (1999). Moral agency and the family: the case of living related organ transplantation. *Cambridge Quarterly of Health Care Ethics* 8/3: 275–87.

Dresser, R. (1995). Dworkin on dementia: elegant theory, questionable policy. *Hastings Center Report* 25/6: 328.

Dunn, L. B., Nowrangi, M. A., Palmer, B. W., Jeste D. V., and Saks, E. R. (2006). Assessing decisional capacity for clinical research or treatment: a review of instruments. *American Journal of Psychiatry* 163: 1323–34.

Dwyer, J. and Vig, E. (1995). Rethinking transplantation between siblings. *Hastings Center Report* 24/5: 7–12.

Elliott, C. (1997). Caring about risks: are severely depressed patients competent to consent to research? *Archives of General Psychiatry* 54: 113–16.

Faden, R. and Beauchamp, T. (1986). *A History and Theory of Informed Consent.* New York: Oxford University Press.

Grisso, T. and Appelbaum, P. S. (1995). The MacArthur treatment competence study. I. Mental illness and competence to consent to treatment. *Law and Human Behavior* 19: 105–25.

Hauerwas, S. (1986). Suffer the retarded: should we prevent retardation? In P. R. Dodecki and R. M. Zaner (eds.), *Ethics of Dealing with Persons with Severe Handicaps.* Baltimore, MD: Paul H. Brooks, pp. 53–70.

McCormick, R. A. (1974). Proxy consent in the experimentation situation. *Perspectives in Biology and Medicine* 18: 2–20.

Nelson, J. L. (1995). Critical interests and sources of familial decision-making authority for incapacitated patients. *Journal of Law, Medicine and Ethics* 23: 143–8.

Nelson, J. L. and Nelson, H. L. (1995). *The Patient in the Family: An Ethics of Medicine and Families.* New York: Routledge.

President's Commission for the Study of Ethical Problems in Medicine and Biomedical and Behavioral Research (1982). *Making Health Care Decisions: The Ethical and Legal Implications of Informed Consent in the Patient–Practitioner Relationship.* Washington: US Government Printing Office.

Smith, A. (1982). *The Theory of Moral Sentiments.* Indianapolis, IN: Liberty Press.

Taylor, C. (1989). *Sources of the Self.* Cambridge, MA: Harvard University Press.

Further reading

Bloch, S., Chodoff, P., and Green, S. (eds.) (1999). *Psychiatric Ethics*, 3rd edn. Oxford: Oxford University Press.

Brody, H. and Bartholome, W. (1988). In the best interests of. . . . *Hastings Center Report* 18/6: 37–40.

Charland, L. (1998). Appreciation and emotion: theoretical reflections on the MacArthur treatment competence study. *Kennedy Institute of Ethics Journal* 8/4: 359–76.

Elliott, C. (2001). Attitudes, souls, and persons: children with severe neurological impairment. In C. Elliott (ed.), *Slow Cures and Bad Philosophers: Essays on Wittgenstein, Medicine and Bioethics.* Durham, NC: Duke University Press, pp. 89–102.

Freedman, B. (1975). A moral theory of informed consent. *Hastings Center Report* 5/4: 32–9.

Lantos, J. (1997). *Do We Still Need Doctors?* New York: Routledge.

Lidz, C., Meisel, A., Zerubavel, E., Carter, M., Sestak, R., and Roth, L. (1984). *Informed Consent: A Study of Decisionmaking in Psychiatry.* New York: Guilford Press.

Murray, T. (1996). *The Worth of a Child.* Berkeley: University of California Press.

National Bioethics Advisory Commission (1998). *Research Involving Persons with Mental Disorders that May Affect Decisionmaking Capacity.* Washington, DC.

President's Council on Bioethics (2005). *Taking Care: Ethical Caregiving in our Aging Society.* Washington, DC. Available at: www.bioethics.gov/reports/taking_care/index.html.

46

Ethics in Nursing Practice

JANET L. STORCH

Introduction

In every health-care workplace, values operate at individual and organizational levels. These values, influenced by societal values, affect the structure of the organization, the organizational resources available to health-care workers, and the interpersonal resources available for practice. The values may be stated or implied and they set the moral climate of the workplace (Rodney and Street 2004). The quality of nurses' work environments is currently a major focus of federal, provincial/state, and local authorities and associations. Work environments have become an issue because the "inappropriate application of knowledge from business and engineering has led to such problems as unsustainable staff reductions and excessive demands on a shrinking number of practitioners" (Austin 2007: 83).

This chapter will focus on the ethical concerns that nurses face working within the moral climate of their health agencies. A brief historical sketch of nursing ethics will be followed by an elaboration on the context of nursing practice and nursing ethics leading to a discussion of the insufficiency of bioethics for addressing everyday ethics. Current research in nursing ethics is utilized in this discussion and the chapter concludes with a focus on the renewal of nursing ethics and desired futures for nursing ethics.

Tracing a History of Nursing Ethics

In almost all traces of early attention to ethics in nursing, in Western and Eastern traditions, nursing values emanate from religious traditions of caring and compassion. In the Western world, there has been the influence of military values as well, including values of order, organization, hierarchy, loyalty, and devotion to duty. Florence Nightingale, considered the founder of secular nursing, instilled these types of values in "her nurses" during the Crimean war (1853–6) and they have been retained in the fabric of nursing. Nightingale also developed principles for nursing, and along with those general principles she emphasized the importance of character and character development in nursing students. She provided student and graduate nurses with practical ethics

based upon putting patients first, listening to them, and upholding their confidentiality (Nightingale 1860).

Nursing texts on ethics, written in the early 1900s (see, for example, Aikens 1935),
provide evidence of the primacy of the person in care as the focus of nurses' work. In
those texts, there was an emphasis on developing trusting relationships with patients,
their families, and friends; of working with patients in a non-judgmental manner;
of trying to imagine the experiences of the patient and learning to see things from his
or her point of view; and of focusing on the ethics of nurses' everyday work. Such
attention to the ethics of the everyday routine found in these early publications is
"striking given our recent rediscovery in nursing of the importance of everyday ethics
versus sensational issue-focused health ethics" (Storch and Kenny 2007: 482).

By the mid-1900s, hospitals began to become a necessary part of the landscape of
health care in ways not previously required. The acquisition of a growing plethora of
medical technology made it imperative that doctors have a place to use this technology in their medical practice. For several decades (and the process continues),
advances in medical technology have driven health care and often seem to drive
health ethics in ways that lead away from the person receiving care. By the late 1970s
nurses responded by promoting an advocacy role of nurses for their patients (Curtin
1979). Nurses' attention was focused mainly on the individual patient and his or
her needs, with limited attention directed toward problems of the wider system. The
diminishing attention to ethics in nursing practice during this period was likely a byproduct of hospital policy, with regulation and custom replacing nursing ethics. The result
was a period when etiquette dominated ethics (Lamb 2004).

With this growth in hospitals and technology came a subsequent backlash from
consumers of care who believed that their rights as patients were being ignored and
often dismissed in health care. It was through a consumer movement in health care
in Canada, for example, that ethical issues began to surface and were taken up via the
medium of rights language. In the early 1980s, I published a text, *Patients' Rights: Ethical
and Legal Issues in Health Care and Nursing*, that utilized patients' rights language as a
way to help nurses understand ethical and legal responsibilities in health care and in
nursing (Storch 1982). As part of an introduction to ethical theory in that text, the
ethical principles of autonomy, beneficence, nonmaleficence, and justice were used.
At the time, their use seemed appropriate for nurses, since teaching by "principles" was
(and, indeed, still is) common in nursing education (for example, principles of asepsis
and principles of communication). Two books on nursing ethics were published
around this time as well, one in the United Kingdom simply entitled *Nursing Ethics*
(Thompson et al. 2006 [1983]) and a joint American-Canadian authored text titled
Nursing Ethics: Theories and pragmatics (Curtin and Flaherty 1982).

During this same period, the bioethics movement took root in North America and
nurses began to focus on approaches to health ethics and nursing ethics as outlined
by leading bioethicists and biomedical ethicists. In large part, this focus included
extensive use of principles of ethics as outlined in the US Belmont Report (National
Commission 1978) and reinforced in the ethics text by Beauchamp and Childress
(2009 [1979]). As noted above, this approach to principles seemed to serve nursing
and helped nurses have a vocabulary in common with their medical colleagues.
However, many nurses began to realize that there seemed to be limited room for the

ethical issues and concerns of nurses in relying only on a "principled approach." Further, many philosophers and bioethicists tended to discount nursing ethics, seeing it (and all nurses' work for that matter) as only a subset of medical work and medical ethics.

The Sociopolitical Context of Nursing and Nursing Ethics

The dismissal of nursing work and nursing ethics has been part of the ongoing struggle of nursing as a primarily female profession. Being female and seeking a career such as nursing in the late 1800s and early 1900s was considered paradoxical, since proper women knew their place and for many it was to be in the home. For women who were in nursing, their adherence to a role of women similar to that taken in a household seemed to be (implicitly) expected in the hospital hierarchy (Johnstone 1999). Even in this century, devaluing of nursing work is common. For example, young women are still advised by some high school counselors that they are too intelligent to go into nursing; and nurses who have continued their studies to achieve a Master's or doctoral degree in nursing are often asked why, with all those years of study, they did not become a physician instead.

Multiple loyalties

The nursing pledge named after Nightingale clearly stated: "With loyalty will I endeavor to aide the physician in his work." Nursing students were taught that their first loyalty was to the doctor and the hospital. By default, patients became of secondary concern. In 1953, the International Council of Nurses (ICN) reinforced this loyalty by stating that nurses were obligated "to carry out physician's orders intelligently and loyally" (ICN 1953, cited in Storch 1982: 199–200). But this demand of loyalty to physicians became a serious point of contention for nurses as they faced (and continue to face) repeated conflicts with regard to this expectation (Mansell 2004). By 1973, the ICN code was changed to state as its first point of principle that "the nurse's primary responsibility is to those people who require nursing care" (ICN 1973, cited in Storch 1982: 201–2).

The fact remains, however, that nurses have multiple loyalties in health care – to the patient, the patient's family and significant others, to physicians, to the hospital, and to the wider health-care system. Nurses have described their role as a moral agent as involving working the "in-betweens," that is "working in-between their own identities and values and those of the organization in which they worked, working in-between their own values and the values of others, and working in-between competing values and interests" (Varcoe et al. 2004: 319). Conflicting loyalties are part of the everyday ethical challenges of nurses and being "in-between" calls for unique ethical knowledge and skills to negotiate and make decisions for the good (Rodney et al. 2002). Hamric (2001) used the term "in the middle" to describe these same dilemmas for nurses in their practice.

Emanating from research on nursing ethics is a rich array of stories from practice that illustrate these in-between struggles. Many examples that follow are drawn from previous and ongoing studies in a research program of Drs Storch, Rodney, Varcoe,

553

Hartrick Doane, Starzomski, and Pauly; articles by these researchers are included in the reference list.

From the neonatal intensive care nurses, instances are cited where the family, physicians, and nurses disagreed on the timing of a decision to discontinue aggressive treatment of a severely compromised neonate. From operating room nurses, concerns were raised about patients coming to surgery who were found to be uninformed about the surgery about to be performed on them. From nurses engaged in long-term care, instances were cited about the neglect of elderly residents because some care aides did not share values of compassionate and ethical care with the nurses. From clinical nurse leaders, stories were shared about the choices they often had to make to speak up at meetings or remain silent. They said they had to pick their battles so that they would not be discounted in (or not invited to) nursing care meetings that focused on nursing policy and practice. From these examples, and others, it is clear that nurses' multiple loyalties and obligations are a part of the social context of nurses' work that can create barriers to ethical practice.

Institutional values

The poor alignment of institutional values and nursing values is well expressed by Austin, who states that health-care environments "are places where value resides in the scientific, the efficient, the economical, the impartial, and the procedural" (2007: 84). Each of these values has an impact on nurses and their ability to enact their moral agency.

Biomedical Science as a Value: The privileging of biomedical knowledge and the scientific process over other types of knowledge and ways of knowing creates a barrier for nurses in having their knowledge understood and their ethical voices heard by others in health care. Nursing education has increasingly evolved to establish a better balance between the biomedical sciences and social sciences in order to create nursing science that fits with nursing practice. These changes have been poorly understood by physicians and the public, many of whom continue to perceive nurses as technical experts who only assist and support medical and surgical physicians' practice.

Efficiency as a value

The move to create more efficient systems based upon business practices led to massive downsizing in hospitals and other health agencies in the late 1980s and early 1990s. Rodney and Street (2004) note that "nursing's historical position as a (primarily) women's occupation in a gender biased culture has made it vulnerable to the economic forces sweeping through health care" (217). There were extensive lay-offs of nurse managers and staff nurses, including nurses who had served their hospitals loyally for decades, as well as hiring freezes and altered work expectations (Weiss et al. 2002). As the lay-offs were announced, at least one chief executive officer communicated to nursing staff that the bottom line expectation was patient safety only. This meant that therapeutic and relational caring was no longer wanted by some of those in charge of health care. The lay-offs had the serious consequence of devaluing nurses and nursing as work that almost anyone could do and as unnecessary in a market economy aimed at greater efficiency in the provision of care. The ensuing lowered standards in patient care in many care facilities, and poor outcomes for patients, are a continuing concern. These lay-offs have had other serious and long-lasting effects. They drastically reduced nursing leadership and have been a major cause of the current system-created nursing shortage. Nurses questioned their loyalty to the institutions they had served faithfully for so many years of their lives and they advised their children and friends' children not to go into nursing.

A less visible but significant impact of these dismissals was the loss of a core group of nurses in a care setting. "In the systems engineering approach, differences in temperament and skills are minimized and human beings are treated as standard units of labor rather than as unique resources for the teaching and advancement of good practice" (Weiss et al. 2002: 103). In their research, Weiss et al. (2002) noted that there was a sudden need for written standards to make up for gaps in the knowledge and continuity needed for high-quality care. These written standards were required because a core group of nurses, working together with common goals and processes, were disrupted. Further, nurses found it difficult to maintain reasonable standards when their unit's stability was diminished. The loss of large numbers of nurses, coupled with the loss of core groups of knowledgeable and experienced nurses, has been a major contributor to the need for a stronger focus on patient safety. This is because those nurses remaining in practice are often less senior and cannot easily rely upon others to compensate for their own lack of experience. Further, there has not been sufficient time or opportunity to build trusting team relationships because of staff turnover, use of part-time and casual staff, and limited orientation of new staff. These factors, along with the constant pressure to do more with less, creates a climate ripe for error and "near misses."

The notion that health care was just a type of business was not adopted by nurses, and nurses individually and collectively reacted to the shortfalls in staffing, equipment, and lack of involvement in decision-making. Yet, the language of evidence-based practice and best clinical practices predominates care today. As with many initiatives, this language can be beneficial as well as problematic. The benefit is to encourage practitioners to become more reflective about their practice and examine the taken-for-granted procedures involved to insure they are for the patient's benefit. The prob-lematic aspect of evidence-based practice is that it fails to take into account qualitative measurement of outcomes, and that it can minimize the importance of embodied nursing knowledge as part of good clinical judgment.

Economics as a value

The economics of health care continue to challenge nurses, as false economies are seen everyday in their practice. Nurses speak about practices that are wasteful of materials, time, and emotional energy; about poor policy-making regarding, for example, early discharges as cause of frequent patient readmissions; of poorly financed and supervised contracted housekeeping as cause of increasing infection rates in hospital; and of the disregard of nurses' voices in helping administrators and policy-makers know what actually happens on the front lines of care.

Nurses express their despair about the economic drivers in health care leading to a business approach that overwhelms a "caring" emphasis. The de-emphasis of caring (nursing care) is augmented by a continuing emphasis on cure and on the use of technologies without question. They see these aspects of their organizations as drivers for the dehumanizing practices, unnecessary suffering of patients, approaches that see some patients as more deserving than others, and failure of the system to deal with incompetence of health professionals.

Objectivity as a value

Also at odds with nursing ethics is the prevailing value of routinization of care, which often requires complete objectivity to the point of emotional detachment. In nursing history, one additional expectation of women engaged in nursing practice was that they were to suppress their emotions while on duty – that is, they were not to become "emotional" about the distress they might experience in caring for those suffering or in dealing with interpersonal situations/relations in the hospital. I well remember the reprimand I received in my early days as a student nurse when I showed some emotion after a woman I was caring for died. Objectivity was demanded, particularly given that science predominated medical knowledge. But, as Little noted, "what one is attentive to is largely a function of the one thing Nightingale does not mention, namely one's affect" (1995: 122).

Objectivity and loyalty as expectations of nursing practice have served as serious barriers to nurses in their understanding and practice of nursing ethics. In some respects the hospital's lack of loyalty to nurses freed them to reflect on their primary values and responsibilities in health care, and to better understand the importance of using their many ways of knowing to provide better patient care. In doing so, many nurses have searched for an understanding of ethics that speaks to the everyday issues of their practice.

The Renewal of Ethics in Nursing: The Insufficiency of Bioethics

"Although contemporary ethical theory is of tremendous value to nursing, the extent to which such theory has been informed by the concerns and practice of nurses has been limited" (Varcoe et al. 2004). In fact, contemporary ethical theory may well have temporarily diverted nurses from meaningful use of ethics in their nursing practice. Only since the 1990s have nurses really discovered (rediscovered) their ethical roots, and only in doing so have they been able to recognize the importance of their own moral agency, of ethical work environments, and of the need for the formation of moral communities in health care (Storch and Kenny 2007).

In the 1980s, Jameton laid the groundwork for considerations of the context of nursing work and introduced terms such as ethical uncertainty and moral distress. In *Nursing Practice: The Ethical Issues* (1984), he addressed nursing issues as opposed to the standard medical ethics issues found in other texts. It took some time, however, before his concepts of moral distress and moral uncertainty became part of nurses' ethics vocabulary, but current nursing ethics research has been heavily focused in this direction.

With the recognition by many that biomedical ethics and bioethics were helpful but limited in practical relevance to nurses, scholars began to delineate ethical issues in nursing (see, for example, Aroskar 1995; Johnstone 1999; Lutzen 1997; Storch 1992; Tschudin 1997; 1999) and to raise questions about the need for a theory of nursing ethics (Fry 1989). Ethical issues experienced by nurses were generally identified as nurses' multiple obligations (and loyalties), their enormous responsibility with limited autonomy, and their 24-hour coverage of patient care. The latter reality means that nurses are present to bear witness to ethical situations in ways that other health-care professionals are not, since most others only visit the units where patients are in care for short periods of time on any given day. Research by nurse scholars and those of other disciplines then began to focus on the ethical conflicts experienced by nurses in providing nursing care. Initially, these studies focused on the ethical dilemmas they faced in their practice, and their moral reasoning processes. But that focus became too limiting, since the everyday ethics of nursing is rarely as simple as involving a true dilemma. Rather, nurses experience ethical concerns in every part of their working day. "Everyday ethics refers to how nurses pay attention to ethics in carrying out their common daily interactions, including how nurses approach their practice and reflect on their ethical commitments to the people receiving care and those with health needs" (CNA 2008).

More recently, the focus has been on moral stress or distress, and the context of work environments that allow nurses to be moral agents in the provision of care. Many studies point to moral stress amongst nurses today (Juthberg et al. 2007; Lutzen et al. 2003), and to the significant moral residue, both affected by the climate in which nurses work (Corley et al. 2005). Although considerable research has focused on nurses' work environments as correlated with nurse turnover, sick and injury time, and patient outcomes, very limited attention has been directed to the moral environment of nursing practice and its impact on the level of moral distress of nurses. Even with attention focused on medical error and client outcomes in the patient safety movement, voices speaking to the significance of an ethical climate for nurses and their subsequent care of patients are mainly absent from the rhetoric of root causes in patient safety (Storch 2005).

Scholars in Sweden, Norway, Israel, Australia, the United States, and Canada have identified many common sources of moral dis-ease or moral distress. These include value conflicts between physicians and nurses, often expressed as nurses' voices not being heard in decision-making about treatment and care plans for patients. In almost all countries noted, end-of-life decision-making is a major area of moral distress for nurses. Given that they remain on the unit to attend to the treatment ordered, while physicians and others leave, it is not surprising that sustaining the lives of people whom nurses hear begging to be allowed "to let nature take its course" becomes a major issue and value conflict. Issues of patient choice and consent in other areas of care also arise, as do issues of social judgment made about people in care. Increasingly, attention is directed to the impact of the moral climate of an organization on nurses' ethics. It seems clear that many of these issues are not unique to nurses. Other health-care professionals, including pharmacists and many physicians, are recognizing similar ethical concerns (see, for example, Sporrong et al. 2006).

Desired Futures

There is a need to widen our understanding of everyday ethics concerns, to engage in relational practice, to open up moral space, and to focus on social justice as well as individual patient care concerns.

Widening the understanding of everyday ethics

The issues of everyday ethics are recognized as impacting all health professionals on the front line of care. Hamric calls attention to the reality that ethics is the business of every practicing health professional. She suggests that to "narrow the gap between ethics and clinical practice" (2002: 177), we must dispel some commonly held beliefs. These include the belief that ethics is simply a matter of intuition, that ethics is a foreign language, and that ethics is irrelevant to clinical practice. She recommends more relevant ethics teaching in medical, nursing, and other health professional/occupational schools and, in practice, including interdisciplinary teaching and learning.

Also suggested is the need for education about the ethics of teams and teamwork (Storch and Kenny 2007). Even though many professions may discuss teamwork in basic education and continuing education programs, the way in which teamwork is understood may differ. For example, all professions may need to answer the questions: What if I am not the captain of the team? How does a team function with shortages of time and resources? How can we make a stronger case for time for teamwork to improve patient care? And, most importantly, how do we work together to address our ethical concerns?

Opening moral spaces

In 1993, Walker made a plea for keeping moral spaces open, suggesting that the work of the bioethicists in organizations should be to make "open, accessible and active moral-reflective spaces in institutional life" (1993: 38) where people can talk about ethical concerns. She urged that times and places be set aside for regular ethics discussions in conferences, consultations, meetings, rounds, lectures and other situations to "propel the moral life of that institution" (ibid.). Such focused sessions can allow staff to develop trusting relationships with each other, as well as with the people receiving care and their families.

End of life decision-making and care is one example of an issue that might be discussed by a wider team if moral space were open for such discussion. When nurses disagree with a physician's orders to continue life-sustaining measures, they often have a difficult time being heard. Sometimes it is because they lack the moral courage to speak to the physician; at other times it is because they speak and take multiple actions, but receive no response. These actions range from speaking to their nurse manager or to another physician, attempting to arrange for a meeting of health team members, urging families to ask questions, or documenting their concerns in a letter to the chief of staff. They often look to their nursing peers and other team members for dialogue and support. In several research studies the desire of nurses to speak to others when dealing with such difficult situations has been noted. In these situations it has been found that many nurses know more about ethics in practice than they realize, but in a difficult situation they may require help to discover what they know and how they can use their knowledge. In Israel (Wagner and Ronen 1996) and in Canada (Rodney et al. 2002), nurses were found to seek support mainly for dealing with ethical issues from their peers. In Norway (Brunch 2001), nurses stated they wanted to discuss ethical issues and were found to be well educated and qualified to find viable solutions to complex ethical and clinical challenges.

Relational practice

The importance of relational practice is a critical element of nursing and nursing ethics (Hartrick Doane and Varcoe 2005). The therapeutic value of nurses and the care they can provide is vital to a system that describes itself as health "care." Weiss et al. note:

> Nursing practice is embedded in human relationships of healing and caring . . . nursing is sustained by institutional structures that allow adequate time for nurses' relational work with patients, families, and colleagues in order to skillfully assess the patient's safety, physiological and emotional needs and to intervene with appropriate timing and care. (2002: 107)

Relational practice is crucial to other health professions/occupations as well. Yet, with the constraints imposed on such ethical practice, health professionals of all types need a place and space to debate ethical concerns in everyday practice. In finding this space, the importance of a moral community cannot be underestimated. A moral community is defined as a workplace where ethical values are clear and shared, where ethical values direct action, and where individuals feel safe to be heard (cf. Rodney and Street 2004). Creating such a space is challenging but vital to addressing concerns of everyday ethics, including moral distress, moral residue, and moral uncertainty. Aroskar described this moral community as "a community in which the welfare of nursing caregivers and patients is explicitly recognized as being interrelated and interconnected" (1995: 137).

Attention to social justice

Because the focus of health care and much of the bioethics literature is on individual patient care, therapeutic relationships, and good clinical practice (including attention to ethics as a good), limited attention has been given to the ethical issues of populations and vulnerable groups in society. An ethical concern raised in nursing, particularly in the past decade, is sensitivity of the individual practitioner to concerns about social justice. Such concerns arise in the discussion of access to health care, recognizing the social determinants of health, and paying attention to the limited choices vulnerable people can make in health care (or in their lives for that matter).

These issues, and a wide range of ethical concerns, arise in the work of public health nurses. Population health disease control, pandemic planning, and other public matters raise many ethical issues. Also, while it is easier to suggest that these public matters are not ones any individual should be required to take up, sensitivity to the part that social determinants of health play in the lives of the patients for whom nurses are providing care makes this, too, an ethical concern for every practitioner. Attention to these matters must increase so that fairness and justice can prevail in health care.

Nursing Leadership in Practice and Policy through Attention Ethics

Research is currently focused on the role of nurse leaders in facilitating nurses' enactment of their moral agency and in assisting them to develop a moral community (Rodney

559

et al. 2006). No matter how well intentioned staff nurses might be, they find it almost impossible to sustain the level of care and attention to everyday ethics that is desirable unless nurse leaders are committed to similar aims.

One of the paradoxes of the focus on quality practice environments for nurses is the current lack of attention to ethics and support for ethical practice. The link between burnout and moral distress and moral residue appears to be direct. Nurses who leave work each day or night feeling that they did not live up to their standards of practice or their ethical commitments leave with a troubled conscience even though responsibility for their failure to meet their goals usually rests with the lack of system supports. Not only do nurse leaders need to pay attention to ethics in nursing practice, but corporate administrators too must give greater attention to ethical practice within hospitals, care homes, and other health agencies.

Summary

In this chapter the ethical concerns of nurses in practice are discussed with particular attention to the ethics of everyday practice. Issues faced by nurses in hospitals and other health agencies are described through tracing a history of nursing ethics and through the lens of current research findings. The sociopolitical context of nursing and nursing ethics is outlined with particular attention to problems created for nurses' enactment of their moral agency due to overriding institutional values that focus on scientific knowledge, efficiency in care delivery, economies of system redesign, and limited time for relational practice in provision of care. Also discussed in this chapter is the insufficiency of bioethics to guide ethical practice in everyday nursing care. There is evidence of the discovery or rediscovery of nursing ethics in current research and writings from many countries.

Finally, desirable futures for nursing ethics and ethical climates in health agencies are outlined with attention given to widening the understanding of everyday ethics to include other health professionals' concerns, to create moral spaces for interdisciplinary teams, to focus on relational practice including developing moral communities, and to attend to issues of social justice in health care. The need for leaders who have the vision to support these desirable futures is critical.

References

Aikens, C. (1935). *Studies in Ethics for Nurses*, 3rd edn. Philadelphia, PA: Saunders.

Aroskar, M. A. (1995). Envisioning nursing as a moral community. *Nursing Outlook* 43/3: 134–8.

Austin, W. (2007). The ethics of everyday practice: healthcare environments as moral communities. *Advances in Nursing Science* 30/1: 81–8.

Austin, W., Lemermeyer, G., Goldberg, L., Bergum, V., and Johnson, M. S. (2005). Moral distress in healthcare practice: the situation of nurses. *HEC Forum* 17/1: 33–48.

Beauchamp, T. L. and Childress, J. F. (2009 [1979]). *Principles of Biomedical Ethics*, 6th edn. New York: Oxford University Press.

Brunch, E. H. (2001). Hidden and emerging drama in a Norwegian critical care unit: ethical dilemmas in the context of ambiguity. *Nursing Ethics* 8/1: 57–67.

CNA (Canadian Nurses Association) (2008). *Code of Ethics for Registered Nurses.* Ottawa: Author.

Corley, M. C., Minick, P., Elswick, R. K., and Jacobs, M. (2005). Nurses' moral distress and ethical work environment. *Nursing Ethics* 12/4: 381–90.

Curtin, L. L. (1979). The nurse as advocate: a philosophical foundation for nursing. *Advances in Nursing Science* 1/3: 1–10.

Curtin, L. L. and Flaherty, M. J. (1982). *Nursing Ethics: Theories and Pragmatics.* Bowie, MD: Robert J. Brady.

Fry, S. T. (1989). Toward a theory of nursing ethics. *Advances in Nursing Science* 11/4: 9–22.

Fry, S. and Johnstone, M.-J. (2002). *Ethics in Nursing Practice: A Guide to Ethical Decision-making*, 2nd edn. Oxford: Blackwell Publishing.

Fry, S. T., Harvey, R. M., Hurley, A. C., and Foley, B. J. (2002). Development of a model of moral distress in military nursing. *Nursing Ethics* 9/4: 373–87.

Hamric, A. B. (2001). Reflections on being in the middle. *Nursing Outlook* 43: 254–7.

Hamric, A. B. (2002). Bridging the gap between ethics and clinical practice. *Nursing Outlook* 50/5: 176–8.

Hartrick Doane, G. and Varcoe, C. (2005). *Family Nursing as Relational Inquiry.* Philadelphia, PA: Lippincott Williams and Wilkins.

ICN (International Council of Nurses) (1953). *International Code of Nursing Ethics.* Geneva: Author.

ICN (International Council of Nurses) (1973). *Code for Nurses: Ethical Concepts Applied to Nursing.* Geneva: Author.

Jameton, A. (1984). *Nursing Practice: The Ethical Issues.* Englewood Cliffs, NJ: Prentice-Hall, Inc.

Johnstone, M.-J. (1999). *Bioethics: A Nursing Perspective*, 3rd edn. Marrickville, Australia: Saunders.

Juthberg, C., Eriksson, S., Norberg, A., and Sundin, K. (2007). Perceptions of conscience in relation to stress of conscience. *Nursing Ethics* 14/3: 329–43.

Lamb, M. (2004). An historical perspective on nursing and nursing ethics. In J. Storch, P. Rodney, and R. Starzomski (eds.), *Toward a Moral Horizon: Nursing Ethics for Leadership and Practice.* Toronto: Pearson Prentice Hall, pp. 20–41.

Little, M. O. (1995). Seeing and caring: the role of affect in feminist moral epistemology. *Hypatia* 10/3: 117–37.

Lutzen, K. (1997). Nursing ethics into the next millennium: a context-sensitive approach to nursing ethics. *Nursing Ethics* 4/3: 218–26.

Lutzen, K., Johansson, A., and Nordstrom, G. (2000). Moral sensitivity: some differences between nurses and physicians. *Nursing Ethics* 7/6: 520–30.

Lutzen, K., Cronqvist, A., Magnusson, A., and Andersson, L. (2003). Moral stress: synthesis of a concept. *Nursing Ethics* 10/3: 312–22.

Mansell, D. J. (2004). *Forging the Future: A History of Nursing in Canada.* Ann Arbor, MI: Thomas Press.

National Commission for the Protection of Human Subjects of Biomedical and Behavioral Research (1978). *The Belmont Report.* Washington, DC: DHEW Publication OS 78-0012.

Nightingale, F. (1860). *Notes on Nursing.* New York: Dover Publications.

Olson, L. L. (1998). Hospital nurses' perception of the ethical climate of their work setting. *Image: Journal of Nursing Scholarship* 30/4: 345–9.

Redman, B. K. and Fry, S. T. (2000). Nurses' ethical conflicts: what do we really know about them? *Nursing Ethics* 7/4: 360–6.

Rodney, P. (1988). Moral distress in critical care nursing. *Canadian Critical Care Nursing Journal* 5/2: 9–11.

Rodney, P. and Street, A. (2004). The moral climate of nursing practice: inquiry and action. In J. Storch, P. Rodney, and R. Starzomski (eds.), *Toward a Moral Horizon: Nursing Ethics for Leadership and Practice*. Toronto: Pearson Prentice Hall, pp. 209–31.

Rodney, P., Hartrick Doane, G., Storch, J. L., and Varcoe, C. (2006). Toward a safer moral climate. *Canadian Nurse* 102/8: 24–7.

Rodney, P., Varcoe, C., Storch, J. L., McPherson, G., Mahoney, K., Brown, H., Pauly, B., Hartrick Doane, G., and Starzomski, R. (2002). Navigating towards a moral horizon: a multisite qualitative study of ethical practice in nursing. *Canadian Journal of Nursing Research* 34/3: 75–102.

Sporrong, S. K., Hoglund, A. T., and Arnetz, B. (2006). Measuring moral distress in pharmacy and clinical practice. *Nursing Ethics* 13/4: 416–27.

Storch, J. L. (1982). *Patients' Rights: Ethical and Legal Issues in Health Care and Nursing*. Toronto: McGraw Hill Ryerson Ltd.

Storch, J. L. (1992). Ethical issues. In A. J. Baumgart and J. Larsen (eds.), *Canadian Nursing Faces the Future*, 2nd edn. St Louis, MO: Mosby Year Book, pp. 260–70.

Storch, J. L. (2005). Patient safety: is it just another bandwagon? *Nursing Leadership* 18/2: 39–55.

Storch, J. L. and Kenny, N. (2007). Shared moral work of nurses and physicians. *Nursing Ethics* 14/4: 478–91.

Storch, J. L., Rodney, P., and Starzomski, R. (2004). *Toward a Moral Horizon: Nursing Ethics for Leadership and Practice*. Toronto: Pearson Prentice Hall.

Storch, J. L., Rodney, P., Pauly, B., Brown, H., and Starzomski, R. (2002). Listening to nurses moral voices: building a quality health care environment. *Canadian Journal of Nursing Leadership* 15/4: 7–16.

Thompson, I. E., Melia, K. M., and Boyd, K. M. (2006 [1983]). *Nursing Ethics*, 6th edn. Edinburgh: Churchill Livingstone.

Tschudin, V. (1997). *Deciding Ethically: A Practical Approach to Nursing Challenges*. London: Bailliere Tindall.

Tschudin, V. (1999). *Nurses Matter: Reclaiming Our Professional Identity*. London: Macmillan Press Limited.

Varcoe, C. and Rodney, P. (2001). Constrained agency: the social structure of nurses' work. In B. S. Bolaria and H. D. Dickinson (eds.), *Health, Illness and Health Care in Canada*, 3rd edn. Scarborough, ON: Nelson Thomas Learning, pp. 102–28.

Varcoe, C., Doane, G., Pauly, B., Rodney, P., Storch, J. L., Mahoney, K., McPherson, G., Brown, H., and Starzomski, R. (2004). Ethical practice in nursing: working the in-betweens. *Journal of Advanced Nursing* 45/3: 316–25.

Wagner, N. and Ronen, I. (1996). Ethical dilemmas experienced by hospital and community nurses: an Israeli study. *Nursing Ethics* 3/4: 294–304.

Walker, M. U. (1993). Keeping moral space open: new images of ethics consulting. *Hastings Center Report* 23/2: 33–40.

Weiss, S. M., Malone, R. E., Merighi, J. R., and Benner, P. (2002). Economism, efficiency, and the moral ecology of good nursing practice. *Canadian Journal of Nursing Research* 34/2: 95–119.

47

Global Trends in Nursing Ethics

VERENA TSCHUDIN

Although many attempts have been made, it has been notoriously difficult to describe exactly what nursing is and what nurses do. As a result, nursing often lacks a clear voice in governments and forums where health is considered in terms of outcomes, economy, and efficacy, rather than individual or professional needs and values. The issues facing nursing in the future are largely dependent on the case that can be made for skilled nursing in a global climate of budgetary constraints.

Professional Issues

The work of nurses varies greatly, from basic care in hospitals to specialisms in a great variety of diseases or procedures, personal care for people in their own homes and in care homes, and being in the frontline with armed forces. Not all tasks demand the same caliber of education. The individualization of Western health care means that more personalized care is needed, demanding a diverse and flexible workforce.

Nursing is branching into many different extensions of its traditional role, including prescribing, anesthetizing patients, carrying out minor operations, and diagnosis. Within neonatology, gerontology, hospice care, mental health, and rehabilitation, entirely nurse-led care of units or areas is growing, with nurses calling on physicians only when necessary. Clinics and health stations in low-income countries have long known this model.

Nurse specialists exist in many hospital departments or clinics. The best known among them include breast-care nurses and stoma (or enterostomal) therapists (specializing in the care of patients with stomas, that is, artificial orifices from the gastrointestinal or urinary tract). Other specialties are in dietetics, diabetes, pediatrics, oncology, geriatrics, and, particularly, in end-of-life care. Many local conditions enable other specialist roles. Such nurses treat patients and have a significant role in the education of families and staff. This has increased good care, but can also lead to acute conflicts of role, where the nurses' professional judgment and autonomy are challenged. In many countries around the world, notably in the United Kingdom, midwives have traditionally been much less dependent on physicians than have nurses.

The more technical that health care becomes, the more that health-care practitioners need to be aware of the fears and anxieties of patients and clients who are dependent on the technology. Good and accessible information needs to be given at every stage to allay worry and gain cooperation. Nurses therefore need not only to be skilled in using increasingly complex technology, but also in relating to and communicating with patients and clients and other health professionals.

Nursing research has been a driver for these developments. Research has also led to the realization that professionalization has resulted in greater accountability, and hence professional and legal responsibility for the care given. The production of codes of professional conduct, the necessity of nurses to adhere to them, the revolution in nurse education, and the need for evidence-based care have all contributed to nursing being more self-assured as a profession. The need for care of one kind or another will always exist; what kind of care is given, how, and by which type of health-care professional is, however, increasingly blurred.

Nurses can, and need to, take the lead in areas such as communication between patients and health-care personnel, maintaining and fostering human rights, using and promoting complementary therapies and other aspects of holistic care, promoting health, and helping the population at large to undertake check-ups and gain information. These are included within the basic caring role of nursing, but they also form part of the ethical role and include aspects of advocacy, confidentiality, and informed consent.

Educational Issues

The move of health care into the community and away from hospitals will influence the type of education that is most fitting for nurses and midwives. Nurses working in community settings need to be familiar with a much wider diversity of care applications than they have probably been educated for until now. This poses challenges for educators, policy-makers and budget-holders.

The education of its practitioners has always been considered a vital element in the practice of nursing, and basic nurse education is now almost universally available in institutes of higher education. The US had university education for most students of nursing by the late 1980s and now has several different levels of education. In Britain, approximately one-third of nursing students graduate with a bachelor degree; the remainder receive a diploma that can be topped up to degree level.

There is still a marked contrast between nurses educated in high-income countries, with the emphasis on prolonging life, and those trained in low-income countries, with the emphasis on preventing illness. Worldwide changes in demographics, and epidemics of HIV/AIDS, TB, and infections due to antibiotic resistance are changing the global need for, and role of, nursing considerably, strengthening the need for largely unskilled personal care in the future in all areas of the world, with hospitals becoming centers for quick specialist interventions only.

The trend worldwide in nurse education is for a core program of basic studies, after which students branch out into a number of specialties. The emphasis in this form of nurse education is on health (rather than illness) and health management, and students are schooled equally in community settings and hospitals. The core curriculum consists of subjects such as health education, ethics, relationships, sociology, and communication, as well as life sciences, pathology, and sociology.

The need to respond to new economic and political pressures is evident in nurse education. Indeed, the shift to higher education has coincided with the trend to a market economy. With no clear focus of direction being pursued by the profession at present, there are strong pressures from outside nursing for more and more of the caring tasks to be carried out by care assistants rather than nurses. This gives nurse education a stronger incentive to prepare its practitioners for taking responsibility in many different settings and circumstances, and indeed in becoming leaders of health-care teams.

University education for nursing students means that there are now no national curricula, but various supranational agreements are in place, as, for example, in the European Union. Nursing is somewhat of a hybrid in that students receive at the same time a degree/diploma in nursing studies and licensure (registration) to practice, although these two elements are granted by separate bodies. The International Council of Nurses (ICN) is the driving force in coordinating the terms of regulation of the nursing workforce worldwide, recognizing that:

> setting and enforcing standards for nursing education and practice is a major responsibility of organized nursing and a key aspect of nursing's progress as a profession. The various means of setting standards are the credentialing (licensing and certification) of nurses and specialists, approval of schools and accreditation of nursing services in hospitals and other settings. . . . [The] ICN has proposed universal guidelines for basic and specialty practice to help the nursing profession wrestling with questions of authority, definition, boundaries, scope of practice and educational standards for nursing specialties. . . . A major regulatory dynamic in many countries has to do with the use of auxiliary and unlicensed personnel in health care. (ICN 2006b)

All nurse education is for critical, reflective, moral, inquiring, and cooperative care. It also needs to be visionary enough to lead health care in its adaptation to different demographic patterns and social settings, and lead the workforce to make these changes possible so that people around the world will have realistic and adequate health care, given with dignity and respect.

All nurses have to work by codes of ethics or practice that are regularly updated, and nurses are urged to contribute to the formulations of such codes. They are familiar with the practice that leads the profession, and the profession needs to regulate its own practice through education.

Policy Issues

Nurse migration

Nurses have always been part of a mobile workforce, but nurse migration has caused major problems for many governments around the world.

In numerous Western countries the nursing workforce significantly diminished in the 1980s because of reductions in nurse training, thus also becoming an aging workforce (Cutliffe and Yarbrough 2007). The globalization of the workforce meant that increasing numbers of nurses from low-income countries were able to move elsewhere and gain financially and professionally. When this proved detrimental to many

565

of the source countries' health systems, the recruitment of nurses from overseas, especially from sub-Saharan Africa, became a key issue in view of global poverty and human development. The nurses defended their personal right to free movement, but source countries were concerned with their populations' right to health care, as few of the nurses who gained experience abroad returned to their home countries (Batata 2005). Nurses became significantly aware of their social responsibilities as citizens; and numerous publications by individuals and organizations spoke out about the perceived inequities, and influenced changes in recruitment policies by governments (see, e.g., Buchan 2005; Chagutur and Vallabhaneni 2005; ICN 2004).

Economic and institutional pressures

The increasing role of market forces in health care has led many nurses to complain that they are not able to exercise professional discretion. The need for economy, efficiency, and effectiveness is not always conducive to professional integrity. Many nurses feel that workplace policies, directions, and other guidance restrict their professional judgment. An analysis of articles published in *Nursing Ethics* between 1994 and 2005 (Tschudin 2006) showed a clear trend among nurses to override the restrictions and work as they judge most appropriate, given that their education trained them for this. The phenomenon of "moral stress" (and distress) caused mainly by such situations continues to be regularly addressed in the nursing press, both academic and journalistic.

Leadership Issues

Nurses as leaders and policy-shapers

There is still considerable lack of visionary and political leadership in nursing. The ICN is increasingly joining other world bodies, such as the World Medical Association (WMA), International Pharmaceutical Federation (FIP), World Dental Federation (FDI), World Health Organization (WHO), and Medicos Na Internet (MNI) in statements of relevance to all these organizations singly and collectively. National and international nursing organizations also sponsor individuals on leadership programs, as the need for leaders is increasingly urgent. (This topic is addressed in chapter 46, "Ethics in Nursing Practice.")

Professional interdependence

One important way forward for health care is for some basic education and training of personnel to happen jointly. Medical, nursing, physiotherapy, pharmacy, and social-work students can be taught together in health sciences, communication, ethics, and sociology, and for discussions of political, economic, and social trends in health care. Joint education removes many of the difficulties created by separate interests and ideologies. Meetings with, and discussions among, a wide variety of professions in the health care and law-enforcement fields help to focus communication between the various groups on their responsibilities toward their clients. When boundaries of work and socialization are maintained, it is easy to forget the patients or clients who should be at the center of care and attention.

Many of the problems faced by nurses in the area of patient-centered care stem from the traditional role of nursing as subordinate to medicine. Nurses claim that they are generally closer to patients and clients, both physically and emotionally, than physicians, and therefore know them better and understand their needs better, but they are frequently not consulted on important decisions, or they are consulted but their concerns are ignored. Conflict between medical and nursing staff over treatments is often sharp and bitter. When nurses can argue on an equal footing with professional peers, especially on issues of ethical relevance, respect between the professions strengthens and reduces tension between nursing and medical staff.

Specific Issues

Keeping professional codes and guidelines

The *ICN Code of Ethics for Nurses* (2006a) is binding on all nurses. In addition, many countries have their own codes, giving more specific guidance. According to the ICN code, "the fundamental responsibility of the nurse is fourfold: to promote health, to prevent illness, to restore health and to alleviate suffering." Problems arise when any of these responsibilities conflict, or when personal values encroach on those demanded by patients or clients, other health-carers, employers, the profession, or society at large. Nurses working in specific settings – for example, prisons – also have to keep to codes and guidelines produced by those institutions, and demands made by one code (e.g., confidentiality) may be contradicted by another (e.g., disclosure of details to police). Codes can be prescriptive only in general terms, and personal interpretation of specific clauses in particular circumstances will vary. If necessary, nurses should consult with senior personnel or with professional bodies in cases of conflict. This in itself can be controversial, as the lines of management may overlap for nurses.

Conflicts of interest

Conflicts are caused by the many demands made on nurses. Problems arise from: conflicts of role and culture; demands for efficiency made by employers; not having enough staff to work to targets demanded by management and one's conscience; professional demands to exercise judgment while being limited by policies; the need to adapt to changes in care with insufficient resources available; demands made by patients and clients for rights to be upheld (to which nurses are often unable to respond due to various restraints); the need to extend into other professional fields, and also to expand practice by deepening existing skills.

The role of caring for people combines both technical and interpersonal skills. This demands a wide range of expertise, experience, and stamina. Conflicts arise because of the various spheres of professional and managerial demands made on nurses. Although both medicine and nursing aim to promote and safeguard the interests and well-being of patients and clients, in a given situation this is often difficult to do. In their area of care, nurses usually become very experienced, but they may have to depend on physicians with less experience to prescribe treatments, or carry out decisions that have been taken without them being consulted. Significantly, nurses have to uphold the law (e.g., report illegal acts), yet are themselves often pushed to illegal acts (e.g., illicit drug-taking) through stress.

Nurses are obliged to care for patients without discrimination. Nurses cannot refuse to care for patients, but in most countries they can claim conscientious objection to taking part in certain procedures that are not considered treatments, such as abortions. When they are confronted with circumstances which they find personally and professionally challenging, conflicts arise that may cause "moral distress." This term was coined specifically for work in nursing "when one knows the right thing to do, but institutional constraints make it nearly impossible to pursue the right course of action" (Jameton 1984) and has since been widely studied.

Advocacy

Nurses have long understood themselves to be the patients' advocates, though this is not mentioned in the *ICN Code of Ethics for Nurses*. However, the American Nurses Association has as the third provision in its code: "The nurse promotes, advocates for, and strives to protect the health, safety, and rights of the patient" (ANA 2001). In the detail for this provision, various issues are discussed that show that nurses must go about their work with independence, judgment, and a critical attitude in the way they foster and maintain the patients' and clients' well-being. How this is done in practice is less clear. Curtin (1979) based a philosophy of nursing on the concept of advocacy, stressing the common humanity, the common needs, and the common human rights of both patients and nurses. This commonality compels nurses to act as advocates. This basic stance defines nurses as carers, but at the same time makes them vulnerable because it is their humanity that is called upon, not simply certain skills.

Advocacy involves more than simply taking sides. It may also entail trying to understand work systems and cultures, values, and what drives people. Conflicts in health care may be exacerbated by not being able to go for promotion for any number of reasons and therefore having lost interest in the work.

The role of caring for people combines many skills, demanding a wide range of expertise, experience, and stamina. When nurses no longer have the possibility to reflect on and in their work, they are no longer able to advocate for others. Unfortunately, too often nurses are then not supported and helped, i.e. no one is willing to advocate for them.

References

ANA (2001). *Code of Ethics for Nurses With Interpretive Statements*. American Nurses Association. Available at: www.nursingworld.org/ (accessed June 4, 2007).

Batata, A. S. (2005). International nurse recruitment and NHS vacancies: a cross-sectional analysis. *Globalization and Health* 1/7. Available at www.globalizationandhealth.com/content/1/1/7 (accessed June 3, 2007).

Buchan, J. (2005). Global shortage in healthcare skills reaches crisis point. *Employing Nurses and Midwives* (February): 4–6.

Chagutur, S. and Vallabhaneni, S. (2005). Aiding and abetting: nursing crisis at home and abroad 2005. *New England Journal of Medicine* 353: 1761–3.

Curtin, L. L. (1979). The nurse as advocate: a philosophical foundation for nursing. *Advances in Nursing Science* 1/3: 1–10.

Cutliffe, J. R. and Yarbrough, S. (2007). Globalization, commodification and mass transplant of nurses: part 1. *British Journal of Nursing* 16: 876–80.

Henderson, V. (1966). *The Nature of Nursing*. New York: Macmillan.

ICN (no date). *Definition of Nursing*. International Council of Nurses. Available at: www.icn.ch/definition.htm (accessed June 4, 2007).

ICN (2004). *The Global Nursing Review Initiative: Policy Options and Solutions*. International Council of Nurses. Available at: www.icn.ch/global (accessed August 10, 2007).

ICN (2006a). *The ICN Code of Ethics for Nurses*. Geneva: International Council of Nurses.

ICN (2006b). *The Global Nursing Shortage: Priority Areas for Intervention*. International Council of Nurses. Available at: www.icn.ch/global (accessed August 13, 2007).

Jameton, A. (1984). *Nursing Practice. The Ethical Issues*. Englewood Cliffs, NJ: Prentice-Hall, 6.

RCN (2003). *Defining Nursing*. London: Royal College of Nursing.

Tschudin, V. (2006). How nursing ethics as a subject changes: an analysis of the first 11 years of publications in the journal. *Nursing Ethics* 13: 65–85.

Watson, J. (2002). *Assessing and Measuring Caring in Nursing and Health Sciences*. New York: Springer.

WHO (2003). *International Nurse Mobility: Trends and Policy Implications*. Geneva: World Health Organization.

Wros, P. L., Doutrich, D., and Izumi, S. (2004). Ethical concerns: comparison of values from two cultures. *Journal of Nursing and Health Sciences* 6: 131–40.

Part XIII

The Teaching and Practice of Bioethics

48

Ethics Committees and Ethics Consultants

JONATHAN D. MORENO

Ethics committees and ethics consultants are among the more interesting phenomena associated with bioethics. Although in some respects both reach back to the ancient origins of medical ethics, in other ways they are reflections of a postmodern society that seeks moral resolutions while remaining agnostic about substantive moral issues. In this chapter, I shall describe the history of ethics committees and ethics consultants, the received view of their functions and uncertainties about their appropriate status. I will conclude with some philosophical remarks about the nature of ethics committees and ethics consultants, as well as their implications for the field of bioethics.

Origins and Development

The relationships of ethics committees and ethics consultants to the history of medicine are quite different. These differences highlight an interesting tension between the two, even though they are both manifestations of the institution of bioethics.

The Hippocratic texts (those attributed to a historical personage Hippocrates or to a cult of male physicians) are explicit about the physician's role as including the projection of a certain moral standing to patients and their families. In this tradition the healer's charisma is closely associated with his (at least apparent) wisdom and personal carriage. The appreciation for the close linkage between the qualities of wisdom and technical proficiency in the healer's art is remarkably persistent both historically and cross-culturally, including in those medical traditions (e.g., Jewish and Islamic) that stem from non-Hippocratic sources. To a large degree, the role of the ethics consultant is an extension of that of the wise physician.

In other respects, however, the ethics consultant is quite a different figure. Most obviously, many modern ethics consultants are not doctors of medicine. In fact, though the Hippocratic authors counseled the use of consultants in hard cases, they did not seem to anticipate a non-physician consultant whose sole function was to provide ethical rather than medical assistance (Ackerman 1989). Further, while the Hippocratic doctors were guided mainly by the values of nonmaleficence and beneficence, today's ethics consultants concern themselves with other values as well, such as autonomy and justice. But though the modern ethics consultant is undeniably a product of the bioethics movement, for which autonomy is the usual ethical "trump," it is possible that this is less often the case at the bedside than it is for bioethicists who operate in more rarefied settings.

It is not clear who the first modern ethics consultants were, but the occupation can be traced in general terms from several antecedents, including hospital chaplains and theologians who taught medical students in the 1960s, academic philosopher-bioethicists who became interested in the clinical setting in the 1970s, and ethics committee members who offered their services for helping with emergent ethical disputes, also during the 1970s (Rothman 1991). Today, ethics consultants often work in tandem with ethics committees, or members of ethics committees who are on call may consider themselves ethics consultants (Wear et al. 1990). However, there is also a small but vigorous movement of professional ethics consultants who work as independent entrepreneurs, usually in positions supported by hospital receipts.

Berkowitz and Dubler (2007) have proposed three models of ethics consultation with differing contextual and institutional value. The individual consultant approach allows for expedient responses to urgent cases and yields fewer logistical difficulties than the others; unfortunately, it necessitates a consultant with a wide breadth of knowledge, and of course lends itself to the consultant's subjective biases. In the team approach, a committee of 6–20 experts performs the consultation, thereby insuring a broad understanding of the issues and incorporating multidisciplinary views. Not suitable for situations requiring expediency of response, this approach requires significant logistical resources, leads to inefficiencies by fragmenting responsibility for the case among its membership, and sometimes intimidates patients and patient families. The small team approach utilizes a group of experts who vary from situation to situation and who share the responsibility of the case. This model is naturally efficient and expedient. It includes a diverse membership and reduces the intimidation associated with large groups; however, the small team approach tends toward group bias and lacks the total efficiency of the individual ethics consultant. This model seems to be the most pragmatic and is preferred in most hospitals (Fox et al. 2007).

While the recent origins of ethics committees are more clear than those of ethics consultants, they are notable for the virtual absence of ancient predecessors. The Hippocratic physician was a solo practitioner who, following apprenticeship, did not seek the moral advice of a committee, and certainly not a committee dominantly comprised of non-physicians. Instead, the ethics committee is a creature of a liberal, Western, and pluralistic society. It is also indebted to the highly bureaucratized institutional structures of modernity, structures that include working groups known as committees. Moreover, ethics committees are mainly identified with secular bioethical theory, which is dominated by "mid-level" principles that seek to avoid reference to a single foundational philosophy or to imply that certain actions are ethical and others not (Beauchamp and Childress 2009 [1979]). Liberal democratic pluralism, committee systems, and mid-level principles all emphasize procedural solutions to social controversy. As a result, ethics committees are process-oriented to the extreme.

The predecessors of ethics committees in the United States were not as determinedly procedural, nor were they at first controlled by non-physicians, though their evolutionary vectors are plain (Moreno 1995). As part of the eugenic movement early in the twentieth century, sterilization committees were composed mainly of those experienced in the management of the mentally ill (trained neurologists complained there were not enough "real experts" on these committees). They made what they took to be objective decisions based on the goal of avoiding the social burdens of inherited "idiocy" through prevention; only much later was it appreciated that few instances of cognitive deficiency are inherited. Until the early 1970s in the United States, abortion selection committees often identified those whose medical or psychiatric condition warranted an elective pregnancy termination. Compared to sterilization decisions, this was a somewhat less "hard science" judgment. Another ancestor of ethics committees was panels for determining which patients suffering from terminal kidney disease should have access to the dialysis machines that were in short supply in the 1960s. Composed in many cases mostly of non-physicians, kidney dialysis selection committees made explicit value choices for the allocation of a scarce life-saving resource. The most famous of these was the "God committee" at Swedish Hospital in Seattle, Washington, which was the subject of major media coverage in the early 1960s. The publicized experience of this committee was for many people their first exposure to the vexing problem of fairness in the allocation of scarce life-or-death resources (Alexander 1962).

In a 1975 law review article, the physician Karen Teel reported that many hospitals used ethics committees to help make difficult decisions. Her article was cited by the New Jersey Supreme Court in its landmark ruling on the case of Karen Ann Quinlan. Quinlan was a young woman who fell into a persistent vegetative state (a condition of irreversible unconsciousness) after collapsing at a party. The court found that if the family requested discontinuation of treatment, and if there was no reasonable possibility of Karen Quinlan returning to a "cognitive, sapient state," and if a hospital ethics committee agreed, then the decision-makers would be immune from civil and criminal liability. The judges' citation of Teel's article was the first great spur for the growth of ethics committees. Ironically, however, the judges seem to have misunderstood the function of ethics committees, confusing them with more traditional and technically driven prognosis committees (Moreno 1995).

Nonetheless, the New Jersey court's decision was the first of a series of events that gave impetus to the ethics committee movement in the United States. Another important development was the Reagan administration's attempt, in the early 1980s, to require aggressive treatment of severely disabled newborns, regulations that included reference to "infant care review committees" (Moreno 1987). The Rudolfo Torres case set the precedent for extramural ethics consultation. In this case, a patient's fall from a hospital bed led to anoxia-caused brain trauma; given the possible liability-related conflict of interest of the ethics consultants from this particular hospital, three chairs of ethics committees at different hospitals were contacted to assess the case and testify in court (Hosford 1986). Extramural ethics consultation is now used by the Veterans Administration Health System and skilled nursing facilities without the means to have an ethics consultant on staff; and they can be used to resolve issues not resolved by ethics committees (Miller 2002). More recently, the Joint Commission for the Accreditation of Healthcare Organizations (JCAHO 1992) has established as a condition for accreditation that hospitals have a mechanism for addressing ethical disputes, and several states have legislated requirements that their hospitals have ethics committees. As a result, virtually all larger hospitals, and most smaller ones, now claim to have ethics committees in place.

In the United States, ethics committees vary greatly in many of their specific features, but it is a given that they must represent various perspectives, including that of the institution's "community," and that they should not be dominated by physicians. This is a reflection of the fact that the ethics committee idea is legitimized as an expression of certain themes of democratic liberalism, including especially the notion that moral controversies are best resolved through a process that takes into account multiple perspectives on the nature of the good life. But while ethics committees have an essentially cosmopolitan aspect, the same is not quite true of the idea of ethics consultation, which retains the option of physician dominance. Today, nurses and physicians usually perform ethics consultations (Fox et al. 2007). I will return to some of the philosophical implications of ethics committees and ethics consultation later.

One obvious near relation of the ethics committee is the committee for the scrutiny of the use of human subjects in medical research. The idea of prior group review of proposals for experiments involving human subjects dates back at least to the late 1940s in the US Atomic Energy Commission's Isotope Distribution Division, though its most famous early manifestation was at the Clinical Center of the National Institutes of Health in Bethesda, Maryland, beginning in 1953 (Advisory Committee for Human Radiation Experiments 1995). But unlike the ethics committee movement, the current system of local review boards owes its growth mainly to a series of well-publicized "scandals." One of these was the infamous Tuskegee syphilis study, in which more than 400 poor African American men were medically monitored by public health officials for decades without being told their diagnosis, even when effective treatment became available (for more on this, see chapter 38). Therefore, in the United States the use of human research subjects is subject to government regulation, and "institutional review boards" have certain codified legal obligations, while ethics committees do not, at least not at the federal level.

The Functions of Ethics Committees and Ethics Consultants

I have noted that human subject review panels were largely a response to allegations of investigators' misbehavior. By contrast, the origins of ethics committees are not nearly so readily identifiable. Thus it is not surprising that their goals are not as clear, for they include assisting physicians in dealing with their ethical dilemmas as well as helping hospitals avoid lawsuits and bad publicity; little reflection is required to register the fact that these goals are not necessarily compatible.

There is broad agreement that ethics committees have three functions: case review, policy advice, and staff education. Beyond these functions, and a membership that includes multiple perspectives, there are wide discrepancies among ethics committees. Some report to the hospital's organized medical staff, others directly to administration; some are passive and de-emphasize bedside consulting, others have active leadership and try to assert a presence on the wards; and some include members who are familiar with the bioethics literature and theory, while the members of others have had virtually no previous experience with ethical analysis. No matter what the composition of the committee is, top-down support is necessary for deft processing and implementation of recommendations issued (Mayle 2006; McGee et al. 2001).

Of the three "classical" functions of ethics committees, case review has received far and away the most attention, staff education the least. This is perhaps because case consultation is the "sexiest" of the functions, but it is also the most potentially volatile and the most labor-intensive. The vast majority of committees have operated on what is known as an "optional-optional" basis for case review. This means that whether or not a case is brought to the committee is optional, as is whether or not the attending physician follows the committee's advice.

Not all the functions of ethics committees were foreseen when they were first organized, and some diverge from the optional-optional model. In some states, ethics committees serve to satisfy certain legal requirements. For example, in New York State there is a law that mandates the consent of the patient or her appropriate surrogate to a physician's DNR ("do not resuscitate") order. In the event of a dispute between the surrogate and the physician, a dispute resolution committee must be formed, and some ethics committees fulfill this function. Dispute resolution mechanisms are also part of some state laws concerning the assignment of durable powers of attorney for health care, and, again, ethics committees can be convenient venues for this role.

Of the two other classical ethics committee functions, staff education is arguably the most important and the most efficient. A staff that is well informed about local advance directive mechanisms and actively encourages their use by patients can thereby prevent many problems that might be presented to an ethics committee. However, the practical conditions under which most in-hospital personnel must work make the provision of such "cognitive" services a low priority.

Policy review and consultation can be of great benefit to the institution's administration, especially if it leads to more reflective and philosophical policy-making than is usually the case when left in the hands of the hospital's attorney. Some committees have drafted truly innovative policies on end-of-life issues, for example, and these efforts have sometimes been made part of a general effort to bring staff together in an educational setting as well. Again, however, these kinds of contribution require a sophisticated ethics committee, which in turn depends upon an initial investment by the institution for the training of committee members. This is especially true of the committee chair, who may also have to be released from some other responsibilities in order to function optimally in this position. If the chair is a physician, this could represent a substantial financial commitment by the institution.

It appears that a large proportion of consultants are trained through direct, formal supervision by an experienced member of an ethics committee; relatively few complete a fellowship or graduate degree program in bioethics (Fox et al. 2007). That the apprenticeship model predominates in the preparation of ethics consultants may indicate that on-the-job experience is much more important than formal training, or simply that institutions fail to support formal education in clinical ethics. In any event, it is essential that ethics consultants and committees have ready access to educational materials, clerical support, training, and continuing education (Berkowitz and Dubler 2007). There is a need for clear standards for ethics consultation practice, for educational resources to assist ethics consultants in implementing those standards, and for tools to evaluate whether those standards are being met.

In my experience as a member and consultant for numerous ethics committees since 1984, the commitment of institutions to ethics committees, and the resulting quality of committees, varies widely. Ethics committees are often created amid great excitement and optimism about their anticipated contributions to institutional culture, education, and morale, but after the first two years they obviously suffer from what the bioethicist John Fletcher called a "failure to thrive" syndrome (Fletcher 1995: 228). In many cases the etiology of this syndrome turns out to be a passive committee style. The more successful committees tend to be those that actively insert themselves into day-to-day clinical and educational activities, creating relationships with staff members and the sense that the committee is a vital resource for everyone concerned.

For all their remarkable growth and undeniable popularity, there are many unanswered questions about ethics committees. For example, what is the legal status of an ethics committee's non-binding recommendations in a court of law? Should hospital lawyers be voting members of the ethics committee? Who should be able to bring a case to the committee? Should a designated patient advocate sit on the ethics committee? What about the hospital's risk manager? Should an ethics committee record its recommendation in the patient's chart, or only that it discussed the case and offered some assistance?

One possible function of ethics committees that was unforeseen in the mid-1970s is that of resource allocation. As the financial pressures on health-care systems worldwide increase, explicit rationing is a looming possibility. An editor of the *Journal of the American Medical Association* once suggested that ethics committees help develop practice guidelines for their institutions to identify when treatment may be withheld on grounds of (so-called) futility (Lundberg 1993).

Ethics consultants may work with ethics committees or as independent actors. In either case there is a lively debate in the United States about how they should operate. According to what might be called the "soft" model, the ethics consultant's job is to bring the parties together, help clarify the issues and arrange a mutually acceptable resolution (Ackerman 1989). This soft model is similar to the "pure facilitation approach" in which consultants solely facilitate consensus among involved parties (ASBH 2003). On the "hard" model, the ethics consultant resembles a consulting physician who performs an assessment of the patient's condition, identifies the relevant medical, social, legal, and ethical facts and issues a recommendation (LaPuma and Schiedermayer 1991). The hard model suggests a more authoritarian approach, wherein the consultant functions as the primary moral decision-maker at the expense of the values of the patient or designated patient advocate (ASBH 2003). The latter model is supported mainly by those who regard formal medical training as a prerequisite for the competent ethics consultant. In their extreme forms, these approaches are both inadequate. A third approach, ethics facilitation, provides a contextual framework in which consultants both identify and analyze the conflict underlying the consultation and facilitate the building of consensus and a balance between the approaches (ASBH 2003).

Although the potential for disciplinary division between physicians and non-physicians within the ranks of ethics consultants is ever-present, so far it has been largely contained. Yet if reimbursement for ethics consultation becomes available, one can imagine that the discussion will become less civil. Similarly, the question whether there should be a certification process for ethics consultants is a flashpoint in the practice.

However one approaches this issue, it is plain that the ethics consultant's role is a terribly complicated one, calling for a remarkable range of skills. At a minimum, the competent ethics consultant must speak the languages of medicine, law, and ethics, must be interpersonally skilled and cognizant of social-psychological issues, and must have the ability to inspire confidence among patients and their families as well as her medical colleagues (Moreno 1991). So described, ethics consultation perhaps deserves the characterization that was once applied to psychoanalysis as "the impossible profession."

Just as there are serious practical questions about the ethics committee phenomenon, so the ethics consultant role is also puzzling. Even apart from the problem of which model of consultation to adopt, there is an inherent difficulty with the notion of ethics consultants who are vulnerable to conflicts of interest when they are salaried by the hospital. Short of a version of academic tenure, or at least long-term contracts, the ethics consultant is in a poor position to take a principled stand that is incompatible with administrative goals. Perhaps this is why most who have performed the ethics consultant role have been members of faculties whose primary association is with some associated academic unit, such as a medical school or a philosophy department. The salaried consultant, compensated from hospital revenues, must exercise unusual self-discipline and independence to retain professional integrity. Although this can be done, it presents such an inherently conflictual role that ethics consultation may always be a marginal activity. Though ethics committees are also made up mainly of hospital workers, the group nature of their discourse may provide some more protection than can be true of the "loan ethicist" on the wards.

One initial obstacle to the establishment of ethics committees and consultants appears to have been dissipated, at least in the United States: the resistance of attending physicians. Especially in the early days of the ethics committee movement, many physicians seemed to take the suggestion of committee involvement as an indictment of their personal moral character. More recently, younger physicians seem to embrace the ethics committee as a source of moral guidance – or, less admirably, as an opportunity to "turf" a complex and legally ominous issue. The latter is a special concern with respect to ethics consultants, who could easily be viewed as providing "ethical cover" in tough cases. Thus, one reason for the popularity of ethics committees and ethics consultants could be that they provide an opportunity to shift responsibility for decisions that are born in ambiguity and which can provoke anxiety among physicians.

It remains to be seen whether ethics committees and ethics consultants will become permanent fixtures of modern health-care decision-making, or whether they are temporary, transitional arrangements while a new and settled consensus on the use of powerful medical technologies sorts itself out. But then, the same question can be asked of bioethics itself.

The Significance of Ethics Committees and Ethics Consultation for Bioethics

As interesting as the phenomena of ethics committees and ethics consultants are in themselves, they also raise provocative questions about the nature of bioethics as an institution. Elsewhere, I have argued at length that bioethics must be understood in the same way social scientists understand any other social institution, namely as a set of social practices (Moreno 1995). That is, the intellectual and academic origins of bioethics should not obscure its sociological functions. Central among these functions is not only to serve as a multidisciplinary forum for raising interesting value questions about health care and the applications of the life sciences, but also to serve as an agent for certain social forces of which it is itself a product.

In particular, bioethics in the clinical setting has functioned partly as a social reform movement, especially insofar as it has participated in the revolution in the way most people think of doctor–patient relations. Surely, no profession has undergone more change in public attitudes in a shorter time than has medicine, and no profession's values have undergone more relentless scrutiny – in spite of the fact that medicine is also the profession that has historically been the most jealous of its prerogatives. Barely 30 years old, the lifetime of bioethics is also the period in which the official values of "paternalistic" medicine have been shattered.

Bioethics has not only been a foremost voice in the emergence of a new social consensus about doctor–patient relations, it has also established itself as an agent for the development of a new consensus about a myriad of moral questions made pressing by the emerging biomedical technologies. Among the vehicles for the creation of this new consensus have been ethics commissions, operating at regional and national levels, and ethics committees and consultants, operating at institutional levels.

As vehicles for consensus creation in institutions, ethics consultants are a mixed bag. What I have called the "hard" ethics consultation model is an instrument of consensus only in the sense and to the degree that people are likely to defer to expertise. But contemporary skepticism of expert consensus is one of the sources of modern bioethics. The "soft" model of ethics consultation, which aims at transforming a morally problematic situation into one of relative moral clarity, is perhaps a more promising source of consensus creation. However, it too is limited by the dynamics of intervention by an individual consultant who is too easily viewed as the "ethics expert." Ethics experts must, it seems, possess several characteristics, including analytical discernment and a knowledge of medical ethical issues and the relevant literature.

Ethics committees are more promising vehicles for institutional consensus creation. In general, well-integrated groups composed of individuals who are respected within the institution are far more powerful agents of change than any lone consultant could be. But for what sort of change should ethics committees strive? What makes one consensus morally superior to another?

Philosophically, this is surely the root problem for ethics committees and ethics consultants: the fact that there is a certain moral consensus does not imply it is a morally sound one. This appears to be an instance of the fact–value problem, and according to standard analytical philosophy it raises notoriously recalcitrant obstacles to the generation of morally adequate conclusions from social decision processes. There seem to be two ways to deal with this dilemma. One is to accept it as insoluble and conclude that moral truth (however one understands this term) and social consensus coincide accidentally, if at all.

An alternative is to reject a simplistic fact–value dichotomy in favor of a naturalistic moral epistemology in which valuation is viewed as emergent from states of affairs. On this view, morally value-laden conclusions are seen as "evaluations," literally, "drawing the value from" state-descriptions. This approach has its *locus classicus* in the work of John Dewey, whose model of "social intelligence" seems uniquely well suited to arrangements like ethics committees. Dewey's model was that of an informed citizenry reaching tentative conclusions (or "hypotheses") together for the solution of common problems, subjecting them to field tests and then revising the hypotheses in light of the results (Dewey 1958).

The concept of social intelligence, a happy corollary of the scientific method, seems to presuppose a shared culture, or at least shared moral values. However, if the value premises differ among deliberators, there is no guarantee that consensus will be reached, even if there is agreement about the empirical premises. Consider two ethics committees faced with problematic cases having identical fact patterns, but with one committee operating in a religiously affiliated hospital that caters to patients of that faith tradition, the other operating in a secular hospital. Though the committees may be similar in all other respects, their value-based differences will often generate divergent results.

A somewhat different problem infects the relationship between the committee and the patient community served by the institution. A value consensus reached by a committee composed mainly of well-educated white males may not be shared by many patients or their families. Even the apparently content-free value of autonomy may not be esteemed or understood the same way in all cultures or subcultures.

Of course, the ethics committee itself faces the challenge of achieving internal consensus on the issues it faces. The fact that ethics committees are themselves subject to small group processes has been the source of much criticism of these committees, since interpersonal relations in any group can distort what should be orderly deliberations. This possibility recommends at least that ethics committee processes should be subjected to empirical study.

Some data about ethics committees is already available, and it has interesting philosophical implications. For example, how shall disagreements within ethics committees be resolved? Under what conditions can it be said that the committee has reached an end to its deliberations on a particular matter? Data collected through self-reporting indicates that the vast majority of ethics committees consider themselves to operate according to "consensus." Moreover, most committees seem to be uncomfortable about taking explicit votes on substantive questions (Hoffman 1991). Moral issues, it seems, are not to be settled by recourse to the usual parliamentary procedures.

It might be expected that there would be consensus among ethics consultants, at least on the basic issues of contemporary bioethics, just as we expect consensus among experts on scientific questions. However, what little data is available on this question suggests that is not necessarily the case. In their survey of ethics consultants, Fox and Stocking (1993) found great disagreement concerning several case scenarios. They surveyed 154 ethics consultants for their reactions to a case of a patient in a persistent vegetative state receiving artificially administered food and fluids. Of the several scenarios in which non-treatment was an alternative, the one that specified that the patient had left instructions that she would not want life-prolonging treatment, and her family agreed, was the only one in which the consultants tended to agree (87 percent) that the patient should not be treated. The other cases, in which the wishes of the patient and the family were varied, received no more than 50 percent agreement to stop treatment.

Conclusion

Ethics committees and ethics consultants are among the most visible manifestations of a highly public, social reform-oriented and multidisciplinary field. Yet for all the enthusiasm and wide acceptance that has greeted them in the past few years, beyond some generalizations there is little that can be said with confidence about their functions and goals. Their future seems closely tied to the further evolution of bioethics, especially whether the field continues to be a vigorous presence beyond the academy.

Acknowledgments

The author expresses his gratitude to Michael Peroski, who provided invaluable assistance in the revision of the previously published version of this chapter.

References

Ackerman, T. (1989). Conceptualizing the role of the ethics consultant. In J. C. Fletcher, N. Quist, and A. R. Jonsen (eds.), *Ethics Consultation in Health Care*. Ann Arbor, MI: Health Administration Press, pp. 37–52.

Advisory Committee for Human Radiation Experiments (1995). *Final Report*. Washington, DC: Joseph Henry Press.

Alexander, S. (1962). They decide who lives, who dies. *Life* (November 9): 102.

American Society for Bioethics and Humanities (2003). Core competencies for health care ethics consultation. In M. P. Ausilo, R. M. Arnold, and S. J. Youngner (eds.), *Ethics Consultation: From Theory to Practice*. Baltimore, MD: Johns Hopkins University Press.

Beauchamp, T. and Childress, J. (2009 [1979]). *Principles of Biomedical Ethics*, 6th edn. New York: Oxford University Press.

Berkowitz, K. A. and Dubler, N. N. (2007). Approaches to ethics consultation. In L. F. Post, J. Blustein, and N. N. Dubler (eds.), *Handbook for Healthcare Ethics Committees*. Baltimore, MD: Johns Hopkins University Press.

Dewey, J. (1958). *Experience and Nature*, 2nd rev. edn. New York: Dover.

Fletcher, J. C. (1995). Bioethics services in healthcare organizations. In J. C. Fletcher, C. A. Hite, P. A. Lombardo, and M. F. Marshall (eds.), *Introduction to Clinical Ethics*. Frederick, MD: University Publishing Group.

Fox, E. and Stocking, C. (1993). Ethics consultants' recommendations for life-prolonging treatment of patients in a persistent vegetative state. *New England Journal of Medicine* 270: 2578–82.

Fox, E., Myers, S., and Pearlman, R. A. (2007). Ethics consultation in United States hospitals: a national survey. *American Journal of Bioethics* 7/2: 13–25.

Hoffman, D. E. (1991). Does legislating hospital ethics committees make a difference? A study of hospital ethics committees in Maryland, the District of Columbia, and Virginia. *Low, Medicine, and Health Care* 19: 111.

Hosford, B. (1986). *Bioethics Committees: The Health Care Providers Guide*. Rockville, MD: Aspen Publishing Corporation.

JCAHO (1992). Patients' rights. In *Accreditation Manual of Hospitals*. Chicago: Joint Commission for the Accreditation of Healthcare Organizations.

LaPuma, J. and Schiedermayer, D. L. (1991). Ethics consultation: skills, roles, and training. *Annals of Internal Medicine* 114: 155–60.

Lundberg, G. (1993). American health care system management objectives: the aura of inevitability becomes incarnate. *Journal of the American Medical Association* 269: 2554–5.

Mayle, K. (2006). Nurses and ethics consultations: between a rock and a hard place. *Journal of Clinical Ethics* 17/3: 257–9.

McGee, G., Caplan, A. L., Spanogle, J. P., and Asch, D. (2001). A national study of ethics committees. *American Journal of Bioethics* 1/4: 60–4.

Miller, R. B. (2002). Extramural ethics consultation: reflections on the mediation/medical advisory model and a further proposal. *Journal of Clinical Ethics* 13/3: 203–5.

Moreno, J. D. (1987). Ethical and legal issues in the treatment of impaired newborns. *Clinics in Perinatology* 14: 325–39.

Moreno, J. D. (1991). Ethics consultation as moral engagement. *Bioethics* 5: 44–56.

Moreno, J. D. (1995). *Deciding Together: Bioethics and Moral Consensus.* New York: Oxford University Press.

Rothman, D. (1991). *Strangers at the Bedside: A History of How Law and Bioethics Transformed Medical Decision Making.* New York: Basic Books.

Teel, K. (1975). The physician's dilemma; a doctor's view: what the law should be. *Baylor Law Review* 27: 6–9.

Wear, S. et al. (1990). The development of an ethics consultation service. *HEC Forum* 2: 75–87.

Further reading

Fletcher, J. C. (1991). The bioethics movement and hospital ethics committees. *Maryland Law Review* 50: 859–94.

Fletcher, J. C. and Hoffmann, D. E. (1994). Ethics committees: time to experiment with standards. *Annals of Internal Medicine* 120: 335–8.

Povar, G. (1991). Evaluating ethics committees: what do we mean by success? *Maryland Law Review* 50: 904–19.

Wolf, S. (1991). Ethics committees and due process: nesting rights in a community of caring. *Maryland Law Review* 50: 798–858.

49

Teaching Ethics in the Health Professions

LYNN GILLAM

Teaching ethics in the health professions, whether to students or working practitioners, is complex and challenging. The challenges go beyond the usual pedagogical concerns of course design and methods of teaching and assessment – though, of course, all these are important in health ethics teaching. The real challenge lies in the fact that teaching ethics in the health professions is ultimately teaching with a vocational purpose. In this context, ethics teaching is inevitably aimed at influencing students' thinking and behavior in their future practice, with the ultimate purpose that they will practice ethically, however this is conceived. This is the rationale for including ethics in the curriculum, and this is how students will interpret the teaching they receive. As others have pointed out (McCullough 2002; Wear 2002), this is very different from teaching bioethics in a humanities or liberal arts context, where there is no specific vocational orientation, little expectation of influencing behavior, and it matters less what views students go on to hold, so long as they have acquired an understanding of ethical theories and the nature of ethical reasoning. For teachers of ethics in the health professional setting, however, it matters very much what students go on to think and do, because this will have very tangible effects on patient care, as well as potentially very serious ramifications for professionals who act contrary to established ethical norms of practice.

Reflection on these practical vocational consequences of ethics teaching raises fundamental questions of moral theory, moral psychology, and meta-ethics. What values, ethical principles, and positions should be promoted, and why? Are these values culturally relative (and hence potentially different in different societies) or universal? Why is it even necessary to teach ethics – isn't the students' innate sense of right and wrong enough? These are very large questions, but in the design of an ethics curriculum they cannot be avoided. The course objectives, the content, the mode of delivery and assessment all necessarily assume a position on these questions. In order to teach health professional ethics in a responsible way, course designers and teachers must be aware of the underlying theoretical issues, and make considered decisions about them. In doing so, they must take into account the foreseeable impacts that their teaching will have on their students, in terms of what messages students will take away, and how they are likely to act. Doing a good job of teaching ethics in the health professions is not only a matter of great practical significance; it is also a major theoretical challenge.

584

Trends in Ethics Teaching in the Health Professions

Over the past several decades, the strong trend in health professional education has been to make ethics an explicit and formal part of the curriculum. The longest history of this is in university medical schools, beginning in the early 1970s. In the US, for example, ethics was part of the formal curriculum in most medical schools by 1990, and the situation was similar in the UK by the mid-1990s (Goldie 2000). As university-based training in other health professions such as nursing and physiotherapy has become established, inclusion of ethics in those curricula has also become quite standard (Mostrom 2005). Prior to explicit ethics teaching, the approach in medical schools involved implicit learning through observation and role-modeling – that is, predominantly bedside teaching of "bedside manner" and professional etiquette. Explicit formalized ethics teaching has a number of obvious advantages over implicit teaching, especially because it is not dependent on which particular practices and role models individual students happen to be exposed to, and what each student manages to make of their own experience. Formal teaching, when done well, encourages independent reflection and critical thinking, rather than unreflective copying. It can build understanding systematically and sequentially. In being formalized, it also gains recognition as an important component of training, with its own knowledge base and core elements. The presence of ethics in the curriculum can be seen by accrediting bodies, and institutions can be held accountable for the quality of their teaching in this area, just as in other, more traditional areas. Of course, this is not to say that implicit teaching and role-modeling no longer happen, or are redundant; simply that they are no longer regarded as sufficient for training new health professionals in ethics.

In the curriculum of a health professional training program, ethics teaching may appear under a number of guises. As well as being labeled as such, ethics may be taught in terms of professionalism, or under medical humanities. It can also form part of communications skills, interviewing, or clinical skills. There may be a focus on ethics in particular content areas of the curriculum, especially palliative care, reproductive medicine (obstetrics and gynecology), and genetics. In some settings it is taught as an aspect of law. One of the reasons that ethics can appear in so many places is the very wide range of views about what constitutes ethics, and how to go about teaching it.

Partly in response to the burgeoning of widely different ethics programs, there have been moves in a number of countries to codify and standardize an ethics curriculum, especially for medicine. In the US, the De Camp conference in the mid-1980s produced a set of basic curricular goals for medical ethics teaching (Culver et al. 1985), which became accepted as the minimum standard for ethics teaching. In the UK, the process of standardization began with the Pond report in 1987 (Boyd 1987), continued in the General Medical Council's document *Tomorrow's Doctors* (GMC 1993), and culminated in the agreed core curriculum in 1998 (Consensus Statement 1998). A similar consensus process led to an ethics core curriculum in Australia in 2001 (Braunack-Mayer et al. 2001).

Theoretical Questions Underlying Curriculum Content

The content of these curriculum documents is quite consistent in terms of content areas. These include ethical theories and basic concepts in medical ethics (such as autonomy and paternalism, patients' rights); informed consent, competence, privacy and confidentiality, and truth-telling; end-of-life decisions; research ethics; genetics, reproduction (including prenatal testing, abortion and artificial reproductive technologies), transplantation, and euthanasia; resource allocation; and ethical issues for students. It is also common to divide an ethics curriculum into the standard educational categories of knowledge, skills, and attitudes. The knowledge component consists of the content areas just listed; skills standardly include skills of ethical reasoning and interpersonal communication; and attitudes include compassion, care, integrity, honesty, and so on. While this may appear to represent a remarkable degree of agreement for an academic discipline known for competing and controversial positions on almost every matter, a closer look quickly shows that this is much more a list of topic areas than an agreement about what substantive positions should be endorsed or taught within these areas. That the compilers of such documents are aware of this can be seen in the emphasis given to critical thinking and ethical reasoning skills. A major aim of ethics teaching is regarded as being to equip and encourage each practitioner to come to his or her own considered decision on ethical matters (Miles et al. 1989).

This sort of schema, commonplace though it is, raises some of the big questions in relation to ethics. Under the surface of these core curricula lurks uncertainty and disagreement about ethical knowledge. Is there any ethical "knowledge," and what is its status? Even having the category of "knowledge" in a curriculum seems to suggest that there is "ethical truth" which can be taught to students (Momeyer 2002), yet many moral philosophers would deny that there is any such thing. Even if educators take some sort of realist or objectivist meta-ethical position, they still have the problem of which normative theory to choose. In teaching on specific matters, such as whether it is ever ethically acceptable to withhold information from patients, it seems that educators must decide whether they are adopting and teaching from a particular normative position, such as Kantianism, liberalism, or preference-utilitarianism, or whether they are laying out a range of possible positions, and inviting (and hopefully equipping) students to choose between them. Both paths have their dangers, however.

The main problem with adopting a particular normative moral theory is that of justification. Hundreds of years of philosophical endeavor have failed to produce convergence in the field of normative ethics, so it cannot be said of any of the major competing theories that it has a great degree of academic authority or overwhelming support. Of course, the teacher may have his or her own well-considered and well-argued reasons for preferring one position over the others and, in a humanities or liberal arts setting, this would be quite an acceptable basis from which to proceed. It would be understood that students are encouraged to challenge and disagree, and arguing for one normative theory is a legitimate pedagogical strategy in teaching students about other theories and how philosophers debate their relative merits. However, in the vocational setting of health professional training, this is not such a tenable position. Students are expecting to be taught how to act ethically in their professional field, and will quite reasonably interpret what they are taught as correct and authoritative. Simply laying out a range of options fails to meet the practical vocational needs of students, who need to know what their profession expects of them, and what the requirements and constraints on their behavior will be in the real world of clinical practice. The ethical smorgasbord approach also runs the very real risk of leaving students with the impression that, in ethics, there is no way of coming to an objective decision, and hence anything is acceptable, just so long as you can find a theory that suits your position. This matters. Educators have moral responsibility for the foreseeable outcomes of their teaching, not just those they intend. It is just not the case that anything goes out there in the real world of health work, and it is wrong to teach in a way that is likely to produce such a belief. Moreover, it is highly unlikely to be a belief that any clinical ethics educator actually holds, so students would end up with a false understanding of their teachers' basic premise in teaching them ethics – namely that there are some sorts of behavior and interactions with patients that are wrong for health professionals to engage in.

This conundrum may explain to some extent the attraction of Beauchamp and Childress's principlism, which is widely used, especially in medical and allied health ethics curricula (less so in nursing, where ethics of care is a more common theoretical basis). In presenting their principles as the agreed ground between competing normative theories, they appear to offer a way around the horns of this dilemma (Beauchamp and Childress 2009). The principles of nonmaleficence, beneficence, autonomy, and justice seem to provide a neutral zone of ethical knowledge, substantive and definitive in one way, and yet not controversial because not adopting any particular position. This approach works well, up to a certain point. Principlism is good for providing some basic ethical boundaries, and a framework or structure in which to organize one's thoughts, observations, and intuitions. For students, it seems to be readily understandable and able to be put into immediate use, at least at a relatively superficial level. However, as has often been noted, principlism is not so good when it comes to resolving issues and making specific decisions. Beauchamp and Childress do provide an account of how to balance competing principles, but it leaves many gaps. Major theoretical disagreements, such as the relative moral weight that should be accorded to acts versus omissions and intended versus foreseeable consequences, are left obscure or unaddressed. Hence, on the most controversial issues there is the least guidance, and the greatest scope is left for individual judgment. While this may be regarded as a merit of principlism in a theoretical sense, it is a definite drawback when it comes to providing some sort of neutral but definitive moral ground.

Beyond this challenge for ethics teachers, another issue remains that neither principlism nor particular normative theories can solve. In this increasingly globalized world, it is impossible to ignore cultural difference. (This is discussed in chapter 3, "Culture and Bioethics.") Students in health professional courses come from a great variety of ethnic and religious backgrounds. Some are overseas students who will return to their home countries to practice, and local students can reasonably expect to work outside their own country at some point in their careers. Of course, students do not have to go beyond their local hospital or community to find great diversity amongst their patients. In this context, cultural difference between health professionals and their patients is to be expected, and must be regarded by teachers of ethics as a standard feature of professional practice. However, the differences in values and beliefs which often accompany cultural variation pose another major challenge for ethics teachers. These differences operate at two distinct, but connected, levels: first, individual cultural difference between patients and health practitioners, and, secondly, difference in moral values and positions between cultures themselves.

Cultural and values distinctions between health professionals and patients can play out in many ways. It is a well-recognized problem in relation to informed consent. Where there is cultural difference, there may be quite separate understandings of who should make health-care decisions for a patient (the patient themselves, the family as a whole, the senior male family member, the doctor, or someone else?), and on what basis (for example, is information about risks required in order for the patient to make a reasoned and informed choice, hence empowering the patient, or will talking about risks actually cause them to occur, and hence harm the patient?). Cultural difference also profoundly affects end-of-life decision-making. A good death may be understood as one where the patient is fully aware of what is happening and is able to complete "unfinished business" and say final farewells; or as one where the patient does not know that death is approaching, feels safe and optimistic, and does not have to deal with distressing thoughts and interactions. Physical suffering at the end of life may be seen as the ultimate evil, to be avoided at all costs, or as a spiritually uplifting experience, which should not be taken away from the patient. How should students in the health professions be taught to understand and deal ethically with these sorts of cultural differences?

A common approach would be to interpret all these situations through the lens of respect for patient autonomy. Respect for autonomy can be taken as implying that a person should be given just the information that they want to have, given whatever their beliefs are. If the patient belongs to a culture in which the family makes the decision, then respect for the patient's autonomy means allowing the patient to use whatever decision-making process he or she chooses, including opting to have someone else make the decision. While this makes sense on a practical level, and permits a way forward that is often acceptable to all parties, there are a number of problematic issues in the background. One is that some cultural practices actually require individual autonomy not to be respected, such as when family members want a diagnosis to be told to them, but not to the patient. The patient cannot sensibly make an autonomous decision not to be told something, without knowing what that thing is, in which case he or she has already been told. More fundamentally, what is actually going on here is that the value of respect for individual autonomy (interpreted in a particular way) is being accorded paramount value from the health professional's perspective, when this is precisely *not* the value that the patient's culture endorses. From another perspective, though, there is the opposite problem that the patient's values are being privileged over those of the health professional. The importance of health professionals' integrity can be seriously underrated by this approach. If health professionals really believe that respect for patient autonomy requires them to tell the patient what his or her diagnosis is, then asking them to set this aside because of the different values of the patient's culture can be experienced as asking them to do something that they strongly believe to be wrong. And it is not at all clear that it would be ethically justifiable to demand this, especially on a relativistic worldview. Relativism holds that there are not universal moral values or standards against which different culturally based values can be judged. So there is no sound reason to take the view that health professionals' values must cede to patients' values in circumstances of cultural difference. Both sets of values have claims to validity in their own context, and no claims to trump other sets of values.

This example indicates that it is not really possible to keep issues of cultural difference confined to the individual level. Teaching ethics in the health professions ultimately runs into the question of whether any ethical values, principles, or rules are universal, or whether all are culturally determined (and hence not necessarily valid or enforceable across different cultures). One of the standard criticisms of principlism is that it is a Western, individualist normative theory arising out of a particular cultural context, illegitimately purporting to be universalist. Its emphasis on the principle of respect for individual autonomy (and the related values of privacy and informed consent) is the major focus of this criticism. Teaching an ethics curriculum based on principlism could then be seen as an act of cultural imperialism – unless, of course, it can be shown that universalism is true, and these particular principles are the correct ones. Unfortunately for the teacher of health ethics, the meta-ethical debate over universalism and relativism is unresolved, just like the debate between competing normative theories. And, this being the case, the same sorts of pitfalls of adopting a particular position, or laying out a range of options, that were described in that context also apply here.

There is a pragmatic solution to fraught problems of cultural and value difference, which offers a way forward, but it does so without actually resolving anything at a theoretical level. The pragmatic approach involves explicitly teaching to the cultural context of the country in which the students are located and will initially practice, without making any claims that the values are applicable in any other context. The justification for this is that students are learning and practicing in that particular context, and must come to understand what will be expected of them in that context. This avoids taking any position, either universalist or relativist, and seems acceptable to students. However, for this approach to be intellectually honest, both for teachers and students, a key element is specific teaching about the debate around cultural relativism and universalism, so that the underlying philosophy of the teaching is transparent. Students should know that there is contention around the universality or otherwise of values, and know what pedagogical strategy their teaching is based on. This leaves them with a very large unresolved question about the universality or otherwise of values, which they may struggle with for the rest of their careers, or put on hold indefinitely. While this may be unsatisfactory in many ways, it is surely better than trying to avoid the whole issue.

In short, then, formulating the content of an ethics curriculum is a theoretically loaded task. There is no neutral way of doing it, and the theoretical questions must be decided in some way. Such decisions may be taken deliberatively and explicitly, or implicitly and by accident. Clearly the former is preferable for the integrity and academic honesty of all involved, but it is also a harder and more challenging course. Teachers of ethics who take on this task can expect their own theoretical positions about meta-ethics and normative ethics to change and develop over time, in the search for a coherent and meaningful theoretical foundation (Tong 2002). What is more, formulating content is only one aspect of the challenge of teaching ethics in the health professions, and is perhaps not the major one.

Ethical Knowledge or Ethical Behavior?

Among the most discomforting moments in the lives of ethics educators are the occasions on which the question of the ultimate outcomes of their teaching is raised. Does ethics teaching actually lead to (more) ethical behavior? The literature is full of evaluations of ethics programs, but the majority of these investigate whether the program has improved students' ability to recognize ethical issues and use ethical reasoning (using, for example, Rest's Defining Issues Test, or the Toronto Ethical Sensitivity Instrument). There have been very few attempts to evaluate the impact on students' actual behavior. This is hardly surprising, given the difficulty of finding a way to collect meaningful data, but it does highlight a very problematic issue for ethics teaching. There is clearly more to ethical *conduct* in the health professions than ethical *decision-making*: health professionals must actually recognize that there are ethical values at stake and a decision to be made, believe that these values are important enough to act on, be able to think effectively about the context-specific matters as well as ethical principles, and actually be willing and able to act on their ethical evaluations and decisions (Guillemin and Gillam 2006). It would seem that ethics education should encompass much more than ethical knowledge and ethical reasoning skills if, in the words of the UK Consensus Statement, it is to "create good doctors who will enhance and promote the health and medical welfare of the people they serve in ways which fairly and justly respect their dignity, autonomy and rights" (Consensus Statement 1998).

It is interesting that some quite influential statements of the aims of medical ethics teaching have shied away from the idea that ethics teaching should directly affect behavior. Miles et al., for example, set out what they regard as the agreed aims of medical ethics teaching. These aims are to give physicians various abilities: to recognize ethical aspects of medicine, to reflect on their own values, to use ethical knowledge in clinical reasoning, and so on (1989: 706). However, they never actually state as an aim that physicians will actually use these abilities, or act in ethical ways. Indeed, they caution that medical ethics education should not be expected to create sound moral character, promote a particular moral viewpoint, or mitigate the dehumanizing effects of excessive workloads during training (1989: 707). While this is understandable in light of the earlier discussions about competing normative theories and meta-ethical positions on universalism, it is arguably too timid and circumscribed for a context where, as described at the beginning of this chapter, the stakes are so high for both patients and health professionals. There *are* behaviors and attitudes in health professionals that many different ethical and cultural value-systems would endorse (care, compassion, putting the patient's interests first, taking care not to cause avoidable harm, for instance). These could legitimately form the basis of a program aimed at influencing and directing what students value and how they act, at least in broad terms, without taking particular positions on controversial matters. Indeed, a health ethics education program which avowed no interest in how its students actually conducted themselves in their professional work would arguably be a contradiction in terms (and would certainly fail to meet the expectations of bodies which accredit the courses).

There are many ethics education programs across the spectrum of health professions that do quite explicitly aim to influence attitudes and behavior. This is done in a great variety of ways. Many programs specifically address ethical issues associated with examining patients primarily for the purpose of learning, rather than providing care, since these are matters that the students will currently be dealing with, and need to handle well. There is also a range of symbolic strategies for sending the message to students that ethics and ethical conduct matter, such as the so-called "white-coat" induction ceremonies held in some US medical schools, the ceremonial swearing of the Hippocratic oath, and so on. There are also explicitly theoretical approaches to inculcating attitudes and fostering ethical behavior. In medicine, for example, Aristotelian virtue ethics can be used as a basis to explicitly identify, and begin to teach, attitudes characteristic of a good doctor (Shelton 1999). In nursing, the ethics of care movement can be understood in a similar way. Ethics of care as the basis for teaching nursing ethics is totally focused on ethical behavior: in particular, ethical relationships between nurses and their patients which operate on a deep emotional level, rather than on ethical knowledge or thinking. Of course, ethics of care differs radically from virtue ethics in that it involves explicit rejection of principles and reasoning; the similarity lies in the focus on the personal character of the health professional.

The medical humanities tradition is yet another approach for encouraging ethical behavior. The fundamental aim of medical humanities is to give students a greater awareness of, and sympathy for, real people's actual experience of life, illness, and suffering, and greater insight into themselves as complex, feeling human beings. Within medical humanities, there is a variety of methods for achieving this: reading literature and poetry (the classics and contemporary personal accounts), being involved in music and theater, and so on. The presupposition is that such literary activities effectively tap into students' emotions in ways that can build ethical character and promote ethical behavior. Narrative ethics (which is seen by some, though not all, as an aspect of medical humanities) is also being increasingly used as a method of promoting ethical mindfulness through a process of students telling and reflecting on their own and each other's stories (Guillemin and Gillam 2006).

The final step in this line of thinking is to give students direct personal experiences, rather than have them read or write about them. Some institutions have innovative programs which provide students with actual personal experience of what it is like to be in hospital, or to be poor or marginalized. Examples include students accompanying patients throughout their hospital stay (Goldie 2000: 117), working as helpers with social service organizations and charities, and being placed in manual labor and production-line workplaces with which they are usually totally unfamiliar, given their generally high socioeconomic status backgrounds. These sorts of programs are of course extremely difficult to evaluate. The effects on students are highly varied and subjective, in spite of the use of journals and other reflective writing processes as part of the program. Despite their powerful potential, they do have the same drawbacks as the old-style implicit learning described earlier.

591

The Hidden Curriculum

Whether the emphasis is on ethical knowledge or ethical behavior, the common feature of all approaches described so far is their focus on the individual health professional. They all assume that ethical behavior depends on the knowledge, skills, and personal qualities of the individual: if these are taught well, health professionals will act ethically. However, there is growing recognition that this assumption gives insufficient weight to the powerful influence of the context – both of health professional education and of practice. Being trained as a health professional, whether as a doctor, nurse, or physiotherapist, is a process of socialization into a complex web of norms and practices, not simply a transmission of knowledge and skills. The powerful messages about values implicit in this process have come to be called the "hidden curriculum." They are conveyed by the structure of the course, the attitudes of all those involved in teaching, and by the hospital environment – particularly by the ways of treating patients and colleagues, and the ways of viewing oneself, that are obviously accepted, even valorized, in that environment. As Hafferty and Franks (1994) have argued so strongly, these implicit messages are often contrary to what is explicitly taught in ethics courses, and are much more influential. If it is the hidden curriculum, rather than ethics classes, that largely determines how students will behave as future practitioners, then this is a major challenge to the whole endeavor of teaching ethics in the health professions.

Dealing with the influence of the hidden curriculum is a work in progress for ethics education. Mere recognition of the problem immediately expands the scope of ethics teaching: it is important for students to at least understand concepts of socialization, and the moral distress and threats to moral agency and integrity that can accompany it. Responding appropriately to the unethical behavior of others, including by whistle-blowing, and being ethical in unethical places, become as important in curriculum content terms as confidentiality and informed consent. But beyond alerting students to what is happening to them and around them, is there anything that can be done to equip students with skills, attitudes, or tools to develop and stand their own moral ground? It is a yet unanswered question as to whether ethics teaching in itself can empower students to act ethically in these environments, or whether change in the cultures of health professions and institutions is a necessary concomitant.

Conclusion

The stakes are high in teaching ethics in the health professions, and the challenges, both theoretical and practical, are many. Such is the level of complexity, that any attempt to provide a straightforward recipe for successful ethics teaching is doomed to over-simplification and ultimate failure. However, I suggest that some guiding principles can be identified. First, the theoretical positions and debates under the surface of apparently agreed-upon ethics curricula need to be acknowledged. Each teacher of ethics should understand the implications of the path they decide to take, and work to counter the known pitfalls of that path. Secondly, transparency and meta-commentary is important: students should be let in on the tough questions and theoretical puzzles so that they can see the rationale for what they are being taught and what assumptions are being made. Thirdly, the hidden curriculum cannot be ignored. Doing so at best renders ethics teaching ineffective, will almost inevitably lead to cynicism about ethics in general when students see that theory does not match practice, and, at worst, exposes students to moral confusion and distress as they see that they cannot do what they have been taught is right to do, and interpret this as their own personal failing.

References

Beauchamp, T. L. and Childress, J. F. (2009 [1979]). *Principles of Biomedical Ethics*, 6th edn. New York: Oxford University Press.

Boyd, K. (ed.) (1987). *Pond Report on the Teaching of Medical Ethics*. London: Institute of Medical Ethics.

Braunack-Mayer, A. et al. Association of Teachers of Ethics and Law in Australian and New Zealand Medical Schools (2001). An ethics core curriculum for Australasian medical schools. *Medical Journal of Australia* 175/4: 205–10.

Consensus Statement (1998). Teaching medical ethics and law within medical education: a model for the UK core curriculum. *Journal of Medical Ethics* 24: 188–92.

Culver, C. M. et al. (1985). Basic curricular goals in medical ethics. *New England Journal of Medicine* 312: 253–6.

Fox, E. et al. (1995). Medical ethics education: past present and future. *Academic Medicine* 70/9: 761–9.

GMC (1993). *Tomorrow's Doctors*. London: General Medical Council.

Goldie, J. (2000). Review of ethics curricula in undergraduate medical education. *Medical Education* 34: 108–19.

Guillemin, M. and Gillam, L. (2006). *Telling Moments: Everyday Ethics in Health Care*. Sydney: IP Communications.

Hafferty, F. and Franks, R. (1994). The hidden curriculum, ethics teaching and the structure of medical education. *Academic Medicine* 69/11: 861–71.

McCullough, L. B. (2002). Philosophical challenges in teaching bioethics: the importance of professional medical ethics and its history for bioethics. *Journal of Medicine and Philosophy* 27/4: 395–402.

Miles, S. H. et al. (1989). Medical ethics education: coming of age. *Academic Medicine* 64: 705–14.

Momeyer, R. (2002). What conception of moral truth works in bioethics? *Journal of Medicine and Philosophy* 27/2: 403–16.

Mostrom, E. (2005). Teaching and learning about the ethical and human dimensions of care in clinical education: exploring student and clinical instructor experiences in physical therapy. In R. Purtilo, G. Jensen, and C. Royeen (eds.), *Educating For Moral Action*. Philadelphia, PA: FA Davis Company.

Shelton, W. (1999). Can virtue be taught? *Academic Medicine* 74/6: 671–4.

Tong, R. (2002). Teaching bioethics in the new millennium: Holding theories accountable to actual practices and real people. *Journal of Medicine and Philosophy* 27/2: 417–32.

Wear, S. (2002). Teaching bioethics at (or near) the bedside. *Journal of Medicine and Philosophy* 27/4: 433–45.

Index